D1613790

Dictionary of Literary Biography

Documentary Series

Yearbooks

Concise Series

Japanese Fiction Writers, 1868–1945

Dictionary of Literary Biography® • Volume One Hundred Eighty

Japanese Fiction Writers, 1868–1945

Edited by
Van C. Gessel
Brigham Young University

A Bruccoli Clark Layman Book
Gale Research
Detroit, Washington, D.C., London

Printed in the United States of America

Published simultaneously in the United Kingdom
by Gale Research International Limited
(An affiliated company of Gale Research)

The paper used in this publication meets the minimum requirements
of American National Standard for Information Sciences–Permanence
Paper for Printed Library Materials, ANSI Z39.48-1984. ⊚ ™

The excerpt from *East Asia: The Modern Transformation* is copyright © 1965 by John K. Fairbank, Edwin O. Reischauer, and Albert M. Craig. Reprinted with permission of Houghton Mifflin Company.
The excerpt from *Japanese Culture,* third edition, by H. Paul Varley is copyright © 1984 by University of Hawaii Press and is used with permission.

Library of Congress Cataloging-in-Publication Data

Japanese fiction writers, 1868-1945 / edited by Van C. Gessel.
  p. cm.–(Dictionary of literary biography; v. 180)
"A Bruccoli Clark Layman book."
Includes bibliographical references and index.
ISBN 0-7876-1069-0 (alk. paper)
1. Japanese fiction–1868–Bio-bibliography–Dictionaries. 2. Novelists, Japanese–20th century–Biography–Dictionaries. I. Gessel, Van C. II. Series.
PL747.55.M63 1997
895.6'3009'03–DC21   97-11573
[B]   CIP

10 9 8 7 6 5 4 3 2 1

Dedicated, with gratitude for their example of meticulous scholarship,
to William H. and Helen Craig McCullough

Contents

Plan of the Series

. . . Almost the most prodigious asset of a country, and perhaps its most precious possession, is its native literary product — when that product is fine and noble and enduring.

Mark Twain*

The advisory board, the editors, and the publisher of the *Dictionary of Literary Biography* are joined in endorsing Mark Twain's declaration. The literature of a nation provides an inexhaustible resource of permanent worth. We intend to make literature and its creators better understood and more accessible to students and the reading public, while satisfying the standards of teachers and scholars.

To meet these requirements, *literary biography* has been construed in terms of the author's achievement. The most important thing about a writer is his writing. Accordingly, the entries in *DLB* are career biographies, tracing the development of the author's canon and the evolution of his reputation.

The purpose of *DLB* is not only to provide reliable information in a convenient format but also to place the figures in the larger perspective of literary history and to offer appraisals of their accomplishments by qualified scholars.

The publication plan for *DLB* resulted from two years of preparation. The project was proposed to Bruccoli Clark by Frederick C. Ruffner, president of the Gale Research Company, in November 1975. After specimen entries were prepared and typeset, an advisory board was formed to refine the entry format and develop the series rationale. In meetings held during 1976, the publisher, series editors, and advisory board approved the scheme for a comprehensive biographical dictionary of persons who contributed to North American literature. Editorial work on the first volume began in January 1977, and it was published in 1978. In order to make *DLB* more than a reference tool and to compile volumes that individually have claim to status as literary history, it was decided to organize volumes by topic, period, or genre. Each of these freestanding volumes provides a biographical-bibliographical guide and overview for a particular area of literature. We are convinced that this organization — as opposed to a single alphabet method — constitutes a valuable innovation in the presentation of reference material. The volume plan necessarily requires many decisions for the placement and treatment of authors who might properly be included in two or three volumes. In some instances a major figure will be included in separate volumes, but with different entries emphasizing the aspect of his career appropriate to each volume. Ernest Hemingway, for example, is represented in *American Writers in Paris, 1920–1939* by an entry focusing on his expatriate apprenticeship; he is also in *American Novelists, 1910–1945* with an entry surveying his entire career. Each volume includes a cumulative index of the subject authors and articles. Comprehensive indexes to the entire series are planned.

The series has been further augmented by the *DLB Yearbooks* (since 1981) which update published entries and add new entries to keep the *DLB* current with contemporary activity. There have also been *DLB Documentary Series* volumes which provide biographical and critical source materials for figures whose work is judged to have particular interest for students. One of these companion volumes is entirely devoted to Tennessee Williams.

We define literature as the *intellectual commerce of a nation*: not merely as belles lettres but as that ample and complex process by which ideas are generated, shaped, and transmitted. *DLB* entries are not limited to "creative writers" but extend to other figures who in their time and in their way influenced the mind of a people. Thus the series encompasses historians, journalists, publishers, book collectors, and screenwriters. By this means readers of *DLB* may be aided to perceive literature not as cult scripture in the keeping of intellectual high priests but firmly positioned at the center of a nation's life.

DLB includes the major writers appropriate to each volume and those standing in the ranks behind them. Scholarly and critical counsel has been sought in deciding which minor figures to include and how full their entries should be. Wherever possible, useful references are made to figures who do not warrant separate entries.

Each *DLB* volume has an expert volume editor responsible for planning the volume, selecting the figures for inclusion, and assigning the entries. Volume editors are also responsible for preparing, where appropriate, appendices surveying the major periodicals and literary and intellectual movements for their volumes, as well as lists of further readings. Work on the series as a whole is coordinated at the Bruccoli Clark Layman editorial center in Columbia, South Carolina, where the editorial staff is responsible for accuracy and utility of the published volumes.

One feature that distinguishes *DLB* is the illustration policy – its concern with the iconography of literature. Just as an author is influenced by his surroundings, so is the reader's understanding of the author enhanced by a knowledge of his environment. Therefore *DLB* volumes include not only drawings, paintings, and photographs of authors, often depicting them at various stages in their careers, but also illustrations of their families and places where they lived. Title pages are regularly reproduced in facsimile along with dust jackets for modern authors. The dust jackets are a special feature of *DLB* because they often document better than anything else the way in which an author's work was perceived in its own time. Specimens of the writers' manuscripts and letters are included when feasible.

Samuel Johnson rightly decreed that ''The chief glory of every people arises from its authors.'' The purpose of the *Dictionary of Literary Biography* is to compile literary history in the surest way available to us – by accurate and comprehensive treatment of the lives and work of those who contributed to it.

The *DLB* Advisory Board

Introduction

DLB 180: *Japanese Fiction Writers, 1868–1945* focuses on the lives and works of twenty-five Japanese authors who achieved prominence and influenced literary development from the beginning of Japan's encounter with the West through the end of World War II. An argument can be made that the most persuasive dividing point between Japan's classical tradition and a quasi-modern consciousness came in the early seventeenth century, when the creation of a mercantile economy and culture led to the establishment of a society that was decidedly secular and up-to-date. But an even more obvious and startling transformation—because it was imposed on Japan from the outside and was not a slow, evolutionary development within the culture—occurred in the last three decades of the nineteenth century, when Japan's closed doors were forced open and a new foreign culture stormed in.

Perhaps the single most dynamic influence on the development of modern Japanese literature has been the interplay between traditional Japanese views of fiction and literary concepts from the West that the Japanese examined and copied and to which they reacted. Dominant throughout the twentieth century as a literary form has been the *watakushi-shōsetsu* (sometimes written *shi-shōsetsu*), the I-novel or personal narrative. The form became the main mode of artistic expression for writers in the first decade of the twentieth century, dominated literary debate and practice in the 1920s, and has demonstrated remarkable endurance ever since. It is safe to say that virtually every important writer of the twentieth century in Japan has had to define his or her literary stance in relation to the I-novel, with many preferring to draw their materials from personal experience rather than from their imaginations. The reasons for this artistic choice include a Japanese preference for "truth" over "fiction," a dependence on literature as one of the few means available for the venting of personal emotion in a highly ritualized society, and a distrust of writers who claim to be able to imagine the thoughts of others. The term *I-novel* itself is somewhat misleading, since many such works are told in the third person; nevertheless, they are still closely modeled after the experiences of the authors. More often than not these narratives, whether told in the first or the third person, limit themselves to the thoughts and experiences of a single consciousness; other characters are little more than sounding boards for the protagonist's feelings. The form was initially a convenient channel for the expression of a Japanese Naturalistic view of the baseness of human experience and the powerlessness of the individual against an unforgiving, all-consuming society; often this attitude was depicted as an opposition between the individual and the family. Later, writers interested in the individual's *shinkyō* (state of mind) used the form in a more positive fashion to explore the ways in which one develops a sense of personal independence and spiritual growth. The I-novel even survived the emotional ravages of the mid-century war and defeat.

Japan's political and cultural encounter with the West, which was initiated by the arrival of Commodore Matthew Perry's "black ships" in 1853, led in 1867 to what the Japanese call the "Meiji Restoration"—the enthronement of the emperor Meiji, who would rule in place of the military warlords who had controlled the country for centuries. This social and cultural revolution ranks in significance with the Ōnin War of 1467 to 1477, which marked the end of aristocratic rule, as one of the two most important turning points in Japan's history. Reform was instituted at virtually every level of the society, and "modernization," synonymous at that time with Westernization, led to the creation of a strong military, a centralized government controlled by oligarchies, and an industrial revolution.

In literature the Japanese had their first true encounter with a non-Asian writing. Though for centuries they had been studying, copying, and altering traditions of Chinese literature even as they developed indigenous forms, their acquaintance with Western literature before the Meiji Restoration seems to have been limited to a translation of Aesop's fables by Catholic priests in the late sixteenth century and portions of the

Odyssey related either by the Christian missionaries or Dutch sailors who were among the few foreigners allowed into Japan during its long period of isolation in the Tokugawa era of 1600 to 1867. What struck the Japanese about Western literature were the breadth of its topics, the freedom of its forms, and the prestige of its authors. Spurred by a nationwide interest in studying and imitating things Western, Japanese writers in the early Meiji era began to experiment with literary forms and styles that had never been a part of their historical tradition.

The earliest translations were free approximations of works by Sir Walter Scott, Edward Bulwer-Lytton, Jules Verne, and Daniel Defoe. Bulwer-Lytton's *Ernest Maltravers* (1837), one of his least-known works in the West, was in 1879 the first full-length novel to appear in Japanese. The Japanese were impressed more by the fact that a novelist could achieve social status as a statesman in England than by any quality that might distinguish the writing. Defoe's *Robinson Crusoe* (1719) was offered as an example of how hard work could transform a backward island nation into a modern civilized society. Works by many other Western writers appeared in rapid succession, giving the rapidly expanding reading audience insights into Western manners and customs. Before long a new literary form, the *seiji shōsetsu* (political novel), emerged with the flowering of freedom and a people's rights movement—flowerings inspired by the glimpses of personal liberty that readers had acquired from their perusal of Western fiction.

In the later years of the Tokugawa regime fiction had generally been considered a debased form of entertainment, pandering to the lowest level of readers with salacious violence and sexuality plastered over with a thin veneer of Confucian morality. The Meiji critic Tsubouchi Shōyō, who achieved a remarkable facility in English (he eventually translated the complete works of William Shakespeare into Japanese), studied and translated Western—particularly British—writing and sensed the need for a new kind of fiction to depict the realities of an essentially new Japan. In his pioneering critical work, *Shōsetsu shinzui* (The Essence of the Novel, 1885–1886), Shōyō argued that realistic fiction, not the sex and gore of the prevailing literary mode, was best suited to express the aspirations and perceptions of contemporary society. He also urged writers to create a written language with the vigor and comprehensibility of the spoken language, since the gap between spoken and literary Japanese at the time

was extremely wide. Relying on Shōyō's theories and personal guidance, Futabatei Shimei, an avid reader of Russian fiction and a sensitive translator of the works of Ivan Turgenev, produced what has been called Japan's first modern novel, *Ukigumo* (Drifting Clouds, 1887–1889; translated as *Ukigumo*, 1965). The story is about a mediocre government clerk whose preference for old-fashioned virtues costs him his job and renders him a pathetic figure both to his opportunistic colleagues and to his fiancée. In his indecisiveness, his inability to find any solid moral basis on which to render a decision, this character is a model for the antiheroes who populate the modern Japanese novel. In the latter third of the novel Futabatei creates a new colloquial language and probes the psychology of his character in ways that are fresh and challenging. After writing *Ukigumo*, however, Futabatei lost faith in his creative talents and, like his protagonist, joined the government bureaucracy. No other author of the time showed his level of understanding of the modern psychological novel.

In the 1890s young writers began to be attracted to the portrait of the liberated individual they discovered in the poetry of the English Romantics; simultaneously, they were attracted to the promise of spiritual freedom that they were taught by Protestant missionaries, and many converted—fleetingly, in most cases—to Christianity. Consequently, a Romantic movement developed in Japan, first in poetry and then in prose. The Romantic writers clustered around the literary journal *Bungakukai* (The Literary World), which was published from 1893 to 1898. The most moving work of fiction to appear in the journal was the novella "Takekurabe" (Comparing Heights, 1895–1896; translated as *Growing Up*, 1956), by a young female author, Higuchi Ichiyō. Higuchi's language retained much of the classical diction and imagery, but the content and sensibilities of her story are clearly modern. Ichiyō describes the loneliness of youth, the confusion that attends maturation, and the choices that must be made as her adolescent characters become part of the adult world.

It was another member of the *Bungakukai* coterie, Shimazaki Tōson, who nudged the novel in the direction of "realistic" fiction, in which he attempted to assert the authenticity of the individual personality. His novel *Hakai* (1906; translated as *The Broken Commandment*, 1974) concerns a young schoolteacher who belongs to an outcast group that has endured discrimination for centuries in Japan. The teacher hides his origins until he concludes that he must divulge his secret if he is to be free of the fetters of tradition and establish himself as a unique individual in the society. The tale represents both Shimazaki's reaction against his conservative family and a probing look at social problems in modernizing Japan. This combination of personal and social concerns makes *The Broken Commandment* a novel of range and depth and establishes a pattern that, had it been followed by other writers, would have produced a quite different history of the modern novel in Japan. Although Japanese literature has traditionally distanced itself from large social or political issues and preferred the lyric to the narrative mode, Shimazaki's novel suggested ways in which the concerns of the individual could be made accessible and relevant to a broader reading audience. But readers and authors in the early years of the twentieth century were evidently more interested in the minute detailing of an individual's inner landscape, and Shimazaki's achievement in producing a thoroughly realistic novel was swept aside as a uniquely Japanese brand of Naturalism was ushered in by Tayama Katai.

Influenced by Emile Zola's emphasis on social and biological destiny but turning quickly from the "scientific" study of humanity to a highly confined examination of the debased self that often produced stark personal confessions, Japanese Naturalism flourished in the early twentieth century. Tayama created a vogue for the confessional I-novel with the publication of his autobiographical *Futon* (1907; translated as *The Quilt,* 1981), in which he describes a writer's sexual yearnings for a young woman who has come to study literature with him. Public reaction to the work was so positive and persuasive that Shimazaki abandoned fiction and retreated into his own private world to write I-novels. His characters, like Tayama's, turn their focus inward; his novels become records—sometimes brutally honest records, as in *Shinsei* (A New Life, 1919), in which he confesses to an affair with his niece—of the survival of the author's identity. Shimazaki's abandonment of social realism bolstered the establishment of personal fiction, with its narrow world of limited alternatives, as the mainstream genre in Japan.

With confession set as the norm for the prose narrative, the development of a mature, realistic novel was left to Natsume Sōseki, an esteemed scholar of English literature who spent nearly three years studying in London. Natsume wrote a series of novels that remain among the most probing fictional accounts of the impact of modernization and individualization on the intellectual class in Japan. His heroes are often men in agony, well educated in Western ways but keenly aware that their learning and their expanding individuality are isolating them from those around them. Time and again Natsume presents characters in triangular relationships that graphically illustrate the ways in which egotistical concerns wound sensitive hearts, destroy friendships, and leave the individual utterly alone. In *Kokoro* (The Heart, 1914; translated as *Kokoro,* 1941), the most popular and influential of Natsume's novels, the hero, unable to overcome his guilt over driving a friend to suicide because of their love of the same woman, kills himself and leaves behind for another friend a chronicle of his fall into isolation and self-loathing. Betrayal and isolation are, for Natsume, the inevitable consequences of the modern self with its egotistical yearnings; and though he would not trade away the freedom that has come through association with Western ideas, Natsume is painfully aware of the emptiness that can result from a misuse of that liberty.

Natsume may be the first modern novelist in Japan who can lay claim to world-class stature as a writer; the Japanese government acknowledged his importance—and legitimized the concerns he expressed about the breakdown of interpersonal bonds in a Westernized Japanese society—when it placed his portrait on the thousand-yen bill in 1984. But some Japanese consider Natsume too modern, too cut off from traditional values, and too isolated, because of his long experience abroad, from what it means to be Japanese. For such readers, Mori Ōgai is the great thinker and writer of the Meiji period. Mori studied medical hygiene in Germany and won initial acclaim with three romantic short stories—"Maihime" (1890; translated as "The Dancing Girl," 1964), "Utakata no ki" (Foam on the Waves, 1890; translated as "Utakata no ki," 1974, and as "A Sad Tale," 1994), and "Fumizukai" (1891; translated as "The Courier," 1971)—about experiences of Japanese living in that country. In "Maihime" about a promising young Japanese bureaucrat studying in Berlin falls in love with a common German dancing girl. The young man finally chooses career over love, casting his lot with the dictates of society over the promptings of the heart, but he does so with bitterness and regret. Many Japanese readers find such resignation more attractive than Natsume's despair. Mori's novels set in contemporary Japan are not as dramatic or affecting as Natsume's, and they do not deal as forthrightly or as profoundly with the issues of modernization and its impact on the individual. But Mori can draw sympathy to the subtle yearnings of commonplace characters in works such as *Gan* (1915; translated as *The Wild Geese,* 1959), in which a usurer's mistress begins to recognize that hers is a life of entrapment, and that the handsome university student who frequently passes by her house is unavailable as a means of escape. Natsume produced complex, pessimistic psychological studies of the modern isolated individual; meanwhile, Mori, frustrated by the conflicts inherent in his dual position as a writer and as surgeon general for the Japanese army, abandoned the contemporary period altogether in his later years to study feudal loyalty and honor in historical and biographical works that can scarcely be called fictional.

Emperor Meiji died in 1912. The subsequent Taishō period, which lasted until 1926, was characterized as a period of "democratization," with the rise of political parties, but the seeds of military expansionism had already been planted; the Peace Preservation Act of 1925 was only one among many attempts to encourage conformity with national aims. The first important development in Taishō literature was the emergence of the Shirakaba (White Birch) School, a name that symbolized Russian and the particular liberal humanism of Leo Tolstoy. Critical of the earlier trends of Naturalism, which focused on the base aspects of human nature, and of aestheticism, which stressed pleasure, the Shirakaba writers believed in the innate goodness and potential of humanity—particularly their own. Though aggressively optimistic in opposition to the dark pessimism of the Naturalists, the wealthy, self-confident Shirakaba authors continued to write autobiographical narratives in the belief that their lives could serve as a model for others. The best-known author of the group was Shiga Naoya, whose self-confidence produced a strong, direct writing style that earned him the title "the god of fiction" and who depicted strong-willed male characters in many short stories and his only full-length novel, *An'ya kōro* (1922–1937; translated as *A Dark Night's Passing,* 1976). The works of Arishima Takeo, whose upper-class origins and exposure to Christianity challenged him with painful moral dilemmas, include *Aru onna* (1919; translated as *A Certain Woman,* 1978).

The I-novel arose in the middle of the Taishō period. With the anti-idealistic traditions of Naturalism as its heritage and the writer as its central character, the I-novel evolved from the Shirakaba School's self-revelations. Eschewing fabrication, these writers took their material from everyday life. Many autobiographical works of fiction were written, and by the mid 1920s a biocritical approach had emerged in Japan that emphasized the connections between an author's personal experience and his or her writings. Few examples of this important genre have been translated into Western languages; thus, the picture one gets of modern Japanese fiction from reading works in translation is distorted.

The best of Japanese fiction written from the 1920s onward touches on a greater range of human experience. This scope is perhaps best exemplified in the works of Tanizaki Jun'ichirō, regarded by some as the most inventive writer of the modern period. In his early novels, such as *Chijin no ai* (A Fool's Love, 1925; translated as *Naomi,* 1985), and *Manji* (Maelstrom, 1931; translated as *Quicksand,* 1993), the deceptions practiced by the characters are metaphors for the deceptiveness of fiction. Tanizaki is constantly mindful of the writer's responsibility to entertain and of the reader's pleasure in being manipulated and deceived. Tanizaki also possesses a rare capacity to articulate through allegory the cultural confusions of modern Japan. In novels such as *Tade kuu mushi* (1929; translated as *Some Prefer Nettles,* 1955) he seeks a sense of continuity amid contemporary uneasiness by turning to the past; the hero of *Some Prefer Nettles* is an indecisive Westernized Japanese man whose marriage has turned loveless and who begins to discover beauty in such traditional arts as the puppet theater.

Akutagawa Ryūnosuke, perhaps the best writer of short stories modern Japan has produced, set many of his stories in the past, which offered him a freedom that the present could not. His "Hana" (1916; translated as "The Nose," 1961), "Jigokuhen" (1918; translated as *Hell Screen,* 1948), and "Yabu no naka" (1922; translated as "In a Grove," 1952)—the basis for the acclaimed Akira Kurosawa film *Rashō-Mon* (1950)—are brilliantly told, combining psychological subtlety and modern cynicism with a fanciful delight in the grotesque. Akutagawa is a representative figure of the Taishō period because of his tenuous sense of reality and a fragility that seems to have come with the sophistication of the freed imagination.

Akutagawa and Tanizaki seemed more at home in the past; similarly, Nagai Kafū remained loyal to the shadowy neighborhoods of Tokyo that still called up memories of the past. The wandering, solitary old man in his *Bokutō kitan* (1937; translated as *A Strange Tale from East of the River,* 1965) is, paradoxically, not a rootless figure but one firmly placed in surroundings that, however changed, retain for him their historical context.

The enthronement of the emperor Shōwa in 1926 ushered in a radically diverse age; the literature of the period traces Japan's course through militarization, war, defeat and occupation, and rebuilding to international stature. With military expansionism writers, like other citizens, became eligible for the draft and were deprived of freedom of expression; imprisonment and torture were used against those who were critical of the government. The most infamous instance of torture was the 1933 murder of the left-wing writer Kobayashi Takiji during police interrogation. Kobayashi's *Kani kōsen* (Crab Cannery Boat, 1929; translated as *The Factory Ship,* 1973) is the best-known Japanese proletarian novel.

Literary modernism, patterned after the experimental writings of European authors, enjoyed a brief popularity in the early Shōwa period with the formation of the Shinkankaku (New Sensibilities) School, which included Yokomitsu Riichi and Kawabata Yasunari. Using vivid, futuristic images, these writers sought to break through the limitations of the individual; but the experiment was short-lived. After the outbreak of war in Manchuria in September 1931, "modernist" literature was denounced for its superficial imitation of Western modes. Between 1926 and 1931 older writers such as Nagai and Shiga again rose in prominence, while Tanizaki attracted new attention with *Shunkinshō* (A Portrait of Shunkin, 1933; translated as "The Story of Shunkin," 1936). Some writers of the 1930s were persuaded by the authorities to write about their conversion from Marxism, while new authors, such as Dazai Osamu and Ishikawa Jun, used their writings to laugh at their own powerlessness—though the laughter was also a criticism of society. Meanwhile, some of the masterpieces of Shōwa literature, including Kawabata's *Yukiguni* (1937; translated as *Snow Country,* 1956), appeared amid the turmoil.

The best full-length works treating Japan's expansionist war in China include Ishikawa Tatsuzō's *Ikite iru heitai* (Living Soldiers, 1937), which was banned for describing the atrocities committed by the Japanese army in northern China, and Hino Ashihei's trilogy, *Mugi to heitai* (1938; translated as *Barley and Soldiers,* 1939), *Tsuchi to heitai* (1938; translated as *Mud and Sol-*

diers, 1939), and *Hana to heitai* (1939; translated as *Flowers and Soldiers,* 1939).

By 1941, with World War II in progress, even those writers who had been critical of the war in China were affected by the notion of the "sacred war." In 1942 the Nihon Bungaku Hōkokukai (Patriotic Association for Japanese Literature) was established, and virtually all writers were compelled to join. The activities of writers during the war ranged from producing propaganda to making lecture tours of the provinces and occupied territories to explain the cultural superiority of Japan. Communist and socialist writers, who had initially opposed the war, changed their views under censorship and police repression, becoming known as *tenkō* (intellectual conversion) writers. As the war intensified, many works were banned; Tanizaki's *Sasameyuki* (Thin Snow, 1944–1948; translated as *The Makioka Sisters,* 1957) was censored not because it was seditious but because it was considered too "frivolous" in a time of national emergency. Literature was made an instrument of the state, and authors were often drafted to write reports from the front.

Throughout this volume the typical Japanese usage has been followed for presenting all Japanese names: the surname is given first, followed by the given name. Every attempt has been made to include in this volume the most important authors of the period covered. Circumstances have, however, resulted in the omission of a few writers who deserved to be treated. The editor especially regrets the absence of an entry on Tayama, who helped establish the I-novel form in the early twentieth century. Though specialists in the field may bemoan a missing favorite or two, the volume is the first book in English to bring together so many biographical studies of modern Japanese fiction writers. The contributors to the volume comprise a group of critics and translators who have pioneered the study of Japanese fiction in the West over the past several decades, as well as a handful of scholars at Japanese universities. The entries of the latter group have been translated into English by the volume editor, who takes full responsibility for any errors or infelicities that may have resulted.

—*Van C. Gessel*

Acknowledgments

This book was produced by Bruccoli Clark Layman, Inc. Karen L. Rood is senior editor for the *Dictionary of Literary Biography* series. Denis Thomas was the in-house editor.

Administrative support was provided by Ann M. Cheschi and Brenda A. Gillie.

Bookkeeper is Joyce Fowler.

Copyediting supervisors are Laurel M. Gladden Gillespie and Jeff Miller. The copyediting staff includes Phyllis A. Avant, Patricia Coate, Thom Harman, and William L. Thomas Jr.

Editorial associate is L. Kay Webster.

Layout and graphics staff includes Marie L. Parker and Janet E. Hill.

Office manager is Kathy Lawler Merlette.

Photography editors are Julie E. Frick and Margaret Meriwether. Photographic copy work was performed by Joseph M. Bruccoli.

Production manager is Samuel W. Bruce.

Software specialist is Marie L. Parker.

Systems manager is Chris Elmore.

Typesetting supervisor is Kathleen M. Flanagan. The typesetting staff includes Pamela D. Norton and Patricia Flanagan Salisbury. Freelance typesetters include Melody W. Clegg and Delores Plastow.

Walter W. Ross, Steven Gross, and Mark McEwan did library research. They were assisted by the following librarians at the Thomas Cooper Library of the University of South Carolina: Linda Holderfield and the interlibrary-loan staff; reference-department head Virginia Weathers; reference librarians Marilee Birchfield, Stefanie Buck, Stefanie DuBose, Rebecca Feind, Karen Joseph, Donna Lehman, Charlene Loope, Anthony McKissick, Jean Rhyne, Kwamine Simpson, and Virginia Weathers; circulation-department head Caroline Taylor; and acquisitions-searching supervisor David Haggard.

Japanese Fiction Writers, 1868–1945

Dictionary of Literary Biography

Akutagawa Ryūnosuke
(1 March 1892 – 24 July 1927)

James O'Brien
University of Wisconsin–Madison

BOOKS: *Rashōmon* (Tokyo: Oranda Shobō, 1917); translated by Takashi Kojima as *Rashōmon and Other Stories* (Tokyo & Rutland, Vt.: Tuttle, 1952);

Tabako to akuma (Tokyo: Shinchōsha, 1917);

Hana (Tokyo: Shun'yōdō, 1918);

Eitōrō (Tokyo: Shun'yōdō, 1920);

Yarai no hana (Tokyo: Shinchōsha, 1921);

Gesaku zanmai (Tokyo: Shun'yōdō, 1921);

Jigokuhen (Tokyo: Shun'yōdō, 1921); translated by W. H. H. Norman as *Hell Screen and Other Stories* (Tokyo: Hokuseido, 1948);

Aruhi no Ōishi Kuranosuke (Tokyo: Shun'yōdō, 1921);

Imogayu (Tokyo: Shun'yōdō, 1922);

Jashūmon (Tokyo: Shun'yōdō, 1922);

Harugi (Tokyo: Shun'yōdō, 1923);

Kōjakufū (Tokyo: Shinchōsha, 1924);

Akutagawa Ryūnosuke shū (Tokyo: Shinchōsha, 1925);

Saihō no hito (Tokyo: Iwanami Shoten, 1927);

Shuju no kotoba (Tokyo: Bungei Shunjusha, 1927);

Bungeiteki na, amari ni bungeiteki na (Tokyo: Iwanami Shoten, 1931).

Collected edition: *Akutagawa Ryūnosuke zenshū*, 8 volumes (Tokyo: Iwanami Shoten, 1927).

Akutagawa Ryūnosuke

Akutagawa Ryūnosuke committed suicide in 1927 at the age of thirty-five, but he accomplished much during his short writing career. Excelling in the finely crafted short tale, Akutagawa also wrote poetry and several acclaimed prose works. After honing his skills on mostly impersonal tales, he composed several hauntingly personal pieces. Only eight years after Akutagawa's death his stature was officially recognized through the establishment of the Akutagawa Prize for literature. Awarded twice a year, this prize recognizes new literary talent and has become probably the most coveted literary award in Japan.

Before turning to his own life for inspiration as a writer, Akutagawa often relied on other literary works. Japanese scholar Yoshida Seiichi has traced 62 of Akutagawa's 150 or so compositions to various kinds of literary sources. A reader with wide tastes, Akutagawa adopted ideas from mod-

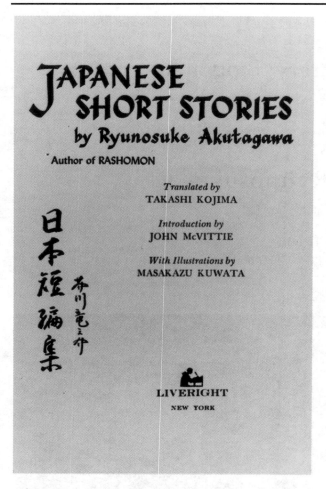

Title page for an American edition of a collection of translated stories that includes Akutagawa's whimsically ironic early piece, "The Nose" (1916)

ern Western writers such as Guy de Maupassant, Edgar Allan Poe, and Nikolay Gogol as well as from collections of medieval Japanese stories. Akutagawa's interest in collections such as the *Konjaku Monogatari* (circa 1120; translated in part as *Tales of Times Now Past* by Marian Ury, 1979) and *Uji Shūi Monogatari* (1210–1220; translated as *A Collection of Tales from Uji* by D. E. Mills, 1970) contributed to a twentieth-century revival of interest in such collections. Well schooled in both Chinese and English, Akutagawa possessed a level of cosmopolitan erudition near that of Natsume Sōseki, an older writer and intellectual who predicted a great future for him.

Akutagawa Ryūnosuke was born in Tokyo, where he remained a lifelong resident. His family name was Niihara (which some scholars also read as Niibara), and Ryūnosuke kept this family name until he was twelve years old, when his mother's family formally adopted him and he became an Akutagawa. At the time of Ryūnosuke's birth, his father was forty-two years old and his mother was thirty-three years old—a combination which, according to a peculiar folk belief that holds these ages to be inauspicious, marked the infant as vulnerable to misfortune. As a protective measure Ryūnosuke immediately had to undergo the ritual of "abandonment and recovery"—that is, to be adopted briefly by another family before being returned to his parents' home. A more serious complication arose when his mother, evidently because she felt responsible for the death of her young daughter, became deranged within a year of Ryūnosuke's birth. Because of his mother's condition, Akutagawa was eventually raised, mainly by a spinster aunt, in his uncle's house. More than a decade after the move, this familial arrangement was officially recognized when Ryūnosuke was formally adopted into the Akutagawa family.

A morbidly sensitive child, Akutagawa was fascinated with books, and his adoptive family provided a nurturing cultural environment for him. Dōshō, his uncle, was an adept composer of haiku, a classical form of poetry containing only three lines and usually consisting of five, seven, and five syllables, respectively. The entire household took instructions in reciting *jōruri,* the texts of the classical puppet theater, and may have encouraged Akutagawa's attachment to ghostly and grotesque tales of the Edo Period. At this stage of his life such Japanese and Chinese stories gave him pleasure; eventually he found similar fare in Western writers such as Ambrose Bierce and Algernon Blackwood.

Akutagawa attended excellent elementary and secondary schools in Tokyo and finished his formal education by majoring in English literature at Tokyo Imperial University, the pinnacle of the Japanese education system. Like so many aspiring authors in Japan, he began by joining like-minded classmates in publishing a magazine. When Akutagawa published a brief tale, "Hana" (1918; translated as "The Nose," 1930), Natsume Sōseki told Akutagawa that he would be without peer in Japanese literary circles if he could produce twenty to thirty such tales, and various commercial magazines began to request that Akutagawa submit work to them. In 1918, the year in which he married, Akutagawa signed a contract with the newspaper *Ōsaka Mainichi Shinbun.* While leaving him free to publish in magazines, this contract prevented him from publishing any of his stories with other newspapers. For his contributions the newspaper paid him an annual stipend as well as a commission, and Akutagawa thus escaped the financial trials that many Japanese writers underwent early in their careers.

Even in his earliest works—as in the title story for *The Nose*, for example—Akutagawa displays a penchant for irony and moralism. The story recounts how a Buddhist priest submits to several painful treatments on his gigantic nose, all of them undertaken in hopes of reducing it to a normal size. When the nose is finally reduced, however, people comment about the change so often that the priest wants it restored to its original size. In this ironic reversal "The Nose" resembles other early Akutagawa tales—"Imogayu" (1922; translated as "Yam Gruel," 1952), for example, or one of two tales titled "Sennin" (1915; translated as "The Immortal," 1988).

In the former work a feckless Heian court official is taken on a long journey after being promised a meal of all the yam gruel he can eat. Although he normally has an insatiable craving for the gruel and even complains about a minute serving that he receives at an annual court banquet, the huge quantities that his principal tormentor prepares for him soon disgust him. After the official has forced down a considerable amount, his tormentor evidently leaves him relieved—and wiser.

In "Sennin" a Chinese itinerant who makes a precarious living by directing an exhibit of performing mice becomes fabulously rich after he meets a Taoist, a member of a Chinese cult that incorporates certain magical practices. In effect, the itinerant trades places with the religious adept, who, in a coda to the tale, expresses his dissatisfaction with immortality. It appears that the monotony of immortal life has instilled in the Taoist a desire for the contingencies of mortality, of human life.

Sudden reversals of fortune often occur in the works of Akutagawa, as in "Hyottoko" (1915; translated as "The Clown's Mask," 1969) and in Rash»mon (1917; translated as *Rashō Gate,* 1930). "The Clown's Mask" presents a theme of self-deception and reveals Akutagawa's interest in the doppelgänger, one that he might have developed from reading Western writers such as Fyodor Dostoyevsky, E. T. W. Hoffman, and Poe. The title refers initially to the clown's mask that the protagonist wears as he dances madly on a festively decorated river barge. As his antics attract attention, the dancer suddenly collapses in a fatal seizure. The narrative then reviews the man's life—and distinguishes between his sober and his inebriated personae. The final paragraph describes the face of the dead man, its pinched and oily surface starkly contrasting with the unchanged expression of his discarded mask, now "turned silently upon the dead man." Akutagawa occasionally enjoyed decadent writing, and such a scene reveals that he was an avid reader of Oscar Wilde: the similarities between Akutagawa's conclusion and the final scene of Wilde's *The Picture of Dorian Gray* (1891) seem beyond question.

Rashōmon is familiar to devotees of the cinema, for *Rashōmon*—the screenplay written by Shinobu Hashimoto and Akira Kurosawa and directed by Kurosawa in 1950—was the first Japanese motion picture to win wide international acclaim. The plot of the movie derives mainly from Akutagawa's story "Yabu No Naka" (1921; translated as "Within a Grove," 1952), but Akutagawa's *Rashōmon* concerns a crucial decision in the life of a male servant who has recently been dismissed by his master. Pondering how to survive in the chaos of the times, the servant is reluctant to follow the obvious course of turning to thievery. However, as he listens to an old woman explain that she plucks the hair from a corpse to make wigs, he begins to lose his scruples. If she must violate another human being to make her living, why should he not do likewise? Turning the woman's self-justification against her, the man strips off her garment and flees into the night with this booty.

The historical settings of these stories by Akutagawa vary considerably—from the Heian capital of the late twelfth century in *Rashōmon* to Akutagawa's contemporary Tokyo in "The Clown's Mask." Occasionally his work focuses on political matters—as, for example, in *Aruhi no Ōishi Kuranosuke* (Ōishi Kuranosuke on a Certain Day, 1921). However, when the settings of his stories are close to his own times, the works usually avoid issues of wide social and political import. Exhibiting a distaste for the mundane, Akutagawa treated contemporary material as fantasy, at least until the later stages of his life. Foreign lands—such as China, which he especially favored—often provide the settings for works in which he unleashes this distaste through fantasy. As he searched the works of earlier writers for inspiration, Akutagawa focused on the specific anecdote or description to refashion his material, as one finds in *Jigokuhen* (1921; translated as *Hell Screen and Other Stories,* 1948). The character and fate of the artist in this story probably come from medieval tales collected in both *Uji Shūi Monogatari* (1210–1220; translated as *A Collection of Tales from Uji,* 1970) and *Kokon Chomonjū*

THE STORY OF YONOSUKE

老え介の話

Woodcut frontispiece by Masakazu Kuwata for an American edition of Japanese Short Stories *(1971)*

(Record of Things Heard, Past and Present), a collection of moral tales compiled by Tachibana Narisue in 1254. *Jigokuhen* illustrates Akutagawa's ability to combine motifs from diverse sources. The motif of the demonic artist, one ready to sacrifice even his most precious possessions for the sake of his art, is evident in many Japanese tales: the *Uji Shūi Monogatari,* for instance, depicts an artist who watches a neighbor's house burn to the ground so that he can paint the figure of Fudō Myōō, the god of fire in esoteric Buddhism.

Hell Screen concerns a tacit rivalry involving Yoshihide, a painter who attempts to paint a picture of hell at the behest of Lord Horikawa, his ruler. An artist of demonic intensity, Yoshihide is one who must first see what he is to paint, and the lengths to which he goes in order to do this—peering closely at rotting corpses, for example—reveal the fascination that Akutagawa, also

as an artist, has with the decadent.

The principal complication of the plot lies in Yoshihide's need to see a carriage set afire, specifically one with "a lovely woman of high birth inside." Lord Horikawa agrees to this request—but he places Yoshihide's own daughter in the carriage. According to the standard interpretation of the story, the lord sacrifices the daughter both to punish the artist for being arrogant and to get revenge against her, for she has rejected the lord's advances.

Having witnessed this horrible immolation of his daughter, the artist completes a screen with an unnatural power that impresses all who see it—including both Lord Horikawa and a rather conventional-minded abbot, representatives of civil and religious authority, respectively. Yet by allowing his daughter to perish for the sake of his art, Yoshihide sacrifices himself as a father: after presenting the completed screen, he immediately takes his own life. "Hell Screen" shows that art transcends all things, including the artist.

Several technical features make this story, a relatively long one by Akutagawa, a complex work. The narrator, who has witnessed the main events and recounts the tale in its entirety, is a servant of Lord Horikawa. This servant, in awe of the lord, nevertheless unwittingly recounts events in ways that undercut his reverential view of his master. By his expressions of humility and ignorance, the narrator seems to assert his credibility, but he proves to be quite unreliable. At best, one can conclude that he, like the lord and the abbot, represents a conventional view of society that only inadvertently acknowledges the supreme authority of art. The presence of a pet monkey with the same name as the artist, Yoshihide, also complicates the narrative—particularly when the monkey invariably acts as a paternal surrogate toward the daughter, while the painter remains deeply engaged in his art.

Another tale published in the same year as *Hell Screen* also presents some fascinating complications of plot and point of view. "Kesa to Moritō" (1918; translated as "Kesa and Moritō," 1956) briefly juxtaposes two dramatic monologues to create a striking reversal of expectations: a wife who has conspired to have her lover kill her husband decides to make herself the victim, a substitution that the lover realizes only after he has committed the crime. Although far briefer than *Hell Screen,* "Kesa and Moritō" also shows Akutagawa experimenting with techniques of indirection and leaving the reader to

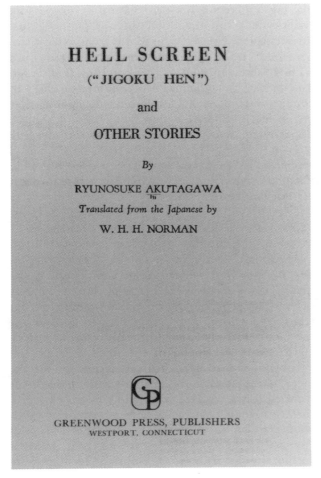

*Title page for an American edition of the translation of Akutagawa's 1921 book, with the illustration
for one of the stories, "Jashumon" (Heresy)*

find the proper bearings for the tale.

During this period Akutagawa was also working intently on purely historical tales. "Chūtō" (1917; translated as "The Robbers," 1964), a long narrative set in the Tokugawa Period, presents sexual jealousy in a manner reminiscent of Prosper Mérimée's *Carmen* (1847), a work with which Akutagawa was familiar. "Ōishi Kuranosuke on a Certain Day" speculatively presents certain doubts that the leader of the forty-seven *rōnin*, or masterless samurai, felt in carrying out a vendetta celebrated both in popular accounts of Tokugawa history and in plays of the Kabuki theater.

Illustrating Akutagawa's practice of remaining eclectic and experimental, two deft sketches from 1918 and 1919 sharply contrast with these lengthy historical pieces. "Kumo no ito" (1918; translated as "The Spiderthread," 1930) shows the author at his ironic best. He begins by depicting a peaceful day in Paradise, with the Buddha stroll-ing about the perimeter of the lotus pond. Happening to glance downward, the Buddha notices excruciating happenings in hell, particularly those involving Kandata, a thief, who has performed one trivial good deed during his life. To recognize this, Buddha lowers a nearby spider thread to allow him to ascend to Paradise. Kandata manages to clamber well above the lake of blood and the mountain of spikes where he and his fellow sinners are being punished. However, when he realizes that these sinners are also following immediately behind him and thus intolerably straining the thread, Kandata characteristically begins shouting and kicking at the other sinners to get them off his rope. The rope tears under this stress, and Kandata plummets back into hell along with his fellow sinners. The Buddha continues his stroll, and the lotus flowers in Paradise give off their usual noontime fragrance.

In "Mikan" (1919; translated as "Tangerines," 1961) the irony is directed at the narrator, seemingly the author's own persona. The sketch opens with the narrator sitting in a railway carriage and waiting for the train to leave the station. Already in a foul mood, he becomes angrier when a peasant girl rushes in at the last moment and, as the train pulls away and enters a nearby tunnel, opens the window by her seat. As smoke pours into the carriage, the narrator becomes furious at the girl. However, when the train emerges from the tunnel and she tosses some tangerines out the window to several boys who are waving farewell to her, he feels ashamed of his earlier contempt for the girl.

The closing moment of remorseful goodwill in this anecdote is hardly typical of Akutagawa. "Hankechi" (1916; translated as "The Handkerchief," 1930), a wicked little sketch, is often read as a satire on Nitobe Inazō, the Japanese educator whose *Bushido: The Soul of Japan* (1900) provided an explanation for the nation's rapid modernization. Nitobe, who was principal of the First Higher School in Tokyo while Akutagawa was a student there, appears in "The Handkerchief" as a law professor who ponders questions such as whether Bushidō, the cult of loyalty followed by the samurai of medieval times, is Japan's spiritual equivalent to Europe's Christianity. The professor also ponders certain things that he has learned about acting from having read August Strindberg's *Dramaturgie* (1911).

A well-dressed, middle-aged woman—the mother of one of his students whom the professor knows has been hospitalized—visits the professor and informs him that her son has in fact recently died, yet she speaks so imperturbably of this that the professor is astonished. Only when he picks up her fan and observes her trembling hands clinging to her handkerchief does he realize how distraught she is. The concluding commentary depicts the professor as perplexed by his encounter with the woman. Although he has spoken favorably of this woman's emotional discipline to his own wife (who happens to be an American, as was Nitobe's spouse), the professor's doubts derive from Strindberg's remark about how well one actress had mastered a certain "mannerism"—that of smiling even as she portrays grief by nearly tearing her handkerchief in two. The professor and the reader are thus left doubting the authenticity of the woman's conduct that afternoon.

During the early 1920s Akutagawa wrote many stories on the topics of doubt and skepticism. "Saigō Takamori" (1917; translated, 1964) leaves the reader doubting whether the author is playing a joke on his protagonist or expressing skepticism about the possibility of knowing historical truth. The story presents a university student on a train, where he gets into a discussion with a stranger who convinces him that Saigō Takamori, the soldier and revolutionary, did not commit suicide in a battle some decades earlier but in fact is asleep on that same train. Although the stranger eventually reveals that the sleeping man is actually an acquaintance who merely resembles Saigō, the student is left deeply shaken about the possibility of discovering truth through historical investigation.

Akutagawa pursued a similar theme four years later in "Yabu No Naka" (translated as "Within a Grove"), which presents a judicial hearing into the circumstances surrounding a death. After four peripheral witnesses testify, the three principals—a man, his wife, and a famous robber named Tajōmaru—recount events that transpired within a grove of cedars. Except for the fact that the man is dead (and must therefore testify from the realm of the dead through the agency of a medium), little is certain about the facts of the case, and so, after each of the three principals has testified, the reader is no closer to the truth than before. Each version that is given conflicts with those given by the other two, and Akutagawa gives no hint as to the truth. In what seems an unwarranted attempt to decide where the author's sympathies lie, certain critics have resorted to biographical interpretation by claiming that Akutagawa's alleged misogyny calls into question the testimony of the wife, at least.

In "Kage" (1920; translated as "The Shadow," 1988) Akutagawa uses the doppelgänger to convey deep-seated doubt and skepticism in a third story. In spite of its sophisticated psychology and symbolism, "The Shadow" has attracted little attention either in Japan or abroad. Suspicious of his young, beautiful Japanese wife, a Chinese businessman living in Japan hires a detective agency to spy on his house. After he telephones that business reasons will prevent him from returning home one evening, he slips back after dark, spies on the house from outside, and eventually breaks into his wife's bedroom to confront her in the company of a lover.

He strangles her but then discovers that the lover is his own double—a revelation which explains why his wife often felt that she was being watched by someone even when her husband was absent. "The Shadow" combines dialogue with tersely worded descriptive passages, the piece suggesting a film scenario. Certain motifs

Dust jacket for an American edition of translated stories including "The Handkerchief," "The Robbers," and "The Kappa"

in the tale strengthen this association with film. The businessman gazes at his wife's illuminated bedroom while standing in the darkness outside; when he approaches the bedroom door, the beam of light from the keyhole suggests the working of a movie projector.

In any event the final passage shifts to a totally different context. A first-person narrator, hitherto absent from the story, now appears in a movie theater sitting next to a woman companion. "So that's how it ends," he remarks, this observation leading to a conversation between the two people which reveals that each has seen a different movie. The woman presently dismisses the puzzle, leaving the reader to ponder the problem.

Akutagawa uses the plains of north China as the initial setting for an even more bewildering tale, "Uma no ashi" (1925; translated as "Horse Legs"). A Japanese soldier, slain in battle during war, is temporarily refused entry into the underworld and sent back to earth by the underworld surgical team that has attended to his wounds. Unfortunately, the only healthy legs available at the time of his surgery have been those of a horse, and, equipped with this new set of legs, the former soldier must keep this fact hidden—even from his wife. He manages to do so even when the two are in bed together, but when the urge to mate rises in him, he cannot resist:

neighing frantically, he rushes from the house and heads toward the Continent.

Akutagawa wrote several tales about Christian belief and practice, his most willful treatment of which occurs in "Hōkyōnin no shi" (1918; translated as "The Martyr," 1952), also a story with highly improbable events. Set in the sixteenth century when many Japanese converted to Christianity, the narrative concerns Lorenzo, a young Japanese Christian. Befriended by a group of Jesuit brothers serving a parish in Nagasaki, Lorenzo impresses everyone with his saintly nature. After some years, however, a girl claims that Lorenzo is responsible for her pregnancy. He denies the accusation but offers no convincing alibi. Rejected by the Jesuits, he is compelled to live as a beggar. His innocence is apparent only in the final scene, when a huge fire breaks out one night in Nagasaki and he rushes into a burning building to rescue the child he has been accused of fathering. As Lorenzo subsequently lies near death from having battled the smoke and flames, the child's mother, overcome with remorse, confesses that she had falsely accused him. Lorenzo's innocence is further confirmed by a discovery that he is in fact a woman.

This story employs a tactic Akutagawa uses in other stories—that is, withholding information that provides a fundamentally different perspective on the narrative until the last possible moment. Indeed, Shiga Naoya, a short-story writer whom Akutagawa greatly admired, complained about the use of this tactic in "The Martyr." Some readers might regard Akutagawa's use of this tactic as deceptive; others, however, might argue that it signals his unremitting interest in the deceptive nature of appearances and the elusive nature of truth.

During the final years of his career Akutagawa wrote fewer historical and mythic works and began writing partly autobiographical stories. From 1922 to 1925 he composed the Yasukichi Tales, a series of ten stories narrated in the third person, as if the author were hesitant about writing autobiographically. The protagonist is Horikawa Yasukichi, a poorly paid English instructor at the Yokosuka naval engineering school and a barely disguised version of Akutagawa. Critics generally found Akutagawa overly tentative in using his life for material in these stories.

If he needed to adopt a bolder approach to writing from personal experience, Akutagawa was ready to do so. Even before he completed the Yasukichi series, Akutagawa in 1924 published "Daidōji Shinsuke no hansei" (The Youth of Daidōji Shinsuke), a set of observations on the upbringing of an aspiring writer. The account is usually taken as autobiographical; certainly each of the six segments presents material closely related to Akutagawa's interests and experience—his omnivorous reading, for example, or the genteel poverty (as he saw it) in which his family's declining fortunes left him. The work aroused critical interest, and Akutagawa promised to continue it.

Yet for whatever reasons, he did not focus exclusively on autobiographical material. Instead, he spent the final two years of his life on works that broadened his pessimistic view of society or offered a concentrated look at his current state of mind. "Tenkibo" (The Death Register, 1926) contains references to dead members of his family: his father and mother (her insanity is unforgettably evoked in the opening section), as well as the sister who had died even before Akutagawa was born. His description of a visit to the family grave hints strongly that he will soon join them.

Although less explicitly autobiographical than "The Youth of Daidōji Shinsuke," "Aru ahō no isshō" (1927; translated as "A Fool's Life," 1970) gives considerable insight into his tribulations. Read as a direct reference to Akutagawa, the title also suggests the nature of any artist's life. The fifty-one sections of the work deal with such matters as illness, insanity, and death.

"Haguruma" (1927; translated as "Cogwheels," 1965) provides a psychological sketch that most vividly reveals Akutagawa's fear that he was on the verge of insanity. Published posthumously, it presents a host of impressions that crowd upon a writer as he visits Tokyo, where, obsessed with his work, he spends much of his time in a hotel room. A series of ominous incidents occurs during this brief time: the writer learns that his brother-in-law has committed suicide, and he remembers an anecdote about a raincoat that seems to foreshadow that suicide. Above all, he has visions of turning cogwheels.

A work of fantasy published that same year provides a philosophic gloss to the visions that Akutagawa presents in "Cogwheels." *Kappa* (1927; translated, 1947) suggests the range of Akutagawa's reading; his inspiration for the work is usually attributed to Anatole France's *L' Ile des pingouins* (1908; translated as *Penguin Island,* 1909), Samuel Butler's *Erewhon; or Over the Range* (1872), and Jonathan Swift's *Travels into Several Remote Nations of the World, in Four Parts, by Lemuel Gulliver* (1726). In Akutagawa's work the protagonist sojourns in the land of the *kappa,* amphibious creatures of grotesque appearance. There Akutagawa's narrator discovers, as does Gulliver, that perspective and custom can change radically from one civilization to another. Women pursue men in the kappa world; aware of the horrible nature of existence, infants have the power of choosing not to be born.

Scholars have determined that Akutagawa considered committing suicide for a year or more. The circumstances surrounding his death show that he undertook his suicide with the same deliberation that he brought to his craft. In his often-quoted "Aru kyūyū e okuru shuki" (1927; translated as "Memorandum to a Certain Friend," 1987) Akutagawa describes how he pondered various methods of suicide before he eventually decided to take an overdose of drugs. He considered this a relatively foolproof method and the one least likely to inflict either physical pain on himself or psychological pain on his family.

Reticent about his ultimate view of the matter, Akutagawa referred merely to a "vague uneasiness" to explain why he had decided to take his life. These words are often interpreted to refer to the historical situation of the late 1920s. The Taishō Period ended in 1926, and the Japanese experiment in democracy often associated with the decade and a half of that era seemed to have reached a dead end. The militaristic tyranny that would gain strength during the 1930s and result in the disaster of World War II was to come.

Any attempt to evaluate the place of Akutagawa Ryūnosuke in modern fiction must acknowledge the radical changes that Japanese literature underwent in the twentieth century. Many argue that the nation exemplifies postmodernism in its highest form, with much of its contemporary literature reflecting this state. Except for such figures as Natsume Sōseki and Kawabata Yasunari, twentieth-century prose writers are constantly exposed to the vagaries of critical opinion.

Yet accounts of Japanese prose invariably stress the historical importance of Akutagawa. Historians often emphasize his role in the so-called plot controversy—a rather mild, inconclusive dispute between Akutagawa and Tanizaki Jun'ichiro over the claims of autobiographical fact and fictionality in literature—rather than his achievement in specific works such as "Hell Screen." Other historians often construe the impact of his suicide as his main legacy to aspiring writers.

Letters:

Akutagawa Ryūnosuke zenshū volumes 7 and 8 (Tokyo: Chikuma Shobō, 1986–1989).

References:

Akutagawa Ryūnosuke, Issatsu no Kōza: Nihon no Kindai Bungaku series (Tokyo: Yuseidō, 1982);

Ebii Eiji and Miyasaka Satoru, eds., *Sakuhinron Akutagawa Ryūnosuke* (Tokyo: Sōbunsha, 1990);

Fukuda Kiyoto and Kasai Akifu, *Akutagawa Ryūnosuke* (Tokyo: Shimizu Shoin, 1969);

Howard S. Hibbett, "Akutagawa Ryūnosuke and the Negative Ideal," in *Personality in Japanese History,* edited by Albert M. Craig and Donald Shively (Berkeley: University of California Press, 1970), pp. 425–451;

Ishiwari Tōru, ed., *Akutagawa Ryūnosuke: sakka to sono jidai* (Tokyo: Yuseidō, 1987);

Kasai Akifu, *Akutagawa Ryūnosuke sakuhin kenkyū* (Tokyo: Sōbunsha, 1993);

Donald Keene, "Akutagawa Ryūnosuke," in his *Dawn to the West* (New York: Holt, Rinehart & Winston, 1984), pp. 556–593;

Kikuchi Hiroshi and others, eds., *Akutagawa Ryūnosuke kenkyū* (Tokyo: Meiji Shoin, 1981);

Makoto Ueda, "Akutagawa Ryūnosuke," in his *Modern Japanese Writers and the Nature of Literature* (Stanford, Cal.: Stanford University Press, 1976), pp. 111–145;

Miyasaka Satoru, ed., *Akutagawa Ryūnosuke: richi to jojō* (Tokyo: Yūseidō, 1993);

Miyoshi Yukio, *Akutagawa Ryūnosuke ron* (Tokyo: Chikuma Shobō, 1993);

Morimoto Osamu, *Shinkō Akutagawa Ryūnosuke den* (Tokyo: Kitazawa Tosho Shuppan, 1971);

Takeuchi Makoto, *Akutagawa Ryūnosuke no Kenkyū,* Kindai Sakka Kenkyū Sōsho series (Tokyo: Nihon Tosho Sentā, 1987);

Uno Kōji, *Akutagawa Ryūnosuke* (Tokyo: Chikuma Shobō, 1973);

Yoshida Seiichi, *Akutagawa Ryūnosuke,* 2 volumes (Tokyo: Ōfūsha, 1979);

Beongcheon Yu, *Akutagawa: An Introduction* (Detroit: Wayne State University Press, 1972).

Arishima Takeo
(4 March 1878 – 9 June 1923)

Leith Morton
University of Newcastle

BOOKS: *Ribingusuton den,* by Arishima and Morimoto Kōkichi (Tokyo: Keiseisha Shoten, 1901; republished, with new autobiographical preface by Arishima, 1919);

Arishima Takeo chosaku shū, volume 1 (Tokyo: Shinchōsha, 1917)–includes "Osue no Shi," translated by Leith Morton as "The Death of Osue," in *Seven Stories of Modern Japan,* edited by Morton (Sydney: University of Australia, 1991); "Shi to sono zengo"; and "Heibonjin no tegami";

Arishima Takeo chosaku shū, volume 2 (Tokyo: Shinchōsha, 1918)–includes "Sengen";

Arishima Takeo chosaku shū, volume 3 (Tokyo: Shinchōsha, 1918)–includes "Kain no matsuei," translated by John W. Morrison as "Descendants of Cain," in *Modern Japanese Fiction,* edited by Morrison (Salt Lake City: University of Utah Press, 1955); "Jikkenshitsu"; and "Kurara no shūkke";

Arishima Takeo chosaku shū, volume 4 (Tokyo: Shinchōsha, 1918)–includes "Hangyakusha" and "Kusa no ha";

Arishima Takeo chosaku shū, volume 5 (Tokyo: Shinchōsha, 1918)–includes *Meiro,* translated by Sanford Goldstein and Shinoda Seishi as *Labyrinth* (Lanham, N.Y. & London: Madison Books, 1992);

Arishima Takeo chosaku shū, volume 6 (Tokyo: Sōbunkaku, 1918)–includes *Umareizuru nayami,* translated by Seiji Fujita as *The Agony of Coming into the World* (Tokyo: Hokuseido Press, 1955); and "Ishi ni hishigareta zassō";

Arishima Takeo chosaku shū, volume 7 (Tokyo: Sōbunkaku, 1918)–includes "An Incident," "Chiisaki mono e," and "Gasu";

Arishima Takeo chosaku shū, volume 8 (Tokyo: Sōbunkaku, 1919)–includes "Aru onna no gurimpusu";

Arishima Takeo chosaku shū, volume 9 (Tokyo: Sōbunkaku, 1919)–includes *Aru onna,* trans-

Arishima Takeo

lated by Kenneth Strong as *A Certain Woman* (Tokyo: University of Tokyo Press, 1978);

Arishima Takeo chosaku shū, volume 10 (Tokyo: Sōbunkaku, 1919)–includes *Daikōzui no mae, Samuson to Deraira,* and *Seisan*;

Ibusen Kenkyu (Tokyo: Daigaku Hyōronsha, 1920);

Arishima Takeo chosaku shū, volume 11 (Tokyo: Sōbunkaku, 1920)–includes *Oshiminaku ai wa ubau*;

Arishima Takeo chosaku shū, volume 12 (Tokyo: Sōbunkaku, 1920)–includes *Tabi suru kokoro*;

Arishima Takeo chosaku shū, volume 13 (Tokyo: Sōbunkaku, 1921)–includes *Jiko no yōkyū* and *Burando*;

Hoittoman shishū volume 1 (Tokyo: Sōbunkaku, 1921);

Arishima Takeo chosaku shū, volume 14 (Tokyo: Sōbunkaku, 1922)–includes *Seiza;*

Hitofusa no budō (Tokyo: Sōbunkaku, 1922);

Arishima Takeo chosaku shū, volume 15 (Tokyo: Sōbunkaku, 1922)–includes *Egakareta hana* and *Sengen hitotsu;*

Hoittoman shishū, volume 2 (Tokyo: Sōbunkaku, 1923).

Collections: *Arishima Takeo zenshū,* 12 volumes, edited by Asuke Soichi and Koizumi Magane (Tokyo: Sōbunkaku, 1924–1925);

Arishima Takeo zenshū, 10 volumes, edited by Oda Masanobu (Tokyo: Shinchōsha, 1929–1930);

Arishima Takeo zenshū, 3 volumes, edited by Arishima Ikuma (Tokyo: Kaizōsha, 1931);

Arishima Takeo zenshū, 16 volumes, edited by Senuma Shigeki and others (Tokyo: Chikuma Shobō, 1979–1988).

Arishima Takeo is one of Japan's most significant twentieth-century novelists. In using romantic and political themes to create psychological dramas almost Gothic in their emotional intensity, his experiments in the *shōsetsu,* or novel genre, are among the most interesting and adventurous produced by his generation. In addition to translating Walt Whitman into Japanese, Arishima also wrote poetry, plays, and essays on various themes and produced much polemical writing on literature, art, and social and political issues. After his death he became known for having been an assiduous diarist. Covering more than twenty volumes, his diary provides an intimate record of his life, a chronicle of his fears and hopes, both for his own future and that of Japan.

His contemporaries regarded Arishima as a thinker and social critic as much as a novelist. In actively discussing religious and political issues such as female emancipation, class conflict, the suitability of Christianity for Japan, the political role of literature, and the role of the intelligentsia in society, he was an idealist in an age when Japan had embarked on an imperialist path that seemed to brook no dissent from intellectuals. His decision in 1922 to give estates he had inherited from his father to peasant farmers marked the peak of his popularity as a social figure; like Count Leo Tolstoy, Arishima was seen as a radical reformer who sought to act in conformity with his principles. Unable to abide the compromises demanded by an increasingly intolerant and authoritarian Japan, he committed suicide in 1923 with a beautiful young journalist married to a prominent businessman, outraging conservatives but adding to his image as a humanist pursuing an ideal of love.

Arishima was born in his father's house in Tokyo, by that time the capital of a thriving, modern state. His father, Takeshi, was from the Satsuma domain in Kyūshū and was a bureaucrat turned banker who moved in the highest official circles. In 1896 he left considerable wealth and estates to Takeo, his oldest son. Yukiko, the boy's mother, was also from a samurai family, and she bore six other children, including the painter Arishima Ikuma and the novelist Satomi Ton. Arishima Takeo grew up in the port city of Yokohama, where his father was head of the customs office, and from an early age he mingled freely with westerners. He attended a mission school until 1887, when he returned to Tokyo to enter the aristocratic Gakushūin, or Peers School, which was established for the children of the Meiji elite. Students from this background normally continued their educations at Tokyo University, but in 1896 Arishima chose to attend the Sapporo Agricultural College on the northern island of Hokkaidō.

Arishima converted to Christianity in Sapporo, and from 1903 to 1907 he made the customary tour abroad, which he spent mainly as a student in the United States. After graduating with a master's degree from Haverford College in Pennsylvania, he returned to Sapporo to teach English and marry Kamio Yasuko, another Christian, who bore him three sons before dying of tuberculosis in 1916. Following the deaths of his wife and of his father in that same year Arishima left his university post and became a full-time writer. His experience in the United States had left Arishima disgusted with the hypocrisy of the Christian church. Socialism, he believed, provided a far more effective conscience than Christianity, and although he retained some Christian ideas throughout his life, he had become unable to accept the doctrine of atonement.

While studying at the Library of Congress, Arishima in 1906 wrote his first major work of fiction, which was eventually rewritten and published as "Kan kan mushi" (Rust-Chipping Grubs) in 1910. He had originally set this tale of rebellion among wharf dwellers in Yokohama, but by 1910 he had shifted the locale to Russia, a change that added political overtones to the events recounted by an anonymous narrator in conversation with his boss, Yakov Ilyich. The story concerns the abortive romance between Ephrahim, a Turkish laborer, and Katya, Yakov's

Arishima in 1908, the year of his marriage (courtesy of the Library of Modern Japanese Literature)

metaphor, he deliberately salts the dialogue of Yakov and Ephrahim with Yokohama working-class slang. The story so strongly reminded readers of Maksim Gorky's blend of romanticism and realism that one of Arishima's friends suggested that Arishima wrote the story as a prank, to tempt critics into arguing that it was a translation of a work by Gorky.

This comment reveals the distance between Arishima and the mainstream of Japanese fiction. The year in which he wrote the story is generally considered to mark the preeminence of naturalism in the Japanese novel. A prevailing mood of gloom, which seemed characteristic of Japanese society following the end of the Russo-Japanese War, distinguished such fiction in Japan. Arishima read Gorky and other writers in translation while he was in the United States, and Gorky and Henrik Ibsen—rather than Katai and Doppo—provided his first literary models.

The story was published in the *Shirakaba* (White Birch) magazine, one of the main sources of information on Western art for the intelligentsia and a journal that challenged the dominance of naturalism by publishing the literature and art criticism of a group of iconoclastic writers from both the bourgeoisie and the aristocracy. The exotic, foreign features of "Rust-Chipping Grubs" comprise parts of a romantic reaction against the naturalists. In 1910 Arishima also expressed his admiration for Gothic art in "Hangyakusha" (Rebels), an article extolling the rebellious spirit of other artists such as Ibsen, Tolstoy, Whitman, Edouard Manet, and Paul Cézanne—who comprised his pantheon of heroes. Arishima claims that the Gothic "beautification of ugliness" paradoxically betokens its revolutionary nature. Arishima extolled paradox in his notions that two contrary impulses, the Apollonian and the Dionysian, oppressed humanity, or that a path of good and a path of evil existed. In "Futatsu no michi" (The Two Paths), another essay published in *Shirakaba* in 1910, he succinctly expressed this belief. He was much given to emotional extremes, as his diary vividly demonstrates, and these extremes began to appear in his fiction from about this time.

"Osue no shi" (1914; translated as "The Death of Osue," 1991), an early story published in *Shirakaba,* presents the unhappy tale of Osue, a fourteen-year-old girl whose family runs a barbershop in Sapporo but is struggling to survive because of an economic depression. Osue's family members, including her father and two brothers, die one after another, and the narrative im-

daughter. Ephrahim's rival for Katya's hand is an accountant, Grigori Petonikov, a "human" rather than a "grub" (the term Yakov uses for the working-class laborers), and the contrast between the lives of the "humans" and the "grubs" whom they oppress is the focus of the work.

Arishima's style is as interesting as the tale. Writing in a mannered tone that is heavy with plicitly links their deaths to their poverty. Overcome with guilt at the possibility that she may have caused her sister's baby to die, Osue eventually commits suicide. But Osue's sense of guilt is also tacitly associated with her emerging sexuality, and Arishima's writing is charged with emotion in portraying the psychic states of Osue and her elder brother.

The same stylistic excess became even more apparent after Arishima decided to quit his academic post in Sapporo in 1917 to become a full-time author. Three stories written in 1917—"Kain no matsuei" (translated as "Descendants of Cain," 1955), "Kurara no shukke" (The Ordination of Clara), and "Jikkenshitsu" (The Laboratory)—all incorporate Gothic stylistic excesses that distinguish his fiction.

"Descendants of Cain," his most well known work published in this year, drew immediate acclaim. This story tells of Hirooka Nin'emon, an itinerant laborer who, with his wife, horse, and baby, arrives at a small village during a fierce Hokkaidō winter. They are oppressed by the harshness of nature; the cruel exploitation of Matsukawa, a landlord; and their own natural allies, the other tenant farmers who come to fear and hate Nin'emon. Failing in his attempt to rouse the other tenant farmers to challenge Matsukawa, Nin'emon eventually loses his child to dysentery, his money to gambling, and his horse to death after its legs are broken. Striding into the icy winter with only his wife at his side, Nin'emon abandons the village.

This protagonist reminds the reader of Ibsen's harsh Pastor Brand (about whom Arishima wrote repeatedly)—defiant until the end, possessed of an almost supernatural energy, and more of a wild, primal force than a man. Nin'emon's irrational, instinctual nature is evident in his brutish affair with the wife of a neighbor: his encounters with her verge on the sadistic, but she responds just as passionately. Arishima's use of dialect, his unvarnished naturalism in descriptions, and his vivid presentation of Nin'emon's perverse sexuality heralded for readers a realism previously unseen in Japanese letters. But the florid rhetoric of Arishima's prose and his concern with the bestial nature of sexual passion are better understood in relation to the Gothic romance of nineteenth-century European fiction—as in the writings of Charlotte or Emily Brontë—or to that in the works of twentieth-century novelists such as D. H. Lawrence. Japanese writers who preceded Arishima, as well as his contemporaries, were affected by this disconcerting mix-

Dust jacket for Aru onna (A Certain Woman, 1919), in which Arishima expressed his anger at sexual inequality in society

ture of naturalism and romanticism. Among those whose writing both attracted Arishima's attention (sometimes negatively) and displayed similar stylistic features were the novelists Kōda Rohan and Izumi Kyōka.

Arishima's deep interests in the psyche and in melodramatic excess are revealed also in "The Ordination of Clara," which relates the events of Palm Sunday, 18 March 1212. The story mainly recounts the dreams of eighteen-year-old Clara Sciffi, who, influenced by the example of Francis Bernardone (later to become Saint Francis of Assisi), flees from her wealthy family and eventually becomes Saint Clara. The young woman is secretly in love with Francis, and her love for him inspires her to take vows. But Arishima's chief concern is the depiction of not only Clara's religious sensitivity but also her sexuality and her mystical Christianity. He presents Clara's psyche mainly through recounting her dreams, which are rich in sexual imagery. For example, one passage from the work recalls Saint Teresa of Avila, as Arishima tells of Clara's mystical experience when

Gabriel thrust his flaming sword deep down between her breasts. The burning sword-tip penetrated to her bowels. In the midst of her agony Clara raised her eyes and looked about. In a dazzling light, the severe figure of Christ hanging on the

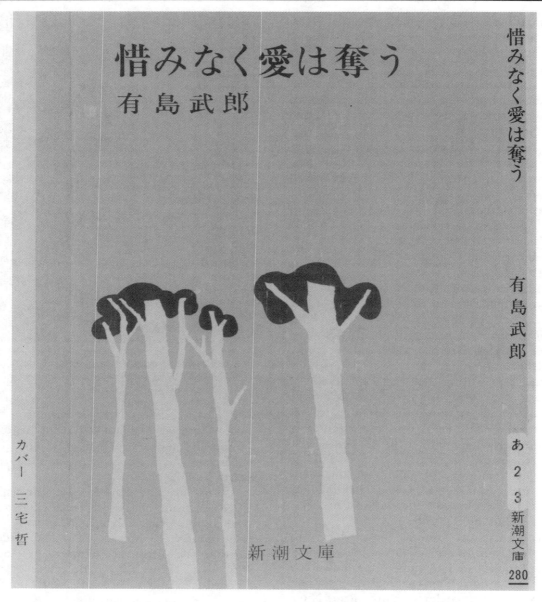

Dust jacket for Oshiminaku ai wa ubau *(Love Deprives Unconditionally, 1920),*
Arishima's essay on the nature of love

cross appeared, shimmering, before her. Clara was in ecstasy.

The last of Arishima's three major works published in 1918 is "The Laboratory," undoubtedly one of his most Gothic pieces. The work resembles Kyōka's "Gekashitsu" (The Operating Room, 1895), in which a surgeon operates on his married lover who refuses an anesthetic, so determined is she to keep their relationship secret. The protagonist of "The Laboratory" is Dr. Mitani, a one-eyed surgeon who performs an autopsy on his wife in order to prove to his colleagues that the cause of her death was tuberculosis and not pneumonia. His relatives vehemently oppose the autopsy, but Mitani proceeds. After being confronted by the grotesque vision of his wife protesting her desecration when he is about to cut open her skull, he cannot go on. But he regains his composure and eventually continues, even though he is assailed by a vision in which the deterioration and death of his wife are depicted in horrifying detail. At this point Mitani stops and entrusts the rest of the autopsy to his subordinates.

Arishima describes this autopsy not with clinical detachment but with melodramatic excess.

When Mitani is about to cut into the skull, the narrative likens the act to ravaging a virgin and calls Mitani's impulses "sadistic." Arishima is interested above all in Mitani's subliminal desires and fears, instinctual drives that are linked, if only metaphorically, with sexuality. The mood of the story is dark, perhaps influenced by Arishima's memories (carefully chronicled in his diary) of the slow and painful death of his own wife from tuberculosis. Critics so disliked the story when it first appeared that Arishima was forced to rewrite it; yet his inattention to conventional characterization and plot demonstrates how committed he was to a different kind of fiction: that of the unconscious.

In 1918 Arishima completed *Umareizuru nayami* (translated as *The Agony of Coming into the World*, 1955), a stylistically complex novel that is one of Arishima's most innovative technical experiments. The first half of the narrative, covering chapters 1 through 4, consists of the first-person narrator's series of recollections about Kimoto, a fisherman to whom the narrator addresses his tale. He recalls how he first met Kimoto when the fisherman was a sixteen-year-old boy interested in painting. The first half of the story recounts events of the narrator's life—the loss of his Christian faith, the birth of his three children, and his decision to become a full-time writer in Tokyo. When ten years have passed after their meeting, Kimoto returns—a self-assured giant of a man, with his own story of how he has been forced to become a full-time fisherman to avoid destitution. Yet all the while he has held on to his dream of becoming an artist.

The second half of the novel, comprising chapters 5 through 9, represents the narrator's imaginative reconstruction of Kimoto's life during the previous ten years. This part of the novel relates a series of episodes that characterize Kimoto as a romantic hero battling the fierce Hokkaidō elements, being lost deep in the mountains, and fighting the giant seas—but always dreaming of art and trying to paint, whatever the circumstances.

The novel thus affords a contrast in narrative modes. Its first half is presented largely through realistic description (although in an almost stream-of-consciousness style), and the second half is presented in a highly mannered, almost rococo style. Yet the fantasy of the second half is most impressive, for it draws attention from the narrator or from Kimoto to the writing itself. The metaphor of realization—the birth of art from privation—invades the very texture of the prose, which attempts to realize Kimoto's life in a rich, stylized rhetoric that mimics the technique employed in Kimoto's paintings.

In June 1918 Arishima published *Meiro* (translated as *Labyrinth*, 1992) in the fifth volume of his *Collected Works*. This novel had been published serially in three parts beginning in 1916, and its first part is so autobiographical that most critics read it more for that reason than for its virtues as fiction. The novel tells the story of A, a young Japanese student studying in the United States and working as a male nurse at a mental asylum. The chief event of this part of the novel is the suicide of Dr. Scott, a patient whom A befriends, and the events described are exactly as they appear in Arishima's diary entries for 1904.

The second part of the novel recounts A's love affair with Mrs. P, the wife of a lawyer with whom he is staying. The novel conveys the sexual desire of A and Mrs. P in language that struck many contemporary readers as contrived. The seduction scenes are much less convincing than those in his masterpiece, *Aru onna* (1919; translated as *A Certain Woman*, 1978), and contrast sharply with the early scenes describing A's life at the mental asylum, a description that succeeds in capturing the emotional and intellectual turmoil of the young intellectual.

One of the most interesting parts of the novel is Arishima's depiction of the racial prejudice that A receives from Americans. While A is working for Professor M, Julia, the professor's daughter, rejects A by reminding him, "You are an Oriental. . . . You haven't forgotten that, have you?" Her question echoes similar words of rejection and self-hatred recorded by other authors such as Natsume Sōseki, Nagai Kafū, and the poet Takamura Kōtarō—all of whom also visited the West and were subjected to prejudice. After Mrs. P has deceived A by making him think that she is pregnant, A becomes almost obsessed with racism; he fears for his child, whom he imagines as an ugly half-caste. After A's socialist friend K informs him of Mrs. P's deception, the story ends with K's death from tuberculosis.

The friendship between A and K—a character based on Kaneko Kiichi, a socialist whom Arishima befriended in the United States—furnishes the background for this bildungsroman. Yet the novel does not achieve the emotional power of "Descendants of Cain" or "The Ordination of Clara," and because the characterization of almost everyone except A lacks impact, the novel has generally been regarded as a failure.

Arishima in 1922, a year before his suicide (courtesy of the Library of Modern Japanese Literature)

Arishima's masterpiece is *A Certain Woman*. The genesis of the novel lies in a novelette, "Aru onna no gurimpusu" (A Glimpse of a Certain Woman), that Arishima wrote in 1911–1913 while he was still teaching in Hokkaidō. He intended to write a sequel to this story as early as 1916, but he did not begin work on it until 1918, when he rewrote the earlier story and added a second half to make it a complete novel, first published in the ninth volume of his *Collected Works* in 1919.

The novel presents the story of Satsuki Yōko—a beautiful, coquettish young woman who, while traveling by ship to Seattle to meet her fiancé, Kimura Sadaichi, falls in love with the purser, Kuraji Sankichi, a coarse, working-class character. Her engagement to Kimura has been orchestrated by her mother, and Yōko has no affection for her fiancé. She is a divorcée whom Arishima depicts as a woman dominated by almost uncontrollable passion. She passionately advocates female emancipation and dreams of America, where she can be free, "without the need of a man's help." Yōko becomes equally passionate about Kuraji, who overwhelms her with his brutish sexuality. In their rather sado-masochistic relationship Yōko's suppressed sexuality surfaces in her savage, brutal encounters with Kuraji, encounters that convey Arishima's theme—that society oppresses female sexuality. Indeed, as he wrote in a letter to a friend three months after publication of the novel, "women are the slaves of men. . . . The war between men and women arises from this."

Tragedy inevitably results from this conflict between Yōko's rebellious nature and bourgeois society. Without setting foot onshore in the United States, she returns with Kuraji to Japan, where the two live as husband and wife in Yokohama. Their relationship becomes a public scandal when the press learns of it, and Yōko learns that Kuraji is a spy for foreign powers—and also that he is already married. After she attempts suicide, she falls ill with a uterine complaint, and the final chapters of the novel are set in darkened hospital rooms. Her family, her friends, and Kuraji all desert her; wracked with pain, she succumbs to a paranoiac hysteria and in the final scene dies in her hospital bed.

Arishima's last novel, *Seiza* (The Constellation, 1922), remained unfinished. In the novel's myriad characters he was attempting to create a fictional world comparable in richness and complexity to that of *A Certain Woman,* but he did not succeed. Yōko remains the culmination of a host of characters; her complex psychology provides glimpses of Dr. Mitani, Clara, Osue, and even Emma Bovary and Anna Karenina, the last two being fictional characters of Gustave Flaubert and Tolstoy that greatly impressed Arishima. In creating Yōko, Arishima was making the first attempt in modern Japanese literature to shape a female character with all the psychological drives that characterize the modern sensibility. Yōko's passion, her sexuality, and her complex psyche remain in the reader's mind long after the weaknesses of the novel have faded from memory. With *A Certain Woman* Arishima contributed much not only to Japanese literature but to the portrayal of the female in modern literature.

In 1920 Arishima suffered a profound crisis: he found himself unable to continue creating fiction as effortlessly as he had. In a letter of 15 September 1920 to Asuke Soichi, a close friend, Arishima wrote: "I cannot write, I cannot! I have never suffered so much as now. And have never been so helpless." Perhaps as a result of this creative block or of his increasingly radical political views, Arishima turned more and more to polemics. His essays on art, religion, politics, women, and other topics grew more prolific but also more despairing. His *Sengen hitotsu* (A Manifesto, 1922) concludes with a declaration that his work cannot be relevant to the working class, that intellectuals such as he were the bastard children of the bourgeoisie and must write only for their own class. In other writings he expressed his admiration for the anarchism of Prince Pyotr Kropotkin and apparently began secretly to give financial support to Japanese anarchists.

In May 1922 he handed over his estate in Hokkaidō to peasant farmers, who were to work it as a communist farm, but he found it almost impossible to gain legal approval for his action. His apparently quixotic gestures concealed a despair over the course of world events. Arishima's idealism and his humanism seemed threatened by the bleak reality of an aggressive, imperialist Japan, and his suicide on 9 June 1923 with Hatano Akiko, who was trapped in an unhappy marriage, did not appear to shock those closest to him. It stunned others, however, and, partly as a result, his writing lost favor with the conservative literary establishment and prewar authorities.

Critical interest in Arishima—whose extravagant, passionate fiction stakes his claim to a much more important position in Japanese liter-

ary history than was previously recognized—has revived. The Gothic excess that characterizes much of his writing led him to create visions of disordered worlds populated by larger-than-life individuals whose lives take on a special intensity. Arishima's fictional creations burn fiercely in every aspect of their personalities—emotional, psychological, and sexual. His distinctive experiments in the novel genre dared readers of his time to contemplate a view of human nature more complex than could be offered by conventional fiction of his day. Readers of Arishima's fiction are even today challenged to encounter the human psyche in extremis—there to recognize truths as uncomfortable as they are profound.

Bibliography:
Sasaki Yasuaki, *Shiryō Arishima Takeo chosaku mokuroku chosaku kaidai* (Tokyo: Man'yōdō, 1978).

Biographies:
Sadoya Shigenobu, *Hyōden Arishima Takeo* (Tokyo: Kenkyusha Shuppan, 1978);
Yasukawa Sadao, *Arishima Takeo: Higeki no chishikijin* (Tokyo: Shintensha, 1983);
Leith Morton, *Divided Self: A Biography of Arishima Takeo* (Sydney: Allen & Unwin, 1988).

References:
Paul Anderer, *Other Worlds: Arishima Takeo and the Bounds of Modern Fiction* (New York: Columbia University Press, 1984);
Egashira Tasuke, *Arishima Takeo no kenkyū* (Tokyo: Chōbunsha, 1992);
Egusa Mitsuko, *Arishima Takeo ron* (Tokyo: Ōfūsha, 1984);
Egusa and Kurita Hiromi, eds., *Arishima Takeo: Ai/Sekushūariti* (Tokyo: Yūbun Shoin, 1995);
Honda Shūgo, *"Shirakaba-ha" no bungaku* (Tokyo: Shinchō Bunko, 1960);
Ishimaru Akiko and Nishigaki Tsutomu, eds., *Arishima Takeo no sakuhin: Jō* (Tokyo: Yubun Shoin, 1995);
Kawakami Minako, *Arishima Takeo to dōjidai bungaku* (Tokyo: Shinbisha, 1993);
Donald Keene, *Dawn to the West: Japanese Literature of the Modern Era—Fiction* (New York: Holt, Rinehart & Winston, 1984);
Kikuchi Hiroshi, *Arishima Takeo* (Tokyo: Shinbisha, 1986);
Kodama Kōichi, *Hikaku bungaku kenkyū: Arishima Takeo* (Tokyo: Asahi Shuppansha, 1978);
Kosaka Susumu, *Arishima Takeo bungaku no shinriteki kōsatsu* (Tokyo: Ōfūsha, 1979);

Miyano Mitsuo, *Arishima Takeo no bungaku* (Tokyo: Ōfūsha, 1974);

Nakamura Miharu, *Kotoba no ishi: Arishima Takeo to geijutsu shi teki tenkai* (Tokyo: Yūseidō, 1994);

Nihon Bungaku Kenkyū Shiryō Kankōkai, *Arishima Takeo* (Tokyo: Yūseidō Shuppan, 1986);

Nishigaki Tsutomu, *Arishima Takeo ron* (Tokyo: Yūseidō Shuppan, 1978);

Niwa Kazuhiko, *Arishima Takeo ron: Kankei ni totte 'Dōjō' towa nani ka* (Tokyo: Furindō, 1987);

Sasaki Yasuaki and Fukuda Junnosuke, eds., *Arishima Takeo no sakuhin: Chū* (Tokyo: Yubun Shoin, 1995);

Senuma Shigeki and Honda Shūgo, eds., *Arishima Takeo kenkyū* (Tokyo: Yūbun Shoin, 1972);

Takayama Ryōji, *Arishima Takeo kenkyū: "Nōjō," "e" e no shiten o chūshin ni shite* (Tokyo: Meiji Shoin, 1972);

Tanabe Kenji, *Arishima Takeo shiron* (Tokyo: Keisuisha, 1991);

Uchida Mitsuru and Egashira Tasuke, eds., *Arishima Takeo to shakai* (Tokyo: Yūbun Shoin, 1995);

Uekuri Wataru, *Arishima Takeo kenkyū: "Aru onna" made* (Tokyo: Yūseidō, 1990);

Uesugi Yoshikazu, *Arishima Takeo: Hito to sono shōsetsu sekai* (Tokyo: Meiji Shoin, 1985);

Yamada Akio, *Arishima Takeo: Shisei to kiseki* (Tokyo: Yubun Shoin, 1973);

Yasukawa Sadao, *Arishima Takeo ron* (Tokyo: Meiji Shoin, 1973);

Yasukawa and others, eds., "Tokushū: Arishima Takeo no sekai," *Kokubungaku: Kaishaku to Kanshō,* special issue on Arishima, 54 (1989).

Papers:

Arishima's manuscripts and other important materials are housed in the Nihon Kindai Bungakkan (Library of Modern Japanese Literature) in Tokyo. Other materials are held by Chikuma Shobō Publishers, which issued the definitive collected works. Papers relating to the Arishima family and the estates are housed in the Arishima Takeo Kinenkan (Arishima Takeo Museum) on the site of the former Arishima estate at Niseko in Hokkaidō.

Futabatei Shimei
(Hasegawa Tatsunosuke)
(4 April 1864 – 10 May 1909)

Tōgawa Shinsuke
Gakushūin University

BOOKS: *Ukigumo,* part 1 (Tokyo: Kinkōdō, 1886);

Ukigumo, part 2 (Tokyo: Kinkōdō, 1888);

Ukigumo, parts 1–3 (Tokyo: Kinkōdō, 1891); translated by Marleigh Grayer Ryan as *Japan's First Modern Novel:* Ukigumo *of Futabatei Shimei* (New York: Columbia University Press, 1967; London: Greenwood Press, 1983);

Sekaigo (Tokyo: Saiunkaku, 1906);

Sekaigo tokuhon (Tokyo: Saiunkaku, 1906);

Sono omokage (Tokyo: Shun'yōdō, 1907); translated by Buhachiro Mitsui and Gregg M. Sinclair as *An Adopted Husband* (New York: Knopf, 1919; London: Hutchinson, 1919);

Karuko shū (Tokyo: Shun'yōdō, 1907);

Heibon (Tokyo: Bun'endō & Nyozandō, 1908); translated by Glenn W. Shaw as *Mediocrity* (Tokyo: Hokuseidō, 1927).

Collections: *Futabatei Shimei zenshū,* 17 volumes, edited by Kōno Yoichi and Nakamura Mitsuo (Tokyo: Iwanami Shoten, 1953–1954);

Futabatei Shimei zenshū, 8 volumes (Tokyo: Chikuma Shobō, 1984–1993).

TRANSLATIONS: Ivan Sergeyevich Turgenev, *Katakoi* (Tokyo: Shun'yōdō, 1896);

Count Leo Tolstoy, *Tsutsu o makura* (Tokyo: Kinkōdō, 1904);

Leonid Andreyev, *Kesshōki* (Tokyo: Ekifusha, 1908);

Turgenev, *Ukikusa* (Tokyo: Kaneo Bun'endō, 1908);

Nikolai Gogol, *Kojiki* (Tokyo: Saiunkaku, 1909);

Vissarion Belinsky, "Bijutsu no hongi," in *Meiji bunka zenshu,* volume 12, edited by Yoshino Sakuzō (Tokyo: Nihon Hyōronsha, 1928).

Although he wrote only three novels during his career and spent most of his life in govern-

Futabatei Shimei

ment service, Futabatei Shimei (the pen name for Hasegawa Tatsunosuke) is credited with having written the first modern Japanese novel. His knowledge of Russian literature, combined with his facility for language and his insistence on a new colloquial style for the fiction of a new age, helped him write a novel that inspired an entire generation of authors. The indecisive, ineffectual protagonist he created became a prototype for Japanese antiheroes throughout the twentieth century.

As the only child of Hasegawa Yoshikazu, a samurai from Owari, and his wife, Gotō Shizu, Hasegawa Tatsunosuke was born at the Ichigaya mansion in Edo, the capital city and present-day Tokyo. His grandmother, Mitsu, who wielded the actual power in the family and dominated Yoshikazu, adopted the child, raised him, and showered love on him. In an autobiographical note, Futabatei described himself at this age as "a lion at home, a mouse abroad." After the Meiji Restoration in 1868, he moved to his parents' ancestral home of Nagoya, where he attended the domainal school, studied French, and picked up rudiments of the Chinese classics. He grew to maturity in Tokyo and Matsue, where his father served as a low-ranking government official. Futabatei studied at the Sōchōsha Academy of Chinese Studies and at a private middle school in Matsue, and the restoration upheavals during his childhood inspired in him a fondness for politics that he labeled his "Restoration patriot's spirit." Stimulated by events such as the public outcry when Japan abandoned its claims to Sakhalin in 1875, he decided that his life's mission was to protect Japan from Russia's southward expansion. In order to achieve that goal he moved to Tokyo in 1878 and applied three times to the army officer training school. Each time, however, he was rejected because of his poor grades and severe nearsightedness, and these rejections prompted him to change his goals and aim for a diplomatic career.

In order to learn about conditions in Russia, Futabatei entered the Russian language department of the Tokyo School of Foreign Languages in 1881. According to a friend, Futabatei was a stalwart student who recited Chinese poetry in a loud voice, and he was fond of kendo fencing. An affable young man, he also liked popular music, especially the romantic ballad-singing style known as *shinnai*. His grades at the school were superior, and he was admired for his talents. He was particularly impressed by the literary training he received from Nicholas Gray, a Russian with United States citizenship and a teacher who used Russian novels as his class texts. This class inspired Futabatei to study such Russian writers as Nikolai Gogol, Ivan Turgenev, Ivan Goncharov, Fyodor Dostoyevsky, and Vissarion Belinsky. The heavy political cast of Russian literature naturally appealed to Futabatei and invigorated his own literary inclinations. He forsook his initial political aim in preventing the southward expansion of Russia and instead became interested in studying cultural criticism and social problems such as those treated by the Russian novelists. At the time he sought to "act independently," to live an "honest" life that was true

to his own ideals—a vision based in the Confucian ethics and the samurai education that he had received as a child and blended with a Western veneration for honesty that he had acquired in his studies of Russian literature, the socialism of Aleksandr Herzen and Ferdinand Lassalle, and such enlightenment works of the early Meiji period as *Saigoku risshihen* (Success Stories of the West), an 1870 translation of Samuel Smiles's *Self-Help* (1859).

The Tokyo School of Foreign Languages was abolished in 1885 as part of school reform procedures, and the Russian language department, which prepared its students for practical employment, was subsumed by the Tokyo School of Commerce. Futabatei was in his fifth and final year at the school when this change was made, and it infuriated him. In January 1886 he quit the school and visited the critic and author Tsubouchi Shōyō, who became a lifelong friend. Futabatei had been inspired by the success of Shōyō, who had become chief advocate for a new Japanese literature through the publication of his *Shōsetsu shinzui* (1885–1886; translated as *The Essence of the Novel,* 1983) and such novels as *Tōsei shosei katagi* (The Character of Modern Students, 1885–1886). Futabatei firmed up his own resolve to become a writer.

In all likelihood Futabatei agreed with Shōyō's fundamental principles, but he doubted their philosophical foundation. He presented these doubts to Shōyō in a critique of *Tōsei shosei katagi,* and in April 1886 the introduction of that critique was published as "Shōsetsu sōron" (Elements of the Novel). In writing his critique of literature, Futabatei was powerfully influenced by the writings of Belinsky, particularly by "The Idea of Art," which Futabatei translated into Japanese. Futabatei emphasized how the "ideologies" (ideas, intentions, fabrications) within "phenomena" (forms, structures, circumstances) were more essential than those phenomena. His theory of the novel is erected on a scaffolding of modern realism that transcends the simple concept of realistic depiction that Shōyō had presented in *The Essence of the Novel.* Basing his arguments on the premise that art acquires its essence (truth) directly from inspiration one finds in all forms of material, Futabatei posits that because the novel is one kind of art, it must present truth not through the abstractions of scholarship but through concrete shapes that are in fact replicas or representations of external reality.

These are the essential features of Futabatei's argument. He deletes from Belinsky's theories the notion of a human personality that develops in conjunction with the will of God and is derived from the "absolute idea of God," and he replaces this notion with static concepts of "volition" and "fabrication." "Elements of the Novel" is thus no mere copy of Belinsky's views but an original synthesis that Futabatei fashions from Belinsky's theories, traditional Japanese concepts of truth, and Neo-Confucian ideas about the duality of *li* (principle) and *chi* (spirit). Perhaps as a result, the essay is somewhat unsophisticated, and some portions are inadequately developed; during Futabatei's life it influenced few others except Shōyō, Saganoya Omuro, Uchida Fuchian, and others among his circle of friends.

Futabatei subsequently translated portions of Turgenev's *Fathers and Sons* (1862) as "Kyomutō katagi" (Character Studies of Nihilists), but it was never published. In summer 1885 he began writing a novel, *Ukigumo* (The Drifting Clouds, 1891), and the first part was published in June 1886, at which time he adopted the pen name of Futabatei Shimei. The book was published under Shōyō's name, with Futabatei's appearing only inside as co-author. Shōyō's preface made it clear, however, that Futabatei was the actual author, and his fame as a writer mounted as acclaim for the novel increased. The second part of *Ukigumo* appeared in 1888, and in that year Futabatei published translations of two Turgenev stories, "Aibiki" (Svidaniye; The Rendezvous) and "Meguriai" (Tri vstrechi; Three Meetings), and solidified his fame as a representative of a new kind of literature. The fresh depictions of nature in his translation of "The Rendezvous," combined with his brilliant use of colloquial language that set a pattern for literary translation in Japan, profoundly influenced the next generation of writers, including Kunikida Doppo, Shimazaki Tōson, and Tayama Katai.

In 1889 Futabatei began serializing a third part of *Ukigumo* in the journal *Miyako no Hana*. The novel is set in Tokyo around 1886, in the home of Sonoda Magobei, who is away on business. Utsumi Bunzō, the young son of a samurai from Shizuoka Prefecture, travels to the capital after the death of his father and moves into his uncle Magobei's house. He graduates from school with excellent grades and obtains a job as a low-ranking government clerk. Bunzō's uncle and aunt implicitly accept the romantic feelings that Bunzō has for their daughter, Osei, but their feelings change dramatically when Bunzō loses his job in a personnel reduction. Omasa, Bunzō's calculating aunt, decides that she would rather have

her daughter marry Honda Noboru, one of Bunzō's coworkers who has abundant knowledge of how to succeed in the world, and she begins treating Bunzō brutally. Osei, who has extolled Westernization under Bunzō's influence and defended him because he is educated, eventually also reveals her "innate flippancy" and moves away from Bunzō, who is shackled by his idealism and his unbending nature.

After Bunzō argues with Noboru, who advises him to get his job back by currying favor with his former boss, Noboru snubs Bunzō, and Osei defends Noboru. Bunzō warns Osei about the dangers of associating with Noboru, but she will not listen to him; Bunzō is left alone in his agony. He comes to believe that the former days of peace in the Sonoda household were no more than a pretense and that in reality the house is a cluster of ugly egoism, but he can do nothing to change it.

This is where the novel ends, and a plan for the book that was discovered in Futabatei's journal makes it clear that the novel was left unfinished. According to Futabatei's notes, Noboru was to make sport of Osei and then abandon her, while Bunzō's despair and unhappiness were to mount until he ruined himself through dissipation and went mad.

Ukigumo was written under the influence of Russian novels such as Goncharov's *The Precipice* (1869). No doubt Futabatei originally intended to caricature the Meiji period's "enlightened" society, the members of which lacked moral bearings after traditional values had collapsed and new codes of conduct remained insubstantial. Midway through part 2 of *Ukigumo,* however, Futabatei's interest shifts to the psyche of Bunzō, as this antihero becomes more of a "superfluous man," and the meaning of the title is transformed to suggest an image of the anxious Bunzō. Futabatei's own anguish is reflected in the novel, as the interest is diverted from presenting a criticism of contemporary civilization to exploring what Futabatei found as a personal problem—that of determining the proper way for an intellectual to live.

In any case, the significance of *Ukigumo* as the first modern Japanese novel is unassailable, as the work draws on the principles of realism that Futabatei expounded in "Elements of the Novel" and examines the distortions of Meiji society and the sufferings of the intellectual. The novel also influenced later generations of fiction writers in its pioneering use of colloquial language: Futabatei learned much from his study of oral storytellers such as San'yutei Enchō, the Edo period satirist Shiktei Samba, and the Russian writers he had read. Futabatei between 1888 and 1894 apparently kept his journal initially to refine his writing style, and it is filled with fragmentary entries that provide a moving glimpse into his agony, his quest for truth, and his groping for meaning, peace, and enlightenment as he wrote the novel. In addition to what may be inferred about Futabatei from his fictional works, the journal is a valuable resource for understanding him.

The intellectual turmoil Futabatei felt while writing the second part of *Ukigumo* and the financial difficulties he encountered after his father had retired forced him to stop writing the novel. In 1893 Futabatei married Fukui Tsune, but, after having two children, the couple divorced in 1896. During this period, after he had ceased writing *Ukigumo,* Futabatei's literary work generally diminished, mostly because of a need to raise money in order to settle with his ex-wife. He took a job with the cabinet office that published *Kampō,* the official government gazette. One source of his intellectual unrest was the conflict between writing novels and living in active pursuit of a realm of ideals in the real world, a conflict that undermined his sense of honesty that he so highly esteemed. Other sources of his anguish included the state of literature as a profession (epitomized by the rise of the Ken'yusha Society, a group of popular writers at the turn of the century who wrote melodramatic love stories in old-fashioned diction) and self-doubts that his garbling of the structure of *Ukigumo* had raised about his talent.

His main duties at the government office included translating English- and Russian-language newspapers and editing a monthly survey of published materials. The atmosphere at the office suited his temperament, and he remained there until the end of 1897. This period is often regarded as his abandonment of literature, but it was a time of withdrawal, as Futabatei sought answers to questions about the purpose of life, about the conflict between the ideal and the real, and about the role of literature in human life. His studies during these years included philosophy, medicine, psychology, Christianity, Buddhism, and many other fields, and his interest in socialism led him to join Yokoyama Gennosuke in studying the lower echelons of society.

The more deeply he studied, however, the greater his doubts became, and ultimately he began to question the value of intellect and reason and to reject philosophical ideals. He became disappointed at being unable to discover any ideals by which to live, and the dark possibility that man lives merely to live in discomfort remained. As a result, he came to regard sensation as the ultimate veracity and sought fulfillment in life through his struggles amid the eddies of reality.

After Futabatei published translations of Gogol's "Portret" (The Portrait) and Turgenev's *Rudin,* some people believed that he would resume his own writing, but he produced no original pieces. He resigned from his position with the government office and began working parttime at the army university and as an editorial clerk for the navy. In 1899 he was hired as a professor at the Tokyo Foreign Language School. Through all these professional changes Futabatei could not conceal that he felt "no peace at any time in my heart." "I have fallen into hell," he wrote in a letter to Tsubouchi Shōyō, and he searched for opportunities to struggle "as a corpse" in the midst of his "real-life business." Russo-Japanese relations had become worse following the Boxer Rebellion, and in an attempt to resolve both his "long-cherished desire" to be involved in Russian affairs and his feelings of emptiness, he resigned from the language school.

In May 1902 he left behind Takano Ryu, whom he had just married, as well as his aging mother and his children in order to travel to the Chinese continent to work at the Harbin branch of the Tokunaga Store, which had headquarters in Vladivostok. He soon became discouraged with Tokunaga, however, and called on a former classmate from the foreign-language school, Kawashima Naniwa, who was director of the police academy in Beijing. Kawashima appointed him to an executive position at the academy, and in this post Futabatei was able to associate with many important figures who visited Beijing. It is likely that he was privy to secret information about the imminent outbreak of war between Japan and Russia, and one might expect that such diplomatic responsibility must have gratified him at finally becoming able to realize his dreams to "subjugate China and Russia."

However, what Uchida Roan describes as Futabatei's characteristic "stubborn rebelliousness" at this time renewed his desire to be an "observer"—in contrast to those years when his livelihood had made him an "observer" who yearned to become a "doer." Futabatei's discordant relations with Kawashima, whose thinking and temperament were opposed to his own, drove Futabatei to resign from the academy, and in July

1903 he returned to Japan in a state of depression.

After the fall of Beijing he hoped to write an essay on the problems of governing East Asia, and he planned a piece on the eastward advance of the Russian forces, but he never wrote it. Through the influence of Naitō Konan, Futabatei was hired as Tokyo correspondent for the Osaka *Asahi Shinbun* newspaper in March 1904. But the paper, which regarded his submissions on East Asia as too sophisticated and complex, never published these pieces. Futabatei was also publishing translations of fiction in other newspapers, and partly for this reason his relations with the directors of the Osaka paper soured—and before long he was encouraged to resign. Ikebe Sanzan, chief writer for the Tokyo *Asahi Shinbun*, intervened as a mediator in this clash of wills, and a sense of obligation to Ikebe and other executives at the Tokyo paper compelled Futabatei to write some fiction for them. In 1906, heralding his return as a fiction writer, he began to publish *Sono omokage* (1907; translated as *An Adopted Husband*, 1919) serially in the Tokyo newspaper.

An Adopted Husband presents the anguish of Ono Tetsuya, a professor at a private university and a man whose ideas, like "the spirits of old books," have gnawed at his heart. Weary of the loveless household that he shares with his wife and mother-in-law, Ono has lost virtually all interest in living. Only the presence of Sayoko, his divorced sister-in-law, who also happens to be a Christian, sustains him. Eventually the two run away together to share their love, but Ono's indecisiveness, born of his ideological bent and his inability to act, as well as Sayoko's suffering over the adultery that she has committed, end their relationship. She disappears, and Tetsuya moves to China, where he wanders hopelessly searching for her and becomes an alcoholic.

In this novel Futabatei continues his deliberations on the proper way for an intellectual to live. Tetsuya and his friend, the realist Hamura Kōsaburō, appear as reincarnations of Bunzō and Noboru from *Ukigumo,* and some critics have therefore criticized the novel for reworking that earlier story. But the essence of *An Adopted Husband* lies in its depiction of a human being who has lost his heart through his idealism and intellectualism. The rejection of the intellectual and a yearning after a vital force that actually moves society represent some conclusions that Futabatei had reached after writing *Ukigumo,* and the narrative offers traces of Futabatei's personal experience between 1894 and 1895 in describing the atmosphere of Tetsuya's household. Just before this novel was published serially, Futabatei had begun and then abandoned work on "Chasengami" (Widow's Weeds), a novel in which he planned to depict the remarriage of a war widow from the Russo-Japanese War, and *An Adopted Husband* was most likely a reworking of this manuscript.

Japanese readers and critics hailed Futabatei's return to writing, and the response to *An Adopted Husband* was positive, but Futabatei did not consider it noble to be regarded as a man of letters. He continued to pursue his dream of being involved in international affairs, and he spent his time working with Russian and Polish revolutionaries such as Bronislav Pilsudski and Leonchii Podpakh and working to popularize the international language of Esperanto by publishing *Sekaigo* (A Language for the World, 1906).

In 1907 Futabatei serialized another novel, *Heibon* (1908; translated as *Mediocrity*, 1927), in the Tokyo *Asahi Shinbun*. Written in an episodic, autobiographical style and including a famous section about a young boy's love for his dog, *Mediocrity* presents Furuya Sekkō, a former writer turned government clerk. Sekkō, who has grown disenchanted with the emphasis that literature places on his imagination, wishes to live "seriously" by basing his life on actual experience, but the demands of reality overwhelm him, and his life ends in mediocrity. This novel was influenced by the popularity of Count Leo Tolstoy's *The Kreutzer Sonata* (1889) and that of personal confession following publication of Tayama Katai's *Futon* (1907; translated as *The Quilt*, 1981); in it Futabatei uses the techniques of linked verse both to express his doubts about literature and to satirize human life. Futabatei's nihilism emerges from beneath the apparently easygoing surface of the work.

After publishing *Mediocrity* and several volumes of conversations, Futabatei seemed to have settled, however unwillingly, into his vocation as a writer. But an opportunity to realize his lifelong dream of visiting the Russian capital appeared during the visit of Russian dramatist Vladimir Nemirovich-Danchenko to Japan. In June 1908 he sailed from Kobe as a special correspondent for the Tokyo *Asahi Shinbun*. He crossed Siberia on his way to Saint Petersburg, and, arriving in the Russian capital, he threw himself into his work as a reporter despite being tormented by insomnia. As Futabatei had promised at a banquet held to honor him before he left for

Russia, he made every effort to increase mutual understanding between the peoples of Russia and Japan in order to prevent another war between the two countries.

In 1909 Futabatei contracted both pneumonia and tuberculosis, and on 10 May he died on board a ship returning him to Japan by way of London. He was survived by his mother, his wife, three sons, and one daughter.

References:

Inagaki Tatsurō, *Bungaku kakumeiki to Futabatei Shimei* (Tokyo: Iwanami Shoten, 1954);

Ino Kenji, *Nihon riarizumu no seiritsu* (Tokyo: Miraisha, 1954);

Kamei Hideo, *Sensō to kakumei no hōrōsha: Futabatei Shimei* (Tokyo: Shintensha, 1986);

Nakamura Mitsuo, *Futabatei ron* (Tokyo: Shiba Shobō, 1936);

Nakamura, *Futabatei Shimei den* (Tokyo: Kōdansha, 1958);

Odagiri Hideo, *Futabatei Shimei* (Tokyo: Iwanami Shinsho, 1970);

Oketani Hideaki, *Futabatei Shimei to Meiji Nihon* (Tokyo: Bungei shūnju, 1986);

Sakamoto Hiroshi, *Futabatei Shimei* (Tokyo: Shibun Shobō, 1941);

Seki Ryōichi, *Kōshō to shiron: Futabatei, Tōkoku* (Tokyo: Kyōiku Shūppan Center, 1992);

Shimizu Shigeru, ed., *Futabatei Shimei* (Tokyo: Kadokawa Shoten, 1967);

Togawa Shinsuke, *Futabatei Shimei ron* (Tokyo: Chikuma Shobō, 1971);

Tsubouchi Shōyō, *Kaki no heta* (Tokyo: Chuō Kōronsha, 1933);

Tsubouchi and Uchida Roan, eds., *Futabatei Shimei* (Tokyo: Ekifusha, 1909);

Uchida, *Omoidasu hitobito* (Tokyo: Shūnjusha, 1925);

Yanagida Izumi, *Futabatei to sono shūi* (Tokyo: Iwanami Shoten, 1954).

Hayashi Fumiko
(31 December 1903 – 28 June 1951)

Joan E. Ericson
The Colorado College

BOOKS: *Aouma o mitari* (Tokyo: Nansō Shoin, 1929);

Hōrōki (Tokyo: Kaizōsha, 1930; revised edition, Tokyo: Shinchōsha, 1939);

Zoku Hōrōki (Tokyo: Kaizōsha, 1930);

Seihin no sho (Tokyo: Kaizōsha, 1933);

Watashi no rakugaki (Tokyo: Keishōdō, 1933);

Omokage (Tokyo: Bungaku Kuōtarisha, 1933);

Chūjo zakki (Tokyo: Okakura Shobō, 1934);

Sanbunka no nikki (Tokyo: Kaizōsha, 1934);

Tabi dayori (Tokyo: Kaizōsha, 1934);

Inaka gaeri (Tokyo: Kaizōsha, 1934);

Nakimushi kozō (Tokyo: Kaizōsha, 1935);

Ningyō seisho (Tokyo: Uedaya, 1935);

Kaki (Tokyo: Kaizōsha, 1935);

Tanpen shū (Tokyo: Kaizōsha, 1935);

Nomugi no uta (Tokyo: Chūō Kōronsha, 1936);

Bungakuteki danshō (Tokyo: Kawade Shobō, 1936);

Aijōden (Tokyo: Miwa Shobō, 1936);

Aijō (Tokyo: Kaizōsha, 1936);

Onna no nikki (Tokyo: Daiichi Shobō, 1937);

Inazuma (Tokyo: Yukōsha, 1937);

Suppon (Tokyo: Kaizōsha, 1937);

Hana no ichi (Tokyo: Takemura Shobō, 1937);

Kōyō no zange (Tokyo: Hangasha, 1937);

Hyōga (Tokyo: Takemura Shobō, 1938);

Watashi no konchuki (Tokyo: Kaizōsha, 1938);

Kawa (Tokyo: Ōru Yomimono, 1938);

Tsukiyo (Tokyo: Takemura shobō, 1938);

Sensen (Tokyo: Asahi Shinbunsha, 1938);

Yushu nikki (Tokyo: Chuō Kōronsha, 1939);

Mippō (Tokyo: Sōgensha, 1939);

Shinkyō to fukaku (Tokyo: Sōgensha, 1939);

Hitori no shōgai (Tokyo: Sōgensha, 1940);

Seishun (Tokyo: Jitsugyō no Nihonsha, 1940);

Akutō (Tokyo: Chuō Kōronsha, 1940);

Joyuki (Tokyo: Shinchōsha, 1940);

Budō no kishi (Tokyo: Jitsugyō no Nihonsha, 1940);

Shokujo (Tokyo: Jitsugyō no Nihonsha, 1940);

Gyokai (Tokyo: Kaizōsha, 1940);

Hayashi Fumiko

Nanatsu no tomoshibi (Tokyo: Murasaki Shuppansha, 1940);

Junenkan (Tokyo: Shinchōsha, 1941);

Rekisei (Tokyo: Kanchō Shorin, 1941);

Zuihitsu (Tokyo: Chippu Shobō, 1941);

Bara (Tokyo: Rikon Shobō, 1941);

Senka (Tokyo: Shinchōsha, 1941);

Hatsu tabi (Tokyo: Jitsugyō no Nihonsha, 1941);

Keikichi no gakkō (Tokyo: Kigensha, 1941);

Shūka (Tokyo: Kaizōsha, 1941);

Nikki I (Tokyo: Tōhō Shobō, 1941);

Ame (Tokyo: Jitsugyō no Nihonsha, 1942);

Nikki II (Tokyo: Tōhō Shobō, 1942);

Den'en nikki (Tokyo: Shinchōsha, 1942);

Onna no fukkatsu (Tokyo: Hakubunkan, 1943);

Ryojō no umi (Tokyo: Shinchōsha, 1946);

Ukigusa (Tokyo: Tankō Shobō, 1946);

Ryokan no baiburu (Tokyo: Ōsaka Shinbunsha, 1947);

Ningen sekai (Tokyo: Eikōsha, 1947);

Rinraku (Tokyo: Kantō Shoin, 1947);

Onna no seishun (Tokyo: Kawabata Shoten, 1947);

Sōsaku nōto (Tokyo: Kantōsha, 1947);

Kagi (Tokyo: Shin Bungeisha, 1947);

Hitotsubu no budō (Tokyo: Nanboku Shoin, 1947);

Maihime no ki (Tokyo: Ozaki Shobō, 1947);

Yume hitoya (Tokyo: Sekai Bungakusha, 1947);

Gan (Tokyo: Fusōsha, 1947);

Kitsune monogatari (Tokyo: Kokuritsu Shoin, 1947);

Ochibo hiroi (Tokyo: Asahi Shinbunsha, 1947);

Pari nikki (Tokyo: Tōhō Shobō, 1947);

Otōsan (Tokyo: Kigensha, 1947);

Shukumei o tou onna (Tokyo: Ozaki Shobō, 1948);

Minamikaze (Tokyo: Rokugatsusha, 1948);

Aru onna no hansei (Tokyo: Miwa Shobō, 1948);

Uzushio (Tokyo: Shinchōsha, 1948);

Kurai yoru (Tokyo: Bungei Shunjusha, 1948);

Jinsei no kawa (Tokyo: Mainichi Shinbunsha, 1948);

Hōrōki dai sanbu (Tokyo: Ryujo Shobō, 1949);

Dai ni no kekkon (Tokyo: Shufu to Seikatsusha, 1949);

Chairo no me (Tokyo: Asahi Shinbunsha, 1950);

Shin Yodogimi (Tokyo: Yomiuri Shinbunsha, 1950);

Kinka (Tokyo: Jitsugyō no Nihonsha, 1950);

Aware hitozuma (Tokyo: Rokkō Shuppansha, 1950);

Ukigumo (Tokyo: Rokkō Shuppansha, 1951); translated by Yoshiyuki Koitabashi and Martin C. Collcott as *The Floating Cloud* (Tokyo: Hara Shobō, 1965);

Ehon Sarutobi Sasuke (Tokyo: Shinchōsha, 1951);

Ore ashi (Tokyo: Shinchōsha, 1951);

Sazanami—Aru onna no techō (Tokyo: Chuō Kōronsha, 1951);

Meshi (Tokyo: Asahi Shinbunsha, 1951).

Collections: *Hayashi Fumiko zenshu,* 7 volumes (Tokyo: Kaizōsha, 1937);

Hayashi Fumiko chōhen shōsetsu zenshu, 8 volumes (Tokyo: Chuō Kōronsha, 1938–1940);

Hayashi Fumiko bunko, 10 volumes (Tokyo: Shinchōsha, 1948–1950);

Hayashi Fumiko zenshu, 23 volumes (Tokyo: Shinchōsha, 1951–1953);

Hayashi Fumiko zenshu, 16 volumes (Tokyo: Bunsendō, 1977).

Hayashi Fumiko was one of the most popular and prolific writers in Japan during the 1930s and 1940s. Much of her work was ostensibly autobiographical, and her portrayals of struggle and perseverance among the dispossessed and disaffected attracted many readers. In the four years before her death in 1951, Hayashi published eleven serialized novels, twenty-two other volumes (mainly novels), and more than thirty short stories, some of which were among her most sophisticated and successful works. Her sole literary prize, the Joryū Bungakushō (Women's Literary Prize), awarded for "Bangiku" (1948; translated as "Late Chrysanthemum," 1956), confirmed her status among the preeminent women writers of the era. Yet because critics continued to categorize her as a *joryū sakka* (woman writer) of *joryū bungaku* (women's literature), this regard for her work ensured that no matter how prominent that oeuvre became, it would still be considered marginal to the canon and would rarely receive sustained critical scrutiny. Moreover, this categorization by gender obscured the salience of her work to literary, social, and political trends.

Hayashi was born in Shimonoseki, a port city on the southwest corner of Honshu, to Miyata Asatarō, her twenty-two-year-old father, and Hayashi Kiku, her thirty-six-year-old mother. He refused to register her as his child, and she was thus listed in her maternal family registry as an illegitimate child. When Miyata brought home a young geisha to live with him in 1910, Kiku left and took her daughter with her. At the age of forty-two Kiku began a relationship with twenty-two-year-old Sawai Kisaburō, a former employee of Miyata, and during the next few years the three traveled around Kyushu peddling various wares.

Hayashi changed elementary schools repeatedly or failed to attend at all. When her family settled in Onomichi (Hiroshima Prefecture), she worked to put herself through Onomichi Public Girls High School, and in 1922 she went to Tokyo to join Okano Gun'ichi, whom she had met in a literary youth group in Onomichi before he became a student in the commercial department at Meiji University. In 1924 she became acquainted with a group of anarchist poets who gathered almost daily in Hongō, in the French café where Hayashi worked as a waitress. Through this group Hayashi met Tanabe Wakaō, a *shingeki* (modern theater) actor, with whom she lived for nearly a year before he took another lover. That summer she and Tomotani Shizue, an

Dust jacket for Hōrōki (Diary of a Vagabond, 1930), Hayashi's portrait of women living on the underside of Japanese society

associate of the anarchist poets, published *Futari* (Two People), a small poetry journal.

Hayashi had a succession of short, generally unhappy relationships with men during this period. In 1926 she was abandoned by the poet Nomura Yoshiya, with whom she had lived for more than a year. Later that year her unstable life became more settled, however, when she met Tezuka Ryokubin, a young sculptor with whom she remained until her death. Although their marriage was not officially registered until 1944, at that time Hayashi adopted a boy and Ryokubin entered Fumiko's family registry as a *yōshi* (adopted husband) and took the Hayashi surname.

Hōrōki (Diary of a Vagabond, 1930), Hayashi's immensely popular, ostensibly autobiographical account of the hardships and travails of an aspiring young writer, was initially serialized in 1928–1930 in *Nyonin Geijutsu* (Women's Arts), a feminist journal. When published as a separate volume in July 1930, it was an immediate and unexpected best-seller. Within two years *Diary of a Vagabond*–combined with *Zoku Hōrōki* (Diary of a Vagabond, Part Two), a sequel also published in 1930–sold six hundred thousand copies. It has been reprinted often and regularly selected for inclusion in many editions of *zenshū* (collections) of modern Japanese literature.

Purporting to be excerpts from an unnamed author's diary, *Diary of a Vagabond* mirrors the structure of a classical *uta monogatari* (poetic tale) by frequently including poetry and letters. The protagonist's drive to write and her unvarnished encounters with an assortment of literary figures reflect the roman à clef style of a *watakushi shōsetsu* (confessional fiction). Yet the originality and power of the work are rooted not so much in a mix of literary allusions as in the clarity and immediacy with which Hayashi conveys the humanity of those occupying the underside of Japanese society. Hayashi memorably portrays women who exist on the margin, with tenuous holds on employment, residence, or relationships from which they are often cut loose and have to scramble to find any means to survive—women whose interests and experiences were neglected by contending political ideologies and ignored by male writers.

Published in November 1930, *Zoku Hōrōki* uses the same structure and language, covers the same period, and reexamines many of the same incidents, but with more graphic elaboration and incriminating detail. Hayashi not only revisited and revised the same events in sequels of *Diary of a Vagabond* but also revised the text when a 1939 edition was published. The language of the first edition is more colloquial, spontaneous, and sometimes melodramatic, exactly as it appeared in its serialized installments in *Nyonin Geijutsu* and in the single installment of the prologue in *Kaizō*, while the language of the revised edition is more standard, composed, and grammatically complex. The longer paragraphs of the later edition make the text seem less staccato as well. Some passages are altered; some are eliminated. The later edition also eliminates subtitles to the diary entries. This serves to present the work as a seamless whole rather than random pieces.

One of the most striking emendations is that of some sixty passages added in classical Japanese grammar (or pseudoclassical grammar, since only the ending of each phrase or sentence is rendered into classical grammar, most often *nari*) to emphasize a distinct perspective on actions or judgments. On one level these passages appear as literary affectations, not only because the subject matter seems far removed from Heian Japan but also because, as a curious grammatical amalgam, they hardly meet standards of proper classical syntax. However, they set the tone by providing an unexpected atmosphere, by conveying a sense of the mundane as elevated, even transcendent.

Hayashi's accounts reveal much of what is known about her life. They reflect her effort to project a public persona as a brash, irrepressible, sometimes flamboyant libertine and, in particular, to depict an early life fraught with hardship. Her biographers tend to accept what she asserts at face value, to treat much of her confessional writing as unadorned autobiography and to correlate episodes from her fiction with incidents in her own life. However, like many male authors, Hayashi was perfectly capable of dissembling her past and recasting herself, successively, to fit the times.

In the afterword to *Onna no nikki* (A Woman's Diary, 1937) Hayashi describes her concerted effort to change her style from that used in the autobiography to that used in her fiction in order "to separate myself from the retching [literally, throwing up bloody vomit] confusion of the autobiographical *Diary of a Vagabond*." *Kaki* (Oyster, 1935), published in *Chūō Kōron* in September 1935, reveals a shift in her style. Told from a man's point of view, the story is not autobiographical or sentimental but rather unvarnished and straightforward in depicting an inept, possibly retarded man unable to adjust to transitions in his workplace or to resolve tensions in his family life. One month after having published "Oyster" and a volume of short stories with the same title, Hayashi flouted publishing industry conventions by organizing and paying for her own celebration in honor of these works. Reportedly in high spirits, Hayashi performed the comic folk dance *dojō sukui* (Scooping Loaches), much to the disdain of some recognized literary people.

In many later works Hayashi would return to the self-referential, lyrical style that characterizes *Diary of a Vagabond*. Several of her ostensibly autobiographical accounts might best be considered as revisions and elaborations or continuations of the personal odyssey that began with her *Diary*. *Hitori no shōgai* (One Person's Life, 1940) begins by describing recent trips to Kyoto and Peking. However, the bulk of Hayashi's *One Person's Life* focuses on those few years in the mid 1920s that she records in *Diary of a Vagabond* but has reorganized more cohesively in this prose narrative. As in *Diary of a Vagabond,* she incorporates free-verse poems in *One Person's Life*. Hayashi also included an account of the trip she took to Europe. She had already recounted in "Santō ryokō no ki" (Record of a Trip by Third Class, 1933) a 1930 tour of Europe she had taken, and she further elaborated both of these tours later in *Pari nikki* (Paris Diary, 1947). *One Person's Life* was one in a series of confessional diaries—*Yushu nikki* (Melancholy Diary, 1939), *Nikki I* (Diary, Part I, 1941), *Nikki II* (Diary, Part II, 1942), and *Den'en nikki* (Rural Diary, 1942)—published in quick succession. Perhaps the most notable of her later autobiographical works was *Hōrōki dai sanbu* (Diary of a Vagabond, Part Three, 1949), which began serialization in May 1947. This

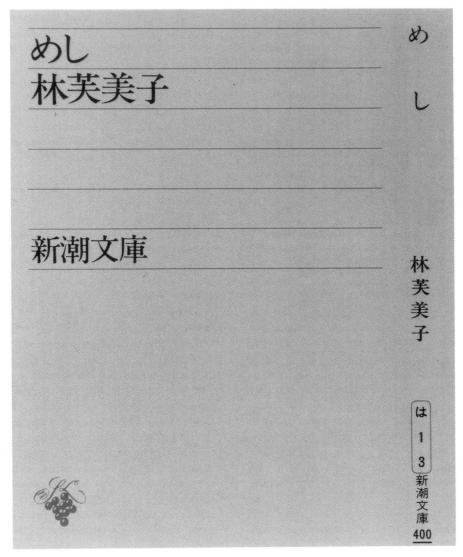

めし
林芙美子

新潮文庫

め
し

林
芙
美
子

は
1
3
新潮文庫
400

Dust jacket for Meshi *(Meal, 1951), the unfinished novel in which Hayashi depicts a troubled, childless marriage*

third version of Hayashi's exploits from her 1920s diary is far more sensational than the first, and it explicitly identifies everyone who had appeared in earlier installments.

Hayashi also suggested that she was revealing personal experiences by using in her titles such terms as *nikki* (diary), *ki* (chronicle), *sho* and *fu* (record), *rakugaki* (scribbling), and *den* (biography), even though these works were clearly fictional. "Senshun fu" (Record of a Shallow Spring), which was serially published in January and February 1931 in *Tokyo Asahi Shinbun,* was the first of such titles; *Sazanami—Aru onna no techō* (Ripples—A Certain Woman's Date Book, 1951) was the last.

Hayashi particularly enjoyed taking—as the basis for a story—an image, often only a title, from a prominent foreign work. During her association with Tanabe, Hayashi attended a reading of August Strindberg's play *Oväder* (Thunder, 1918), translated into Japanese as *Inazuma* (Lightning), and wrote that it inspired her story *Inazuma* (1937), based largely on her mother's unhappy marriage. Her titles offer other examples of this pattern: *Onna no nikki* is taken from Octave Mirbeau's *Le Journal d'une femme de chambre* (1900), and *Omokage* (Vestiges, 1933) is likewise taken from a volume of European poetry translated by Mori Ōgai in 1889. Hayashi also took her titles from prominent works of Japanese fiction: her *Ukigumo* (1951; translated as *The Floating Cloud,* 1965) from the work of Futabatei Shimei (1887–1889; translated as *Japan's First Modern Novel: Ukigumo of Futabatei Shimei,* 1967), or her *Gan* (Wild Geese, 1947) from the novel by Mori Ōgai (1911).

Hayashi borrowed titles and imagery from other recognized works, but her stories were usually wholly unlike their namesakes or sources of inspiration, and her work was not simply imitative. For example, Futabatei's *Ukigumo* focuses on the life of Utsumi Bunzō, an ordinary man who finds his dreams of marriage crushed when he loses his low-level government job; Hayashi's *Ukigumo* describes the malaise and rootlessness of postwar Japanese society, as seen in the ill-fated relationship of Yukiko and Tomioka after they are repatriated from French Indochina. Hayashi's story has a strong, more fully developed female protagonist whose plight and social milieu are far more bleak than those of Futabatei's protagonist.

In December 1937 Hayashi received considerable notoriety when, writing for a Mainichi newspaper, she was the first Japanese woman to enter Nanking after it had fallen to Japanese troops. Yet her newspaper articles failed to note any atrocities and hardly made any observations whatsoever about Nanking; the initial article that presented her often-repeated claims of being first in Nanking recounted her experiences from an earlier trip to Taiwan in 1930. Nevertheless, Hayashi's renown as a war reporter was assured, and in 1938 she and Yoshiya Nobuko were two women whom the Ministry of Information included in the first "Pen Squadron"—a group of popular writers who were to tour the front and write about the circumstances and sacrifices of soldiers for readers in Japan. Later that year, after slipping away from the rest of the squadron and the supervision of its leader, Kikuchi Kan, Hayashi hitched a ride on an *Asahi* newspaper truck and again received much publicity, this time for being among the first Japanese to enter the city of Hankow. Hayashi and the other Pen Squadron writers also toured extensively as speakers—in Japan, among military units, and in the Japanese communities in Korea, Manchuria, and China.

Hayashi's reportage of this tour—*Sensen* (Battle Front, 1938) and both "Hokugan butai" (Northern Bank Platoon) and *Hatō* (Rough Seas) published in *Chūō Kōron* in January 1939—included poetry and brief vignettes recounting the difficulties and perseverance of soldiers as well as emphasizing the minutiae of her own travels and

travails. Essentially daily entries in a diary format, these works detail how she traveled, usually at some considerable distance behind the front lines. They offer no descriptions of battle per se, refer infrequently to any Chinese, and describe the landscape (when it is described at all) mostly by focusing on the muck through which she had to travel. These works have received little critical notice and are largely dismissed, not only for their politics but also for their rather uninspired obsession with Hayashi's mundane experiences.

Her collaboration with state-sponsored wartime propaganda was the focus of much postwar criticism. She was singled out in a 1946 editorial of *Akhata,* a Communist Party newspaper that condemned the wartime collaboration of writers. Sata Ineko, who had joined Hayashi on tours of Manchuria and Southeast Asia, wrote postwar accounts such as *Kyogi* (Falsehood, 1948) and *Hōmatsu no kiroku* (A Record of Foam, 1948), in which she agonized over how former associates were condemning her participation in government-defined roles and her attempts to maintain a commitment to her former political beliefs. Hayashi, however, never rationalized her actions or apologized for her participation in the war effort.

When the war was over, Hayashi returned to Tokyo. Just as she had seemed to join in the general enthusiasm for the war effort, she began to voice her opinion against the death and misery caused by war. In the early years of the occupation two of her short stories, "Ame" (Rain, 1946) and "Uruwashiki sekizui" (Splendid Carrion, 1947), were explicitly antiwar, although neither seems to draw on any personal observations from her battlefront tours. Both are set in postwar Japan and center on the dilemmas of repatriated soldiers—unwelcomed, rootless, and lost. *Uzushio* (Swirling Eddies, 1948), serialized in the *Mainichi Shinbun,* was the first work of long fiction to appear in postwar newspapers. It focused on the problems of the women widowed by the war and left to fend for themselves, often after fleeting relationships with their spouses. Hayashi's depictions of their wandering, abandonment, bare subsistence, and disillusioned intimacy tempered by irrepressible resiliency reveal much of what was best in her earlier works. This postwar fiction captured the imaginations of a generation, who found their experience reflected in it.

In "Dauntaun" (1949; translated as "Downtown," 1956, and as "Tokyo," 1961) Riyo, a young woman from the countryside, comes to Tokyo to peddle tea door-to-door in order to support herself and her son. Torn between her

Writers Hayashi, Uno Chiyo, Yoshiya Nobuka, and Sata Ineko at Yoshiya's house in 1936

obligation toward her absent husband, who she assumes is still stranded in Siberia, and the prospect of establishing a relationship with a generous and sympathetic laborer, Riyo first regretfully stifles her desires, rejects his advances, then hesitates and finally yields to a new love. When she and her son arrive at his hut for a visit, she is staggered to learn of his death in a truck accident.

"Bangiku" (1948; translated as "Late Chrysanthemum," 1956) presents the sour end to a relationship between Kin, a remarkably well-preserved former geisha more than fifty years old, and Tabe, a once-dashing young officer who has returned embittered and destitute from the war. Hayashi effectively evokes the weary disillusionment of the times through the succession of false hopes that each character embraces. The contrast between fairy-tale endings and the fortunes of Kin and Tabe is bitterly apparent to both of them, and yet Hayashi suggests that even in their disgust for each other, their emotions mix and confuse illusions about themselves with memories that they can no longer clearly recall. When the end of their relationship comes, it comes not simply from a cold calculus of self-interest or a steely rejection of sentimentality but

from the passage of time and distance that have inevitably altered both of them.

Ukigumo, Hayashi's last complete novel, recounts an affair between Yukiko and Tomioka in the wartime highlands of Indochina and their rocky relationship in postwar Japan. After Tomioka's wife dies, he is posted to remote Yakushima, an island south of Kyushu, and amid ceaseless downpours of rain Yukiko dies there following a botched abortion. She is the only female protagonist to die in all of Hayashi's work. Tomioka is deeply moved at her death, but he also feels profoundly relieved, freed from the oppressive burden of a relationship that had dragged on. This freedom, however, has its own price: he is left rootless and with no direction. As Donald Keene observes, Tomioka "will live like a drifting cloud, the traditional metaphor for an aimless life."

Much of Hayashi's most successful postwar work adopts a dark tone in portraying individuals, mostly women, confronting bleak circumstances and unpleasant choices. But unlike other nihilistic authors who also write of desperate poverty and disillusionment, Hayashi stands out in presenting the feints and false starts that fractured personalities suffer. Her characters internalize the ambiguities and conflict that characterize the uncertainties of the era, but they still embody some of the resiliency that was such a hallmark of the characters in Hayashi's *Diary of a Vagabond*. Through their interior monologues Hayashi captures their conflicting desires; how they struggle with these desires, rather than what they do or how low they descend, is what elicits the reader's sympathy.

Meshi (Meal, 1951), an unfinished novel, depicts the rather prosaic struggles that accompany an unexceptional, childless marriage. Having married for love, a man of modest yet reasonably secure income finds his marriage falling apart after five years. The circumstances and the dilemmas are far more ordinary and conventional than those in the lives of most of Hayashi's characters in previous stories. Hayashi admitted that the title is a bit enigmatic, but it refers to cooked rice, a staple of the Japanese diet, and could also imply a *meshi bukuro* (useless life). The title may symbolize this unglamorous institution of marriage, a center of the simple necessities of life. The word *meshi* often appears on signs outside inexpensive eateries in Osaka and alludes to the basic concerns of working people.

"Suisen" (1949; translated as "Narcissus," 1982) is representative of Hayashi's postwar fiction in demonstrating her growing sophistication in using language and her tightness of narrative. "Narcissus" presents the irreconcilable differences and bitter recriminations between a mother and her son. The unrelenting petty insults and bickering between two selfish, vain, and irresponsible characters sets a bleak tone and conveys an especially dark, pessimistic assessment of human relations. The story chronicles the growing rift between Saku and Tamae, the mother's growing detachment from her son, and her reaction to the eventual breakup with him. Despite her transparently hollow denials, the mother from the outset broaches her desire for separation. Her shiftless twenty-two-year-old son finally secures an offer of a job in a coal mine in Hokkaidō, and they prepare for what will be a final separation. She declares that she will not write and will not hear of him returning, even if she becomes ill or dies. Unlike Hayashi's early work, this story lacks even a hint of sentimentality: at the final parting of the two characters, the mother thinks that her son looks pathetic, and he quickly releases her hand. For her, the final parting is a liberation.

Edward G. Seidensticker heralds this closing scene from "Narcissus" as among the most memorable of postwar literature. Writing in a special issue of *Bungei* devoted to Hayashi in 1957, Mishima Yukio considers "Narcissus" to have been his favorite among Hayashi's later works; with it she reaches "the level of mature art." In contrast to the rigid conformity of any governmentally orchestrated *ryōsai kenbo* (good wife, wise mother) perspectives or any didactic moralizing of *katei shōsetsu* (household or domestic fiction), "Narcissus" depicts a world bereft of righteousness. By focusing on the most common and revered of personal relations, Hayashi reveals a dark underside of ordinary life, and she suggests that, however resilient the human spirit, the real exercise of free will is in choosing between distasteful choices.

In "Narcissus" and her other postwar fiction Hayashi departs from the lyrical sentimentality that characterizes earlier work such as *Diary of a Vagabond*. In these later works her language reveals some of the standard, composed, and complex grammatic constructions evident in her revisions of *Diary*. Perhaps the most striking change in her style, however, is in her shift from a fragmented, discontinuous narrative that leaves many incidents either partially or wholly unresolved to a structure that is more clearly delineated, with a standard beginning, middle, and end, and that unfolds to reveal a tightly rendered story. Even in purportedly autobiographical later works such as *Paris Diary*, Hayashi presents incidents in a continuous narrative, in chronological order, and within a discrete time frame.

The continuities in Hayashi's work, taken as a whole, are also striking. Her characters, predominantly women, embody a dogged determination, perseverance, and resilience in spite of the unrelenting woes that besiege them. Most of Hayashi's work illuminates the lives of an underclass, catch-as-catch-can world that is often drab or desperate. If her comparatively comfortable working family in her last, unfinished novel occupies a lower-middle-class station, its members still feel the powerlessness that marks the lives of her earlier characters. But Hayashi infuses a humanity in the lives of all these characters and conveys their unextinguished aspirations and anxieties among the debris of their broken dreams. The world presented in Hayashi's fiction is *minshuteki* (of the people), but not from any ideological commitment or motives of political correctness. Hayashi drew her portraits within a small social milieu: descriptive depictions of *shomin no seikatsu* (everyday life). Yet her point of view was not restricted to a particular social class or gender.

Hayashi's career was shadowed by the notion that she was a "woman writer," but this designation also advanced it. Through *Nyonin Geijutsu,* the women's journal, Hayashi found a publication outlet that would allow free rein for the originality of *Diary of a Vagabond* and its successful blend of idioms and themes of classical women's diaries along with portraits of figures in impoverished circumstances. After *Diary* had made Hayashi a public figure, she wrote for an audience that wanted to learn more about her. She used all the opportunities—tours, lectures, and even airplane relays—that her prominence as a woman writer could afford in order to acquire and preserve a celebrity status and to garner offers for publication. As she tried to establish herself as a writer of serious fiction in mainstream presses and literary journals, Hayashi also continued to publish ostensibly autobiographical works that catered to the expectations of her audience. Her embrace of this identity as a woman writer secured her a status capable of providing security solely through her publications for more than twenty years.

Biographies:

Itagaki Naoko, *Hayashi Fumiko no shōgai: uzushio no jinsei* (Tokyo: Raifusha, 1965);

Fukuda Kiyoto and Endō Mitsuhiko, *Hayashi Fumiko: hito to sakuhin* (Tokyo: Shimizu Shoin, 1966);

Hirabayashi Taiko, *Hayashi Fumiko* (Tokyo: Shinchōsha, 1969);

Onomichi Dokusho Kai, ed., *Onomichi to Hayashi Fumiko—arubamu* (Onomichi: Onomichi Public Library, 1984), pp. 163–168;

Takemoto Chimakichi, "Ningen-Hayashi Fumiko (1): tsuminokoshi—Nomura ron," *Hiuchi,* 7 (1986): 94–113.

References:

Bungei, special issue on Hayashi, 14 (1957);

Itagaki Naoko, Afterword to her *Hayashi Fumiko shū* (Tokyo: Kadokawa, 1953), pp. 405–420;

Donald Keene, "The Revival of Writing by Women," in his *Dawn to the West,* 2 volumes (New York: Holt, Rinehart & Winston, 1984), I: 1113–1166;

Muramatsu Sadataka, "Hayashi Fumiko no dansei henreki," in his *Sakka no kakei to kankyō* (Tokyo: Shibundō, 1964), pp. 202–217;

Nakamura Mitsuo, "Hayashi Fumiko bungaku nyūmon," *Bungei,* 14 (1953): 20–27;

Edward G. Seidensticker, "Hayashi Fumiko," translated by Saeki Shōichi, *Jiyu,* 5 (1963): 122–131;

Tamiya Torahiko, "Kaisetsu," in *Meshi,* by Hayashi (Tokyo: Shinchōsha, 1982), pp. 217–221;

Victoria Vernon, "Between Osan and Koharu: The Representation of Women in the Works of Hayashi Fumiko and Enchi Fumiko," in her *Daughters of the Moon: Wish, Will, and Social Constraint in Fiction by Modern Japanese Women* (Berkeley: University of California Press, 1988), pp. 137–169;

Yukiko Tanaka, "Hayashi Fumiko," in her *To Live and to Write: Selections by Japanese Women Writers* (Seattle: Seal, 1987), pp. 99–104.

Hirabayashi Taiko
(3 October 1905 – 17 February 1972)

Lin Shu-Mei
Bunkyō University

BOOKS: *Seryōshitsu nite* (Tokyo: Bungei Sensensha, 1928);

Naguru (Tokyo: Kaizōsha, 1929);

Fusetsu ressha (Tokyo: Nihon Hyōronsha, 1929);

Sekken kōjo no dōshi (Tokyo: Shiokawa Shobō, 1930);

Kōchi (Tokyo: Kaizōsha, 1930);

Shinsen Hirabayashi Taiko shu (Tokyo: Kaizōsha, 1932);

Hanako no kekkon, sono ta (Tokyo: Keishōdō, 1933);

Kanashiki aijō (Tokyo: Naukasha, 1935);

Hirabayashi Taiko senshū (Tokyo: Banrikaku, 1947);

Kō yu onna (Tokyo: Chikuma Shobō, 1947);

Watashi wa ikiru (Tokyo: Itagaki Shoten, 1947);

Jinsei jikken (Tokyo: Yakumo Shoten, 1948);

Onna no kaidō (Tokyo: Sankō Shorin, 1948);

Chiitei no uta (Tokyo: Bungei Shunjō Shinsha, 1949);

Tsuyu no inochi (Tokyo: Bungei Shunjō Shinsha, 1949);

Onna oyabun (Tokyo: Seiseidō Shuppanbu, 1949);

Taiko Nikki shō (Tokyo: Itagaki Shoten, 1949);

Jōnetsu kikō (Tokyo: Kōdansha, 1950);

Haru no mezame (Tokyo: Chūō Kōronsha, 1950);

Eiyo fujin (Tokyo: Bunko, 1950);

Yume miru onna (Tokyo: Daikō Shuppansha, 1950);

Honoo no ai (Tokyo: Minato Shobō, 1951);

Fūfu meguri (Tokyo: Shufu no Tomosha, 1952);

Momoiro no musume (Tokyo: Yomiuri Shinbunsha, 1953);

Aijō ryokō (Tokyo: Shinchōsha, 1953);

Owareru onna (Tokyo: Mainichi Shinbunsha, 1954);

Onna hitori (Tokyo: Kōdansha, 1956);

Nagurareru aitsu (Tokyo: Bungei Shunjū Shinsha, 1956);

Onna futari (Tokyo: Kindai Seikatsusha, 1956);

Utsumuku onna (Tokyo: Shinchōsha, 1956);

Onna wa dare no tame ni ikiru (Tokyo: Murayama Shoten, 1957);

Hirabayashi Taiko

Ai araba (Tokyo: Yayoi Shobō, 1957);

Sabaku no hana, part one (Tokyo: Kōbunsha, 1957);

Sabaku no hana, part two (Tokyo: Kōbunsha, 1957);

Tsuma wa utau (Tokyo: Mainichi Shinbunsha, 1957);

Honoo no onna: Datsuhi no Ohyaku, Hanai Oume, Takahashi Oden (Tokyo: Shinchōsha, 1958);

Nikumaremondō (Tokyo: Kōbunsha, 1959);

Otokotachi (Tokyo: Shinchōsha, 1960);

Ai to kanashimi no toki (Tokyo: Bungei Shunjū Shinsha, 1960);

Hōman seijo (Tokyo: Kadokawa Shoten, 1960);

Jōnetsu no ichi (Tokyo: Kōdansha, 1960);

Jidenteki kōyūroku: Jikkantekit sakkaron (Tokyo: Bungei Shunjū Shinsha, 1960);

Fumō (Tokyo: Kōdansha, 1962);

Gendai no teijo (Tokyo: Kōdansha, 1965);

Ai to maboroshi (Tokyo: Kōdansha, 1966);

Watashi no rirekisho (N.p., 1966);

Mahiru no yōjutsu (Tokyo: Sankei Shinbun Shuppankyoku, 1967);

Sakka no tojiito (Tokyo: Haga Shoten, 1968);

Himitsu (Tokyo: Chūō Kōronsha, 1968);

Hayashi Fumiko (Tokyo: Shinchōsha, 1969);

Tetsu no nageki (Tokyo: Chūō Kōronsha, 1969);

Miyamoto Yuriko (Tokyo: Bungei Shunjū, 1972).

Collection: *Hirabayashi Taiko zenshū,* 12 volumes (Tokyo: Ushio Shuppansha, 1976–1979).

"I am the daughter of a peasant from Suwa in Shinshū province," writes Hirabayashi Taiko in the introduction to *Watashi no rirekisho* (My Life, 1966), her series of autobiographical essays. "My grandfather was involved in Itagaki Taisuke's Freedom Party, but the silk reeling factory he ran at the time went out of business because of fluctuations in the silver market, and he died an ill man. My father, who had been adopted into the family, liquidated the company and became a farmer."

Hirabayashi was born in the village of Nakasu, Suwa-gun, in Nagano Prefecture. The silk industry flourished in that area, but following the death of her grandfather, a businessman who dabbled in politics, the once-wealthy family declined and turned to farming and operating a general store on the side. In her youth Hirabayashi recalls that she assisted her mother by tending the tiny shop where, "thanks to this business, I first learned some things about the world." In 1918 she enrolled in the Suwa Higher School for Girls, operated by Nagano Prefecture. These higher schools for girls, which provided secondary education to women in prewar Japan, primarily trained women of middle-class and higher status to become "good wives and wise mothers." As a result, course content—with emphasis placed on homemaking skills such as sewing and housework—differed significantly from that offered at schools for boys. Around 1918 only a few young women—about 6 percent of those who graduated from normal elementary schools—continued their educations at these higher schools. In the village where Hirabayashi

grew up, many young women from good families ended up working in the silk factories, as her two older sisters had done. Although Hirabayashi's mother opposed having her, as the daughter of an impoverished family, continue her education, in the end Hirabayashi's strong will prevailed. Yet the education she obtained after having sought it so eagerly only discouraged her.

Hirabayashi demonstrated her strong will not only in seeking an education. In "Shisō to dansei o henreki shita seishun" (My Youth, When I Made the Rounds of Ideas and of Men, 1965) she recalls that she had "ardent demands" that continued to drive her life for many years. Even in her youth one of those demands had been the urge to become a writer, but in 1918, as the end of World War I spurred a rapid growth of capitalism in Japan, Hirabayashi was not satisfied merely with an opportunity to pursue her interest in literature.

The end of the war came only a year after the Russian Revolution, and the impact which that revolution had on social philosophy, the labor movement, and intellectuals in Japan marked the beginning of a new era. Demands for freedom and the rise of a new middle class of white-collar workers had been produced by a wartime expansion of the economy in the mid-Taishō period, and this was to be the age of the "Taishō Democracy." The expanding social roles of the intelligentsia and the working class also encouraged a surge in socialist activities, and in 1920 the Japan Socialist League was formed. This organization included socialists with the diverse political and economic interests of anarchists and labor-union activists, as well as the broad social interests of philosophers, students, and literary men and women.

Hirabayashi Taiko began her literary studies at a girls' school that seemed designed to discourage women from continuing their educations, but near the age of fifteen Hirabayashi had grown increasingly interested in social matters. She read Christian labor activist Kagawa Toyohiko's best-seller, *Shisen o koete* (Crossing the Death Line, 1920), and Ikuta Chōkō's extremely flawed partial translation of Karl Marx's *Das Kapital,* published in 1919, and she was still in her fifteenth year when she sent her first letter to Sakai Toshihiko, a socialist renowned since the Meiji era. In 1921 she picked up her first copy of the pioneering journal of the Japanese proletarian literary movement, *Tane Maku Hito* (The Sower), and she recalled in "Bungaku-teki jijoden" (A Literary Autobiography, 1935) that "The intense excitement and surprise I felt from that single slim volume bound me immediately to socialism."

At the age of sixteen she wrote her first work of fiction, "Aru yoru" (One Night, 1922), and submitted it to a magazine. It is a brief piece in which a young Buddhist nun, upon learning that the master of her hermitage has died, feels that his death has freed her to live a "human life." On the day of Hirabayashi's graduation, just one month after this story was published in *Bunshō Kurabu,* she had secured a job at the Tokyo Central Telephone Company and set off for Tokyo in search of freedom.

Hirabayashi's job of supervising switchboard operators at the company was one of few high-quality jobs available for women, but she had no ambition to become a workingwoman. No doubt she wished to use the freedom that her new opportunity in Tokyo provided to discover some new identity as a member of Japanese society. One manifestation of that desire was certainly behind her move to Tokyo, in what she later wrote was her belief that her "duty lies less in literature than in the actual revolutionary movement itself."

The year that Hirabayashi moved to Tokyo was a period of intense conflict between the Bolshevik and anarchist factions of the socialist movement following the breakup of the Socialist League, which had provided a common ground for various ideological camps. The peak of the strife, a disagreement over the principles of organization, occurred at a congress held in September 1922 to create a coalition of labor unions. The congress proceeded without resolving the conflict between the two camps, and afterward the anarchist faction was excluded from the Japanese socialist movement.

Hirabayashi arrived in Tokyo during the verbal war between the two factions, and this conflict was important both to her and to her writing. Sakai Toshihiko, a Marxist critic, helped her get a job at a German bookstore after the telephone company fired her, and initially she associated mostly with members of the Bolshevik faction. But her upbringing as a daughter of the crumbling middle class filled her with antipathy toward conventional morality and the constraints of custom, and she ultimately sided with the anarchists, who rejected all forms of authority and sought to expand the prerogatives of the individual. Although Hirabayashi never became involved in any of the labor movements led by anarchist factions, her "ardent demands" were shaped during this period. While working at her new job in the bookstore in January 1923, she met Yamamoto Torazō, a young anarchist with whom she began to live shortly thereafter.

All of the people who had helped to look after Hirabayashi following her arrival in Tokyo were opposed to her association with this young anarchist, but, as she wrote in "My Youth, When I Made the Rounds of Ideas and of Men,"

> the more people opposed our relationship, the closer we became. My rebellious nature was drawn toward a man who had no worldly qualifications, who had nothing but a collection of negative factors to recommend him. My feeling at the time was that I wanted to reject everything affirmed by the society, and to affirm everything they rejected.

At the age of eighteen Hirabayashi thus began to affirm everything that society rejected. She and Torazō—a naive, weak-willed young man only a year older than she—began an impulsive life together, playing at being anarchists without any real prospects for effecting social change or artistic achievement.

In September 1923 Hirabayashi and Yamamoto were arrested during the period of martial law following the Kantō earthquake and were ordered to leave Tokyo. Living in Tokyo had facilitated their anarchist interests, and after leaving Tokyo they moved to Dalian in Manchuria. At the time—January 1924—Hirabayashi was pregnant. Her life in Manchuria during the ensuing ten months was harsh and dismal, and she gave birth to, and lost, her child. After Torazō had been imprisoned for lèse majesté, she returned by herself to Tokyo. Her colonial experiences in Manchuria, however, became the basis for two excellent stories that she wrote in 1925, when she was completely unknown as a writer: "Nagesuteyo!" (Give Up!, 1927) and "Seryōshitsu nite" (In the Charity Ward, 1927). These stories recount how her lover is arrested for a trivial matter, and, suffering from malnutrition, she gives birth in a charity hospital to a child who dies almost immediately. Although the situations she presents are tragic, her aim is not to portray the pathos of her experience, but rather to depict the passion that had helped her survive the fate that she had chosen.

Only a few months after her return to Tokyo, Hirabayashi became sexually involved with three different men. This profligacy perhaps resulted not from her desire for men so much as from her impatience to find something that would continue to stimulate her yearning to oppose the world around her. She writes of this time in *Watashi no rirekisho* that "because I was a woman, there was one aspect within myself that had to be opposed. . . . I opposed my own chastity." She freely chose these sexual liaisons, all of which involved young Japanese rebels, fledgling artists whose opposition was linked to the arts: Takamizawa Chūtarō (later known as Tagawa Suihō), Okada Tatsuo, and Iida Tokutarō were all leaders of the avant-garde movement that flourished briefly after the Kantō earthquake. Takamizawa and Okada were painters and members of the influential "Mavo" group at the forefront of many avant-garde fields, while Iida was a member of the coterie that produced *Damudamu,* the journal of Dadaist writing.

The artistic movement driven by these rebels aimed at overturning all prevailing aesthetic values and was also a plan for social insurgency. The men associated with Hirabayashi belonged to a group known as the "black criminals," a term used in a declaration published in *Aka to Kuro* (Red and Black), the first anarchist magazine to be published, in January 1923, and one which Itō Sei, in his *Shōwa bungaku seisuishi* (A History of the Rise and Fall of Shōwa Literature, 1958), has used to characterize their belief that their activities were essential in creating Shōwa literature. Hirabayashi wrote many proletarian works of fiction, and one must recall that her literary origins lay in this avant-garde mixture of anarchism and Dadaism.

Her relationship with Iida Tokutarō began around March 1925 and continued for about one and one-half years, but her life with this man, whose one desire was to scorn social institutions, was miserable. He made her work as a waitress in a café and even forced her into prostitution with acquaintances so that he could borrow money from them. While working at the café Hirabayashi met Hayashi Fumiko, a poet who was also working there and whose lover was also an anarchist. The two women were among the first female intelligentsia to appear during this era, and in her reminiscences in "Himawari" (Sunflower, 1931–1932) Hirabayashi wrote of her association with Hayashi that "the path which the two of us had trod up until that point in time was a path from which women can seldom escape—a path upon which women have no money or physical beauty, but where they yearn for some kind of freedom."

During the time Hirabayashi lived with Iida, she wrote "Azakeru" (1927; translated as "Self-Mockery," 1987), a superb story that she published two years later. Set in the metropolis,

this story presents a corrupt, transient woman who invites the antipathy of strangers she passes on the street. This woman, who tells the story in the first person, recounts her experiences as a prostitute, a woman whose body has been transformed by urban life into a marketable commodity. She also wrote several detective stories at about the same time, and the social content of her works in this genre, which depict the obliteration of all traces of the individual by the masses of the city, are not far different from what Hirabayashi presents in "Self-Mockery."

In January 1927 Hirabayashi married Kobori Jinji, a Marxist who was associated with the leftist journal *Bungei Sensen* (Literary Battlefront) and was introduced to her by Yamada Seizaburō, the editor of the journal. Having closed out the turbulent period of her life through marriage, Hirabayashi began an active period of writing. In the following year she attracted attention and became recognized as an influential writer of proletarian literature after she published "Yokaze" (Night Wind), which describes the bitter lives of peasants, and "Naguru" (Beating). Disputes between the Japanese Communist Party and the Laborers and Peasants' Party caused repeated shifts in sympathies and allegiances among proletarian writers of the day, but Hirabayashi and her husband steadfastly supported the workers and peasants and criticized the political manipulations of the so-called "NAPF," the Japan Proletarian Artists' Federation. Her commitment to anarchism ended when she married, but it is unclear whether her marriage also betokened her philosophical conversion to Marxism. Her anarchism had been essentially motivated by emotion, and Hirabayashi does not seem to have been inspired by philosophical considerations.

Life with her socialist husband was a struggle, but the two endured the difficulties with love and cooperation despite the complications. When Kobori and other leftists were arrested in February 1937 during a roundup known as the Popular Front Affair, Hirabayashi was also confined for eight months for having attempted to stop the police from taking her husband away. She contracted tuberculosis in jail, and this condition kept her in a sickbed until 1944. Her physical condition was serious, and Kobori cared for her and raised money to pay for her convalescence by translating works and serving as a civil engineer. Hirabayashi was grateful for his care, but in 1955 the demands of her life as a writer and her husband's infidelities led to their divorce.

After the end of the war Hirabayashi published a series of memorable short stories. "Hitori iku" (I Go Alone, 1946) provides an autobiographical depiction of the trials she endured in the 1930s. "Kō iu onna" (This Kind of Woman, 1946), "Mekura Chūgokuhei" (1946; translated as "Blind Chinese Soldiers," 1980), "Kishimojin" (1946; translated as "The Goddess of Children," 1952), and "Watashi wa ikiru" (I Mean to Live, 1947) established her as one of the most active female authors in postwar Japan. Despite some criticism of the change in her political stance from the prewar era and some censure of her various political pronouncements, she continued her many literary activities. The works that she published on female writers Hayashi Fumiko in 1969 and Miyamoto Yuriko in 1972 are invaluable studies of her literary contemporaries.

References:

Abe Namiko, ed., *Hirabayashi Taiko* (Tokyo: Nichigai Associates, 1985);

Itagaki Naoko, *Hirabayashi Taiko* (Tokyo: Raifusha, 1956);

Kurabayashi Taira, *Hirabayashi Taiko* (Tokyo: Nanshin Nichinichi Shinbunsha, 1975);

Teshirogi Haruki, ed., *Hirabayashi Taiko tsuitō bunshū* (Tokyo: Hirabayashi Taiko Kinen Bungakukai, 1973);

Toda Fusako, *Moete ikiyo: Hirabayashi Taiko no shōgai* (Tokyo: Shinchōsha, 1982).

Ibuse Masuji

(15 February 1898 – 10 July 1993)

Anthony V. Liman
University of Toronto

BOOKS: *Shigotobeya* (Tokyo: Shun'yōdō, 1931);
Kawa (Tokyo: Egawa Shobō, 1932);
Zuihitsu (Tokyo: Shii no Kisha, 1933);
Tōbōki (Tokyo: Kaizōsha, 1934);
Den'enki (Tokyo: Sakuhinsha, 1934);
Kataguruma (Tokyo: Noda Shobō, 1936);
Seiyashi (Tokyo: Mikasa Shobō, 1936);
Keirokushū (Tokyo: Takemura Shobō, 1936);
Yakuyoke shishū (Tokyo: Noda Shobō, 1936);
Shūkin ryokō (Tokyo: Hangasō, 1937);
Jon Manjirō hyōryūki (Tokyo: Kawade Shobō, 1937); translated by Hisakazu Kaneko as *John Manjiro, the Castaway: His Life and Adventures* (Tokyo: Hokuseidō, 1941);
Sazanami gunki (Tokyo: Kawade Shobō, 1938); translated by David Aylward and Anthony Liman as *Waves: A War Diary,* in their *Waves: Two Short Novels* (Tokyo: Kodansha International, 1986);
Kamokudo (Tokyo: Hangasō, 1938);
Rōkō no uta (Tokyo: Shun'yōdō Shoten, 1938);
Kinsatsu (Tokyo: Takemura Shobō, 1939);
Kawa to tanima (Tokyo: Sōgensha, 1939);
Oroshabune (Tokyo: Kinseidō, 1939);
Fuzoku (Tokyo: Modan Nihonsha, 1940);
Shiguretō jokei (Tokyo: Jitsugyō no Nihosha, 1941);
Shiki shishū (Tokyo: Sangabō, 1941);
Natsu no kitsune (Tokyo: Shun'yōdō Shoten, 1941);
Fūbō shisei (Tokyo: Shun'yōdō Shoten, 1942);
Ibuse Masuji shū (Tokyo: Kaizōsha, 1942);
Chūshū meigetsu-shishū (Tokyo: Chiheisha, 1942);
Chushu meigetsu-techō bunko (Tokyo: Chiheisha, 1942);
Ichiro heian (N.p., 1942);
Gojinka (Kyoto: Kōchō Shorin, 1944);
Tange-shi-tei (Tokyo: Shinchōsha, 1945);
Magemono (Tokyo: Kamakura Bunko, 1946);
Wabisuke (Tokyo: Kamakura Bunko, 1946); translated by Aylward and Liman as *Isle on the Billows,* in their *Waves: Two Short Novels;*

Ibuse Masuji

Oihagi no hanashi (Tokyo: Shinchōsha, 1947);
Ibuse Masuji senshū, 9 volumes (Tokyo: Chikuma Shobō, 1948);
Yofuke to ume no hana (Tokyo: Shinchōsha, 1948);
Sanshōuo (Tokyo: Shinchōsha, 1948);
Kashima ari (Tokyo: Kamakura Bunko, 1948);
Shi to zuihitsu (Tokyo: Kawade Shobō, 1948);
Shibireike kamo (N.p., 1948);
Warui nakama (Tokyo: Chikuma Shobō, 1949);
Kakū dōbutsufu (Tokyo: Chikuma Shobō, 1949);
Botan no hana (Tokyo: Chikuma Shobō, 1949);
Shiken kantoku (N.p., 1949);

Nihon shōsetsu daihyōsaku zenshū, by Ibuse, Kawabata Yasunari, and Mamiya Shigesuke Henshu (Tokyo: Koyama Shoten, 1949–1951);

Horidashimono (N.p., 1950);

Ibuse Masuji shū (Tokyo: Shinchōsha, 1950);

Yōhai taichō (Tokyo: Kaizōsha, 1950); translated by Glenn Shaw as *A Far-Worshipping Commander* (Tokyo: Shinchōsha, 1955); translated by John Bester as *Lieutenant Lookeast* (Tokyo & Palo Alto, Cal.: Kodansha International, 1971; London: Secker & Warburg, 1971);

Kawazuri (Tokyo: Iwanami Shinsho, 1952);

Kikkyō no uranai (N.p., 1952);

Ibuse Masuji sakuhinshū, 6 volumes (Tokyo: Sōgensha, 1953);

Tenteki (N.p., 1953);

Genta ga tegami (Tokyo: Sōgensha, 1954);

Hyomin Nanakamado (N.p., 1955);

Zaisho kotoba (N.p., 1955);

Hakuchō no uta (N.p., 1955);

Hyōmin Usaburō (N.p., 1956);

Yane no ue no Sawan (Tokyo: Kadokawa Shoten, 1956);

Ekimae ryokan (Tokyo: Shinchōsha, 1957);

Kanreki no koi (N.p., 1957);

Nanatsu no kaido (N.p., 1957);

Chinpindo shujin (Tokyo: Chūō Kōronsha, 1959);

Nihon no fudoki (Tokyo: Hōbunkan, 1959);

Tsurishi; Tsuriba (Tokyo: Shinchōsha, 1960);

Ibuse Masuji shū (Tokyo: Shinchōsha, 1960);

Kinō no kai (N.p., 1961);

Shuzai ryokō (N.p., 1961);

Ibuse Masuji (Tokyo: Kadokawa Shoten, 1962);

Bushū hachigatajō (Tokyo: Shinchōsha, 1963);

Mushinjō (Tokyo: Shinchōsha, 1963);

Gendai bungaku taikei (N.p., 1966);

Bamen no kōka (Tokyo: Daiwa Shobō, 1966);

Kurumi ga oka (Tokyo: Bungei Shunjūsha, 1966);

Kuroi ame (Tokyo: Shinchōsha, 1966); translated by John Bester as *Black Rain* (Tokyo: Kodansha International, 1969);

Nihon bungaku zenshū 41; Ibuse Masuji shū (Tokyo: Shueisha, 1967);

Nihon bungaku zenshū 22; Ibuse Masuji (Tokyo: Shinchōsha, 1967);

Waga shi waga tomo (Tokyo: Chikuma Shobō, 1967);

Nihon bungaku zenshū 70; Ibuse Masuji shū (Tokyo: Chikuma Shobō, 1967);

Shūkin ryokō (N.p., 1969);

Nihon bungaku zenshū 23; Ibuse Masuji (Tokyo: Kawade Shobō Shinsha, 1969);

Nihon bungaku zenshū 43; Ibuse Masuji (Tokyo: Chikuma Shobō, 1970);

Tsuribito (Tokyo: Shinchōsha, 1970);

Shincho nihon bungaku (N.p., 1970);

Nihon bungaku zenshū 15; Ibuse Masuji (Tokyo: Shinchōsha, 1971);

Waseda no mori (N.p., 1971);

Hito to hitokage (Tokyo: Mainichi Shinbunsha, 1972);

Nihon bungaku zenshū gōkaban 41; Ibuse Masuji shū (Tokyo: Shueisha, 1973);

Gendai nihon bungaku zenshū 70; Ibuse Masuji shū (Tokyo: Chikuma Shobō, 1973);

Nihon no bungaku 53; Ibuse Masuji (Tokyo: Chūō Kōronsha, 1973);

Gendai bungaku taikei 44; Ibuse Masuji shū (Tokyo: Chikuma Shobō, 1976);

Gendai junin no sakka 4; Ibuse Masuji no jisen sakuhin (Tokyo: Futami Shobō, 1976);

Sugare oi (Tokyo: Chikuma Shobō, 1977);

Gendai bungaku taikei 44; Ibuse Masuji shū (Tokyo: Chikuma Shobō, 1979);

Ogikubo fudoki (Tokyo: Shinchōsha, 1982);

Nihon no meizuihitsu 18; Natsu (Tokyo: Sakuhinsha, 1984);

Yakimono zakki (Tokyo: Bunka Shuppankyoku, 1985);

Tomonotsu chakaiki (Tokyo: Fukutake Shoten, 1986);

Toto to iu inu (Tokyo: Bokuyōsha, 1988);

Dazai Osamu (Tokyo: Chikuma Shobō, 1989).

Collections: *Ibuse Masuji zenshū,* 14 volumes (Tokyo: Chikuma Shobō, 1964–1975);

Ibuse Masuji jisen zenshū, 13 volumes (Tokyo: Shinchōsha, 1985–1986).

Ibuse Masuji's writing career spanned most of this century. Through seventy years of his remarkably consistent literary work, Ibuse contributed significantly to most literary genres—short stories, novellas, novels, poems, essays, and translations. His writing expresses the painful struggle of the Japanese people for identity and documents their most shattering experience of this century—the atomic bombing of Hiroshima.

Ibuse is renowned above all for experimenting radically with styles and for becoming the voice of the *shomin* (common people). Saeki Shōichi, one of the most influential critical authorities in Japan, places Ibuse's achievement at the peak of one end of the range of aesthetic, social, and political concerns in modern Japanese literature, with Kawabata Yasunari at the opposite end. In Saeki's view Kawabata is the modern representative of the classical *monogatari* (Heian "tales") and *nikki* (diary) tradition, with their emphases on emotional subtlety, fragile nature-lyricism, and an intimate if somewhat monologuic narrative voice. Ibuse, on the other hand, wrote in the more robust classical genre of the *zuihitsu*, essays or sketches written by learned Buddhist monks, and the tradition of the historical novel practiced by writers such as Mori Ōgai. Ibuse was also keenly interested in the oral literature of the medieval period, especially the so-called *gunki monogatari* (martial chronicles). Using the rich resources of these literary traditions, Ibuse expanded the limits of the Japanese novel by grafting an epic quality onto the ancient stock of romantic nature-lyricism and by enlivening the somewhat self-centered and monologuic technique of the conventional *watakushi shōsetsu* (I-novel) with the polyphonic energy of colloquial Japanese.

Even when Ibuse treated the most solemn themes, he did so with a light, bittersweet humor often missing from modern Japanese prose. Modern Japanese literature and its critical categories were defined in Meiji through the influence of a Western center of cultural power and because Ibuse never allowed these imported concepts to shape his writing, he was rejected by both Marxist and Western-influenced humanist critics during the first half of his career. Only in the last quarter of the twentieth century or so, as Japan gradually repossessed her indigenous cultural values, has Ibuse become recognized as one of the most important modern Japanese novelists. He received the highest literary awards in Japan and was repeatedly nominated as the Nobel Prize candidate from Japan during the last years of his life.

Ibuse was born in Kamo, a small rural town in Hiroshima Prefecture. His ancestors were independent farmers of the middle *jinushi* (landowner) rank who had lived in the area since the sixteenth century. Because Minzaemon, Ibuse's grandfather, had no male descendants, Minzaemon married his daughter Miya to a *muko* (adopted husband), a younger son of a farming family in the neighboring Okayama Prefecture. Ikuta, Ibuse's father, had pronounced cultural interests: he subscribed to literary magazines and new book series from Tokyo, and he translated Chinese poetry as a hobby. He was, however, of fragile health and died when Masuji was only five years old. Ibuse's cultural tastes and deep interests in Japanese history were undoubtedly shaped by his eccentric grandfather, who was an avid reader of classical Chinese and Japanese literature and a collector of pottery and antique curios. He frequently took the boy to auctions at castles or feudal mansions, and the precisely ob-

Ibuse, around thirty-four years old (courtesy of Chūgoku Shinbun)

served detail of Ibuse's historical descriptions owes much to these youthful excursions.

After a childhood spent in this remote countryside, rich in folklore and characterized by a pronounced melodious dialect, Ibuse was sent to a prestigious high school in nearby Fukuyama. The school was rather old-fashioned in emphasizing calligraphy, the study of oriental classics, and Japanese history. When he graduated from high school, Ibuse briefly thought of becoming a painter, but after being rejected by Hashimoto Kansetsu, a master painter in Kyoto, he decided to begin literary study at Waseda University in Tokyo.

A whole new world opened to the shy country boy in Tokyo, where he arrived in late summer 1917. For the first two or three years Ibuse was just trying to get his bearings in the metropolis, and he finally settled on the study of French literature. As did so many modern Japanese writers, he spent more time trying to gain access to the literary coterie than pursuing his official studies. Among his early literary acquaintances were men such as the naturalist Iwano Hōmei, whose dissipated way of life and fairly crude prose style failed to attract the young writer; Ibuse's early writing appealed to Tanizaki Seiji, the writer and critic who was the younger

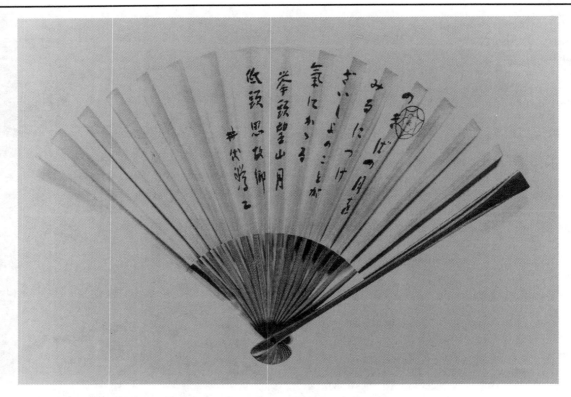

Japanese fan with calligraphy by Ibuse, lines from "Quiet Night Thoughts" by Chinese poet Li Po: "Lifting my head I watch the bright moon, lowering my head I dream that I'm home . . ."
(collection of Anthony V. Liman)

brother of famous novelist Jun'ichirō. Seiji served as Ibuse's tutor and was a harsh but fair critic for some time. Ibuse later presented "Koi" (1926; translated as "Carp," 1971), one of his first stories, to the poet Satō Haruo, who encouraged him and helped him start developing his style.

At the university Ibuse also befriended Aoki Nanpachi, who had translated into Japanese many works by French authors such as Théophile Gautier, Charles-Louis Philippe, Charles-Pierre Baudelaire, and others. Aoki served not only as a sympathetic reader but also, perhaps, as Ibuse's first editor. The first stories Aoki saw were all animal sketches, most likely executed in the *shaseibun* (nature-sketching) tradition. However, his first work—published as "Yūhei" (Confinement, 1923) but better known under its revised title, "Sanshōuo" (1926; translated as "Salamander," 1971)—is a complex story that is more than a simple animal sketch and uses a personification technique that is rare in Japanese literature.

The protagonist is a giant salamander whose head has grown so large that he is forever trapped in his cave. To alleviate the loneliness of his existence, he captures a frog, who is forced to share his confinement. This story was inspired by Anton Chekhov's "The Bet," in which a student wagers with a banker that the student can give up the pleasures and temptations of the world and spend twenty years in a cell. Ibuse's version of this confinement theme presents a multilayered parody of prevailing artistic and political pretensions as well as a merciless self-caricature of the debuting young artist. In a cultural milieu increasingly dominated by imported Marxist dogmatism, on the one hand, and the obsessive quest for truth by the naturalists and the I-novelists, on the other, Ibuse parodies the watakushi shōsetsu writers' personal laments and the assorted Romantic notions of love and the Wertherian self. Ibuse employs a deliberately stilted style that juxtaposes *yamatokotoba* (Japanese words) with high-flown Sino-Japanese compounds. This technique resembles the awkward style of direct translation from Western languages and expresses the detached viewpoint of the personified animal-speaker. The story codified Ibuse's rejection of Romanticism and helped him to assert his skepticism about life and establish a detached narrative voice. Focused on a grotesque animal, the third-person narration not only allowed radical self-caricature but enabled Ibuse to experiment boldly with norms of nature description and modes of self-expression.

In several important stories written after "Salamander," Ibuse switched to an urban setting, particularly that of Waseda University. The most noteworthy among these stories is "Koi" (Carp, 1926), an elegy for Aoki Nanpachi, Ibuse's deceased friend. The white carp of the story is a gift that Masuji received from his late friend, and the Japanese title "Koi" has also the double entendre of *koi*, or love. As an important cultural and literary symbol, the carp is featured in *koinobori* during the boys' festival, when streamers symbolizing will, strength, health, and long life are hoisted for each son in the family. The story is about boys, and the robust health of the carp sharply contrasts with Aoki's fragility and short life. Rather than serving merely as a symbol of the boys' friendship, the carp almost becomes Aoki, and the protagonist refuses to share this living embodiment of his dead friend with anybody.

In some classical stories the fish often becomes the abode of the human soul. Yet Ibuse goes beyond such an analogy in symbolically representing technical problems that he confronted as an artistic novice. He refers deliberately to French art, especially to fin de siècle symbolism, and some of the artist's polemic about the limits of symbolic expression appears in the story. Cast in first-person form, the narrative superficially reminds one of the watakushi shōsetsu by fictionalizing the artist's intense emotions.

Ibuse's early city stories were generally less successful than those inspired by the rural countryside, but this does not mean that his writing leaned toward any pastoral mode. Other twentieth-century Japanese writers found it hard to present the milieu of Tokyo because it changes so quickly in adopting many imported moods and fashions. Tokyo differs from the modern Western metropolis—in which the city is the traditional center of culture, not only in political but also in spiritual and ecclesiastical authority. In prewar Japan the countryside or the provincial towns had preserved some important features of Japanese cultural and spiritual identity, most notably the local *matsuri* (festivals).

In the late 1920s Japanese authors who resisted the pressure of a proletarian literature movement found it almost impossible to publish. Since Ibuse's family did not approve of his decision to leave the university and become a freelance writer, he could not afford to wait silently for this politicized period to pass. Avoiding the best-selling leftist publications, he kept publishing in little-known artistic journals. Moreover, he parodied the superficial, ill-digested Marxist ideology of the proletarian literature movement in several satiric stories such as "Masuji e no tegami" (A Letter to Masuji, 1930) and "Banshun" (Late Spring, 1930).

When most of the *bundan* (literary circle) influence swayed politically from the extreme Left to an equally extreme nationalist Right in the early 1930s, Ibuse remained aloof. Turning from the turbulent political arena of Tokyo, he again reached for settings and topics of his native countryside, and critics agree that this encouraged the flowering of Ibuse's creative talent. It resulted in a cycle of short stories and novellas that include several of his masterpieces, such as "Tange-shi-tei" (1931; translated as "Life at Mr. Tange's," 1971) and "Kawa" (The River, 1932). These stories are not motivated by rural nostalgia but by an interest in the mentality of the Japanese peasant, a member of a class that is far more representative of the Japanese popular psyche than is the urban proletariat.

The best among these stories is "Life at Mr. Tange's," which presents a couple of colorful rustics, a master and his servant, living in a rather unconventional household. Old Ei, the aging servant, is a foundling; Mr. Tange, his employer, is a cultured old eccentric of the landowning class. The story shows the relative sophistication of this class in southern Japan, where its members often sponsored traveling artists and poets, collected antiques and items of local history, and frequently became unofficial historians of their areas. Rather than analyzing class and power relationships, Ibuse presents the paternalistic symbiosis of master and servant that was so typical of prewar Japanese life.

In 1932 Ibuse completed the serial publication of a novella, *Kawa,* in which he attempted to capture the soul of his beloved river scenery in the manner of traditional oriental landscape painting. Yet one of its four installments was called "Sono chiiki no rokēshon" (The location of that area), and the word *location* is particularly apt: like many young writers of his generation, Ibuse was interested in the possibilities of a new medium—the motion picture. Chinese and Japanese landscape paintings are only in part the bases of his pictorial interest; he also seeks to give the narration a cinematic quality.

The outline of this story looks simple: the description of a river flowing from a spring high

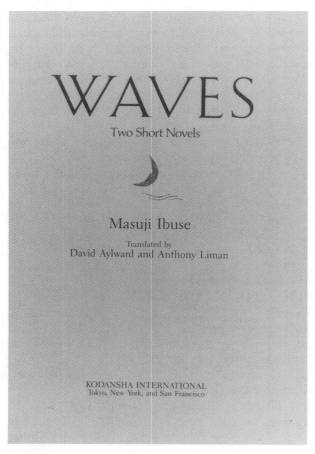

*Title page for a translation of two short novels that present the
social and personal tragedies that wartimes had brought to
pre-Meiji Japan*

in the mountains provides episodic snapshots of the fauna and flora along the banks as it flows down to the sea. A central theme of this story is the élan vital of the river and all the living forms beside it. Differences between organic and inorganic matter, between animate and inanimate life, disappear as these phenomena are presented more in holistic than in qualitative terms. This theme enables Ibuse mainly to infer that the plot is naturally given and not a result of any coincidence of fate and man's free will.

In the early 1930s the growing power of the Japanese military led to a series of expansionist adventures and eventually to World War II. Ibuse felt acutely the increasing anxiety of this era and the darkening days that lay ahead. He wanted to write about war, for war was in the air. He knew it must be an authentic, personal account, but he did not want to write from the position of a helpless modern intellectual, for his voice would have easily slipped into the wailing tone of the watakushi shōsetsu. It was also in-

creasingly dangerous to criticize directly the "national interest" of Japan, for strong antimilitary sentiment was not welcome amid the growing patriotic jingoism of the country. So Ibuse turned to historical fiction–not to escape pressing contemporary problems and find an ideal world in the past, but to cast the most urgent, most personal concerns into a classical context where they would acquire an epic breadth and an elegance that contemporary work could hardly provide.

Among these stories on historical themes the novella *Sazanami gunki* (1938; translated as *Waves: A War Diary,* 1986) stands out. Ibuse needed about ten years to complete this work–much longer than he spent on novels three or four times its length–because he had to develop both as an artist and as a human being to handle it adequately. He intended this novella–which he began writing on the eve of the Manchurian Incident and finished on the eve of World War II–to dramatize the initiation of a young boy into a cruel world at war and to show how quickly one must grow up in such a situation. The boy, young Tomoakira of the Heike clan, does age quickly–almost too fast, since the story covers only ten months or so. From being a pampered, aristocratic youth whose roughest pastime has been a game of *kemari* (a ritualized slow-motion version of soccer), he is forced to become a leader of desperate marauders, to run away from the familiar, civilized world of the capital to a wilderness of rough fishing villages and camps in the forest.

Yet even when Ibuse parodies lyrical accounts of the glory of the Heike clan and softens the pathos of their downfall, the ancient images still carry enough power and luster to give an essentially modern story the sad elegance of bygone days. Furthermore, the historical disguise–on which Ibuse had depended to provide the safe distance he needed in treating topical issues of the present–allows him to maintain better aesthetic control and perhaps even overcome some of his habitual weaknesses. Ibuse was contending with two powerful influences in writing at this time: the watakushi shōsetsu technique that was the prevailing mode of Japanese writing, on the one hand, and leftist political pressures from the literary establishment, on the other.

He had tried using Western narrative techniques before writing *Waves* and had even worked out a reasonable compromise between traditional Japanese ways of handling the first-person narrative and Western ways of doing so. Yet he was too serious an artist to imitate foreign modes when viable native ones could be modified to achieve expectations of his readers. He could not dismiss the confessional mode altogether, for he felt that it provided an authentic, credible voice that could speak intimately to a reader living in a confused age in which the objective, wide-ranging narration of an omniscient writer had lost much of its authority.

Unlike the familiar self-pitying I-novelists, Ibuse manages to preserve a considerable distance between himself and the "I" of his young narrator: he inserts another "I" (that of the translator-editor) between the two while he maintains the close focus, fine perception, and convincing subjective experience of the Japanese first-person narrative. Moreover, by placing his story—so remote in time—in the familiar landscape of his childhood, Ibuse can indulge in a lyrical excursion into the favorite scenery of his own past without being too obviously nostalgic. Many of Ibuse's personal dilemmas are symbolically represented in the painful process that his protagonist undergoes in coming of age. The boy is forced to become a man faster than he likes, and he badly needs a father figure with whom he can identify. His own father has unattractive qualities that disqualify him from serving in this role, and the boy must turn either to the staunch and brave but hopelessly rustic Miyaji Kotarō (who appears almost foolish in his sincerity) or to Miyaji's foil, Kakutan, the well-read and ingenious, if somewhat cynical, monk. These figures provide two models of courage, two "ways of the warrior" that young Tomoakira may choose to follow: the good-natured, conservative representative of the countryside; or the cooler, more efficient urban intellectual.

This was the kind of decision that Ibuse had been forced to make as a young man. Should he remain in his native village and become a provincial gentleman-farmer who dabbles in the arts? (Innoshima, the fictional Miyaji's native island, is close to Ibuse's birthplace and was one of his favorite islands.) Or should Ibuse go to the bohemian milieu of Tokyo and become a modern artist? As an extended metaphor, Tomoakira's choice between these two possible models of identity may betoken the Japanese situation at the outset of World War II, a historical crossroads for that country. Just as the young boy—whether he likes it or not—eventually chooses to act as Kakutan does (because Kakutan's way is the more efficient and "modern"), while gallant old Miyaji dies heroically, so Japan emerged from the war with a more cynical identity than it had maintained before the war (as embodied in the slightly naive figure of Miyaji).

The lofty historical theme and the diary format helped Ibuse avoid the pitfalls of the I-novel and also enabled him to develop the classical poise and aesthetic control he needed to restrain the turmoil he must have felt when virtually all his literary friends had joined the popular proletarian literature movement in the late 1920s and he—ironically the only one among those intellectuals who was genuinely interested in the common people—was left isolated. One feels a loneliness and longing for communication with human beings outside Ibuse's own class throughout *Waves*, yet these feelings do not become ideological motifs.

Waves is one of those rare, completely successful works of art that artists create once or twice in their lifetimes. A wealth of meaning blends with precise, realistic detail; colorful images of the heroic past are imbued with contemporary significance; and an entire poetic tradition is subjected to loving parody and thus to critical reinterpretation, as the best of a tradition is welded with modern, enlightened skepticism.

As xenophobia focusing mainly on Anglo-American "barbarians" grew stronger among the Japanese people, in 1937 Ibuse adopted another source of historical material—the well-known story of Nakahama Manjirō—which he used in writing *Jon Manjirō hyōryūki* (translated as *John Manjiro, the Castaway: His Life and Adventures*, 1941), his semidocumentary novella. Born in 1827 as a son of a poor fisherman in Shikoku, Manjirō is shipwrecked on an island at the age of fourteen with a party of fishermen and later rescued from there by an American whaler. The skipper, William H. Whitfield, grows fond of the intelligent boy, whom he nicknames "John" during the long voyage to Hawaii, and Whitfield invites him to the United States. At Fairhaven, Massachusetts, the captain sends Manjirō to school and later helps him become a skipper of his own whaling schooner.

What is remarkable about Ibuse's story was its time of publication: a historically true account of the close friendship between an American and a Japanese was coming out in 1937, just when the wave of hysterical xenophobia was peaking in Japan. At a time when peaceful communication between the two nations was breaking down, Ibuse rewrote and published a true story about human communication between Americans and Japanese. In troubled times and faced with real issues of life and death, Ibuse seemed to be saying, peoples of different colors and cultures who

MASUJI IBUSE

winner of Japan's highest literary award,
the Noma Prize,
of whose novel "Black Rain"
C.P.SNOW said:

"If I were thinking of, say, ten novels
of high class written in the last
twenty-five years ... I should
include this one."

IBUSE

MASUJI IBUSE

LIEUTENANT
LOOKEAST AND OTHER STORIES

LIEUTENANT LOOKEAST

by the same author as "Black Rain"

*Dust jacket for the translation of a collection of stories in which Ibuse satirizes the foibles of the
Japanese military establishment during and after World War II*

do not understand a word of each other's languages can communicate surprisingly well.

This adventure examines the possibility of human communication and explores Japanese identity–above all, linguistic identity–in posing significant questions. What happens when insular people are exposed to a foreign culture? How viable is their cultural identity in an emergency situation? At a time when Japan was about to embark on its boldest confrontation with the outside world, these were timely questions. In "Tajinko mura" (1937; translated as "Tajinko Village," 1971) Ibuse again presents this cultural identity theme, but in this story, instead of sending his protagonist on a long overseas voyage or into a hopeless flight through the turmoil of civil war, Ibuse sets his narrative in the center of the Japanese heartland, a peaceful small town in rural Shikoku. The narrator of the story is Kōda, a village policeman who keeps records of all the memorable incidents he faces in his career. The novella looks like a eulogy to a vanishing way of life, but it accurately portrays the hidden tensions and contradictions of a Japanese village, a microcosm of Japanese society.

Some critics attacked Ibuse for presenting a nostalgic vision of an idealized "nipponese" way of life, but in fact Kōda observes all the vices and conflicts within a Japanese community. By placing his narrator in the central position of a policeman, Ibuse reminds readers of the traditional role that the *shōya* (head man) played in the village community. The multiple strands of village stories and events meet in the hands of the policeman as he attempts to arrange them into a coherent narrative, and he also acts in resolving many of the villagers' problems. Thus, the narrative fulfills one of Ibuse's continuing aims: it presents a narrator who tells a complex story while maintaining some objectivity and distance (as a policeman must manage to do), as well as a man who is one of the common people whose lives he touches and whose language he speaks. Seemingly marginal episodes–such as that of Granny Okinu hanging herself because she does not want to impose on the village anymore, or that of Gankai, the Zen priest, sending young men to a distant battlefield with a sentimental song and dance–present devastating if subtly oblique critiques of the sentimentality and brutality lurking beneath the placid surface of Japanese social life.

In December 1941 the themes of war, forced exile, shipwreck, and drifting that Ibuse had used through the 1930s suddenly became frighteningly personal. Drafted into the Imperial Army on 22 November as a war correspondent, Ibuse left Kobe harbor for an unknown destination somewhere in the South Seas. His unit was eventually sent to Malaya, where he came to know the brutality of war firsthand. He describes his experiences in several diaries, most notably in "Nankō taigaiki" (Records of a Southern Voyage, 1943) and "Chōyōchū no koto" (During My Draft, 1980). A comparison of these two works shows Ibuse retelling in expanded form and in much greater detail what he could not reveal during the war, when he published the first chronicle. "During My Draft" is the longest serialized work of Ibuse's later years, and his concentration and skill in organizing the elusive material of memories reveal how seriously he was concerned to leave a truthful, objective account of the most painful period that both he and his people suffered.

On the transport ship and during the Malayan campaign Ibuse met some fanatical officers whom he transformed into characters in satiric postwar stories such as *Yōhai taichō* (1950; translated as *A Far-Worshipping Commander,* 1955, and as *Lieutenant Lookeast,* 1971). In this work Ibuse presents an army lieutenant who, following an accident in Malaya, has become deranged and believes that the war has not ended. His mind is frozen in the war years, and he responds to an entirely different language and with different emotions from those of the postwar period. His part of the village is referred to as *kōchi ga megeru* (ruptions over here), which correlates with the fractured state of his mind—it is split between the here and now of the postwar village and the distant battlefields of Malaya. In his "normal" state, he believes he is stationed at home; during his fits, he thinks he is on the war front. In symbolic terms, the "ruptions over here" run not so much through any remote village in the south as through the mind of the Japanese Everyman.

Another remarkable story of Ibuse's postwar period is *Wabisuke* (1946; translated as *Isle on the Billows,* 1986), which he finished writing just one day before the first United States jeep arrived in his village of Kamo in Hiroshima Prefecture, where he was staying in his parents' house to escape the raids and the famine in Tokyo. That Ibuse wrote the story at this particular time is significant: the war had ended at last; most Japanese cities were smoldering rubble; the exhausted population was starving; and the survivors of the atomic bombing of Hiroshima were still painfully shocked throughout Ibuse's native

prefecture. Ibuse had seen enough of the war—at close range—through his service as a war correspondent during the fall of Singapore. He had not liked being inducted into the army, and he liked even less what he saw during his service in Malaya. Although many of his literary colleagues had written patriotic articles praising the heroism of the Japanese soldier or supporting the official ideology of the Greater East Asia Co-prosperity Sphere, Ibuse had never done so. He returned from war service as an angry man, critical not only of the military clique but also of the ruling bureaucracy of institutions.

Ibuse expressed this anger in several powerful stories. *Isle on the Billows* is less a satire on the army and its tyranny over the common people than *Lieutenant Lookeast,* but it caricatures the samurai bureaucracy. *Isle on the Billows* conveys Ibuse's conviction that the world of the common people has almost nothing to do with that in which their superiors lived, as many intimations in the imagery of the story suggest. For instance, Hadakajima, the name of the island, is written with three characters meaning "High-Wave Island" and has a double entendre of "Naked Island," which suggests that this penal colony is a microcosm of Japanese society, with its power structure baldly exposed. A chain of bureaucrats stretches from the top of the social hierarchy, in which the well-meaning shogun and his religious adviser overzealously administer law, down to the ambitious warden of a small penal colony. By aping their superiors, these political climbers seek to reach the exalted status of their betters.

In contrast to these bureaucrats, who can easily replace each other, the common people (and especially their representative in the story, Wabisuke the Bird-Catcher) each possess individual crafts and skills. Anyone can become a warden and copy the refined way of beating prisoners by drumming on their backs, but no one can catch four sparrows with one thrust of the fowling rod, or tell at a glance what kind of bird is nesting high in the branches of a tree, as Wabisuke can. Although Ibuse does not idealize him—he is an earthy workingman, inarticulate and socially clumsy at times—Wabisuke's name combines connotations that suggest he is more than a simple Everyman. *Wabisuke,* which translates as "companion in solitude," is also the name of a modest yet elegant variety of camellia.

In 1956 Ibuse published *Hyōmin Usaburō* (Usaburō the Drifter), one of his rare longer works. This novel continues the themes of shipwreck and drifting from earlier stories and novellas,

Dust jacket for the translation of Ibuse's novel documenting the bombing of Hiroshima

and it explores again the question of Japanese identity vis-à-vis the rest of the world. Unlike Nakahama Manjirō, Usaburō is a marginal historical figure about whom little is known, although his adventures were extraordinary. Before spending some years in Russia and in Hawaii, he was shipwrecked in the northern seas of Japan and rescued by an American whaler. The novel explores the clash of linguistic identities by using a carefully stylized dialogue in which the foreigners speak broken Japanese and the Japanese respond in broken foreign languages. The narrative reveals Ibuse's sense of how his insular, sheltered mother-tongue will increasingly be exposed to the onslaught of world languages and how the Japanese "cocoon mentality" must gradually adjust to cultures abroad.

Throughout his career Ibuse pursued his favorite hobby of fishing, a pastime that complemented his writing. Even after leaving his native countryside, Ibuse needed to maintain his rapport with nature and its creatures, and in pursuing his hobby he also collected material for his stories by familiarizing himself with the rural locales that he wished to use as settings. *Kawazuri* (River Fishing, 1952) was the first collection of his fishing stories and essays, and it contains stories such as "Shiraga" (White Hair) and "Wasabi nusubito" (Wasabi Thieves). In 1960 he published *Tsurishi; Tsuriba* (Fishermen; Fishing Holes), another collection of essays, and this was followed by another, *Tsuribito* (Anglers), in 1970. Ibuse probably owes to his fishing expeditions the precision and economy of his marvelous landscape descriptions. Mountain fishing, its elaborate etiquette, and the presence of healthy fish in clean streams came to represent symbolically for Ibuse the moral and ecological health of Japan through the postwar period. Most of his fishing stories feature his favorite figure of the *rōjin* (wise old man), a character who embodies Ibuse's philosophy, expresses the soul of Japan, and bears its identity through the trials of the late twentieth century.

The most memorable in this gallery of elderly men is Shizuma Shigematsu, the protagonist of Ibuse's greatest work, *Kuroi ame* (1966; translated as *Black Rain,* 1969). In taking the atomic bombing of Hiroshima as his theme in *Black Rain,* Ibuse undoubtedly accepted the greatest challenge of his career. He completed much research in preparing to write this book; in an interview with Kawamori Yoshizō, Ibuse talked about the overwhelming volume of documentary material he had to examine in Hiroshima.

Critics have suggested that in writing *Black Rain,* Ibuse paid a debt to the Chūgoku region that he had left to take up a writing career in Tokyo. Ibuse was not born in Hiroshima, as the dust jacket of the translated edition of the novel states, but in a nearby village, yet the book represents both a symbolic return to his birthplace and a return to his most familiar theme through its recounting of how, in an instant, half a million people were reduced to castaways floating on an ocean of nonsense. As Ibuse reveals, the people of Hiroshima lose their community in a faster flash than does the young boy in *Waves* or *John Manjirō,* for they live in an age of more advanced technology. The task of rebuilding their community is far more formidable than that of the protagonists in those earlier works. What the people of *Black Rain* have to rely on are the oldest gestures of village mutuality, the bits of superstition and half-forgotten provincial remedies, the memories of life-celebrating *matsuri* (festivals), the branches and fruit from the old trees of their *furusato* (hometowns), and a special kind of remembering and organizing the experience: the chronicle that Shigematsu keeps, the way of recording things for posterity that the head man of the village uses.

Ibuse modeled his protagonist, Shizuma Shigematsu, on a Mr. Shigematsu from the actual village of Kobatake. The only concession to fiction Ibuse made was to switch the standard order of Japanese family and given names: the real-life Shigematsu Shizuma became Shizuma Shigematsu in the novel. The real Mr. Shigematsu did keep a diary and record his memories of the bombing in a lively, expressive style. In the novel Shigematsu goes fishing with his friends, just as Ibuse had gone fishing with the real Mr. Shigematsu. When Ibuse heard the story of how the real Mr. Shigematsu's niece, like so many young girls in Hiroshima, had been exposed to radiation and consequently had diminishing chances of getting married, Ibuse asked if he could look at Mr. Shigematsu's diary.

Mr. Shigematsu loaned Ibuse his diary and urged him to make the story of his niece into a novel. This was probably what inspired Ibuse to write the novel as a montage of diaries, and comparing the Shigematsu diary in Ibuse's novel with Mr. Shigematsu's actual diary reveals an imaginative and stylistic reworking of the latter. In addition to the indomitable Dr. Iwatake, Ibuse introduces several characters who appear under their real names. Mr. Satō Susumu, a friend of Ibuse, was for some years a respected member of the prefectural parliament. Satō and others recalled how for several months Ibuse walked the streets of Hiroshima and measured the widths of its streets, the positions of its buildings and temples, and the lengths of its many bridges.

The novel has a sound documentary basis, although many survivors have commented that the reality of the bombing and its aftermath were far more gruesome than the novel represents them to have been. But Ibuse avoids depicting the disaster in its totality and instead sets the beauty of the southern landscape, the ancient customs of the people, their colorful foibles, and the everyday details of their lives against the absurd brutality of the holocaust. All his previous thematic interests and artistic techniques served him well as he wrote this novel. He displays his characteristic sympathy for the simple life and his knowledge of popular lore as well as the calm detachment of the chronicler that he had become through his earlier historical writings.

As an elegy for a city and its people, *Black Rain* differs from many sentimental and political accounts of the bombing, and it is a central work in Ibuse's oeuvre. He maintained a wholesome vision of life through rather dark times not by inserting a verbal screen between himself and reality but by writing in accord with what he believed: that writing—no matter how polished—is one of life's meaningful chores, an activity rooted in the records of the lives of his people.

Ogikubo fudoki (Ogikubo Chronicles, 1982) was published when Ibuse was eighty-four years old and had been living in the Ogikubo district of Tokyo continuously for fifty-five years—except for short fishing trips and the year of wartime service in Singapore. Like the authors of the old *fudoki*, or ancient local "histories of natural features," Ibuse records those features of his community, but he does so in a modern, playful way. He offers his readers a loving evocation of some features of the city's ward, the aura of its past, and the origins of its local names, for all these express the soul of the locale. He does not project nostalgic images of his old country home into the reality of the present urban landscape. Having established his local milieu and placed himself firmly at its center, Ibuse then sums up his writing career with apparent nonchalance. With a little of the Japanese *akirame* (old age resignation) along with Ibuse's honesty and humanism, this late narrative presents a witty, relaxed, and revealing autobiographical summary of his life.

Bibliography:
Ibuse Masuji bungaku shoshi (Tokyo: Nagata Shobō, 1985).

References:
Arthur G. Kimball, "After the Bomb," in his *Crisis in Identity and Contemporary Japanese Novels* (Rutland, Vt. & Tokyo: Tuttle, 1973);

Robert J. Lifton, "Black Rain," in his *Death in Life: Survivors of Hiroshima* (New York: Simon & Schuster, 1967);

Anthony V. Liman, "Ibuse's Black Rain," in *Approaches to the Modern Japanese Novel,* edited by Kinya Tsuruta and Thomas E. Swann (Tokyo: Sophia University Press, 1976);

J. Thomas Rimer, "Tradition and Contemporary Consciousness: Ibuse, Endō, Kaikō, Abe," in his *Modern Japanese Fiction and Its Traditions* (Princeton: Princeton University Press, 1978);

John W. Treat, *Pools of Water, Pillars of Fire* (Seattle & London: University of Washington Press, 1988).

Iwano Hōmei

(20 January 1873 – 9 May 1920)

Richard Torrance
Ohio State University

BOOKS: *Yūshio* (Tokyo: Hidaka Yūrindō, 1904);
Hiren hika (Tokyo: Hidaka Yūrindō, 1905);
Shinpiteki hanjūshugi (Tokyo: Sakuma Shobō, 1906);
Shintaishi no sahō (Tokyo: Shūbunkan, 1907);
Yami no haiban (Tokyo: Hidaka Yūrindō, 1908);
Shin-Shizenshugi (Tokyo: Hidaka Yūrindō, 1908);
Tandeki (Tokyo: Ekifūsha, 1910);
Hōrō (Tokyo: Tōundō, 1910); enlarged as part of *Hōmei gobusaku sōsho* (Tokyo: Shinchōsha, 1919);
Hatten (Tokyo: Jitsugyō no Sekaisha, 1912); enlarged as part of *Hōmei gobusaku sōsho*;
Bonchi (Tokyo: Shokuchiku Shoin, 1913);
Sumiya no fune (Tokyo: Okamura Shoten, 1913);
Kindai shisō to jisseikatsu (Tokyo: Tōadō, 1913);
Dokuyaku o nomu onna (Tokyo: Suzuki Miekichikata, 1914); enlarged as part of *Hōmei gobusaku sōsho*;
Kindai seikatsu no kaibai (Tokyo: Kōbunkan, 1915);
Kakei Hakase no Ko-Shintō no taigi (Tokyo: Keibunkan, 1915);
Akumashugi no shisō to bungei (Tokyo: Tengendō, 1915);
Koi no sharikōbe (Tokyo: Kinfusha, 1915);
Seifuku hiseifuku (Tokyo: Shun'yōdō, 1919);
Hōmei gobusaku sōsho: Hōrō, Hatten, Dokuyaku o nomu onna, Dankyō, Tsukimono (Tokyo: Shinchōsha, 1919);
Moeru juban (Tokyo: Nihon Hyōronsha, 1920);
Hitsū no tetsuri (Tokyo: Kōbunkan, 1920);
Setsuna tetsugaku no kensetu (Tokyo: Kōbunkan, 1920).
Collections: *Hōmei zenshū*, 18 volumes (Tokyo: Kokumin Tosho Kabushiki Kaisha, 1921–1922);
Iwano Hōmei zenshū, 16 volumes (Kyoto: Rinsen Shoten, 1994–1996).

TRANSLATION: Arthur Symons, *Hyōzō-ha no bungaku undō* (Tokyo: Shinchōsha, 1913).

SELECTED PERIODICAL PUBLICATIONS—UNCOLLECTED: *Dankyō* [serialized novel], *Mainichi Denpō* (January–March 1911); enlarged as part of *Hōmei gobusaku sōsho*;

Iwano Hōmei

Neyuki [serialized novel], *Shinshōsetsu* (May–July 1912); enlarged as part of *Hōmei gobusaku sōsho*.

The many writers associated with Japanese naturalism during its period of greatest influence from 1906 to 1910 each found different ideas and motives borne by it. As a national literary movement that drew support from the provinces and transformed linguistic, intellectual, and artistic sensibilities, naturalism underlay the "bourgeois individualism" of Shimazaki Tōson, the Wordsworthian Romanticism in the nature descriptions of Kunikida Doppo, the leveling and simplifying of style advocated by Tayama Katai, the nihilism of Masamune Hakuchō, the nationalism of Hasegawa Tenkei, and the aestheticism of everyday life in the works of Shimamura Hōgetsu. Iwano Hōmei, in both his life and his writing, was the author who most thoroughly embodied these diverse and at times contradictory ideas and motives.

With the possible exception of Shimamura Hōgetsu, Hōmei was the most intellectually consistent and philosophically grounded theorist of Japanese naturalism, and his thinking has continued to influence Japanese literary, political, and philosophical discourse. Perhaps modern historians have not readily acknowledged the debt owed to Hōmei because many of his actions and convictions—his scandalous treatment of women, his praise for the salutary effects of war, his advocacy of the imperial office, his belief in Nietzschean superheroes—offend contemporary orthodoxies. Ōsugi Sakae, the well-known anarchist, wrote in 1915 that Hōmei was a magnificent fool—"Hōmei wa idai naru baka da!"—and many readers still find this to be an apt characterization.

Iwano Hōmei was born Iwano Yoshie, the oldest son of a low-ranking samurai of the Tokushima domain. After the Meiji Restoration of 1868, his father, Tadao, became a constable in what later became Tokushima Prefecture, and Tadao held this position until 1888, when he and his family moved back to Tokyo. Brought up by a family with few financial resources in a domain torn by factional strife, Hōmei had few pleasant memories of his childhood, but his father managed to provide him with an education, the only route to success for male children of former samurai deprived of hereditary incomes in the new Meiji state. In 1887 Hōmei began studying English at a Protestant missionary academy in Osaka, and he was baptized that same year. The following year he rejoined his family in Tokyo and enrolled at Meiji Gakuin, a Christian college where Tōson, who became his literary rival, also was studying.

Until 1906 Hōmei was merely an intellectual surviving on the margins of an expansive growth in publishing and education in Japan. He was a student in political economics at Senshū Gakkō, Japan's first private law and business college; a student and instructor at Tōhoku Gakuin, a Christian college in Sendai; and an instructor at private academies and night schools after he returned to Tokyo in 1894. He married Takenokoshi Kō in 1895, took a series of editing

and translating jobs for small magazines, and established himself as a poet with journals associated with the Christian romanticism of Kitamura Tōkoku. Although Hōmei's gradual disillusionment with Christianity began several years after his conversion, he was still translating Methodist hymns into Japanese for John Carrol Davidson, a Protestant minister, in 1895. The depth of Hōmei's engagement with Christianity is most apparent in *Shinpiteki hanjūshugi* (Mystic Demianimalism, 1906), which expresses his rebellion against the universal ethics of Ralph Waldo Emerson, Emanuel Swedenborg, Maurice Maeterlinck, and Arthur Schopenhauer.

Despite the bombast of its title, this essay helps one understand Hōmei's later intellectual development and the continuing influence of naturalism, for the text presents a mode of argument that has been repeated in nationalistic reactions against Westernization—for example, in the "transcendence of modernity" debates of the 1930s or in the neoromanticism of Mishima Yukio. Hōmei's essay focuses on resolving dichotomies established by Western philosophy. Following Emerson and Swedenborg, Hōmei maintains that the individual is one with nature, that every person is a microcosm of the universe, and that each universe is a living poem. Nature is a physical manifestation of spirit (*shizen-soku-shinrei*), and phenomena in themselves exist not as material ends but as symbolic language in a story: each symbol in that story is infinitely interchangeable, for the distinction between symbol and symbolized is a false dichotomy. Individual identity is theoretically impossible, a mere fiction. Existence is a mutable symbolic order.

After Hōmei has acknowledged the influence of these existential Western thinkers, he then accuses them of not following their arguments to logical conclusions. Religious, philosophical, or moral systems offer no salvation from the relativity of identity and the nonreferentiality of language. The "world of will" in Schopenhauer or the moral hierarchies of nature that in Emerson and Swedenborg form ladders to transcendence are derived from Plato's doctrine of ideas or "forms" and must be rejected as methodological hypocrisy (*gizenteki ronpō*): "I long to face and inform them that if they were just to honestly examine their own positions," Hōmei writes, "they would realize 'will' itself is a purposeless symbol as well." Hōmei's insistence that language and nature have no ultimate aim or purpose reveals something distinctly contemporary and postmodern, and although he critiques

Western metaphysics with unrelenting severity, his essay is far less persistent and thorough in treating Japan.

For Hōmei, all human relations, most particularly those of love between men and women, are based on a struggle for power. The function of the state is to legitimate the victors and provide the cocoon from which the "great man," the hero, emerges. The greatest of great men in Japan is, of course, the emperor, and in justifying Japan's "unique Imperial institution," Hōmei finds a wonderful analogy in Swedenborg. The emperor, like Swedenborg's God, is a movable symbol that pervades the living bodies of all Japanese. The central, mutable identity of the emperor enables the individual to manifest the totality of the entire system. Those who are not Japanese are simply outside the circle of signification. Hōmei's imperial institution (*kokutai*) is not a universal, and the ultimate expression of universal love can be established only through war with the other, the sole means by which power relationships are established beyond doubt.

Hōmei embraced the most masculine, individualistic aspects of Japanese naturalism, and the title of his work, "Mystic Demianimalism," suggests the direction in which his career moved. The "demianimal" refers to the centaur—half-man, half-beast—and signals Hōmei's aim of overcoming the dichotomy between the spiritual and the physical. In Hōmei's thought the unity of mind and body engenders the unity of symbolism and realism (*shajitsu*). According to the peculiar way in which Hōmei defines symbolism, realism is necessarily the representation of all reality immediately experienced, at the moment of truth:

> The symbol in this world of mystery has no purpose. Thus the symbol cannot be systematized or allegorized. The genius must portray immediately the workings of his pain, the source of his inspiration. Since nature is spirit, my view of the world as a succession of symbolic moments is realism (*shajitsushugi*). Realism is the depiction of the universe realized in the moment.

This 1906 essay marks Hōmei's change from being a poet associated with Christian romanticism to being an icily nihilistic novelist and critic advocating an idiosyncratic doctrine of naturalism. By assuming an objective high ground in critiquing the metaphysical underpinnings of the Western existential tradition while incorporating that tradition to bolster Japanese nationalism, he prefigured a genre of Japanese political philosophy and literary criticism. "Mystic demianimalism" established Hōmei's reputation as a leading theorist of naturalism, and for the rest of his life he continued to mine the ideas he articulated in this essay.

As a literary theorist Hōmei in 1913 translated Arthur Symons's *The Symbolist Movement in Literature,* which may have influenced critics such as Kobayashi Hideo and Kawakami Tetsutarō. One of Hōmei's most influential essays, "Gendai shōrai no shōsetsu-teki hassō o isshinsubeki boku no byōsha ron" (My Theory of Narrative That Should Revolutionize Our Conception of the Novel in the Present and Future, 1918), advanced a "theory of one-dimensional narrative perspective" that provided a catalyst for critical thinking about the nature of narrative in modern Japanese literature and an argument for a fixed, unified point of view in prose fiction. As a nationalist, Hōmei continued to expand and clarify his ideas on symbolism and on the nature of the emperor's position in works such as "Ko-Shintō no taigi" (The Great Cause of Ancient Shinto, 1915), and he founded a journal, *Shin-Nipponshugi* (New Japanism; retitled *Nipponshugi,* Japanism, in 1916), to promote consciousness of the national will and mission. As a man of action Hōmei insisted that his literature and life were one, and he incorporated this conviction into all his major novels. It was also apparent in the pages of newspapers, which published accounts of his failed attempt as an entrepreneur and his various scandalous love affairs and marriages.

Hōmei's first successful work of fiction, *Tandeki* (Dissipation, serialized, 1909; book publication, 1910), concerns a love affair with a provincial geisha, and he dedicated the novella to Tayama Katai, whose *Futon* (1907; translated as *The Quilt,* 1981) was the most frankly autobiographical Japanese novel until that time. The two works are superficially similar. Both have protagonists clearly identifiable with the author (the first-person Tamura Yoshio in *Dissipation;* the third-person Takenaka Tokio in *The Quilt*), and both concern the "women troubles" of the two writer/intellectual protagonists. The social statuses of the women presented in each novel differ, however. Yokoyama Yoshiko in Tayama's *The Quilt* recalls Gustave Flaubert's Emma Bovary, a character educated in Western romance, brought up under Christian influence, and lost in self-delusion. Tayama's portrayal of Yokogama is equivocal and ambivalent; in *Dissipation* Hōmei presents a stock figure, a purely mercenary prostitute, from Japanese drama.

The novella opens with the hero, Tamura, lodged by the sea in Kōzu, where he is working on a play that he hopes will establish his literary reputation. The owner of a nearby restaurant sends his slow-learning son to study conversational English phrases such as "come in," "do you want beer?," and "do you want a geisha?" in order to be able to communicate with occasional foreign guests. At one of his lessons, the boy announces that the geisha employed at the restaurant wants to study English conversation, and Tamura later concludes that this has been the start of a campaign to deceive him.

Love is a power struggle with clear winners and losers, and Tamura is the loser. Kichiya is tall and has a handsome face, but except for her body she does not possess one attribute to recommend her. She is lazy, unfaithful, a little dirty, and almost illiterate. She speaks a rough provincial dialect that Tamura imitates to amuse himself, gives laughably inept performances of traditional dance and song, and is so dark complected that she is known as the "crow geisha." Yet her sluttish, animal sexuality draws Tamura to her: "My mind had become a hairy beast," he says, "and I felt its sharp nose sniffing at the rump of another beast." Indulging in this dissipation, however, has a price, and the intellectual Tamura's ill-considered promise to make Kichiya an actress in Tokyo traps him in social obligations that are enforced by Kichiya's scheming parents and the family who owns the local restaurant. Tamura ultimately has to call his wife to save him. Leaving her as a kind of hostage, he returns to Tokyo to pawn her clothing and send a sum of money to buy Kichiya's contract. When Kichiya moves to another demimondaine house in Tokyo, Tamura yields to the strong attraction of dissipation and visits her. After he discovers that she has changed her name and is now plagued with a serious eye ailment caused by venereal disease, Tamura leaves, freed from his obsession.

Hōmei's belief in the unity of life and art inspired strange, and often humorous, works of fiction. Yet read in the context of his critical writings, the descriptions Hōmei provides of crude male desires and transparent calculations about the prostitute make one admire the way his ideas about "man's animal nature" were removed from the parlor-game realm of intellectual discourse and translated into a familiar, universal realm of lust and greed, in which mind and body really are unified. Though he was one of the most sophisticated Japanese theorists of naturalism, Hōmei did not privilege the position of the intellectual. Playing out his theories in real life often required that Hōmei cast his alter ego as a quixotic figure, and he seemed enthusiastic in playing this role.

In the middle of the success he enjoyed as a leading theorist and writer of naturalism following *Dissipation,* Hōmei suddenly departed for Sakhalin to start a crab cannery. This business venture was a complete failure. After being jeered during a talk at a middle school in Hokkaido, he declared that he was emperor of the universe—indeed, that he was the universe itself—and walked off the stage. Such behavior raised rumors that he had lost his mind, and several days later he and his lover Masuda Shimoe attempted suicide by jumping off a bridge. Their fall was broken by a snowdrift, and they returned to Tokyo without injury.

Shortly afterward Hōmei began a relationship with the feminist Endō Kiyo, and the two began living together in November 1909. He divorced Takenokoshi Kō, his long-suffering wife, in 1912, formally married Endō in 1913, and in 1915 left Endō to begin another new life with Kanbara Fusae, another member of Seitō (Bluestocking), the women's suffrage group. Both Kanbara and Hōmei were still legally married to other partners, however, and the ensuing scandal placed Hōmei's name in the news once more. In 1915 and 1916 he was embroiled in various scandals and litigation. While he was negotiating with his first wife for support and custody of their children, Endō was suing him for desertion and was publishing her own account of their love affair, and Hōmei was suing a literary critic for having published an allegation that Hōmei was sexually abnormal.

In 1910 Hōmei had begun writing a series of novels based on the tumultuous events of 1908 and 1909, and this series ultimately included five major autobiographical novels. In 1917 he began rewriting and enlarging these works from a unified perspective and with a single hero, the familiar Tamura Yoshio, and beginning in 1919 these rewritten versions were published as *Hōmei gobusaku sōsho* (Hōmei's Pentalogy): *Hōrō* (Wandering), *Hatten* (Development), *Dokuyaku onna* (Poisonous Woman), *Dankyō* (Broken Bridge), and *Tsukimono* (The Possessed). In maintaining his view of the unity of art and action, he continued through the last decade of his life to publish fiction based on his complicated love affairs.

Hōmei's theoretical works on symbols and narrative, on the overarching narrative by which the emperor was legitimated, on his own life, and on ways an author should approach his material probably make Hōmei worthy of continued attention from literary and cultural historians and literary theorists. In "My Theory of Narrative That Should Revolutionize Our Conception of the Novel in the Present and Future," his response to the moral and philosophical chaos of proliferating points of view in the literature of naturalism, Hōmei advocated *ichigen byōsha* (one-dimensional description) as a means of unifying works through a single narrative perspective without unnecessary authorial interpretation. He wrote:

> Just as the author should examine his or her actual life as if he or she were an independent, different person, so the author in the literary work should decide on one character to whom to transfer his or her subjective outlook, or at least on a single character who directly participates in that subjective outlook. An author who does not do so cannot avoid including concepts and explanation in his or her description. The author must become as one with the feelings of a single character (if character A, then let it be character A) and portray life as A sees it.

Many writers in 1918 objected that Hōmei's theory would turn fiction into a monological wasteland, but he raised questions about the nature of narrative and contributed to the theoretical justification for autobiographical fiction for years to come.

Hōmei was hospitalized for symptoms of typhoid fever on 8 May 1920, and he died in the hospital the next day following an abdominal operation. Shortly after Hōmei's death Tokuda Shusei wrote that Hōmei alone had maintained the confidence and ambition to take on his own shoulders the intellectual trends of a generation, and by doing so he created many enemies. This animosity meant that he had to go through life in a crouch, constantly wary of potential attackers. This is probably a fair assessment. Hōmei articulated what he knew to be the historically significant ideas of his age, and he integrated these ideas into his life. This is what makes him a fascinating historical figure—and a "magnificent fool."

Bibliographies:

Shōwa Joshi Daigaku Kindai Bungaku Kenkyū-shitsu, *Kindai bungaku kenkyū sōsho,* volume 19 (Tokyo: Shōwa Joshi Daigaku, 1962), pp. 231–256, 286–359;

Sugimoto Kuniko, ed., "Nenpu" and "Sankō bunken," in Hōmei's *Hōmei shū,* volume 71 (Tokyo: Chikuma Shobō, 1965), pp. 429–443.

References:

Ban Etsu, *Iwano Hōmei: "gobusaku no sekai"* (Tokyo: Meiji Shoin, 1982);

Funabashi Seiichi, *Iwano Hōmei den,* 2 volumes (Tokyo: Aoki Shoten, 1938);

Donald Keene, *Dawn to the West,* 2 volumes (New York: Holt, Rinehart & Winston, 1984), I: 288–295;

Ogawa Taketoshi, ed., *Tokuda Shūsei to Iwano Hōmei: Shizenshūgi no saikentō,* volume 16 (Tokyo: Yūseidō, 1992);

Ōkubo Tsuneo, *Iwano Hōmei* (Tokyo: Nanbokusha, 1963);

Ōkubo, *Iwano Hōmei no jidai* (Tokyo: Tōjusha, 1973).

Izumi Kyōka

(4 November 1873 – 7 September 1939)

Charles Shirō Inouye
Tufts University

BOOKS: *Iki ningyō* (Tokyo: Shun'yōdō, 1893);
Nanigashi (Tokyo: Shun'yōdō, 1895);
Kanmuri Yazaemon (Tokyo: Tanaka Sōeidō, 1896);
Yushima mōde (Tokyo: Shun'yōdō, 1899);
Teriha kyōgen (Tokyo: Shun'yōdō, 1900);
Fūryūsen (Tokyo: Shun'yōdō, 1904);
Zoku fūryūsen (Tokyo: Shun'yōdō, 1905);
Chikai no maki (Tokyo: Hidaka Yūrindō, 1906);
Kusa meikyū (Tokyo: Shun'yōdō, 1908);
Onna keizu zenpen (Tokyo: Shun'yōdō, 1908);
Kōya hijiri (Tokyo: Sakura Shobō, 1908); translated by Charles Shirō Inouye as *The Tale of the Wandering Monk* (New York: Limited Editions Club, 1995) and as *The Holy Man of Mt. Kōya,* in his *Japanese Gothic Tales* (Honolulu: University of Hawaii Press, 1996);
Onna keizu kōhen (Tokyo: Shun'yōdō, 1908);
Shirasagi (Tokyo: Shun'yōdō, 1910);
Uta andon (Tokyo: Shun'yōdō, 1912); translated by Stephen W. Kohl as "The Song of the Troubadour," in *The Saint of Mt. Koya and The Song of the Troubadour* (Kanazawa: Takakuwa Bujutsu Insatsu, 1990);
Kunisada egaku (Tokyo: Shun'yōdō, 1912); translated by Mark Jewel as "The Kunisada Prints," in his *Aspects of Narrative Structure in the Work of Izumi Kyōka* (Ann Arbor: University Microfilms International, 1985);
Nihon bashi (Tokyo: Senshōkan, 1914);
Shakuyaku no uta (Tokyo: Shun'yōdō, 1919);
Yukari no onna: kushigeshū (Tokyo: Shun'yōdō, 1921);
Usu kōbai (Tokyo: Chūō Kōronsha, 1939).
Collections: *Kyōka shū,* 5 volumes (Tokyo: Shun'yōdō, 1910–1918);
Kyōka zenshū (15 volumes, Tokyo: Shun'yōdō, 1925–1927; 29 volumes, Tokyo: Iwanami Shoten, 1973–1976; Tokyo: Chickuma Shobō).

PLAY PRODUCTIONS: *Yashagaike,* Tokyo, Hongōza, July 1916;

Izumi Kyōka

Tenshu monogatari, Tokyo, Shinkyo Enbujō, November 1951.

OTHER: Gerhart Hauptmann, *Die versunkene glocke,* translated by Kyōka and Tobari Chikufū as *Chinshō* (Tokyo: Shun'yōdō, 1908).

Izumi Kyōka (given name, Kyōtarō) was a prolific novelist and playwright who, at a time when Japanese writers were finding inspiration in the realistic European novel, chose to write in a lyrical, imagistic vein that owed much to Edo-period precedents. "How glad I am to owe nothing to [Count Leo] Tolstoy," he insisted in declaring his indifference to those Western narrative conventions that redefined Japanese literature during the Meiji and Taishō periods. Although he was relegated to a place outside the literary mainstream of his own day, he of course could not altogether avoid some contemporary trends. With the naturalists he shared an obsession with the self, yet he rejected the notion of a transparent linguistic medium that would supposedly make possible an undistorted representation of reality. Preferring to use the connotative force of literary language as it had developed in symbiosis with the visual arts, he set about to create a wildly imaginative, mythopoeic world beyond the confines of the plausible and the quotidian.

His rejection of positivism was not firmly grounded in a well-articulated philosophical position. Rather, it derived from his need for literary ritual and for the ability of literature to address feelings of loss and fear—of death, disease, dogs, and thunder—that plagued him throughout his life. Kyōka needed to believe that language and literature could imaginatively effect a trespass into the realm of the dead, where one could experience the possibilities of unconditional love and salvation. His work was marginalized in his own day; yet the eccentric and even bizarre nature of his masterfully crafted stories and plays continues to attract audiences. During his lifetime he enjoyed the support of some ardent admirers, including influential members of the younger generation such as Akutagawa Ryunosuke, Tanizaki Jun'ichirō, Kawabata Yasunari, and others. After his death in 1939, his work received the attention of Mishima Yukio, whose prediction of a Kyōka revival turned out to be prophetic. In the 1970s a reevaluation of his work began, led by performances of his plays and by adaptions of his work for motion pictures, and his reputation seems still to be growing.

Kyōka, the oldest of four children, was born in Kanazawa, a castle town on the Japan Sea coast that was home to many important literary figures, such as Murō Saisei and Tokuda Shūsei. His father, Izumi Seiji, was a fashioner of fine metals; his mother, Nakata Suzu, was the daughter of a Nō musician. The changes effected by the Meiji Restoration of 1868 severely limited the demand for the articles of Seiji's craft, and consequently the Kyōka family was never prosperous. When Kyōka was nine years old, his mother died—an event that later fueled his desire to create through his writings the figure of a

sexually attractive yet maternal female savior. His desire to leave Kanazawa for Tokyo was also partly driven by this loss, for Nakata Suzu was born in Edo, and Kyōka had always associated the city with her.

His main reason for going to the capital, though, was to meet Ozaki Kōyō, who was one of the leading writers of the day. Kyōka arrived at the Shinbashi station on 31 November 1890, but the clamor of the crowds and the size of the city drained his courage, and he did not meet Kōyō until 19 October 1891. The details of Kyōka's year of wandering between Tokyo and Kamakura are hard to recover, but vague suggestions have been made that, in his extreme need, Kyōka resorted to picking pockets and possibly even working as a prostitute. Whatever the truth about such rumors might be, his knowledge of poverty and hunger certainly helped make him sympathetic to the plight of the poor.

The impecuniousness of a young man and the nurturing and sacrificing of an older woman form the thematic center of "Giketsu kyōketsu" (Noble blood, heroic blood, 1894), Kyōka's first major work, which was published in the newspaper *Yomiuri Shinbun*. Kyōka's heavily corrected manuscript shows how much the young writer, who had finally met Kōyō and become one of his students, owed to his mentor's willingness to work closely with his disciples. Because of literary conventions at the time, this novella was published jointly, and many assumed that this story about Murakoshi Kin'ya and Taki no Shiraito was Kōyō's. The figure of Shiraito, a woman who sacrifices all so that Kin'ya can pursue a law degree, is clearly Kyōka's creation, however: she is one of many women whose roles as saviors held Kyōka's interest for decades.

The work was quickly adapted for the stage, and the resourceful, sacrificing Shiraito immediately became an icon of Meiji culture. Kyōka, however, became widely recognized only later, following the publication of two short pieces, "Yakō junsa" (The Night Patrol, 1895) and "Gekashitsu" (1895; translated as "The Surgery Room," 1996). These stories, called *kannen shōsetsu* (conceptual novels) by Shimamura Hōgetsu, dealt critically with certain social ideas. In the latter work, for instance, Kyōka presents the double suicide of Countess Kifune and Doctor Takamine, who burn passionately for each other even though she is married to another man. Beautiful in death as her red blood flows over her white skin, the countess plunges Takamine's scalpel deep into her chest and dies on

Izumi Kyōka at age thirty

the operating table. To the very end she remains true to love, an absolute value in the system of morality that Akutagawa later called an "ethics based on poetry." Railing against the institution of marriage that made slaves of women who submitted to matrimony and whores of those who did not, Kyōka placed the concept of romantic love on a collision course with the paternalistic authoritarianism that was developing during the reactionary sociopolitical milieu of life in Japan during the 1890s.

Critics appreciated Kyōka's evaluations of Meiji society and called for more. But utterly disregarding their wishes and knowing that his readers had in fact misread his intention, Kyōka set out to write a series of stories in which the principal male figures are always young boys. Some literary historians suggest that he was following the lead of Higuchi Ichiyō, a woman writer whose *Takekurabe* (1895–1896; translated as *Growing Up,* 1956) was winning the praise of all. But in writing about children Kyōka was following an established path of development that eventually allowed him to satisfy his thirst for love and to gain reprieve from feel-

ings of paranoia and loss that were beginning to compromise his daily activities.

"Kechō" (A Bird of Many Colors, 1897) is a story that clearly presents his apotheosis of the mother figure. Gazing at a river on a rainy day, the young protagonist recounts an incident when he was about to drown but was plucked from death by a giant bird with brilliantly colored wings. He suspects that this mysterious bird was his mother, but its identity remains a mystery. Wanting to know the truth of the matter, he feels the seductive pull of the river—a traditional image of violence, death, and metamorphosis. Knowing that his mother will save him once again, the boy in this early story risks its danger.

This strangely fractured, image-laden story was not well received. Many critics thought that Kyōka had taken a wrong path and that his obsession with metamorphosis and monstrosity was out of place in an age of realism and reason. Just as a new aesthetic based on realistic principles was forming, Kyōka switched to a new colloquial idiom that had developed as a part of *genbun itchi* (melding of literary and colloquial) movement, while making his style richly figural. He resolved the dissonance caused by these simultaneous moves in opposite directions only in 1900, with his writing of *Kōya hijiri* (1908; translated as *The Tale of the Wandering Monk,* 1995).

In this account of the trials of a wandering monk, Kyōka presents an archetype that had been slowly developing, one in which a young (or otherwise sexually hesitant) male passes through water in order to encounter an alluring yet maternal female figure. This event also marks a trespass into the realms of death, violence, and mystery. Aided by the woman, who sacrifices herself for his sake, he returns from this journey and learns something important about himself and about the meaning of love.

The outlines of this archetypal narrative generally conform to the plot of *The Tale of the Wandering Monk,* which sets the important images—water, man, woman, forest, and mountain—into their proper relationships with each other. The careful clarification of these images breaks down, however, at the climactic moment in Kyōka's story when the monk, having survived a harrowing night in the woman's mountain hut, gazes at a waterfall and sees the woman's body being torn apart like a flower and mixed with the rushing currents of the pounding stream. The lyrical, highly visual style that prevails in this passage became the mode by which Kyōka continued to express this metastory in his fiction. Once he es-

Dust jacket for a 1992 edition of Kōya hijiri *(The Tale of the Wandering Monk, 1908), the novel
that provided Kyōka with images and narrative archetypes that shaped his later works*

tablished meanings of the principal images for his mythology by finding places for them in the archetype, he used them as a shorthand to connect his future works with this archetype. By doing this he allowed the imagery to develop his stories rather than allowing the story to develop the images. His best works after *The Tale of the Wandering Monk* are often compressed and fragmented tales that, like Nō librettos, use many flashbacks, multiple narrators, and a poetic prose with a polysemic visual texture to pull the past into the present. Having discovered what he wanted most to say, Kyōka concentrated on the process of writing at the level of the word.

Early examples of Kyōka's mature style appear in works such as "Chūmonchō" (The Order Book, 1901), a story that works out poetic connections between images such as snow, mirror, and knife as it presents narrative connections that link characters such as Owaka, the geisha who is possessed by the vengeful spirit of Onui, and Wakiya Kinnosuke, the handsome nephew of Onui's former lover. Masamune Hakuchō, who disliked the work, saw the narrative connections as being little more than coincidental. Clearly, the gap between Kyōka's standards of plausibility and those of the realists derives largely from a mythopoeic foundation that Kyōka found believable but that in 1903 many naturalist writers who flourished after Kōyō's death regarded as little more than outdated aesthetic nonsense.

No longer having the support of Kōyō and assailed by the naturalists, Kyōka's ability to find publishers for his work began to fade. Moreover, the death of Meboso Kite, his grandmother who had cared for him following his mother's death, contributed to his rapid mental and physical decline. He and Itō Suzu, his lover, left Tokyo for Zushi, a quiet town on the Shōnan Coast, where they lived for the next four years. Kyōka described himself as being "able to eat nothing but gruel" and "living in a dream, unable to tell night from day."

In this state of confusion he wrote some of his more masterful stories, including "Shun-chū"/"Shunchū gokoku" (Spring at Midday, 1906; translated as "One Day in Spring," 1996) and "Kusa meikyū" (The Grass Labyrinth, 1908), both of which use Zushi as the setting. In the former, an extended contemplation of Chuang-tzu's famous butterfly dream (which presents the boundary between dream and reality as being unknowable), a certain visitor to the area goes to a temple tucked high in the hills overlooking the sea. From the lonely priest who presides over the dilapidated temple, he hears an engrossing story about passion and madness and later encounters Tamawaki Mio, the beautiful temptress about whom he has just heard. The protagonist, identified simply as "the wanderer," represents one of three incarnations of the same man. Kyōka uses the possibilities of doppelgänger in this story and in others to underline how love and passion can fracture and multiply one's sense of identity.

Less disconcerting but no less mesmerizing is "The Grass Labyrinth," another tale of yearning and wandering. In this narrative Hagoshi Akira, the protagonist, has been searching for five years to hear the song that his dead mother once sang. His travels bring him to Zushi and finally to a deserted mansion, which has been abandoned as a place of misery and death. Despite the dangers Hagoshi dares to trespass here, even at the risk of losing his life, and spirits assail him. Yet the purity of his motives spares him from the destruction that would normally result.

This story closely follows the *jo, ha, kyū* (introduction, development, climax) structure of a classical Nō play. In the concluding scene the room in which Hagoshi sleeps is turned into a brocade of words, as many spirits sing the sought-after song while batting a ball back and forth between them. At issue in this fabulous show of language are Kyōka's profound sense of loss and his compulsion to provide answers to the question of what one can and cannot gain

through believing in words and relying on narrative ritual. As an integral part of his highly figurative rhetoric of transformation, the reality of *bakemono* (monsters) is essential; in answer to realism and its reliance on an empirical model of reality, Kyōka insisted upon the possibility of believing as seeing.

Not all of Kyōka's works written while he lived at Zushi are filled with spirits and monsters. *Onna keizu zenpen* (A Woman's Pedigree, 1908) was published in two parts as a story presenting Meiji society without such metaphors. Based on Kyōka's romance with Itō Suzu, this narrative dares to divulge the resistance that the two of them met from Kōyō, who regarded Suzu as an inappropriate partner for his most promising student. Kyōka first met her at a New Year's party attended by Kōyō and other writers of the Ken'yūsha school. Her professional name was Momotarō, but her real name was the same as Kyōka's mother, Suzu. Because of this and because she was also a true Edoite, knowledgeable about the manners of the pleasure quarters to which Kyōka was drawn, he disobeyed Kōyō and continued his romance, even though he could not hide it successfully.

This long, poorly structured novel concerns much more than this conflict between mentor and protégé, but the tension between these two proved to be the most engaging part of the book. Indeed, the adaptation of this story that was soon made for the Shinpa stage focuses directly on this conflict. Kyōka was asked to write "Yushima no keidai" (The Yushima Temple Grounds), the scene in which Hayase Chikara (modeled after Kyōka) and Otsuta (modeled after Suzu) bid each other a bitter farewell. This scene, a synecdoche for the entire play, has become a signature piece in the Shinpa repertoire and is still regularly performed as such.

Involvements such as this allowed Kyōka to develop relationships with actors and playwrights, and these in turn eventually led to his extraordinary activity as a playwright during the Taishō period. Kyōka found in the space that the stage afforded many of the same things that William Butler Yeats sought when he embraced Nō: a realm for the supernatural and for the ritual presence of lyrically conjured meanings. To establish such a space even in fiction had always been an important concern for Kyōka, for his best work had succeeded in establishing just that sacred, magical sphere, an idiosyncratic world that Akutagawa deemed "Kyōka sekai" (Kyōka's World). *Uta andon* (A Song by Lantern Light,

Hida, the setting for The Tale of the Wandering Monk

1912; translated as "The Song of the Trouba- dour," 1990), written just before Kyōka shifted to writing plays, is perhaps his best work and provides an excellent example of his creation of a memorable space in fiction. As a story about estrangement and reconciliation, "The Song of the Troubadour" is especially notable for the skill with which Kyōka interweaves its scenes, di- vided between two places and two different sets of characters. Inspired by the sight of moonlit Kuwana, he wrote the novella quickly and with a master's skill.

Some have found the shifting point of view in "The Song of the Troubadour" to be cine- matic, an implication that Kyōka learned much from his frequent visits to the movie theater. Certainly the frequency with which his stories and novels were adapted for the stage or for mo- tion pictures indicates that his ways of writing had always incorporated something dramatic and visually engaging. What is notable about the plays is how they do not simply follow the exam- ple of earlier adaptations but depart in wildly ex- perimental ways from dramatic conventions. His best plays are those such as *Yashagaike* (Demon Pond, 1916) that meander along the border be- tween the familiar and the strange, the believable and the incredible.

The drama of this play focuses on a legend

that has lost a place in the modern imagination. According to a local legend, if a bell is not rung faithfully, once in the morning and once at night, a demon that has been contained in a lake situ- ated above a mountain village will escape and thus destroy the village in a flood. The central conflict is between those few who believe and the many who do not, and in the end the believ- ers—including two anthropologists, Hagiwara Akira and Yamazawa Gakuen (modeled after Yanagita Kunio, Kyōka's friend)—are overcome by those who do not believe: no one rings the bell, and a flood occurs as the demon of the lake takes advantage of this lapse and flees to her lover in another pond. Only Gakuen survives.

Kyōka's most famous play, *Tenshu monogatari* (The Castle Keep, 1917), also mediates between the supernatural and the mundane. With an ele- gant retinue of ladies-in-waiting, beautiful young women who fish for butterflies by baiting hooks with flowers, Princess Tomi dwells in a castle away from the heartlessness of men. Her castle tower provides a space for the dispossessed, a sphere that looks down upon the barbarous. The play exploits the potential of the stage as a place of mystery and death by establishing it as an un- abashedly strange and otherworldly milieu. Prin- cess Tomi's dwelling place is not a place where men can survive, but Zushonosuke, one young

Dust jacket for the second volume of Kyōka zenshū *(Collected Stories, 1996)*

warrior who is driven there by fear, breaches it and discovers the power of love. This trespass shapes the narrative not only of this play but of practically everything that Kyōka wrote.

The bizarre nature of plays such as *The Castle Keep* has delayed their production. *Demon Pond* was produced shortly after it was written, but *The Castle Keep* was not performed until 1951, and another excellent play, "Yamabuki" (Wild Roses, 1923), has yet to be produced. That a play such as *The Castle Keep* has stimulated interest in Kyōka's work says as much about postmodern Japan and its capacity for visual opu-

lence as it does about anything that might be said about the relevance of the themes of his play. At a time when changes in the Japanese language have made challenging, difficult writers all but impossible to decipher, the appearance of Kyōka's work on the stage and in motion pictures has encouraged reevaluation of his oeuvre.

Central to this revival is the *onnagata* (female impersonator) Bandō Tamasaburō, who, after performing the major female roles in plays such as *Demon Pond* and *The Castle Keep,* turned to making films that are either based on or inspired by Kyōka's work. Since the so-called Kyōka boom began in the 1970s, Tamasaburō has remained one of Kyōka's most important interpreters. He shares Kyōka's abiding interest in the pursuit of a feminine ideal, that of the suffering-yet-heroic Japanese woman who has won both appreciation and criticism from feminists.

The intensity of this quest for such an ideal is expressed no more eloquently than in two works written near the end of the Taishō period, when Kyōka's main interest in writing prose resumed. *Yukari no onna* (Women of Acquaintance, 1921) is one of his more comprehensive and satisfying rehearsals of his metastory. This novel about returning to Kanazawa represents a significant time in his career: practically all the women who were important to him—his wife, Suzu; his mother; his cousin, Meboso Teru; and his childhood sweetheart, Yuasa Shige—became models for the unusually large number of main characters in this story. Asagawa Reikichi, the male protagonist who is a thinly veiled proxy for Kyōka himself, makes it possible for all these characters to appear in this narrative. Loved by these women who are joined by *yukari*, a karmic connection, he stands at the center of these relationships, and together they struggle with the weak and against the politically powerful, ever critical of the essentially unfair and unfeeling nature of modern Japanese society.

The same ethos prevails in "Baishoku kamonanban" (Prostitution Duck Noodles, 1920; translated as "Osen and Sōkichi," 1996). As a remembrance of Kyōka's penniless year of wandering aimlessly in Tokyo, the story resembles his treatment of a woman's dedication to and sacrifice for an otherwise helpless young man in *Noble Blood, Heroic Blood*. Osen, who prostitutes herself in order to provide clothing and shelter for Sōkichi, literally gives him her soul: she blows her breath into a folded paper crane that, so inspired by her, takes to the air and leads him to the gate of the wealthy family that eventually takes him in and helps him become a famous physician. Many years later Sōkichi meets Osen by chance while they are both waiting for a train, delayed by unseasonably heavy spring rains. She has lost her mind and is being taken to a mental institution, but Sōkichi, now a famous doctor, takes her instead to his own hospital. There he brings a razor to her bedside, and together they end their lives in a double suicide, an event patterned after the example of Kyōka's early "The Surgery Room."

As depicted by Tanizaki Jun'ichirō, Kyōka became largely forgotten by the end of his ca-

reer. Critical tastes had shifted away from his poetic, highly figurative craft. Yet he continued to enjoy the support of a small number of ardent fans, and he could always rely on the financial backing of Minakami Takitarō and the patronage of the Shun'yōdō house, which published his collected works in 1925. Many of Kyōka's most enthusiastic readers happened to be women, who appreciated his depictions of female suffering. Another subset of readers consisted of some younger writers who, in their dissatisfaction with the tenets of naturalism, came to see the eccentric Kyōka as a rallying figure for their cause of reform. In addition to Tanizaki, Akutagawa and Kawabata, who came to dominate Japanese letters in a way that Kyōka never did, wrote enthusiastically about his work. In 1925 Akutagawa wrote a preface for Kyōka's collected works and an important critical essay, published in the *Tokyo Daily News*. These pieces depict him as a beaten yet unvanquished foe of the coarser sentiments of realism and have guided criticism of his work ever since.

Perhaps for this reason Japanese scholars often overlook the fact that Kyōka's sensibilities coarsened during the final decade or so of his career. His last masterpiece was "Mayu kakushi no rei" (The Ghost of Matrimony, 1924), an engaging story about a traveler's encounter with the uncanny. Perhaps no other story so clearly expresses his desire to transcend reality and reach a more profound state of being. The gradual, steady accumulation of imagery destabilizes this narrative, powered as it is by protagonist Sakai Sankichi's masochistic fear of becoming prey to the woman/bird figure that looms throughout, and this destabilizing signals both the fullness of the metastory and the beginning of its deterioration. To the extent that the seduction that occurs is horrible yet unbearably attractive, Kyōka's male characters have matured considerably, but this maturation brings about a crisis. If they are no longer boys—beings of intense desire and yearning who are nevertheless sexually hesitant in their actions—how can the structure of the archetype continue to preserve them?

The metastory eventually breaks down. No longer guided by it, late works such as "Sankai hyōbanki" (Of the Mountains and the Sea, 1929) and "Yuki yanagi" (The Snow Willow, 1937) lack the coherence of the earlier works. However fragmented those early pieces may seem, they still hold together in ways that the works Kyōka wrote during his final decade do not. Minakami Takitarō described the aged Kyōka as a man try-

Kyōka, at age sixty-one

ing to retain sexual vigor at all costs, a man whose usual fineness of sensibility suffered as a result. Whatever the reasons may have been, Kyōka's attempts to write about sexually aggressive men in his later narratives are hard to defend.

Kyōka must have sensed the futility of this detour from the aesthetic path that had served him well for so many years. In the final months of his life and against the protestations of Suzu, who knew the physical toll that writing took on Kyōka, he managed to grind out one last story, "Rukōshinsō" (The Heartvine, 1939), which stands as a final memory of Kanazawa and of a horrible moment when Kyōka, as a young man, had nearly committed suicide by throwing himself into the black waters of the castle moat. His father had just died, leaving the family penniless, and Kyōka, called back from Tokyo and fearing that his dream of becoming a writer had been shattered, had considered ending his life. Kōyō wrote an impassioned letter berating him for entertaining thoughts of death and encouraging him to endure the trials that would someday make him a great writer. Yet Kyōka probably would have killed himself if Meboso Teru, a cousin who apparently had discovered him missing from his bed, had not run to the moat to rescue him. Another possibility is that he was saved by a young woman who threw herself into the moat just as he was about to do the same. Just as he was beginning his career, Kyōka had written of such an event in "Shōsei yahanroku" (The Night Bell Tolls, 1895), a minor story, and it seems fitting that his last work should return to this setting and situation.

Kyōka died in Tokyo shortly after finishing

"Rukōhinsō." During his long career he wrote at least three hundred stories, novels, and plays. Mishima Yukio, who believed that the supernatural was indispensable to fiction, praised him as perhaps the only genius of his time. To Mishima, Kyōka was a "garden of blossoming peonies among the desert of modern Japanese literature." A literary prize established in Kyōka's name is awarded annually. Among contemporary Japanese authors who openly express indebtedness to Kyōka's work are Kōno Taeko and Tsushima Yūko.

Bibliographies:

Kindai Bungaku Kenkyū Sōsho series, volume 45 (Tokyo: Shōwa Joshi Daigaku Kindai Bunka Kenkyusho, 1977);

Tanaka Reigi, "Izumi Kyōka sankō bunken mokuroku (zasshi no bu)," *Dōshisha Kokubungaku,* 13 (1978): 102–136;

Tanaka, "Izumi Kyōka sankō bunken mokuroku (zasshi no bu) hoi," *Izumi Kyōka kenkyū,* 5 (1980): 72–83;

Tanaka, "Izumi Kyōka sankō bunken mokuroku (zasshi no bu) hoi 2," in *Ronshū Izumi Kyōka,* edited by Kasahara Nobuo, Tōgō Katsumi, Mita Hideaki, and Muramatsu Sadataka (Tokyo: Yūseidō, 1987), pp. 223–261;

Tanaka, "Izumi Kyōka sankō bunken mokuroku (zasshi no bu) hoi 3," in *Ronshū Izumi Kyōka* (Tokyo: Yūseidō, 1991), pp. 224–247.

References:

Akutagawa Ryunosuke, "*Kyōka zenshū* ni tsuite," in *Kyōka ron shūsei,* edited by Tanizawa Eiichi and Watanabe Ikkō (Tokyo: Rippu Shobō, 1983), pp. 199–201;

Juliet Carpenter, "Izumi Kyōka: Meiji-Era Gothic," *Japan Quarterly,* 32 (1984): 154–158;

Charles Shirō Inouye, *Japanese Gothic Tales by Izumi Kyōka* (Honolulu: University of Hawaii Press, 1996);

Inouye, "Kyōka and Language," *Harvard Journal of Asiatic Studies,* 56 (1996): 5–34;

Kasahara Nobuo, *Hyōden Izumi Kyōka* (Tokyo: Hakuchisha, 1995);

Kasahara, *Izumi Kyōka: bi to erosu no kōzō* (Tokyo: Shibundō, 1976);

Kasahara, *Izumi Kyōka: erosu no mayu* (Tokyo: Kokubunsha, 1988);

Kawabata Yasunari, "Izumi Kyōka no *Kushigeshū* nado," in *Izumi Kyōka ron shūsei,* pp. 204–207;

Donald Keene, "Izumi Kyōka," in his *Dawn to the*

West, volume 1 (New York: Holt, Rinehart & Winston, 1984), pp. 202–219;

Kobayashi Hideo, "Kyōka no shi sono ta," in *Bungei Tokuhon Izumi Kyōka,* edited by Mita Hideaki (Tokyo: Kawade Shobō Shinoha, 1981), pp. 15–19;

Mishima Yukio, "Kaisetsu," in his *Ozaki Kyō, Izumi Kyōka* (Tokyo: Chūō Kōronsha, 1969);

Mita Hideaki, *Izumi Kyōka no bungaku* (Tokyo: Ōfusha, 1976);

Muramatsu Sadataka, *Ajisai kuyōshō–waga Izumi Kyōka* (Tokyo: Shinchōsha, 1988);

Muramatsu, *Izumi Kyōka* (Tokyo: Bunsendō, 1966);

Muramatsu, *Izumi Kyōka jiten* (Tokyo: Yuseidō, 1982);

Muramatsu, *Izumi Kyōka kenkyū* (Tokyo: Tōjusha, 1974);

Noguchi Takehiko, *Izumi Kyōka* (Tokyo: Shinchōsha, 1985);

Noguchi, ed., *Shinchō Nihon bungaku arubamu Izumi Kyōka* (Tokyo: Kadokawa, 1982);

Tanizaki Jun'ichirō, "Junsui ni 'Nihonteki' na 'Kyōka sekai,'" in his *Tanizaki Jun'ichirō zenshū,* volume 22 (Tokyo: Chūō Kōronsha, 1968), pp. 336–338;

Tanizawa Eiichi and Watanabe Ikkō, eds., *Kyōka-ron shūsei* (Tokyo: Rippū Shobō, 1983);

Teraki Teihō, *Hito, Izumi Kyōka* (Tokyo: Nihon Tosho Sentā, 1983);

Tōgō Katsumi, ed., *Izumi Kyōka* (Tokyo: Yūseidō, 1981);

Tōgō, ed., *Izumi Kyōka* (Tokyo: Shōgakkan, 1992);

Tōgō, ed., *Izumi Kyōka: bi to gensō,* Nihon Bungaku Kenkyū Shiryō Shinshū series, volume 12 (Tokyo: Yūseidō, 1991);

Waki Akiko, *Gensō no ronri: Izumi Kyōka no sekai* (Tokyo: Kōdansha, 1974);

Yoshimura Hirotō, *Izumi Kyōka geijutsu to byōri* (Tokyo: Kongō Shuppan Shinsha, 1970);

Yoshimura, *Izumi Kyōka no sekai: gensō no byōri* (Tokyo: Makino Shuppan, 1983);

Yoshimura, *Makai e no enkinhō: Izumi Kyōka ron* (Tokyo: Kindai Bungeisha, 1991).

Papers:

Most of Kyōka's manuscripts are held in the Rare Book Room of the new Keiō University Library on the Mita campus of Keiō University in Tokyo. A replica of Kyōka's study, which includes portions of his library, has been built in the old Keiō library, also on the Mita campus. A smaller number of manuscripts than that held at the new Keiō University Library, along with certain personal effects and letters, are at the Ishikawa Prefecture's Museum of Modern Literature in Kanazawa. Izumi Natsuki, Kyōka's adopted daughter, keeps the bulk of the author's notebooks, photographs, and personal effects at her residence in Zushi. Other collections are at the Kindai Bungakukan, the Chūō Tōritsu Toshokan, and the Kokkai Toshokan, all in Tokyo.

Kasai Zenzō

(16 January 1887 – 23 July 1927)

Kamiya Tadataka
Hokkaidō University

BOOKS: *Ko o tsurete* (Tokyo: Shinchōsha, 1919);
Funōsha (Tokyo: Shinchōsha, 1919);
Bafunseki (Tokyo: Shun'yōdō, 1920);
Nisemono (Tokyo: Shun'yōdō, 1921);
Kanashiki chichi (Tokyo: Kaizōsha, 1922);
Akuma (Tokyo: Kinseidō, 1923);
Shii no wakaba (Tokyo: Shinchōsha, 1924);
Kasai Zenzōshu (Tokyo: Shinchōsha, 1951).
Collections: *Kasai Zenzō kansō shū* (Tokyo: Kaizōsha, 1934);
Kasai Zenzō zenshū, 6 volumes (Tokyo: Bunsendō, 1974);
Kasai Zenzō zenshū, 4 volumes (Aomori: Tsugaru Shobō, 1974–1975).

Kasai Zenzō, at his house in Tokyo, about a year before his death

The history of modern fiction in Japan is inextricably tied to the "I-novel," an autobiographical, often confessional genre that developed early in the twentieth century as both an extension of the traditional Japanese preference for lyrical narratives and a native reinterpretation of Western naturalism. Of the many authors who produced I-novels of various sorts, perhaps the one whose work is most closely identified with the capacity of this genre for expressing personal pain, and whose chaotic life was that of a writer who struggles to define himself through his work, was Kasai Zenzō. The self-portrait that Kasai provides in his stories is of an artist apparently bent on self-destruction through dissipation, yet one who uses literature to give voice, and thereby significance, to his torment. His life of anguish and self-loathing helped to forge the image that modern Japanese readers have of the novelist.

Kasai Zenzō was born in Hirosaki, Nakatsugaru-gun, in Aomori prefecture, at the northern tip of the island of Honshu, just across the Tsugaru Straits from Hokkaidō. His father ran a rice brokerage, but operating the firm became difficult, and when Zenzō was three years old, his father moved the family to Hokkaidō, where he attempted to set up a new business. He failed at this, however, and two years later the family returned to Aomori.

After graduating from elementary school, Kasai spent two years taking supplementary courses, until at the age of fourteen he became a shopboy at a multiservice agency that undertook deliveries, repairs, and other miscellaneous work. At age sixteen Kasai went to Tokyo and delivered newspapers while he attended night school, but his mother became ill and he returned to his family home. She died after suffering complications from a miscarriage when she was forty-one years old.

In 1904 Kasai and two of his friends moved to Hokkaidō, where he worked as a railroad conductor and as a woodcutter for the regional forestry office. The two years he spent in Hokkaidō stirred a passion for literature in the young man, and at the age of nineteen he returned to Tokyo, where he enrolled in the general education program at Tōyō University. There he became an auditing student two years later, and he continued his broad reading of literary works.

In 1909 Kasai married Hirano Tsuru, a twenty-year-old woman from his hometown.

Shortly after the wedding he left her at her parents' home and went alone to Tokyo, where he began to study fiction writing under the tutelage of novelist Tokuda Shūsei. He made regular visits to Aomori and, with financial assistance from his father-in-law, continued his literary studies at Waseda University. The couple became parents of a son in 1910.

In 1912 Kasai joined Hirotsu Kazuo, a writer whom he had met at Waseda, and Tanizaki Seiji, the younger brother of Tanizaki Jun'ichirō, in founding the coterie magazine *Kiseki* (Miracle), in which Kazai published "Kanashiki chichi" (The Sad Father) that same year. In this story the protagonist is a writer residing in Tokyo with his wife and four-year-old son. When their lives become increasingly strained, he sends the two to stay with her family, but he makes no progress in his writing and eventually falls ill. When a holiday comes, he stares at the goldfish that he had bought for his son and ponders what a sad father he is, unable even to live with his family. Yet he tells himself, "My noble son surely can get along without having his father right there with him," and he determines that "I must seek my own way, no matter where it may lead, pursue it, and then finally die." He concludes that he must continue to write, even if it means sacrificing his family. The story won recognition as a model for the Japanese I-novel.

Kasai's second story, "Akuma" (The Demon, 1912), clearly expresses his view of literature. The protagonist of this story lives as a pauper while he writes his fiction. One day while he and a writer friend are sitting at a bar and discussing their determination to be novelists, the protagonist insists:

> We can acquire the authority and power to rise up in arms against others in all seriousness only after we have devoured ourselves. Let us be destroyed! Then we will live anew. We must not brood over life. The day will come when we can no longer eat; when that day arrives, the pathway to a better life will be open and waiting for us. That is a fact. It's obvious. We can breathe in the most splendid life possible only after we have dropped to the depths. This is no vain imagining. It is the truth. Those who die believing in this truth have nothing to regret. This same idea is eloquently described in the Bible. Only after we reject all things and destroy all things can we arrive at the true and absolute homeland.

Kasai at the Kamakura Kenchō Temple, circa 1920

In these lines Kasai expresses sentiments of romanticism, of what might be called a belief in the ultimate supremacy of literature. This belief in sacrificing one's life for literature has the force of religion, and it influenced the self-destructive I-novelists—such as Dazai Osamu, for example—who followed Kasai and modeled their work on his.

Kasai's colleagues at the coterie magazine praised him as a novelist, but his income from writing was insufficient. He therefore worked as a reporter for *Orimono Taimusu* (Textile Times) and at a grain brokerage firm, and for about five years he tried to live with his family on his meager earnings. The couple by this time had three children, and they took turns living in his wife's family home and in Tokyo. His reading through this period included works by Fyodor Dostoyevsky, Guy de Maupassant, Gustave Flaubert, Leo Tolstoy, and August Strindberg.

Kasai first gained literary fame by publishing the short story "Ko o tsurete" (With Children on My Hands, 1918) in the literary magazine *Waseda bungaku* when he was thirty-two years old. The story opens with the protago-

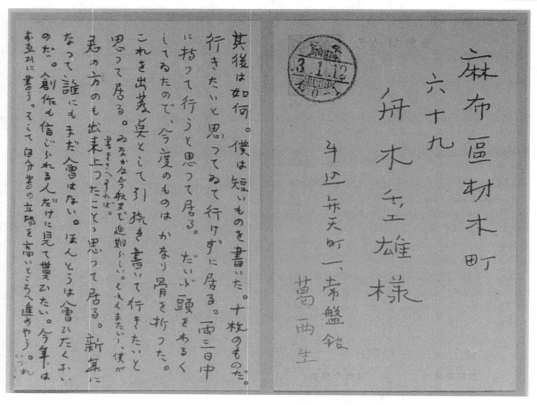

Letter to Funaki Shigeo in which Kasai mentions his difficulty in finishing a ten-page story and his reluctance to let others see his work (collection of Itō Yūko)

nist—a novelist living with two of his children, an eight-year-old son and a six-year-old daughter—being told that he must either pay his rent or vacate the house in which they live. His wife has already returned to her family home with another daughter, and he has depended on the money that she sends him. In order to support himself and the two children he has with him, the protagonist has also been borrowing money from a writer friend, but after his friend leaves the city to escape the summer heat, no one is left to lend him money. As the novelist walks around the city searching for a new house to rent, he runs into a police superintendent who had attended the same preparatory school with him.

He begs the officer to intercede and help him get his eviction date extended, but the policeman's refusal leaves the novelist hopeless. When the appointed hour arrives for the protagonist and his two children to vacate, he sells his household furnishings to a secondhand dealer and, with his children in tow, wanders the night streets. As he treats his children to a meal and drinks some sake, he thinks, "It's true. The life of an artist who has lost his inspiration is a terrible life, more horrible than

the life of a farmer or a ricksha driver or someone even worse off. It's truly an awful life."

He goes to the lodgings of a friend who is traveling and pleads to have his family housed there. Although he gets permission, his daughter weeps at her father's pitiful figure. The story ends as the three board a train late at night and head off in search of another place to stay. Kasai's reputation was established after the publication of "With Children on My Hands," which won praise from various readers. "The protagonist of this story," wrote one, "is the original 'natural man' mistakenly finding himself in the grip of the modern economic system, like a sailor walking across the desert"; this reader saw Kasai as "a man who cannot live a lie, a man who cannot live a haphazard life, a man who cannot live a life of deception." By 1918, when this story was published, the rapid growth of capitalism in Japan had widened the gap between the rich and the poor, and in that same year rice riots and strikes had erupted all over the country.

In 1919 Kasai began to receive more requests for manuscripts from trade magazines, and he finally was able to make a living from his writing. As his writing came to occupy more of his time, Kasai sent his wife and children back to her family and rented a room for himself at the Kenchōji Temple in Kamakura. He remained in Kamakura from 1919 to 1924, and there he met Asami Hana, a woman thirteen years his junior. She was the daughter of the owner of a restaurant in front of the temple, and she was responsible for bringing meals to Kasai three times each day. Although Kasai's wife does not appear often in his stories, Osei, a character modeled on Asami, appears in many stories—for example, in "Kurai heya nite" (In a Dark Room, 1920), "Furō" (Vagrancy, 1921), "Furyōji" (Bad Child, 1922), "Osei" (1923), and "Ugomeku mono" (Wriggling Things, 1924). About two years after Kasai met Asami they became lovers, and in 1925 she gave birth to a daughter, Yūko.

For Kasai, Asami was the source of creative power, and his attachment to her fictional counterpart, Osei, is presented in his portrait of the Snow Maiden in another of his stories, "Yuki onna" (Snow Maiden, 1917): "The Snow Maiden descends from Heaven on nights of blinding snowstorms. She stands dejected in the blizzard, with a pure whiteness and a beauty not of this world, clutching a newborn infant to her breast. And she says, 'Would you please hold this child for just a brief while?' But one must not hold the child. Any man who takes the child into his arms will drop dead on the spot."

In "Wriggling Things" Osei blames the protagonist for the death of her stillborn child, and this use of a child to attack another person is part of Kasai's conception of the Snow Maiden, who carries a child with her from the outset in "Snow Maiden." If the Snow Maiden—who had lived as an image in Kasai's mind and was an image that he found incorporated in Osei or Asami, the woman before him—inspired in him an urge to create, then the abundant creativity of his final years perhaps came from his discovery of the evil that the character of Osei embodied. Osei certainly becomes prominent in Kasai's stories after her pregnancy.

Almost immediately after Kasai's death in 1927, his story "Kohan shuki" (Lakeside Notebook, 1924) gained recognition as his masterpiece. Uno Kōji, another writer, praised this story highly and claimed that Kasai "is greater than any philosopher, greater than any Buddhist priest, greater than any other artist." In September 1924 Kasai had traveled to the hot

Asami Hana, Kasai's lover, who appears as "Osei" in many of his stories

springs at Oku Nikkō, where he had remained until November composing "Lakeside Notebook." The opening passage reveals the autobiographical background for his writing of the story: "I had finally escaped to this place. But now what was going to happen? What did I plan to do? From my chair on the second floor of the inn, I looked out at the melancholy colors on the surface of the lake, and day after day, time after time, I sighed the same soliloquy."

In July 1924 Kasai had taken Asami to Aomori and introduced her to his wife. His wife's antagonism and the fact that Asami was pregnant with a second child encouraged what the story describes as the protagonist's "escape" to the resort. The realizations that he had infuriated his wife, that Asami was going to have another baby, and that he had fathered another child on his limited income made Kasai feel cornered, and his motives behind this story were in his desires to apologize to both his wife and Asami. "Today I was supposed to attend the publication party in Tokyo for one of my close friends," he continues in "Lakeside Notebook," and yet

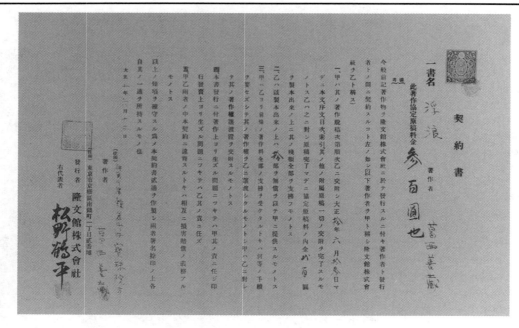

Kasai's contract for the magazine publication of "Furō" (Vagrancy, 1921)

I can't do that. I can't do this. Everything is out of the question. If I continue like this, all my friends will desert me, life will desert me, I'll become—what? a living corpse? Or maybe a dead corpse, one or the other. What a fool—racing around, raising pitiful cries! I can't bear to look at myself in such a pitiful state.

At Mount Shirane
A sea of clouds
In the glow of sunset
When I think of my wife
My heart aches.

When I bite into the redness
Of an oleaster fruit
It tastes sour, astringent.
Sad that it has seeds.
Osei, too, is sad.

In writing of his own pathos, Kasai frees himself by portraying his wife and Osei in these haiku verses and merging the two women with the natural setting. "Lakeside Notebook" concludes:

In another two or three days a month will have passed. Everything around me – the mountains, the lake, the hot springs, the women – everything has vanished from my emotions. Just like my family, my wife and children, Osei, my sad friends, everything here infuses me with dark feelings and

torment. What has become of that initial charm that made me into something like a poet and caused me to cry out, "O wife! Intoxicate me more powerfully than liquor!"? My feelings evaporate like foam. But, the intoxication that comes from liquor, narcotics – I am totally addicted to both.

These lines suggest that, at least initially at the hot springs, the natural environment and the women working at the spa had consoled Kasai. But his torment had deepened, and he came to realize that drinking sake and torturing himself were acting on him as intoxicants. "Lakeside Notebook," which depicts Kasai's feelings in abandoning his attempt to find consolation in nature and in realizing that he is irredeemably alone, marks the zenith of the I-novel in Japan.

Readers have generally asserted that the quality of Kasai's writing declined after "Lakeside Notebook," a decline evident in his eschewal of novelistic techniques in his works that followed. In "Shimogare sakka no hanashi" (Tale of a Desolate Writer, 1925) Kasai writes stories using a technique of oral dictation that ignores matters of structure. Magazine editors recorded what Kasai related orally to them, because his alcoholism had rendered him unable to pick up a pen. In spite of his illness and because of his economic distress and the two families that he

Kasai holding his daughter, Yūko, born to Asami in 1925

had to support, Kasai had to continue earning money by selling manuscripts.

In his *Shōsetsu no hōhō* (Techniques of the Novel, 1947) Itō Sei, assessing the significance of Kasai's emergence as a writer in Japan, explains that "Zenzō lived solely within the literary world. The unique lifestyle of this unique society made it possible for him to experiment with pure ideas within his own life. His life itself became a work of art."

Funaki Shigeo, who worked with Kasai at the magazine *Kiseki,* adds that through Kasai's final years from around 1925

His health declined progressively, and the problems of illness, his difficulty in explaining himself, and the trials of his family combined to torment him, and his life became a shambles. He began to drink in the daytime, and he often would get dead drunk and start screaming, behaving violently, creating troubles for his family and even throwing

the neighborhood into turmoil. Even though he had no money, he would order *sake* and drink to his heart's content; when all the money was gone, he would summon a scribe and dictate a manuscript. An old man named Maruyama, who ran a liquor store in the neighborhood, was captivated by Kasai's character and would provide him all the *sake* he wanted for free. He seems to have been attracted to the fact that Kasai had no desires other than toward his writing, and to the natural virtues that derived from him being a simple, primitive child of nature.

Nonetheless, a small group of devout readers admire both the life and the writings of Kasai Zenzō, a writer who gave everything for his art.

References:

Funaki Shigeo, *Kasai Zenzō Senshū,* volume 2 (Tokyo: Koizōsha, 1948);

Itō Sei, *Shosetsu no hōhō* (Tokyo: Kawade Shobō, 1948);

The Kasai Zenzō "Snow Maiden" literature monument erected at Meoto Daki Park, Ashibetsu, Shijō, in 1986

Kamada Satoshi, *Kasai Zenzō no shōgai* (Tokyo: Kōdansha, 1994);

Kamiya Tadataka, *Yuki onna no bigaku: Kasai Zenzō ron* (Sapporo: Kyōbunsha, 1992);

Ōmori Sumio, *Kasai Zenzō no kenkyū* (Tokyo: Ōfusha, 1970);

Tanizaki Seiji, *Hōrō no sakka: Kasai Zenzō hyōden* (Tokyo: Gendaisha, 1955).

Papers:

Some of Kasai Zenzō's papers are located at Aomori Kindai Bungakukan in Aomori shi and at Hosi no Furusato Kinenkan, at Ashibetsu in Hokkaido.

Kawabata Yasunari
(14 June 1899 – 16 April 1972)

Van C. Gessel
Brigham Young University

BOOKS: *Kanjō sōshoku* (Tokyo: Kinseidō, 1926);
Izu no odoriko (Tokyo: Kinseidō, 1927); translated by Edward G. Seidensticker and others as *The Izu Dancer and Others* (Tokyo: Harashobo, 1964); republished as *Ei-Wa taishō Izu no odoriko* (Tokyo: Hara Shobō, 1968); republished as *The Izu Dancer, and Other Stories* (Tokyo & Rutland, Vt.: Tuttle, 1974);
Kawabata Yasunari shū, Shinshin Kessaku Shōsetsu Zenshū series (Tokyo: Heibonsha, 1929);
Boku no hyōhonshitsu, Shinkō Geijutsuha Sōsho series (Tokyo: Shinchōsha, 1930);
Hana aru shashin, Shinkō Geijutsuha Sōsho series (Tokyo: Shinchōsha, 1930);
Asakusa kurenaidan (Tokyo: Senshinsha, 1930);
Keshō to kuchibue (Tokyo: Shinchōsha, 1933);
Suishō gensō, Bungei Fukkō Sōsho series (Tokyo: Kaizōsha, 1934);
Kawabata Yasunari shū (Tokyo: Kaizōsha, 1934);
Jojōka (Tokyo: Takemura Shobō, 1934);
Kinju (Tokyo: Noda Shobō, 1935);
Junsui no koe (Tokyo: Sara Shoten, 1936);
Hana no warutsu (Tokyo: Kaizōsha, 1936);
Yukiguni (Tokyo: Sōgensha, 1937); translated by Seidensticker as *Snow Country* (New York: Knopf, 1957);
Musumegokoro (Tokyo: Takemura Shobō, 1937);
Josei kaigan (Tokyo: Sōgensha, 1937; revised edition, Tokyo: Eikōsha, 1947);
Kyūchō no tantei (Tokyo: Chūo Kōronsha, 1937);
Otome no minato (Tokyo: Jitsugyō no Nihonsha, 1938);
Tampenshū, Hakushoku Sōsho series (Tokyo: Sunagoya Shobō, 1939);
Kawabata Yasunari shū, Shin Nihon Bungaku Zenshū series (Tokyo: Kaizōsha, 1940);
Shōgatsu sanganichi (Tokyo: Shinseikaku, 1940);
Negao, Yūkō Meisaku Senshū series (Tokyo: Yūkōsha, 1941);
Shōsetsu no kōsei (Tokyo: Mikasa Shobō, 1941);
Aisuru hitotachi (Tokyo: Shinchōsha, 1941);
Bunshō (Tokyo: Tōhō Shobō, 1942);

Kawabata Yasunari in 1968

Kawabata Yasunari shū, Saidai Meisaku Zenshū series (Tokyo: Kawade Shobō, 1942);
Utsukushii tabi (Tokyo: Jitsugyō no Nihonsha, 1942);
Kōgen (Tokyo: Kōchō Shorin, 1942);
Ai (Tokyo: Bitokusha, 1945);

Komadori Onsen (Tokyo: Shōnan Shobō, 1945);

Asagumo (Tokyo: Shinchōsha, 1946);

Hijaku (Tokyo: Shinkigensha, 1946);

Yūbae shōjo (Tokyo: Tanchō Shobō, 1946);

Onsenyado (Tokyo: Jitsugyō no Nihonsha, 1946);

Gakkō no hana (Tokyo: Shōnan Shobō, 1946);

Chirinuru o (Tokyo: Maeda shūppansha, 1946);

Issō ikka (Tokyo: Seiryusha, 1948);

Kawabata Yasunari shū, 2 volumes (Tokyo: Hosokawa Shoten, 1948);

Shiroi mangetsu (Tokyo: Rotte shūppansha, 1948);

Aishū (Tokyo: Hosokawa Shoten, 1949);

Nihon shōsetsu daihyōsaku zenshū (Tokyo: Koyama Shoten, 1949);

Asakusa monogatari (Tokyo: Chūō Kōronsha, 1950);

Kageki gakkō (Tokyo: Himawarisha, 1950);

Shin bunshō tokuhon (Tokyo: Akane Shobō, 1951);

Maihime (Tokyo: Asahi Shimbunsha, 1951);

Kawabata Yasunari shū (Tokyo: Shinchōsha, 1951);

Shōsetsu nyūmon (Tokyo: Kaname Shobō, 1952);

Sembazuru (Tokyo: Chikuma Shobō, 1952); translated by Seidensticker as *Thousand Cranes* (New York: Knopf, 1958);

Tenohira no shōsetsu hyappen (Tokyo: Shinchōsha, 1952-);

Saikonsha (Tokyo: Mikasa Shobō, 1953);

Kawabata Yasunari shū, Shōwa Bungaku Zenshū series (Tokyo: Kadokawa Shoten, 1953);

Hi mo tsuki mo (Tokyo: Chūō Kōronsha, 1953);

Matsugo no me (Tokyo: Sōgensha, 1953);

Kawabata Yasunari shū, Chōhen Shōsetsu Zenshū series (Tokyo: Shinchōsha, 1953);

Kawa no aru shitamachi no hanashi (Tokyo: Shinchōsha, 1954);

Kawabata Yasunari shū, Gendai Bungō Meisaku Zenshū series (Tokyo: Kawade Shobō, 1954);

Yama no oto (Tokyo: Chikuma Shobō, 1954); translated by Seidensticker as *The Sound of the Mountain* (New York: Knopf, 1970);

Meijin (Tokyo: Bungei Shunjū Shinsha, 1954); translated by Seidensticker as *The Master of Go* (New York: Knopf, 1972; London: Secker & Warburg, 1973);

Dōyō (Tokyo: Tōhōsha, 1954);

Kawabata Yasunari shū, Nihon Shōnen Shōjo Meisaku Zenshū series (Tokyo: Kawade Shobō, 1954);

Izu no tabi (Tokyo: Chūō Kōronsha, 1954);

Niji ikutabi (Tokyo: Kawade Shobō, 1955);

Shin'yū (Tokyo: Kaiseisha, 1955);

Tōkyō no hito, 4 volumes (Tokyo: Shinchōsha, 1955);

Mizuumi (Tokyo: Shinchōsha, 1955); translated by Reiko Tsukimura as *The Lake* (Tokyo & New York: Kodansha International, 1974; London: Peter Owen, 1977);

Kawabata Yasunari shū (Tokyo: Tōzai Bunmeisha, 1955);

Shōsetsu no kenkyū (Tokyo: Kaname Shobō, 1955);

Tamayura (Tokyo: Kadokawa Shoten, 1955);

Tsubame no dōjo (Tokyo: Chikuma Shobō, 1955);

Kawabata Yasunari shū, Gendai Nihon Bungaku Zenshū series (Tokyo: Chikuma Shobō, 1955);

Onna de aru koto, 2 volumes (Tokyo: Shinchōsha, 1956–1957);

Fuji no hatsuyuki (Tokyo: Shinchōsha, 1958);

Kaze no aru michi (Tokyo: Kadokawa Shoten, 1959);

Nemureru bijo (Tokyo: Shinchōsha, 1961); translated by Seidensticker as "House of the Sleeping Beauties," in *House of the Sleeping Beauties, and Other Stories* (Tokyo & New York: Kodansha International, 1969; London: Quadriga, 1969);

Koto (Tokyo: Shinchōsha, 1962); translated by J. Martin Holman as *The Old Capital* (Berkeley, Cal.: North Point Press, 1987);

Jūnin hyakuwa (Tokyo: Mainichi Shimbunsha, 1963);

Kawabata Yasunari tampen zenshū (Tokyo: Kōdansha, 1964);

Koto no fu (Tokyo: Yuyudō, 1964);

Utsukushisa to kanashimi to (Tokyo: Chūō Kōronsha, 1965); translated by Howard Hibbett as *Beauty and Sadness* (New York: Knopf, 1975; London: Secker & Warburg, 1975);

Kataude (Tokyo: Shinchōsha, 1965); translated by Seidensticker as "One Arm," in *House of the Sleeping Beauties, and Other Stories*;

Kawabata Yasunari shū, Nihon Bungaku Zenshū series (Tokyo: Kawade Shobō, 1966);

Kawabata Yasunari jisenshū (Tokyo: Shūeisha, 1966);

Rakka ryūsui (Tokyo: Shinchōsha, 1966);

Kawabata Yasunari shū, Gendai Nihon Bungakukan series (Tokyo: Bungei shunjū, 1966);

Kawabata Yasunari shū, 2 volumes, Nihon Bungaku Zenshū series (Tokyo: Shūeisha, 1966–1967);

Kawabata Yasunari, 2 volumes, Karāban Nihon Bungaku Zenshū series (Tokyo: Kawade Shobō, 1967–1970);

Gekka no mon (Tokyo: Yamato Shobō, 1967);

Kawabata Yasunari sakuhinshū (Tokyo: Chūō Kōronsha, 1968);

Kawabata Yasunari shū, Gendai Nihon Bungaku series (Tokyo: Chikuma Shobō, 1968);

Kawabata Yasunari shū, Shinchō Nihon Bungaku series (Tokyo: Shinchōsha, 1968);

Kawabata Yasunari shōnen shōjo shōsetsu shū (Tokyo: Shinchōsha, 1968);

Utsukushii Nihon no watakushi—sono josetsu (Tokyo: Kōdansha, 1969); translated by Seidensticker as *Japan, the Beautiful, and Myself: The 1968 Nobel Prize Acceptance Speech* (Tokyo & New York: Kodansha International, 1969);

Kawabata Yasunari, Gendai Chōhen Bungaku Zenshū series (Tokyo: Kōdansha, 1969);

Kawabata Yasunari, Nihon Bungaku Zenshū series (Tokyo: Shinchōsha, 1969);

Kawabata Yasunari, Gendai Nihon no Bungaku series (Tokyo: Gakushū Kenkyūsha, 1969);

Bi no sonzai to hakken, translated by V. H. Viglielmo as *The Existence and Discovery of Beauty* (Tokyo: Mainichi Shimbunsha, 1969);

Kawabata Yasunari shū, Akatsuki Meisakukan Nihon Bungaku Shiriizu series (Tokyo: Akatsuki Kyōiku Tosho, 1970);

Kawabata Yasunari, Nōberu Bungaku Zenshū series (Tokyo: Shūfu no Tomosha, 1971);

Teihon Yukiguni (Tokyo: Bokuyōsha, 1971);

Kawabata Yasunari, Nihon Bungaku Zenshū series (Tokyo: Shūeisha, 1971);

Taidan nihon no bungaku (Tokyo: Chūō Kōronsha, 1971);

Aru hito no sei no naka ni (Tokyo: Kawada Shobō Shinsha, 1972);

Tampopo (Tokyo: Shinchōsha, 1972);

Nemureru bijo / Yukigunishō (Tokyo: Horupu shūppan, 1972);

Take no koe momo no hana (Tokyo: Shinchōsha, 1973);

Nihon no bi no kokoro (Tokyo: Kōdansha, 1973);

Honehiroi: Terohira no shōsetsu (Tokyo: Yumanite, 1975);

Tenju no ko (Tokyo: Shinchōsha, 1975);

Sansai ryokuyū kaiyū, by Kawabata, Tanikawa Tetsuzō, and Narasaki Shōichi (Tokyo: Chūō Kōronsha, 1976);

Tokoname atsumi sanage, by Kawabata, Tanikawa, and Narasaki (Tokyo: Chūō Kōronsha, 1976);

Shigaraki bizen tamba, by Kawabata, Tanikawa, and Narasaki (Tokyo: Chūō Kōronsha, 1976);

Seto minō, by Kawabata, Tanikawa, and Narasaki (Tokyo: Chūō Kōronsha, 1976);

Nāshissasu (Tokyo: Tōjusha, 1977);

Konrei to sōrei (Tokyo: Sōgensha, 1978);

Maihime no koyomi (Tokyo: Mainichi Shinbunshe, 1979);

Umi no himasturi (Tokyo: Mainichi Shinbunsha, 1979).

Collections: *Kawabata Yasunari senshū,* 9 volumes (Tokyo: Kaizōsha, 1938–1939);

Kawabata Yasunari zenshū, 16 volumes (Tokyo: Shinchōsha, 1948–1954);

Kawabata Yasunari senshū, 10 volumes (Tokyo: Shinchōsha, 1956);

Kawabata Yasunari zenshū, 12 volumes (Tokyo: Shinchōsha, 1959–1961);

Kawabata Yasunari zenshū, 19 volumes (Tokyo: Shinchōsha, 1969–1974).

Collection in English: *Palm-of-the-Hand Stories,* translated by Lane Dunlop and J. Martin Holman (San Francisco: North Point Press, 1988; Tokyo: Tuttle, 1988; London: Picador Classics, 1989).

OTHER: *Gendai jidō bungaku jiten,* edited by Kawabata, Ogawa Mimei, and Furuya Tsunatake (Tokyo: Hōbunko, 1955);

Mizuumi, edited by Kawabata (Tokyo: Yuki Shobō, 1961);

Kyōto jiten, edited by Kawabata (Tokyo: Jinbutsu Ōraisha, 1967);

Gakushū shin kokugo jiten, edited by Kawabata and Saeki Umetomo (Tokyo: Kōdansha, 1968);

Aesop, *Isoppu,* translated by Kawabata (Tokyo: Fureberu-kan, 1968–);

Bunshō no gihō, edited by Kawabata, Hisamatsu Sen'ichi, and Endō Yoshimoto (Tokyo: Meiji Shoin, 1970);

Ōchō monogatarishū, 2 volumes, edited by Kawabata (Tokyo: Kawade Shobō Shinsha, 1971–1972).

Kawabata Yasunari was the first (and, until 1994, the only) Japanese author to achieve international status through receiving the Nobel Prize for Literature, which came to him in 1968. His writings attracted a worldwide audience who saw in them expressions of the traditional beauty and aesthetic values of Japan as well as some of the exoticism that it hoped to find in books about the country. Yet Kawabata's work is much more complex and multidimensional than such a reading suggests. His works, particularly those of the postwar years, certainly celebrate the rich cultural heritage of Japan, but a careful reading reveals that his preoccupation with the past resulted less from a desire to preserve tradition than from a desire to indulge in the pleasures of the past precisely because they were unattainable. One motif common to most of Kawabata's works is that of distancing: characters rush away from becoming involved with others; men and women, though always attracted to one another, seem like identical magnetic poles in pushing away from those for whom they yearn. Only if one admires beauty from a distance can it remain unspoiled, and both one's appreciation of that remote beauty and one's resignation in recognizing that it can never be intimately embraced can preserve such unspoiled beauty. The intricate, sometimes enigmatic aesthetic values in Kawabata's writings are intriguing, but they, like his characters, are not easily approached and apprehended.

As one of two Kawabata children (Yoshiko, a sister, was four years older than he), Kawabata Yasunari was born in Osaka. His family, while not particularly well-to-do by the time of his birth, could trace its heritage to the third military regent of Japan in the early thirteenth century, and this gave the family some status in the village. His ancestors had erected a temple of the Obaku Zen sect of Buddhism in town, and Yasunari's father had obtained a medical license and become assistant director of a clinic in Osaka. His father had also studied Confucian philosophy, Chinese poetry, and painting in addition to pursuing his medical interests, but he was a man of feeble constitution, and his children inherited his respiratory problems. Kawabata wrote that his family was convinced he would not survive childhood. His father succumbed to tuberculosis when Yasunari was only two years old, and less than a year later his mother died from the same illness. Yoshiko was taken to live with her maternal aunt, and Yasunari joined his grandparents in a farming village on the outskirts of Osaka.

Kawabata's grandfather was essentially blind by this time, but he encouraged the boy to pursue his interest in painting. In fall 1906 Kawabata's grandmother died, the third close relative that the boy had lost in five years. Three years later his sister Yoshiko died at age fourteen. Kawabata had seen her only twice in the seven years since they had been separated, and he felt detached when the news of her death arrived. Living alone with his blind grandfather, Kawabata developed a lifelong habit of staring into the faces of people around him, often to the dismay of those who did not understand the reason for his stares. He also became a voracious reader, even struggling through demanding Heian period (794–1185) classics such as Murasaki Shikibu's *The Tale of Genji* and *The Pillow Book of Sei Shōnagon* and reading every volume in the library of his elementary school by his last year. Kawabata

later claimed that his reading of these ancient texts by women had profoundly influenced his use of language and his literary sensibilities.

Kawabata entered the Ibaraki Middle School in 1912, and before long he decided to become a writer rather than a painter, a shift in career interests that pleased his sightless grandfather. His grandfather soon had his grandson write a letter to an uncle who was providing them with a monthly stipend from the estate: Grandfather, the letter said, was surviving on a few swallows of soup each day, and the boy was contributing to his own sickly nature by eating pickled plums by day and vegetables before bedtime. Kawabata also began writing essays and poetry, the latter in the new style and colloquial diction popularized by Shimazaki Tōson.

In spring 1914 Kawabata's grandfather, his last surviving relative, was confined to his bed, and during the final month of the old man's life Kawabata began writing a diary recounting his ministrations to the dying man. The toll on the psyche of the sixteen-year-old boy was heavy, and at times he would flee from the house and abandon the old man until after dark. The respite was fleeting, however, for Kawabata then felt guilty that his grandfather might die while he was absent. On the evening of the state funeral for the widow of Emperor Meiji in late May 1914, Kawabata's grandfather died. Following all the deaths of his family members, others began to apply the title "master of funerals" to Kawabata. The boy spent a short time with an uncle and then the following January moved into the middle-school dormitory, where he remained until he graduated.

At school he began to read contemporary Japanese and Russian literature, but he remained under the sway of *The Tale of Genji*. A small local paper published some of his poems, essays, and short pieces of fiction, and after the unexpected death of his English teacher, Kawabata wrote "Shi no hitsugi o kata ni" (With Our Teacher's Casket on Our Shoulders), his first story to be published in a literary journal. During his final year at the school he had a fleeting homosexual affair with another young man in his dormitory, a relationship that Kawabata claimed had "warmed and purified and saved me," presumably from his loneliness.

Partly in the hope that he could at least pursue a career as a literary scholar if he were unable to succeed as a writer, Kawabata applied for admission to and was accepted by the English Literature Department of the First High School in Tokyo, one of the most prestigious public schools in the country. But he paid virtually no attention to the study of his major subject and in fact read mostly the works of Fyodor Dostoyevsky and other Russian authors. Lacking confidence in his writing talents, loathing his new dormitory environment in Tokyo, and feeling sorrow at the end of his homsexual affair convinced Kawabata that his personality had been warped by what he called his "orphan's disposition."

To assuage his grief, in late autumn 1918 he set out on a shank's mare journey across the Izu Peninsula, where he encountered a troupe of traveling entertainers and spent several days in their company. Judging from "Izu no odoriko" (The Izu Dancer), the story he eventually wrote about the experience, the time he spent with these simple but honest country folk restored his sense of self-worth and his desire to continue his literary pursuits. The following year Kawabata published an account of his journey in the high-school journal, and he began frequenting a Tokyo restaurant known for its attractive young waitresses. He quickly developed a crush on one waitress, and by 1920, when he moved on to the English Literature Department at Tokyo Imperial University, he had fallen desperately in love with her.

There he and a group of colleagues founded their own literary magazine with the support of Kikuchi Kan, an important editor of *Bungei shunjū*. Kikuchi praised highly the first story that Kawabata published in this coterie journal, and the editor continued to be an important literary and personal supporter of the young writer. Kawabata repaid this support by publishing much of his fiction in *Bungei shunjū,* and Kikuchi also introduced Kawabata to Yokomitsu Riichi and several other writers who became his close friends and literary allies throughout his career.

Romance had fully bloomed, however, and although his intended had only recently become fifteen years old, Kawabata was determined to marry his waitress. Kikuchi promised to provide some financial support; Kawabata visited the father of his fiancée in the "snow country" of northern Japan to gain his permission for the match; and all preparations were completed when the young woman sent Kawabata a letter announcing that an unspecified "catastrophe" had occurred and that she could never see him again. He was crushed, for through his relationship with her Kawabata had hoped to regain the "heart of a child" that he had lost through the deaths of his family members. He avowed

Kawabata (center) with two literary friends at Ibaraki Middle School

throughout his relationship with the girl that their relations had always been pure, that he had "never laid so much as a finger on the girl," and one of his closest friends corroborated this by insisting that Kawabata "did not have a whit of sexual passion, sensuality, or carnality in him."

Taking refuge in his writing, Kawabata started publishing reviews of contemporary fiction in a well-known monthly magazine, a pursuit that he continued for twenty years. Although other writers were founding and joining ideological and artistic camps and praising only their comrades, Kawabata became one of the most generous, unbiased critics of the modern period. By joining so many diverse groups that none could claim his undivided loyalties, he remained aloof from literary factionalism and wrote his reviews based on what he saw as the intrinsic merits of the writing rather than on any affiliations of the author.

After a year in the English Literature Department, Kawabata switched his major to Japanese literature—primarily, he claimed, because the Japanese Literature Department required less of its students and the professors never took roll. But by this time he had published translations of some stories by John Galsworthy, Lord Dunsany, and Anton Chekhov. Three years of study was the usual amount of time required to graduate from college, but after four years Kawabata still lacked enough credits in his major field to graduate. His professors took pity on him, and, perhaps hoping that he might develop into a writer, they allowed him to receive a diploma in 1924.

Soon after Kawabata had left the university, he and his friend Yokomitsu launched *Bungei jidai*

Love Suicides

A letter came from the woman's husband. It had been two years since he had taken a dislike to his wife and deserted her. The letter came from a distant land.

"Don't let the child bounce a rubber ball. I can hear the sound. It strikes at my heart."

She took the rubber ball away from her nine-year-old daughter.

Again a letter came from her husband. It was from a different post office than the first one.

"Don't send the child to school wearing shoes. I can hear the sound. It tramples on my heart."

In place of shoes, she gave her daughter soft felt sandals. The girl cried and would no longer go to school.

Once more a letter came from her husband. It was posted only a month later than the previous letter, but his handwriting suddenly looked old.

"Don't let the child eat from a porcelain bowl. I can hear the sound. It breaks my heart."

The woman fed the girl with her own chopsticks as if she were three years old. Then she remembered the time when the girl really was three years old and her husband had spent pleasant days at her side. The girl went to the cabinet on her own and took out her bowl. The woman quickly snatched it from her and dashed it against a rock in the garden: the sound of her husband's heart breaking. Suddenly the woman raised her eyebrows. She threw her own bowl against the rock. Wasn't *this* the sound of her husband's heart breaking? The woman tossed the small dinner table out into the garden. What about this sound? She threw her whole body against the wall and pounded with her fists. She flung herself at the paper partition like a spear and tumbled out on the other side. And what about this sound?

"Mommy, Mommy, Mommy!"

The girl ran toward her, crying, and the woman slapped her. Oh, listen to this sound!

Like an echo of that sound, another letter came from the woman's husband. It had been sent from yet another post office in a new distant land.

"Don't make any sound at all. Don't open or close the doors or sliding partitions. Don't breathe. The two of you mustn't even let the clocks in the

(continued on back flap)

NORTH POINT PRESS · SAN FRANCISCO

Palm-of-the-Hand Stories

Yasunari Kawabata

Palm-of-the-Hand Stories
by Yasunari Kawabata

Translated from the Japanese
by Lane Dunlop and J. Martin Holman

Dust jacket for an American edition of a translation of sketches that Kawabata likened to the poems that young poets produce

(The Age of the Literary Arts), a bold new literary journal that they hoped would be an outlet for a new kind of writing that followed the modernist experiments in Europe. The first issue of the journal appeared in October 1924, and the writing was so fresh and challenging that critics labeled the coterie as members of the *Shinkankaku-ha* (Neo-Perceptionist School). The authors associated with the movement had wearied of the dull, quasi-confessional narratives by writers of the Naturalist School and were yearning for new ways to express feelings and present human interactions. Although the movement was short-lived and produced only a few enduring works (mostly by Yokomitsu), the influence of this movement on Kawabata's work was tremendous.

In the form of what he called "palm-of-the-hand" stories, brief sketches of human experience that he compared to the poetry that most authors produce in their youth, Kawabata published his earliest significant fiction in *Bungei jidai*. Throughout his career he continued to write these stories, which total more than 140, and he also published a recast version of his account of his grandfather's death as "Jūrokusai no nikki" (Diary of My Sixteenth Year,

1925). As his fame increased, Kawabata also moved about with great frequency between Tokyo and a hot springs resort on the Izu Peninsula. His literary colleagues, noting his proclivity for spending only a few months in any particular residence, began referring to him as an eternal traveler (*eien no tabibito*), a characterization that also metaphorically describes the fluid relationships between Kawabata's literary characters and between the shapes of his narratives. Stylistically he is known as an elliptical, even surrealistic, writer whose work is governed more by a desire to evoke mood than by an interest in plot, structure, logical development, and so many of the other features often associated with the writing of fiction. Some critics have attributed these stylistic features to his interests in the literature written by women of the court in the tenth century, particularly in the masterpieces such as *The Tale of Genji*, but the influences of European modernistic technique on Kawabata's style and approaches to writing are also worth considering.

In May 1925 Kawabata met Matsubayashi Hideko, a young woman with whom he soon began living in what became a common-law marriage until 1931, when the two finally registered formally as husband and wife. Around this time Kawabata was also writing a script for a motion-picture agency of the Neo-Perceptionist School, and critics regard this work, "Kurutta ippeiji" (A Crazy Page, 1926), as a landmark in the impressionist motion-picture movement in Japan. The work, which was directed by Kinugasa Teinosuke and follows the actions of a man who has taken a job at an insane asylum so that he can observe the wife whom he has driven to madness, was named one of the best motion pictures of the year.

In 1926 Kawabata also published "The Izu Dancer," the story that is typically regarded as his maiden work (and Kawabata once declared any author's "maiden work" to be his masterpiece). While recounting fairly faithfully Kawabata's journey around the Izu Peninsula in search of consolation following the many disappointments and losses of his youth, this story of an intelligent student joining a group of traveling performers regarded as social outcasts seems on the surface to be a straightforward look at youthful love. The reader first sees the student racing up a rain-swept mountain and hoping that he can catch up with the players whom he has seen from a distance in order to get a closer look at the beautiful dancing girl. Kawabata lets the reader think that this young man's aim in pursuing the girl is commonplace—that he is hoping for an opportunity to fulfill his sexual yearning for the young woman.

But the student makes an early discovery in one memorable scene of the story. When the young woman is soaking in an outdoor bath of an inn, she spots the student, leaps from the water, and stretches her naked body to its full length to wave at him and call his name. He quickly realizes that she cannot be more than twelve or thirteen years old, that she has been made up to appear much more mature on occasions when he has seen her previously. Readers might expect the student to feel disappointed and frustrated, but Kawabata surprises them by presenting the joyous relief that this young man feels at no longer finding a barrier of sexual tension separating him from these performers. He can draw emotionally close to them on a level untainted by desire, and they in turn can accept him as a "good person"—words that he hears from the dancing girl and that he had thought he would never hear again.

In representing the intense but passionless purity that becomes the ideal for many of Kawa-

bata's characters, the story gained a wide popular readership and was adapted as a motion picture at least five times following its publication. But the financial success it brought Kawabata was not immediate, and even when Kanjō sōshoku (Decorations of Sentiment, 1926), his first collection of palm-of-the-hand stories, was published, Kawabata was forced to sell a copy of this collection to a used bookstore in order to have enough money to take a train into town to negotiate with a money lender.

Kawabata's wife gave birth to a daughter in June 1927, but the infant died before she could be named. The couple never again attempted to have children, and Kawabata publicly expressed his fear of taking on the responsibility of parenting, which he described as an "audacious experiment." He distanced himself from the emotions attending family relationships in much the same way that his fictional characters struggle to remain aloof while still participating in life.

After publishing The Izu Dancer, another collection of stories, Kawabata, who had been making his home at one of the hot springs resorts on the Izu Peninsula, traveled to Tokyo in April 1927 to attend Yokomitsu's wedding. There he decided that he and his wife should settle permanently in the city, where he could be close to the bustle of literary activity. One of his favorite undertakings was that of serving as a staff member of coterie magazines, and he was probably correct in estimating that he belonged to more editorial staffs at small magazines than any other writer of his day. His involvement in such enterprises widened his circle of contacts among literary figures, further expanded his associations with authors of different camps and persuasions, and gave him a chance to promote the careers of struggling writers who, without his support and encouragement, would have run into barriers of prejudice and disfavor from the establishment. He fostered the careers of writers such as Okamoto Kanoko and Hōjō Tamio, a young leper whose stories Kawabata was able to get published and whose collected works Kawabata arranged to have printed after Hōjō's death. The most famous of Kawabata's literary disciples was Mishima Yukio, who survived a couple of scathing reviews of his first collection of stories partly through Kawabata's support.

After settling in Tokyo, Kawabata began to frequent the many cafés and revue theaters in the Asakusa district, where he made friends with dancers and artists who provided him with a wealth of materials for journals. He later pub-

Dust jacket for the first American edition of the translation of Kawabata's Meijin *(1954), drawing on his newspaper reports of Go matches in 1938*

lished these in *Asakusa kurenaidan* (The Asakusa Crimson Gang, 1930), a work that succeeded in putting his favorite nightclub on solid financial ground for the first time. He collected so much material for stories that he attempted several sequels to *Asakusa kurenaidan,* but none was ever completed.

Kawabata lectured on literature once a week at the Bunka Gakuin school between 1930 and 1934, not because he necessarily enjoyed the classroom but because his friend and mentor Kikuchi Kan had been appointed to head the department of literature there. Visitors to Kawabata's home at this time were astonished at the small menagerie of animals with which he had surrounded himself. Among these were nine dogs and so many birds that he was occasionally seen tossing a dead bird into a cupboard. In 1933 a misanthropic bird lover appeared as the protagonist of his story "Kinju" (translated as "Of Birds and Beasts," 1969).

In the fall of 1933 *Bungakukai,* a literary journal destined to become influential, was launched, and Kawabata joined its staff. *Bungaku-*

kai was especially interesting to Kawabata because it was the first Japanese literary journal to be free of intimate ties to any literary clique, and as such it provided Kawabata and other writers with opportunities to discuss and publish pieces from across the spectrum of literary approaches. His subsequent literary activities reflect some of the difficult choices facing Japanese writers in the mid 1930s. Though Kawabata could not be considered an eager collaborator with various government agencies that worked to suppress seditious thought and writing as Japan moved closer to world war, he seemed to feel that any responsible writer ought to attempt to have a say in those associations that the government was establishing to oversee literary affairs. In January 1934 he joined a literary discussion group organized by a former head of the Public Security Division of the Home Ministry.

A more felicitous endeavor began after Kikuchi Kan used *Bungei shunjū* to establish a literary prize in honor of writer Akutagawa Ryunosuke, his friend who had committed suicide in 1927. The Akutagawa Prize was designed then, and continues today, to recognize and encourage the talents of budding writers, and both Kawabata and Yokomitsu were asked to serve on the selection jury for the biannual prize when it was introduced in 1935. This gave Kawabata yet another opportunity to promote the work of young authors, although in the first year that the prize was to be awarded some young writers may have felt that he was using his position to thwart their ambitions. Dazai Osamu was all but frantic to receive the first Akutagawa Prize, and he was furious when Kawabata dashed his chances by obliquely suggesting that Dazai's drug addiction hampered his writing abilities. After Dazai had mounted letter-writing campaigns to gain the support of Kawabata and another member of the jury but still failed to win recognition in being considered for two subsequent prizes, Dazai stormed over to the house of the other juror and, in an excess of frustration, threw rocks at his house.

In 1935 Kawabata began to write and publish parts of *Yukiguni* (1937; translated as *Snow Country*, 1957), one of his best-known works. He did not conceive of this work as a long, unified narrative, but after having written an initial short story for a magazine, Kawabata felt what he called a "lingering feeling" for the characters and their situation, and he produced a second story for a different magazine with a later publication deadline. The narrative of *Yukiguni* continued in this fashion, with Kawabata adding a new story as the whim struck him, until finally a collection of these connected stories was published as *Snow Country*. He was never completely satisfied with the way the work ended, and finally, only three months before his death, Kawabata produced a brief palm-of-the-hand condensation of it.

The setting and imagery of *Snow Country* are ideally suited to the kind of story Kawabata enjoyed relating. His male protagonist, Shimamura, is a critic of Western ballet and a peculiar dilettante who refuses to corrupt his idealized conception of that art form by actually viewing a performance of it. Shimamura is comfortable in his relationship with Komako, the vibrant hot springs geisha, only because he can maintain a geographical distance between himself and her: in order to visit her, Shimamura travels from his home in Tokyo through a long, dark tunnel (like a passageway leading into a fairy-tale land) that crosses the frozen borders of the "snow country" in northern Japan. As the renowned opening passage of the novel presents Shimamura returning through the tunnel to visit Komako, mist from

Kawabata addressing the International P.E.N. Conference in Japan, 1957

the steam has settled over the windows of the train, and when Shimamura swipes his finger across the glass he is startled to find a female eye appearing on its mirrorlike surface. That disembodied eye represents the only kind of relationship in which Shimamura is comfortable—one in which he is free to sit back and observe without suffering any messy emotional entanglement, to objectify women and other aesthetic pleasures in his life, and to maintain his distance so that he does not have to see all the details that might spoil his fantasies.

Shimamura continues to visit Komako, but when she becomes too real for him to remain comfortable, his mind shifts toward the beautiful, enigmatic Yōko—a woman who has been caring for her terminally ill lover and whom he has seen on the train. The novel ends indeterminately with Yōko critically injured—or perhaps killed—in a fire and with Shimamura convinced that it is time to break off his relationship with Komako.

In 1937 the initial collection of *Snow Country* stories was published, and Kawabata celebrated its success by purchasing a second home in the resort town of Karuizawa, where he spent his summers throughout the war years. He seemed to withdraw more and more from society as the Japanese military tightened its control of the nation by censoring speech and published materials and by interrogating and imprisoning those accused of seditious thoughts. In summer 1938 Kawabata accepted a request from newspapers in Tokyo and Osaka to record the *go* matches in which Honnimbō Shūsai, the master player, was

Dust jacket for the first American edition of the translation of Yama no oto (1954), one of Kawabata's later novels

participating. Kawabata revised and restructured these accounts during a period of twelve years throughout and after the war until he finally produced *Meijin* (1954; translated as *The Master of Go,* 1973), which he regarded as his only completed work.

During the war Kawabata also served as a judge of young people's compositions, helped elderly author Shimazaki Tōson edit a collection of his writings, and devoted much time to writing stories for children and popular audiences. Another means by which he sought to set aside the unpleasantness of the contemporary period was that of reading and rereading classical Japanese literature. Especially during the last two years of the war, as fire bombings of Tokyo mounted, Kawabata began rereading *The Tale of Genji* at every possible opportunity. His mind focused upon the days of ancient Japan, and he took pains to preserve and study copies of the tale during the calamitous warfare in the capital. Because *The Tale of Genji* had acquired so much personal significance for him, he began to regard himself as a vessel through which the traditions

of the past could be safely preserved during the war and for the future.

In the spring of 1941 a Japanese newspaper published in occupied Manchurian territory invited Kawabata to visit. He attended a *go* tournament there and then traveled to meet Japanese writers living in the colony. In September that year he returned again, this time under the official sponsorship of the Japanese government, and although he acceded to the request of the military that he deliver some lectures on the superior values of Japanese culture, he was most eager to travel around China and collect folktales. These he edited into a collection called *Manshukoku kaminzoku sōsaku senshū* (A Collection of Folk Writings from Manchukuo, 1942–1943). He cut his travels short in late November when rumors of an imminent crisis forced him to return to Japan just a few days before the bombing of Pearl Harbor. The wartime pursuit for which Kawabata is best remembered consists of the compiling that he made of the writings left by those who had died in battle and the commentary that he provided on these. Published at the end of 1942 and throughout 1944, this series was "Eirei no ibun" (Posthumous Writings of the Spirits of Fallen Heroes).

In spring 1943 Kawabata and his wife adopted a young woman named Masako, the daughter of a maternal cousin. Before long, he dug an air-raid shelter in his garden and spent nights patrolling the neighborhood as part of a fire prevention initiative. In April 1945 he was assigned to visit a naval airbase at the southern tip of the main islands, and there he spent a month with soldiers preparing to become kamikaze pilots. Kawabata wrote one story, "Seimei no ki" (The Tree of Life, 1946), about his observations there, but generally he seems to have been dispirited by the experience.

Three months before the end of the war, in yet another attempt to preserve something of the culture that he daily saw going up in flames around him, Kawabata contacted many established writers living in Kamakura and asked them to donate books to a lending library he wished to establish. His efforts succeeded, and he was able to set up the Kamakura Bunko library, which quickly moved into publishing after the war and began reprinting affordable editions of some of the best-known works of modern Japanese literature. The rapid resurgence of interest in reading and writing literature after the war, despite all the devastation and poverty, resulted partly from the efforts of the Kamakura Bunko publishers. By January 1946 the firm, which continued to contribute significantly to Japanese literature until it ceased operations in 1950, also launched its own literary magazine, *Ningen* (Humanity), to introduce the work of new writers—and in this journal Kawabata arranged for the publication of a story by an unknown writer, Mishima Yukio.

Kawabata's enthusiasm for the publishing operations of Kamakura Bunko was obvious; he contributed his own stories to *Ningen* and published a new story for the *Snow Country* series in the May 1946 issue of the journal. Beneath his flurry of activity, however, Kawabata clearly mourned the many lives and vestiges of culture that the war had destroyed. As a writer, he felt deeply the need to perpetuate traditions of beauty in Japan that were in danger of being lost. He remarked that what remained for him in the postwar years was to return to the ancient mountains and rivers and to produce elegies for the lost Japan. Nakamura Mitsuo, an astute Japanese critic, has suggested that Kawabata "sensed within the defeated people of Japan the same orphaned condition that had been his own in the past." As if to certify his position as a "master of funerals," Kawabata delivered the eulogies of many of his close literary friends, including Yokomitsu and Kikuchi.

Surrounding himself with cultural relics in the postwar years just as he had cluttered his house with birds and beasts in prewar days, Kawabata became an art collector and built up a reputable collection of eighteenth-century paintings and contemporary works by Japanese as well as Western artists. He attempted to produce modern versions of two works of classical Japanese literature, both *The Tale of Genji* and another Heian tale, *Torikaebaya monogatari,* but he was unable to complete either.

In 1947 the "completed" version of *Snow Country* was published and received considerable acclaim, although Kawabata maintained reservations about it. Publication of a sixteen-volume set of his collected works began that year, and in June 1948 he was elected fourth president of P.E.N. Japan, a position that enabled him to foster and influence profoundly literary activities in Japan as well as to encourage the translation of Japanese works into other languages so that other people might begin to appreciate them. Kawabata served as president of P.E.N. Japan for seventeen years, through a period in which Japanese literature began to gain international recognition. Because of Kawabata's new stature on the

literary committee of this organization, a newspaper invited him to attend a session of the Tokyo War Crimes trials and publish what he observed, and on two subsequent occasions he was invited to Hiroshima to view the atomic bomb destruction. As president of P.E.N. Kawabata published statements in favor of nuclear disarmament and world peace, and in 1950 he sponsored a P.E.N. conference in Hiroshima on World Peace and Literature.

He also struggled to regain a sense of direction in his writing. Between 1948 and 1952 he wrote *Shōnen* (Boys; first published in the 1948–1954 collected works), a fictional reminiscence of his youthful encounter with the Izu dancer and his homosexual romance during his school days. Despite its direct connection with Kawabata's experience, however, the work lacks the power and grace of his other writings and perhaps suffers from its lack of the "distance" that characterizes his best work.

One of Kawabata's most creative periods was in 1949 when he began to publish serially both *Sembazuru* (1952; translated as *Thousand Cranes,* 1958) and *Yama no oto* (1954; translated as *The Sound of the Mountain,* 1970). Both of these serialized works are similar to *Snow Country* in their structure and manner of composition, but Kawabata neither took as long to complete them nor continued to expand them later, as he had done with *Snow Country.* Both *Thousand Cranes* and *The Sound of the Mountain* comprise not "novels" as much as they do two series of vignettes, each bound by common characters and natural imagery. Some critics have compared Kawabata's mode of composition to that of a master in the *renga,* a medieval poetic form of linked verse in which one verse simultaneously terminates and transmutes the flash of imagistic inspiration in the preceding one—and thereby creates an amorphous form described as a "plotless narrative." In some ways Kawabata's work creates the same kinds of poetic effects and betrays the expectations of Western readers, who expect something to happen in the way of beginning and ending a story. Kawabata seldom provides such tidy moments for his readers, and in that sense his work is both Japanese in temperament and strikingly modern, or even postmodern, in its literary orientation.

As another indication of Kawabata's concern for the passing of old Japan, *Thousand Cranes* concerns what Kawabata saw as the degradation of the tea ceremony in contemporary Japan. Yet the high point of his late fiction—in the words of

Dust jacket for an American edition of the translation of Nemureru bijo *(1960–1961), a collection of stories incorporating Kawabata's familiar themes of love and loneliness, youth and aging*

Yamamoto Kenkichi, the "very summit of postwar Japanese literature"—was *The Sound of the Mountain*. "The Izu Dancer" is unquestionably the purest work of his youth, and *Snow Country* is the finest expression of a middle-aged author contemplating, but not fully resigned to, the distances separating him from others. But *The Sound of the Mountain* presents the vision of a wise but wounded man sensing the approach of death, recognizing that he grows increasingly distant from the world around him, and finding a retreat into his memories to be his only solace.

Shingo, the aging protagonist, has begun to forget what has happened recently but recalls the distant past with surprising clarity. Kawabata presents, in a way that Shingo cannot understand, an aging man who in postwar Japan is surrounded by tokens of his failure as a husband, father, and employee, one who only by hastening into a past that he has idealized as an alternative to this present reality can find peace. This character replicates something that Kawabata must have felt as he saw the passing of an ancient cul-

ture that he so loved, yet *The Sound of the Mountain* transcends Kawabata's personal recognition by drawing readers into the mind of Shingo as he struggles to prepare for his own death.

Amid all Shingo's disappointments—in his wife, whom he sees as plain and coarse in contrast to her deceased sister, whom he loved in the distant past; in his children, who seem incapable of sustaining relationships with him or with their spouses; and in his work, which is drab and unfulfilling—the only present comfort Shingo can find is in his associations, both real and imagined, with Kikuko, his daughter-in-law. He can sustain an ideal image of her precisely because she is unattainable, as are his memories of the dead sister-in-law whom he had hoped to marry. He thus cherishes the inapproachability of both Kikuko and the dead woman he once loved, and he grows increasingly weary of and removed from the unpleasant realities of the present. Except for Kawabata's depiction of the natural milieu, he presents almost everything about postwar Japanese life as depressing, and from the way Kawabata manipulates imagery, only Shingo and—at least until the end of the novel—Kikuko clearly seem to have any sensitivity to or interest in nature. In the flowers and shrubbery of Shingo's garden Kawabata mirrors the emotions of his characters.

As the novel opens, Shingo hears the sound of the mountain behind his house, a sound that he comprehends as foreshadowing his death. By the end of the work Shingo has decided that he must return to his native Shinshū and see the brilliant reds of the autumn maple leaves that his memories have always associated with his late sister-in-law. But the sound with which the novel ends, as Shingo tries to communicate his feelings to Kikuko, is the sound that she makes in washing the dishes, and she cannot hear his voice. That, perhaps, is as close as Kawabata could come to providing an "ending" for the work: for Kawabata, to kill Shingo might have entailed killing a part of himself.

Having written this exceptional elegy, Kawabata again began to struggle for direction in his writing. Around 1954 he became addicted to sleeping pills, and the quality of his work suffered. Much of his time was devoted to writing serialized novels in newspapers and women's magazines that were aimed at a popular audience. He wrote scripts for two dance dramas, but much of the time that he might have spent on his writing was directed into activities on behalf of his profession, as he continued to labor for

YASUNARI KAWABATA, born in 1899 in Osaka, Japan, was orphaned at the age of two and soon lost his grandparents as well. While still a student at Tokyo Imperial University he joined writer Yokomitsu Riichi in starting *Bungei Jidai* (*The Artistic Age*), a journal that became the organ of the Neo-Impressionist school with which Kawabata was early associated. His first major work, *Izu no odoriko* (*The Izu Dancer*), appeared in 1925; works such as *Yukiguni* (*Snow Country*) led Kawabata to be recognized as one of the major writers of the prewar years. In the postwar period he produced *Sembazuru* (*Thousand Cranes*), *Yama no-oto* (*The Sound of the Mountain*), and *Koto* (THE OLD CAPITAL). On receiving the Nobel Prize for Literature in 1968, he said that in his work he sought a harmony among man, nature, and emptiness. He committed suicide in 1972.

NORTH POINT PRESS · SAN FRANCISCO

Dust jacket for an American edition of the translation of Koto *(1962), a novel set in postwar Kyoto, which was once the capital of Japan*

P.E.N. This work largely culminated in 1957, when the twenty-ninth international conference of P.E.N. was held in Japan.

The insularity of modern Japanese literature had begun to break down only a few years before, as a handful of Kawabata's works paved the way by being translated into English and European languages. The extraordinary time and care that Kawabata spent in preparing for the P.E.N. conference did more to open Japanese literature to a world audience than anything else might have done. In jetting to Europe for an executive committee meeting to make the original preparations, meeting with writers such as François Mauriac and T. S. Eliot to elicit their support, and bustling throughout Europe, Scandinavia, and Asia to extend personal invitations to the conference, Kawabata had traveled for months before the gathering. As a result, the conference prefigured in international cultural affairs what the 1964 Tokyo Olympics did in international relations: it provided the world with a view of a revitalized postwar Japan and attracted a wide assortment of writers, critics, and translators from all over the world.

International contacts were initiated between writers, between writers and translators, and between writers and publishers, and interest in Japanese literature exploded. Translations of works by Kawabata, Mishima, Jun'ichirō Tanizaki, and other contemporary writers began to appear in many languages, and after Kawabata secured copyrights and intervened with other assistance, Donald Keene published *Modern Japanese Literature: An Anthology,* the first collection of twentieth-century Japanese stories. For his efforts in organizing the conference and for making Japanese literature accessible, Kawabata was awarded the Kikuchi Kan Prize. He was also elected an international vice president of P.E.N. and was awarded the Goethe Medal at the P.E.N. convention in Frankfurt in 1958.

These activities on behalf of his literary colleagues, combined with a gallstone attack that put Kawabata into a hospital for more than half a year in 1958, reduced the time he spent on his writing, but following his recovery he published a final masterpiece, *Nemureru bijo* (1961; translated as *House of the Sleeping Beauties, and Other Stories,* 1969). The implications of the story are chilling even in simple outline, and they provide a fitting coda to Kawabata's continuing literary depictions of human isolation. The "house" of the title is in fact a peculiar brothel—where physically perfect young women are drugged so that, for a fee, impotent elderly men can lie naked beside them for a night. Bringing together a desire for intimate association and an inability to consummate the yearning, this portrait of pathetic loneliness reiterates a familiar motif of Kawabata's writings, but nowhere else is that desire expressed with such hopeless sorrow. The same longing with no possibility of fulfillment also appears in Kawabata's last story, "Kataude" (1963; translated as "One Arm," 1967). In this surrealistic story a man desires to possess his lover but can approach her only as if she were a physical object; understanding his need and the incapacity he has, she allows him to remove her arm and take it home with him for the night. He embraces it passionately but is filled with horror after he has used only a portion of her body to satisfy his longing for human contact.

While he was still serializing *Koto* (1962; translated as *The Old Capital*, 1987) and *Utsukushisa to kanashimi to* (1965; translated as *Beauty and Sadness*, 1975), Kawabata received yet another honor—the Medal of Culture (Bunka Kunshō), the highest award that the Japanese government confers upon writers. Yet signs of his physical and creative decline were already appearing. His addiction to sleeping pills marred the writing of *The Old Capital*, and when he once tried to break his dependence on them after he finished the novel, he lapsed into a coma from which he did not emerge for ten days. Most of the rest of the long pieces that he tried to serialize for the next several years remained unfinished. Despite these difficulties Kawabata continued to work on behalf of other writers and in efforts to preserve literary tradition in Japan. In Tokyo he was instrumental in establishing the Nihon Kindai Bungakukan (Museum of Modern Japanese Literature), a library and museum for which he helped design plans and raise construction funds. When the museum was finished in 1967, he became an honorary adviser and later its honorary director.

Kawabata also continued to participate in P.E.N., as he attended its international conferences in São Paolo and Oslo, but in October 1965 he resigned as president of the Japan chapter of the club. Only a month later the people of the Izu Peninsula honored his first work by unveiling a statue depicting the dancing girl and the student at the Yugano hot springs resort.

Early in 1966 Kawabata spent three months in the hospital with a liver disorder. In 1968 he served as campaign chairman for Kon Tōkō, an old school friend and writer who was running for election to the Japanese Diet. That October he was notified that he had been chosen as the first Japanese writer to receive the Nobel Prize in Literature, and Kawabata graciously invited Edward G. Seidensticker, his primary English translator, to join him for the award ceremonies in Stockholm and to translate his acceptance speech, "Japan, the Beautiful, and Myself." A surge of acclaim followed: he received a commendation from the Japanese Diet; was elected as an honorary member of the American Academy and Institute of Arts and Letters; received an invitation in spring 1969 to lecture at the University of Hawaii, where he was also given an honorary doctoral degree; and was honored in London by the Japanese consulate, which mounted a public exhibition on him and his writings. The Association for the Study of Kawabata Literature was organized in 1970, the same year that a fifth edition of his collected works was published.

Kawabata was doing very little writing, however, and in November 1970 he suffered a serious blow to his morale when Mishima, his brightest protégé, committed seppuku. Kawabata was attending funeral services for another friend when the news of Mishima's sensational act reached him, and he rushed to the Self-Defense headquarters but was not permitted to see Mishima's body. When asked to write about Mishima's suicide a couple of months later, Kawabata could not comment. Only thirteen days before his own death could Kawabata write of this event to his publisher in New York: "I am not free for a single moment from the grief and sorrow I feel over Mishima's deplorable death."

Yet Kawabata continued to pursue nonliterary activities. He campaigned for another friend who was running for election and helped arouse interest in an international conference on Japanese studies, but the only significant writing that he did in the last months of his life was an essay appropriately titled "Dreams Are like Phantoms."

Kawabata kept an apartment in the Hayama district where he did his writing, and there he was found, apparently having taken his own life by gas poisoning. Some of his friends cling to a belief that his death was accidental since he left no suicide note and had given none of them any indication of his intention to die. The Japan P.E.N. Club joined the Japan Writers Association and the Museum of Modern Japanese Literature

Kawabata (third from the left) at the wedding reception for his protégé, Mishima Yukio, in 1958

to sponsor his funeral. His favorite fountain pen, a hundred sheets of blank manuscript paper, his pipe and glasses, a volume of his writings, a kimono, and the purple ceremonial *hakama* he wore to accept the Nobel Prize were placed beside his body in his casket. Exhibitions honoring his work toured the nation for eight months following his death; a memorial society was founded in his honor; and a reading room was named for him in the Museum of Modern Japanese Literature.

References:

Furuya Tsunatake, *Hyōden Kawabata Yasunari* (Tokyo: Jitsugyō no Nihonsha, 1960);

Van C. Gessel, *Three Modern Novelists: Sōseki, Tanizaki, Kawabata* (Tokyo: Kodansha International, 1993);

Hasegawa Izumi, *Kawabata Yasunari ronkō,* third expanded and revised edition (Tokyo: Meiji Shoin, 1984);

Kawashima Itaru, *Kawabata Yasunari no sekai* (Tokyo: Kōdansha, 1969);

Donald Keene, *Dawn to the West,* volume 1 (New York: Holt, Rinehart & Winston, 1984);

Masao Miyoshi, *Accomplices of Silence: The Modern Japanese Novel* (Berkeley: University of California Press, 1974);

Nakamura Mitsuo, *Ronkō Kawabata Yasunari* (Tokyo: Chikuma Shobō, 1978);

Ōoka Makoto, Takahashi Hideo, and Miyoshi Yukio, eds., *Kawabata Yasunari,* Gunzō Nihon no Sakka series, volume 13 (Tokyo: Shōgakkan, 1991);

Shindō Junkō, *Denki Kawabata Yasunari* (Tokyo: Rokkō shūppan, 1976).

Papers:

In addition to papers and memorabilia of Kawabata Yasunari held by the Museum of Modern Japanese Literature in Tokyo, which Kawabata helped found, there are extensive collections of his papers, letters, and personal belongings at the Kawabata Yasunari Kinenkan (Memorial Museum), established at his home in the Hase district of Kamakura City.

Kobayashi Takiji

(13 October 1903 – 20 February 1933)

Hidaka Shohji
Kanagawa University

BOOKS: *Kani kōsen* (Tokyo: Senkisha, 1929); translated as "The Cannery Boat" in *The Cannery Boat, and Other Japanese Short Stories* (New York: International, 1933; London: Lawrence, 1933); translated by Frank Motofuji as "The Factory Ship" in *"The Factory Ship" and "The Absentee Landlord"* (Seattle: University of Washington Press, 1973; Tokyo: University of Tokyo Press, 1973);

Fuzai jinushi (Tokyo: Nihon Hyōronsha, 1930); translated by Motofuji as "The Absentee Landlord" in *"The Factory Ship" and "The Absentee Landlord"*;

1928 nen 3 gatsu 15 nichi (Tokyo: Senkisha, 1930); translated as "The Fifteenth of March, 1928" in *The Cannery Boat, and Other Japanese Short Stories*;

Kōjō saibō (Tokyo: Senkisha, 1930);

Puroretaria bungakuron (Tokyo: Tenninsha, 1931);

Higashi Kutchankō (Tokyo: Kaizōsha, 1931);

Orugu (Tokyo: Senkisha, 1931);

Numajiri-mura (Tokyo: Nihon Puroretaria Sakka Dōmei Shuppanbu, 1932);

Hiyorimi shūgi ni taisuru tōsō (Tokyo: Nihon Puroretaria Sakka Dōmei Shuppanbu, 1933);

Tenkeiki no hitobito (Tokyo: Kaizōsha, 1933);

Chiku no hitobito (Tokyo: Kaizōsha, 1933);

Kobayashi Takiji nikki shū (Tokyo: Naukasha, 1936);

Tōseikatsusha (Tokyo: Minshu Shobō, 1947);

Bōsetsurin (Tokyo: Nihon Minshu-shugi Bunka Renmei, 1948).

Collections: *Kobayashi Takiji shokan shū*, 3 volumes (Tokyo: Naukasha, 1935);

Kobayashi Takiji zuihitsu shū (Tokyo: Shomotsu Tembōsha, 1937);

Teihon Kobayashi Takiji zenshū, 15 volumes (Tokyo: Shin Nihon Shuppansha, 1968–1969);

Kobayashi Takiji Bungakukan (Tokyo: Horupu Shuppan, 1980);

Kobayashi Takiji zenshū, 7 volumes (Tokyo: Shin Nihon Shuppansha, 1982);

Kobayashi Takiji

Kobayashi Takiji shū (Tokyo: Shin Nihon Shuppansha, 1987–1988).

Kobayashi Takiji wrote powerful and acclaimed works one after another during a few years between the late 1920s and mid 1930s, the height of the socialist movement in Japan. Especially as social reverberations from the Russian Revolution reached their homeland, Japanese who had experienced Western-style democracy during the Taishō Period (1912–1926) gradually awoke to Marxist doctrine, began to oppose government policies of building a "wealthy nation and strong army"—the motto of the Meiji government's reform policies—and sought to liberate the masses. Of the many writers who joined the battle lines of the socialist movement, the author who stood in the middle of the fray and embodied the vitality of the uprising was Kobayashi Takiji.

Many of Kobayashi's works are set in Hokkaidō, the new frontier opened by pioneering farmers during the Meiji Period (1868–1912). As one who had migrated to Hokkaidō and had observed closely how the region had been exploited by capital ventures from the main island, Kobayashi decided early in his career that he would write about the miserable, tragic reality of this exploitation. As he gradually became aware of Marxist views of history, he knew that his main themes must concern the control of wealth and the liberation of the working class.

Mesmerized by Charlie Chaplin's films and charmed by Dorothy and Lillian Gish, Kobayashi was an unparalleled fan of motion pictures. In the films of his day Kobayashi witnessed many innovations: American director D. W. Griffith introduced close-up and montage techniques that contributed to a grammar of the cinema, and Soviet film director Sergey Eisenstein also contributed to this epoch-making age of motion pictures. Kobayashi's fascination with these new ideologies and techniques thus provided him with a background from which he could make a brilliant appearance as a Japanese writer. His interests in Marxist philosophy and in the grammar of filmmaking provided him with models of how to think about and depict the masses.

Kobayashi was born in a collapsing farmhouse in Kawaguchi, Shimokawazoi Village, Kita Akita-gun, in Akita Prefecture. His father, Suematsu, was thirty-nine years old at the time of Kobayashi's birth; Seki, his mother, was thirty. Takirō, an older brother; Machi, an older sister; and Tsune, a step-grandmother, were also members of the growing household, which eventually included three more siblings younger than Kobayashi—Tsugi, Sango, and Sachi. In November 1907 the family moved to Otaru in Hokkaidō, and there, with assistance from an uncle who ran a bakery plant, they were able to open a bread store at Wakatake-chō. The neighborhood was filled with poor fishermen at that time, but Kobayashi soon was spending his early years surrounded by manual laborers working on major construction projects such as the building of a dike and the laying of railroad tracks.

▲413　小林多喜二　小樽高商卒業のころ。

Kobayashi soon after his graduation from Otaru Commercial School

At the age of twelve Kobayashi graduated from elementary school in April 1916, and with assistance from his uncle he entered the Otaru Commercial School operated by the Hokkaidō government. He helped with the work in his uncle's bakery and, dropping off orders on the way to his classes, commuted to school in the bakery delivery truck. Under the influence of Taishō democracy the Otaru Commercial School maintained an open atmosphere, and Kobayashi organized a circle of friends there to draw pictures and exhibit their work. The group produced watercolor paintings, Kobayashi's being characterized by thick lines and colors filled with dark shadows. He excelled at composition and began writing Chinese-style poems, Japanese verses, and stories that he submitted to magazines such as *Bunshō Sekai* and *Chūō Bungaku*.

In April 1921 he advanced to the Commercial High School in Otaru, and he commuted from his home in Wakatake-chō. The school was at the top of a hill that the students

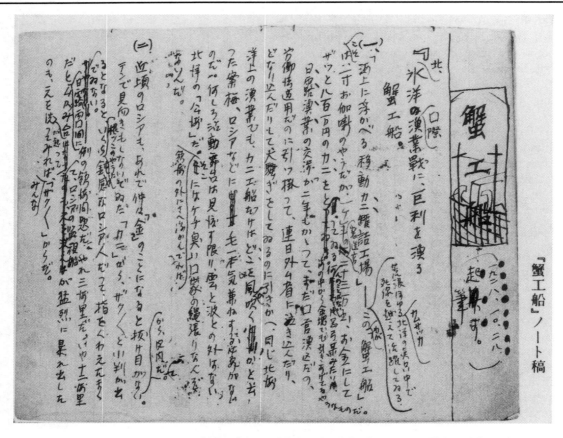

Manuscript for an early version of The Cannery Boat, *dated October 1928 in Kobayashi's notebook*
(location unknown)

had named "Hell Slope," which afforded a view of the city and harbor of Otaru and of the Sea of Japan, and the open expanse created an atmosphere of literary and philosophical freedom. A cadre of excellent young teachers had gathered at the school, and they added to the freshness Kobayashi sensed in his studies of economics and other subjects. The three years he spent at the school strongly aroused his interests in literature. He developed a deep interest in the works of August Strindberg, Fyodor Dostoyevsky, and Anton Chekhov, and he read the fiction of Shiga Naoya. With some friends he formed *Kurarute,* a coterie journal named in honor of Henri Barbusse's Clarté movement, an organization of pacifist and internationalist thinkers with proletarian sympathies. Kobayashi thus began to write in the company of others such as Itō Sei, who was a young poet a year behind him at the school.

In March 1924 Kobayashi graduated from the high school and took a job in the Otaru branch of the Hokkaidō Colonial Bank. Trade in items from the sea was flourishing in Otaru, and the banks, shipping companies, and warehouses of the city made it the "Wall Street of Hokkaidō," the center of the northern Japanese economy. Yet it was also filled with poor, oppressed people, one of whom was Taguchi Taki, a young woman whom Kobayashi met two months after his father had died in August. Kobayashi decided to rescue her and took her into his home in 1926, but, without telling him where she was going, she fled from the house and disappeared from Otaru. A central theme of his writing thereafter concerned the question of how people in miserable circumstances can carry on, and he began to grope for ways to alter unpleasant social realities.

Deeply moved in September 1926 by reading Hayama Yoshiki's "Imbaifu" (Prostitute), Kobayashi discovered a literature informed by a new social consciousness, and his reading of Maksim Gorky deepened his interests in proletarian literature. When tenancy disputes in Furano erupted on a farm run by Isono Susumu, the head of the chamber of commerce in Otaru, Kobayashi aided the sharecroppers by provid-

『蟹工船』(「戦旗」昭和4年5月、6月)

Pages from the May/June 1938 issue of Senki *(Battle Flag), the journal published by the proletarian artists' organization.* The Canning Boat *was first published in this issue.*

ing them with information that the bank held. In November he joined the Vanguard Artists Association, the proletarian artists' league of Japan, and began making notes for some works of fiction.

In December 1927 Kobayashi began writing *Bōsetsurin* (Snowbreak, 1948), a novella set against the violent natural background of Hokkaidō and depicting the pathetic lives and the rebellion of the cultivators along the Ishikari River. This was the first work into which he poured his full energies, and his notes for it were discovered only in 1947.

In February 1928 the first general election under the universal suffrage act was held, and Kobayashi, representing the Vanguard Artists Association, campaigned for Yamamoto Genzō, a Communist Party member who was the candidate on the Workers and Farmers Party ticket. For the first time revolutionary forces gained strength in this election, and on 15 March, after the polling, authorities across the nation responded with repressive action. Five hundred laborers, farmers, and intellectuals in Otaru alone were rounded up during two months and jailed. Kobayashi recounts his experiences from this time in *Higashi Kutchankō* (Eastern Kutchankō, 1931).

Following this attempt to suppress them, the proletarian artists formed the All-Japan Proletarian Artists Association (NAPF), a consolidated organization that began publishing *Senki* (Battle Flag), a journal for which Kobayashi became the Otaru secretary. In May he went to Tokyo to meet with Kurahara Korehito, the leader of the proletarian literary movement, and Kurahara became Kobayashi's mentor in theoretical matters. After returning to Otaru, Kobayashi immediately began writing *1928 nen 3 gatsu 15 nichi* (1930; translated as "The Fifteenth of March 1928," 1933), which recounts the suppression that had occurred and depicts the masses of people who had courageously struggled against their oppressors. The story was published in the November and December issues of *Senki,* where the spirited response to it made Kobayashi known throughout Japan. An excerpt from the work was translated into Russian and published in *World Revolutionary Literature,* a journal published in Russia by the World Revolutionary Writers Association, and other translations in English, German, and French were also published.

In October, Kobayashi began writing *Kani kōsen* (1929; translated as "The Cannery Boat," 1933), a story about one of the ships in the fleet operating in the northern sea fisheries off

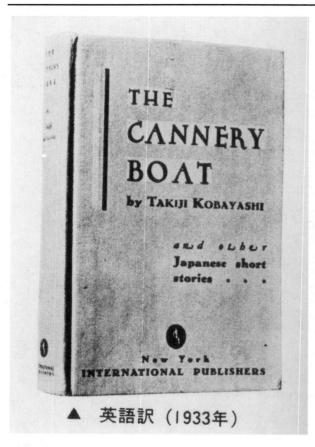

Dust jacket for the first English translation of Kani kōsen
(1929), Kobayashi's first novel

the coast of Hokkaidō. This fleet maintained facilities on the deck of its mother ship to can crabs, an industry that was exceeded in size only by the production of raw silk among Japanese export ventures. Working conditions aboard these ships were recognized as particularly harsh, as newspapers frequently reported mistreatment of the laborers. Kobayashi was especially interested in these workers, for many of them came from poor farming families in northeastern Japan, the region where he had been born. From former classmates at the Otaru Commercial High School he gathered information about their situation, and his painstaking investigation convinced him that some reprehensible national interests involving the armies of the Japanese empire were being served by this industry.

Based on his findings, *The Cannery Boat* reveals the ways in which, as part of a scheme of Japanese capitalist economics, Hokkaidō was being exploited as a domestic colony. Using techniques such as close-ups and montages that Kobayashi had learned from his interests in motion pictures, the novel conveys fresh, powerful impressions to its readers. He completed the story in five months, and in 1929 it was published serially in the May and June numbers of *Senki,* where it provoked a response even more enthusiastic than that of "The Fifteenth of March 1928." Translated into Russian, English, German, and French, *The Cannery Boat* made Kobayashi's name internationally known.

In July 1929 he began writing *Fuzai jinushi* (1930; translated as "The Absentee Landlord," 1973), a work in which he aimed to expose absentee landlords who owned vast tracts of land in Hokkaidō. In this novel Kobayashi explores a broad range of relationships involving tenant sharecroppers—between farmers and immigrants, farmers and banks, farmers and soldiers—and he incorporated into the story some of the information to which he had been privy through his position in the Hokkaidō bank. The novel was first published serially in *Chūō Kōron,* an influential journal that published the work of major contemporary Japanese writers. Despite the fact that the journal published its version only after excising the second half of the piece, one result of its publication was that Kobayashi, after having worked at the bank for more than five and one half years, was fired from his job there. Even after this dismissal, however, Kobayashi continued to write: in 1930 *Kōba saibō* (Factory Cell), a story of the efforts of a union organizer working in a factory, was serially published in the April through June numbers of *Kaizō.* At Harkov in November of that year the second International Congress of Revolutionary Writers praised this piece.

Kobayashi moved to Tokyo in 1930 and began a series of arduous activities. In May he traveled to Kyoto and back to Osaka to give lectures, and he was arrested when he returned to Osaka. After being released, he was again arrested in June. During his incarceration he was deeply moved by his first readings of works by Charles Dickens and Honoré de Balzac.

Even after being released on bail in January 1931, Kobayashi showed no regrets or apprehensions, and he set to work writing *Orugu* (The Organizer, 1931), a sequel to *Factory Cell.* Immediately after having finished this story, he proposed marriage to Taguchi Taki, with whom he had been reunited since May 1930, but she rejected the proposal because of responsibilities she owed to her family—and because of concerns that her presence might impede the difficult work that lay ahead for Kobayashi.

Memorial to Kobayashi on a hilltop overlooking the ocean, near Otaru. The inscription reads: "When winter comes to a close, I think about my beloved countryside, and I'm deeply moved."

In July 1931 he brought his mother to Tokyo from Otaru and set up a house for her, his younger brother, and himself in the Suginami district, where he began writing *Tenkeiki no hitobito* (People of a Transition Era, 1933). This novel on a majestic scale is set in Otaru and depicts the entire Japanese liberation movement between 1925 and 1928. In October, Kobayashi joined the outlawed Japan Communist Party and became a member of the party's league of writers. When the Japanese war of aggression began in China, additional restrictions of speech and writing were instituted, and Kobayashi had to go underground, moving from house to house in continuing his writing and the cultural activities for the party.

In March 1932 Kobayashi wrote *Numajiri-mura* (Numajiri Village), his second novel on the farming class. This work presents the realities of wartime agricultural villages near the coal mines of Hokkaidō as the village farmers struggled with crop failures, and it also provided him with an opportunity to begin expressing antiwar sentiments in his work. After four months in hiding he married Itō Fujiko, and in August he completed *Tōseikatsusha* (Party Member, 1947), a novel about both the political struggles occurring in a munitions factory and the underground activities of those who resist the severe

prohibitions and restrictions that officials place on their lives. As "Tenkan jidai" (Age of Change), it was eventually published only after Kobayashi's death—in the April and May 1933 numbers of *Chūō Kōron*. In newspaper advertisements for the serialization of this novel, the editor of *Chūō Kōron* declared that it was a privilege to be able to publish it.

In January 1933 Kobayashi wrote *Chiku no hitobito* (People of the Region), which appeared in the March number of *Kaizō*. In this work he used techniques he had learned during his reading of Dickens, and the piece may provide some indication of ways in which his writings might have developed—especially in his use of a realistic style to explore his times.

On 20 February, even before it began to appear in print, Kobayashi was apprehended by "special police" from the Tsukiji station, and he died in jail that night while he was being tortured. Funeral services were held for Kobayashi at the Tsukiji Little Theatre on 15 March, and people from abroad (such as Romain Rolland and Lu Hsun) as well as from Japan sent many letters of outrage and condolence. After Kobayashi's death many writers connected with the socialist movement were forced, either under the threat or the infliction of torture, to declare publicly their "conversion" from seditious beliefs.

Since the publication of three volumes of Kobayashi's collected works in 1935, his writings have been republished frequently, and many different editions of his collected works have appeared.

References:

Eguchi Kan, *Sakka Kobayashi Takiji no shi* (Tokyo: Shobō Goorosu, 1946);

Hashizume Ken, *Takiji gyakusatsu* (Tokyo: Shinchōsha, 1962);

Hidaka Shohji, *Bungaku tekusuto no ryōbun* (Kyoto: Hakujisha, 1995);

Hirano Ken, *Waga sengo bungakushi* (Tokyo: Kōdansha, 1969);

Kurahara Korehito, *Kobayashi Takiji to Miyamoto Yuriko* (Tokyo: Kawade Shobō, 1953; enlarged edition, Tokyo: Kokumin Bunko, 1975);

Kurahara and Nakano Shigeharu, eds., *Kobayashi Takiji kenkyū* (Tokyo: Kaihōsha, 1948);

Miyamoto Kenji, *Bungei hyōron senshū*, volume 2 (Tokyo: Shin Nihon Shuppansha, 1966);

Nakano Shigeharu, *Kobayashi Takiji to Miyamoto Yuriko* (Tokyo: Kōdansha, 1972);

Odagiri Hideo, *Kobayashi Takiji* (Tokyo: Shin Nihon Bungaku Kai, 1950; enlarged edition, Tokyo: Yushindō, 1969);

Ogasawara Masaru, ed., *Shinchō Nihon bungaku arubamu: Kobayashi Takiji* (Tokyo: Shinchōsha, 1985);

Tezuka Hidetaka, *Kobayashi Takiji* (Tokyo: Chikuma Shobō, 1958);

Tezuka, *Nihon bungaku arubamu: Kobayashi Takiji* (Tokyo: Chikuma Shobō, 1955);

Udō Toshio, *Bungaku, shinjitsu, ningen* (Tokyo: Kōwadō, 1976).

Papers:

The Otaru Literary Library in Hokkaidō holds a collection of Kobayashi Takiji's papers.

Kōda Rohan

(23 July 1867 – 30 July 1947)

Kyoko Kurita
Pomona College

BOOKS: *Fūryūbutsu* (Tokyo: Yoshioka Shoten, 1889);

Hazueshū (Tokyo: Shun'yōdō, 1890)–includes "Tai dokuro," "Kidanji," "Ichisetsuna," and "Shin bijin";

Tsuyu dandan (Tokyo: Kinkōdō, 1890);

Shingon himitsu Seitensama (Tokyo: Yoshioka Shoten, 1891);

Ninomiya Sontoku Ō (Tokyo: Hakubunkan, 1891);

Shin Hazueshū (Tokyo: Shun'yōdō, 1891)–includes "Tsuji jōruri" and "Nemimi deppō";

Shichihenge (Tokyo: Shun'yōdō, 1891);

Isanatori, 2 volumes (Tokyo: Aoki Kōzandō, 1891–1892);

Takara no kura (Tokyo: Gakureikan, 1892);

Obanashū (Tokyo: Aoki Kōzandō, 1892)–includes "Kekkōsei" and "Gojū no tō"; translated by Sakai Shioya as *The Pagoda* (Tokyo: Ōkura Shoten, 1909); translated by Chieko T. Mulhern as "The Five-Storied Pagoda," in her *Pagoda, Skull, and Samurai* (Ithaca, N.Y.: China-Japan Program, Cornell University, 1982);

Shin Saiyūki (Tokyo: Gakureikan, 1893);

Chintō sansui (Tokyo: Hakubunkan, 1893);

Nichiren shōnin (Tokyo: Hakubunkan, 1894);

Yūfuku shijin (Tokyo: Shun'yōdō, 1894);

Sasabune (Tokyo: Aoki Kōzandō, 1895);

Kiku no hamamatsu (Tokyo: Aoki Kōzandō, 1896);

Hitorine (Tokyo: Aoki Kōzandō, 1896);

Kumo no sode (Tokyo: Aoki Kōzandō, 1896);

Hige otoko (Tokyo: Hakubunkan, 1896);

Gyōkō (Tokyo: Hakubunkan, 1897);

Suijō goi (Tokyo: Chitokukai, 1897);

Shin Hagoromo monogatari (Tokyo: Murai Kyōdai Shōkai, 1897);

Kohagishū (Tokyo: Shun'yōdō, 1899);

Inō Tadataka (Tokyo: Hakubunkan, 1899);

Miho monogatari (Tokyo: Aoki Kōzandō, 1901);

Yuki funpun (Tokyo: Shun'yōdō, 1901);

Rangen (Tokyo: Shun'yōdō, 1901);

Chōgo (Tokyo: Shun'yōdō, 1901);

Kōda Rohan

Motsure ito (Tokyo: Aoki Kōzandō, 1902);

Takara no yama (Tokyo: Shun'yōdō, 1902);

Takara no kura (Tokyo: Shun'yōdō, 1902);

Rohan sōsho (Tokyo: Hakubunkan, 1902);

Kokoro no ato: Shutsuro (Tokyo: Shun'yōdō, 1905); translated by Jirō Nagura as *Leaving the Hermitage* (London: Allen & Unwin, 1925);

Shiomachigusa (Tokyo: Tōadō Shobō, 1906);

Fuzōan monogatari (Tokyo: Kyōnandō, 1906);

97

Chūshaku "Futsuka monogatari" (Tokyo: Tōadō Shobō, 1906);

Sora utsu nami, 3 volumes (Tokyo: Shun'yōdō, 1906-1907);

Harusame shū (Tokyo: Tōadō Shobō, 1907);

Kagyūan yadan (Tokyo: Shun'yōdō, 1907);

Tamakatsura (Tokyo: Shun'yōdō, 1908);

Shōhin jusshu (Tokyo: Seikō Zasshisha, 1908);

Yoritomo (Tokyo: Tōadō Shobō, 1908);

Futsū bunshōron (Tokyo: Hakubunkan, 1908);

Bungakujō ni okeru Kōbōdaishi (Tokyo: Sokudaishiposha, 1909);

Rohan sōsho, 2 volumes (Tokyo: Hakubunkan, 1909);

Doryoku ron (Tokyo: Tōadō Shobō, 1912);

Shukusatsu doryoku ron (Tokyo: Tōadō Shobō, 1913);

Senshin roku (Tokyo: Shiseidō Shoten, 1914);

Risshi rikkō (Tokyo: Tōadō Shobō, 1915);

Etsuraku (Tokyo: Shiseidō Shoten, 1915);

Hakuro kōro (Tokyo: Shun'yōdō, 1916);

Shukusatsu Shūsei ron (Tokyo: Tōadō Shobō, 1916);

Kōda Rohan biji meiku shū (Tokyo: Kyōbashidō, 1917);

Yūjōki (Tokyo: Ōkura Shoten, 1919); republished as *Yūhiki* (Tokyo: Kaizōsha, 1925);

Rohan bunshū (Tokyo: Seikadō Shoten, 1919);

Kōrōmu, 3 volumes, Kokuyaku Kanbun Taisei series (Tokyo: Kokumin Bunko Kankōkai, 1920-1922);

Shiomachigusa (Tokyo: Tōadō Shobō, 1921);

Go to shōgi (Tokyo: Kokushi Kōshukai, 1922);

Bashō haiku kenkyū (Tokyo: Iwanami Shoten, 1922);

Suikoden, 3 volumes, Kokuyaku Kanbun Taisei series (Tokyo: Kokumin Bunko Kankōkai, 1923-1925);

Zoku Bashō haiku kenkyū (Tokyo: Iwanami Shoten, 1924);

Fuyu no hi shō (Tokyo: Iwanami Shoten, 1924);

Yūhiki (Tokyo: Kaizōsha, 1925);

Gamōshi-gō Taira no Masakado (Tokyo: Kaizōsha, 1925);

Nawa Nagatoshi (Tokyo: Hakuyōsha, 1926);

Yoritomo, Tametomo (Tokyo: Kaizōsha, 1926),

Zokuzoku Bashō haiku kenkyū (Tokyo: Iwanami Shoten, 1926);

Senshin Kōroku (Tokyo: Shiseidō Shoten, 1926);

Doryoku ron (Tokyo: Chūseidō, 1926);

Ryuūshi dashi (Tokyo: Kaizōsha, 1927);

Haru no hi, Arano shō (Tokyo: Iwanami Shoten, 1927);

Fūryūbutsu, Ikkōken (Tokyo: Iwanami Bunko, 1927);

Kōda Rohan hen, Meiji Taishū Bungaku Zenshū series, volume 6 (Tokyo: Shun'yōdō, 1928);

Bokushi, Iwanami Kōza: Sekai Shichō series, volume 5 (Tokyo: Iwanami Shoten, 1928);

Hisago, Sarumino shō (Tokyo: Iwanami Shoten, 1929);

Sumidawara, Zoku Sarumino shō (Tokyo: Iwanami Shoten, 1930);

Yoritomo, Taira no Masakado (Tokyo: Shun'yōdō Bunko, 1932);

Dōkyō ni tsuite (Tokyo: Iwanami Shoten, 1933);

Yoritomo, Tametomo (Tokyo: Kaizō Bunko, 1934);

Bancha kaidan, Shōnen Sekai Bunko series, volume 1 (Tokyo: Koyama Shoten, 1936);

Dōkyō shisō (Tokyo: Iwanami Shoten, 1936);

Tarō bō, hoka sanpen (Tokyo: Iwanami Shoten, 1936);

Hyōshaku Sarumino (Tokyo: Iwanami Shoten, 1937);

Unmei (Tokyo: Iwanami Shoten, 1938);

Ikkan shogi, Kyōgaku Sōsho series, volume 3 (Tokyo: Kyōgakukyoku, 1938);

Kangen, Toyamabō Hyakka Bunko series, volume 69 (Tokyo: Toyamabō, 1939);

Chikutō (Tokyo: Iwanami Shoten, 1939);

Shibusawa Eiichi den (Tokyo: Shibusawa Seien-ō Kinenkai, 1939; Tokyo: Iwanami Shoten, 1939);

Susuki no (Tokyo: Chūō Kōronsha, 1939);

Gamō Ujisato (Tokyo: Kaizō Bunko, 1939);

Ryushi dashi (Tokyo: Kaizō Bunko, 1939);

Doryoku ron (Tokyo: Iwanami Bunko, 1940);

Chōgo (Tokyo: Toyamabō, 1940);

Gendan (Tokyo: Nihon Hyōronsha, 1941)—includes "Gendan," "Yuki tataki," and "Renkanki";

Kagyūan renwa (Tokyo: Chuō Kōronsha, 1943);

Hyōshaku Fuyu no hi (Tokyo: Iwanami Shoten, 1944);

Dogū mokugū (Tokyo: Yōtokusha, 1945);

Hyōshaku Haru no hi (Tokyo: Iwanami Shoten, 1946);

Imo no ha (Tokyo: Iwanami Shoten, 1946);

Kottō (Tokyo: Tōkyo Shuppan, 1946);

Rongo, Etsuraku Chūjo (Tokyo: Chūō Kōronsha, 1947);

Hyōshaku Hisago (Tokyo: Iwanami Shoten, 1947);

Yūjin (Tokyo: Tōkyo Shuppan, 1947);

Aigo shōja zappitsu (Tokyo: Yōtokusha, 1947);

Bōjuki (Tokyo: Tokyo Shuppan, 1948);

Shiwa (Tokyo: Tokyo Shuppan, 1948);

Chichi Rohan no nikki, edited by Koda Aya (Tokyo: Jij Shinpō, 1948);

Hyōshaku Arano, 2 volumes (Tokyo: Iwanami Shoten, 1948-1949);

Kagūyan nikki (Tokyo: Chūō Koronsha, 1949);

Kagyūan kushū (Tokyo: Chūō Koronsha, 1949);

Kikuzu (Tokyo: Kaizōsha, 1949);

Shūtaian monogatari (Tokyo: Asahi Shinbunsha, 1949);

Fūryū emma den (Tokyo: Kadokawa Shoten, 1950);

Rohan no shokan (Tokyo: Kōbundo, 1951);

Yuki tataki, hoka nihen (Tokyo: Kadokawa Shoten, 1951);

Gachō (Tokyo: Kawade Shobō, 1952);

Rohan shōhin (Tokyo: Kawade Shobō, 1952–1953);

Rohan Kagyūan kabun (Tokyo Chūō Kōronsha, 1955).

Collections and editions: *Rohan shu,* 2 volumes (Tokyo: Shun'yōdō, 1911);

Kōda Rohan shū (Tokyo: Kaizōsha, 1927);

Rohan zenshū, 12 volumes (Tokyo: Iwanami Shoten, 1929–1930);

Rohan shiden shōsetsu shū, 2 volumes (Tokyo: Chuō Kōronsha, 1942–1943);

Kōda Rohan shū, edited by Saitō Mokichi (Tokyo: Tōhō Shokyoku, 1947);

Rohan zenshū, 42 volumes (Tokyo: Iwanami Shoten, 1950–1958);

Rohan Kagyūan goi, edited by Kōda Aya (Tokyo: Shinchōsha, 1956);

Rohan ishū (Osaka: Yukawa Shobō, 1978);

Rohan shōsetsu, 6 volumes (Tokyo: Iwanami Shoten, 1988);

Rohan zuihitsu shū, 2 volumes (Tokyo: Iwanami Shoten, 1993).

OTHER: *Kyōgen zenshū,* edited by Rohan (Tokyo: Hakubunkan, 1903).

Along with Natsume Sōseki, Mori Ōgai, and Ozaki Kōyō, Kōda Rohan is one of four chief literary figures of the mid Meiji Period. He and Kōyō offered a neoclassicist and idealist alternative to the realism favored by Tsubouchi Shōyō and others, especially during the "Age of Koyo and Rohan." His literary achievements during six decades, from his debut in 1888 until his death, cover a range of genres: he was a novelist, poet, essayist, critic, linguist, philologist, and historian. He wrote commentary on poetry and on historical records, and he published moral tales, stories for youth, and travel essays. His initial contribution to modern Japanese literature was in laying a basis for the development of Romanticism, and his debut as a writer coincided with a turning point for Japanese society around 1887, when the fusions and clashes of old and new, East and West, encouraged cultural evolu-tion. Rohan enhanced the Romantic spirit and the literary quality of the political novel during the second decade of the Meiji Period. He addressed the pressing issues of his day with a mix of Western liberalism, Confucian morality, Taoist cosmology, scientific interest in pattern and logic, Buddhist resignation, and Christian Unitarian activism. He was a true multicultural-ist who created a conceptual niche beyond East and West and whose contribution to world lit-erature transcends space and time.

A torrent of works by Rohan and Kōyō in the first few years after Rohan's debut in 1889 offered alternatives to Shoyo's call for a modern realistic novel, *Shōsetsu shinzui* (The Essence of the Novel, 1885). Despite the popularity of Futabatei Shimei's experiment with a colloquial and realist style in *Ukigumo* (1887–1891; translated as *Japan's First Modern Novel:* Ukigumo *of Futabatei Shimei,* 1967), the work of Rohan was widely popular until the ascendancy of the Naturalist School fol-lowing the turn of the century. After the late Meiji Period, naturalist tenets have generally dominated the literary criticism and the writing of literary history in Japan, and although Ro-han's vast knowledge and literary talent have been universally recognized, his reputation has suffered strangely: he has been praised but ig-nored.

One reason that readers have misunder-stood Rohan's fiction is his prose style, which both combines and diverges from classical Japa-nese and classical Chinese. Most Meiji writers moved away from using these highly literary, traditional styles. They eagerly participated in the *genbun itchi* movement, which favored clos-ing the gap between the spoken and written languages. Among writers of this movement, form was more important than content, and the strength of this movement has made it difficult to appreciate Rohan's skillful and implicit in-corporation of Western influences. Tanizaki Jun'ichirō predicted that understanding the full scope of Rohan's achievement would take a century. Near the end of the twentieth century Rohan's fiction remains largely unstudied; the rest of his literary work, invisible.

Rohan was born in Edo in the last year of the Edo Period. Because of confused record-keeping when dating of events changed from following the traditional lunar calendar to fol-lowing the Western calendar, even he never knew whether his birthday was 23 July (20 August by the new calendar) or 26 July. His childhood name was Tetsushirō; his legal name

Kagyū-an (Snail house), Rohan's Tokyo home, where he lived for about a decade following 1897

was Shigeyuki. He was the fourth of eight children (six sons and two daughters) born to Kōda Shigenobu and his wife, Yū, both of whom came from families of Buddhist samurai priests in charge of protocol at Edo Castle. Rohan was raised with discipline in a family burgeoning with literary and musical talent.

The comfortable life that the family had enjoyed during Edo years began to deteriorate with the Restoration and the anti-Buddhist movement in the Meiji era, and Rohan's education was therefore sporadic. After he graduated from Tokyo Normal School, an elementary school, at age thirteen, he entered Tokyo First Middle School in Kanda in 1879, but he withdrew after about a year because of the family's financial difficulties. He then entered Tokyo English School instead and acquired a knowledge of English. From there he withdrew the following year and joined a tuition-free private academy that was committed to Chinese learning and run by Kikuchi Shōken, a neo-Confucian scholar. Rohan frequented the only public library then in Tokyo to prepare for discussion and to read widely.

After three years of study at the academy, Rohan decided to obtain practical skills in order to support himself, and in 1883 he became one of the first students at the new School of Telegraph Technology, which the Telegraph Bureau had established. Rohan excelled in practical studies such as mathematics and remained keenly interested in science throughout his life. After a year of schooling he worked as an intern at the central office of the Telegraph Bureau, and in July 1885 he was assigned to three years of service at Yoichi in Hokkaidō.

While working as a telegraph engineer, Rohan lived as a frontiersman in this uncultivated land rich in natural resources: he fished, hunted animals, and rode horses. He also studied various possibilities for business and industry and made recommendations to local residents. He finished reading a box full of Chinese classics that he had brought with him, and he read Buddhist texts borrowed from Eizenji, the nearest temple. He also began to frequent the licensed quarter in the town and to acquire a taste for liquor and tobacco.

In August 1886 Rohan suddenly and secretly left Yoichi for Tokyo; his trip back to his parents' home required more than a month, for he had left Yoichi without much money. "Tokkan kikō" (The Journal of a Desperate Journey, 1887) recounts the hardships of this trip, and a haiku that he composed on the way reveals the origin of his pen name, "Rohan" (companion of the dew): "Sato tōshi / iza tsuyu to nen / kusamakura" (Far from villages, / I shall sleep with the dew, / on a pillow of grass). Rohan, who had broken his contractual commitment and had been fired, was not welcomed by his family, whose members had also significantly changed their lives: his father had lost his job at the Ministry of Finance and had converted the rest of his family to Christianity. For about a year Rohan's life was frustrating, as he performed various chores at home and worked at the paper shop that his father opened.

During his free time Rohan frequented Tokyo Library, and, wishing to gain recognition, he wrote after his family had gone to bed. Awashima Kangetsu, a literary student with whom Rohan became acquainted at Tokyo Library, introduced him to Yoda Gakkai, a prominent Sinologist and writer, in December 1888. When Rohan brought the manuscript for "Tsuyu dandan" (Dewdrops Falling, 1890) to Gakkai, the latter was impressed with it. He wrote an introduction for the book and recommended it to Kinkōdō, a well-known publisher, who bought the manuscript for fifty yen—more than twice what Rohan had been earning per month as a telegraph engineer—and serialized it in *Miyako no Hana* from February to August 1889. It was well received and was published as a book in 1890.

Dewdrops Falling was meant to be paired with *Yuki funpun* (Snowflakes Swirling, 1901), a tragic story about Ainus, but serialization of the latter in the *Yomiuri Shinbun* in 1890 was interrupted, and it was not completed until ten years later. When the two stories are read together, their political orientation becomes apparent. Both advocate freedom and popular rights, even for women and racial minorities; they also attack hypocritical Japanese attitudes toward stronger as well as weaker nations.

Dewdrops Falling, which should be read in the context of the development of the Meiji political novel, is an ambitious work in terms of structure and style. The larger part is written in dialogues, which satisfied readers' increasing demands for work written in a colloquial style. It incorporates various genres of literature: haiku by Matsuo Bashō for chapter titles, classical Chinese poems, Japanese free verse, a poetic passage presented as a translation from a

piece by William Wordsworth, a letter, and a newspaper advertisement. It also introduces some scientific novelties: a planetarium, a cobalt ink that becomes visible only when heated, and a mathematical game involving the magic square. This game, known to ancient Chinese and to Western contemporaries, demonstrates Rohan's belief in the essential unity of Eastern and Western learning.

The basic structure of *Dewdrops Falling* is borrowed from "The Story of the Brilliant Sen Mistakenly Marrying the Friend of a Phoenix," a Ming Dynasty vernacular novella. However, Rohan's narrative is set in America and presents a romantic story of two Americans: Rubina, a beautiful and intelligent daughter of Bunseimu, an American millionaire; and Shinja, a dedicated Unitarian minister. The American setting of this story is unusual for a supposedly Oriental writer such as Rohan, and this early work shows his synthetic and transcendental bent: *American* was his synonym for *universal,* and he intended to write about universal ideals, about overcoming all differences and limitations in cultural and linguistic heritage.

The years after Rohan's debut were his most prolific as a writer. *Fūryūbutsu* (The Image of Beauty, 1889) had solidified his reputation, and a few months after its publication he was invited to become a guest writer for the *Yomiuri,* the most prestigious newspaper of the time. *The Image of Beauty* presents Shūun, a young traveling sculptor who falls in love with Otatsu, a kind, beautiful young woman who sells salted flower blossoms for tea. Just before their wedding Otatsu is kidnapped in Tokyo by her father, who had abandoned her and her mother to go abroad and had become successful as a government official after he returned. In despair, Shūun carves a life-size sculpture of Otatsu. The sculpture seems to come alive, falls on him, and knocks him unconscious, and in this state he is reunited with Otatsu. The narrator continues, relating how this figure of Otatsu began to appear all over Japan in different images that corresponded to the social and professional status of their viewers. To noblemen she appeared as a noblewoman; to fishermen, as a fisherwoman.

The concept Rohan elaborated in this novel and continued to develop is that of *fūryū,* which he used to denote the spiritual beauty of aspiring for one's ideal or goal rather than to denote the aesthetic appreciation of Nature. Furthermore, the *butsu* of *Fūryūbutsu* does not

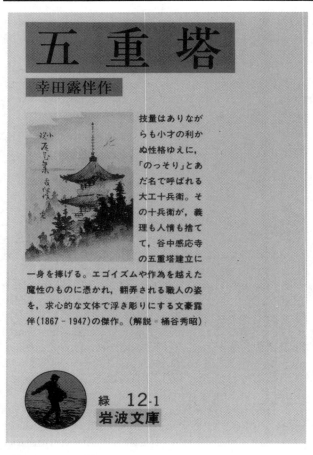

技量はありなが
らも小才の利か
ぬ性格ゆえに、
「のっそり」とあ
だ名で呼ばれる
大工十兵衛。そ
の十兵衛が、義
理も人情も捨て
て、谷中感応寺
の五重塔建立に
一身を捧げる。エゴイズムや作為を越えた
魔性のものに憑かれ、翻弄される職人の姿
を、求心的な文体で浮き彫りにする文豪露
伴(1867‐1947)の傑作。(解説＝桶谷秀昭)

Dust jacket for Gojū no tō *(The Five-Storied Pagoda, 1891-1892), in which two competitive builders must reconcile their personal differences while constructing a temple pagoda*

connote religious images of the Buddha but pluralistic, multifarious images that individuals project in their different dreams and ambitions. Through a message as liberating as Fukuzawa Yukichi's famous line, "Heaven created no man above or below another," Rohan implies that any icon, symbol, or index is shaped and interpreted by the experience and background of the reader and that no such device can be valued more than another. What is real or important differs from person to person, so that there cannot be one single representation of the truth. Rohan's early work delivered a general warning to society, which was rapidly growing centralized again after two decades of relative freedom and social mobility.

Other important projects of Rohan's early years are the novellas "Tai dokuro" (1890; translated as "The Encounter with a Skull," 1985) and "Dokushūshin" (Venomous Vermilion Lips, 1890), which were first published in journals and were later republished together in yet another journal as "Dai shijin" (The Great Poet, 1897). The structure of "The Encounter with a Skull" follows that of a two-part Nō play. Lost at dusk in the snowy mountains, Rohan, the protagonist, seeks lodging for the night in a hut where Tae, a beautiful woman, lives alone. When she offers to share her bedding, he resists this sexual temptation by reciting a Buddhist sutra. They agree to stay up together, and Tae tells him her tragic life story. After hearing it, Rohan wakes up and finds a white skull beside him, and a villager tells him of a deranged woman with leprosy who used to roam about the area. Tae, whom the narrator has met, is thus an apparition; the skull is her skull. Both the graphic, detailed description of advanced leprosy and the earlier scene of sexual temptation are memorably presented. Although Rohan was often criticized for lacking a sense of the dark side of life, writers such as Tanizaki Jun'ichirō appreciated his ability to combine opposite features such as beauty and deformity or Eros and Thanatos.

Much of "Venomous Vermilion Lips" is a monologue by a reportedly beautiful female protagonist who lives alone in the mountains. A man who has heard of her and is interested in marrying her goes to see her one day and talks with her over a drink. The nameless woman tells him how "in love" she is with the Buddha, whom she considers to be the ultimate poet and whose words she considers to be the most beautiful poetry. When she realizes that the man to whom she has been talking has become totally mystified and has fallen asleep, she disappears like a ghost.

"The Encounter with a Skull" is Rohan's only fiction in which the protagonist bears his own pen name, but its fantasy kept readers from considering it an early I-novel, which became a popular genre around the start of the twentieth century. Although "The Encounter with a Skull" and "Venomous Vermilion Lips" may seem classical in form and content, their Romantic focus on the experience of the great poet differs dramatically from the realism of Tsubouchi Shōyō and his followers, who believed that contemporary literature should represent believable emotions and conduct and be written in colloquial language. For Rohan, what was truthful or realistic was not bound by mundanity of content or the proximity of spoken and written languages: he sought a metaphorical, symbolic representation of his ideas. In

"Hannya shingyō dai ni-gi chū" (A Secondary Commentary on the Heart Sutra), written in 1890 but not published in its entirety until 1947, Rohan borrowed the Buddhist concepts of *kū* (emptiness) and *shiki* (substance) to explain his views on the relations between form and content, language and meaning.

By 1890 literary circles acknowledged the advent of the *Kō-Ro jidai* (The Age of Kōyō and Rohan). This fame, however, did not please Rohan; on the contrary, he went through a difficult period in 1890 and reevaluated his interpretation of *fūryū*. "Jigoku-kei nikki" (Diary of Hell Valley), which he wrote during his seclusion in the Akagi Mountains in June, records his mood at the time. To Shōyō he also wrote a long letter that, published as "Zyka to bungaku" (Nature and Literature) in the newspaper *Yūbin Hōchi*, praised Ihara Saikaku and Matsuo Bashō and deprecated *Arabian Nights* and Kyokutei Bakin's *Hakkenden* (The Parable of the Eight Dogs, 1814–1842), Shōyō's bête noire. Rohan's reorientation disrupted publication of *Hige otoko* (The Bearded Samurai), his first historical novel, which began serialization in July 1890. Although the first five installments of this work were well received, it remained uncompleted for another six years.

The novels that Rohan published during the following year show that he began to incorporate some of Shōyō's realism, to delineate psychologically complex characters who were not mere representations of moral values or abstract ideas. In Rohan's Romanticism *Tsuji jōruri* (The Wandering Balladeer, 1891) and its sequel, *Nemimi deppō* (Surprise Gunshot, 1891), mark a new stage that the influential poet Kitamura Tōkoku and some other critics, who were expecting him to contine in a heroic and dramatic vein, did not much appreciate. These works present the enigma of Dōya, a kind of superman or a Faustian figure endowed with artistic talent, intelligence, and good looks—yet who cannot find spiritual satisfaction. Through this protagonist Rohan asks what art really is or what makes a person an artist.

In 1891 Rohan also published half of *Isanatori* (The Whaler, 1891–1892), his first long novel; *Gojū no tō* (translated as *The Pagoda*, 1909, and as "The Five-Storied Pagoda," 1982), his best-known novel; as well as shorter fictional works, essays, and a play. *The Whaler* has a circular temporal structure based on the idea of karmic cycles. The most memorable scenes of the book concern the protagonist's double murder of his adulterous wife and her lover and the protagonist's demonic attack on a whale. Even the confessional novels so popular in the late Meiji Period did not address actions as grave as those of murder. To depict the whaling scenes Rohan studied "Isanatori ekotoba" (Pictures and Stories on Whaling), a scroll he saw at the Tokyo Library; he probably also knew of Herman Melville's *Moby-Dick; or, The Whale* (1851).

"The Five-Storied Pagoda," a story about an artisan, is generally considered Rohan's representative work. Jubei is a talented carpenter-architect, but, because of his uncouth appearance and unassuming personality, no one notices him. The story recounts his struggle to overcome various obstacles that keep him from completing a five-tiered pagoda that he has designed. In a scene that presents the most well known passage in Rohan's fiction, a fierce storm severely tests his pagoda, a structure that boldly challenges Heaven. The pagoda here serves as a spiritual symbol for the Meiji Period rather than as a Buddhist religious structure.

In celebrating the powers of human imagination and creation over those of Nature, this work was a sweeping success. It incorporated the idea that "Where there's a will, there's a way," a main theme of *Saigoku risshi hen* (Ambition in the West, 1870–1871), an influential condensed translation by Nakamura Masanao of Samuel Smiles's *Self-Help* (1859). In "The Five-Storied Pagoda" Rohan celebrates the rights and freedoms of individuals to pursue their ideals and encourages them to understand and accept the ambitions of others.

Powerful male protagonists such as Jubei are attractive and memorable, and predominantly male readers and critics have determined which of Rohan's works are best. Yet he was supportive of Higuchi Ichiyō, one of the most outstanding female writers of the Meiji Period, and his writings present many memorable female characters. During 1890, for example, among nineteen short stories that Rohan wrote, more than half present female characters who are rational, articulate, and brave souls whose lives comprise the media for his messages. In "Myō shichijō" (Seven Delicate Emotions) the wife who burns an expensive chessboard that her husband cherishes in order to reprove him for being obsessed with a mere game is as attractive as any of Rohan's male heroes.

Dust jacket for Kumo no kage / Binbō no setsu, *a 1994 collection of thirty of Rohan's essays*

From 1895 to 1897 he wrote novellas that incorporate basic features of famous legends: "Shin Urashima" (New Urashima), "Shin Ikutagawa" (New Ikuta River, later republished as "Yumiya no ie," The House of the Bow and Arrows), and *Shin Hagoromo monogatari* (New Heavenly Maiden Story, 1897). The original narratives of these legends end rather tragically, and Rohan's concern for the sanity of the modern intellectual class adds pessimistic notes to his versions of these works. These novellas are classic in form, but the modernity of their themes inspired Ōgai, Sōseki, and other writers to use some of the same legends in their works.

Near the end of the century Rohan wrote two works exhibiting a notable pessimism: "Chōchūsho" (Behind the Curtain)–usually known under its republished title, "Fūryūma" (The Bane of Faith, 1898)–and "Wankyu monogatari" (The Story of Kyūbei, the Potter, 1899–1900), both of which present artists who succumb to their weaknesses and fail. In these works Rohan continues to explore the insuperability of one's attachments to the self and to worldly affairs that appears in "Kono ichinichi" (This One Day, 1898, the first half of "Futsuka

monogatari," A Tale of Two Days, in *Chūshaku "Futsuka monogatari,"* A Tale of Two Days, with Commentary, 1906). Masaoka Shiki, a haiku poet who believed in *shasei,* a realistic portrayal of what the eyes behold, criticized Rohan's style in this novel, although others praised its stylistic sophistication. Tanizaki, who generally admired Rohan's works, ranked the quality of "A Tale of Two Days" as second only to that of "The Encounter with a Skull." Yet critics favored Masaoka's opinion, as a new style of writing that valued colloquial quality over Chinese characters and Sino-Japanese literary tradition rapidly gained influence.

After "A Tale of Two Days" received mixed reviews, Rohan began to write fewer works of fiction than he had. Some feel that he had exhausted his literary ingenuity; others attribute his diminishing amount of writing to his happy marriage. In any case, he realized how far popular literary tastes were diverging from his own, and he deliberately suspended his fiction writing.

Formal and stylistic considerations have weighed heavily in assessing Rohan's place in Japanese literary history. His unwillingness to abandon the classical Sino-Japanese heritage sets his work apart from that of others. Even *Unmei* (Destiny, 1938), Rohan's historical masterpiece published late in his career, is written in *kanbun,* a hybrid Sino-Japanese classical style that most Japanese fiction writers had abandoned a decade or more earlier. Furthermore, he did not hesitate to depart from the facts in his historical novels such as *Destiny.* Historians of China generally believe that Emperor Kenbun of the Ming dynasty was killed in a rebellion by his scheming uncle, King En, but Rohan chose to base the last part of his novel on the popular but unfounded story that the emperor in fact survived the rebellion and traveled like an itinerant monk until he became ninety years old. Rohan's belief that historical narrative is a kind of fiction and his desire to rewrite history in creating his story were misunderstood as degradations of the status of both history and fiction.

The power and sophistication of Rohan's fiction are inseparable from the poetic qualities of his prose, as some works read almost like epic poetry rather than prose. Contemporary writers of Rohan's time remembered and recited as poetry famous passages from his prose. In 1904 he turned briefly from writing poetic prose to composing *Kokoro no ato: Shutsuro* (1905; translated as *Leaving the Hermitage,* 1925), a rather colloquial long piece that is Rohan's only poetic work published in book form. He had not intended to publish "Kokoro no ato" (Records of Thoughts), a collection of poems that he had been writing for many years, but he decided to publish the portion called "Shutsuro" (Leaving the Hermitage) because at the time of the Russo-Japanese War he felt moved to express his thoughts publicly. This metaphysical, engaging poem passionately acknowledges the poet's involvement in the world, even in a dreadful war of which he does not approve, by asserting the inseparability of reality and imagination, politics and poetry, nation and individual.

Rohan had a personal interest in this war: Gunji Shigetada, his older brother, was a lieutenant in the Japanese navy and was sent on an exploratory mission to the Chishima Islands. When Shigetada was captured by the Russians and held for two years, the Rohan family deeply felt the consequences of the war and of the turbulent political circumstances. Rohan interrupted the serial publication of his *Sora utsu nami* (Waves Dashing against Heaven,

1906–1907), which was half completed in the *Yomiuri Shinbun* in 1903–1904, and instead began to serialize *Leaving the Hermitage,* which dealt more directly with contemporary themes. Despite requests from readers, Rohan left *Sora utsu nami* unfinished.

Dogū mokugū (Clay Doll, Wood Doll, 1945), a novella that was first published in *Nihon* in 1905 and that resembles "The Encounter with a Skull," marks the end of one phase of Rohan's career. The differences between these two stories reveal how, at the end of his most productive period of fiction writing, Rohan was focusing on worldly affairs, the invisible workings of psyche, and fate. The traveling artist in "The Encounter with a Skull" is able to see beyond time and space, and he resists the deathly lure of the other world; the cynical protagonist in *Clay Doll, Wood Doll* acknowledges the operation of karma and confirms the dual structure of past-in-present through his relationship with a woman he has met in a reverie. As the Naturalist movement was gaining influence, *Clay Doll, Wood Doll* received little attention when it first appeared. Rohan's mysticism had little in common with the Naturalists' passion for copious description or with the trand toward the confessional, and he ceased writing fiction for some time.

When Rohan reduced his literary work, people began to treat him as a retired authority on literature and history. Because of his accomplished style and vast knowledge of traditional culture, no one could ignore his presence. He was invited to join the faculty of Kyoto University as a visiting lecturer, for the university acknowledged his expertise in Japanese literature even though he lacked formal credentials. After deliberating, he accepted the offer in 1908, but he resigned the following year. The Ministry of Education awarded him a doctorate in literature in 1911, the same year in which Sōseki declined such recognition.

During the next one and one-half decades Rohan lost many close family members, the first of whom was his wife, Kimiko, in 1910. Before his only son died in 1926, his first daughter as well as his father, mother, and two brothers also died. Awashima, Rohan's old friend who had contributed much to his debut, also died in 1926. The Great Kantō Earthquake in 1923 and his unhappy second marriage added to a series of misfortunes he suffered, but throughout these difficult years Rohan continued to write, mainly a wide range of essays

Rohan in later years

and commentaries. His pieces on Bashō's haiku are particularly well known.

For his accomplishments as a literary scholar rather than as a novelist Rohan was elected to membership in the Japan Academy in 1927. As if to declare the end of his career, publishers eagerly produced volumes of his collected works, and Iwanami Shoten published the first complete edition in 1929 and 1930. In 1937 Rohan became one of the first recipients of the Order of Culture medal and, along with his sister, Nobu, one of the initial members of the Imperial Academy of Arts. In 1938 he resumed fiction writing. As his daughter Aya recalls, Rohan had ceased publishing not because he lacked ideas, but because he had grown indifferent about publishing. He wrote both "Gendan" (Fantastic Tales) and "Yuki tataki" (Knocking off Snow) only after editors had appealed for new works. Based on third-party accounts, the stories in *Fantastic Tales* (1941) tell

of fantastic experiences—one on the Matterhorn, the other on the waters of Edo Bay. Both of these suggest the Hegelian unity of mental constructs and visual images.

"Knocking off Snow" is a profound, masterly piece written in Rohan's late style. The story tells of a feudal retainer who learns about the adultery of a merchant's wife. The protagonist is a cynical character who disdains human nature and has been embittered by the disloyalty that his fellow retainers have shown toward his former lord, and the story exposes the interlocking interests and emotions of different people. Kizawa, the protagonist, realizes that he cannot remain pure. His interests are closely woven into the conflicting interests of the society in which he lives.

"Renkanki" (The Chain Link, 1940), Rohan's last fictional work, tries to unravel the interrelatedness of all individuals in a collection of short stories that develop sequentially. "The Chain Link" is a historical piece that begins with the story of Kamo no Yasutane in the Heian Period. Mushanokōji Saneatsu and Saitō Mokichi considered it to represent the culmination of Rohan's career.

After Japan entered World War II in 1941, Rohan moved from Tokyo to Itō, and from there he continued to publish a commentary on a collection of Bashō's haiku. He had been publishing this piece in installments, and he finished it five months before his death. These essays are collectively known as "Hyōshaku Bashō shichibu shū" (Commentaries on the Verse of Bashō, 1947). Shiotani San, Rohan's last disciple, notes in his biography of the master that Rohan had planned to write yet another work of fiction after he finished his commentary on Bashō.

Other works suggest the range of Rohan's interests as both a literary and a social critic. The first essay he ever published, "Sakushisha to sakkyokusha to no chii no taitōnarubekikoto o uttauru no bun" (An Appeal for Equal Status for the Lyricist and the Composer, 1889), discusses the inseparability of sound from language and the need to correct the Japanese tendency to underestimate the importance of melody. His family background may well have shaped his interests in this essay: members of the Kōda family were known for generations to excel in music, and at a young age both of his sisters, Nobu and Kō, were musicians whom the government sent to study in the United States and in Germany. In "Ikkoku no shūto"

(The Capital of a Nation, 1899, 1901) Rohan passionately appeals to both nationalistic and cosmopolitan sentiment by articulating the cultural significance that a capital holds for a nation and for the world. In "Bungei ni okeru chihōshoku no shōchō" (The Rise and Fall of Local Color in Literature, 1913), he examines the relationship between the places of origin that writers have and the characteristics of their style and philosophy. He also predicts that local characteristics will gradually disappear as a world culture brings them to the attention of world readers.

Rohan's daughter Aya survived him and became a writer following his death. She wrote memoirs of him at first, and her accounts of her struggles with Rohan's temperament and strong emotions illuminated the energy that the man maintained behind his public literary work. As if forming another link in a chain, Aya's daughter, Aoki Tama, has also written memoirs of her grandfather and her mother.

Letters:

Kōda Aya, ed., *Rohan no shokan* (Tokyo: Kōbundō, 1951).

Biographies:

Yanagida Izumi, *Kōda Rohan* (Tokyo: Chūō Kōronsha, 1942);

Kōda Shigetomo, *Bonjin no hansei* (Tokyo: Kyōritsu Shobō, 1948);

Takagi Taku, *Ningen Rohan* (Tokyo: Tanchō Shobō, 1948);

Shiotani San, *Rohan-ō kago* (Tokyo: Asahi Shinbunsha, 1948);

Kobayashi Eiko, *Rohan seidan* (Tokyo: Kinu Shobō, 1949);

Kōda Aya, *Chichi–sono shi* (Tokyo: Chūō Kōronsha, 1949);

Kōda, *Konna koto* (Tokyo: Sōgensha, 1950);

Kōda, *Misokkasu* (Tokyo: Iwanami Shoten, 1951);

Kōda, *Chigiregumo* (Tokyo: Shinchōsha, 1956);

Kobayashi Isamu, *Kagyūan hōmonki* (Tokyo: Iwanami Shoten, 1956);

Kōda, *Otōto* (Tokyo: Chūō Kōronsha, 1957);

Shiotani, *Kōda Rohan*, 3 volumes (Tokyo: Chūō Kōronsha, 1965);

Nihei Aizō, *Wakaki hi no Rohan* (Tokyo: Meizendō Shoten, 1978);

Shimomura Ryōichi, *Bannen no Rohan* (Tokyo: Keizai Ōraisha, 1979);

Aoki Tama, *Koishikawa no ie* (Tokyo: Kōdansha, 1994).

References:

"Botsugo sanjūnen 'Kōda Rohan ten' hajimaru," *Nihon Kindai Bungakkan,* special issue on Rohan (September 1977);

Bungaku, special issue on Rohan, 46 (November 1978);

Fukumoto Kazuo, *Nihon runessansu shiron kara mita Kōda Rohan* (Tokyo: Hōsei Daigaku shūppankyoku, 1972);

Hiraoka Toshio, "Kōda Rohan no hyōka no kijiku," *Kokubungaku,* 10 (1965): 40–46;

Hiraoka, "Rohan no isō," in *Nihon bungaku kōza,* volume 6, edited by Izu Toshihiko (Tokyo: Taishūkan, 1987), pp. 153–170;

Hiraoka, "*Yuki funpun* no mondai," *Bungaku,* 46 (1978): 1388–1404;

Hirata Yumi, "Kindai bungaku ni okeru romanesuku no keifu," *Kokugo Kokubun,* 54 (1985): 1–16;

Ikari Akira, *Kōda Rohan to Higuchi Ichiyō* (Tokyo: Kyōiku shuppan Sentā, 1983);

Ino Kenji, "Rohan, mō hitotsu no 'kindai,'" *Bungaku,* 38 (1970): 1041–1053;

Katanuma Seiji, *Kōda Rohan kenkyū josetsu* (Tokyo: Ōfūsha, 1989);

Kawamura Jiro, "*Renkanki* o megutte," *Bungaku,* 46 (1978): 1377–1385;

Kokubungaku, special issue on Rohan (March 1974);

Kokubungaku Kaishaku to Kanshō, special issue on Rohan, 43 (May 1978);

Kurita Kyōko, "Rohan no shuppatsu to seiji shōsetsu," *Nihon no Bungaku,* 2 (1988): 156–176;

Maeda Ai, "Rohan ni okeru risshin shusse shugi," *Kokugo to Kokubungaku,* 45 (1968): 36–45;

Maeda, "Sakka ni miru nashonarizumu: Kōda Rohan," *Kokubungaku Kaishaku to Kanshō,* 36 (1971): 46–49;

Mikame Tatsuji, "Kōda Rohan," in his *Meiji rekishi shōsetsu ronsō* (Tokyo: Shintensha, 1962), pp. 164–188;

Chieko Mulhern, *Kōda Rohan* (Boston: Twayne, 1977);

Nihei Aizō, *Rohan: fūryū no ningen sekai* (Tokyo: Tōensha, 1988);

Noborio Yutaka, "*Isanatori* ron," *Bungaku,* 46 (1978): 1405–1417;

Noborio, "Sakuhin ron no shin shikaku: Kōda Rohan: *Fūryūbutsu* ron," *Nihon Bungaku,* 22 (1973): 56–65;

Noborio, "Tai dokuro ron," *Bungaku,* 44 (1976): 1044–1058;

Noyama Kasho, "Kindai shōsetsu shinkō, Meiji

no seishun–Kōda Rohan, Fūryūbutsu,"
Kokubungaku Kaishaku to Kyōzai no kenkyū, 36
(October–December 1991): 140–144,
148–152; 37 (January–March 1992):
146–150, 154–159;

Okazaki Yoshie, "Rohan no fūryū shisō," in his
Nihon Geijutsu Shichō, volume 2 (Tokyo:
Iwanami Shoten, 1948), pp. 3–131;

Saitō Mokichi, *Kōda Rohan* (Tokyo: Senshin
Shorin, 1949);

Sasabuchi Tomoichi, "Kōda Rohan," in his
Rōman shūgi bungaku no tanjō (Tokyo: Meiji
Shoin, 1958), pp. 645–727;

Sasabuchi, "Rohan to *Bungakkai* dōjin," in his
Meiji Taishō bungaku no bunseki (Tokyo:
Meiji Shoin, 1970), pp. 134–149;

Seri Hiroaki, *Bunmei hihyōka toshite no Rohan* (Tokyo: Miraisha, 1971);

Seri, *Rohan–Shizen, Kotoba, Ningen* (Fukuoka:
Kaichōsha, 1993);

Seri, *Rohan to Dōgen* (Fukuoka: Sōgensha, 1986);

Seri, *Rohan to gendai* (Fukuoka: Sōgensha, 1989);

Shinoda Hajime, *Kōda Rohan no tame ni* (Tokyo:
Iwanami Shoten, 1984);

Shiotani San, *Rohan no ma* (Tokyo: Nihon
Tosho Sentā, 1984);

Shiotani, *Rohan to asobi* (Tokyo: Sōjusha, 1972);

Takagi Taku, *Rohan no haiwa* (Tokyo: Kōdansha, 1990);

Takemori Ten'yu, *"Kangadan," Kokubungaku
Kaishaku to Kanshō,* 44 (1979): 93–97.

Kunikida Doppo
(12 August 1869 – 23 June 1908)

Hiraoka Toshio
Gunma Prefectural Women's University

BOOKS: *Doppo gin* (Tokyo: Min'yūsha, 1897);
Musashino (Tokyo: Min'yūsha, 1901);
Doppo shū (Tokyo: Kinji Gahōsha, 1905);
Unmei (Tokyo: Sakura Shobō, 1906);
Tōsei (Tokyo: Saiunkaku, 1907);
Aitei tsūshin (Tokyo: Sakura Shobō, 1908);
Doppo shū daini (Tokyo: Saiunkaku, 1908);
Byōshōroku (Tokyo: Shinchōsha, 1908);
Nagisa (Tokyo: Saiunkaku, 1908);
Azamukazaru no ki (Tokyo: Sakura Shobō, 1908–1909).
Edition in English: *River Mist, and Other Stories,* translated by David Chibbett (Tokyo & New York: Kodansha International, 1983; Tenterden, England: Norbuy, 1983).

In the early years of the twentieth century Japanese authors redefined the Western literary concept of naturalism in various ways, but perhaps the work of no author more clearly and intensely seeks a place for Man in the natural world than does that of Kunikida Doppo. In his early years as a lyric poet, in his embrace of Christianity because of its emphasis on individual freedom, and in the dark, cruel fate that haunts his later stories, Doppo consistently sought (and often found wanting) in Nature a refuge from the wounds of human interaction. His pen name, Doppo, means "one who walks alone," and as a solitary poetic figure he left his mark on Japanese literature of the early twentieth century.

Kunikida Doppo (whose given name was Tetsuo and whose childhood name was Kamekichi) was born in Chōshi, in Chiba Prefecture. His father, Kunikida Senpachi, was a samurai from the Tatsuno domain in Banshū (Hyōgo Prefecture); his mother, Awaji Man, was a native of Chōshi. When a ship from Tatsuno was wrecked off the coast of Chōshi, Senpachi was one officer who was rescued from the disaster, and while he was recuperating in the Yoshinoya inn at Chōshi, he met Man, a servant at the inn. Doppo was

Kunikida Doppo

born of that association, although some questions remain about his parentage. According to the family register, Doppo was born to Man and a man named Masajirō; his mother then took the infant with her when she married Senpachi, and the date of Doppo's birth is recorded as 12 August 1869. The wreck of a ship from Tatsuno domain is recorded in 1868, and one source suggests that Senpachi, hearing of the shipwreck, came to Chōshi in March 1869. Today, it is informally accepted that Doppo was actually Senpachi's son and was born in 1869.

Senpachi had another wife, Toku, and other

children in Tatsuno, but in 1874 he left them and moved to Tokyo, where he brought Man and her son (known as Kamekichi) from Chōshi when he began a job with the municipal court. As an active child, Kamekichi was so rough that he was nicknamed "Gari-Game," which means "Clawing Tortoise." He was also said to have been a master at tree-climbing, and his poetic recollections in *Doppo gin* (Doppo's Songs, 1897) present both his early fondness for nature and his early feelings upon leaving Chōshi to live in Tokyo: "Freedom dwells in the mountains and the forests," he wrote, and "Where is my dear home? / There I was a child of the mountains and forests." A large natural stone tablet engraved with those words has been placed at Kurohae Beach in Chōshi.

When Senpachi was transferred to the Yamaguchi city courthouse in 1876, Man and Kamekichi again went with him. In Yamaguchi, Senpachi divorced Toku, officially entered Man and the boy into his family register, and publicly declared Kamekichi to be his heir. The family settled in Iwakuni, in the eastern part of the prefecture, where they remained until 1893. This region influenced Doppo profoundly, and it became the foundation for his literature. His father crossed the Kintai Bridge every day on his commute to the Iwakuni district court, and Kamekichi began attending the Nishimi Elementary School, which was reserved for children of the warrior class. One of his classmates, Nagata Shinnojō, recalls in *Shōnen jidai no Doppo* (Young Doppo, 1908):

> The bright skies of southern Japan; the fresh, clear air; the warm sun-light: I don't believe that the influence which these elements had on the heart of a young poet were minimal... Aside from the famed Kintai Bridge, the Iwakuni River, which collects the drops of water that fall from the overhanging pines and then flows through the crevices of the smooth white granite rocks, churning over a sudden deep pool or brimming over a gulf as it finally circles through the city of Iwakuni, has a clarity and a beauty of which those accustomed only to the vast muddy waters rushing through the Tokyo area cannot even conceive.

Many scholars in Chinese studies and writers of poetry and prose came from the domain, and Nagata asserts that in these disciplines young Kamekichi ranked first or second in his elementary school. He was also the leading mischiefmaker in his class, and because of his small stature the boy grew long fingernails and clawed at

his opponents, behavior that earned him the nickname "Clawing Kame." He was also called "Red Monkey," because his complexion was ruddy and his hair was tinged with brown.

"E no kanashimi" (The Sadness of Drawings, 1902), included in *Unmei* (Fate, 1906), is a first-person narrative that recounts his elementary school days in Iwakuni. The schoolboy narrator, who ranks first in both unruliness and scholarship, enters a school competition in drawing, which he has loved since his childhood. The narrator sketches a horse, and a fellow student, Shimura, creates a chalk portrait of Christopher Columbus that becomes the hit of the exhibition. Shimura is a white-skinned, mild-mannered, almost girlish young student whose quiet ways attract the sympathies of the principal, the teachers, and the several hundred other students. Although the narrator is a handsome young man, he is by contrast rough, haughty, and quick to pick fights. His brutality grates on his classmates; his pride irritates his teachers; his popularity suffers; and he loses the competition to Shimura.

Weeping loudly, the narrator gets some chalk and goes off alone to sketch a waterwheel. When he arrives at the site, however, Shimura is already there and intently drawing the waterwheel. The narrative recalls that "The shadows of the purple willows covered his entire body from the rear, leaving only a faint light that spilled between the willow branches and gently lit his face and shoulders." Doppo unites youth and nature in this passage, and the two boys use this opportunity to become fast friends. Their lives go in separate directions, but years later when the narrator returns to his hometown and learns that Shimura had died young, he is overcome by a deep sorrow. "The sadness of drawings" is filled with the natural environment of Iwakuni and with Doppo's recollections of his youth.

Another work set in Iwakuni is "Kawagiri" (1898; translated as "River Mist," 1983). Ueda Toyokichi, the protagonist, spends twenty years in Tokyo before returning to his hometown of "Iwa—." Namiki, an old man who is from the samurai residence, is known as "the bearded man from Suginomori," and, just as he has prophesied, Toyokichi has failed and returned home. Toyokichi stands watching as another boy standing beneath the purple willows—their long, green leaves glittering in the sunlight—drops a fishing line into the river. Toyokichi, who watches as one who has failed in life, thinks through his tears: "It's here. This is the place where I was born. This is where I will also die. Ah, I'm so happy. I'm so relieved."

The townspeople welcome Toyokichi's return and even establish a private school for him, but the day before the school is to open, he boards a riverboat, sails downstream through the mist, and never again returns to the village. Perhaps Toyokichi cannot die in his birthplace because he embodies the feelings of Doppo, who continued to seek his own hometown.

When Doppo and his family moved to Yamaguchi, it was then a village. There he began attending the Imamichi Elementary School, where he was profoundly influenced by Nakayama Shin'ichi, the principal. He lived along with several other students at the principal's house, and he attended classes and studied kendō fencing. Nakayama may have been a model for Ōshima Shin'ichi, the elementary school principal who appears in "Hi no de" (Sunrise, 1903). In this story Kodama Shingo, a powerful reporter for a Tokyo newspaper, is surrounded by colleagues who brag about their degrees from Oxford University, Harvard University, Tokyo University, Keiō University, or Waseda University. Kodama announces proudly that he is a graduate of Ōshima Elementary School in his hometown. Kodama tells these others how Mr. Ōshima's father had once encouraged Ikegami Gonzō, a young man who was contemplating suicide, to "Behold the sunrise!" on a New Year's Day. Gonzō took this encouragement, worked diligently, and never forgot the inspiration of the sunrise as he constructed an elementary school that he presented to Shin'ichi, his benefactor's son. Animated by the spirit of the sunrise, Shin'ichi also threw himself into guiding the lives of young people. The story presents a stinging critique of Meiji society, which was rapidly turning into one that valued only superficial academic background.

Kuwabara Shin'ichi writes that the difference between Doppo's mentor, Nakayama Shin'ichi, and the fictional Ōshima Shin'ichi of "Sunrise" is that Nakayama realized in his own life and inspired in others the "salutary spirit of Suō and Nagato—a spirit inherited from the pioneers of these provinces who carried out the noble work of the Restoration, a spirit of constant, heartfelt service to the nation." That Doppo was eager for political fame can be seen in "Ambishon" (Ambition, 1889), but his wish was simply to be free to determine the course of his own life rather than to achieve the social recognition represented in the sunrise spirit.

In 1885 Doppo passed the entrance examination for Yamaguchi Middle School with a rank as the eleventh of thirty-three who were accepted, and he moved into the dormitory there. While he attended the middle school, which allowed students to read any books they chose in addition to their assigned texts, Doppo also read popular contemporary political novels such as Yano Ryūkei's *Keikoku bidan* (Inspiring Instances of Statesmanship, 1883–1884) and Tōkai Sanshi's *Kajin no kigū* (Chance Meetings with Beautiful Women, 1885–1897), which brought him under the influence of the popular-rights movement. The supporters of this, the first democratic movement in Japan, opposed the Meiji oligarchy set up under the control of the Satsuma and Chōshū domains (modern Kagoshima and Yamaguchi Prefectures), and in Yamaguchi, the center of the Meiji government, the movement gained many followers. Doppo's father had come from Tatsuno province, which supported the shogunate in the civil wars, and he was forced to retire from public service without being able to rise through the ranks of the government bureaucracy.

Doppo dropped out of the Yamaguchi Middle School in 1888 apparently because his father's position as an assistant judge was suddenly eliminated in the bureaucratic reforms of 1887. Although he was not fired, he had no hope of transferring to another position, and his monthly salary was cut to one-third its previous level. This austerity made life severe for the Kunikida family. Encouraged to move to Tokyo by Imai Chūji, a close friend, Doppo hoped to begin studying law and politics so that he could get a position and take care of his parents. Furthermore, even if he were somehow to have remained in school and graduated, Doppo would have needed to enter a university, and that also would have required an impossible expense of time and money for the Kunikida family.

One story based on Doppo's days in Yamaguchi is "Bajō no tomo" (Friend on Horseback, 1903). It opens with battleship lieutenant Nomura telling a newspaper reporter about Itoi Kuninosuke, a friend who is presently serving as purser of a transport ship. Nomura tells how he had met Itoi at a livery stable and learned how he had been forced to quit school after completing his elementary program because of the old-fashioned ideas of his father. After the Restoration, his father had lost his position as horse riding trainer for the domain and had been forced to open the stable. The lieutenant recalls the young man washing horses in a pond at the base of a lake that autumn day, while the lieutenant was bathed in sunlight. In depicting warriors sinking into poverty and young Itoi, who pursues his studies despite adversity, finally rising to become purser of a great ship, the story illuminates hidden sociopolitical consequences of life in Yamaguchi Prefecture, the center of the Meiji government.

In April 1888 Doppo moved to Tokyo, and in May 1889 he was admitted into the English Department at Tokyo Senmon Gakkō. The school proclaimed the independence of learning and aimed to provide an open atmosphere for study. In 1889 Doppo dropped his childhood name of Kamekichi, adopted the name of Tetsuo, transferred to a department where politics was taught in English, and there threw himself into debates over current affairs. When he published a handwritten journal in which he candidly criticized the university authorities and teachers, he was once ordered to stop distributing it. In January 1891 he was baptized as a Christian by Protestant minister Uemura Masahisa; at the same time he became a member of the school reform committee and joined in a strike to remove Hatoyama Kazuo from office as the president of the school. By the end of March Doppo officially withdrew from the school.

Doppo's acceptance of Christianity marked a significant shift in his life—into religion and away from politics, as the popular-rights movement waned. In 1885, a year after the dissolution of the Freedom Party that had been the core of the popular-rights movement, 168 Christian churches claiming to have 11,000 converts existed in Japan. But those numbers had increased to 206 churches and 23,000 believers by 1891. Christianity provided one source of Doppo's early encounters with Western culture, and "Ano jibun" (Those Days, 1906) recounts an early experience with Christianity while attending Tokyo Senmon Gakkō.

After leaving the school Doppo returned to Ogō village in Kumage-gun, Yamaguchi, where his parents were living, in May 1891. As his ship passed through the Inland Sea he saw people gathering something on a tiny island and later wrote about the experience in "Wasure-enu hito-bito" (1898; translated as "Men I Shall Never Forget," 1910, and as "Unforgettable People," 1972). After returning to Yamaguchi he read the works of Yoshida Shōin, one of the founders of Chōshū province, and visited the remains of the Shōka Sonjuku private academy that Shōin had established at Hagi. Many important people had studied there, and Doppo presents Tominaga

Yūrin, one of its unfortunate teachers left behind by the times, in "Tomioka Sensei" (Mr. Tomioka, 1904). Taking the Shōka Sonjuku academy as his model, Doppo established the Hano English School, where he taught English and mathematics. After he received no support from the villagers, he closed the school, and his family moved to Yanai. In June 1892 Doppo took Shūji, his younger brother, with him to Tokyo. He showed no interest in returning to the college, but he began publishing a periodical, *Seinen Bungaku* (Literature for Youth), and in February 1893 he began keeping a journal, "Azamukazaru no ki" (An Honest Record).

In September 1893 Doppo was hired as a teacher by the Tsuruya School in Saiki (Saeki) in Oita Prefecture. There he taught English, mathematics, and history, and the year that he spent in this tiny castle town surrounded by beautiful scenery allowed him to glory in the harmony between man and nature. These were feelings that reaffirmed his Christian faith and his reading of the poetry of William Wordsworth, as his one desire was to feel "wonderment" at the incomprehensibility of nature.

Doppo's experiences in Saiki provided the bases for his first story, "Gen oji" (1897; translated as "Old Gen," 1956), and others such as "Haru no tori" (1904; translated as "Bird of Spring," 1983) that were heavily influenced by his reading of Wordsworth's works. "Bird of Spring," which tells of Rokuzō, a retarded boy who chases birds until one day he falls from a stone wall and dies, shares with Wordsworth's "There Was a Boy" a theme of returning to the bosom of nature, but the closing appearance of the bird and the mother of the boy presents a tragic ending that is typical of Doppo's writing.

Doppo and Shūji left Saiki on 1 August 1894, the same day that Japan declared war on China. On 17 September Doppo took a job with the Min'yūsha publishing company headed by Tokutomi Sohō, and in October he boarded the battleship *Chiyoda* to serve as a naval war reporter for the *Kokumin Shinbun* newspaper. His first piece of reportage was "Nenshō shikan" (A Youthful Officer), in which Doppo rejects the notion that the lives of rear admirals and captains are more valuable than those of ensigns and lieutenants junior grade, and he argues that the people and political leaders should respect these young officers, who embody the hopes of the future for the nation. Doppo's wartime communiques, opening with "Dearest Brother!" and addressed as though written to Shūji, were acclaimed and later published as *Aitei tsūshin* (Communiques to a Dear Brother, 1908).

On 5 March 1895 the *Chiyoda* docked at the naval port of Kure, and Doppo joined his parents, who were now living in Tokyo. There he began editing *Kokumin no Tomo* (The Nation's Friend), a magazine published by Min'yūsha. On 9 June Sasaki Toyoji, a vice president of the Women's Christian Temperance Union, and her husband, Honshi, a physician, sponsored a dinner party in honor of the war correspondents, and at this party Doppo first met their seventeen-year-old daughter, Sasaki Nobuko.

A romantic relationship rapidly developed between the two, and Doppo, who planned to move to Hokkaidō and begin farming, dreamed of taking Nobuko with him and starting a family there. In September he went to Hokkaidō and looked for a promising site in the vicinities of Utashinai and Sorachigawa. Doppo had spoken of his plans to Nobuko's father, but when her mother learned of the romance she went into an intense rage and encouraged Nobuko to commit suicide. Instead, Nobuko wrote to Doppo to declare that she intended to travel to the United States, and he hurriedly returned to Tokyo. Tokutomi Sohō of the Min'yūsha company mediated, and in 1895 Christian minister Uemura Masahito married Doppo and Nobuko.

The newlywed couple began life together in a room rented at the Yanagiya, a former inn on Zushi Beach in Kanagawa Prefecture. Lacking a regular job and a fixed income, Doppo initially supported his new family by writing two pieces—biographies of Benjamin Franklin and of Abraham Lincoln—for Min'yūsha's juvenile readers. The new couple lived frugally, and they remained in Zushi only three months, until Doppo's father became ill and the two returned to Tokyo. On 12 April 1896 Nobuko suddenly left, in part because she had been raised free of want and had come to realize that she was unable to endure a life of poverty, and also because the romantic dreams of life with Doppo—who could display a selfish, short-tempered personality—had faded. Her departure and the subsequent divorce hurt Doppo badly, and acquaintances felt that he distrusted women throughout the rest of his life. He also had not known that Nobuko was pregnant at the time she left him, and on 20 February 1897 she gave birth to a daughter, whom she named Urako because the child was delivered in the Urashima Hospital.

On the day Urako was born, Doppo published several poems in the journal *Kokumin no Tomo*. These were republished later that year as *Doppo gin,* and while he was living in Nikkō he also published his first short story, "Old Gen," the piece that launched his literary career.

In August 1898 Doppo married Enomoto Haruko, and in 1901 *Musashino* (The Musashi Plain), his first short-story collection, was published. The title story, which sketches in a fresh, colloquial style the scenery on the outskirts of Tokyo, is an essay more than a work of fiction. Doppo had been inspired by Futabatei Shimei's translation of "Svidaniye" (The Rendezvous; translated as "Aibiki," 1896), Ivan Turgenev's description of a Russian forest blanketed with fallen leaves, and in "Musashino" Doppo in turn presents the beauty of fallen leaves in the forests of the Musashi plain.

Doppo's activities, interests, and feelings up to the conclusion of the Russo-Japanese War in September 1905 are presented in *Doppo shū* (A Collection by Doppo, 1905), his second collection. According to the prefatory essay, "Yo no sakubutsu to ninki" (My Writings and My Popularity), his works from this period were not popular, but he did not believe them to be of poor quality, and he was not concerned with being popular but with performing his labor as well as he could. The collection includes works such as "Bird of Spring" and "Mr. Tomioka," which are among his finest. One story from the collection that presents a part of Doppo's philosophy is "Gyūniku to jagaimo" (translated as "Beef and Potatoes," 1983), in which the "beef" party, who are the realists, and the "potatoes" party, who are the idealists, debate each other. Okamoto, the protagonist, ultimately cannot side with either group, because he retains a desire to feel a "wonderment" that neither can provide.

The treaty ending the Russo-Japanese War on 5 September 1905 shocked the Japanese people, a shock well documented by Doppo's "Gōgai" (Newspaper Extra, 1906). In this story Baron Katō, dressed in tattered clothes and known as "Mr. Extra," laments that everyone had been caught up in the fighting, eager to know whether Japan would defeat or would be defeated by Russia, and had grown frenetic whenever a newspaper would publish an extra edition, but that after the treaty was signed, the nationalism that had united the people collapsed. In the wake of the Russo-Japanese War, Baron Katō insists that Japan has become a society of individuals, each focusing on his or her own desires.

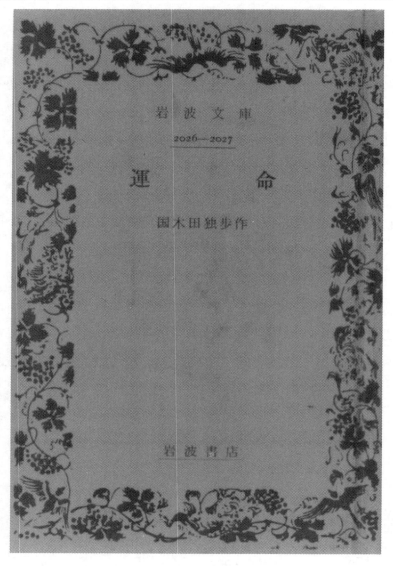

Cover for Doppo's Unmei *(Fate, 1906), a collection of stories that express his fatalistic views in the wake of the Russo-Japanese War*

At this time Doppo published *Unmei,* his third collection, and the journal *Waseda Bungaku* noted that this collection, along with Shimazaki Tōson's *Hakai* (1906; translated as *The Broken Commandment,* 1974) and Natsume Sōseki's *Yōkyoshu* (Drifting in Nothingness, 1906) accurately expressed the new social ethos in Japan after the war. Although every story included in *Fate* had been published before the war, each work met the needs of people in postwar Japan, and the collection was welcomed as postwar literature. *Waseda Bungaku* ventured that every story presented a subjectivity and an autobiographical approach. The most representative work in the collection is "Unmei ronsha" (The

Fatalist), in which the protagonist, who has unwittingly married his half-sister, remarks, "I don't suppose a man has any way of escaping the power of fate." Some critics insisted that "The Fatalist" emphasizes the mysteries surrounding Doppo's own parentage, but others assert that the two shocks of being divorced by Nobuko and of later learning that she had secretly given birth to their daughter moved him to write the story.

During the Russo-Japanese War, Doppo had edited *Kinji Gahō* (Current Events in Pictures), a journal later renamed *Senji Gahō* (Wartime in Pictures). After the war he revived the Kinji Gahō company as Doppo Publishers and began a new career in publishing. This enterprise went bankrupt in 1907, and he developed a serious case of tuberculosis. Stories such as "Hirō" (Exhaustion, 1907) and "Kyūshi" (Death in Misery, 1907) were published after *Tōsei* (The Sound of Waves, 1907), the last collection of his stories that he lived to see, had been published, and these two stories vividly present Doppo's pathetic circumstances at this time. "Death in Misery" is a particularly painful story of Bunkō, who suffers from tuberculosis and has no family on whom to rely—and with whom Doppo no doubt empathized. "I can't bear any of it any longer," Bunkō cries, and he throws himself in front of a train.

In autumn 1907 Doppo moved to Minatomachi in Ibaraki Prefecture to convalesce, and in January 1908 he published "Take no kido" (Bamboo door) and "Ni Rōjin" (Two Old Men). In February he entered the Nangoin Hospital in Chigasaki, Kanagawa Prefecture. Tayama Katai and several other friends compiled *Nijūhachinin shū* (A Collection by Twenty-Eight Writers) and presented it to him.

Following his death in June, ceremonies were held at the Aoyama Funeral Hall in Tokyo, and he was buried at the Aoyama Cemetery. In July *Doppo shū daini* (A Second Doppo Collection), his fifth collection of stories, was published. "Take no kido" (The Bamboo Door), included along with "Death in Misery" in this collection, is another representative story. In "The Bamboo Door" a poor gardener's wife often passes through a bamboo door to draw water from a well, but one day she is caught stealing charcoal and hangs herself. "Ni Rōjin" (Two Old Men) presents two old gentlemen whom the narrator encounters on a park bench, and its portrayal of the common man makes it a representative Doppo story.

In November 1908 *Nagisa* (The Waterside), a compilation of various works by Doppo, was published. It includes "Okamoto no techō" (Oka-

moto's Notebook), which expounds Doppo's philosophy of "wonderment"; "Bōfū" (The Storm), a fragment of an unfinished, full-length novel; a translation of Turgenev's "Bretior" (The Duellist); and the title story, a series of letters that Doppo sent to a friend to describe what he saw and heard while he was convalescing at Nakaminato. A quotation from the opening of *Nagisa* has been engraved into a memorial tablet that stands in Nakaminato (Hitachi Minato): "Here there are blood and flesh, life and death, love and hatred, and sorrow." It is a quotation that fittingly describes Doppo's life and writings.

Biographies:

Ono Shigeki, *Wakaki hi no Kunikida Doppo* (Tokyo: Aporonsha, 1959);

Tanibayashi Hiroshi, *Seinen jidai no Kunikida Doppo* (Tokyo: Yanai Shiritsu Toshokan, 1970);

Kuwabara Shin'ichi, *Kunikida Doppo: Yamaguchi jidai no kenkyū* (Tokyo: Kasama Shoin, 1972);

Hiraoka Toshio, *Tanpen sakka Kunikida Doppo* (Tokyo: Shintensha, 1983).

References:

Ashiya Nobukazu, *Doppo bungaku no kichō* (Tokyo: Ōfūsha, 1989);

Kitano Akihiko, *Kunikida Doppo no bungaku* (Tokyo: Ōfūsha, 1974);

Kitano, *Miyazaki Koshoshi, Kunikida Doppo no shi to shōsetsu* (Tokyo: Izumi Shoin, 1993);

Nakajima Reiko, *Kunikida Doppo: Shoki sakuhin no sekai* (Tokyo: Meiji Shoin, 1988);

Takitō Mitsuyoshi, *Kunikida Doppo ron* (Tokyo: Hanawa Shobō, 1986);

Yamada Hiromitsu, *Kitamura Tōkoku to Kunikida Doppo: Hikaku bungaku-teki kenkyū* (Tokyo: Kindai Bungeisha, 1990);

Yamada, *Kunikida Doppo ronkō* (Tokyo: Shinseiki, 1978).

Miyamoto Yuriko
(13 February 1899 – 21 January 1951)

Eileen B. Mikals-Adachi
University of Notre Dame

BOOKS: *Mazushiki hitobito no mure* (Tokyo: Genbunsha, 1917);

Hitotsu no mebae (Tokyo: Shinchōsha, 1918);

Nobuko (Tokyo: Kaizōsha, 1928);

Chūjō Yuriko shū / Uno Chiyo shū (Tokyo: Heibonsha, 1930);

Atarashiki Shiberia yokogiru (Tokyo: Naigaisha, 1931);

Chibusa (Tokyo: Chikuson Shobō, 1937);

Asu e no seishin (Tokyo: Jitsugyō no Nihonsha, 1940);

Asa no kaze (Tokyo: Kawade Shobō, 1940);

Sangatsu no daiyon nichiyō (Tokyo: Kinseidō, 1940);

Watakushitachi no kensetsu (Tokyo: Jitsugyō no Nihonsha, 1946);

Shinjitsu ni ikita joseitachi (Tokyo: Sōseisha, 1946); republished as *Shinjitsu ni ikita josei* (Tokyo: Shin Nihon Shuppansha, 1989);

Fūchisō (Tokyo: Bungei Shunjūsha, 1947);

Banshū heiya (Tokyo: Kawade Shobō, 1947);

Utagoe yo, okore (Tokyo: Kaihōsha, 1947);

Atarashii fujin to seikatsu (Tokyo: Nihon Minshu Shugi Bunka Renmei, 1947);

Kōfuku ni tsuite (Tokyo: Onkeisha, 1947);

Sakka to sakuhin (Tokyo: Sanne Shoten, 1947);

Fujin to bungaku (Tokyo: Jitsugyō no Nihonsha, 1947);

Dōhyō, 3 volumes (Tokyo: Chikuma Shobō, 1947–1950);

Onna kutsu no ato (Tokyo: Takashimaya Shuppanbu, 1948);

Futatsu no niwa (Tokyo: Chūō Kōronsha, 1948);

Josei no rekishi (Tokyo: Fujin Minshu Shinbun Shuppanbu, 1948);

Shiroi kaya (Tokyo: Shinkyō Geijutsusha, 1948);

Fujin no tame ni (N.p., 1949);

Watashitachi mo utaeru (N.p., 1949);

Heiwa no mamori (Tokyo: Shin Nihon Bungakukai, 1949);

Mosukuwa no inshoki (Tokyo: Tōkyō Minpō Shuppansha, 1949);

Jūninen no tegami (Tokyo: Chikuma Shobō, 1950);

Nihon no seishun (Tokyo: Shunjūsha, 1951);

Miyamoto Yuriko

Heiwa o warera ni (Tokyo: Iwasaki Shobō, 1951);

Wakai josei no tame ni (N.p., 1951);

Miyamoto Yuriko (N.p., 1951).

Collections: *Chūjō Yuriko shū* (Tokyo: Kaizōsha, 1931);

Miyamoto Yuriko bunko, 8 volumes (N.p., 1949–1951);

Miyamoto Yuriko zenshū, 15 volumes (N.p., 1951–1953); 30 volumes (Tokyo: Shin Nihon Shuppansha, 1979–1986);

Miyamoto Yuriko shū, edited by Yoshida Akira (Tokyo: Chikuma Shobō, 1954);

Miyamoto Yuriko hyōron senshū, 4 volumes (1964–1965).

OTHER: *Bungaku no shinrō* (Tokyo: Kōzan Shoin, 1941);
Watakushitachi no seikatsu (Tokyo: Kyōryoku Shuppansha, 1941);
Bungei hyōronshū (Tokyo: Kindai Shisōsha, 1949).

Miyamoto Yuriko stands as an important figure in the history of both the literature and the women of Japan. Her fame is not attributable to her being an innovator of any new literary technique but to her participating in the proletarian literature movement and in vividly presenting the life of one woman in the troubled society of Japan during the first half of the twentieth century. Determined to reconstruct facts in a realistic fashion, Miyamoto used her own experiences as the core of her writing and, through her style, unveiled to her readers the new and fascinating perspective of a humanist turned proletarian writer. Today her works are invaluable sources of information on Japanese society, the position of women in the early 1900s, and modern Japanese literature as a means of political expression.

During the height of militarism in Japan, Miyamoto openly joined both the Japan Proletarian Writers' Association and the Japan Communist Party, and she boldly stepped forward to express what were considered to be radical ideas. She was repeatedly imprisoned and tortured for her political beliefs between 1932 to 1942, and although these abuses ruined her health, nothing could destroy her fighting spirit. Until her death at the age of fifty-one, Miyamoto continued to write significant works of literature and literary criticism and to advocate freedom and the rights of women. She wrote a variety of novels and short stories and many impressionistic, introductory works on the Soviet Union, yet she is best remembered for her autobiographical works: *Mazushiki hitobito no mure* (A Flock of Poor People, 1917), *Nobuko* (Nobuko, 1928), *Fūchisō* (Weathervane Plant, 1947), *Banshū heiya* (The Plains of Banshū, 1947), *Futatsu no niwa* (Two Gardens, 1948), *Dōhyō* (Road Sign, 1947–1950), and *Jūninen no tegami* (Letters of Twelve Years, 1950). These are the works that trace her life and her struggle to liberate herself from her conventional background as she worked for human welfare, and these works attest to her beliefs amid the turmoil and intellectual trends of her times.

Miyamoto Yuriko was the first child of Chūjō Seiichirō, a Cambridge-trained architect, and his wife, Yoshie, the daughter of Nishimura Shigeki, one of the leading intellectuals in the Meiji period. She was born in the Koishikawa section of Tokyo, but the family soon moved to Hokkaidō, where she spent the first three years of her life. Although she later traveled extensively, both domestically and internationally, she generally considered herself to be a resident of Tokyo. Given the name Yuri at birth, young Miyamoto grew up in a comfortable middle-class home with all the freedom she could possibly want. Five of her eight siblings died from natural causes, and one of her brothers committed suicide; this left only Miyamoto, another brother, and a physically weak sister to enjoy the luxuries that the family could afford. Miyamoto was therefore able to attend the most prestigious private schools and to spend summers at her grandmother's villa in Fukushima Prefecture. Life was comfortable for her, and this bourgeois upbringing nurtured her independence and sense of freedom that moved her to express herself so openly in a society that traditionally taught women to suppress their feelings.

While the views that Miyamoto developed were clearly leftist, they were not aroused by bitter feelings toward her parents or her background. Although Chūjō Seiichirō spent much time away from the family on business, Miyamoto still felt close to and respected her father. Following his death, Chūjō was unexpectedly found to have fathered an illegitimate child, but in her autobiographical writing Miyamoto presents her father as a wonderful, loving person without a fault to his name. On the other hand, she presents her mother, whom she describes as unsophisticated, less flatteringly than she presents her father. This deprecation of her mother is perhaps a mere projection of the frustration she felt toward a mother bound by traditions, for Yoshie, who acted more like an older sister than a mother, actually provided the support and encouragement that Miyamoto needed in her literary endeavors. Unable to exhibit her own artistic talent, Yoshie clearly wanted Miyamoto to have opportunities that the mother had not been afforded, and she did her best to ensure that Miyamoto could have such advantages.

As a precocious child, Miyamoto began writing when she was still in elementary school. Her first novel, set at the seaside, was a romantic story about two young lovers, and Miyamoto's parents were overcome with joy when they saw their daughter's work hand-bound in a cover painted with flowers and tied in ribbon. After en-

Dust jacket for Nobuko *(1928), Miyamoto's autobiographical novel that draws on events in her life during 1918–1919*

tering the renowned Ochanomizu Women's High School in 1910, she wrote five novels—the last of which, *Nōson* (A Farming Village, 1916), became her first published work after she had revised and condensed it. Young Miyamoto was an avid reader of modern novels and of the classics, both Japanese and foreign, and her craving for knowledge developed into an obsession for reading that frequently took her to the library rather than to the classroom. Miyamoto's mother never suspected that the daughter for whom she held such high expectations nearly failed such subjects as mathematics.

In April 1916 Miyamoto entered the English Department of Nihon Women's University. After publishing *Mazushiki hitobito no mure* in the prestigious magazine *Chūō Kōron* in September of that year, she left the university and never returned. Her parents fully supported her decision to become a writer, and their support contributed to the success of her literary debut. As the first reader of *A Flock of Poor People,* Yoshie delivered her daughter's manuscript to Tsubouchi Shōyō, a friend of Miyamoto's father and one of the leading early writers of modern Japanese literature. He recommended that it be published, and the efforts of Miyamoto's parents were rewarded

when literary critics had only praise for their daughter, a "seventeen-year-old genius."

Set in a remote village in Fukushima Prefecture, *A Flock of Poor People* is based on material gathered during the summers that Miyamoto had spent in that area. The story concerns the close relations she had maintained with the poor farmers living in the village below her grandmother's villa, which was symbolically on the top of a hill, and the book presents the narrator's awakening to the meaning of class differences. Miyamoto's sympathies tend to be with the "poor people," and yet her goal is to relate the facts, not to make judgments. As she presents a young girl of good fortune trying to help poor farmers with their daily struggles, Miyamoto contrasts the lives of people living at opposite ends of the social structure. The innocent way in which she describes various incidents, such as that in which the protagonist gives her pocket money to the farmers to get food and then finds that they have spent it for a night on the town, helped make the book an instant success.

Publication of *A Flock of Poor People* increased Miyamoto's incentive to become a writer, but her more immediate purpose in leaving the university was to accompany her father on a business trip that had been scheduled to New York in 1916. Although the trip was postponed until 1918, Yoshie at the end of Miyamoto's first semester met with Professor Matsuura, chair of the English Department at the university, and proudly explained that her daughter was withdrawing from the university to study English literature abroad. Some critics believe that Miyamoto decided to travel to escape the pressure of a domineering mother; others feel that her motive for traveling was merely to fulfill her deep interest in the West. Whatever Miyamoto's reasons may have been, Professor Matsuura never lived to see that he was wrong in insisting that for her to leave Japan without having received a basic Japanese education would hurt her career as a writer, nor did Yoshie find that what Miyamoto brought back from the United States was what the mother liked.

As Miyamoto eagerly waited for her departure date, she continued to publish many short stories, including the collection *Hitotsu no mebae* (One Seedling, 1918), about her brother's illness. Her only involvement in literary circles at this time was in meeting writers such as Akutagawa Ryūnosuke. Her main interest was her trip abroad, and she gathered materials for her writing until September 1918, when she and her father left for the United States.

World War I ended shortly after they arrived in New York, and Miyamoto set out to become a great writer in a new era. Through a favor from an art professor whom her father knew, Miyamoto was allowed to audit classes at Columbia University and to live in one of the dorms. Given a private language tutor, she studied how to translate the Japanese classics into English. During their stay in New York, Miyamoto and her father met Araki Shigeki, a specialist in ancient languages and a researcher who had lived in the United States for fifteen years and had helped Asians visiting the country.

After her father returned to Japan, Miyamoto began to date Araki. As the two had completely different backgrounds and personalities, their relationship might have seemed doomed from the beginning, but the twenty-one-year-old Miyamoto was infatuated with Araki, who was fourteen years older than she. Although she dreaded being an ordinary woman or an average housewife and merely wanted to be a free human being, she still regarded marriage as an important part of her future. She refused, however, to follow the conventional Japanese pattern of having an arranged marriage, and in a modern fashion she soon took the initiative and boldly proposed. Araki accepted and agreed to Miyamoto's stipulation against their having any children, so that she could remain free to pursue her career as a writer. Despite opposition from her tutor and almost everyone she knew, Miyamoto and Araki were married in New York in August 1919.

In December that year Miyamoto returned to Japan to be with her diabetic mother, who was about to give birth to another child. Araki joined Miyamoto four months later, when he returned to Japan unemployed and proved to be far from the son-in-law that Yoshie wanted. Her disapproval of Miyamoto's marriage was evident from the start, as Yoshie criticized Araki's every move. The couple tried living with Miyamoto's parents, but the friction grew as Araki tried to adjust to a life quite different from his own and struggled to support his wife by lecturing at many universities. Caught between her mother and her husband, Miyamoto found the pressure unbearable, and writing became impossible. After Yoshie practically kicked the couple out of the Chujō home, the two lived alone for awhile, but in summer 1924 their four-year marriage ended in divorce. In the September number of *Kaizō* Miyamoto soon afterward published the first part of her next major, and perhaps best known, work—*Nobuko*, a novel that was serialized in ten parts, the last of which was published in 1926.

Nobuko is an autobiographical novel that provides a clear picture of her life during and immediately after her stay in New York. In addition to recounting the stresses of her marriage to Araki, Nobuko presents one of the first female protagonists in Japanese literature to choose her own way of life in this story of a woman trying to become independent, both mentally and financially. Because the life of Miyamoto's protagonist parallels her own, the information presented about Nobuko's growth as a writer and as a woman is invaluable. Nobuko is married, as was Miyamoto, to a middle-aged man who seems exhausted with life, although she feels as if she has just begun to live. While he seems to believe in taking life as it comes, Nobuko wants to shape her own destiny. Miyamoto was full of this same vitality, and when she realized that it was time to move on, she decided to dissolve her marriage. In spring 1924 Miyamoto had befriended Yuasa Yoshiko, a woman scholar of Russian literature and a person whose developing relationship with Miyamoto may have contributed to her divorce from Araki.

It is not clear that Miyamoto's relationship with Yuasa went beyond friendship, but the two lived together in Tokyo for some time after her divorce and then in the Soviet Union for two and a half years during 1928–1930. They were also companions during a six-month trip through Europe, so the two were together away from Japan for a total of three years. Miyamoto found that her years living with Yuasa, unlike those years she spent with Araki, left her able to write—even if what she wrote were mainly essays such as *Atarashiki Shiberia yokogiru* (Crossing over the New Siberia, 1931) about the Soviet Union. For political reasons Miyamoto's writing was later banned during World War II, and only in her later years was she able to return to writing in her autobiographical mode and reveal, in her novel *Two Gardens,* details about her life after her divorce and about her relationship with Yuasa before their departure for Moscow.

In contrasting the households and the relationships that Miyamato and Yuasa had maintained with those involving her father and brothers, *Two Gardens* focuses on how Miyamoto is able to move freely between these two "gardens." By reintroducing the character of Nobuko in a kind of sequel to that 1928 novel, Miyamoto reveals how her protagonist develops her independence and an awareness of her position as a woman. *Two Gardens* also reveals the socialist and feminist stances that Miyamoto adopted after she had been exposed to Marxism in Europe—on a trip that her father had both arranged and paid for.

After she returned to Japan in 1930, Miyamoto immediately joined the All-Japan Proletarian Artists' Association (NAPF); a year later she coordinated the Women's Committee of NAPF and became editor of its journal, *Hataraku Fujin* (Working Women). In 1931 she also became a member of the Japan Communist Party, in which she met Miyamoto Kenji, a literary critic ten years younger than she and a man who was to become her husband. In addition to writing fiction Yuriko began writing literary criticism after she joined the proletarian movement, and she also began lecturing and organizing for her political party. During her participation in this crusade to better the world for the poor, laborers, and women, she fell in love with young Kenji, and their marriage in February 1932 ended her relationship with Yuasa.

While it seemed that Yuriko had finally found happiness in her relationship with Kenji, only two months after their marriage she was ar-

rested, and Kenji was forced to go underground because of their political beliefs. Yuriko was repeatedly arrested between 1932 and 1945, and her refusal to give up her political beliefs only increased the torture and hardships she experienced. To add to her woe, Kenji was eventually arrested and sentenced to life imprisonment after a long trial that was attended by no party member except Yuriko. The couple thus spent the first thirteen years of their marriage living apart, but Yuriko's love for Kenji never died.

Her parents were extremely distressed by her political activities, which caused Ochanomizu Women's High School to remove her name from their list of alumni. She became a disgrace to the family name. Her mother blamed Kenji for the change that had occurred in her daughter, and Yoshie pleaded to get Yuriko to divorce him. Each of the times that Yuriko was arrested, however, Seiichirō silently rescued his daughter by going to the authorities to beg for her release. Both of her parents painfully waited for the return of the daughter they knew, but they both died—Yoshie in 1934 and Seiichirō in 1936—with Yuriko refusing to abandon the one man whom she felt would let her be her true self.

Yuriko and Kenji were finally reunited on 9 October 1945, after the Occupation forces freed all political prisoners in Japan and revoked the Maintenance of Public Order Act that had been in effect during the war. This occasion is recorded in the beginning of *Weathervane Plant,* which recounts Yuriko's life with Kenji after he was liberated. *The Banshū Plains* tells of that period of their marriage before his release, and together these two novels in 1947 were awarded the Mainichi Publishing Culture Award, recognizing Miyamoto's skill as an autobiographical novelist. This honor could not have come at a more appropriate time, for she was at the peak of her career. After the restrictions that the military had imposed on her were lifted, she was again able to write freely. As if all that she had kept inside came gushing forth, the period from 1945 to 1951, the year of her death, proved to be her most active and productive.

As a writer, Miyamoto in 1945 helped form the Shin Nihon Bungakukai (New Japanese Literature Association), a group of writers who maintained an anti-imperialist view and continued to write fiction. As a social and political activist, she was the founder of the Fujin Minshu Kurabu (Women's Democratic Club), and after she added to the array of articles on women and women writers about whom she had written during the war, Miyamoto collected and published these essays in *Fujin to bungaku* (Women and Literature, 1947).

Although Miyamoto's contributions, both literary and political, are thus varied, she is renowned for her writing. Her earliest accomplishments in writing include a fine assortment of short stories, such as "Koiwai no ikka" (1934; translated as "The Family of Koiwai," 1982), "Chibusa" (Breasts, 1935), "Hiroba" (Plaza, 1940), and "Sangatsu no daiyon nichiyō" (The Fourth Sunday in March, 1940); yet her best works are drawn from her personal experience. *Letters of Twelve Years,* the collection of letters that she and Kenji had exchanged during his long years in prison, and *Road Sign,* the novel that recounts her experiences in the Soviet Union, became the final chapters of her own life story, for soon after Miyamoto completed the book she died suddenly on 21 January 1951.

Many gathered to mourn Miyamoto's death, and many continue to see in her life a model of the independence that Japanese women also can attain. While much of her literature has been translated into Russian, little has been made available in English. Yet her works are widely read in Japan, where she is respected as one of the great writers of the early twentieth century and as a woman who, in finding her own identity, was able to expand the horizons of modern Japanese literature.

References:

Okuno Takeo, *Joryū sakkaron* (Tokyo: Daisan Bunmeisha, 1974);

Sakagaki Naoko, *Meiji, Taishō, Shōwa joryū bungaku* (Tokyo: Ōfūsha, 1967);

Yamamoto Kenkichi, *Shōwa no joryū bungaku* (Tokyo: Jitsugyō no Nihonsha, 1957);

Yoshida Seiichi, ed., *Nihon joryū bungaku shi kinsei kindai hen* (Tokyo: Seikyōsha, 1969).

Mori Ōgai

(17 February 1862 – 9 July 1922)

Yamazaki Kuninori
Hanazono University

BOOKS: *Minawashū* (Tokyo: Shun'yōdō, 1892);
Tsukikusa (Tokyo: Shun'yōdō, 1896);
Kagegusa (Tokyo: Shun'yōdō, 1897);
Nishi Amane den (Tokyo: Nishi Shinrokurō, 1898);
Shinbi shinsetsu (Tokyo: Shun'yōdō, 1900);
Jinshu tetsugaku kogai (Tokyo: Shun'yōdō, 1903);
Kōkaron kōgai (Tokyo: Shun'yōdō, 1904);
Uta nikki (Tokyo: Shun'yōdō, 1907);
Ichimakumono (Tokyo: Ekifūsha, 1909);
Tōkyō hōganzu (Tokyo: Shun'yōdō, 1909);
Gendai shōhin (Tokyo: Ōkura Shoten, 1910);
Kenteki (Tokyo: Shinchōsha, 1910);
Ōgonhai (Tokyo: Shun'yōdō, 1910);
Zoku ichimakumono (Tokyo: Ekifūsha, 1910);
Enjin (Tokyo: Shun'yōdō, 1911);
Yūrei (Tokyo: Shun'yōäō, 1911);
Miren (Tokyo: Momiyama Shoten, 1912);
Seinen (Tokyo: Momiyama Shoten, 1913); translated by Shoichi Ono and Sanford Goldstein as *Youth* (Honolulu: University of Hawaii Press, 1994);
Iji (Tokyo: Momiyama Shoten, 1913);
Bunshin (Tokyo: Momiyama Shoten, 1913);
Shin ichimakumono (Tokyo: Momiyama Shoten, 1913);
Ka no yō ni (Tokyo: Momiyama Shoten, 1914);
Tenpo monogatari (Tokyo: Hōmeisha, 1914);
Sakai jiken (Suzuki Miekichi, 1914);
Gan (Tokyo: Momiyama Shoten, 1915); translated by Kingo Ochiai and Goldstein as *The Wild Geese* (Tokyo: Tuttle, 1959); translated by Burton Watson as *The Wild Goose* (Ann Arbor: University of Michigan Press, 1995);
Chirihiji (Tokyo: Senshōkan, 1915);
Sara no ki (Tokyo: Oranda Shobō, 1915);
Mōjin mōgo (Tokyo: Shiseidō, 1915);
Takasebune (Tokyo: Shun'yōdō, 1918);
Kaeru (Tokyo: Genbunsha, 1919);
Umoregi (Tokyo: Iwanami bunko, 1927).
Collection: *Ōgai zenshū,* 35 volumes (Tokyo: Iwanami Shoten, 1936–1939).

Mori Ōgai

Edition in English: *The Historical Literature of Mori Ōgai,* 2 volumes, edited by David Dilworth and J. Thomas Rimer (Honolulu: University of Hawaii Press, 1977).

PLAY PRODUCTIONS: *Tamakushige futari Urashima,* Tokyo, Ichimura-za Theater, 2 January 1903;
Nichiren Shōnin tsujizeppō, Tokyo, Kabuki-za Theater, 1 April 1904;
Kamen, Tokyo, Shintomi-za Theater, 1 June 1909;
Ikutagawa, Tokyo, Yūraku-za Theater, 23 May 1910;

Onnagata, Tokyo, Teikoku Gekijō Theater, 1 October 1912;

Sōga kyōdai, Tokyo, Teikoku Gekijō Theater, 26 February 1914;

Shizuka, Tokyo, Teikoku Gekijō Theater, 26 March 1921.

TRANSLATIONS: Hans Christian Andersen, *Sokkyo shijin* (Tokyo: Shun'yōdō, 1902);

Henrik Ibsen, *Jon Gaburieru Borukuman* (Tokyo: Gahōsha, 1909);

Gerhart Hauptmann, *Sabishiki hitobito* (Tokyo: Kaneo Bun'endō, 1911);

Ibsen, *Yūrei* (Tokyo: Kin'yōdō, 1911);

Jūjin jūwa (Tokyo: Jitsugyō no Nihonsha, 1913);

William Shakespeare, *Makubesu* (Tokyo: Keiseisha, 1913);

Ibsen, *Nora* (Tokyo: Keiseisha, 1913);

Shokoku monogatari (Tokyo: Kokumin Bunko Kankōkai, 1915);

Johann Wolfgang von Goethe, *Gyottsu* (Tokyo: Momiyama Shoten, 1916);

August Strindberg, *Perikan* (Tokyo: Zenbunsha, 1921).

Along with Natsume Sōseki, Mori Ōgai is one of the literary giants of the modern age. Not only did Ōgai help create a new literature for the Japanese people as the country endured the pains attending the birth of the modern nation, but he also expounded on a wide spectrum of issues and worked to enlighten the backward consciousness of the Japanese. Although he manifested a pedantic streak as a young man, his concern for the awakening of his country was striking, and it produced significant results in the evolution of modern Japan.

Ōgai, whose real name was Mori Rintarō, was the son of the official physician in the domain of Tsuwano, a tiny western province. From his youth he excelled in educational pursuits, and his intelligence led his teachers at the Yōrōkan, the fief school, to have high hopes for his future. In 1872 the boy accompanied his father to Tokyo, and he never returned to his birthplace. In Tokyo Ōgai enrolled immediately in the Shinbun Gakusha, a school where he continued his studies with a particular emphasis on the German language. In 1877 he was formally admitted into the medical school at Tokyo University, from which he graduated with superior grades in 1881. Following graduation he joined the army medical staff, and in 1884 the Medical Affairs Bureau of the army selected and assigned him to study hygiene in Germany.

For nearly four years thereafter Ōgai studied in cities such as Berlin, Leipzig, Dresden, and Munich, and after acquiring a vast knowledge of many subjects he returned to Japan in September 1888. Elise, a young German woman, followed Ōgai back to Japan, but when she found his family and associates strongly opposed to her hopes of developing a relationship with Ōgai, she returned to Germany. Distressed at this incident, Ōgai's parents arranged for him to marry Akamatsu Toshiko, the daughter of a colleague of Nishi Amane, his benefactor, in March 1889. Shortly after the birth of a son in 1890, however, the marriage ended in divorce. In all his writing Ōgai never acknowledges any reasons for his divorce, but starting with "Maihime" (1890; translated as "The Dancing Girl," 1975), the first three stories that he wrote are based on his experiences in Europe and on the emotional torment that those experiences engendered.

Ōgai's first public statements about literature after his return from Germany were published in "Shōsetsu ron" (On the Novel), which appeared in the *Yomiuri Shinbun* on 3 January 1889. There he criticized the "experimental novel" of Emile Zola, whose novels had overwhelmed readers throughout Europe. In "Ima no shoka no shōsetsuron o yomite" (Reading Contemporary Essays on the Novel), which was published in *Shigarami zōshi* on 25 November 1889, Ōgai further elucidated his position on Zola's literary technique by remarking that the French novelist "attempts to observe nature, and copies down the results on paper without adding even a bit of subjectivity to his observations. . . . This is nothing other than forgetting one's purpose for the sake of the technique." Ōgai adds that "The achievements that come from analyzing and dissecting [human behavior] are the special accomplishments of the writer. The techniques by which these talents are employed should come solely through creative imagination." Ōgai clearly separates the materials from the techniques involved in the writing of fiction, and he insists that the imagination performs an important role in creating through the use of those techniques.

Among other reflections on Zola's techniques for producing fiction, Ōgai remarks that writers or critics have already recognized the value of the psychological novel. However, psychological observation is only a technique in the creative writing process, not the end thereof. Consequently, in order to defend the borders of

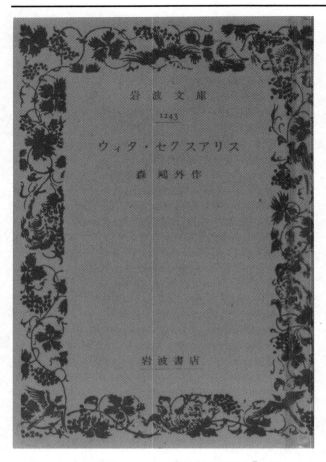

Cover for Vita sekusuarisu *(1909), Ōgai's scandal-arousing examination of the limits of human sexual desire*

art, one must somewhat restrain one's energies, and by means of the creative functions purify the natural stains, and construct one's work as driven by inspiration and possessed by the imagination.

His own methodology is clear: observation is a technique, a means to an aesthetic end, and the essence of art lies in the creative functions and in the artist who is "possessed by the imagination." These ideas are rooted in the work of Rudolf von Gottschall and Eduard von Hartmann.

"Reading Contemporary Essays on the Novel" was published around the time that Ōgai was planning and writing "The Dancing Girl," so this essay is of great significance in fully appreciating his first three stories. Around the same time Ōgai was also working with Miki Takeji to translate Pedro Calderón de la Barca's *El alcalde de Zalamea* (The Mayor of Zalamea, circa 1643; translated as *Shirabe wa takashi gitarura no hitofushi,* 1889), and thereafter he trans-

lated many works. Most of his translations originally appeared in journals or newspapers, and were later published in collections of Ōgai's works.

Ōgai's first published collection of works, *Minawashū* (A Collection of Bubbles, 1892), includes the seventeen stories he had written during the three years after he had returned from Germany, along with many translations. In addition to "The Dancing Girl" and two other stories set in Germany, it contains translations of works such as Alphonse Daudet's "Le Cabecilla" (The Warring Priest) and Friedrich Hackländer's "Zwei Nächte" (Two Nights). An understanding of the nature of this collection is essential to any consideration of Ōgai's early ideas about fiction.

Matsuki Hiroshi suggests that the notion of a literary technique involving both a "single-layer story" and a "multiple-layer story"—a notion that Ōgai considers in his "Reading Contemporary Essays on the Novel"—was influenced by Paul Heyse, one of the leading writers of German literature at that time. Matsuki asserts that all seventeen of the stories in *Minawashu* are written as single-layer stories, in which, according to Ōgai,

> One writes about events in the life of a single individual, or of several individuals, while at the same time extending one's consideration to the state of the nation and the circumstances of the society. Alternately, one writes about events in the life of one or more individuals, while considerations of national and social circumstances are largely eliminated; or, even if they are described, one merely glances over semblances of their forms.

Matsuki adds that, in a work on children's stories and short stories, Gottschall remarked that single-layer story techniques "must converge" in a single "element of chance." Matsuki finds that Heyse and Gottschall influenced Ōgai's early views on fiction in two respects: in the emphasis these theorists placed on the short story rather than the novel; and on the value of works that contain a "turning point based on external chance."

In January 1890 Ōgai began to write "The Dancing Girl," a story that presented an unusual topic in Japanese literature of the time: the tragic love between individuals from different lands. Seita Fumitake notes that Ōgai had just finished translating Leo Tolstoy's "Lyutsern," and the influence of this experience on Ōgai's style in writing "The Dancing Girl" is obvious in his multiple uses of exclamations, antithetical expressions, repeated negations, and variations on the diary form. "The Dancing Girl" owes much of its originality to such experiments in bringing a new European style of expression to Japanese literature, but most important in the story is the presentation of the first young intellectual nurtured in the new Japan.

Ōta Toyotarō, the protagonist, sets the pattern for such a character, and, along with Bunzō in Futabatei Shimei's *Ukigumo* (The Drifting Clouds, 1887–1888; complete edition, 1889), Ōta is the model for the modern intellectual who wonders how he should live and agonizes about the role he has been assigned in a nation just beginning to define a cultural identity as one of many other nations. For many readers the focus of the story becomes the discord between Ōta, a member of the young elite, and the youthful country around him; the disjuncture between the individual and the state; the problem of the formation and collapse of the "modern self"; and the fragility of the modernization occurring in Japan. The notion of a "true self" that the story presented to young men living in the formative years of modern Japan was both a great end to be pursued and a cloud floating in the sky, and these mixed conceptions of the "true self" afforded the bases of the first great spiritual battle waged in the pages of modern Japanese literature.

Yet if one reads "The Dancing Girl" straightforwardly, the story does not raise merely the question of a "modern self" but also questions about the love between Toyotarō and Elise. It is reasonable to read the story as a single-layer story, a tragedy of two young people in love, and to ignore what Ōgai called "considerations of national and social circumstances."

At the opening of "The Dancing Girl" Ōta Toyotarō is aboard a ship at Saigon and about to return to Japan. Although the other passengers have gone ashore to see Saigon, he is "locked away in [his] cabin" and tortured by a "pain that feels as though [his] bowels were being wrenched nine times each day," as his "mind is tormented by a hidden regret." The narrative foregrounds the spiritual sufferings of a young man with its exaggerated expression of Toyotarō's present agony. The flashbacks that follow then summarily recount details of his "hidden regret," which he promises that he will "try to record in outline." Following his return from Europe, Ōgai had experienced the pain of sending his Elise back to Germany after she had crossed the ocean to be with him, and that suffering becomes a motif of his story.

What causes Toyotarō to feel such regret is his betrayal of Elise. He cannot forgive himself for refusing to return her love, and he torments himself for using and then abandoning her. Ōgai remarked that Toyotarō "does not know true love," and when he and Elise first meet, Toyotarō recounts how his relationship begins with pity for this "girl who showed up at my lodgings to thank me" and continues to be "innocent" until he loses his job and his mother dies. After these events he and Elise became "inseparable," as "at that time . . . my feelings of love for her suddenly intensified" and the young woman's "beautiful, pathetic appearance struck my mind, which was not in its normal state because of the assaults of profound pain, and I wondered how I had reached such a state in the midst of such enchantment."

Toyotarō's state of mind at the time is "not normal," and the two come together in the midst of "enchantment." Yet Ōgai foreshadows his protagonist's inability to return Elise's love, as Toyotarō confesses that he has a "cowardly heart" that cannot be overcome merely by the power of any "enchantment" he feels. Elise eventually becomes a burden to Toyotarō, and, faced with her pregnancy and the letters she sends him while he is working in Russia, he subordinates his feelings for her to his increasing "thoughts of home and the yearning after fame."

Ultimately Count Amakata, who is visiting Europe, and Aizawa Kenkichi, a good friend, succeed in persuading Toyotarō to return to Japan, and his heart is overcome with guilt: "My head was filled with the thought that I was an unredeemable criminal," he recalls. This sense that he is a criminal signals his recognition that he has wounded another human being, and his feeling that he has used and then abandoned her during a time of personal stress leaves him suffering as he appears on the ship in Saigon at the start of the story. "The Dancing Girl" presents the tragedy of a young man who cannot truly love another and must live with the pain and guilt borne by his recognition of that fact.

"Utakata no ki" (1890; translated as "A Sad Tale," 1974) is a mellow, sweet, and pathetic tale divided into three parts and set in Munich, in the southern region of Germany where Ōgai had lived for about a year. In the first part Kose, a Japanese art student, meets

Cover for a translation of the novel in which Ōgai begins to examine Japanese life during the 1880s in order to understand the rapid cultural changes that were reshaping Japan by 1911

Marie, a violet seller, at the Café Minerva, and his second encounter with her is also described. In the second part Marie, who has begun working as a model at an art school, visits Kose's apartment, where she tells of her colorful career. In the final section Marie and Kose go to Lake Starnberg, where their feelings for each other deepen, but the story ends with Marie tragically dying. In this work Ōgai takes the tragic story of Marie and Kose (who is modeled after Ōgai's friend Harada Naojirō), adds to it the story of King Ludwig II (who had drowned while Ōgai was studying in Germany), and includes an imagined illicit affair between the king and

Marie's mother. The resulting narrative provides a drama reminiscent of the European theater.

Particularly dramatic is the scene in which Kose and Marie ride in a carriage toward Lake Starnberg. Both have been hesitant in their relationship until that time, but in the hooded carriage their hearts incline toward each other:

> The pathway beneath the trees was dark. The smell of the grasses—heated beneath the summer sun, then steamed in the rain—blew into the carriage, and the two inhaled the aroma like parched souls drinking water. . . . Then Marie put her arms around Kose's neck and leaned the weight of her body against him. Her face, illuminated by the flashes of lightning that filtered through the trees, wore a smile as they gazed into each other's eyes. They forgot themselves, forgot the carriage in which they rode, forgot even the world outside the carriage.

Yet tragedy soon follows. As the two ride in a boat near the shore of Lake Starnberg, mad King Ludwig II mistakes Marie for her mother, whom he had loved, and he cries out as he approaches them. Surprised by his shouts, Marie tumbles into the lake and drowns. The king dies in an attempt to save her, and even his aged physician Gudden perishes. Marie's death amplifies the tragic notes she has sounded about the evanescence of human life in her earlier remarks during the carriage ride: "Today! Today! What can be done with yesterday? Tomorrow, and the next day—they are merely empty names, useless sounds." Marie's impulses to live for the moment define her character. The emotions of the moment and intimate exaltation followed by an overwhelming sense of emptiness are the feelings that echo through "A Sad Tale," and the twilight and the white flowers that bloom beside the gloomy lake into which Marie tumbles symbolize these conflicting emotions.

"Fumizukai" (1891; translated as "The Courier," 1971) differs from Ōgai's two earlier stories in its representation of Kobayashi, a young officer whom the story presents as a narrator only intermittently, rather than as "The Dancing Girl" and "A Sad Tale" present Toyotarō and Kose as the principal figures in those stories. Kobayashi, who has returned to Japan after studying in Germany, reports on his European experiences before a gathering at the Hoshigaoka Teahouse, to which he has been invited by a prince. Kobayashi decides to tell the dramatic story of how Ida, a noble lady whom he had met while he was participating in military exercises with the Saxon army in Dresden, avoids a loveless marriage.

Ida is one of five daughters of Count von Bülow, master of the castle at Döben, where Kobayashi spends one night. Kobayashi is attracted to Ida, who has black hair and always dresses in black, and he readily agrees to perform the favor that she asks of him—that of delivering a letter to her aunt, the wife of a government minister, at the palace in Dresden. Although Ida has a secret fiancé, Baron von Meerheim, whom her parents have selected for her, she does not love him, and she wishes to reject the match. In the letter that Ida wishes Kobayashi to deliver for her, she asks an aunt to arrange for her to take a position among the ladies at court.

Ida does not wish to marry von Meerheim, who is traveling with Kobayashi, because the baron is a shallow man who lives solely through the influence of his social position. Another character who is enamored with Ida is a young harelipped man whom she had rescued as a boy and who has continued to love her since then. Although Ida is not cold toward him, she will not allow him to see her in person, for, Ōgai writes, she has a strongly independent nature that makes her take "a profound dislike to any who hung about her with excessive familiarity."

This disposition may betoken Ida's yearning for an unconstrained life and for her rejection of a social system that assigns value to family pedigree. Ōgai presents the plight of Ida, tightly bound by concerns of pedigree, in the following manner:

> Seeing her father in a good mood on one occasion, she attempted to discuss her torment with him, but with only a look at her countenance he interrupted her. "The selfish behavior so common among the lower classes is unthinkable for one born to the nobility. Individual rights are sacrificed to the rights of heredity. Although I am an old man, . . . I have preserved the honor of this family, which has not been tainted with a single drop of base blood for several hundred years."

In response to her father's emphasis on the luxury of hereditary rights Ida insists that "though I was born the child of nobility, I too am a human being."

Stubbornly defending her independence, Ida refuses to follow the dictates of her parents and takes a position at the palace, yet the glimpse that Kobayashi provides of the court's unattractive women, for whom "the spring of their lives had long since passed," painfully pre-

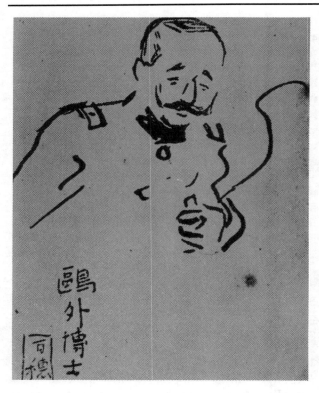
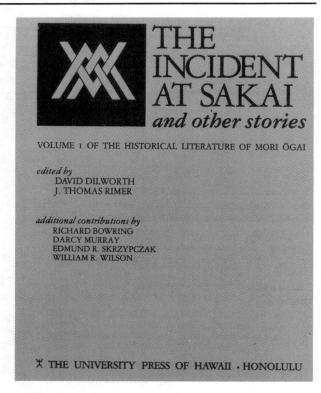

Frontispiece and title page for an American translation of a collection of Ōgai's historical narratives. The title story recounts an incident in 1868, when French authorities at Sakai demanded the ritual suicide of twenty Japanese men as reparation for a conflict between French and Japanese soldiers near Osaka.

figures Ida's future. Although "The Dancing Girl" and "The Courier" seem different stories at first glance, both examine the sacrifice of youth and humanity to emotional, psychological, and social pressures. Written soon after Ōgai's divorce from Toshiko in September 1891, "The Courier" relates a young man's experiences in the West, although by telling this story to a "certain prince" in Japan, Kobayashi makes vividly real this tale of an escape from marriage. That, too, was surely part of Ōgai's intention.

From the late 1880s and into the 1890s, a time often described as Ōgai's period of attempts at "aggressive enlightenment," he pursued various activities aimed at bringing what he had learned in Europe to a backward Japanese society. Some colleagues in the Army Ministry criticized Ōgai's writing of fiction after he had published his first three stories, and for a time he stopped writing altogether. After "The Courier" he published "Somechigae" (Separate Dyes, 1897), representing the morals of the pleasure quarters and written in a classical idiom that recalls the work of Ihara Saikaku, a seventeenth-century author, but years passed before he resumed writing prose in "Asane" (Late

Riser, 1906) and "Yurakumon" (Yuraku Gate, 1907), in neither of which did he display much enthusiasm for creative writing. In October 1889 Ōgai founded *Shigarami Zōshi,* a critical journal that became the forum in which he presented his arguments on literary theory. His vigorous literary debates with critics such as Ishibashi Ningetsu and Tsubouchi Shōyō are well known. Around this time Ōgai also wrote many medical articles based on principles of hygiene that he had learned in Europe, and he contributed significantly to the practice of medicine in Japan.

In 1899 Ōgai was transferred to the Twelfth Division of the army in Kokura on the island of Kyūshū, where he became the chief medical officer. In 1902 he married twenty-three-year-old Araki Shige (or Shigeko), a woman whom his mother, Mineko, had chosen to become his second wife. At the outbreak of the Russo-Japanese War in 1904 Ōgai was serving as chief medical officer of the First Division in Tokyo, and from there he was transferred to northeastern China to head the medical unit of the Second Division. He returned to Tokyo at the conclusion of the war in January 1906.

He displayed no desire to return to writing

prose at the end of the war, but his participation in the Tokiwa-kai poetry society, created by the statesman Yamagata Aritomo, encouraged him to resume his literary work. In November 1907 Ōgai realized his dream of becoming surgeon general at a rank corresponding to that of lieutenant general, and at the age of forty-five he simultaneously took over as head of the Bureau of Medical Affairs for the War Ministry. He was particularly gratified to achieve the top post in the Bureau of Medical Affairs, if only as some recompense for all the suffering he had endured while being criticized for pursuing the dual paths of literature and medical administration within the War Ministry.

After a lapse of nearly eighteen years during which he had written no fiction, he published "Hannichi" (1909; translated as "Half a Day," 1973), and the decade beginning in 1910 marked Ōgai's most productive period of writing. Kinoshita Mokutarō sees this return to literary work as Ōgai's "age of abundance," for the security of Ōgai's professional position, his drive to compete with Natsume Sōseki, and the creation of *Subaru* (The Pleiades), a new literary journal in 1909 motivated his efforts. Ōgai was also struggling with family problems. In 1908 Tokujirō, his younger brother, died, and his death was soon followed by that of Fritz, Ōgai's young son. Ōgai also stood in the middle of an abrasive psychological battle between his mother and his new wife, and perhaps all these events and situations moved him to resume writing literature.

The stabilization of his position as head of the Bureau of Medical Affairs provided the occasion for an outburst that had built up inside him following a string of misfortunes. The spark was perhaps provided by the violence inflicted on him by a newspaper reporter on 2 February 1909. At a social gathering with reporters who covered the Ministry of War, Murayama Teikei, a reporter for the *Asahi Shinbun,* denounced Ōgai, who was involved in selecting a successor to head the Red Cross Hospital. The two got into a fight and fell from the porch, and Ōgai injured his hand. With his mother and wife waging a cold war in the background and Murayama's public insult, Ōgai appeared unable to suppress his anger over this encounter with the reporter, and in May 1909 he re-created the incident in "Konshinkai" (Social Gathering).

Ōgai also wrote openly about the strife between his mother and wife in "Half a Day," which focuses on half a day in the life of Dr.

Takayama Shunzō, who has to call on the imperial palace for a ceremony commemorating the reign of Emperor Kōmei. The psychological warfare between his wife and mother starts early in the morning, and Dr. Takayama ultimately abandons his plan to visit the palace.

Critics such as Kobori Keiichirō regard this work as an expression of Ōgai's "tenaciously critical spirit" and as "the new generation's view of the family." Yet the background of the story makes it a lively piece that exhaustively praises the mother and disparages the wife. Ōgai wrote the story to invite his wife to engage in some self-reflection, and he was wary of having his story degenerate into the kind of naturalistic exposé that he generally disliked. It represented an attempt to heal the bitterness within his household.

In his next story, "Tsuina" (1909; translated as "Exorcising Demons," 1971), Ōgai presents an excuse for having written a personal exposé in "Half a Day," and "Exorcising Demons" also declares his belief in the autonomy of the writer to choose and to write about subjects in certain ways: "the notion that a novel must treat certain situations in a certain way is itself a very enslaved notion. I would offer the opinion, derived from my 'thoughts at night,' that a novel ought to be able to depict anything at all in any manner at all."

During this period he published many works—from "Masui" (Hypnotism, 1909) to *Vita sekusuarisu* (1909; translated as *Vita Sexualis,* 1972)—on controversial subjects. The events presented in "Hypnotism," which is based on one of the experiences of Ōgai's wife, question whether a man's wife has been abused while she is under hypnosis during a doctor's examination at a clinic. *Vita Sexualis* recounts Ōgai's own feelings of passion during his youth. It is a valuable document for studying the lives of young intellectuals during the first decade of the Meiji era, yet, as Ōgai expected, government censors banned the number of *The Pleiades* in which the work was published. For a high-ranking official as well known as Ōgai, there was perhaps too much risk attending the publication of works such as "Half a Day," "Hypnosis," and *Vita Sexualis.* He wrote the works with a full awareness of what he was doing, and following the banning of *Vita Sexualis* the reprimand he received from Vice Minister Ishimoto Shinroku, whom he disliked, was a considerable insult.

Even before publishing *Vita Sexualis* Ōgai wrote "Daihakken" (The Great Discovery,

1909), a rather didactic story about the "great discovery" that a character makes—that Westerners pick their noses. After *Vita Sexualis* Ōgai continued to describe trivial incidents from his own experience, and this incorporated a wry tone into many works. In "Asobi" (1910; translated as "Play," 1994), for example, Ōgai writes:

> Kimura was a man of letters. At the government office, he did painstaking, lifeless, unimportant work for others, and even though his hair had started to thin, his activities had had absolutely no influence on anyone. But as a man of letters, he was known to a fair number of people. He had written nothing of any merit, but he was known to people.

When the banning of *Vita Sexualis* obstructed Ōgai's fierce determination to "depict anything at all in any manner at all" and forced his energy inward, he plunged into self-trivialization. Kimura in "Play" can be regarded as a representative of Ōgai, who must have felt at this time that he "had written nothing of any merit."

In "Mōsō" (1911; translated as "Daydreams," 1994) Ōgai wrote, "I feel as though the things I do are no different than an actor appearing on a stage and playing a certain part. . . . But I can't imagine that this role is actual life itself. I feel that something that lies hidden in the background is real life." In "Hyaku monogatari" (1911; translated as "Ghost Stories," 1994) he adds, "Even though I have stood on the stage of life, I have never played a role that seemed like a true role." When obstacles precluded Ōgai's living and working independently, the falsehood that he felt was imposed on his life became magnified, and a sense of trivialization distinguished his thinking around 1910. In the years before he began writing historical novels and biographies, such an awareness of the trivial provided Ōgai with one of his distinct stylistic methods.

In "Yo ga tachiba" (My position, 1909) Ōgai remarks, "To my way of thinking, I am myself, and it is up to me to do the things I want to do. That satisfies me." Ōgai adds that "I feel as though it doesn't matter to me that the writings of Tayama Katai, Masamune Hakuchō, and Shimazaki Tōson are better than mine." Evidently the quality of the work of naturalist writers bothered Ōgai, yet his dissatisfaction became another source of his own approach.

His technique was to stand back from the events occurring around him and to observe them from a distance. In "Ghost Stories" he writes, "I was a born onlooker," and "I became an onlooker because I had received formless wounds that never healed." This perspective engendered a contemplative literary viewpoint, and after the banning of *Vita Sexualis* much of Ōgai's fiction was written with this meditative point of view.

"Niwatori" (Chicken, 1909) is based on Ōgai's experiences after his transfer to Kokura. Major Ishida avoids becoming part of the human interactions around him, as he distances himself from others and attempts to remain an observer. Those who observe from a distance are ironically able to see very well. "Kinka" (1909; translated as "The Gold Coin," 1994) is the story of a stupid thief who follows three army officers to their quarters, hides in their garden, and spends an entire night observing every move of those inside. When everyone has fallen asleep, he sets about his crime, grossly blunders in his attempt at theft, and is captured. The first half of "Konpira" (Konpira Shrine, 1909; translated, 1994) describes the contemplative stance of Professor Ono as he visits the Konpira Shrine on the island of Shikoku. The latter half, set at the deathbed of his dying son, is most striking in its presentation of the professor's icy demeanor. Ōgai writes that "It was horribly unpleasant to be standing there as an onlooker."

"Gyunabe" (Pan of Beef, 1910) recounts the behavior of a man, a woman, and a girl who are eating beef from a pan, and their actions are described as though a camera had been set up to record the action. "The pan boiled steadily," the story opens, as it unemotionally presents the three different people gathered around the pan. The description of the woman's "eternally parched eyes" as they gaze on the man becomes a refrain throughout the story, which is both a realistic and a philosophical description. The contemplative orientation of Ōgai's writing, viewing life from a low, restrained perspective, illuminates the truths of human existence to be found in the most trivial details.

Ōgai mixes his contemplation of human life with a set of values that places great importance on everyday life. In "Kazuisuchika" (1911) he writes: "I realized that my father devoted his entire soul to the most meaningless daily activities. I came to see, albeit vaguely, that my father's attitude of *resignation,* as he interacted at ease with the doctors at the post town, was close to the dignity attained by those who have come to know the Way. It was at that time that I suddenly developed a respect for my father."

The words of Ōmura in *Seinen* (1913; translated as *Youth,* 1994) share the same respect for the mundane: "Even though [Count Leo] Tolstoi was a great man, he too was an ascetic. He had to promptly run up against daily life. . . . There is something Apollonic about his ability to be immersed in daily life while still firmly maintaining his freedom of spirit and not compromising one whit." Jun'ichi, the protagonist of *Youth,* is a cheerless young man, a naturalistic youth who despises everyday undertakings, as do Takenaka Tokio in Tayama Katai's *Futon* (1907; translated as *The Quilt,* 1981) or Suganuma Kenji in Masamune Hakuchō's *Doko e* (*Quo Vadis?,* 1908). The novel can be read as a tale of this young man turning toward the kind of life Ōgai advocated in lauding his "ability to be immersed in daily life while still firmly maintaining his freedom of spirit."

"Sakazuki" (The Sake Cup, 1910; translated as "Cups," 1971) and "Kodama" (An Echo, 1910) are unusual works of this period. Many of Ōgai's works after "Half a Day" depict trivial events from his own surroundings, but these two works are allegorical prose poems. Seven girls who come to drink at a pure spring of water each carry a silver cup engraved with the word "nature." An eighth girl with golden hair and blue eyes appears, and she says, "My cup is not very large. But I will take some water into my cup." Takemori Ten'yu compares the seven girls to the constellation Pleiades, for which the Japanese name, *Subaru,* is also the name of the literary magazine that was founded by young anti-naturalist writers and for which Ōgai wrote these stories. In broader terms these figures may suggest Ōgai's feelings of independence from the naturalist literary movement.

"An Echo" is also an unusual story that Ōgai published under the pseudonym of Takugo Yajin. Whenever Franz calls out "Hello!," the word echoes back to him, but one day he hears no echo and concludes that the echo has died. This troubles him, and one night he sets out for the mountain. There seven children call out, and, when the echo answers their call, Franz thinks, "The echo hasn't died. But I will no longer call out to it. If I were to call again, it might answer. But I will not call again." Kobori considers these seven children to represent new

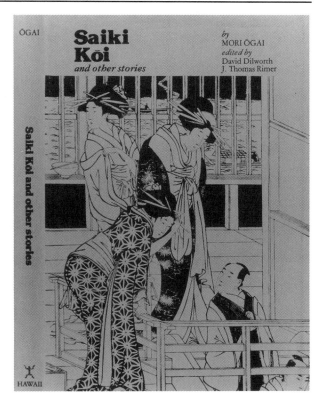

Dust jacket for a 1977 translation of stories by Ōgai. In the title story, written in 1917, he identifies himself with a rake of the Tokugawa Era.

poets such as Kinoshita Mokutarō and Kitahara Hakushū, who were members of the *Subaru* coterie, and he speculates that Ōgai "may have wanted to consign his hopes to the younger generation and suggests his intention to retreat from the literary scene."

In November 1909 Ōgai formally became a member of the Mitsukoshi Ryūkōkai, an association of the leading men of culture. Ōgai wrote stories such as "Saezuri" (Chirping, 1911) and "Ryūkō" (Fashion, 1911) for the in-house bulletin of the Mitsukoshi Department Store, which sponsored the group and catered to a distinguished clientele. These stories were written in recognition of the growing popularity of department stores.

On 1 June 1910 Kōtoku Shūsui and twenty-six conspirators were arrested by the police and charged with plotting to assassinate Emperor Meiji. In a closed trial they were found guilty of the crime of lèse majesté, and two conspirators received fixed prison terms, while twenty-four were sentenced to death. On the following day twelve of the condemned group had their sentences commuted to life imprisonment. During the pretrial hearings Ōgai published

"Chinmoku no tō" (1910; translated as "The Tower of Silence," 1994), his reaction to "Dangerous Western Books"—a series of articles published between 16 September and 4 October in the *Asahi Shinbun,* which warned readers about the "dangerous ideologies" to be found in the works of Guy de Maupassant, Henrik Ibsen, Pyotr Kropotkin, Gustave Flaubert, and others.

In "The Tower of Silence" Ōgai criticizes the ignorance that led authorities to conjoin works of naturalist and socialist literature in condemning them as dangerous books. "The values accepted by art lie in the breaking down of convention," he wrote. "Works which dawdle about within the bounds of convention are commonplace works. If one examines art through the eyes of convention, every form of art begins to appear dangerous."

In this piece Ōgai, whose political position was likely to make the authorities uneasy, emphasizes the fundamentally revolutionary nature of art. The de facto leader of the Meiji government who pressed these charges of treason was Yamagata Aritomo, and Ōgai, who was closely tied to Yamagata in the Tokiwa-kai poetry society, had to comment circumspectly. Ōgai was not sympathizing with the alleged conspirators, and he could not countenance the destruction of social order that might have resulted from the assassination of the emperor. He felt strongly that government officials must not undermine the values of art in the name of perpetuating conventional social order. This he makes clear in "Bungei no shugi" (The Principles of the Literary Arts, 1911): "It is lamentable that the State, in order to expel anarchy and the socialist doctrines that sprouted alongside it, should oppress the arts by slapping on them the abstract label of 'individualism.'" In "Shokudō" (1910; translated as "The Dining Room," 1994) the characters describe the defendants in the treason trial as "a frightening bunch" and oppose the death penalty for them, but the story also warns against haphazardly regarding these men as heroes.

Another ideological story is *Ka no yō ni* (1914; translated as *As If,* 1925), which raises a question about the legitimacy of the descent of imperial rule from fourteenth-century Japan, in which two rival courts had vied for power. This question arose following the treason trials, as in Ōgai's day the government-sanctioned textbooks used in primary and secondary schools considered both the northern and southern courts, which had coexisted for sixty-one years, to have

been legitimate. Gojō Hidemaro, the protagonist of *As If,* conveys Ōgai's personal views on contemporary events, and Ōgai opposed the attempt by the Japanese government to establish the southern court as the sole legitimate power. "If we do not consider things that do not exist *as if* they did exist, then morality cannot be established," Ōgai insisted in shaping his "as if" philosophy, by which he sought to find some way to accommodate the claims of both "fact" and "the system."

In the novella "Kaijin" (1911–1912; translated as "The Ashes of Destruction," 1994) Ōgai tries to critique and poke fun at the government's misdirected attempts to control newspapers as a means of controlling freedom of speech. As Ōgai begins to direct his attention toward the behavior of politicians in this story, he uses Setsuzō to criticize those who manipulate the media in order to bury stories that present those figures and their actions unfavorably and to turn all reportage in their favor.

Two works, "Sōmatō" (Kaleidoscope) and "Bunshin" (Alter Ego), were jointly published in June 1913 as part of *Bunshin,* a collection that also included "Hebi" (translated as "Snake," 1971), "Fuji tomoe" (Wisteria Crest), "Shinjū" (Double Suicide), "Hyaku monogatari" (Ghost Stories), "Nezumizaka" (Nezumi Slope), "Hatori Chihiro," and "Nagashi" (Sink). In this collection, which presents people and events as if they were scenes shaped and viewed in a kaleidoscope, Ōgai examines various events that he was observing. "Nezumi Slope" examines the evils that Japanese businessmen with political connections commit on Manchurian battlefields. "Sink" is based on the sad diaries of Ōshita Tōjirō, the young watercolor artist. Ōgai's notion of an "alter ego," which provides the title story for this collection, derives from his dual identity as a public figure and as a writer.

Emperor Meiji died on 30 July 1912, and the passing of this emperor who led Japan into the modern age deeply shocked many writers such as Natsume Sōseki and Ōgai. The state funeral was held on 13 September at the Aoyama Cemetery, and on that day Gen. Nogi Maresuke and his wife committed suicide in order to follow their master in death. Ōgai had respected General Nogi from his years in Berlin, and he was especially shocked and moved by the suicides of the general and his wife. After returning from their funeral, he began writing his first work of historical fiction, "Okitsu Yagoemon no isho" (1912; translated as "The Last Testament of Okitsu Yagoemon," 1971), which he submitted to *Chūō Kōron*.

The story concerns Okitsu and Yokota, retainers of Lord Hosokawa Sansai, who are sent to Nagasaki to buy scented wood for use in their master's tea ceremonies. They argue over the high price of the scented wood: the pragmatic Yokota finds it imprudent to spend too much money for "something like scented wood," while Okitsu insists that they must obey every order given by their lord. Yakota provokes Okitsu into a sword fight, and after Okitsu has killed Yakota, he reports what he has done to Lord Hosokawa. Okitsu fully intends to commit seppuku, but Hosokawa praises and pardons him. Okitsu feels deeply grateful to his master, and he becomes determined to follow Hosokawa in death. When his master dies, Okitsu then commits suicide.

Ōgai's story emphasizes the value of loyalty above practical concerns, and it conveys his respect for General Nogi, an officer who had lost a military flag during the Satsuma Rebellion. Emperor Meiji had pardoned Nogi for this, and the general had felt for the emperor the same gratitude that Okitsu feels for Lord Hosokawa. Both General Nogi and Okitsu were choosing to follow their masters in death.

In *Shibue Chūsai* (1916; translated as *The Woman in the Crested Kimono,* 1985) Ōgai writes: "After I began searching for materials for this piece in the past, due to various circumstances in my immediate surroundings, I started looking for pieces of evidence in the Tokugawa period." One can understand why Ōgai had to be careful about his "surroundings," his positions as surgeon general of the army and as close associate of Yamagata Aritomo, and he set his materials in the past when he incorporated political issues into his writing.

"Abe ichizoku" (1913; translated as "The Abe Family," 1977) is another work based on past events. Just before Hosokawa Tadatoshi, the lord of Higo, dies, many of his retainers request and receive his permission to commit suicide in order to be with him. Among the retainers of a master, permission to die with the master is an honor that assures the stability of their households for many generations, and, both as individuals and as families, those who are forbidden to kill themselves and are compelled to remain alive must bear the shame. Tadatoshi, believing that one of his retainers, Abe Yaichiemon, "somehow or other doesn't get along well with others," refuses to grant him permission to

commit suicide. After Tadatoshi has died, Yaichiemon is therefore forced to live in humiliation, and he eventually commits seppuku without receiving any official sanction. Mitsuhisa, the new ruler of the clan, and Hayashi Geki, the head surveillant of vassal conduct, severely censure Yaichiemon's act, and the entire Abe family is annihilated.

Ōgai concludes that "So long as government is consistent, no one can blame them for their decisions. But once treatment out of the norm is permitted, the question of who made the decision arises." Tadatoshi, Mitsuhisa, and Geki are all figures responsible for making political decisions, and Ōgai observes that when politicians make a wrong decision, people become victims and that he has borne this belief since the writing of *Vita Sexualis* and "The Tower of Silence."

"Sahashi Jingorō" (1913) tells how the arbitrary and inconsistent judgments of a ruler, Shogun Tokugawa Ieyasu, force Jingorō, a faithful follower, into the rebellious act of fleeing. Another tale, "Kuriyama Daizen" (1914), recounts the suffering of a retainer following the mistaken judgment of a ruler, Kuroda Tadayuki, who neglects his governmental duties. "Ōshiro Heihachirō" (1914) tells of Heihachirō, a former leader who can no longer endure the "successive years of famine, and the destitution of the common people." In league with his followers in Ōsaka, he attacks the offices of two magistrates in whom power is concentrated, but his rebellion is ultimately quelled, and he dies tragically.

Heihachirō's actions are haphazard, but, as Ōgai writes in his afterword,

> If Heihachirō had been able to rely upon the national or local governments and could have devised a method of deliverance [for the peasants] while still supporting the contemporary political order, he surely would have put in place some kind of social policy.... Ōsaka by this time had achieved a certain level of development as an independent political entity, and if there had been allowance for Heihachirō to utilize his skills, the rebellion most likely would never have broken out. Because these two alternatives were closed off to him, Heihachirō attempted to achieve his aims by destroying the contemporary order. His beliefs were an as-yet unawakened form of socialism.

Ōgai does not excuse or support Heihachirō's rebellion, but he clearly sees the political leaders in Ōsaka as the motives for Heihachirō's actions.

Sakai jiken (1914; translated as *The Incident at Sakai*, 1977) also presents of a conflict between political leaders and soldiers or commoners. In 1868 French sailors come ashore at Sakai Harbor without receiving official permission, and there they confront soldiers responsible for guarding the port. The citizens of Sakai are plunged into chaos, and in an attempt to restore order the Tosa officer in charge orders his men to fire their rifles. Thirteen French sailors are killed. The new Meiji government, bowing to pressure from French authorities seeking reparation, accept every demand that the French make, and twenty soldiers from Tosa are also condemned to die by being decapitated.

When these soldiers, chosen by the drawing of lots, beg for permission to commit seppuku, their request is finally granted. Ōgai movingly presents a protest by these common soldiers thrust before the authorities, as one of the soldiers cries out: "We are all convinced that what we did in Sakai was meritorious and in no way criminal. What sort of crime did we commit? Please explain it to us in a little more detail." Yet in other works Ōgai presents a model political leader, a figure such as Masamichi of "Sanshō Dayū" (1915; translated as "Sansho the Steward," 1951)—a work that, as Ōgai wrote, he had composed "in an attempt to separate myself from history."

Immediately after writing "Sansho the Steward" Ōgai published "Rekishi sono mama to rekishibanare" (1915; translated as "History As It Is and History Ignored," 1977), an essay in which he explained that his aim in writing historical novels had been "to examine the historical sources and respect the depiction of life 'as it really is' found in them." His reliance on historical materials seems suitable as a technique for criticizing political figures; yet as Ōgai continued to voice his disapproval, he apparently reached a time when he wished to "separate [himself] from history." His interests and sensitivities were thereafter warmly directed toward the common people living in the city, and this change accompanied his resignation from his position as head of the Bureau of Medical Affairs in April 1916.

As he aged, his attitudes grew increasingly tranquil and tolerant. *Takasebune* (1918; translated as *The Boat on the River Takase*, 1971) and "Kanzan Jittoku" (Han-shan and Shih-te, 1916) present his philosophical views during the final years of his life. "The Boat on the River Takase" is based on Kamizawa Teikan's "Okina-

gusa," and it addresses the issues of serenity and euthanasia. Kisuke, who is being exiled to an island for having helped his younger brother commit suicide, tells Shōbē, the constable in custody of him as they ride in a boat on the Takase River, that he "feels content." Shōbē, whose life is filled with discontent, is astonished to see Kisuke so grateful for the two hundred copper coins he has received from the authorities. The freshness of Ōgai's portrait of Shōbē is, no doubt, also a self-portrait.

"Kanzan Jittoku" is taken from the preface to a treatise on Han-shan's poetry written by Hakuin, a Zen priest. Ōgai pokes fun at Lü Ch'iu-yin, the Chinese keeper of records, who lives "like a blind man, respecting things he cannot see," and his portraits of Han-shan, the beggar priest, and of the self-indulgent Shih-te are stirring.

From the time he had written "The Dancing Girl," Ōgai had been forced to serve as a member of the government bureaucracy while he continued his search for his "true self." In his final years of life Ōgai intensely scrutinized himself and acknowledged the exhaustion he felt in having tried to live as both a public servant and a writer, an individual. *Shibue Chūsai* is an attempt to advance his studies of historical documents in order to find "history as it is" as well as to locate, in the figure of Chūsai, an idealized portrait of himself in his declining years. Chūsai (1805–1858) had also been both a doctor in the Hirosaki domain and a textual critic, and Ōgai's identification with him adds to the richness of this work.

Ōgai's *Izawa Ranken,* a monumental and exhaustive biography that presents Ranken as Chūsai's teacher, was serialized in the newspaper *Nichinichi Shinbun* in 1916–1917. While Ōgai presents his own views of Chūsai and his wife, Io, in the former work, he wrote *Izawa Ranken* with what he describes as "an attitude-less attitude." Because he refused to express his personal views about Ranken, the biography was repeatedly criticized as "pointless" even while it was being serialized.

After resigning in 1916 as head of the Bureau of Medical Affairs, a position that he had held for about nine years, Ōgai assumed a post as director of the Imperial Museum and Library. In his last years he suffered from a kidney condition, which eventually proved to be fatal.

Biographies:
Mori Rui, *Ōgai no kodomotachi: Ato ni nokosareta*

mono no kiroku (Tokyo: Kōbunsha, Kappa, 1956);

Mori Mari, *Chichi no bōshi* (Tokyo: Chikuma Shobō, 1956; expanded edition, Tokyo: Kōdansha Bungei Bunko, 1991);

Kobori Annu, *Chichi: Bannen no Mori Ōgai* (Tokyo: Hōbunkan, 1957);

Kobori, *Wakaki hi no Mori Ōgai* (Tokyo: Tokyo Daigaku Shuppankai, 1969).

References:

Richard John Bowring, *Mori Ōgai and the Modernization of Japanese Culture* (Cambridge: Cambridge University Press, 1979);

Hasegawa Izumi, *Mori Ōgai ronkō* (Tokyo: Meiji Shoin, 1962);

Hasegawa, *Ōgai bungaku no isō* (Tokyo: Meiji Shoin, 1974);

Hasegawa, *Ōgai "Vita sekusuarisu" kō* (Tokyo: Meiji Shoin, 1968);

Hasegawa, *Zoku Ōgai 'Vita sekusuarisu' kō* (Tokyo: Meiji Shoin, 1971);

Inagaki Tatsurō, *Mori Ōgai no rekishi shōsetsu* (Tokyo: Iwanami Shoten, 1989);

Kobori Keiichirō, *Mori Ōgai: Bungyō kaidai (hon'yaku-hen)* (Tokyo: Iwanami Shoten, 1982);

Kobori, *Mori Ōgai: Bungyō kaidai (sōsaku-hen)* (Tokyo: Iwanami Shoten, 1982);

Kobori, *Mori Ōgai no sekai* (Tokyo: Kōdansha, 1971);

Koizumi Kōichirō, *Mori Ōgai ron–Jisshō to hihyō* (Tokyo: Meiji Shoin, 1981);

Marvin Marcus, *Paragons of the Ordinary: The Biographical Literature of Mori Ōgai* (Honolulu: University of Hawaii Press, 1993);

Seita Fumitake, *Mori Ōgai bungei no kenkyū–chūnenki-hen* (Tokyo: Yūseidō, 1991);

Seita, *Mori Ōgai bungei no kenkyū–seinenki-hen* (Tokyo: Yūseidō, 1991);

Shibukawa Gyō, *Mori Ōgai: Sakka to sakuhin* (Tokyo: Chikuma Shobō, 1964);

Takemori Tenyū, *Ōgai sono mon'yō* (Tokyo: Ozawa Shoten, 1984);

Yamazaki Kazuhide, *Mori Ōgai: Rekishi shōsetsu kenkyū* (Tokyo: Ōfūsha, 1981);

Yamazaki, *Mori Ōgai: Shiden shōsetsu kenkyū* (Tokyo: Ōfūsha, 1982);

Yamazaki Kuninori, *Mori Ōgai: Kisōteki ronkyu* (Tokyo: Yagi Shoten, 1989);

Yamazaki, *Mori Ōgai: Urami ni ikiru* (Tokyo: Kōdansha, Kōdansha Gendai Shinsho, 1976);

Yamazaki, *Ōgai–Mori Rintarō* (Tokyo: Jinbun Shoin, 1992);

Yamazaki, ed., *Mori Ōgai: Haha no nikki* (Tokyo: San'ichi Shobō, 1985);

Yamazaki, ed., *Mori Ōgai o manabu hito no tame ni* (Tokyo: Sekai Shisōsha, 1994);

Yamazaki Masakazu, *Ōgai: Tatakau kachō* (Tokyo: Kawade Shobō Shinsha, 1972).

Nagai Kafū
(3 December 1879 – 30 April 1959)

Sakagami Hiroichi
Meiji University

BOOKS: *Yashin* (Tokyo: Biikusha, 1902);
Jigoku no hana (Tokyo: Kinkōdō, 1902);
Yume no onna (Tokyo: Shinseisha, 1903);
Joyū Nana (Tokyo: Shinseisha, 1903);
Koi to yaiba (Tokyo: Shinseisha, 1903);
Amerika monogatari (Tokyo: Hakubunkan, 1908);
Furansu monogatari (Tokyo: Hakubunkan, 1909);
Kanraku (Tokyo: Ekifūsha, 1909);
Kafū shū (Tokyo: Ekifūsha, 1909);
Sumidagawa (Tokyo: Momiyama Shoten, 1909); translated by Donald Keene as "The River Sumida," in *Modern Japanese Literature,* edited by Keene (New York: Grove, 1965), pp. 159–200;
Reishō (Tokyo: Sakura Shobō, 1910);
Botan no kyaku (Tokyo: Momiyama Shoten, 1911);
Kōcha no ato (Tokyo: Momiyama Shoten, 1911);
Shinkyō yawa (Tokyo: Momiyama Shoten, 1912);
Sangoshū (Tokyo: Momiyama Shoten, 1913);
Chiruyanagi mado no yūbae (Tokyo: Momiyama Shoten, 1914);
Natsu sugata (Tokyo: Momiyama Shoten, 1915);
Shinpen Furansu monogatari (Tokyo: Hakubunkan, 1915);
Hiyori geta (Tokyo: Momiyama Shoten, 1915);
Saiyū nisshi shō (Tokyo, 1917);
Danchōtei zakkō (Tokyo: Momiyama Shoten, 1918);
Udekurabe (Tokyo: Shinbashidō, 1918); translated by Kurt Meissner and Ralph Friederich as *Geisha in Rivalry* (Tokyo & Rutland, Vt.: Tuttle, 1963);
Okamezasa (Tokyo: Shun'yōdō, 1918);
Edo geijutsuron (Tokyo: Shun'yōdō, 1920);
Mitsugashiwa kozue no yoarashi (Tokyo: Shun'yōdō, 1921);
Aki no wakare (Tokyo: Shun'yōdō, 1922);
Futarizuma (Tokyo: Tōkōkaku Shoten, 1923);
Azabu zakki (Tokyo: Shun'yōdō, 1924);
Shitaya sōwa (Tokyo: Shun'yōdō, 1924);
Kafū bunkō (Tokyo: Shun'yōdō, 1926);

Nagai Kafū, after receiving the Imperial Cultural Decoration in 1952

Tsuyu no atosaki (Tokyo: Chūō Kōronsha, 1931); translated by Lane Dunlop as *During the Rains* (Stanford, Cal.: Stanford University Press, 1994);
Fuyu no hae (Tokyo: Privately published, 1935);
Kihen no ki (Tokyo: Seitōsha, 1936);
Bokutō kitan (Tokyo: Iwanami Shoten, 1937); translated by Edward G. Seidensticker as "A Strange Tale from East of the River," in

his *Kafū the Scribbler, The Life and Writings of Nagai Kafū, 1879–1959* (Stanford, Cal.: Stanford University Press, 1965);

Omokage (Tokyo: Iwanami Shoten, 1938);

Kunsai manpitsu (Tokyo: Fuzanbō, 1939);

Towazugatari (Tokyo: Fusō Shobō, 1946);

Raihōsha (Tokyo: Chikuma Shobō, 1946);

Hikage no hana (Tokyo: Chūō Kōronsha, 1946);

Ukishizumi (Tokyo: Chūō Kōronsha, 1947);

Risai nichiroku (Tokyo: Fusō Shobō, 1947);

Kunshō (Tokyo: Fusō Shobō, 1947);

Kafū nichireki (Tokyo: Fusō Shobō, 1947);

Kafū kushū (Tokyo: Hosokawa Shoten, 1948);

Henkikan ginsō (Tokyo: Chikuma Shobō, 1948);

Odoriko (Tokyo: Chikuma Shobō, 1949);

Zassōen (Tokyo: Chūō Kōronsha, 1949);

Katsushika miyage (Tokyo: Chūō Kōronsha, 1950);

Ratai (Tokyo: Chūō Kōronsha, 1954);

Katsushika koyomi (Tokyo: Mainichi Shinbunsha, 1956);

Azumabashi (Tokyo: Chūō Kōronsha, 1957);

Nagai Kafū nikki (Tokyo: Tōto Shobō, 1957–1958);

Danchōtei nichijō (N.p., 1959).

Collections: *Kafū zenshū,* 6 volumes (Tokyo: Shun'yōdō, 1918–1923);

Kafū zuihitsu, (Tokyo: Chūō Kōronsha, 1933);

Kafū zenshū, 24 volumes (Tokyo: Chūō Kōronsha, 1948–1953);

Kafū zenshū, 28 volumes (Tokyo: Iwanami Shoten, 1962–1965);

Kafū zenshū, 30 volumes to date (Tokyo: Iwanami Shoten, 1992–).

PLAY PRODUCTION: *Katsushika jōwa,* libretto by Kafū, Tokyo, Asakusa Kōen Rokku Opera-kan, 17 May 1938.

Nagai Kafū wrote many poetic essays as well as stories that, although infused with realism, retain their lyricism. He battled the coarseness of the world around him through the way he chose to live, continually at odds with the modernization of Japan. Kafū initially began as a naturalist writer under the influence of Emile Zola, but he flourished as an antinaturalist author whose work represented an aesthetic mode. He was deeply drawn to the culture of the Edo period and reflected that interest in his writings, and he adopted features of the life of an Edo man of culture into his own. Unlike the many writers who collaborated with the military government during World War II, Kafū was one of a handful of authors who coldly turned his back on the war effort.

Nagai Kafū (whose given name was Nagai Sōkichi), the eldest son of Kyūichirō and Tsune, was born in 1879 at Kanatomi-chō, Koishikawa, in the hilly Yamanote district of Tokyo. Other artists born in the same year included the naturalistic author Masamune Hakuchō and the realist poet Nagatsuka Takashi; Kafū was a year younger than both Arishima Takeo of the Shirakaba-ha group and Yosano Akiko, the romantic woman poet. Although Kafū had little personal association with these authors and Masamune's style and theoretical orientation differed from Kafū's, Masamune understood Kafū's works because of their shared generational experience, and at times the two writers engaged in literary debates.

The Nagai family's ancestors had been vassals of Ieyasu, the first Tokugawa shogun, and Kafū's family had become wealthy in the Owari region (the present Aichi Prefecture). Kafū's father had studied Confucian ethics with Washizu Kido, a scholar at the Meirindō academy operated by the Owari domain, and being drawn toward Chinese poetry Kyūichirō had attained fame for his poetic compositions in Chinese and published ten volumes of Chinese poetry under the pen name of Kagen. In 1870 the Owari domain sent him to Tokyo, where he enrolled in the school that became Tokyo University. The following year he was ordered to travel to the United States, where he studied at Princeton and other universities. After returning to Japan, Kyūichirō took a post with the Ministry of Education, where he poured his energies into the founding of libraries and museums.

In 1878 he married Tsune, the daughter of his Confucian teacher Kido, and began working in the Public Health Bureau of the Ministry of Home Affairs. Until his retirement from government service in 1898, he served as a high-ranking bureaucrat in the Ministry of Education; when he left that position, he became branch director of the Shanghai and Yokohama offices of the Japan Mail Lines corporation. The successful Kyūichirō was often the object of the young Kafū's fear and rebellion, but many of Kafū's writings reveal a profound respect for his father's education and the manner in which he combined Asian and Western qualities in his life.

A glimpse of the family home where Kafū spent his childhood can be found in his story "Kitsune" (The Fox, 1909). Three samurai residences belonging to retainers of the Tokugawa shogunate were purchased and remodeled into a spacious mansion on an estate with an ancient

Kafū's family, at Okubo, Tokyo, in 1902: his mother, Kafū, his father, and his brothers, Teijirō and Isaburō

well and a grove of trees, where foxes were said to come and go. Nearby was the Denzūin Temple that the Tokugawa family revered. Kafū's essay "Denzūin" (1910) reveals that his romantic nature was fostered by the puppet shows, storytelling festivals, and other popular events held just outside the gate of the mansion.

Kafū's mother was also fond of plays and artistic performances, and she was proficient at *nagauta* (song-stories) and in playing the koto. In the story "Kangokusho no ura" (Behind the Prison, 1909) Kafū fondly recalls being taken by his mother to enjoy play performances and oral tales illustrated with woodblock prints painted on long strips of brocade. When a brother was born in 1883, maternal relatives in Shitaya, in the downtown Shitamachi district of Tokyo, took Kafū for a time, and there he began attending a nursery school affiliated with the Ochanomizu Women's College. The family house at Shitaya, a samurai mansion decorated with swords and armor, is described in "Shitaya no ie" (The House at Shitaya, 1911). Miyo, Kafū's grand-

mother, later converted to Christianity, and she continued to influence Kafū's mother and his younger brothers.

In 1891 Kafū enrolled in the middle school operated by the secondary education program at Kanda Hitotsubashi College, and such essays as "Gakki" (Musical Instruments, 1911), "Natsu no machi" (The Town in Summer, 1910), "Jūroku-shichi no koro" (When I Was Sixteen or Seventeen, 1934), and "Mokusei no hana" (Sweet Osmanthus Flowers, 1947) recount his experiences during these days. One of his classmates at the school was Terauchi Juichi, who later became a general in the Japanese army and once roundly criticized Kafū for writing an article in praise of extravagance and publishing it in the school's alumni magazine.

In 1894 Kafū was hospitalized for treatment of a tubercular boil in the Tokyo University Hospital, where he fell in love with a nurse named O-ren. It has been suggested that he derived his pen name, Kafū (meaning "breeze in the lotus"), from its association with her name,

The Nagai family house in Okubo

ren, which is another name for lotus. Kafū's physical condition grew worse after a cold, and he continued to recuperate in a hospital at Odawara and in a cottage at Zushi until the middle of 1895. During this time his reading—of the Chinese epic tales *The Water Margin* and *Tale of Three Kingdoms,* the Japanese tale *Hakkenden* (Biographies of Eight Dogs, 1814–1841), and English novels—fostered his interest in literature. His mother encouraged this interest, and he also learned to play the *shakuhachi* (bamboo flute) during his recovery.

In March 1897 he failed the entrance exam to the First Higher School, the elite school from which graduates advanced to Tokyo University, and this failure infuriated his father, who had hoped that Kafū would pursue the elite course. As Kafū recalls in his essay "Kugatsu" (September, 1910), however, the despair that the young man felt following this failure ironically drew him to the life of ease enjoyed by social outcasts. During that autumn Kafū joined his parents and younger brother on a visit to Shanghai, where his father was managing the shipping company,

and the young man wrote of those experiences in "Shanghai kikō" (A Trip to Shanghai, 1898). Partly motivated by his enjoyment of that sojourn, Kafū in November entered the Chinese language department at the School of Foreign Languages, where he studied until he was expelled in December the following year.

Because his father remained working in Shanghai until February 1900, Kafū enjoyed a profligate adolescence in the unsupervised atmosphere at home: he frequently visited the pleasure quarters at Yoshiwara and Susaki. In fall 1898 he became a literary disciple of Hirotsu Ryūrō, a member of the Ken'yūsha, a literary society that was forming around Ozaki Kōyō, a popular writer who had gained fame by writing novels that realistically presented the dark side of contemporary society. Following Hirotsu's lead, Kafū published a series of stories—"Oboroyo" (Misty Night, 1899), "Enkoi" (Opium Addict, 1900), and "Hanakago" (Flower Basket, 1899)—in the Ken'yūsha mode. Leading the life of a disciple at the bottom of the social scale, he also began studying *rakugo* (comic storytelling).

Kafū in Shanghai, on an 1897 visit that he described in "Shanghai kikō" (A Trip to Shanghai, 1898)

In June 1900 Kafū apprenticed himself to study writing with Fukuchi Ōchi, a leading playwright at the Kabuki theater. There he did every kind of work, from cleaning rooms to welcoming guests, and even learned to beat the wooden clappers that announced the beginning of a performance. He also joined the Thursday Literary Society headed by Iwaya Sazanami, another member of the Ken'yusha circle, and there he developed friendships with other young writers.

When Fukuchi was appointed chief writer for the *Yamato Shinbun* newspaper in April 1901, Kafū followed him as a correspondent for the paper, and there he published a serialized novel, *Shin umegoyomi* (The New Plum Calendar). In September, Kafū was fired without warning, and he then began attending night school to study French at the Gyōsei Gakkō. As an employee of the Kabuki theater, he had already learned something about French literature and Zola's works, which had been imported into Meiji literature as pieces representing French naturalism and had launched a period of Zolaism. Kosugi Tengai took the lead in the new movement by imitating Zola's emphasis on heredity and environment in

works such as "Hatsusugata" (Debutante's Finery, 1900) and "Hayariuta" (Popular Song, 1902). Following Kosugi's example Kafū also became a representative writer of the Zola school.

The first of such works that Kafū published was *Yashin* (Ambition, 1902), which recounts how the heir to an old shop, in his attempts to make it into a modern department store, goes bankrupt through his high-handed attitudes. The work that brought him instant fame was *Jigoku no hana* (The Flowers of Hell, 1902), a novel in which a female tutor, after witnessing the collapse of the upper-class home where she works, begins her search for a new freedom. In his epilogue to the work Kafū presents striking evidence of his understanding of Zola's essay "The Experimental Novel." Another work by Kafū, "Shinnin chiji" (New Governor, 1902), describes the vainglorious activities of a husband and wife who will adopt any means in order to achieve the goal of the day, *risshin shusse* (to rise in the world). The model for this ambitious protagonist was Kafū's uncle, who became governor of Fukui Prefecture; after the story was published, he severed all ties with Kafū.

Kafū's third novel, *Yume no onna* (The Woman of the Dream, 1903), presents the life of the daughter of a samurai family, a woman who begins as a mistress, then becomes a licensed prostitute, and finally manages to become the owner of her own assignation house. Kafū avoids becoming ideological in this novel, and his depictions of the scenery are lyrical. Other stories he wrote around this time include "Yami no sakebi" (Cry from the Darkness, 1902), "Yoru no kokoro" (Heart of the Night, 1903), and "Tōka no chimata" (Town of Lights, 1903), all of which oppose conventional morality and express yearnings for freedom.

Disturbed by his son's activities, Kyūichirō in September 1903 sent Kafū to study in the United States, where he hoped that Kafū would acquire some practical business sense. Kafū had been attracted to Western culture for some time and had dreamed of visiting France, so he acquiesced with his father's plans—in hopes of realizing his own dreams. The outlines of Kafū's activities are recorded in his "Saiyū nisshi shō" (Leaves from a Journal of My Western Excursion, 1917).

He first settled in Tacoma, Washington, where he lived in the home of one of his father's acquaintances, the manager of the Furuya Store, and enrolled at Stadium High School. He was deeply moved by the natural beauty of the

United States and touched by the miserable lives of Japanese migrant laborers in the Northwest, and he expressed these feelings in several works. Gradually his sensibilities began to change, as his sympathies shifted from the work of Zola and toward the writings of Guy de Maupassant and Alphonse Daudet.

Kafū left Tacoma in October 1904 to attend the World Exposition held that year in Saint Louis, Missouri, and then started auditing classes at Kalamazoo College in Michigan. As his admiration for France grew, he wrote several pieces heavily influenced by his reading of de Maupassant. In June 1905 he traveled to New York, where he met Nagai Matsuzō, a cousin who worked at the Japanese consulate. He discussed his plans to travel to France with Matsuzō and moved into the Japanese legation office in Washington, D.C., where he worked to raise money for this journey. When his father opposed these plans to travel to France, a disappointed Kafū met Edyth, an American prostitute with whom he spent the next two years in a life of dissipation. After the signing of the peace treaty to end the Russo-Japanese War, Kafū was discharged from his position by the legation office. He returned to Kalamazoo for a while, and his father soon ordered him to take a trainee job that he had arranged for Kafū at the New York branch of the Yokohama Specie Bank. Throughout these experiences Kafū continued to write, and many of his pieces were collected later in *Amerika monogatari* (Tales of America, 1908). He also achieved some of his artistic goals by attending many concerts, plays, and especially operas.

When Kafū's father arranged for him to be transferred to the Lyon branch of the Specie Bank in July 1907, the young writer realized his dream of visiting France. Toward the end of that month he journeyed from the port of Le Havre to Paris and then to Lyons. His heart was not in the business of banking, however, and in March 1908 he resigned his position. Shortly thereafter he received a letter from his father, who ordered him back to Japan. At the end of the month he left Lyon and spent two months in Paris before heading back to Japan at the end of May.

During his stay in Paris, Kafū generally spent his days visiting famous tourist sites or cemeteries, and at night he went to the opera or the theater. His time in Paris, unlike his gloomy sojourn in Lyon, was filled with a feeling of emancipation, and he therefore found his departure from Paris, as "Pari no wakare" (Farewell to Paris, 1908) records, to be painful. His stay in

Cover for the unauthorized edition of Kafū's third novel, Yume no onna *(The Woman of the Dream, 1903)*

France, for which he had so desperately yearned, was all too short in comparison with the three years that he had resided in the United States. He learned that the stories he had been sending to Iwaya Sazanami while he was still in America had been published in various journals, and, perhaps anticipating that his pieces might be collected together in *Tales of America,* he spent his last two months enjoying a rush of activities in Paris as a means to add to his experiences and to his confidence as a writer.

The experiences that Kafū had in the United States and France nurtured the individualism that characterized his life. He was not blinded by the superficial display of Western culture, but he was attuned to the foundations of individual freedom and independence that sustained the material surfaces of that culture, and even after he returned to Japan, Kafū resolved that he would seek to establish his own life on those foundations. In a Japan buttressed by the imperial institution and the patriarchal family, however, this determination could create only conflict with his native culture, which was con-

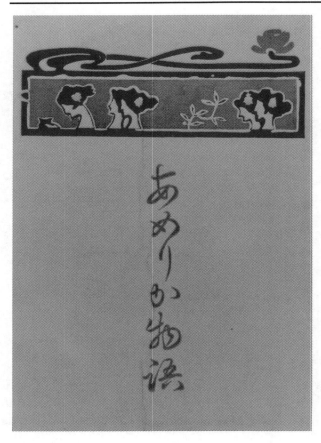

Cover for Amerika monogatari *(Tales of America, 1908),*
Kafū's narrative of his travels in the United States,
1903–1907

stantly directed toward marginalizing such a way of living. Yet Kafū boldly severed his ties with his surroundings (with his relatives and later with his journalistic fraternity), chose a way of living that took money as its means, and carried on with his liberated but isolated artistic life.

By traveling from America to France, Kafū had also become aware of the fact that older traditions continued to thrive in the midst of modern civilization, and he was able to observe a judicious harmony between cultural tradition and a spirit of modernization. In returning with such a vision to the Japan of the Meiji period, he was particularly disturbed to see the ugly realities of a Tokyo in disarray during an age of transition, as though this disarray were a symbol for that of all Japan at the time, and Kafū's disgust aroused the vicious critiques of culture that became such hallmarks of his work. To Kafū the essential characteristics of Meiji culture were nothing more than a vanity, a duplicity, and a utilitarianism born in a superficial attempt to mimic the West. Each work Kafū published following his return

to Japan evidences those beliefs.

He returned in July 1908, and *Tales of America,* which included a total of twenty-four works that he had sent to Iwaya Sazanami from his days in the United States and France, was praised for its fresh sensibilities, its elegant style, and its rich evocation of foreign moods. Among its mix of short travel accounts and fictional tales, some works recount the bleak lives of Japanese living overseas; some reveal the tragicomic fates of men who become martyrs to pleasure; some condemn the feudal paternalism of the Japanese family and extol the familial love enjoyed in free lands; and others present night scenes of brothels and narrow alleyways. The contents of the collection are varied, and one can detect in these works a shift away from the influence of Zola and toward the influence of de Maupassant and Charles Baudelaire. Naturalist critics responded favorably to the stories, which they praised highly for depicting the dark side of life and for doing so with a nihilistic tone.

Furansu monogatari (Tales of France, 1909), published the following February, was banned by government censors as injurious to public morals, and in November 1915 a reconstituted edition was published. Composed of twenty-one stories and essays, the first edition includes the story "Hōtō" (Dissipation); the personal essays "Furansu nikki" (France Diary), "Tochi no ochiba" (Fallen Chestnut Leaves), and "Kaerimichi" (The Path Home); a play, "Ikyō no koi" (Love in a Foreign Land); and four critical essays on music and drama. Many of the works are lyrical impressions based on Kafū's experiences in France. The collection is filled with beautifully cascading expressions of poetic melancholy and weariness. Works such as "The Path Home" betray Kafū's mounting hatred of modern Japan.

Kafū's power peaked in 1909, as he produced the following works in succession: "The Fox," which uses memories of childhood to attack the patriarchal system and the hypocrisy of adults; "Fukagawa no uta" (Song of Fukagawa), containing expressions of Kafū's nostalgic longing for what remains of the old in the chaotically modernized city of Tokyo and in the Shitamachi district of Fukagawa; "Donten" (Overcast Sky), which expresses how out of place and helpless he felt upon returning to his homeland; "Behind the prison," bemoaning the constraints of familial ties and Kafū's sense of isolation; "Shukuhai" (A Toast), which acknowledges his indulgences as a young man; "Haru no otozure" (The Arrival of Spring) and "Hana yori ame ni" (From Flowers to Rain), two works that vividly depict the Japanese natural environment as seen by a native traveler returning from a foreign land; "Kanraku" (Pleasure), in which Kafū, while recounting his experiences with women, acknowledges his stance as an artist to be that of a pleasure seeker; and "Botan no kyaku" (translated as "The Peony Garden," 1965), expressing his feelings of exhaustion and ennui as he sets out with a geisha to view the peonies. Although the censors also banned *Kanraku*, the collection in which these stories appeared, for being dangerous to public morality, Kafū came to be seen as the champion of the aesthetic school of writers who opposed the mainstream Naturalists.

Kafū then published "Kichōsha no nikki" (Diary of a Man Back from Overseas, 1909), a biting critique of the vulgarity and confusion of Japanese civilization in the Meiji period, and the lyrical "Sumidagawa" (1909; translated as "The River Sumida," 1956). This latter work, set in the environs of the Sumida River and allowing Kafū to include fresh descriptions of nature, is a tale about the lamentable first love of a young man and presents Kafū's feelings toward those left behind by modernization. In "Reishō" (Sneers, 1909–1910) Kafū employs the words and actions of five characters, each a manifestation of a part of himself, to critique modern culture and to express his yearning for the Edo period. *Waseda Bungaku,* the journal that was the base for Naturalistic writers of the day, praised each of these works.

In February 1910, upon the recommendations of Ueda Bin and Mori Ōgai, the latter of whom was the most powerful figure in Japanese literature at that time, Kafū was appointed as a professor of literature at Keiō University. In May he initiated publication of *Mita Bungaku,* a journal that fostered the talents of influential new writers such as Kubota Mantarō, Minakami Takitarō, Satō Haruo, and Horiguchi Daigaku, a group that became known as the Mita School. Kafū also heaped praise on Tanizaki Jun'ichirō, then an unknown writer whom he ceremoniously thrust into the center of literary circles. In *Mita Bungaku* Kafū published the essays later collected in *Kōcha no ato* (After tea, 1911), which express his growing distaste for present reality and admiration for the culture of the Edo age.

In 1910 and 1911 several anarchists, including Kōtoku Shusui, were charged with grand treason and executed for plotting the assassination of Emperor Meiji. During the closed trial many writers responded sensitively to the alleged

Wedding picture of Kafū and Yone, his first wife, in 1912

plot, but as Kafū recalled in "Hanabi" (Fireworks, 1919), he was shocked to witness the procession of wagons carrying the accused conspirators through the streets of Tokyo, and he concluded that if a writer such as he could not publicly take a stand on such matters of conscience, then he could only surrender his qualifications to be a modern writer and respond as the *gesaku* writers of the Edo Period had done—by producing only comic or romantic fiction in an age of repression. Works such as "Shōtaku" (The Kept Woman's House, 1912), his geisha romance novel, and stories such as "Kaketori" (The Bill Collector, 1912) or "Kazegokochi" (Coming Down with a Cold, 1912), which were collected in *Shinkyō yawa* (Night tales from Shinbashi, 1912), were inspired by such feelings.

Although Kafū had long maintained plans for living as a hedonist and had continued to frequent the high-class pleasure quarters at Yanagibashi and Shinbashi after his return from France, in September 1912 he consented to an arranged marriage with Yone, the daughter of a lumber merchant at Hongō. Their personalities did not mesh, however, and Kafū was staying at Hakone with Yaeji, a Shinbashi geisha, when he received

Kafū's painting of the Henkikan (Eccentricity House) in Azabu, where he lived from 1920 until 1945 (from Edward G. Seidensticker, Kafū the Scribbler, *1965)*

news of his father's death. He eventually sought a divorce from Yone and formally married Yaeji in August 1914, but shortly thereafter Yaeji, dissatisfied with Kafū's womanizing, left him and filed for divorce. Kafū was involved with many women during subsequent years, but he never again married.

Kafū's love for French literature did remain strong, and he channeled some of that affection into translating works of modern French poets such as Paul Verlaine and Baudelaire. He trans-

lated thirty-eight poems and several works of prose and added critical writings on de Maupassant and Pierre Loti in *Sangoshū* (Coral Anthology, 1913), which young Japanese poets found to be an influential collection. At the same time his nostalgia for the Edo period, which served as a counterpart to his attachment for France, also deepened, and he published works such as "Gesakusha no shi" (The Death of a Frivolous Writer, 1913). In this piece Ryūtei Tanehiko, a representative *gesaku* writer of the late Edo period, is the protagonist who becomes a tragic victim of the evil administrative policies of the shogunate during the era of the Tenpō Reforms in the 1840s. Kafū also produced many essays on ukiyo-e, Edo theater, and *kyōka* (mad verse) of the Edo period, all of which were collected in *Edo geijutsuron* (The Arts of Edo, 1920). Hoping to locate the traces of neighborhoods surviving from the Edo age, he stuck a map of old Edo into his kimono, strolled throughout Tokyo, and published a record of his findings in "Hiyori geta" (Fair-Weather Clogs, 1915).

Citing ill health but in fact increasingly at odds with the administration at Keiō University, Kafū resigned from the faculty in February 1916. He then remodeled his residence, which he named the Danchōtei (Dyspepsia House), in Ōkubo and undertook more gesaku-writer activities, such as starting up the journals *Bunmei* and *Kagetsu*. In *Bunmei* he published "Yahazugusa" (Japanese Clover, 1916), recollections of his affair with Yaeji; *Saiyū nisshi shō*, recording his experiences in the United States; and the serialization of *Udekurabe* (1918; translated as *Geisha in Rivalry*, 1963).

At first *Geisha in Rivalry* was privately published, but after several parts of the text were cut, the book was published in a popular edition. The main character is Komayo, a Shinbashi geisha surrounded by businessmen, actors, and writers who are fickle representatives of the new age, and by an old-fashioned drama critic who has formerly been a professional storyteller and is the present owner of a geisha house. In presenting the connections between money and sex, the novel critiques the underside of the flowery world of the Shinbashi pleasure quarters that Kafū knew so well. Kafū skillfully represents subtle shifts in the seasons, and the work is infused with his poetic sentiment.

Okamezasa (Dwarf Bamboo, 1918), first serialized in *Kagetsu,* is set in the second- and third-rate prostitution districts that lacked the elegance of Shinbashi. As something of a social satire, this novel presents another array of characters: a famed but snobbish artist and his wayward son; a cunning art dealer and a high-ranking bureaucrat desperate for fame and fortune; and the protagonist, a banal artist who manages to achieve an unexpected happiness.

Drawn to the old *shitamachi* downtown district of Tokyo, Kafū sold Dyspepsia House and lived for a time at Tsukiji, but in May 1920, tormented by blaring record players and other annoyances in his surroundings, he moved into a two-story painted house that he built in Western style at Azabu and that he named Henkikan (Eccentricity House). Here he lived alone until this house was burned to the ground in Allied air raids during March 1945. Eccentricity House was a chateau that helped Kafū sustain the rational, individualistic life that he had chosen.

The period through the 1920s and until the publication of *Tsuyu no atosaki* (1931; translated as *During the Rains,* 1994) marked a time of stagnancy in Kafū's career. He published little fiction worth mentioning during these years–except for "Ame shōshō" (1921; translated as "Quiet Rain," 1964), which is filled with lyrical passages expressing the sadness of a man living in seclusion and the regrets he feels about the changes in the world around him; and "Yukige" (Thaw, 1922), which recounts the feelings of a ruined man when he meets a young woman who has become a geisha. Kafū's interests in Edo culture became far more than a pastime during this period; they absorbed him.

He published *Aki no wakare* (Farewell in Autumn, 1922), a collection of Kabuki scripts, and *Azabu zakki* (Azabu Miscellany, 1924), a collection of nostalgic essays. Influenced by the biographical novels being published by Mori Ōgai, whom he had long respected as a teacher, Kafū wrote *Shitaya sōwa* (Shitaya Gleanings, 1924), a series of biographical accounts of Washizu Kidō, Kafū's grandfather, and Ōnuma Chinzan, one of Kidō's relatives who wrote poetry in Chinese and whose personality and life, Kafū finds, were similar to his own. After publishing this work, Kafū used one of his several pen names in the title for his *Kunsai manpitsu* (Random Jottings by Kunsai, 1939), which included biographies of Ōta Nampo and others. Ōta, known by his pen name of Shokusanjin, had been an erudite man of the mid Edo period and a writer not only of comic skyōka verse but also of Chinese poetry and prose. Kafū admired Ōta more than any other individual.

On 1 September 1923 the Great Kantō Earthquake destroyed every remaining trace of the old Edo from Tokyo, and the city that was rebuilt on those ruins was profoundly changed into a modern metropolis shaped by a craze for American things. Kafū viewed these transformations critically, but he was also intrigued by the new features of the city. The new cafés of the Ginza replaced the pleasure quarters as places where he sought amusement, and he studied the lives of the waitresses there with the eyes of a nihilistic spectator who occasionally initiated relationships with some of these women. The fruits of these observations came with his publication of *During the Rains*.

Readers' interests during these times were dominated by proletarian literature, on the one hand, and by European modernism, on the other, and the popularity of established Japanese writers was generally low. Kafū and his work were on the verge of oblivion, but he managed to publish a handful of stories that sustained the readers he had held until he published *During the Rains*. These works include "Chijirashigami" (Frizzled Hair, 1925), in which a young man learns that his lover once had an affair with his father; "Kashima no onna" (Woman in the Rented Room, 1926), about a beautiful prostitute who, proud of her body, is able to flit from one man to another; and "Ajisai" (1931; translated as "Hydrangea," 1961), which depicts the life of a geisha who loses her life through her willingness to respond to the advances of any man. Replaced by the arid gaze of a writer who gives prominence to the physical body, the poetic emotions that had characterized Kafū's early works disappear from these stories.

In *During the Rains* Kafū presents Kimie, a café waitress from the Ginza, as his heroine, and he coolly reveals her dissolute character and actions, the attitudes of the customers who seek her out, and the state of the world represented by the Ginza after dark. A nihilistic mood about the transiency of life underlies this novel, which marks the bounds of Kafū's writing completed after the Great Earthquake. Tanizaki Jun'ichirō praised *During the Rains,* and the novel marked a revival in Kafū's writing. His next novel, *Hikage no hana* (Flowers in the Shade, 1946), concerns an unlicensed prostitute and an ineffectual husband who relies on her for his livelihood as the two of them flee from the police and live resignedly "in the shade." The natural settings through which Kafū had created an air of lyricism in his earlier works are virtually absent from this novel, the

Illustration by Kimura Shōhachi for Bokutō kitan *(1937; translated as* "A Strange Tale from East of the River," *1965)*

focus of which remains the desolate lives of individuals driven into a corner, and this approach betokens some revival of the influence of French naturalism that had so attracted Kafū in his early work.

Around 1935 Kafū, who had enjoyed strolling the outskirts of Tokyo for many years, began to frequent the Tamanoi district populated by many unlicensed prostitutes, and these excursions provided the experiences he incorporated in *Bokutō kitan* (1937; translated as "A Strange Tale from East of the River," 1965), which was serialized between April and June 1937 in the *Asahi Shinbun* newspaper. Modeled after Kafū, the aging writer in the story wanders the streets of Tamanoi in search of materials for his work, and there he comes to know Oyuki, the streetwalker. She knows nothing about this writer whom she begins seeing, and when she earnestly begins to love him, he stops coming to see her and seeks to avoid any deeper involvement. The plot is interwoven with poetic descriptions of the changes of the seasons and with depictions of the manners of the day, and the fictional and essaylike features of the story skillfully balance each other. A work of fiction that the protagonist is busily writing is also included in the work, and some critics have detected the influence of André Gide in the three-dimensional solidarity that this technique adds to the novel.

Kafū next planned to write a story set in the Yoshiwara pleasure district, and he began visiting the area—but he never produced a work about Yoshiwara. Instead, he took daily strolls around Asakusa, where he was fond of attending performances at the opera house, and he wrote his story "Omokage" (Traces, 1938) and the opera libretto "Katsushika jōwa" (Katsushika Love Story, 1938) from these experiences. The latter work was performed at the opera house to sell-out audiences.

Japan had invaded China in 1937, and, as fascist power had been growing steadily in Japan, many writers were becoming willing to collaborate with the war effort. Kafū, however, showed no desire to cooperate with military authorities, and, because he was increasingly regarded as an unpatriotic author, opportunities to publish his work diminished. In fact, following the outbreak of World War II he lost all avenues for publishing in December 1941. This only increased his urge to write, however, and he vented his defiance by writing several works that were published almost immediately after the war had ended.

Postwar journalists hailed this stream of works—*Raihōsha* (The Visitor, 1946), *Towazugatari* (A Tale No One Asked For, 1946), *Kunshō* (The Decoration, 1947), *Ukishizumi* (Sinking and Swimming, 1947), and *Odoriko* (The Dancing Girl, 1949)—that Kafū had written with no hope of publishing during the war years, and a craze for his work ensued. Both "The Decoration" and "The Dancing Girl" are set in Asakusa and concern an old restaurant deliveryman who frequents the theaters and enjoys the wild lives of the young women who hope to become dancers on the stage. "The Visitor" mingles ghost stories with a fictional narrative of the immoral activities of two young writers. The first-person narrator of *A Tale No One Asked For* relates without feeling the romantic history of a painter, the protagonist of the novel, and *Sinking and Swimming* recounts the experiences of a wandering woman as war is about to begin. Kafū continued to write short stories and scripts for light stage entertainments at Asakusa; yet many of his works also reflect the gravity of postwar times in Japan in their descriptions of the food shortages and of the prostitutes who openly wandered through urban streets. These latter are portrayed with a nihilistic view of humanity.

Kafū's work reached a pinnacle with *Strange Tale from East of the River*. The renewed attention that he received in the years following the war can be attributed to the publication of *Danchōtei nichijō* (Dyspepsia House Days), the diaries that he had begun keeping in 1917 and finally published in 1959. In this diary Kafū records the weather, his responses to the seasons, his criticisms of the times and of the customs of Tokyo, his reactions to what he is reading, his associations with others, and his relationships with women—all of which he recounts in an elegant style and without displaying any regrets about his individualistic life.

In 1952 Kafū received the highest literary award in Japan, the Bunka Kunshō (Order of Culture), but this prestigious honor failed to alter Kafū's iconoclastic activities that might easily have been misinterpreted as eccentricity. Suffering with a hemorrhaging stomach ulcer, he died

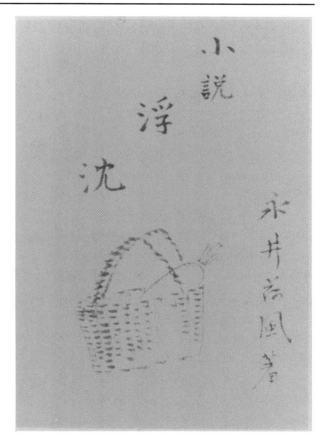

Cover designed by Kafū for Ukishizumi *(Sinking and Swimming, 1947)*

on 30 April 1959 alone at his house in Ichikawa, Chiba Prefecture, where he spent his final years.

Some critics have called for a reevaluation of Kafū's work, in part to reconsider the connections between his individualistic life and the influence of rationalism. Others are interested in reexamining Japanese attitudes toward Edo and Tokyo. They regard Kafū both as the most acute critic of Tokyo in transition—the writer who most perspicaciously described the ugly realities of the city—and as the writer who described Tokyo's cultural features that never should have been, but ultimately were, forever lost.

References:

Akiba Tarō, *Kafū gaiden* (Tokyo: Shun'yōdō, 1979);

Akiba, *Kōshō: Nagai Kafū* (Tokyo: Iwanami Shoten, 1966);

Amino Yoshihiro, *Kafū bungaku to sono shūhen* (Tokyo: Kanrin Shobō, 1993);

Amino, *Nagai Kafū* (Tokyo: Shimizu Shoin, 1985);

Iijima Kōichi, *Nagai Kafū ron* (Tokyo: Chūō Kōronsha, 1982);

Isoda Kōichi, *Nagai Kafū* (Tokyo: Kōdansha, 1979);

Kafū Sensei Shinobu Kai, *Kaisō no Nagai Kafū* (Tokyo: Kasumigaseki Shobō, 1961);

Kojima Masajirō, *Ōgai, Kafū, Mantarō* (Tokyo: Bungei Shunjō, 1965);

Matsumoto Hajime, *Nagai Kafū no Tokyo kukan* (Tokyo: Kawade Shobō Shinsha, 1992);

Miyagi Tatsurō, *Nagai Kafū* (Tokyo: Meiji Shoin, 1965);

Miyagi, ed., *Nagai Kafū no bungaku* (Tokyo: Ōfusha, 1973);

Nakamura Mitsuo, *Hyōron: Nagai Kafū* (Tokyo: Chikuma Shobō, 1979);

Nakamura Shin'ichirō, ed., *Nagai Kafū kenkyū* (Tokyo: Shinchōsha, 1956);

Nihon Bungaku Kenkyū Shiryō Kankōkai, *Nagai Kafū* (Tokyo: Yuseidō, 1971);

Noguchi Fujio, *Waga Kafū* (Tokyo: Shueisha, 1975);

Oketani Hideaki, *Tenshin, Kanzō, Kafū* (Tokyo: Ozawa Shoten, 1976);

Sakagami Hiroichi, *Hanshizenshūgi no shisō to bungaku* (Tokyo: Ōfusha, 1988);

Sakagami, *Nagai Kafū nōto* (Tokyo: Ōfusha, 1978);

Sakagami, ed., *Nihon bungaku kenkyū taisei: Nagai Kafū* (Tokyo: Kokusho Kankōkai, 1989);

Sasabuchi Tomoichi, *Nagai Kafū: "Daraku" no bigakusha* (Tokyo: Meiji Shoin, 1976);

Satō Haruo, *Kafū zakkan* (Tokyo: Kunitachi Shoin, 1947);

Satō, *Shōsetsu Nagai Kafū* (Tokyo: Shinchōsha, 1960);

Suzuki Fumitaka, *Wakaki Kafū no bungaku to shisō* (Tokyo: Ibunsha, 1995);

Takeda Katsuhiko, *Kafū no seishun* (Tokyo: Mikasa Shobō, 1973);

Tsukamoto Yasuhiko, *Romanteki dansō: Kafū no koto nado* (Tokyo: Musashino Shobō, 1991);

Yoshida Seiichi, *Nagai Kafū* (Tokyo: Yagumo Shoten, 1947).

Natsume Sōseki

(5 January 1867 – 9 December 1916)

Yoko McClain
University of Oregon

BOOKS: *Wagahai wa neko de aru,* 3 volumes (Tokyo: Ōkura Shoten & Hattori Shoten, 1905–1906); translated by Katsue Shibata, Motonari Kai, and Harold W. Price as *I Am a Cat: A Novel* (Tokyo: Kenkyusha, 1961); translated by Aiko Itō and Graeme Wilson as *I Am a Cat* (Rutland, Vt.: Tuttle, 1972);

Yōkyoshū (Tokyo: Ōkura Shoten, 1906);

Nihyakutōka (Tokyo, 1906);

Bungakuron (Tokyo: Ōkura Shoten, 1907);

Uzurakago (Tokyo: Shun'yōdō, 1907)–includes *Botchan,* translated by Yasotaro Mori as *Master Darling* (Tokyo: Ogawa Seibundo, 1918) and by Alan Turney as *Botchan* (Tokyo: Kodansha International, 1972; London: Peter Owen, 1973), and *Kusamakura,* translated by Turney as *The Three-Cornered World* (London: Peter Owen, 1965; Chicago: Regnery, 1965);

Kofū (Tokyo: Shun'yōdō, 1908); translated by Jay Rubin as *The Miner* (Stanford: Stanford University Press, 1988);

Gubijinsō (Tokyo: Shun'yōdō, 1908);

Kusa awase (Tokyo: Shun'yōdō, 1908);

Sanshirō (Tokyo: Shun'yōdō, 1908); translated by Jay Rubin as *Sanshiro: A Novel* (Tokyo: University of Tokyo Press, 1977; Seattle: University of Washington Press, 1977);

Bungaku hyōron (Tokyo: Shun'yōdō, 1909);

Sorekara (Tokyo: Shun'yōdō, 1910); translated by Norma Moore Field as *And Then* (Tokyo: University of Tokyo Press, 1978; Baton Rouge: Louisiana State University Press, 1978);

Mon (N.p., 1910); translated by Francis Mathy as *Mon* (Tokyo: Tuttle, 1972; London: Peter Owen, 1972; New York: Putnam, 1982);

Shihen (Tokyo: Shun'yōdō, 1910);

Kirinukichō yori (Tokyo: Shun'yōdō, 1911);

Asahi kōen shū (Tokyo: Asahi Shinbunsha, 1911);

Higan sugi made (Tokyo: Shun'yōdō, 1912); trans-

Natsume Sōseki, 1912

lated by Kingo Ochiai and Sanford Goldstein as *To the Spring Equinox and Beyond* (Rutland, Vt.: Tuttle, 1985);

Shakai to jibun (Tokyo: Jitsugyō no Nihonsha, 1913);

Kōjin (Tokyo: Ōkura Shoten, 1914); translated by Beongcheon Yu as *The Wayfarer* (Detroit: Wayne State University Press, 1967);

Kokoro (Tokyo: Iwanami Shoten, 1914); translated by Ineko Sato as *Kokoro* (Tokyo: Japan Writers' Society, 1941); translated by Edwin McClellan as *Kokoro, A Novel* (Chicago: Regnery, 1957; London: Peter Owen, 1967);

Garasudo no naka (Tokyo: Iwanami Shoten, 1915); translated by Iwao Matsuhara and E. T. Iglehart as *Within My Glass Doors* (Tokyo: Shinseido, 1928);

Shikichō (Tokyo: Shinchōsha, 1915);

Michikusa (Tokyo: Iwanami Shoten, 1915); translated by Edwin McClellan as *Grass on the Wayside* (Chicago: University of Chicago Press, 1969);

Kongōso (Tokyo: Shiseidō, 1915);

Meian (Tokyo: Iwanami Shoten, 1917); translated by V. H. Viglielmo as *Light and Darkness* (Honolulu: University of Hawaii Press, 1971; London: Peter Owen, 1971);

Sōseki haiku shū (Tokyo: Iwanami Shoten, 1917);

Sōseki shishū (Tokyo: Iwanami Shoten, 1919);

Eibungaku keishiki ron (Tokyo: Iwanami Shoten, 1924);

Sōseki no Osero (Tokyo: Tettō Shoin, 1930);

Mokuseiroku (Tokyo: Iwanami Shoten, 1932).

Collections: Sōseki zenshū (Tokyo: Iwanami Shoten, 1917);

Natsume Sōseki zenshū (Tokyo: Meiji Bungaku Kankōkai, 1948–1949);

Natsume Sōseki zenshū, 7 volumes (Tokyo: Sōgeisha, 1953–);

Sōseki bungaku zenshū, 10 volumes, edited by Ara Masatō (Tokyo: Shueisha, 1970–1974);

Natsume Sōseki zenshū, 16 volumes, edited by Yoshida Seiichi (Tokyo: Chikuma Shobō, 1973);

Natsume Sōseki zenshū, 11 volumes, edited by Etō Jun and Yoshida Seiichi (Tokyo: Kadokawa Shoten, 1975);

Meicho fukkoku Sōseki bungakukan, 25 volumes (Tokyo: Nihon Kindai Bungakukan, 1975);

Sōseki zenshū, 35 volumes, edited by Komiya Toyotaka (Tokyo: Iwanami Shoten, 1978–1980);

Natsume Sōseki iboku shū, 6 volumes (Tokyo: Kyuryudō, 1979–1980);

Sōseki zenshū (Tokyo: Iwanami Shoten, 1993–).

Natsume Sōseki is probably the most well known and widely read novelist in Japan; so well known is he that his portrait is currently featured on the 1,000-yen bill. Near the end of the Meiji Period writers who were masters of Western literary form began to appear in Japan, and of these novelists, Sōseki was perhaps the most profound and versatile. His lighthearted, satiric tone in early works such as *Wagahai wa neko de aru* (1905–1906; translated as *I Am a Cat*, 1961) and the humorous *Botchan* (The Little Master, 1907; translated as *Botchan*, 1972) turned serious in his later novels such as *Kōjin* (1914; translated as *The Wayfarer*, 1967) and *Kokoro* (The Heart, 1914; translated as *Kokoro*, 1941), as Sōseki poignantly voiced a sense of human alienation and loneliness long before existentialism became a popular form of literary expression in Europe.

Sōseki was the youngest of eight children of a wealthy and influential landlord, Natsume Shōbei Naokatsu, and his wife, Chie. Although he was named Kinnosuke at birth, he assumed the pseudonym Sōseki in 1889 and later adopted it as his pen name. Because Sōseki's father was fifty-three and his mother, at age forty, was old-fashioned enough to feel ashamed rather than pleased to deliver a child so late in her life, the infant was not welcomed into such a large family. Great sociopolitical changes were sweeping Japan at the time, and the fortunes of the family were also beginning to decline. The newborn Sōseki was therefore soon placed in a foster home, and two years later he was adopted by Shiobara Shōnosuke and Yasu, a couple who were acquainted with his family and who tried to buy the young boy's love by showering him with material things. In *Michikusa* (1915; translated as *Grass on the Wayside*, 1969) Sōseki later wrote about his unhappy childhood with his adoptive parents, whose marriage ended in divorce when he was nine years old. Sōseki then returned to his biological parents' home, although he did not know for some time that they were his real parents. In *Garasudo no naka* (1915; translated as *Within My Glass Doors*, 1928) he writes that, having heard this truth from a maid in the house, he was grateful for her kindness in sharing the story with him.

Although he was pleased to leave his adoptive parents, whose constant quarreling had been a source of great pain, the declining fortunes of his birth family cast a shadow on his homecoming, for Sōseki again became a burden to his father, who had never felt any affection toward the boy. Sōseki had warm feelings toward his mother, but she died only four years after his return. Some critics believe that the memory of his unfortunate infancy and childhood greatly influenced the thinking of the mature writer. Having been deserted by his parents at an early age, Sōseki never knew the satisfaction of love, and memories of his childhood may have led him to reflect seriously in his writing on problems such as human egoism.

He was surely also influenced by the times in which he lived, for the Meiji Era was an epoch-making period in which a backward, feudal

Sōseki at his writing desk, 1914

Japan emerged as a modern nation after more than two centuries of isolation. Sōseki, as soon as he was old enough to understand the age in which he lived, was swept up by the widespread conviction that his homeland was extremely backward in comparison with the West. The veracity or the inaccuracy of this notion is perhaps less important than the fact that most Japanese intellectuals of his age subscribed to it.

Sharing this conviction, Sōseki shouldered the responsibility of a young intellectual in a rapidly developing country. One concern of young Meiji intellectuals was to serve their country in some worthy fashion that would enable Japan rapidly to become a modern nation by Western standards. Deeply concerned about his country's future as well as his own, Sōseki was consumed with difficult problems: how to learn Western culture and yet preserve Japanese traditions, how to fuse Japanese and Western ideas, and how to live ethically between the old and the new. His works provided him a venue for addressing such questions.

In his youth Sōseki had a keen interest in Chinese studies. At age fourteen he attended a private school in which only classical Chinese studies were taught. After spending about a year at this institution, Sōseki began questioning the value of his classical studies, which followed the old traditions of reverence for Chinese learning, in the midst of Japanese modernization that extolled Western learning as its model for a new order. He soon realized he needed a university education in order to contribute effectively to the task of modernization, but in order to enter a university he had to know English. In fall 1883 he left his old-fashioned institution and entered a modern secondary school in which most subjects were taught with English textbooks. Although he changed his course of study to Western learning, Chinese literature remained his love throughout his life. He wrote many classical Chinese poems—an avocation that gave him great pleasure—and many Chinese scholars consider these poems to be outstanding.

With little background in English, Sōseki worked diligently to acquire a reading knowledge of the language. A school friend bought him two books, Matthew Arnold's *Literature and Dogma* (1873), and William Shakespeare's *Hamlet* (1603), and that purchase permitted Sōseki's first experience reading *Hamlet,* a work that he found completely incomprehensible. During these preparatory school years he also became acquainted with Masaoka Shiki, under whose influence Sōseki began writing haiku. As a preparatory school student Sōseki first used his pen name—*sōseki* comes from an old Chinese source meaning "being stubborn"—in a commentary that he wrote on young Shiki's *Nanakusashu* (Collection of Seven Grasses), a collection of haiku, essays, and Chinese poems.

Sōseki apparently acquired a fairly good command of English at this school, and he soon entered the preparatory school for the university. When he began to consider his future during his third year of study, he wanted to pursue a profession that involved being creative and that responded to the demands of society, and he initially chose architecture. Yet a philosopher friend whom he greatly respected pointed out that in Japan no architect could create a magnificent structure, such as Saint Paul's Cathedral, that would elicit centuries of admiration, for Japan was simply not ready for that kind of building. Sōseki reacted swiftly. He decided to study English literature, wanted to become a writer in the English language, and hoped someday to show his great works to westerners—a spirit that was widely shared among young intellectuals during the Meiji years.

In 1890 Sōseki entered the Department of English at Tokyo Imperial University (now Tokyo University), where he wrote and published several articles and translations within three years. In his second year he translated *Hōjōki* (1213; translated as *An Account of My Hut*) into English, an achievement indicating that he had already attained a mastery of the English language at that early stage of his career. James Dickson, a lecturer in English at Tokyo Imperial University, used this translation in presenting "Chōmei and Wordsworth: A Literary Parallel," at a meeting of the Nihon Asia Society in 1892, and this translation was later published along with Dickson's paper in *Nihon Asia Society Bulletin*. In *Tetsugaku Zasshi* (Journal of Philosophy), a periodical published by the university, Sōseki also translated into Japanese two other papers—"The Poet Tennyson" by Augustus Wood, another lecturer in English at the university, and a speech, "Hypnosis," by Ernest Hart, M.D. He wrote two essays—"Rōshi no tetsugaku" (Philosophy of Lao Tzu), on Oriental philosophy, and "Chūgaku kairyōsaku" (A View on Improving Japanese Middle School Education), on pedagogy—and in a third article, "Bundan ni okeru byōdōshugi no daihyōsha, 'Uoruto Hoittoman' Walt Whitman no shi ni tsuite" (On the Poems of Walt Whitman, a Representative Poet of Egalitarianism), he praised Whitman's poetry as "revealing a truly free man, who, bound only by his own conscience, could calmly live and act amidst the evil of the world." Sōseki has been credited with introducing Japanese readers to the work of Whitman.

Between March and June 1893 Sōseki serialized "Eikokushijin no tenchisansen ni taisuru kannen" (Ideas on Landscape Held by English Poets), the last article he wrote during his university days, in *Tetsugaku Zasshi*. This article deserves attention because of what it reveals of Sōseki's disposition at the time. Following his lonely childhood, nature had become his warmest, most comforting friend, and he recalled a time when he had enjoyed looking at hanging scrolls of old southern Chinese landscapes and finding a temporary sanctuary from his loneliness in such representations of nature. As he prepared to graduate from the university, Sōseki expressed his love for nature by examining the attitudes that several English poets presented about nature. He discussed poems by such writers as Alexander Pope, Oliver Goldsmith, Thomas Cowper, James Thomson, Robert Burns, and Wordsworth—the last of whom, Sōseki believed, found vitality in nature through meditation on it. He reflected on his own emotional state in writing poetry and tried to learn more from Wordsworth.

After three years at Tokyo Imperial University, Sōseki, the second person to major in English literature there, graduated in 1893 with an outstanding academic record. He immediately proceeded to graduate school, and there, although the faculty and his fellow students considered him a bright student, he was dissatisfied with his own accomplishments. He felt that he had learned little about English literature or literary study after three years. He complained that students were forced to learn only such insignificant facts as the birth dates of various writers and the publication dates of their works. He felt very empty. Holding a university degree—a prestigious honor at that time—but dissatisfied and disillusioned with his accomplishments, he secured a teaching position at the Tokyo Normal College for about two years while he continued his graduate studies.

During this time Sōseki decided to practice Zen in order to achieve mental and emotional peace. Through his university days Sōseki had often experienced agonizing bouts of depression, as he felt constantly driven by something and could not seem to settle down. His rational disposition did not allow him to turn to most religions, which postulate that only faith in a supreme being such as the Christian God or Buddha might lead him to salvation, and he became most interested in Zen, the essential principle of which is salvation through one's own meditative effort. He went to the Engakuji, a Zen temple in Kamakura, to achieve mental equilibrium, and he later incorporated his experience there in *Mon* (The Gate, 1910; translated as *Mon,* 1972).

Finding no solace in Zen meditation and still depressed, Sōseki finally decided to leave Tokyo. As a highly regarded graduate of a prestigious university, there was no apparent reason for him to leave such a setting and move to a remote small town. Some critics have suggested that his action may betoken a spiritual decision he made, for this self-imposed exile occurred four months after his visit to the Zen temple. Others intimate that his leaving Tokyo was perhaps a response to some unrequited love, but no certain explanation for his departure exists. In any event, Sōseki took a teaching position at a high school in Matsuyama on the island of Shikoku. There his outstanding academic background ensured that he was treated well, and he received an even higher salary than the principal. This setting of Matsuyama later provided the background of *Botchan,* in which he humorously presents the adventures of a simpleminded young man who honors justice.

With first-person narration this story uses the spirited, vigorous, and somewhat crude everyday speech of Edoites, those born and raised in the old district of Tokyo. The title, which means "Little Master," is taken from the way in which Kiyo, the old family maid, addresses the protagonist. She persists in believing that he will be a success one day and adores him for his honesty and simplicity, even though his own parents have never regarded him highly, and Botchan never seems to regret the early death of his parents. With a little inheritance money he finishes college and takes a teaching post at a boys' high school in Matsuyama. He finds no pleasure there, however, for the students are rough and abusive; some teachers are cunning and unscrupulous; and the small town atmosphere offers no stimulation. Particularly disgusted with the intrigues of a senior teacher and his follower, Botchan soon resigns his post and returns to Tokyo, where he finds a job as an assistant engineer and returns to his life with Kiyo.

The story seems pointless, but it is still said to be the most popular of all Sōseki's works among Japanese readers, who are probably attracted to its brisk, lively style as well as to Botchan, who is an ideal hero. Though he is not very intelligent, he respects honesty and justice,

Nakane Kyōko in 1895, before her marriage to Sōseki

endures the evil machinations of his superiors, and exhibits capacities for gentleness, thoughtfulness, and loyalty toward Kiyo, his faithful maid. Moreover, Botchan's disregard for high positions pleases Japanese readers: still required to respect the conventions of a hierarchical system, they tacitly envy Botchan's almost reckless behavior as courageous.

One of the important events of Sōseki's stay in Matsuyama was a two-month visit with Shiki, his old friend who had been born in Matsuyama. Sōseki found this renewal of their relationship to be inspiring, and even after Shiki had returned to Tokyo, Sōseki wrote many haiku that he sent to Shiki for criticism. He tried various poetic experiments using this seventeen-syllable form, and its precision, brevity, and objectivity influenced the prose style Sōseki later developed.

After a year of teaching in Matsuyama, Sōseki assumed a position with the Fifth National College in Kumamoto, Kyushu, the southernmost island of Japan, where he stayed for more than four years until he was sent to England by the

Japanese government. Although he began his career as a teacher, he apparently did not enjoy it and wanted to do something more personally satisfying. He was apparently a devoted teacher at this college, however, as he offered an extra class on the works of Shakespeare to those who were interested and assisted several students financially even though he was not well off.

While he was in Kumamoto, Sōseki married Nakane Kyōko, to whom he had become engaged during his earlier stay in Matsuyama. She was the eldest daughter of Nakane Jūichi, the chief secretary of the House of Peers, and Nakane had heard of Sōseki from those who had known him at Tokyo Imperial University. He had become interested in arranging a marriage between Sōseki and his daughter, and after exchanging pictures and arranging a formal meeting both parties had been satisfied. The engagement had been made in December 1895 in Tokyo, while Sōseki had been visiting for the New Year holidays, and in June 1896 Nakane accompanied his daughter to Kumamoto, where she and Sōseki were married. In her *Sōseki no omoide* (Memories of Sōseki, 1928) Kyōko writes that Sōseki's first words to her after their marriage were not promising: "Because I am a scholar, I have no time for you. Please understand this." Their marriage, which lasted twenty years, was not an easy one, but the first four years that they spent in Kumamoto seem to have been the most peaceful.

During their first year in Kumamoto, Sōseki was happy with his small household and composed almost five hundred haiku. The following year he wrote fewer of these, and, with advice and criticism from an excellent Chinese scholar among his colleagues, Sōseki instead began writing many Chinese poems. According to Kyōko's memoirs, he began to follow some new Japanese literary trends. For example, he was impressed with Higuchi Ichiyō's *Takekurabe* (1896; translated as *Child's Play*, 1981), a novel by a young woman of the time, but he disliked Ozaki Kōyō's *Konjiki yasha* (1896; translated as *A Demon of Gold and Love*, 1968–1971), which he found to be only mawkish, although his contemporaries enthusiastically approved of it. Sōseki was by this time well known as a haiku poet, and he also published "Torisutoramu shandei" (1897), a critique of Laurence Sterne's *The Life and Opinions of Tristram Shandy* (1759–1767); "Eikoku no bunjin to shinbun zasshi" (English Literary Men and Newspapers and Magazines, 1899); and "Shōsetsu Ei-

ruin no hihyō," a critique of Walter Theodore Watts-Dunton's novel *Aylwin* (1899).

From Kumamoto, Sōseki traveled to nearby provinces, visited his friends, and enjoyed nature walks on mountain paths. Using those mountain walks as a backdrop, he later wrote *Kusamakura* (1907; translated as *The Three-Cornered World*, 1965), a work in which a Tokyo painter seeks something profound while visiting the mountain villages of Kyushu. Sōseki uses a *haibun* style, in which the prose is written in the way one composes haiku: the author objectively stands back and views things without emotion. As Sōseki remarks, the aim of this style is "to leave an impression of beauty in the reader's mind"—an ephemeral beauty.

In September 1900 Sōseki sailed for England as a student supported by the government. In his journal he records that he visited Cambridge University immediately upon his arrival, but he found that the emphasis on social life there was too much for a poor government student such as he. Therefore, instead of enrolling either at Cambridge or Oxford (both of which, he presumed, were alike in their emphasis on social life), he stayed in London and regularly attended the University College of London University. He soon found the lectures too boring and mechanical and stopped attending. Then for about a year he studied privately with William J. Craig, a Shakespeare scholar, and although he read voraciously, after a year he realized that the number of books which he had not read far exceeded the number of those he had. He was alarmed by his unsystematic methods, and he realized that he still could not distinguish what English literature was.

Because he had studied Chinese intensively in his early years, he felt he could appreciate Chinese literature. Although he had read as many books in English as he had in Chinese, he simply could not appreciate English literature, and he wondered whether some fundamental difference between English and Chinese literatures existed. In London he decided to resolve the question by trying to define scientifically what literature is. He tried to identify common elements between Oriental and Western literatures, between Chinese or Japanese and English literatures. He realized that the problem he had posed was monumental, and he knew that he could never complete his research during the remaining year. He later wrote that he had never studied as conscientiously as he did through the next six or seven months. Confining himself to his boardinghouse room for months and eating only water and biscuits, he concentrated on his studies, and this frantic dedication to his work ruined his health: he spent most of his small government allowance purchasing books instead of buying proper food, and he reportedly showed signs of either a nervous breakdown or severe depression.

In spring 1901 Sōseki wrote epistolary essays about his life in London and sent them to comfort Shiki, for his friend was bedridden with tuberculosis. Delighted with the essays, Shiki titled them "Rondon shōsoku" (London News, 1901) and published them in *Hototogisu* (Cuckoo), originally a haiku magazine edited by Takahama Kyoshi, Shiki's disciple. Following Sōseki's return to Japan in 1903 this magazine also published "Jitensha nikki" (Bicycle Diary), in which he recounts his experience of learning how to ride a bicycle in England.

Sōseki published his findings after returning from his studies in London—first in the form of lectures at Tokyo Imperial University and then in *Bungakuron* (Theory of Literature, 1907). This book, which Sōseki later called "a deformed child of literature," was not a successful work, and its failure seems to result chiefly from the fact that he had adopted the orientation of the sociologist as his theoretical perspective by approaching literature as only one of many social phenomena that he had sought to analyze. His study in London was not entirely wasted, however, because in struggling to resolve the question of what literature is, Sōseki had constructed his own literary perspective. The prevailing thinking in Japan at that time was that anything Western was better than anything Japanese, but Sōseki believed that constructing his own view and not blindly adopting a Western perspective was the only way for the Japanese to create their own literature.

After he had returned to Japan in January 1903, he took two positions—one teaching English at the First National College, the other lecturing in English literature at Tokyo Imperial University. At the latter institution he replaced Lafcadio Hearn, who had resigned. Most students found his lectures on the theory of literature to be too difficult, partly because they were used to the poetic lectures given by Hearn.

Sōseki was still teaching at Tokyo Imperial University in 1904 when Takahama Kyoshi asked him to write a piece for *Hototogisu,* and although he had never written any fiction, he decided to try to do so, for it would be an essential attempt to fuse what he had learned from both Western and traditional Japanese works. Besides

Sōseki (left) with his daughter Fudeko and one of his protégés, Matsune Tōyōjō, circa 1910

books on haiku and Chinese poetry, in which he was particularly interested, Sōseki apparently read extensively in classical Japanese works such as the *Man'yōshū,* the oldest anthology of Japanese poetry; *Genji Monogatari* (translated by Arthur Waley as *The Tale of Genji,* 1925–1933) and *Ise Monogatari,* romances of the Heian Period; stories of Takizawa Bakin and Ihara Saikaku; and dramas of Chikamatsu Monzaemon, of the Edo Period. In addition to English and Chinese he studied German and French, and he read extensively from translations of Latin, Greek, Slavic, Scandinavian, and Italian literatures. Drawing on these diverse readings, he tried to create something new by combining Western ideas with traditional Japanese thought. He stressed that a true understanding of Western culture would lead to a true understanding of Japanese culture.

He published his first work of fiction—"Wagahai wa neko de aru" (I Am a Cat)—for *Hototogisu* in January 1905. He had not planned to write a full-length novel, but the reception given the appearance of this first piece was so great that Kyoshi asked Sōseki to continue. He complied by eventually writing ten more chapters forming a collection of isolated short stories that were serially published during the next year and a half. Each story depicts everyday occurrences around the Kushami (meaning "sneeze") household. Mr. Kushami is a high-school English teacher, and the stories are told by his tomcat, who satirizes the vanity and pretense of human beings. The style and expressions are uncomplicated, so children of junior-high-school age can easily enjoy the collection; adults can also enjoy the humor and satire as well as the scholarly structure infused with both Western and Oriental thought. Perhaps because his first fictional work was easily understood by the public, Sōseki came to be appreciated by people of various intellectual capacities; his later works are philosophically much more difficult than this first collection of stories.

One cannot help wondering, however, why these stories were so enthusiastically received. After one reads a few chapters, the episodes lose their freshness, and the enjoyable, lighthearted humor that characterizes the first few chapters becomes caustic. This may be explained as a result of some depression Sōseki may have suffered around that time. In any case, naturalism, an influential movement in modern Japanese literature, was still flourishing when I Am a Cat was published in 1905–1906, and this movement generally emphasized real-life settings rather than the fantasy milieus of dreams. In contrast to the rather gloomy, prevailing naturalistic mode of literature, I Am a Cat showed a light, humorous side of life, and this might also explain why it was so well received. The book brought Sōseki fame, and, along with Botchan, it remains his most widely read work in Japan. Although many Japanese readers mistakenly consider both works to be representative of Sōseki's writings, his later pieces include none of the satire or humor that characterizes these two early books.

During the same month that I Am a Cat began being serially published in Hototogisu Sōseki also published "Rondon tō" (1905; translated as "Tower of London," 1991) in Teikoku Bungaku and "Kārairu hakubutsukan" (Carlyle Museum, 1905) in Gakutō. "Tower of London" is a travel narrative based on his visit to the Tower, and in several scenes he colors the history of the Tower of London with romantic tones. This piece and the narratives of I Am a Cat are thus characterized by entirely different styles, the former in a

more ornate style and the latter a realistic work in a plain, objective style.

From 1905 through early 1907, while Sōseki lectured at the university in courses such as "Theory of Literature," "A Critique of Eighteenth Century English Literature," and "Shakespeare," he grew prolific in his writing. Among his many works during this period were The Three-Cornered World and the novel Nihyakutōka (Typhoon, 1906), in the latter of which the volcano Aso in Kyushu provides the backdrop. Sōseki uses a rich, elaborate style in the former work, while in Typhoon he uses simple, colloquial speech throughout the novel. In Typhoon Kei, the main character, attacks the rich and the upper class for abusing their power and oppressing others, and he tries to improve Japanese society. Since his idea of reform is presented abstractly, however, the novel is unconvincing.

In Nowake (Autumn Wind, 1907), his next novel, Sōseki continues to address the social problems borne of the economic and class differences between the rich and the poor, and in this work he first attempts to write about the loneliness of modern Japanese, a familiar theme in his later novels. Three young men, all college graduates, are the chief characters. Nakano, the fortunate one who has been raised in a wealthy family and has a beautiful fiancée, does not comprehend the suffering of the poor. In contrast, Takayanagi, Nakano's friend, has to work hard for a living and is frustrated because he cannot devote more time to his writing. Shirai, Takayanagi's friend, is an idealist who follows his beliefs and is generally oblivious to the social consequences. While Takayanagi is unhappy about his circumstances, Shirai accepts his lot; both are equally lonely in their own ways. The novel is not as skillfully written as Sōseki's later works, but it provides a first glimpse of his treatment of the loneliness of modern man.

Until 1905 Sōseki had been a professor and a haiku poet known only in limited circles, but with satiric and humorous fiction such as I Am a Cat, Botchan, and various short stories with different styles and content, his fame as a writer became solidly established. This recognition earned him an offer of employment from the Asahi Newspaper Publishing Company, and, when Sōseki resigned his two teaching positions to accept the offer in 1907, his action apparently caused an uproar. Being a member of a newspaper staff was a lowly position at that time, and it was unthinkable for anyone to relinquish a post in the highest academic institution in Japan for such an un-

Natsume Soseki

BOTCHAN

'One of the most important Japanese writers of the modern period'
—Times Literary Supplement

Natsume Soseki was born in Tokyo in 1867 and was educated at the Tokyo Imperial University where he studied English literature. In 1900 he was sent to England as a Government Scholar. He returned to Japan in 1903 and succeeded Lafcadio Hearn as lecturer in English literature at the Imperial University. In 1907 he became a full-time writer, producing a group of carefully written novels treating the spiritual torment of Japan's urban intellectuals. He died in 1916.
It is only since 1965, when Peter Owen published *The Three Cornered World*, that his work has become widely known in England.

PETER OWEN

Dust jacket for the British translation of Botchan *(1907), featuring a naive, idealistic young protagonist whose disregard for social conventions made the novel popular with Japanese readers*

prestigious position. Yet two motives prompted Sōseki to accept this newspaper job: one was financial—the *Asahi* offer paid well. The other was the opportunity to concentrate on creative writing that such a position would permit. Sōseki was to supervise the literary columns and to write a novel for serialization in the paper each year. All his novels written after 1907 were thus first published in *Asahi*.

The first of his works to appear in *Asahi* was "Bungei no tetsugakuteki kiso" (The Philosophical Basis of Literature, 1907), which he originally gave as a lecture at an art school in March 1907. In this lecture Sōseki attacked the naturalists "for valuing truth too highly as the objective of literature to the detriment of beauty, goodness, and sublimity." By publishing this essay, he hoped to make his literary stand public for future readers.

His first novel to appear in *Asahi* was *Gubijinsō* (Red Poppy, 1908), which was serially published from June through October 1907. In this melodramatic novel almost all the characters are stereotypes, and Sōseki uses each to make his di-

dactic point: if one disregards morality in life, one will be punished. Sōseki later detested this work, written in an ornate style, and was embarrassed that he had written it. He vehemently declined one offer for it to be translated into German. Yet this was his first long novel after he had joined the *Asahi,* and because readers were anticipating much from him, he apparently tried too hard. He did not repeat this mistake again.

Kōfu (1908; translated as *The Miner*, 1988), his next novel, has remained perhaps the least familiar of all Sōseki's novels in Japan, even though some scholars have claimed that it represents one of Japan's most innovative contributions to contemporary fiction and is notable for its early use of a stream-of-consciousness narrative technique. Written in a tough, colloquial vernacular, the objective style of *The Miner* contrasts with that of *Red Poppy,* a subjective work with a labored style, and while the latter is dramatic, *The Miner*—another experimental piece in which Sōseki was using entirely new techniques—has neither a definite plot nor concrete characterization. The story is presented as a series of first-person recollections of the protagonist, a young man from a good family. Suffering from a failed love affair, he leaves his home in Tokyo, is soon picked up by a procurer of cheap labor, and is sent to the Ashio copper mine. By using a stream-of-consciousness technique the novel delves into the protagonist's mind and reveals that something amorphous is hidden beneath the surface of man's consciousness. In *Yume jūya* (Ten Nights of Dreams, 1908), published shortly after *The Miner,* such levels of hidden consciousness appear in dreams.

Sanshirō (1908; translated as *Sanshiro: A Novel,* 1977), was Sōseki's next serialized novel, published from September through December 1908, and it presents the first part of a trilogy that consists also of *Sorekara* (1910; translated as *And Then,* 1978) and *Mon.* Sanshiro, the protagonist, is a naive young man who has just graduated from a national college in a province of Kyushu and is on his way to enter Tokyo Imperial University. On the train he meets Hirota, an older man who eventually becomes his mentor. Through a family acquaintance Sanshirō meets Mineko, a sophisticated and attractive woman of the same age as he, and Sanshiro becomes attracted to her. Although she shows some interest in him, she wisely chooses for her future husband an older, more mature man whom she can respect as well as love. The story ends with Sanshirō facing this as well as other sources of disappointment: midway through the story the reader has learned that the detachment of his mentor from society stems from the secret of Hirota's birth, and the reader senses that Sanshiro will someday even more fully become heir to Hirota's distrust of society.

And Then was serialized in 1909, and before the first installment of this novel was published, Sōseki explained that he gave this title to this novel as an indication that this work was to be read as a further study of what happens to the kind of protagonist, the young university student, who appears in *Sanshirō.* In *And Then* Sanshirō is replaced by a more mature protagonist who suffers a strange fate, but nothing is said about what lies in store for him, and in that respect, Sōseki wrote, the novel presents a recounting of what happens "then."

Daisuke, the main character, is thirty years old and unmarried. He is intelligent and in good health, but he does nothing for a living and depends on a monthly allowance from his father, a successful businessman. Daisuke excuses his idle lifestyle by blaming the country, where most people live in selfish, dishonest, hypocritical ways in which his conscience will not permit him to live. Daisuke had once loved Michiyo, but when Hiraoka, his best friend, had confided that he was also in love with her, Daisuke surrendered Michiyo to him, for he believed that it was the heroic thing to do. However, three years later when he finds Michiyo unhappy because Hiraoka has been unfaithful to her during her prolonged illness, he decides to ask Hiraoka to give up Michiyo. Furious with Daisuke's dishonorable behavior, his father ostracizes him, and Daisuke must look for a job for the first time. In addition to developing a theme of socially inexcusable love, the novel criticizes both the Japanese society that nurtures men such as Daisuke and those intellectuals who talk but do not act honorably.

Within a week of completing *And Then* in mid August, Sōseki suffered an attack of acute stomach pain from which he did not recover for months. Yet his poor health did not keep him from traveling through Manchuria and Korea for more than a month at the invitation of Nakamura Zekō, an old school friend who was president of the Manchurian Railroad. When he returned home, Sōseki wrote *Mankan tokorodokoro* (Manchuria and Korea, Here and There, 1909), a narrative of his travels that he serialized for about two months, from October through December, shortly after the serialization of *And Then* had ended. Although the title indicates that Korea was included in these travels, Sōseki wrote only about his experiences in Manchuria, and although he was frequently bothered by stomach pain during his trip, he apparently enjoyed reminiscing with many of his old friends who lived in these countries. For this reason, the essays more often recount recollections of Sōseki's youth than present a pure travel narrative.

In *Mon,* a sad but warm novel that comprises the final part of Sōseki's trilogy, Sōsuke, the protagonist, is suffering a fate similar to that which Daisuke, who has been ostracized for having taken the partner of his best friend, suffers in *And Then.* Sōsuke and Oyone, his wife, are a middle-aged, childless couple who live quietly in a shabby rented house at the end of a muddy alley. He is a humble civil servant whose income barely supports the two of them, and their ostracism, despite the loneliness it imposes on them, does enable them to share a quiet intimacy. When Sōsuke hears that Yasui, his friend, may visit their landlord's house, he becomes disturbed and goes to a Zen temple, where he tries to find peace of mind through meditation. Being neither

"One of the most important Japanese writers of the modern period."
—Times Literary Supplement

"A writer to be judged by the highest standards. His stories create, after the fashion of all great writers, a new and completely individual reality."
—Spectator

"The most widely read Japanese writer in modern times, whose work is a byword in Japanese life."
—P.E.N. International Bulletin of Selected Books

ISBN 0-698-11144-3

I AM A CAT

SOSEKI I AM A CAT

NATSUME SOSEKI

COWARD McCANN & GEOGHEGAN

Dust jacket for an American translation of Sōseki's first novel, Wagahai wa neko de aru *(1905–1906), which features a cat as its narrator*

a religious nor a contemplative man, however, he fails to find reassurance and returns home. Sōseki's narrative never reveals whether Yasui actually has visited with Sōsuke's landlord or not, but nothing seems to have happened by the time Sōsuke returns.

At the end Oyone, looking out from the window on a bright, sunny day, remarks cheerfully, "Spring is finally here." In a bittersweet ending typical of Sōseki's works, Sōsuke replies, "But it will soon be winter again." Spiritual peace, if one ever achieves it, is fleeting. *Mon* is not generally considered to be Sōseki's best novel, but its detailed description of the surroundings and the warmth and gentle loneliness of its main characters distinguish it from his other works, and near the end of his life Sōseki was said to have liked this novel best of all his works.

While he was writing *Mon,* Sōseki was frequently plagued with the same stomach pain that he had suffered while traveling in Manchuria and Korea, and after completing this novel he entered a hospital for tests in mid June and was diagnosed with an ulcer. After being hospitalized for

about forty days, he went to Shuzenji, the hot springs resort town south of Tokyo, to recuperate. His condition worsened, however, and on 24 August he vomited blood and lay briefly in a coma. His attendants feared for his life, but he revived.

Many scholars consider this experience of his "grave illness at Shuzenji" to mark a spiritual turning point for Sōseki. Some conclude that he attained a state of tranquility after this serious illness and that his work changed afterward, but others disagree. In October, Sōseki was allowed to return to Tokyo, where he remained in the hospital until the end of February. During his convalescence he wrote *Omoidasu kotonado* (Things I Remember, 1910), a short prose work in which he wrote about his illness, among other topics, and expressed his deep gratitude to those who cared for and were concerned about him.

While he was still in the hospital in February, the Ministry of Education granted Sōseki an honorary doctor's degree. He rejected it, however, and insisted that he had been Mr. Natsume until that time and had no desire to become Dr. Natsume. He explained that he felt offended by

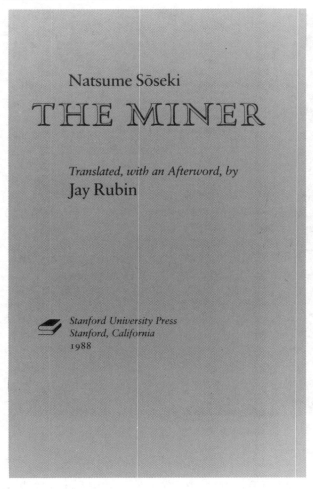

Title page for an American translation of Kofū *(1908), in which Sōseki experiments with the stream-of-consciousness narrative technique*

lowing his illness in 1910. In this work Sōseki experimented with a new format by seeking to make his collection of short stories into one long novel. His use of such an approach in this work was not as effective as it was to prove in his later novels, for although he sought to use parts of the first few chapters of *To the Spring Equinox and Beyond* to foreshadow themes, readers of this work feel that such devices in these chapters are not crucial to the entire scheme.

The story begins with Keitarō as the main protagonist, but later Sunaga, an introspective, alienated intellectual who tries to live according to his conscience, becomes the central character. Although he loves Chiyoko, he cannot express his love for her honestly, because complicated circumstances surround a secret of his birth. After much agonizing, he goes on a trip, and while calmly observing his surroundings, he attains a harmonious state of mind. Sōseki's typical open-ended conclusion, however, appears in Keitarō's final remarks: "What will happen to this drama from now on?" Scholars often categorize this novel, along with *The Wayfarer* and *Kokoro*, as Sōseki's second trilogy, mainly because these three works share the same format: each is a collection of short stories made into a long novel.

In December 1913 *Kōjin* (translated as *The Wayfarer*, 1967) began appearing in *Asahi*, although publication temporarily ceased the following March when Sōseki suffered another relapse of his ulcer condition. That same spring he also suffered from an acute neurotic disorder that had troubled him occasionally ever since he had returned from England. From symptoms apparent in his writing as well as from the comments of others, modern psychiatrists suggest that he must have been suffering from severe depression. If so, then Sōseki wrote *Kōjin* during one of his most physically and mentally difficult periods. Nevertheless, serialization of *The Wayfarer* resumed in September and was completed in November. In this work Sōseki used the same format that he had followed in *To the Spring Equinox and Beyond*—that of combining four episodes into one story—but this time the episodes are well connected.

Jirō, the narrator of the novel, is the younger brother of Ichirō, the protagonist—an alienated scholar who spends most of his time in his study. As a consequence of his isolation, no one in his family feels close to him. Although he is married, for instance, Ichirō feels that he cannot comprehend what kind of woman Nao, his wife, is. He is utterly lonely, not knowing how

the high-handedness of the government, which had sought to give him the degree without first asking him. Following Sōseki's rejection of this award, a messenger from the Ministry of Education visited him several times to urge him to accept it, but each time he flatly rejected the offer.

During 1911 ill health kept Sōseki from publishing a novel in *Asahi,* but after he became well enough he lectured several times in Nagano and in Kansai, where he criticized the notion of modern civilization. Following one of those lectures in August he had a relapse in Osaka, where he was again hospitalized. After recovering, he returned to Tokyo, where he underwent hemorrhoid surgery.

In November 1911 Hinako, his youngest child, died suddenly, and Sōseki recounted this tragic event in his next novel, *Higan sugi made* (1912; translated as *To the Spring Equinox and Beyond,* 1985), the first long novel that he wrote folto love Nao and yet desperately wanting her to love him. He even suspects that she might love Jirō, and he asks his brother to test Nao's fidelity. Jirō is naturally unwilling, and, when he is eventually forced to go on a short trip with his sister-in-law, nothing happens and they both return. As Ichirō's suspicions continue to weigh heavily on him, he feels that his only escape from loneliness is in death, insanity, or religion. He cannot choose. In the end Ichirō is found sleeping in a mountain house, and it is clear that his struggle will begin again as soon as he awakes.

In *Kokoro* the technique of combining short stories into a novel succeeds, and the tales are skillfully and tightly knit so that each is essential to the one that follows it. *Kokoro* is perhaps the most widely read and loved work of Sōseki's profound novels. Only three characters appear in the novel, two main characters—Sensei (maestro) and a young student identified as "I."—and Okusan, a subordinate character who, as Sensei's wife, remains important to the plot.

The student meets Sensei on a beach one summer and is somehow drawn to him. Friendship develops, but the student soon notices that Sensei maintains a remoteness that defies intimacy. Perplexed by Sensei's reserved manner, the student discusses it with Okusan, who also cannot explain it. Only in the closing chapter do readers discover the truth about Sensei in a letter that he writes and addresses to the student. As the only son of a wealthy provincial family, Sensei lost both his parents when he was still a student. His uncle, whom he trusted, swindled him of his inheritance, and Sensei lost his faith in people after that, although he still believed in his own trustworthiness.

However, when K, Sensei's best friend, confides his love for Okusan, the daughter of their landlady, Sensei betrays his friend because he also loves Okusan. Beset with jealousy, he behaves maliciously toward K and drives him to suicide. Recognizing his own dishonesty and acknowledging that he is no different from his uncle and all others, Sensei despairs. Even though he marries Okusan, whom he loves, he cannot be happy. Nor can he share the truth about what has happened to K, because this will also bring grief to her. His guilt and resulting loneliness torment him.

When Emperor Meiji dies and General Nogi commits suicide, Sensei, who has lived entirely in the Meiji Era, also feels that it is time for him to commit suicide, for he can no longer

Title page for an American translation of Sorekara *(1910), the second novel in Sōseki's trilogy about male-female relationships from youth to old age*

bear the loneliness. He writes down the details of his life and shares the note with the student, the only one whom he has trusted, and then kills himself to atone for the wrong he committed against K.

After completing *Kokoro* Sōseki presented "Watashi no kojinshugi" (My Individualism) as a lecture at Gakushūin University. In this address he clarified the term *kojinshugi*, which he defined as one's refusal to sacrifice others to his own advantage. On the contrary, he claimed, when one values himself, he also esteems others. If one respects his own freedom, one must also respect that of others. When feudal ideas such as *giri* (obligation) were still actively being practiced at this time, Sōseki's formulation was a strikingly fresh idea in consonance with modern democracy. In the *Asahi* newspaper he also published *Garasudo no naka,* a series of essays in which he

Title page for an American translation of Kōjin *(1914), a collection of interconnected short stories*

discusses his childhood, his mother, and his personal life. Then he began *Michikusa* (1915; translated as *Grass on the Wayside*, 1969), a new autobiographical novel that covers only the period from 1903, shortly after he returned from England, through 1905, when he was teaching at the universities and beginning to write *I Am a Cat*.

In *Michikusa*, Sōseki's last completed novel, Kenzō returns from abroad and spends days busily lecturing at the university and trying his hand at writing. One day he meets Shimada, his adoptive father, on the street, and this meeting revives memories of his unhappy childhood. After this first meeting Shimada, a brassy man who is not afraid to press his adopted son for money, comes to Kenzō's home several times to ask for financial help. During this time Kenzō's relationship with Osumi, his wife, is neither peaceful nor easy to sustain. Although they care for each other, the pride and stubbornness of each creates a barrier between them. In the end Kenzō gives Shimada a substantial sum of money and severs all ties with him. Osumi is relieved, but Kenzō is

pessimistic, and his last words are that "nothing in this life is settled. Things that happened once will go on happening."

Sōseki began to write *Meian* (1917; translated as *Light and Darkness*, 1971), his last novel, in May 1916, but it remained unfinished at the time of his death in December of that year. He became critically ill in November, but since he had written a few chapters in advance of their serial publication dates, the last story appeared on 14 December, five days after his death. Although the novel is unfinished, several scholars consider this work to be one of his masterpieces. Yet it lacks the warmth of Sōseki's other works. His lonely modern men are always appealing, but almost all the characters in *Light and Darkness* are self-centered, and their unpleasant personalities fail to arouse the reader's sympathy.

The story concerns a couple who have been married for six years. Tsuda, the husband, had a girlfriend, Kiyoko, before he married Onobu, but Kiyoko suddenly left him with no explanation and married another man. Being possessive by nature, Onobu tries to get Tsuda's love by resorting to artifice, but this behavior drives Tsuda away. As the novel begins, Tsuda has gone to a hot springs resort to recuperate from surgery, and an acquaintance arranges an encounter between him and Kiyoko there. The two meet, but the story ends there, as Sōseki left no notes or clues indicating his plans for any conclusion. The novel examines such human weaknesses as egoism, conceit, and vanity, all of which Sōseki presents in minute detail through several self-centered characters. This may explain why the work lacks human warmth; the story does not charm as do his other works, instead presenting lonely, agonized figures.

In working on *Light and Darkness*, Sōseki typically wrote in the morning and composed Chinese poetry or painted pictures in the southern Chinese tradition in the afternoon. Composing Chinese poetry or painting, he claimed, helped purify his mind, which was soiled by thoughts of the fictional world he was creating.

Sōseki died on 9 December 1916 from severe internal hemorrhaging brought on by a fifth recurrence of his ulcer condition in November. During the ten years from the time Sōseki assumed his position with the *Asahi* until he died, he wrote ten novels, many essays, and works of literary criticism, Chinese poetry, and haiku. In 1917 *Sōseki zenshū*, the first complete edition of his works, was published by Iwanami Shigeo, one of Sōseki's former students affiliated with the

The "CHRYSANTHEMUM"
A Japanese brush sketch by Soseki Natsume.

The author was accomplished in every way:
Not only was he a scholar and a novelist,
but also he could paint and compose *haiku*
poetry, and do many things else. Here is a
characteristic example of his artistic ability
in painting.

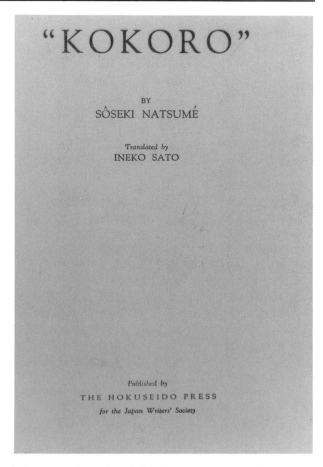

"KOKORO"

BY
SÔSEKI NATSUMÉ

Translated by
INEKO SATO

Published by
THE HOKUSEIDO PRESS
for the Japan Writers' Society

Frontispiece and title page for Kokoro *(1914), Sōseki's novel about a tragic conflict of ethics between two generations*

Iwanami Publishing Company in Tokyo.

As a novelist, critic, scholar, haiku poet, classical Chinese poet, and even a southern Chinese–style painter, Sōseki was a versatile man. Yet he was a novelist above all else. After *I Am a Cat,* his first work, had made him famous, Sōseki honed his technique in each subsequent work he wrote, and he also matured in thought. His early works were characterized by attacks on the injustice and unfairness of the world; in his later works he grew increasingly introspective. His agony, or struggle, arose from his experience as a Japanese who faced the difficult task of modernizing himself while a part of him and of his country still belonged to the world shaped by Confucianism and Buddhism. His writings eventually addressed the eternal inner struggle of a man who tries to see the value of human existence in modern society, and in writing such works he created novels with a universal theme.

Sōseki learned much from the West, added it to his traditional Oriental background, and created a new style of Japanese literature. He showed that it was possible to fuse the literary currents of East and West. This, together with his strong sense of justice, his depiction of the loneliness of modern man, and his versatile style, are the qualities that have made Sōseki's works so widely read in Japan.

Biographies:

Akagi Kohei, *Natsume Sōseki* (Tokyo: Shinchōsha, 1917);

Takahama Kyoshi, *Sōseki-shi to watashi* (Tokyo: Arususha, 1918);

Natsume Kyōko, *Sōseki no omoide* (Tokyo: Kaizōsha, 1928);

Matsuoka Yuzuru, *Sōseki sensei* (Tokyo: Iwanami Shoten, 1934);

Komiya Toyotaka, *Natsume Sōseki* (Tokyo: Iwanami Shoten, 1938);

Uchida Hyakken, *Sōseki sanbō no ki* (Tokyo: Chichibu Shobō, 1941);

Yoshida Rokurō, *Sakka izen no Sōseki* (Tokyo: Kobundō, 1942);

Morita Sōhei, *Natsume Sōseki,* 2 volumes (Tokyo: Kōchō Shorin, 1942–1943);

Tsuda Seifu, *Sōseki to jūdeshi* (Tokyo: Sekai Bunko, 1949);

Natsume Shinroku, *Chichi: Natsume Sōseki* (Tokyo: Bungei Shunjū Shinsha, 1956);

Ara Masatō, *Hyōden: Natsume Sōseki* (Tokyo: Jitsugyō no Nihonsha, 1960);

Ara, *Sōseki kenkyū nenpyō* (Tokyo: Shueisha, 1984);

Shima Tameo, *Natsume san no hito oyobi shisō* (Tokyo: Nihon Tosho Senta, 1990).

References:

Aihara Kazukuni, *Sōseki bungaku no kenkyū–sono hyōgen o jiku to shite* (Tokyo: Meiji Shoin, 1988);

Aihara, *Sōseki bungaku–sono hyōgen to shisō* (Tokyo: Hanawa Shobō, 1980);

Akiyama Kimio, *Sōseki bungaku kōsetsu: shoki sakuhin no hojosei* (Tokyo: Ōfūsha, 1994);

Akiyama, *Sōseki bungaku ronkō–Kōki sakuhin no hōhō to kōzō* (Tokyo: Ōfūsha, 1987);

Bessatsu Kokubungaku: Natsume Sōseki hikkei, special issue on Sōseki, 2 (May 1982);

Ward Biddle, "The Authenticity of Natsume Sōseki," *Monumenta Nipponica,* 28 (1973): 4;

Chiya Shichirō, *Sōseki no byōseki–byōki to sakuhin kara* (Tokyo: Keisō Shobō, 1963);

Deguchi Yasuo, *Natsume Sōseki to Rondon o aruku* (Tokyo: PHP Kenkyujo, 1993);

Deguchi, *Rondon no Natsume Sōseki* (Tokyo: Kawade Shobō Shinsha, 1981);

Doi Takeo, *Sōseki no shinteki sekai* (Tokyo: Shibundō, 1969); translated by William J. Tyler as *The Psychological World of Natsume Sōseki* (Cambridge: Harvard University Press, 1976);

Etō Jun, *Natsume Sōseki* (Tokyo: Shinchōsha, 1974);

Etō, *Sōseki ronshū* (Tokyo: Shinchōsha, 1992);

Etō, *Sōseki to Asa-ō densetsu* (Tokyo: Tokyo Daigaku Shuppankai, 1975);

Etō, *Sōseki to sono jidai,* 3 volumes (Tokyo: Shinchōsha, 1970–1993);

Etō and others, eds., *Kōza Natsume Sōseki,* 5 volumes (Tokyo: Yuhikaku, 1981–1982);

Fujii Hidetada, *Hototogisu no jidai: Suitei no Sōseki to seinentachi* (Nagoya: Nagoya Daigaku Shuppankai, 1990);

Fukae Hiroshi, *Sōseki chōhen shōsetsu no sekai* (Tokyo: Ōfūsha, 1981);

Fukuhara Rintarō, *Natsume Sōseki* (Tokyo: Aratake Shobō, 1973);

Furukawa Hisa, *Sōseki no shokan* (Tokyo: Tōkyōdō, 1970);

Gamō Yoshirō, *Sōseki o yomu* (Tokyo: Yōyōsha, 1984);

Van C. Gessel, *Three Modern Novelists: Sōseki, Tanizaki, Kawabata* (Tokyo, New York & London: Kodansha International, 1993);

Handō Kazutoshi, *Sōseki sensei zo na moshi,* 2 volumes (Tokyo: Bungei Shunju, 1992–1993);

Hasumi Shigehiko, *Natsume Sōseki ron* (Tokyo: Seidōsha, 1978);

Hirai Tomio, *Shinkeishō Natsume Sōseki* (Tokyo: Fukutake Shoten, 1990);

Hirakawa Sukehiro, *Natsume Sōseki–Hiseiyō no kutō* (Tokyo: Shinchōsha, 1976);

Hirakawa and Tsuruta Kinya, eds., *Sōseki no "Kokoro" o dō yomu ka, dō yomarete kita ka* (Tokyo: Shin'yōsha, 1992);

Hiraoka Toshio, *Sōseki josetsu* (Tokyo: Hanawa Shobō, 1976);

Hirata Tsugisaburō, *Natsume Sōseki* (Tokyo: Kawade Shobō, 1948);

Honma Kenshirō, *Natsume Sōseki: A Comparative Study* (Hirakata: Intercultural Research Institute, Kansai University of Foreign Studies, 1990);

Horibe Isao and Murata Yoshiya, eds., *Sōseki kankei kiji oyobi bunken* (Tokyo: Ōfūsha, 1991);

Ihara Mitsuo, *Sōseki no nazo o toku "Higansugi made" ron* (Tokyo: Keisō Shobō, 1994);

Iida Rigyo, *Shin'yaku Sōseki shishū* (Tokyo: Kashiwa Shobō, 1994);

Iijima Takehisa and James M. Vardaman Jr., *The World of Natsume Sōseki's Works* (Tokyo: Kinseidō, 1987);

Imanishi Junkichi, *Sōseki bungaku no shisō* (Tokyo: Chikuma Shobō, 1988);

Inagaki Mizuho, *Natsume Sōseki to Rondon ryūgaku* (Tokyo: Azuma Shobō, 1990);

Inagaki Tatsurō, *Natsume Sōseki* (Tokyo: Fukumura Shoten, 1952);

Inoue Kent, *Sōseki-teki sekai no otoko to onna* (Tokyo: Nihon Tosho Kankōkai, 1994);

Ishikawa Masaichi, *Sōseki: Marui wa no ue de* (Tokyo: Kanazawa: Noto Insatsu Shuppanbu, 1991);

Itagaki Naoko, *Sōseki bungaku no haikei* (Tokyo: Masu Shobō, 1957);

Itō Sei, ed., *Natsume Sōseki: Kindai Nihon bungaku kanshō kōza 5* (Tokyo: Kadokawa Shoten, 1958);

Iwagami Jun'ichi, *Sōseki nyumon* (Tokyo: Chūō Kōronsha, 1959);

Japanese National Commission for UNESCO, *Essays on Natsume Sōseki's Works* (Tokyo: Japanese Society for the Promotion of Science, 1972);

Kaga Otohiko and others, *Natsume Sōseki* (Tokyo: Shōgakkan, 1991);

Kajiki Takeshi, *Natsume Sōseki ron* (Tokyo: Keisō Shobō, 1976);

Kamiyama Mutsumi, *Natsume Sōseki ron—josetsu* (Tokyo: Kokubunsha, 1980);

Kamiyama, *"Sorekara" kara "Meian" e* (Tokyo: Sunagoya Shobō, 1981);

Karaki Junzō, *Natsume Sōseki* (Tokyo: Shūdōsha, 1956);

Karatani Kōjin, *Sōseki o yomu* (Tokyo: Iwanami Shoten, 1994);

Karatani, *Sōseki ron shusei* (Tokyo: Daisan Bunmeisha, 1992);

Kataoka Ryūichi, *Natsume Sōseki no sakuhin* (Tokyo: Kōbunsha, 1952);

Donald Keene, *Dawn to the West*, 2 volumes (New York: Holt, Reinhart & Winston, 1984);

Kinya Tsuruta and Thomas E. Swann, eds., *Approaches to the Modern Japanese Novel* (Tokyo: Sophia University Press, 1976);

Kitagaki Ryuichi, *Sōseki no seishin bunseki*, revised edition (Tokyo: Kitazawa Shoten, 1968);

Kitayama Takashi, *Natsume Sōseki no seishin bunseki* (Tokyo: Okakura Shobō, 1924);

Komashaku Kimi, *Sōseki: Sono jikohon'i to rentai to* (Tokyo: Yagi Shoten, 1970);

Komiya Toyotaka, *Sōseki no geijutsu* (Tokyo: Iwanami Shoten, 1942);

Komori Yōichi, *Natsume Sōseki o yomu* (Tokyo: Iwanami Shoten, 1993);

Kosaka Susumu, *Sōseki no ai to bungaku* (Tokyo: Kōdansha, 1974);

Makoto Ueda, *Modern Japanese Writers* (Stanford, Cal.: Stanford University Press, 1976);

Masao Miyoshi, *Accomplices of Silence: The Modern Japanese Novel* (Berkeley: University of California Press, 1974);

Matsui Sakuko, "East and West in Natsume Sōseki: The Formation of a Modern Japanese Novelist," *Meaning Quarterly*, 3 (1967): 282–294;

Matsui, *Natsume Sōseki as a Critic of English Literature* (Tokyo: Tokyo Center for East Asian Cultural Studies, 1975);

Matsumoto Hiroshi, *Sōseki no jikken: gendai o dō ikiru ka* (Tokyo: Chōbunsha, 1993);

Matsuoka Yuzuru, *Sōseki: Hito to sono bungaku* (Tokyo: Chōbunkaku, 1941);

Yoko Matsuoka McClain, *Mago musume kara mita Sōseki* (Tokyo: Shinchōsha, 1995);

McClain, "Natsume Sōseki: A Tragic Father," *Monumenta Nipponica*, 33 (1978): 461–469;

McClain, "Sōseki and Oliver Goldsmith," *Waseda Journal*, 7 (1985): 32–45;

Edwin McClellan, "An Introduction to Sōseki," *Harvard Journal of Asiatic Studies*, 22 (1959): 150–208;

McClellan, *Two Japanese Novelists* (Chicago: University of Chicago Press, 1969);

Meiji Taishō Bungaku Kenkyū: Tokushū: Natsume Sōseki, special issue on Sōseki, 6 (November 1951);

Meiji Taishō Bungaku Kenkyū: Tokushū: zoku Natsume Sōseki, special issue on Sōseki, 7 (June 1952);

Miyai Ichirō, *Natsume Sōseki no koi* (Tokyo: Chikuma Shobō, 1976);

Miyai, *Sōseki no sekai* (Tokyo: Kōdansha, 1967);

Miyoshi Yukio, *Ōgai to Sōseki—no etosu* (Tokyo: Rikitomi Shobō, 1983);

Miyoshi, *Sōseki bungei no sekai* (Tokyo: Ōfūsha, 1973);

Mori Shinobu, *Sōseki e no sokuen—"Sorekara," "Mon," "Kōjin"* (Tokyo: Keisō Shobō, 1988);

Nakajima Kunihiko, *Natsume Sōseki no tegami* (Tokyo: Taishukan Shoten, 1994);

Nakamura Hiroshi, *Sōseki kanshi no sekai* (Tokyo: Daiichi Shobō, 1983);

Nakamura Mitsuo, *Sōseki to Hakuchō* (Tokyo: Chikuma Shobō, 1979);

Nihon Kindai Bungaku, special issue on Sōseki, 5 (November 1965);

Nishigaki Tsutomu, *Sōseki to Shirakaba-ha* (Tokyo: Yuseidō, 1990);

Ochi Haruo, *Sōseki to Meiji bungaku* (Tokyo: Ōfūsha, 1983);

Ochi, *Sōseki shiron* (Tokyo: Kadokawa Shoten, 1971);

Ogura Shūzō, *Natsume Sōseki—William James juyō no shūhen* (Tokyo: Yūseidō, 1989);

Okazaki Yoshie, *Sōseki to sokuten kyoshi* (Tokyo: Iwanami Shoten, 1943);

Oketani Hideaki, *Natsume Sōseki ron* (Tokyo: Kawade Shobō, 1972);

Ōoka Shōhei, *Shōsetsuka Natsume Sōseki* (Tokyo: Chikuma Shobō, 1988);

Ōtani Masanori, *Natsume Sōseki ronkō* (Tokyo: Ōfūsha, 1988);

William Plomer, "The English Mind: A Japanese Judgement. A Note on Sōseki Natsume," *New Adelph*, 3 (1929): 49–54;

Z. N. Popoff, "Introduction to Modern Japanese Literature: Natsume Sōseki as Pioneer of the Modern Literature," *Cultural Nippon*, 3 (1935): 595–601;

Jay Rubin, "Sōseki on Individualism: Watakushi no kojinshugi," *Monumenta Nipponica,* 34 (1979): 21–48;

Sakamoto Hiroshi, *Natsume Sōseki–Sakuhin no shinsō sekai* (Tokyo: Meiji Shoin, 1979);

Sako Jun'ichirō, *Natsume Sōseki ron* (Tokyo: Shinbisha, 1978);

G. W. Sargent, "Two Meiji Novels on Youth," *Journal of the Oriental Society of Australia,* 6 (1968–1969): 104–111;

Sasabuchi Yūichi, *Natsume Sōseki–Yume jūya ron hoka* (Tokyo: Meiji Shoin, 1986);

Sasaki Hideaki, *"Atarashii onna" no tōrai* (Nagoya: Nagoya Daigaku Shuppankai, 1994);

Sasaki Mitsuru, *Sōseki suikō* (Tokyo: Ōfūsha, 1992);

Satō Yasumasa, *Natsume Sōseki ron* (Tokyo: Chikuma Shobō, 1986);

Senuma Shigeki, *Natsume Sōseki* (Tokyo: Tokyo Daigaku Shuppanbu, 1962);

Shimizu Chūhei, *Sōseki ni miru ai no yukue* (Tokyo: Garafusha, 1992);

Donald Shively, ed., *Tradition and Modernization in Japanese Culture* (Princeton: Princeton University Press, 1965);

Sukegawa Noriyoshi, *Sōseki to Meiji bungaku* (Tokyo: Ōfūsha, 1983);

Takada Mizuho, *Natsume Sōseki ron–Sōseki bungaku no konnichiteki igi* (Tokyo: Meiji Shoin, 1984);

Takagi Fumio, *Sōseki bungaku no shichū* (Tokyo: Shinbisha, 1971);

Takagi, *Sōseki no dōtei* (Tokyo: Shinbisha, 1966);

Takagi, *Sōseki sakuhin no uchi to soto* (Osaka: Izumi Shoin, 1994);

Takizawa Katsumi, *Natsume Sōseki* (Tokyo: Mikasa Shobō, 1943);

Tamai, *Natsume Sōseki ron* (Tokyo: Ōfūsha, 1976);

Alan Turney, *Sōseki's Development as a Novelist until 1907* (Tokyo: Tōyō Bunko, 1985);

Uchida Michio and Kubota Yoshitaro, eds., *Sakuhinron: Natsume Sōseki* (Tokyo: Sōbunsha Shuppan, 1976);

V. H. Viglielmo, "The Hero in Natsume Sōseki's Novels," *Journal-Newsletter of the Association of Teachers of Japanese,* 4 (1966): 1–18;

Viglielmo, "An Introduction to the Later Novels of Natsume Sōseki," *Monumenta Nipponica,* 19 (1964): 1–36;

Yamada Teruhiko, *Natsume Sōseki no bungaku* (Tokyo: Ōfūsha, 1984);

Yamoto Sadatomo, *Natsume Sōseki–sono eibungaku-teki sokumen* (Tokyo: Kenkyusha, 1971);

Yamoto, *Sōseki no seishin* (Tokyo: Akitaya, 1948);

Yoneda Toshiaki, *Watashi no Sōseki* (Tokyo: Keisō Shobō, 1990);

Yoshida Atsuhiko, *Sōseki no yume no onna* (Tokyo: Seidosha, 1994);

Yoshida Rokurō, *Sōseki bungaku no shinriteki tankyu* (Tokyo: Keisō Shobō, 1970);

Yoshida, *Wagahai wa neko de aru ron* (Tokyo: Keisō Shobō, 1968);

Yoshikawa Kōjirō, *Sōseki shi chu* (Tokyo: Iwanami Shoten, 1967);

Beongcheon Yu, *Natsume Sōseki* (New York: Twayne, 1969).

Nogami Yaeko
(6 May 1885 - 30 March 1985)

Yoko McClain
University of Oregon

BOOKS: *Ningyō no nozomi* (Tokyo: Jitsugyō no Nihonsha, 1914);

Atarashiki inochi (Tokyo: Iwanami Shoten, 1916);

Shōsetsu muttsu (Tokyo: Kaizōsha, 1922);

Kaijinmaru sono ta (Tokyo: Kaizōsha, 1924); translated by Ryōzo Matsumoto as "The Neptune," in *The Neptune and The Foxes* (Tokyo: Kenkyūsha, 1957);

Ningen sōzō (Tokyo: Iwanami Shoten, 1926);

Ōishi Yoshio (Tokyo: Iwanami Bunko, 1926);

Machiko (Tokyo: Tettō Shoin, 1931);

Nyūgakushiken otomo no ki (Tokyo: Koyama Shoten, 1933);

Wakai musuko (Tokyo: Iwanami Shoten, 1933);

Yōseien (Tokyo: Chūō Kōronsha, 1936);

Wakaki tomo e no tegami (Tokyo: Tōkō Shoin, 1936);

Akikazechō (Tokyo: Sagami Shobō, 1937);

Ohanashi (Tokyo: Iwanami Shoten, 1940);

Fuji (Tokyo: Kōchō Shorin, 1941);

Ōbei no tabi, 2 volumes (Tokyo: Iwanami Shoten, 1942);

Onō no monogatari (Tokyo: Shōgakkan, 1943);

Sansōki: Nihon sōsho (Tokyo: Seikatsusha, 1945);

Zoku sansōki: Nihon sōsho (Tokyo: Seikatsusha, 1946);

Yamabiko (Tokyo: Seikatsusha, 1947);

Meigetsu (Tokyo: Tokyo Shuppan Kabushikigaisha, 1947);

Kusawake (Tokyo: Koyama Shoten, 1947);

Kin no ringo (Tokyo: Shōgakkan, 1947);

Meiro: Part 1 (Tokyo: Iwanami Shoten, 1948);

Meiro: Part 2 (Tokyo: Iwanami Shoten, 1948);

Onō monogatari (Tokyo: Shōgakkan, 1948);

Obāsan to kobuta (Tokyo: Chūō Kōronsha, 1949);

Meiro: Part 3 (Tokyo: Iwanami Shoten, 1952);

Meiro: Part 4 (Tokyo: Iwanami Shoten, 1952);

Wakaki shimai yo ika ni ikubeki ka (Tokyo: Iwanami Shoten, 1953);

Meiro: Part 5 (Tokyo: Iwanami Shoten, 1954);

Wakaki sedai no tomo e (Tokyo, 1954);

Wakaki josei to kataru (Tokyo: Kadokawa Shinsho, 1955);

Nogami Yaeko

Meiro: Part 6 (Tokyo: Iwanami Shoten, 1956);

Watakushi no Chūgoku ryokō (Tokyo: Iwanami Shinsho, 1959);

Hideyoshi to Rikyū (Tokyo: Chūō Kōronsha, 1964);

Kijo sambōki (Tokyo: Iwanami Shoten, 1964);

Fue; Suzuran (Tokyo: Iwanami Shoten, 1966);

Ichiguno ki (Tokyo: Shinchōsha, 1968);

Mukashi gatari (Tokyo: Horupu Shuppan, 1972);

Hana (Tokyo: Shinchōsha, 1977);

Nihon jidōbungaku taikei (Tokyo: Horupu Shuppan, 1978);

Nogami Yaeko nikki – shinsai zengo (Tokyo: Iwanami Shoten, 1984);

Mori (Tokyo: Shinchōsha, 1985).

Collections: *Nogami Yaeko senshū,* 7 volumes (Tokyo: Chūō Kōronsha, 1949–1952);
Nogami Yaeko zenshū, 26 volumes (Tokyo: Iwanami Shoten, 1980–1982).

OTHER: Thomas Bulfinch, *The Age of Fable,* translated by Nogami as *Densetsu no jidai* (Tokyo: Shōbundō, 1913);
Johanna Spyri, *Heidi,* translated by Nogami as *Haiji* (Tokyo: Katei Yomimono Kankōkai, 1920);
Selma Lagerlöf, *Gösta Berlings Saga,* translated by Nogami as *Gesuta Beruringu* (Tokyo: Katei Yomimono Kankōkai, 1921);
Anne Charlotte Löffler, *Sonya Kovalevski,* translated by Nogami as *Sonya Kobarefusukaya* (Tokyo: Iwanami Shoten, 1924).

At the age of twenty-two Nogami Yaeko made her literary debut with "Enishi" (The Ties of Love, 1907) and thereby began what has been the longest writing career of any author in Japan. Writing for many years does not mean that one is a great writer, but with each new work she steadily matured both in technique and insight. Many critics consider *Hideyoshi to Rikyū* (Hideyoshi and Rikyū, 1964), the historical novel that she completed when she was seventy-eight years old, one of the masterpieces of modern Japanese literature. After finishing this work Yaeko wrote several short stories, miscellanies, and many essays of social criticism. At the age of eighty-seven she published the first installment of *Mori* (The Forest, 1985), her autobiographical novel, in the literary magazine *Shinchō,* and through her perseverance and diligence she was nearly able to complete the final chapter of this work before her death.

Yaeko was born as Kotegawa Yae, the daughter of Kotegawa Kakusaburō, a wealthy wine maker in Usukine-machi in Ōita Prefecture in Kyushu. Her given name, written in *katakana,* was Yae, but after 1907 she used Yaeko, written in Chinese characters, for her pen name. Both her father, a progressive businessman with political and financial power, and her mother, Masa, who had little formal education and wanted more educational opportunities for her daughter, were willing to allow Yaeko to pursue her studies, and this was a rare privilege for a young girl in the late nineteenth century.

Since children had few sources of entertainment in those days, the only thing Yaeko could do was go to a private teacher to read. She usually went there on the way home from school, but, walking in the dark with a paper lantern in her hand, she sometimes even went in the morning before school. She read *Shiki,* the four Chinese classics, and also such Japanese classics as *Kokin wakashū* (Japanese Poems, Ancient and Modern), *Makura no sōshi* (Pillow Book), and Murasaki Shikibu's *Genji monogatari* (translated as *The Tale of Genji,* 1925–1933). Just as children memorize popular songs today, she memorized many of the poems from *Genji.* After completing her primary education, she started studying English with a private teacher.

At the age of fifteen she left home to study in Tokyo, where Kotegawa Toyojirō, her uncle, lived. Her uncle, seventeen years older than she, was a hunchback and an eccentric man, but he was extremely bright and had an independent mind, and her parents apparently felt that Yaeko could live safely under his supervision. Her father had been sympathetic to his younger brother's affliction, and, because Toyojirō's deformity had kept him from being permitted to enter a Japanese university or college, Yaeko's father had supported him for six years when he had gone to study in the United States. There he had earned a Ph.D. degree in economics from the University of Michigan in the late 1800s, and after he had returned to Japan, he had become a banker. During the 1920s Yaeko wrote several short stories—"Sumiko" (1923), "Junzō to sono kyōdai" (Junzō and His Siblings, 1923), and "Kurutta tokei" (Out-of-Order Clock, 1925)—based on his life.

Soon after Yaeko settled in Tokyo she entered Meiji Jogakkō, or Meiji Women's School, a progressive Christian school that cultivated intellect as well as independence of thought in its students. The school's leaders believed that a woman must first develop a personality of her own before she could be a good wife and a good mother. More important than an ability to follow authority and observe the formalities or customs of society was a woman's ability to think for herself. Yaeko acknowledged that the education she received at this school helped her to cultivate intellectual independence.

This educational background must have both encouraged her to proceed at her own pace without being concerned about the productivity of other writers and given her the strength to not be discouraged by occasionally negative critical comments. This school also provided Yaeko with a good command of English—particularly in reading, because all the textbooks were in English, and the students were made to read "by looking

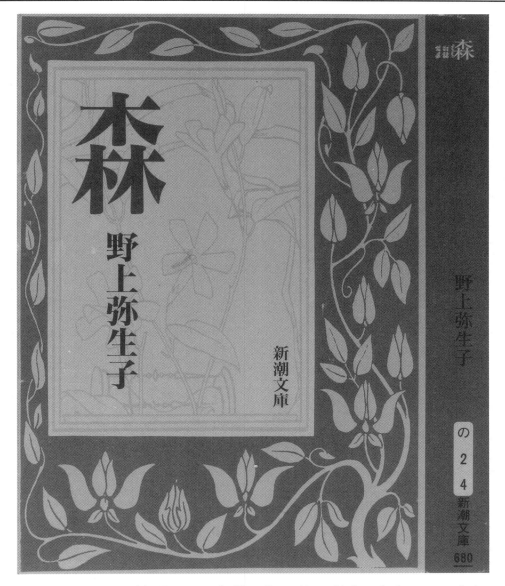

森

野上弥生子

新潮文庫

野上弥生子

の
2
4
新潮文庫
680

Dust jacket for Mori *(The Forest, 1985), Nogami's autobiographical novel whose protagonist is among the women educated in increasing numbers in Japan during 1900–1903*

up words in the dictionary." Because of this intense language training, Yaeko was later able to translate into Japanese many Western literary works, such as Thomas Bulfinch's *The Age of Fable* (1913), Swedish novelist Selma Lagerlöf's *Gösta Berlings Saga* (1921), and Anne Charlotte Löffler's *Sonya Kovalevski* (1924), the life of a Russian mathematician.

In 1905, a year before she graduated from Meiji Jogakkō, Yaeko married Nogami Toyoichirō, an English student at Tokyo Imperial University. He was two years older than she, and he had also come to Tokyo from Ōita. Toyoichirō was interested in creative writing, and he was already a student of Natsume Sōseki. He was also

an understanding husband, and he supported Yaeko's endeavors to become a writer by taking "Meian" (Light and Darkness), her first attempt at short-story writing, to his teacher in January 1907 for comments.

Sōseki responded with both general and specific advice in his letter of 17 January 1907 to Yaeko. He criticized the fact that several of the characters lacked naturalness and the sequence of events was abruptly handled. If Yaeko wanted to become a writer, he advised, she should live every day with this aim in mind and not let years pass without a definite goal. He encouraged her to continue writing and suggested that her shortcomings were not results of her lack of talent but rather of her youth, her lack of experience and philosophical thinking. He predicted that if she read her "Light and Darkness" ten years later, she would understand what he was saying. Yaeko treasured this letter, which was written on rolled Japanese paper more than one-and-one-half meters long, and she conscientiously followed his advice in her later works. She acknowledged that if Sōseki had given neither encouragement nor kind advice to her at that time, she probably would not have become a writer.

Following Sōseki's recommendation the journal *Hototogisu* published "Enishi" (The Ties of Love, 1907), her first story to appear in print. Soichi, her first son, was born in 1910; Mokichirō, her second son, followed in 1915; and Yōzō, her third, was born in 1918. Yet even during those years while the children were still toddlers, Yaeko persevered in her writing by never letting a year pass without producing some work. Taking advantage of her position as a mother, Yaeko observed her children closely and wrote several heart-warming stories about the physical and psychological growth of children as well as the joys and the pains of young, inexperienced parents. Many scenes in these pieces—of sibling quarrels, a young child's imitation of older siblings, a mother's depression after scolding a child, and her pride in watching her children mature intellectually—are familiar to those with children.

She also translated Johanna Spyri's *Heidi* (1920), the children's classic, and wrote many children's stories based on both Japanese sources and on Greek and Roman mythology. As an intellectual mother she wanted to write books of high literary quality that Japanese children could understand and enjoy, and her three sons all became successful scholars. Soichi was a professor of Italian literature at Kyoto University; Mokichirō and Yōzō were both professors of physics at Tokyo University.

One of her most important early works is "Kaijinmaru" (1922), a short story that was apparently the first work with which she was especially satisfied, because she felt that it was more a novel than a schoolgirl composition. *Kaijinmaru* is the name of a small oceangoing cargo boat that becomes damaged by a violent storm that leaves its crew stranded. The story recounts the adventures of its four-man crew—the captain, his young nephew, and two seamen. When the supply of food for the crew runs out, the two seamen—one a rough laborer and the other a simpleton—cannot endure hunger any longer and finally

decide to cannibalize the young boy. Faithfully heeding Sōseki's warning to avoid making the action too abrupt, Yaeko presents events in ways that gradually and powerfully build toward the climactic scene of the boy's brutal murder. The two men split the head of the young boy with an ax, but then they find that they cannot eat him.

After being adrift for fifty-nine days, the boat is finally found by a big cargo ship on its way to Yokohama. The men are picked up, and one of the seamen dies before they reach land. When officials interrogate the captain about his nephew's fate, he exonerates the surviving seaman by reporting that the boy died from illness. This ending may reflect some Christian conception of forgiveness that Yaeko had acquired during her years at Meiji Jogakkō.

According to Yaeko, "Kaijinmaru" is based on a true story that her brother had heard directly from a captain, and from this narrative she created a psychological drama apart from the middle-class world that had been her principal domain. The story is tightly constructed from beginning to end; its characters are well delineated; and its style is forceful but never sentimental or emotional, and these stylistic features frequently give an impression that the author of the story is a male. In fact, this lack of a so-called feminine quality distinguishes Yaeko's later and better works, such as *Meiro* (The Maze, 1948–1956) and *Hideyoshi to Rikyū*.

More ambitious than "Kaijinmaru," her next important work, *Machiko* (1931), involves many more characters and incidents and was first published serially from 1928 through 1930. As an intelligent young woman from an upper-middle-class family, Machiko is provoked by the vanity, hypocrisy, and ostentation of her social class. As a student auditing a sociology class at Tokyo Imperial University, she meets Yoneko, the daughter of a bankrupt farm landlord from the north and a politically active participant in the Socialist movement. Through Yoneko, Machiko meets Seki, a revolutionary youth to whom she is attracted, and she considers giving up her comfortable life to work for the revolutionary cause. Meanwhile, she also meets Kawai, a wealthy, Oxford-educated anthropologist, through her family connections. When Kawai eventually proposes to her, Machiko refuses him and instead chooses Seki as her husband. Just as she is about to marry Seki, however, Machiko learns that Yoneko is pregnant with Seki's child. Infuriated with Seki's insincerity and irresponsibility toward both Yoneko and herself, Machiko concludes that without maintaining high

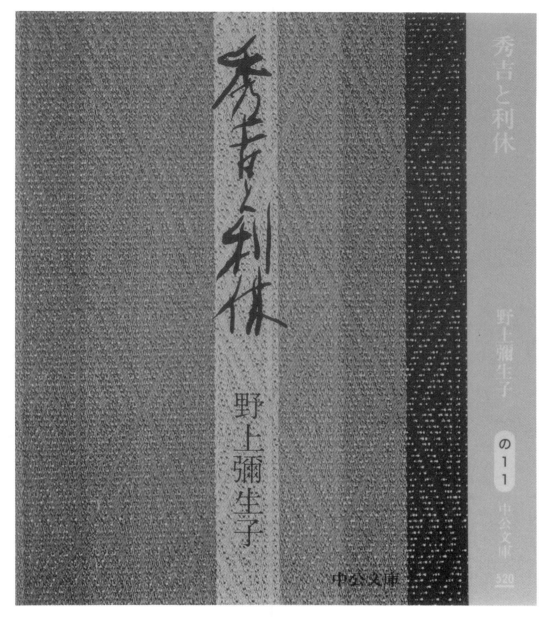

Dust jacket for Hideyoshi to Rikyū *(Hideyoshi and Rikyū, 1964), Nogami's historical novel about a feud between a sixteenth-century ruler and his tea master*

personal standards of morality, those who espouse the ideals of Communism, such as helping the poor and bringing equality to everyone, are voicing meaningless principles. When Kawai, the suitor whom Machiko had earlier rejected and who has relinquished much of his wealth for the workers of his family-owned company, reappears at the end to again propose to Machiko, she realizes that she loves him and agrees to marry him.

Although Yaeko was sympathetic toward socially concerned youth, whose serious thinking often caused them to lean politically toward Social-ist reforms, she disapproved of revolutionary ideas at the cost of human compassion. She clearly despised the affectation and hypocrisy of the rich, although she approved of upper-middle-class people as long as they possessed good sense, fine sensibility, and human warmth. Through the characters and events of *Machiko* both social extremes are rejected, and common sense prevails at the end. The main characters—Machiko, Kawai, and Seki—are psychologically and physically well presented, as are some supporting characters, such as Machiko's sister and brother-in-law in addition to several snobbish, upper-middle-class women. The psychological realism with which Yaeko develops these characters creates a story that reveals the foibles of human nature.

In 1932 Yaeko published another short story with a similar theme, the anguish of a young man who is from a good family and joins the leftist movement in opposition to his mother's pleas. Like *Machiko,* "Wakai musuko" (The Young Son) presents the thinking and behavior of many youths early in the Shōwa Period. Yaeko's oldest son was in college around this time, and because her husband was a professor, she probably witnessed many students, some undoubtedly her son's close friends or her husband's students, whose motives for turning politically to the Left were mainly those of their youthful idealism and passion. Her handling of these youthful characters is more sympathetic than critical, and she probably believed that they would mature and become more understanding adults.

The Maze, a later novel that Yaeko began writing in 1936 and was unable to finish until wartime restrictions on freedom of speech had been removed, presents the same themes through the life of a young man who is expelled from Tokyo Imperial University because he joins a radical group. She rewrote the first part and published it in 1948 in *Sekai,* which continued the serialization of chapters in 1949. In the epilogue of *The Maze,* Yaeko relates that her many years of work on this novel of more than one thousand pages was due not to laziness but to the fact that the political situation in Japan had not permitted her to make the characters behave as she had felt they should. Following the defeat of Japan, she felt that her pen was no longer as restrained by the influence of military authorities as it had been.

The Maze is very much an antiwar work, but it is not a simple, crude criticism of the war. Her views of the years from 1936 through 1944 are woven into the complex plot, and the actions of her characters subtly express her philosophy. It is a long, thoughtfully written work, her most ambitious undertaking, and she received the Ninth Yomiuri Literary Award for it in 1957, a year after she completed it. Because it involves many people with varied backgrounds, interests, and experiences, this novel defies easy summarization.

The story chiefly concerns Shōzō, a sensitive and good but weak young man who proceeds through life constantly wondering what course he should take. An elegant, beautiful, extremely sensuous viscountess seduces him. His attractive cousin, a childhood companion and the extravagant daughter of a wealthy businessman, expresses her affection toward Shōzō but cynically marries a millionaire to enjoy a life of luxury. Kizu, one of his college friends, is a brilliant young man who is expelled from school near the same time that Shōzō is. An uneducated, tyrannical sergeant shows open hatred toward the educated. These are among the many memorable characters in *The Maze.*

The last part of the novel concerns Shōzō's life in China during the war, when atrocities are committed. Even Shōzō, who has tried to abide by his conscience, kills Chinese guerrillas by throwing a hand grenade, an act that horrifies him. Soon afterward he meets Kizu, an old friend who, disguised as a member of a covert military agency, secretly advises him to flee from the Japanese army and join an antiwar organization that has been started in Yenan by an exiled Japanese communist leader. Shōzō hesitates, but when he realizes that a sergeant might order him to behead an innocent Chinese cook who has been charged with distributing anti-Japanese propaganda leaflets, Shōzō finally decides to act. On the night he is scheduled for guard duty he frees the cook, and the two flee together, but Shōzō injures his foot and cannot keep up with the cook. After Shōzō urges the cook to escape without him, the pursuing Japanese soldiers shoot him, and the story ends with Shōzō lying unconscious, only two hundred meters from the village that he had hoped to reach. The novel ends inconclusively, with his fate still unknown.

Yaeko's presentation of army life in the last chapters is surprisingly vivid, and it is hard to believe that these were written by an elderly woman who had never experienced army life. She explained that a young friend, a painter, had supplied her with his notes and drawings, and using these materials she presents the brutal atrocities of war with her characteristic force and objectivity. Yet she also discusses topics such as dialectical materialism, religion, and classical Japanese literature in her presentations of Shōzō's contemplations, and these erudite reflections give her novel an intellectual depth that constitutes another dimension of her work.

Hideyoshi and Rikyū, her next novel, was serialized in *Chūō Kōron* from January 1962 through 1963 before the complete work was published in 1964, the year in which Yaeko received the Third Women's Literary Award. Although written by an author almost eighty years old, the whole story possesses a youthful vigor and is narrated with intensity. The novel concerns Hideyoshi, the sixteenth-century dictator, and Rikyū, his tea master, and their interactions—their mutual dependence and their fatal feud—during the last three years of Rikyū's life.

The seventy-year-old Rikyū recognizes with resignation that an apology to Hideyoshi is his safest and most advantageous course of action, but he cannot bring himself to apologize. He wistfully recalls his earlier days with Hideyoshi, who is also painfully aware of how much he misses Rikyū, the man whom he expelled from the palace in a violent verbal tirade. In spite of their regret, pride prevents both from initiating a truce, and, outraged by Rikyū's arrogance in not begging to be forgiven, Hideyoshi impulsively orders him to commit seppuku. The feud between these two headstrong geniuses eventually culminates with Rikyū fulfilling Hideyoshi's command.

Yet even during the last moments before his death Rikyū knows that Hideyoshi has taken nothing from him. Everything Rikyū has created has been ostensibly for Hideyoshi, but in truth it has been all for himself. Rikyū knows that even a small shōji in a teahouse will remind Hideyoshi of him after Rikyū has committed seppuku, and he therefore finds final satisfaction as an artist and with calm reserve disembowels himself: "The head, carefully cleaned, was beautiful. The neatly shaved head had a good shape, and the white neck bone, cut flat, surrounded by pink flesh looked like the stamen of a flower."

This historical novel is Yaeko's masterpiece. Every incident and every character are essential to its development, and the novel presents the complexity of the individual characters. For example, Hideyoshi, who is often shown to be a tyrant, also is shown to be gentle toward his invalid brother and tractable in yielding to several plans that his aging mother proposes. Two supporting characters—Sōji, an honest, faithful, and almost clumsy tea master, and Kisaburō, a supposed third son of Rikyū—are both memorable, and their disapproval of Rikyū's crafty political maneuvers highlights that part of his character.

Following *Hideyoshi and Rikyū* Yaeko wrote several short stories, miscellanies, and essays that reveal those qualities that distinguish her craft as a writer. Her keen observation, for example, is evident in the almost childlike curiosity with which she observes things around her. Another characteristic, her intellectual capacity, marks her as one of the more thoughtful of modern Japanese writers. Western philosophy was always one of her interests, and for ten years Yaeko, beginning

Nogami Yaeko

shortly before her seventieth birthday, had taken a private course in philosophy from Tanabe Hijime, a well-known philosophy professor who had retired from Tokyo University. Ironically, however, this philosophical orientation may be one reason that her works are not as widely read as those of some writers: for many young readers, her work can be intellectually strenuous rather than merely entertaining.

In 1972 she began to publish *Mori,* her final novel, in a periodical, and by publishing one or two chapters a year she had nearly completed the last chapter, which appeared in the January 1984 issue of *Shinchō,* before her death on 30 March 1985. Although the conclusion was never published, one can infer what she planned as the ending to her story by examining the manuscript that she left. The novel concerns the years from 1900 to 1903 when Kikuchi Kane, the young protagonist, attends Meiji Jogakkō. Kane is no doubt modeled after Yaeko, but the novel is not merely a fictional autobiography; in fact, it aims to recount a moment in the cultural history of intellectual women amid some prominent men of letters, religion, and politics in Japan at the turn of the century. Despite Yaeko's age at the time she was fictionally re-creating her memories of men and women intellectuals, the educational system, and the family structure of Japanese life during the early years of this century, her work shows no signs of deterioration in her intellectual or writing abilities.

Throughout her career Nogami Yaeko worked steadily and diligently as she developed her skills with each new work. Even after completing her masterpiece, *Hideyoshi and Rikyū,* when she was almost eighty years old, she remained indefatigable until the day before her death. The works of many writers more popular than Yaeko have been enjoyed and forgotten, but readers continue to admire Yaeko for her eighty years of intellectual pursuit and her perseverance that have provided a legacy of literary works that remains of enduring value.

Biographies:

Miyamoto Yuriko, *Fujin to bungaku* (Tokyo: Jitsugyō no Nihonsha, 1948);

Yuasa Yoshiko, "Sanjunen no kōyū," in *Nogami Yaeko / Miyamoto Yuriko, Geppō* (Tokyo: Kawade Shobō, 1951);

Murakami Aya, *Nogami Yaeko no furusato* (Tokyo: Fundōkin Shōyu Kabushikigaisha, 1965).

References:

Ara Masatō, *Shimin bungaku ron* (Tokyo: Aoki Shoten, 1955);

Itagaki Naoko, *Meiji, Taishō, Shōwa no joryūbungaku* (Tokyo: Ōfusha, 1949);

Yoko McClain, "Nogami Yaeko: A Writer as Steady as a Cow?," *Journal of the Association of Teachers of Japanese,* 17 (1982): 153–172;

Sukegawa Noriyoshi, *Nogami Yaeko to Taishōki kyōyōha* (Tokyo: Ōfūsha, 1984);

Watanabe Sumiko, *Nogami Yaeko no bungaku* (Tokyo: Ōfūsha, 1984).

Sata Ineko
(1 June 1904 –)

Hasegawa Kei
Women's College, Jōsai University

BOOKS: *Kyarameru kōba kara* (Tokyo: Senkisha, 1930);

Kenkyūkai sōwa (Tokyo: Kaizōsha, 1930);

Kitō (Tokyo: Shinkō Shobō, 1932);

Ichi fujin sakka no zuisō (N.p., 1934);

Botan no aru ie (Tokyo: Chūō Kōronsha, 1934);

Hyōronshō (Tokyo: Naukasha, 1934);

Kurenai (Tokyo: Chūō Kōronsha, 1938);

Hitofukuro no dagashi (Tokyo: Sanwa Shobō, 1939);

Seishun in'ei (Tokyo: Shūn'yōdō, 1939);

Suashi no musume (Tokyo: Shinchōsha, 1940);

Suashi no onna (N.p., 1940);

Onna sannin (Tokyo: Jidaisha, 1940);

Utsukushii hitotachi (Tokyo: Kinseidō, 1940);

Josei no kotoba (Tokyo: Takayama Shoin, 1940);

Kigi shinryoku (Tokyo: Shinchōsha, 1940);

Yume ōki hokori (Tokyo: Gakugeisha, 1941);

Tobira (Tokyo: Kōchō Shorin, 1941);

Kisetsu no zuihitsu (Tokyo: Banrikaku, 1941);

Shiki no kuruma (Tokyo: Bungei Shūnjūsha, 1941);

Onna no kataru hanashi (Tokyo: Futami Shobō, 1941);

Hibi no hanryo (Tokyo: Jidaisha, 1941);

Kokoro kayowamu (Tokyo: Gakugeisha, 1941);

Ka ni niou (Tokyo: Shōrinsha, 1942);

Zoku: Josei no kotoba (Tokyo: Takayama Shoin, 1942);

Kizukazariki (Tokyo: Zenkoku Shobō, 1943);

Josei to bungaku (Tokyo: Jitsugyō no Nihonsha, 1943);

Wakaki tsumatachi (Tokyo: Katsuragi Shoten, 1944);

Tatazumai (Tokyo: Banrikaku, 1946);

Ryojō (Tokyo: Asuka Shoten, 1947);

Kigi no sayagi (Tokyo: Ozawa Shoten, 1947);

Aru onna no koseki (Tokyo: Jitsugyō no Nihonsha, 1948);

Watashi no Nagasaki chizu (Tokyo: Gogatsu Shobō, 1948);

Hirakareta tobira (Tokyo: Yagumo Shoin, 1949);

Watashi no Tokyo chizu (Tokyo: Shin Nihon Bungaku Kai, 1949);

Sata Ineko kansō shū (Tokyo: Hakurinsha, 1949);

Gendai Nihon meisaku sen (Tokyo: Chikuma Shobō, 1953);

Kiiroi kemuri (Tokyo: Chikuma Shobō, 1954);

Moyuru kagiri (Tokyo: Chikuma Shobō, 1955);

Kodomo no me (Tokyo: Kadokawa Shoten, 1955);

Yoru no kioku (Tokyo: Kawade Shobō, 1955);

Kikai no naka no seishun (Tokyo: Kadokawa Shoten, 1955);

Midori no namikimichi (Tokyo: Shin Hyōronsha, 1955);

Chie no wa (Tokyo: Gendaisha, 1956);

Kaze to seishun (Tokyo: Kadokawa Shoten, 1956);

Yoru o se ni hiru o omote ni (Tokyo: Tōhōsha, 1956);

Itoshii koibitotachi (Tokyo: Bungei Shunjō Shinsha, 1956);

Kokoro no tana (Tokyo: Gendaisha, 1956);

Onna no isshō (Tokyo: Sakai Shoten, 1956);

Kaji o waga te ni (Tokyo: Tōhōsha, 1956);

Tsumi tsukuri (Tokyo: Gendaisha, 1957);

Karada no naka o kaze ga fuku (Tokyo: Kōdansha, 1957);

Ningyō to fue (Tokyo: Shuppan Shoshi Patoria, 1957);

Ai to osore to (Tokyo: Kōdansha, 1958);

Hataraku josei no ikikata (Tokyo: Chiseisha, 1959);

Ningyohime (Tokyo: Kōdansha, 1959);

Baanbaan (Tokyo: Shinchōsha, 1959);

Haguruma (Tokyo: Chikuma Shobō, 1959);

Haiiro no gogo (Tokyo: Kōdansha, 1960);

Furimuita anata (Tokyo: Kōdansha, 1961);

Hitotsu yane no shita (Tokyo: Chūō Kōronsha, 1962);

Yoru to hiru to (Tokyo: Kadokawa Shoten, 1962);

Onna no yado (Tokyo: Kōdansha, 1963);

Onna chawan (Tokyo: Sangatsu Shobō, 1963);

Keiryū (Tokyo: Kōdansha, 1964);

Ane to imōto (Tokyo: Tōhōsha, 1964);

Ikiru to iu koto (Tokyo: Bungei Shunjū Shinsha, 1965);

Onnatachi (Tokyo: Kōdansha, 1965);

Onna no michizure (Tokyo: Kōdansha, 1966);

Sozō (Tokyo: Kōdansha, 1966);

Kaze ni najinda uta (Tokyo: Shinchōsha, 1967);

Ato ni ikiru mono e: Waga kokoro no inori o komete (To-
    kyo: Seishun Shuppansha, 1969);
Hitoriaruki (Tokyo: Sangatsu Shobō, 1969);
Aware (Tokyo: Shinchōsha, 1969);
Omoki nagare ni (Tokyo: Kōdansha, 1970);
Juei (Tokyo: Kōdansha, 1972);
Hitoritabi futaritabi (Tokyo: Hokuyōsha, 1973);
Zuihitsushū futo kikoeta kotoba (Tokyo: Kōdansha,
    1974);
Toki ni tatsu (Tokyo: Kawade Shobō Shinsha,
    1976);
Watakushi no Tōkyō chizu (N.p., 1978);
Yukari no ko (Tokyo: Shinchōsha, 1978);
Kinō no niji (Tokyo: Mainichi Shinbunsha, 1978);
Tōku chikaku (Tokyo: Chikuma Shobō, 1979);
Toki to hito to watashi no koto (Tokyo: Kōdansha,
    1979);
Nennen no tegotae (Tokyo: Kōdansha, 1981);
Natsu no shiori: Nakano Shigeharu o okuru (Tokyo:
    Shinchōsha, 1983);
Nenpu no gyōkan (Tokyo: Chūō Kōronsha, 1983);
Zuihitsu shū deatta en (Tokyo: Kōdansha, 1984);
Yosooi (Tokyo: Sakuhinsha, 1985);
Tsuki no en (Tokyo: Kōdansha, 1985);
Chiisai yama to tsubaki no yama (Tokyo: Kōdansha,
    1987);
Omou dochi (Tokyo: Kōdansha, 1989);
Ato ya saki (Tokyo: Chūō Kōronsha, 1993).
Collections: *Sata Ineko sakuhin shū,* 15 volumes (To-
    kyo: Chikuma Shobō, 1958–1959);
Sata Ineko zenshū, 18 volumes, edited by Ōe
    Kenzaburō (Tokyo: Kōdansha, 1977–1979).

"It was a path of suffering, of disappointment, and of frantic searching for something," Sata
Ineko writes of her life. "When I look back at the
path I have walked, all I can say is that I gave it
my very best. I suppose, with life being such a difficult path to follow, that's the only way there is to
live." Perhaps the life of such a woman who has
ceaselessly collided with harsh reality is a work of
art that illuminates the struggles of women.

Sata Ineko's life was initially shaped by the
natural environs of Nagasaki and her childhood
there. She was born of a youthful romance between Tajima Masafumi, a middle-school student,
and Yuki, a young female student. Her birth was
such an embarrassment to her relatives that she
was initially entered into the family registry of her
great-uncle, Tanaka Umetarō. Her parents, however, overcame opposition from their families and
married one another; her mother dropped out of
school, and her father, who was in no position to
inherit his grandfather's medical practice, also
abandoned his education after finishing middle

school and took a job as a clerk at the Mitsubishi Shipbuilding Company in Nagasaki.

Soon after the birth of Masahito, Ineko's
brother, her mother contracted tuberculosis and
died in the same the year that Ineko entered elementary school. Unsophisticated and bereft of his
wife, Ineko's young father sank into a life of dissipation and then became so absorbed with his second wife that he gave no thought to his children.
Ineko was constantly in trouble with Taka, her
lively, hardworking grandmother, who took over
raising the two children. The emotional strain of
these experiences on young Ineko was so severe
that she became ill with a case of juvenile nervous
prostration. But her turbulent childhood produced
a woman sensitive to the feelings of others and a
spirit filled with maturity and independence. A
bright child, she always served as president of her
class in elementary school, and she tenderly looked
after friends who had come from unfortunate circumstances. In the sunny climate of Nagasaki she
developed a strong vitality, and she spent her
young days as a wild, active tomboy.

When Ineko was eleven years old, her father,
who had failed in his second marriage and had
squandered the family estate, decided to turn over
a new leaf, and with no specific plans in mind he
collected his children and headed for Tokyo,
where they rapidly fell into the depths of poverty.
The precipitous collapse of her family smothered
Ineko's exuberant personality and transformed her
into a young woman of intense self-restraint. She
became profoundly introspective and was constantly forced to consider her relationships with
others as she sought to make her own way in life.
The tumultuous changes in her circumstances also
equipped her with eyes to discern, interpret, and
anticipate the inner workings of individuals, and
these abilities contributed to her development as a
writer. At the same time these experiences prepared her for an awakening of class consciousness
that finally led her into the proletarian literary
movement.

Because her father was unable to secure fixed
employment, Ineko had to take on the financial
burdens of the family. She quit school during the
fifth grade and worked first in a caramel factory
and later as a waitress in Chinese and Japanese
restaurants. Although her father was able to land a
position with the Harima Shipbuilding Company at
Aioi in Hyōgo Prefecture, he had to live at the
company by himself, and he sent no allowance to
his children, who were consequently forced to live
and work at a knitting mill. Ineko was so distressed at their poverty that she considered selling

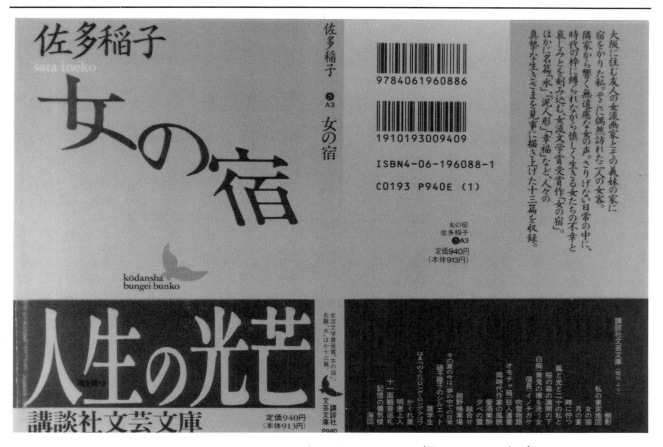

Dust jacket for Sata's 1963 short-story collection, Onna no yado *(Women's Quarters). The title reflects her sympathy for the common people.*

herself as a geisha. She could never free herself from a sense of being in financial adversity, and she constantly felt as though she "concealed within the depths of [her] heart another Self about whom [she] could never speak."

Her resentment and chagrin at being unable to go to school gave birth to a burning desire for learning that was deflected into literature, and she began writing short prose and poetic pieces that she submitted to journals such as *Shōjo no Tomo* (A Girl's Friend) and *Jogaku Sekai* (The World of Learning for Women), where some were published. Her father was a regular reader of magazines such as *Chūō Kōron* and *Manchōhō,* and Ineko had become an avid reader while she was still living in Nagasaki. In addition, her uncle Sata Hidemi (whose surname Ineko adopted after World War II and who lived with the family in Tokyo until he died at a young age), who had studied at Waseda University, joined Shimamura Hōgetsu's Geijutsuza Theatre troupe and wrote drama criticism and fiction. No doubt this uncle also influenced the secret fondness that Ineko, as a young girl, developed for literature.

In 1921 she decided to quit her job as a waitress at the Seiryotei Restaurant at Ueno, where she could find no satisfaction in the chic atmosphere of the district. Hoping to be a part of the cultural world that would quench her thirst for reading, she took a job at the Maruzen Bookstore at Nihonbashi, where she read literary works from both the East and the West. Begrudging even the time it took her to commute to and from the bookstore, she became a model employee in her devotion to her duties. Ultimately, however, she grew frustrated at finding others judging her worth only on the basis of her formal schooling and socio-economic status: with her monotonous, confining job and impoverished situation, she felt she had no hopes of falling in love, and she became nihilistic and began fantasizing about suicide.

She shaped and redirected these feelings into literary channels, and to *Shi to Jinsei* (Poetry and Life), a coterie journal published by Ikuta Shungetsu, she sent her expression of these dark murmurings of a youth wracked by self-doubt and pessimism. The journal published her work and made her an associate member of the coterie. As she continued to search for some way to ameliorate her stifling life, an officer from the bookstore volunteered to arrange a marriage for her, and she agreed to wed Kobori Kaizō, a student at Keiō University and heir to a wealthy family. She entered the marriage with hopes of escaping her impoverished life and of becoming able to satisfy her literary yearnings, but her husband's jealousy tormented her, and her dreams of personal development were shattered. Frustrated at her own shallowness in seeking escape from her confinement solely through a mundane marriage and overwhelmed in the depths of self-hatred, she made several attempts to commit suicide.

The failure of her marriage, however, became a turning point toward a new way of life. With an infant to care for, she made up her mind that "No matter what anyone thinks, I can no longer care about their opinions." She began working at Kōroku, a café at Hongo Dōzaka, where she met the writers associated with *Roba* (Donkey), a coterie magazine that had the support of authors such as Muroo Saisei and Akutagawa Ryūnosuke and that became a source of her literary inspiration. Members of the coterie, which included Nakano Shigeharu, Hori Tatsuo, and Kubokawa Tsurujirō, were all young literati who had cast off social conventions and customs in an attempt to live in accordance with their own definitions of truth. They were filled with a spirit of humanism that found beauty in the most insignificant of objects, refused to look down on poverty, cherished those who labored with modesty, and valued the individual. Their literary spirit moved Sata and awakened her to a new kind of life and literature.

For Ineko, who had been forced to terminate her education, this coterie became her "university" and marked the dawn of a new life. She married Kubokawa and started her "youth" afresh. She eventually published poetry in *Roba;* read the works of Karl Marx, Friedrich Engels, and Vladimir Lenin under the influence of the left-wing writers in the coterie; and was converted to socialist ideology. This philosophy provided her with a class perspective and a rational explanation of the discontent she had felt as a result of her painful experiences and the vagaries of society and guided her toward a new maturity. She became a writer born and reared within the proletarian literary movement.

With the encouragement of fellow coterie member Nakano Shigeharu and the support of Kubokawa, in 1928 Sata wrote *Kyarameru kōba kara* (From the Caramel Factory), her first short story, which dealt with her youthful work experience.

Having found her mode of expression in fiction, Sata wrote many proletarian works, including "Resutoran Rakuyō" (The Restaurant Rakuyō, 1929) and five stories about female factory workers: "Kyōsei kikoku" (Forced Return, 1931), based on the strike at the Tokyo Muslin Company; "Kanbu jokō no namida" (The Forewoman's Tears, 1931); "Shōkanbu" (Minor Executives, 1931); "Kitō" (Prayer, 1932); and "Nani o nasu beki ka" (What Should We Do?, 1932).

She joined the Proletarian Writers' League and with Miyamoto Yuriko and others helped edit *Hataraku fujin* (Working Woman), the journal published by the Proletarian Culture League. For this journal she wrote editorials as well as articles of practical advice. Following the Manchurian Incident in 1931 and the Shanghai Incident in 1932, the Japanese government increasingly suppressed left-wing activities, and Sata fought tenaciously to support the radical revolutionary movement. When Kubokawa was arrested in the assaults on the Culture League and her father went insane, Sata was left to care for her grandmother, her young son, and a daughter with whom she was then pregnant. Taking up semilegal activities in complete devotion to her sociopolitical ideals, she joined the Japan Communist Party and, with her infant strapped to her back, headed for street-corner meetings with Kobayashi Takiji, Miyamoto Kenji, and others in the movement.

In February 1934, however, the government finally succeeded in suppressing some reformist efforts by disbanding the Proletarian Writers' League, and a season of painful resistance ensued. Authorities pressured avowed communists, one after another, to renounce their beliefs, and as suppression of speech became relentless, Sata was left with only the power of her pen to resist the currents of the times. Her eyes, which had been directed toward ideology, turned to focus on the sociopolitical contradictions she saw around her, and she wrote *Botan no aru ie* (A House with Peonies, 1934), tracing the demise of the landed farmer, and "Tetsukuzu no naka" (Amid Scrap Iron, 1935), depicting the cruel realities in the life of a laborer. She also shifted her focus to a concern nearest her own experience, the lives of women, and wrote her first full-length novel, *Kurenai* (Crimson, 1938), which established her reputation and heralded her maturity as a writer.

Her marriage, meanwhile, reached a crisis as her husband took a lover, and this caused her to suffer the contradictions that *Crimson* recounts in presenting the circumstances of her life in this period. It describes a married couple who hope to achieve a new kind of relationship between the sexes by fighting together to further the revolutionary movement but whose relationship collapses as writers are pressured to renounce their ideological beliefs. Yet the main theme of the novel may be found in the cries of a woman torn by the contradictions of "loving her husband, while desiring the freedom to live on her own." *Crimson* remains one of Sata's representative works, and it stands beside Miyamoto Yuriko's *Nobuko* (1928) in its narrative of a woman's progress toward independence and liberation.

Near the time of the outbreak of war with China, Sata's husband began an affair with Tamura Toshiko, a writer who was their close friend, and the marital relationship between Sata and Kubokawa became even more dismal. *Haiiro no gogo* (Gray Afternoons, 1960) treats these events, as it charts the thoughts and torments of a woman whose body is transformed into that of an "insect with sharp feelers" through her suspicions about her husband's infidelity, yet who, bereft of trust in her husband, paradoxically desires him all the more. The novel explores Sata's own self-destructive attitudes, and her sufferings during this period inspired a string of superb resistance writings as she defied the dark mood of the times. One such work is "Chibusa no kanashimi" (The Sorrow of My Breasts, 1937), in which a mother who has left her daughter to live with her parents tries to justify the way of life she has chosen; another is *Kigi shinryoku* (The Fresh Leaves of the Trees, 1940), which recounts her own intellectual awakening that had begun when she met Tsuru-jirō. Another important work, *Suashi no onna* (Barefoot Woman, 1940), tells of her youth and her concealed yearnings to live an earnest life and, from the perspective of a woman's sexual liberation, presents a fresh story of an adolescent's awakening to passion.

With the outbreak of the Pacific War in 1941, militarism grew and continued to restrict freedoms in Japan, and Sata, philosophically restrained as she also agonized in her collapsing marriage, gradually lost the power to resist the socially imposed wartime order. At the urging of newspaper companies and military authorities, and sometimes under military order, she began traveling to Manchukuo, China, and the South Pacific to "comfort the troops." She published reports on her tours, and some have construed these as words and acts of her collaboration with the Japanese military. Yet the causes of her surrender to contemporary political currents were in her own search for an escape from the emptiness she felt amid the ruins of her marriage and in the sorrow that she shared with soldiers headed to the front lines and their family members. She thoroughly understood the day-to-day emotions of the common people, and, unable to bear her loneliness as the masses raced into war and driven by a political system that took advantage of her capabilities as a woman in times of military emergency, she undertook activities that appeared to constitute collaboration.

Just before the Japanese surrender in 1945, Sata divorced Kubokawa and took her two children with her to begin a new phase of her life. Her postwar era began with an examination of her own wartime responsibility. Because of her wartime statements and activities, she was excluded from the group of writers who founded the left-wing New Japanese Literature Association (Shin Nihon Bungaku Kai), and this brought her new feelings of postwar self-recrimination. Yet her scrutiny of her flaws and deviations from her principles brought greater depth to both her character and her writing. In the currents of the new postwar age she rejoined the Communist Party and participated in activities sponsored by the Women's Democratic Club (Fujin Minshu Kurabu), but her attempt to purge herself of the stigma of collaboration by a self-examination marked the heart of her postwar activities.

Her first step in this reexamination came with the publication of her postwar novel *Watashi no Tokyo chizu* (My Map of Tokyo, 1949), in which she traces her life in relation to the lives of the masses. This self-inspection led her to recognize what she shared with the masses and resulted in a novel replete with depictions of the lives of the common people. The novel suggests that Sata was able to demolish the illusions she had held about herself, and that as a result she was able to gain a clear view of reality. In her self-realization of past errors that this novel presents are ideas similar to those in Nakano Shigeharu's *Mura no ie* (House in the Village, 1935). With the aid of this "discovery," which forms the core of Sata's postwar thought, she was able in works such as "Kyogi" (Deception, 1948) and "Hōmatsu no kiroku" (Account of Froth, 1948) to begin coping with the activities that were seen as having provided "comfort to the troops" and to begin looking into her wartime responsibility.

Having undertaken such self-examination, Sata was able to return to a new consideration of her days in the proletarian movement, the root of her ideology, in *Haguruma* (Cogwheels, 1959). This novel is her paean to her youth, and in it she con-

Dust jacket for the 1990 edition of Sata's 1983 short-story collection, Natsu no shiori *(A Guide of Summer)*

fronts the gulf separating the masses from those in the vanguard of the prewar revolutionary movement. For example, the forms of cross-examination that occur in times of danger, such as her doubts about self-awakening that Sata presented in *Crimson,* appear in *Cogwheels* as doubts about her awakening to class-consciousness and are presented as problems deriving from the separation of the revolutionary movement from the common people. Moreover, in *Gray Afternoons,* the title of which suggests the full scope of Sata's life during the mid 1930s, she searches for the causes of her wartime collaboration in her deteriorating marital relationship and again identifies the essence of her collapse.

While conducting her merciless self-examination, Sata continued to doubt the ways in which the Japanese Communist Party pursued the question of war responsibility, because of the "vagueness with which they defined responsibility." She gradually transformed these doubts into questions about the overall structure of the revolutionary movement following the so-called "1950 Crisis," an ideological split in the Japanese Communist Party that resulted from criticisms that the Comin-

tern directed toward it. In the midst of this intraparty strife in 1951 Sata was expelled from the orthodox wing of the party. Four years later at the party congress held to reunify the dissidents and orthodox members, she was unconditionally readmitted. Sata recounted these events in *Yoru no kioku* (Memories of a Night, 1955) and *Keiryū* (Mountain Torrent, 1964). *Mountain Torrent,* written the year before she was ousted from the Communist Party for a second time during disagreements about the treaty on limited nuclear testing, is a work distinguishing her own path from that of the party in the postwar years just before she adopted a definitive stance opposing that of the party. Her aim in this novel is to establish her independence from all institutions. In writing *Sozō* (Clay Figures, 1966) two years after her second expulsion, Sata bid a decisive farewell to the party and declared her own independence.

Perhaps at the heart of Sata's philosophy of independence lies the belief that she "stands where [she] is, in Japan, dealing with Japanese problems," a view rooted in the realities of the lives of the nameless Japanese masses. By continuing to question herself about her own wartime responsibility,

Sata Ineko established herself as a writer who shared the sufferings of the Japanese common people. If her prewar path lay in finding a route of escape from the dark realities of Japanese society, then her postwar position may be read as an attempt to return to the masses. *Juei* (Shadows of the Trees, 1972), written after Sata had separated herself from the party, clearly betokens this stance.

Shadows of the Trees is a novel that locates the terminus of Sata's postwar philosophy. It presents the wounds of bombed-out Nagasaki through recounting the love and death of an ill-fated Japanese artist with a family to support and the overseas Chinese woman with whom he becomes infatuated. A further departure for Sata came with the publication of *Toki ni tatsu* (Standing Still in Time, 1976), a novel of self-discernment that maps the heart of Sata after more than seventy years of life. This work questions the purpose of a revolutionary movement in an age when the postwar Marxist democratic movement has ended. In the novel Sata clearly recognizes that the days when the revolutionary workers had been united in a beautiful bond of solidarity have ended, but through that recognition she gains the means to reconsider human existence as it is, and she seems to set out to find a more comprehensive awareness of human beings. In addition to her autobiographical works in the postwar period Sata also wrote many excellent short stories, including "Mizu" (Water, 1962), and those of *Onna no yado* (Woman's Quarters, 1963), *Aware* (Sorrow, 1969), and *Yukari no ko* (A Related Child, 1978). These stories, portraying the joys and sorrows of the common people as they struggle through life, fully characterize Sata as a writer of the people.

Starting with her debut as a writer of proletarian literature, Sata Ineko always stood socially and politically with the laborers and the weak, as she sought to invigorate the feelings of those who have no means of self-expression. The core of Sata's literature can be found in her affirmation of life, in her quest to live not confined in the private room of ideas but unconfined as a woman and a mother, in her search to be a human being before being a writer, and in her battles for the liberation of the masses. The essence of Sata Ineko, as a writer, may be found in the comments of Aono Suekichi, who calls her "a self-critical author," and of Nakano Shigeharu, who remarks that "The world at large seems to detect a softness of touch and a delicacy of texture in this writer, and while I do not disagree with that view, I am more inclined to call it a robust spirit."

References:

Hasegawa Kei, "Sakka annai: Sata Ineko: Onna no shinsō e no manazashi," in Sata's *Toki ni tatsu* (Tokyo: Kōdansha Bungei Bunko, 1992);

Hasegawa, *Sata Ineko ron* (Tokyo: Orijin Shuppan Sentā, 1992);

Hirano Ken, "Sakka to sakuhin: Sata Ineko," in *Sata Ineko shū* (Tokyo: Shūeisha, 1967);

Kindai joryū bungaku (Tokyo: Yūseidō Shuppan, 1983);

Kobayashi Hiroko, "Kaisetsu: Chinmoku no ronri to haji no rinri," in Sata's *Toki ni tatsu* (Tokyo: Kōdansha Bungei Bunko, 1992);

Kobayashi, ed., *Jinbutsu shoshi taikei 28: Sata Ineko* (Tokyo: Nichigai Associates, 1994);

Kurenai, special journal on Sata, 1–7 (June 1969–April 1990);

Miyamoto Yuriko, *Fujin to bungaku: Kindai Nihon no fujin sakka* (Tokyo: Jitsugyō no Nihonsha, 1947);

Nakajima Kenzō, *Sata Ineko no kussetsu* (Tokyo: Chikuma Shobō, 1960);

Nakano Shigeharu, "Kaisetsu," in Sata's *Kurenai* (Tokyo: Shinchō Bunko, Shinchōsha, 1952);

Nakayama Kazuko, "Sata Ineko: 'Teikō' no imi," in *Shōwa bungaku no kansei: Hirano Ken to sono jidai* (Tokyo: Musashino Shobō, 1988);

Odagiri Hideo, "Sata Ineko," in *Nihon kindai bungaku no shisō to jōkyō* (Tokyo: Hōsei Daigaku Shūppankyoku, 1965);

Okuno Takeo, "Kaisetsu," in *Sata Ineko shū* (Tokyo: Shinchōsha, 1971);

Sakagami Hiroshi, "Kaisetsu: Sata Ineko-shi no tanpen ni yosete," in Sata's *Onna no yado, Mizu, Ningyō to fue* (Tokyo: Ōbunsha Bunko, Ōbunsha, 1976);

Sasaki Kiichi, "Sata Ineko," in *Gendai sakka ron* (Tokyo: Miraisha, 1966).

Shiga Naoya

(20 February 1883 – 21 October 1971)

Cecilia Segawa Seigle
University of Pennsylvania

BOOKS: *Yoru no hikari* (Tokyo: Shinchōsha, 1918);

Araginu (Tokyo: Shun'yōdō, 1921);

Juju (Tokyo: Kaizōsha, 1922);

An'ya kōro, Part I (Tokyo: Shinchōsha, 1922; 7 volumes, Tokyo: Kaizōsha, 1937); Part II (8 volumes, Tokyo: Kaizōsha, 1937; 1 volume, Tokyo: Iwanami Shoten, 1938), translated by Edwin McClellan as *A Dark Night's Passing* (Tokyo & New York: Kodansha International, 1976);

Amagaeru (Tokyo: Kaizōsha, 1925);

Zauhō (Tokyo: Zauhō Kankōkai, 1926);

Juraku (Tokyo: Zauhō Kankōkai, 1930–1933);

Manreki akae (Tokyo: Chūō Kōronsha, 1936);

Tanpen daiisshū (Tokyo: Kaizōsha, 1937);

Tanpen daiyonshū (Tokyo: Kaizōsha, 1937);

Tanpen dainishū (Tokyo: Kaizōsha, 1938);

Tanpen daisanshū (Tokyo: Kaizōsha, 1938);

Tanpen daigoshū (Tokyo: Kaizōsha, 1938);

Chūhen nihen (Tokyo: Kaizōsha, 1938);

Zuihitsu shokan sonota (Tokyo: Kaizōsha, 1938);

Shiga Naoya ryokō kibunzui, edited by Mikami Hidekichi (Tokyo: Daiichi Shobō, 1939);

Eizankō (Tokyo: Kusakiya Shuppanbu, 1940);

Shiga Naoya shū (Tokyo: Kawade Shobō, 1941);

Shiga Naoya shū (Tokyo: Kawade Shobō, 1942);

Sōshun (Tokyo: Koyama Shoten, 1942);

Asa no shishakai (Tokyo: Mikasa Shobō, 1951).

Collection: *Shiga Naoya zenshū,* 16 volumes (Tokyo: Kaizōsha, 1931).

Editions in English: *Morning Glories,* translated by Allen Say and David Meltzer (Luton, U.K.: Mackintosh, 1975);

A Late Chrysanthemum: Twenty-One Stories from the Japanese, translated by Lane Dunlop (San Francisco: North Point Press, 1986).

OTHER: *Gardens of Japan: A Pictorial Record of the Famous Palaces, Gardens and Tea-gardens,* edited by Shiga and Notoi Hashimoto (Tokyo: Zauho, 1935).

Shiga Naoya, 1937

By 1935 Shiga Naoya had been extolled as the "God of Fiction," and his preeminence as the most revered of modern Japanese writers was established by the late 1930s. The body of Shiga's work probably equals that number of works annually published by a contemporary popular writer, but, as Agawa Hiroyuki writes, although Yu Ta-fu has called Shiga "the most laconic writer in Japan, every work he produced was a gem." Shiga's *An'ya kōro* (1922–1937; translated as *A Dark Night's Passing,* 1976) and Natsume Sōseki's Meiji Era works are among the most widely read modern classics even among young people, and it is the only novel from the Taishō Era to be so honored.

On occasion, however, critics contend that Shiga ceased to write major works after the late 1930s and that his post–World War Two works were limited to brief personal and occasional essays. Nakamura Mitsuo even goes so far as to say that Shiga ceased to create after 1929. But even the detractors recognize Shiga's stylistic excellence and his distinction as the most influential of prewar modern Japanese writers. Despite the high regard that writers such as Akutagawa Ryunosuke and Kobayashi Takiji held for stylistic individuality, they imitated Shiga and failed to reach their own standards, for his lucid, terse style that won admiration and tempted imitation does not permit anyone to succeed in adopting it. The efforts of mid twentieth-century writers after Shiga have been struggles either to overcome his influence or to better his style. The power of his writing comes from his ability to penetrate the heart of a matter without making the reader conscious of the process. Both writers and critics have recognized his ability to draw unforgettable images with a bare-bones economy of words.

Shiga Naoya is an important figure in literary history, for he was the leading member of the *Shirakaba* (White Birch) magazine coterie from 1910 through 1923. In the late Meiji Era, when the literature was dominated by Japanese Naturalism, *Shirakaba* members were drawn together by liberalism and idealism to adopt an anti-Naturalist stance without advocating theoretical tenets. In content and style they demonstrated independent spirits that defied unity or ideology; their activities were generated from spontaneous desires and a need to shape their exuberant affirmation of life. At the same time the group helped introduce into Japanese literature much that was new from European writing.

Mostly drawing his material from what he had experienced or heard, Shiga excelled as a short-story writer and perfected his style during his *Shirakaba* days in the 1920s. Some knowledge about his life enhances an understanding of his work, but even a New Critic can appreciate his works, as lacunae of information increase the impact of his writing. Shiga's work presents reactions to specific incidents and emotional experiences, for he usually let several years pass between the time of his actual experience and that of his subsequent writing about it, a process that

allowed him to objectify his perceptions and emotional reactions. He then further pared his drafts to their absolute essence and thus crystallized his works into minimalist pieces. Through a discriminating reading of his works the reader can separate facts from fiction and arrive at fairly accurate information about the man and the writer, for Shiga Naoya was a figure whose life and art coincided.

As the second child of thirty-one-year-old Shiga Naoharu and his twenty-one-year-old wife, Gin, Shiga Naoya was born on 20 February 1883 in Ishimaki-chō, Miyagi Prefecture. Naoyuki, their firstborn son, had died in 1882 at the age of two and a half, and his early death caused Naoya's grandparents, Shiga Naomichi and Rume, to take the two-year-old Naoya away from his parents and keep him until he was full grown. The boy consequently absorbed their sense of values and norms of conduct, and he maintained an unadulterated affection and respect for his grandparents throughout his life.

Shiga wrote many times that he respected and loved his grandfather more than anyone else in his life. Information about Shiga Naomichi comes from "Sofu" (Grandfather, 1955–1956), the short story that Shiga Naoya wrote after Naomichi's fiftieth memorial service. This story was based on Shiga's memories of his grandfather and on a short portion of Naomichi's diary, the greater part of which had been destroyed shortly after Naomichi's death, as the old man had wished.

Shiga Naomichi's ancestors had served the Sōma clan in Rikuzen Nakamura (Sōma, Fukushima Prefecture, at present) in the hereditary office of magistrate of construction. In 1854 Naomichi became a student of Ninomiya Sontoku, the renowned agrarian scholar and philosopher, and he was profoundly influenced by Sontoku's highly ethical and pragmatic philosophy. When the restructuring of the government began in 1868, Naomichi was appointed to several successive bureaucratic positions and eventually became deputy governor of Fukushima Prefecture. When the position was eliminated in 1872, his former lord Sōma, now with the new title of viscount, begged him to return and manage his household, which was in dire financial straits. Naomichi would have had more success in the new government or in the burgeoning business world, but his loyal samurai spirit made him accept the humble position, and he reconstructed the ailing finances of the family virtually by himself. He persuaded Sōma to invest in the Ashio

Cover for Shiga's first novella, a bildungsroman that draws on many of his youthful spiritual crises

copper mines, which he operated with Furukawa Ichibei, the industrialist. Yet while the Sōma family recovered its fortune and Furukawa built his through the mines, the moralist Naomichi took no advantage of the situation and remained extremely poor.

In Tokyo Naoya lived with his grandparents on the Sōma estate and entered the Gakushuin elementary division in 1889. Through the following years Naomichi encountered many difficulties. The Ashio copper mines created extensive pollution that affected the Watarase River and devastated the surrounding agricultural land. This pollution became a major political issue and a basis for serious disputes for many years among members of the Shiga family, and these differences deeply affected both the relationship Naoya developed with his father and the literary career he pursued.

Father-son relationships had not developed ideally in the Shiga family for more than one generation. Naomichi, although he was the second son, had succeeded as the head of the family, while Naokazu, the firstborn, retired early and assumed the position of Naomichi's adoptive father.

Naoharu, Naoya's father, was raised from the age of six as the adoptive son of Naokazu, the retired uncle, and his wife, and Naoharu never grew to love his natural parents. Naoya had noted his father's remoteness toward Naomichi and the extraordinary display of devotion and love that his father maintained for Uncle Naokazu at the time of the latter's death. "I realize that this [upbringing] was one cause of discord between my father and me," Naoya writes in "Grandfather," "and that the two generations had repeated the same error."

A year before Naoya was brought to Tokyo, Nishigori Gōsei, a retainer of the Sōma clan, had charged Shiga Naomichi and three others with incarcerating and poisoning Viscount Sōma, who had gone insane. For ten years until this so-called Sōma Incident was completely resolved in 1893, the Shiga family was beleaguered, but no one who knew Naomichi had believed him to be guilty of the conduct charged by Nishigori. The situation surrounding this episode is described, though not in detail, in Shiga's "Omoidashita koto" (What I Have Remembered, 1912) as well as in "Grandfather." In 1893, during the worst persecution, Naomichi and five others were imprisoned, while Nishigori, an opportunist, became a celebrity by demagoguery.

Ultimately the body of Sōma Nobutane was exhumed, and his alleged poisoning was disproved. Finally exonerated, the grandfather returned home, where eleven-year-old Naoya hid behind the door while others gathered to congratulate Naomichi. When the grandfather inquired about Naoya the boy was brought out, and he burst into tears.

The summer after Naoya graduated from the elementary school, he was at the seaside resort of Katase. When he received his grandfather's letter informing him that his mother was expecting a baby, he was elated because he had envied his classmates who had brothers and sisters. Wishing to "reward" his mother for her achievement, he bought her a special gift—a set of mother-of-pearl hair ornaments and comb. Yet when he returned to Tokyo, she was sick in bed. She took out Naoya's gifts one by one from a wooden box and gazed into it. By the next morning her memory was gone, and she asked him when he had come back. In "Haha no shi to atarashii haha" (Mother's Death and the New Mother, 1912) Naoya writes that

Grandmother told me to show my face to her. I stuck my face over hers as she gazed at the ceiling in a daze. By my side, Grandmother said, "Do you know who this is?" Mother focused her eyes on my face and concentrated for a while. Soon her face was distorted as though she were on the verge of crying. My face became distorted, too. Then Mother said, falteringly, "Even if his complexion is dark and his nose is crooked, as long as he's healthy. . . ."

Naoya's mother died soon afterward, at age thirty-three. When he entered the Gakushuin middle school in the fall, his father married twenty-four-year-old Kō. Naoya vividly recounts her arrival as his new mother as well as the death of his mother in this same story and in "Jitsubo no tegami" (Letters of My Real Mother, 1948) and "Shiroi sen" (White Line, 1956). Gin, Shiga's mother, was a good woman whom he missed, and Kō, his stepmother, also proved to be admirable. She supported him and mediated the discord between him and his difficult father, and she is often also described with affection and appreciation in Shiga's works.

At the Gakushuin middle school in 1896 Naoya and his friends formed a literary group and began to circulate a magazine. Four years after he had failed in his third year of middle school, he was persuaded by the family's *shosei,* or student houseboy, to go to a Christian church, where he met Uchimura Kanzō, the founder of the Non-Church Sect (Mukyōkai-ha) and an individual whose influence on Naoya was exceeded only by that of his grandfather. Naoya was baptized, and his stories suggest that Uchimura's influence was more charismatic than religious or philosophical; for the next seven years he followed the profoundly magnetic personality he had discovered in Uchimura. His novella *Ōtsu Junkichi* (1912) presents Junkichi, a young sport-loving protagonist who respects a swarthy, large-featured, friendly pastor who seems to resemble Friedrich Nietzsche and Thomas Carlyle. Junkichi says, "In the sense that [Ludwig van] Beethoven was the handsomest man in Europe, I was convinced all by myself that my mentor had the best face in all of Japan."

Naoya recognized Uchimura's noble spirit, and he later acknowledged that Uchimura had made him "yearn after the just and hate the unjust and false." The young protagonists in *Ōtsu Junkichi* and in "Nigotta atama" (Muddled Head, 1910; rewritten, 1911) suffer a terrible conflict between their sexual desires and their Christian minister's strong injunction against fornication. Trying to control his desires and impulses by "jabbing a knife through his thigh" or "putting

burning matches on his thigh," the young man in "Muddled Head" agonizes daily.

Under the influence of Uchimura, who publicly joined other Christians, scholars, and Socialists in decrying the Ashio mining pollution, Naoya became interested in this political issue, which had grown increasingly important since Diet member Tanaka Shōzō had presented a first report indicting the mining company at a congressional session in 1891. Meetings were held, and Furukawa's mining company was accused of poisoning rice paddies and fields, ruining river fishing, and causing mothers' milk to stop flowing. Between 1897 and 1899 thousands of peasant demonstrators were arrested in confrontations with the police.

Uchimura had spoken at one public meeting held in support of Tanaka and the victims of pollution, and farmers had asked the audience to visit the polluted villages in order to observe the devastation. Naoya excitedly came home and told his family of his plan to visit the damaged area. As the managing director and comptroller of Sōbu Railroad Company and also an executive of other companies, Naoya's father was by then amassing a fortune, and he absolutely forbade Naoya to participate in the visit. He said that his son's support of the antimine movement would put him in an embarrassing position in his relationship with Furukawa. In "Grandfather" Naoya recounts how he and his father began a fierce quarrel as the young man's grandfather looked on:

> My grandfather was sitting where he always sat, leaning against the pillar, with his eyes closed. From beginning to end, he never opened his mouth; at that time I never thought about his feelings, but much later, I remembered that grandfather was a disciple of Sontoku and had an unusual interest in agricultural matters. In those days, the Kasumichō area where the municipal tram now runs used to be rice paddies, and every autumn my grandfather sent Kumakichi (our gate keeper, who used to be a farmer) to check the crop conditions in the area. Such a man now had to listen to the arguments between his son and grandson over the problems of peasants suffering from the poison from the Ashio mine. His feelings must have been extremely complex.

In the end Naoya did not go to the village, but his grandmother and mother prepared care packages for the victims, and his confrontations with his father subsequently took other forms. His passionate hostility against his father's lack

Shiga Naoya (right) with Tanizaki Jun'ichiro shortly after the end of World War II

of understanding gave energy and impetus to his creativity.

In 1902 Naoya failed middle school again, and by staying in the sixth year of the school he met Mushanokōji Saneatsu, a man who became the third major influence in his life. At the age of twenty-one Naoya began his first serious literary activity with the publication of "Nanohana to komusume" (1904; translated as "The Little Girl and the Rapeseed Flower," 1987), his first short story of some merit. In January 1906 Grandfather Naomichi died, and six months later Naoya, in sixteenth place among twenty-two students, graduated from the Gakushuin school and entered the English Literature section of the Department of Letters at Tokyo Imperial University.

In 1908 Naoya began publishing *Bōya* (Vista of Fields), a small literary magazine, with friends such as Mushanokōji, Kinoshita Rigen, and Ogimachi Kinkazu from the Gakushuin, and he began to write short stories more assiduously. He nominally transferred from the English to the Japanese Department but soon afterward withdrew entirely from the university. Two years later *Bōya* and two other magazines at the Gakushuin, *Mugi* (Wheat) and *Momozono* (Peach Gar-

den), joined forces to create the *Shirakaba* (White Birch) magazine. *Mugi* had been founded by Satomi Ton, the younger brother of writer Arishima Takeo and artist Arishima Ikuma. Shiga and Ikuma had been good friends at the Gakushuin, but their friendship later foundered, and Shiga wrote about this in "Mushibamareta yujō" (Decayed Friendship, 1947). When Ikuma went to Paris to study painting, Satomi Ton formed an off-and-on friendship with Shiga.

Shiga lived a whimsical, irregular life with his free-spirited friends from affluent families in the *Shirakaba* coterie. His short stories such as "Nijudai ichimen" (A Phase of the Twenties, 1912; rewritten, 1922) and "Torio no byōki" (Torio's Illness, 1909; rewritten, 1910) depict a group of seemingly aimless young men carousing at all hours. The *Shirakaba* group gave Shiga the perfect milieu for friendship as well as for publishing, and he brought the magazine fame and prestige with his successful stories. His willfulness and egotism hurt *Shirakaba* leader Mushanokōji and its editor Ogimachi, and when some disagreements, quarrels, and love-hate relationships with such friends occurred, Shiga recorded these experiences in his works with his typical subjectivity.

Between 1909 and 1912 Shiga wrote short stories at a prolific pace, and in 1912 he received his first remuneration of one hundred yen from *Chūō Kōron* for *Ōtsu Junkichi,* his biographical novella, an unpolished but powerful and revealing work. The protagonist, Junkichi, is a young man who becomes interested in Christianity because of the magnetic Mr. U, the minister to whose care Junkichi has "safely entrusted" his faith since he was seventeen years old. But Junkichi suffers from indefinable, unpronounceable desires, and once he abstractly expresses his agony at a meeting in Mr. U's church. During a discussion of resurrection he timidly remarks, "I would be hard put if I resurrect with my entire body. If I can't be only with my head, heaven and this world won't be any different." The other members of Mr. U's inner group ignore him completely. On another occasion Junkichi is distressed when Mr. U says that fornication is as sinful as murder.

Five or six years later Junkichi is a melancholy, unsociable young man who is vaguely in love with a young Eurasian girl. He attends a farewell party for her brother, who is going to study in Dresden, and then another party, a dance at her home. He is extremely awkward—alienated, glum, and angry most of the time—in these social situations. Although he is a member of the upper-class society in which the parties take place, he feels estranged and antagonistic. However, he exchanges photographs with the Eurasian girl.

With his anger and resentment undirected, Junkichi becomes rebellious toward his grandmother, the only one in his family whom he loves. When he speaks harshly to her, she is injured and scolds him for his indolence, and he responds with insolence. He gradually grows interested in Chiyo, the teenage maid whom he believes can give him the solace that no one else can, and he concludes that he must be in love with her. He agonizes over his feelings, because somehow he knows that "she may not be a woman who understands me or my work," and she is completely different from the beautiful woman with whom he had imagined that he would someday fall in love and marry. Nevertheless, his compassion for her makes him much more sympathetic toward employees.

When Junkichi returns from a two-week trip with his grandmother, he asks Chiyo whether she would marry him if he were to propose. Chiyo faints as he kisses her and puts on her finger a gold ring that had belonged to his late mother. However, when he calls another maid to bring a glass of water, he removes the ring from Chiyo's finger and puts it away, a symbolic act that foreshadows the conclusion of this affair. Yet for Junkichi, as Shiga writes in "Kako" (The Past, 1926), "to disclose his love to a woman was to propose to her," and he resolutely announces his engagement to his family. His father wholly disapproves, and Junkichi is on the verge of renouncing his Christian faith. The indoctrination of the church on chastity is deeper than he realizes, however, and Junkichi cannot imagine undertaking any form of sexual union except through the sanctity of marriage. He is unaware of the subconscious nature of sexual feelings, and these feelings need an outlet.

Shiga's actual proposal to someone unknown whom his diary identified only as C, his announcement of his intentions to his family, and his father's strong disapproval were recorded in entries during July and August 1907. He wrote that his father "intends to look for an appropriate bride for me after my study abroad," but on that same night, the determined Shiga added of his relationship with C, "We became husband and wife."

The fictional Chiyo is sent home shortly after Junkichi makes love to her. Surrounded by opposition, Junkichi vents his anger and frustration at night by throwing a large barbell on the floor, and in this act of aimless retaliation he suddenly sees comedy. He imagines the "round-nosed, sallow-complexioned new student houseboy, a country bumpkin who lives downstairs, suddenly rising bolt-upright from his sleep at the tremendous thud right above his head. An irrepressible laughter rose and I chuckled alone." The novella ends with Junkichi freely unleashing his anger in an emotional letter to his friend, a painter modeled on Arishima Ikuma, in Paris.

Junkichi's confusion and the opaqueness of *Ōtsu Junkichi* reveal Shiga's youth and the relative proximity between the time of Shiga's affair with C and his writing of the novella. He had not yet resolved his animosity toward his father, and he had not been able to objectify his emotional reactions. His narrative transition from the story of his relationship with a Eurasian girl to that of Junkichi's affair with Chiyo becomes structurally illogical and incoherent. However, the two disparate parts seem to be a question and answer: the protagonist's youthful struggle with and attempt at resolution of his carnality, which has been prepared by his shrouded confession at the church gathering.

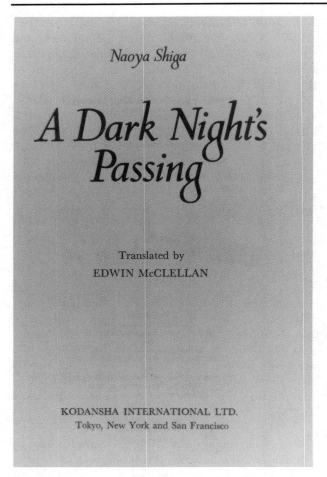

Naoya Shiga

A Dark Night's Passing

Translated by
EDWIN McCLELLAN

KODANSHA INTERNATIONAL LTD.
Tokyo, New York and San Francisco

Title page for the translation of An'ya kōro (1927–1937),
Shiga's only novel

According to the details presented in "The Past," the protagonist and Chiyo maintained a correspondence for some time—as did Shiga and his beloved. Even when the protagonist's love for her begins to wane, he swears that he intends to marry her, and from his meager allowance he sends her the financial means to attend a high school in her region, where he hopes to educate her. But his disillusionment at her ignorance and vulgarity and at the triteness of her insincerity are too great, and ultimately the protagonist does not marry Chiyo. Shiga's affinity also ended, but his affair with the maid had added yet another layer of anger toward his father.

As an unpolished but powerful work, *Ōtsu Junkichi* shocked many young writers outside Shiga's class. Ordinary young men regarded as strangers the socially prominent men's sons who went to the Gakushuin. The uncondescending determination that Shiga had expressed to marry a servant was a refreshing revelation and gave moral support to young writers, who were mostly poor. Arahata Kanson, the Socialist writer and critic, praised *Ōtsu Junkichi* in the journal *Kindai Shisō*, and Itō Sei, having read the book without knowing Shiga, was deeply moved and recommended it to his friends. Ozaki Kazuo was so inspired that he became a writer and Shiga's lifelong disciple.

When Shiga had expressed his wish to marry C, he had sincerely believed that he was moved by egalitarian feelings, but this was not really so. What he had, instead, was a certain amount of innate pride or arrogance. His senses of justice and basic human equality were first nurtured by his humanitarian grandfather, strengthened by Uchimura, and probably confirmed by his brush with socialism and close friendship with the humanist Mushanokōji. Humanism and a sense of decency were almost inherent in Shiga's family, even in his hardheaded businessman father. Despite his youthful confusion, Naoya always expressed and acted in accord with what he believed—the ethical code by which he lived. When some members of the lower class have come to fetch Chiyo, Ōtsu Junkichi expresses his contempt and anger not toward the class but toward the vulgarity of individuals: "The lowly Murai, to whom I don't even speak when I see him, and his wife made me feel terribly insulted by having any say about our fate. And now even the maids gave me an irretrievable sense of humiliation and I grew furious." Junkichi feels that his innate fastidiousness and adherence to purity and integrity are threatened by vulgarity and commonness. Agawa writes that Shiga admitted to his total lack of interest in mingling with lower-class people, but he was devoid of class consciousness and treated with warmth and friendliness those individuals who dealt with him.

After a quarrel with his father in fall 1912, Shiga declared his independence, moved to Onomichi, and began to work on a semi-autobiographical novel. The manuscript bore no title and featured a prototype of Tokitō Kensaku, the hero of *A Dark Night's Passing*. Shiga agonized over the novel, but the only substantive piece he wrote during this sojourn in Onomichi was "Seibei to hyōtan" (1913; translated as "Seibei and His Gourds," 1987). This story, about a twelve-year-old boy who becomes absorbed in making sake flasks from gourds and infuriates his father, was written in defiance of his father's objection to his art and choice of profession. It is often used in school texts.

Shiga's first collection, *Rume*, was published in January 1913, and, while maintaining his pension room in Onomichi, he returned to Tokyo temporarily. In 1912 he had written "Seigiha" (Righteous Men), a story about the death of a little girl hit by a tram car, and on an August night during a stroll with Satomi Ton, Shiga was hit by a train of the Yamanote circle line and hurled about ten feet. He received severe injuries to his head and back, and it is ironic that, on that same morning, he had written another story of a tram car accident, "Dekigoto" (translated as "An Incident," 1987), in which a little boy is saved by a safety-net device. These two tram accident stories are quite different, not only in the fates of the two children but in the tone each develops toward those involved in the incidents. In "Righteous Men" Shiga shows the laborers of the tram company who witness the death of the little girl and testify to the police that the conductor has been responsible for the accident. The excited workers, burning with a sense of justice, are left only with loneliness and frustration, because they are not the representatives of power.

Unlike the third-person, objective "Righteous Men," "An Incident" is a first-person narrative told by a tram passenger on a stiflingly hot July day, and it presents the reactions of various passengers and the cold, uninterested tram conductors. Eventually the tram resumes its operation, and everything returns to normal on the hot afternoon. In its evocation of mood the story clearly shows Shiga's sharpening powers of observation and description.

Two months after his accident Shiga went to the Kinosaki Hot Spring to recuperate. There, his thoughts on the deaths of small animals crystallized in "Kinosaki nite" (1917; translated as "At Kinosaki," 1987), an introspective masterpiece that is often cited as representative of Shiga's prose in regard to its direct, sparse, and elegant style. After a life-threatening accident and many hours of forced rest and inactivity, Shiga considered the ordinary deaths of a wasp, a captured rat, and a newt as he philosophically reflected on the significance of his own near-fatal accident in writing this exemplary *shinkyō shōsetsu* (state-of-mind novel).

Following his recovery Shiga decided to leave his Onomichi pension and return to Tokyo. During this period his association with members of *Shirakaba*, especially with Satomi Ton, reached a frenzied level, as they frequently visited the pleasure quarters. His dissipation and quarrels with Satomi are described, though obscurely, in *A Dark Night's Passing*. Shiga severed

his association with Satomi, and the two did not resume a close friendship until 1923.

In 1914 Shiga moved to Kyoto and married Kadenokōji Sadako, a cousin of Mushanokōji and the daughter of Kadenokōji Sukekoto and Sakakura Tsuru. Both Mushanokōji and Kadenokōji were from old Kyoto families whose descent can be traced to the Fujiwaras of the Heian period. Shiga's father, who upheld conventional values, did not approve of this marriage: Sadako, although she was the daughter of a viscount, was a poor widow with a five-year-old daughter, and Shiga's father offered him a monthly stipend of one hundred and fifty yen if he would agree to marry a young lady from a suitable family. This angered Shiga even more than his father's disapproval of Sadako, and Shiga resolutely married her. In "Kumoribi" (A Cloudy Day, 1926), a story that presents Sadako and her daughter shortly before the marriage, Shiga reveals the resentment of the little girl toward the man who, as her prospective father, threatens the security of her life with her mother.

Shiga legally severed relations between himself and his family following the establishment of his own new family, and various works express his animosity toward his father even when Shiga's personal quarrels with him are not major issues in those stories. Examples include "Sobo no tameni" (For Grandmother, 1911), "Ko o nusumu hanashi" (A Tale of Kidnapping, 1914), "The Past," "A Cloudy Day," "Yamagata" (Yamagata, 1926), and *Asa no shishakai* (Screening in the Morning, 1951).

Naoya and Sadako first lived in the suburbs of Kyoto before moving to Kamakura in May 1915. By that time Sadako was suffering from severe neurosis under the strain of Shiga's relationship with his father, so he decided to move to Mount Akagi for her health, had a cottage built, and lived there for the summer. The couple's life is described in the limpid, serene short story "Takibi" (Bonfire, 1920). As another of Shiga's masterpieces, it presents the beauty of the lake and mountains and the carefree enjoyment of the environment by the couple and their friends. "Akagi nite rakujitsu" (Setting Sun at Mount Akagi, 1920) is also based on his days in the mountains.

In fall 1915 Yanagi Muneyoshi, Shiga's *Shirakaba* friend and founder of the Tokyo Folk Art Museum, and his wife persuaded Shiga to buy a house, sight unseen, in the village of Abiko near Tokyo. Mushanokōji and Bernard Leach, the ceramic artist, also moved to Abiko, and the area

Dust jacket for a 1987 translation of stories by Shiga

took on an appearance of a *Shirakaba* community. In December 1913 Shiga had ceased writing after Natsume Sōseki, literary editor of the Asahi newspaper, had asked him to write a novel for the newspaper. Shiga had agreed and had gone to Matsue to write, but, after he found it impossible to write a full-length novel, he had gone to see Sōseki in 1914 to decline his request. Still feeling obliged to honor his original agreement with Sōseki, Shiga fastidiously forbade himself to write for any other publication.

Three years later, at the insistence of Mushanokōji and perhaps because Sōseki had died in December 1916, Shiga began to write again. In 1917 he wrote important short stories such as "At Kinosaki," "Sasaki no baai" (The Case of Sasaki), "Shōhin itsutsu" (Five Pieces), "Kōjinbutsu no fūfu" (A Good-Natured Couple), "Akanishi Kakita" (translated as "Akanishi Kakita," 1987), "Kugenuma-iki" (A Trip to Kugenuma), and "Araginu" (Raw Silk). In August he finally reconciled with his father, after the strong egos of these two men had been strained for years through quarrels over mining pollution, a proposal of marriage to a maid, a choice of career, and finally the marriage with Sadako. The resolution was motivated by Shiga's concern about the health of his grandmother and perhaps by his own maturity, and his stepmother also played an important role in the reconciliation by persuading him to approach his father with an apology. In his exhilaration Shiga wrote the novella *Wakai* (Reconciliation) immediately after this reunion took place.

Reconciliation is a discourse on a monthlong peacemaking process, without any reference to the causes of disharmony between the father and the son. The work is a *shi-shōsetsu* (I-novel), or rather a *shinkyō shōsetsu* (state-of-mind novel), dealing strictly with Shiga's emotional reactions during each step toward reconciliation. Its concentrated energy, vitality, warmth, and narration of the resolution to long disputes with his father give the reader a sense of participating in the protagonist's jubilation. The reader feels the positive side of being a member of a Japanese family in its most traditional, feudal form. *Reconciliation* is a masterpiece that defies the conventional concept of a novel.

In 1920 Shiga took up the theme of father-and-son discord in another work, "Aru otoko, sono ane no shi" (A Man and His Sister's Death), a part-biographical, part-fictional work. The protagonist, the older brother of the narrator, severs his relationship with his stubborn father, and from the narrative perspective of the younger brother, Shiga presents the psyches of his protagonist (modeled on Shiga himself) and his father by using the younger brother as an objective narrator equally distant from the quarreling father and son.

The narrator's brother leaves home at the age of eighteen because his businessman father objects first to the son's desire to travel, then to his desire to become a writer. The father gives the son five hundred yen to publish his book and tells him to leave home and become independent. The narrator describes his flustered state when the father finds out that his older son has actually left home: "Witnessing my father, who was so tender in his feelings, I felt a deep affection. And I suddenly felt anger rising against my brother's obstinacy."

This sentiment differs from that of other Shiga protagonists, whose anger slowly increases its intensity through a series of arguments with the father. For example, in *Ōtsu Junkichi* the reader feels the young protagonist's explosive anger, and in *Sōsaku yodan* (1928) Shiga writes that *Ōtsu Junkichi*, *Reconciliation*, and "A Man and His Sister's Death" were three branches that grew from the same tree, although the last work was half fiction and the other two were biographical. In "A Man and His Sister's Death" the narrator's sympathy for the two obstinate but affectionate men shows how Shiga felt under the influence of the passage of time (for he had written the first version of this conflict in 1912) and how he had gained objectivity on these events by using a more objective observer to provide his narrative perspective in 1920. However, this later work is not necessarily the more satisfying, as Shiga called it a "dried-up product, whereas *Ōtsu Junkichi* and *Reconciliation* were fresh."

Between 1917 and 1921 Shiga wrote many excellent short stories such as "Jūichigatsu mikka gogo no koto" (translated as "Incident on the Afternoon of November Third," 1987), "Ryūkōsei kanbō" (Influenza), "Kozō no kamisama" (translated as "The Shopboy's God," 1987), *Yuki no hi* (A Snowy Day, 1948), "Bonfire," and "Mana-

zuru." "Kensaku no tsuioku" (Kensaku's Remembrances)—the prologue of his only novel, *A Dark Night's Passing*—was also published in *Shinchō* in January 1920.

On 16 August 1921 his grandmother, the woman whom Shiga loved most and who had influenced him more than any other woman, died at the age of eighty-six. She appears in short stories such as "Aru asa" (One Morning, 1908), "For Grandmother," "A Trip to Kugenuma," and in both *Ōtsu Junkichi* and *Reconciliation*. In 1923 Shiga, his wife, and three daughters (another girl and one boy had died shortly after birth) moved to Kyoto. Following the great earthquake of September 1923 the magazine *Shirakaba* ceased publication.

In 1925 Naokichi, Shiga's only son to survive infancy, was born. Shiga moved to Nara, where, favoring the beauty and serenity of the small city, he built a comfortable home that has since become a museum. In Nara Sadako gave birth to two more daughters, and Shiga's most important task was that of nearly completing *A Dark Night's Passing*. Divided into four parts of unequal length, the novel consists of a prologue as part 1, and the remaining three parts were initially published in *Kaizō*. The first two parts (volume one) were completed in 1920, but the last two parts (volume two) took from 1921 to 1937 to complete, because Shiga found it difficult to write the last half of part 4.

The first volume recounts how, ever since childhood, Tokitō Kensaku has had uneasy feelings about his father's coldness and his mother's sternness toward him. One of his early memories is that of seeing his grandfather for the first time and finding him to be vulgar and unlikable. In adulthood Kensaku's suspicion deepens when his marriage proposal to the sister of a friend is unexpectedly rejected by the friend's mother, who has been almost a surrogate mother to him after the thirteen-year-old Kensaku had lost his own mother. He falls into a pattern of meaningless frivolity with friends at restaurants, teahouses, and bars, where he befriends attractive women. Tormented by unrequited desires, he finally visits a brothel and begins a life of dissipation.

Once he begins to indulge his sexual needs, he becomes attracted to Oei, a much older woman who was his grandfather's concubine until his grandfather died. After she moves into Kensaku's house and looks after him for awhile, he decides to flee from the stifling home, partly to test the authenticity of his feelings.

Kensaku settles in Onomichi by the Inland Sea and there tries to write a biographical novel, but he is continually troubled. He feels he has to act honestly about his feelings for Oei, and the only honorable conduct would be to marry her. He writes to his older brother about his plan to marry her, but by return mail his brother discloses the secret of Kensaku's birth: Kensaku was born while his father was abroad and is actually the son of his mother and her father-in-law. This revelation devastates Kensaku, as he understands why the mother of his friend has rejected Kensaku as a prospective son-in-law when he proposed to marry her daughter. Kensaku feels more than ever that he is totally alone. He suffers much and thinks about women—about the sins of several women of whom he has heard as well as and about the sins of his own mother. He falls back into a life of dissipation.

In the second volume Kensaku visits Kyoto, where he gradually recovers his equilibrium and humility by coming into contact with the ancient art and architecture of the old city. He decides to find a house in Kyoto, and, in the process of house hunting, he sees a young woman, Naoko, whose wholesome, serene beauty captivates him. Through observing her on several occasions he confirms his feelings, and he proposes to her through an aristocratic friend whose old family retainer is an acquaintance of the girl's uncle. When Kensaku reveals his birth secret to Naoko and her uncle, they accept him without any qualms, and Kensaku feels reborn, cleansed, and even spiritually ennobled by the prospect of marrying Naoko. He feels strong love for her, and he seeks legally to sever his own family connections with his father and brother by marrying Naoko and starting a new family with her.

However, after a period of happiness Kensaku is plunged into despair again. First, the couple's newborn baby dies. Then Naoko, following the pattern of Kensaku's mother in behaving unfaithfully, commits adultery. While Kensaku is in Korea to help Oei escape the clutches of an exploitative cousin, Naoko seduces Kaname, her own cousin and childhood friend. After Kensaku returns he feels a difference in Naoko and extracts her confession. She asks him to forgive her, and although Kensaku says that he does, his own sense of integrity is irrevocably damaged and he cannot reconcile himself to her betrayal.

Deeply suffering from his cruelty and lack of generosity toward Naoko, Kensaku escapes by traveling. At the holy mountain of Daisen he observes the flora and fauna and the simple people of the temple where he is lodging, and gradually he recovers his equanimity and faith. He is moved deeply by the story of Take, who forgives his adulterous wife, and on the way to climb Mount Daisen, Kensaku falls ill. Weakened from diarrhea as he lies in the grass, he witnesses a sublime sunrise:

He felt his exhaustion turn into a strange state of rapture. He could feel his mind and his body both gradually merging into this great nature that surrounded him. It was not nature that was visible to the eyes; rather, it was like a limitless body of air that wrapped itself around him, this tiny creature no larger than a poppy seed. To be gently drawn into it, and there be restored, was a pleasure beyond the power of words to describe. . . . It was so still a night, even the night birds were silent. If there were lights in the villages below, they were quite hidden by the mist that lay over the rooftops. And all that he could see above him were the stars and the outline of the mountains, curved like the back of some huge beast. He felt as if he had just taken a step on the road to eternity. Death held no threat for him. If this means dying, he thought, I can die without regret. But to him then, this journey to eternity did not seem the same as death.

He must have slept for some time as he sat there, his elbows resting on his knees. When he opened his eyes again, the green around him had begun to show in the light of early dawn. The stars, though fewer now, were still there. The sky was soft blue—the color of kindness, he thought. The mist below had dispersed, and there were lights here and there in the villages at the foot of the mountain. . . . All aspects of the scene changed rapidly with dawn's hurried progress. When he turned around, he saw the mountaintop outlined against a swelling mass of orange light that became more and more intense; then the orange began to fade, and suddenly everything around him became clearer. The wild grass grew shorter here than it did down below; and in its midst were large wild asparagus, standing singly and far apart from each other, their flowers dotting the landscape near and far. . . . As the mountain range jutting into the water on the other side of the bay began to take on color, the outline of the white lighthouse in the straits became more clearly etched. The sun now reached Daikonjima Island, stretched out like a huge stingray across the bay. . . . [T]here was no sign of activity yet in the villages immediately below, which lay still and dark in the shadow of Daisen. Kensaku then saw for the first time the sharply delineated outline of this shadow in the distance as it retreated from the bay and crept toward him over land, allowing the town of Yonago to emerge in the light. It was like a great dragnet being pulled in; or it was like the caressing shadow of a passing cloud. And so Kensaku watched with emotion this rare sight—the shadow of the proud mountain, the greatest in central Japan, etched boldly across the land.

Because Kensaku is a man of probity and intuitive sensibilities, he has expected purity of heart and honesty from others. He has had a need for a strong sense of self, and his identity and self-confidence have been destroyed, first by the discovery of the secret of his birth and then by his wife's betrayal. But here, surrounded by the dawn of the great mountain, he feels humble and cleansed in the embrace of nature.

The personality and temperament of Kensaku are among the autobiographical features that Shiga incorporates in this novel. Yet many fictional details are also added, such as the secret of Kensaku's birth, the infidelities of his mother and his wife, and the existence of a brother and of Oei. Shiga no doubt had difficulty in shaping this fiction while revealing himself to the extent that he did.

The novel is not perfect in its construction: the structure is not well conceived; the plot lacks dramatic events; and, except for the hero, the characters are not clearly delineated. Of Kensaku's life Shiga provides virtually no familiar details, such as the professions of his friends and family members or the sources of their affluence. Nevertheless, the characters give a clear sense of presence, and Kensaku's psychological pilgrimage through misery and melancholy is compelling. Kensaku is a man who wants to live true to himself as much as possible, despite all the impediments he encounters. His difficulties are not those of poverty, which are familiar among heroes in naturalist novels. He is not accountable for the misfortunes that befall him; he is merely a victim of the actions of the two women closest to him. What is convincing is Kensaku's effort to come through the darkness and find a path on which he can live with dignity.

While writing *A Dark Night's Passing* in 1924, Shiga fell in love with a waitress-maid at a Gion teahouse in Kyoto, and he faithfully recounted this affair in four short stories: "Saji" (Trifling Incident, 1925), "Yamashina no kioku" (1925; translated as "A Memory of Yamashina," 1987), "Chijō" (1926; translated as "Infatuation," 1987), and "Banshu" (Late Autumn, 1926). In "Infatuation" this waitress appears as "a large woman, twenty or twenty-one years old, who had nothing spiritual in her, a woman like a man. He [the hero] did not understand why he was so attracted to her." These brief stories were written and published without the introduction of

Shiga Naoya

other material, and this attests to the depth of Shiga's middle-age crisis.

The protagonist admits that his preoccupation was purely sexual, and although Shiga had been tortured by sexual desires in his youth, following his marriage he had guarded against any involvement with another woman because of his love for his wife and family. In fact, the affair with the teahouse maid was his sole deviation from fidelity during his marriage, and Sadako suffered much from his affair. The hero in "Infatuation" perceived in his uneducated, somewhat vulgar maid a "fresh fruit-like taste that had long been lost in his wife," a "breath that smelled like the breath of his children," and "flesh found in the claws of crabs caught in the northern sea." In "A Memory of Yamashina" the protagonist has repeatedly lied to his wife in order to see the woman. Yet when his wife discovers his infidelity and accuses him, he keeps assuring her that "this has nothing to do with you. . . . [M]y feelings towards you haven't changed a bit." When the wife answers, "How is it possible? What used to be whole is divided now; naturally feelings are reduced by what goes to the other person." The husband answers weakly, "Emotion isn't arithmetic."

> She claims that she can stand any poverty, but she cannot bear her husband's infidelity. . . . He had an excuse in the fact that his feelings toward that

woman were genuine, but if he was serious, it was all the worse for his wife. She was by nature generous to a fault, and he had vaguely hoped that she might show the same generosity in this matter, but now he knew that this was impossible.

In *Shiga Naoya ron* (1954) Nakamura Mitsuo expresses his amazement at the naiveté of the husband who can talk and act from such self-centered logic. He sees in the protagonist "a total lack of the political sense that is minimally required where a husband and wife are concerned."

At the end of the argument, the protagonist reluctantly promises not to see the other woman again, but when she responds, "Promise me that you would never do this sort of thing again," the husband says only, "I wouldn't know. Something that wasn't supposed to happen happened; so I can't guarantee it." Viewed from another perspective, the protagonist's amazing straightforwardness and honesty appear as insufferable as his self-justification and self-indulgence. Yet when Shiga so guilelessly exposes the almost comic "lack of political sense" that his protagonist displays, it impresses even Nakamura as "a certain psychological truth" about the male gender.

The protagonist in "Late Autumn" knows well that he has no intention of parting with his other woman. Yet he is aware that she tolerates him only as a client, that his infatuation is like influenza, and that by allowing it to run its natural course he will eventually recover from it. He is unable to produce a story he has promised to submit to a magazine, and he reluctantly sends a manuscript which he has written earlier and in which he describes his continuing affair. He knows that when the story—"Trifling Incident"—is published it will upset his wife, so he warns her not to read it. When the magazine arrives, his family and friends are careful not to bring up the subject, but the truth comes out from an unexpected source, and his wife is extremely disturbed. Yet, the author says, "he did not care how she [the other woman] felt about him. . . . As long as he knew his love was one-sided, he had no complaint; if he thought she cared for him too, then she would be the source of all kinds of displeasure." With a logic that verges on foolishness this protagonist distinguishes a passing infatuation from his sacrosanct but unexciting marital love. It is difficult to find another writer who reveals himself knowingly with such simplicity and candor.

From 1925 to 1937 Shiga and his family lived in Nara, where he enjoyed his family life and associations with friends. During these years his presence attracted many writers and artists to move to Nara and form an artistic and literary colony around him, just as a colony had sprouted around him in Abiko around 1915. Many simple short stories such as "Nichiyōbi" (Sunday), "Sōshun no tabi" (A Trip in Early Spring), "Ike no fuchi" (The Rim of the Pond), "Asa hiru ban" (Morning, Noon, Night), and "Suekko" (The Youngest Child) describe his daily life with his family and friends during these years, when his affection for his son and five daughter and his sharp observation of life comprise the focal points of these works. In 1938, for the sake of his son Naokichi's schooling at the Gakushuin, Shiga moved back to Tokyo.

During World War II Shiga did not publish at all, except a brief comment on "the spiritual and technical superiority of the Japanese army" at the time of the fall of Singapore. The war years marked the last of three periods of such silence: the first, from 1914 until 1917, when he could not write a novel for Natsume Sōseki; the second, from 1929 for about five years, when he was annoyed by the preponderance of Marxist proletarian literature; and this last, from early 1942 to the summer of 1945. After the war he wrote no long works, but some brief essays increased the beauty and simplicity of his writing. "Haiiro no tsuki" (1945; translated as "A Gray Moon," 1987), "Usagi" (Rabbit, 1946), "Neko" (Cats, 1947), "Yamabato" (Turtledove, 1949), "Jitensha" (Bicycle, 1951), and "Mōki fuboku" (Blind Turtle and Floating Wood, 1963) are examples of his fine postwar essays. In 1949 he received the Order of Cultural Merit medal from the Japanese government.

Nakamura Mitsuo calls the postwar Shiga a "cinder" and says that this postwar work "may show his weakness as a writer but [has] nothing to add to his prestige." Following the war Shiga also made some strange statements: he advocated adopting French as the official language of Japan and building a statue of Gen. Tōjō Hideki to ensure that his evil deeds during the war would not be forgotten. Such bizarre announcements were politely ignored, but his postwar activities such as judging beauty contests became controversial. Some of essays still moved the public. As president of P.E.N., Shiga wrote a speech for the opening of the Japan P.E.N. Conference in June 1947, although he could not attend. His message urged young writers to maintain high spirituality and ideals in order to rebuild a first-rate culture, because the third- or fourth-rate culture into which Japan had plummeted did not deserve to exist. The audience was greatly touched and aroused. Shiga was aware of the anti-Shiga movement that had become fashionable after the war, and in January 1956 he wrote in "Shiroi sen" (White Line):

> Generally my works that please critics and publishers are what I wrote in my youth, in which I am losing interest. Those works that I wrote in my old age and which I myself feel have greater depth seem to receive criticism as though I were dried up as a writer. This seems to have become a fixed idea which everyone repeats mechanically. I don't think such people really understand me. As I have always said, critics are, except for a few who are my friends, completely useless creatures. Such critics are living parasitically on works of writers.

While Shiga became less active as a writer than he had been, his personality continued to attract writers, critics, and artists. Many people visited his Atami house and, subsequently, his new Tokyo residence. He usually had many New Year guests, and on 29 January 1951 an amazed Shiga wrote in his diary that he had entertained eighty-eight visitors since the first of the month.

Shiga traveled to Europe only once—in May 1952 with artist Umehara Ryūsaburō, Yanagi, and Hamada Shōji. When he fell ill in London during July, he altered his itinerary and returned to Japan. He enjoyed his old age. Remaining with his wife in his new house, which was built in 1955 to his specifications for simplicity, practicality, and aesthetic pleasure, Shiga wrote short essays from time to time. He fell ill in 1970, and after about a year of bouts with various illnesses he died at the age of eighty-eight.

Shiga Naoya was endowed with great talent and was able to fulfill his creative wishes because of his relative freedom from financial pressure and responsibilities. Except for his early lack of support from his father, he was able to pursue his career because of his firm belief in himself and his inability to live by any practical means other than writing. His strong emotional reactions toward his father did not harm him but instead inspired his early creative activities. In the formation of his personality the tacit influence of his grandmother, the matriarch, was just as important as that of his grandfather. During his childhood her position of power in the household and Naoya's position as her favorite grandchild were recognized by everyone in the family.

When he outgrew the dominant-dependent relationship with his grandmother in his adulthood, he fused his *amae* (dependency) into a domineering posture and maintained a one-way communication with everyone.

This psychological background explains the personalities of many of Shiga's protagonists who resemble the author. They have a strong sense of self, but they are often motivated by their mood of the moment, as Shiga was wont to be. His works are encoded with frequent mood words: "mood," "feeling," and various likes and dislikes are dominant motives for his protagonists' actions or inactions. In "Aru ippēji" (A Certain Page, 1909; rewritten, 1911) Shiga tells of pampering his whims and temper. Intending to live in Kyoto for at least several months, the protagonist leaves Tokyo with large bundles, and his friends give him a big departing celebration at the station. In Kyoto, however, he cannot find a desirable apartment, so he turns around and goes back to Tokyo without having spent even a night.

Often Shiga's moods shaped his moral judgments of situations and people, for these judgments were based on first impressions that were frequently determined by his state of mind. His extraordinary intuition, however, often permitted him to form uncannily accurate impressions. In "Abashiri made" (1908; translated as "As Far as Abashiri," 1987), one of his celebrated early short stories, the narrator meets a young mother with a little boy and a baby whom she carries on her back. The narrator forms an opinion of the little boy from his first impression: "The boy gave me an unpleasant look. I thought he was a bizarre boy with a bad complexion, with a big head that opened at the top. I had a nasty feeling."

The boy's mean, willful behavior only confirms the narrator's impression, and such behavior in turn makes the narrator sympathetic toward the boy's gentle mother, who is having a difficult time with him. From this intuition the narrator imagines the unhappy life that the woman is probably suffering with an abusive drunkard as a husband. This utterly believable, touching story is based on a mother and her children whom Shiga happened to see on a Tōhoku Line train, but it also brings up inevitable questions about Shiga's intuitive method. Might the author's first impression have caused the narrator to augment the unpleasantness of the child? Or did the behavior of the child make the author exaggerate the boy's visible horridness? Could Shiga have sustained his impartiality?

In early works such as "Kamisori" (Razor, 1910), "Kurōdiasu no nikki" (Claudius's Journal, 1912), and "Han no hanzai" (1913; translated as Han's Crime, 1997) Shiga's mood leads to moral and epistemological questions of where truth lies when human beings are dealing with their emotions and their consciences. In "The Shopboy's God," after performing a genuine act of charity, the protagonist feels ambivalent, left with a sense of shame and hollowness. Each story bears Shiga's hallmarks—his clear focus and succinct style, his skillful storytelling, and his thematic universality.

Ranging from vague displeasure and resentment to an explosive fulmination, Shiga expressed and wrote about his moods freely. His heroes are often aware of their own moodiness, and their emotional reactions are accompanied sometimes by shame or a sense of guilt, sometimes by a full confidence in the judiciousness of their anger. Such idiosyncrasy has caused critics to speculate about the relationship between Shiga's psyche—his creativity—and his moods. In "Shiga Naoya" (1929) Kobayashi Hideo was the first to point out that Shiga Naoya was a writer who permitted no abstraction, that his work represented not his consciousness but the very corporeal self. For Shiga, what made him feel good was good, and what gave him a bad feeling was bad. The basic attitude of Shirakaba writers toward life had the simplicity conveyed by the line from John Keats's "Ode on a Grecian Urn" (1819): "Beauty is truth, truth beauty." No one embodied that attitude better than Shiga Naoya.

Saeki Shōichi sees the epitome of Shiga's typical way of patterning his narratives in his short story "Aru asa" (One Morning, 1908), in which the protagonist's bad humor quickly culminates in actions of fulmination, release, and final reconciliation. He sees this pattern in Shiga's major works such as Reconciliation and finds it appearing with variations in A Dark Night's Passing, but "One Morning" stands as a prototype that contains layers of paradoxes. This extremely short work excludes all the extraneous details, as it concentrates on the mounting frictions and the psychological battles between the grandmother and the spoiled grandson before it finally reveals the depth of the bonds of affection between them. Thus, Shiga's mood shapes the construction of his story.

As is typical of a moody person, Shiga dealt only with matters that appealed to him, and his temperament determined the content and style of his works; conventional dramatic paradigm meant nothing to him. However, he was aware of his whimsical self-indulgence and had a capacity to mock his arrogance. "Yadokari no shi" (The Death of a Hermit Crab, 1914) illustrates this in its presentations of easy changes of moods ranging between despair and confidence. In this work a hermit crab seeks a larger and larger conch shell in which to live and aspires to grow large in order to fill it. As the crab always finds a larger conch, however, it discards with humiliation and vexation the last conch it has occupied. Disheartened in having abandoned its attempt to secure a new habitat, it goes about naked, and its soft underbelly painfully rubs against the rough sea bed. Finally it dies of gloom. When its corpse is netted by oceanographers, the surprised scientists decide that the hermit crab had grown too large for a shell. The face of the dead crab shows the agony it had felt, but the scientists cannot fathom the depth of its despair. In this moody seeker of an ever greater truth to appropriate and dwell in, it is easy to see Shiga's mockery of himself.

What he considered an ideal, ultimate literary form was that of "a work that transcends its creator"—a work such as the statue of Kuan-Yin in the Yumedono (Hall of Dreams) at the Hōryuji temple in Nara, a work that makes one forget the existence of its sculptor. "If I should ever be able to achieve such work of literature," Shiga insisted, "I would not dream of putting my name on it."

The literary reputation of Shiga Naoya has been fully restored in Japan, as critics and writers have paid him impressive tribute. Tanigawa Tetsuzō, a critic and friend, has said, "Shiga's literature is great, but the greater is Shiga, the man." One of his many admirers was the abbot of Tōdaiji Temple, a man whom Agawa has quoted as claiming that "Shiga was a better and greater man than any figure in the contemporary Buddhist world." Admirers of his literature speak of the beauty of his personality and of his childlike honesty and generosity that coexisted with his terrible temper, which Shiga typically directed at his beloved wife. They compare meeting Shiga to performing their ablutions, but his literature also has the same refreshing effect.

Kōno Toshirō has offered Honda Shugo's capsule assessment of Shiga's accomplishments and significance in Japanese literature:

As we review [Japanese] literary history chronologically, as one reaches Shiga, the text brightens remarkably. It is not only that the forms are clear and fresh, the rhythms of his thoughts and emotion are perfectly united and there is no sediment in his words. As we retrace contemporary novels back to Shiga, for example his *Reconciliation*, we feel that all the cells of the writer's entire body are awake and alive. . . . We feel that the entirety of one human being exists here. We feel that contemporary novels describe only a small part of a part. Shiga described only one protagonist [in his life] and influenced generations of literature.

Letters:

Mushanokōji Saneatsu, ed., *Shiga Naoya no tegami* (Tokyo: Yamamoto Shoten, 1936).

References:

Agawa Hiroyuki, *Shiga Naoya*, 2 volumes (Tokyo: Iwanami Shoten, 1994);

Bungei tokuhon Shiga Naoya, special issue on Shiga (September 1976);

Hirano Ken, *Shiga Naoya to sono jidai* (Tokyo: Chūō Kōronsha, 1977);

Honda Shūgo, *Shiga Naoya* (Tokyo: Iwanami Shoten, 1990);

Ikeuchi Teruo, ed., *Shiga Naoya: Jiga no kiseki* (Tokyo: Yūseidō, 1992);

Imamura Tahei, *Shiga Naoya ron* (Tokyo: Chikuma Shobō, 1973);

Iwagami Jun'ichi, *Shiga Naoya* (Tokyo: Yakumo Shoten, 1949);

Kōno Toshirō, ed., *Kanshō Nihon gendai bungaku: Shiga Naoya* (Tokyo: Kadokawa Shoten, 1981);

Machida Sakae, ed., *Shiga Naoya* (Tokyo: Kokusho Kankōkai, 1992);

Frances Mathy, *Shiga Naoya* (New York: Twayne, 1974);

Nakamura Mitsuo, *Shiga Naoya ron* (Tokyo: Bungei Shunjusha, 1954);

"Shiga Naoya hito to sakuhin," *Bungakkai,* special issue on Shiga (December 1971);

"Shiga Naoya, hito to sakuhin," *Kaishaku to Kanshō,* special issue on Shiga (July 1972);

"Shiga Naoya no sōgō kenkyū," *Kokubungaku,* special issue on Shiga (August 1957);

"Shiga Naoya o saihyōka suru," *Kaishaku to Kanshō,* special issue on Shiga (January 1987);

"Shiga Naoya-shi no seikyo o itannde," *Sekai,* special issue on Shiga (December 1971);

"Shiga Naoya Tokushū," *Hyōron,* special issue on Shiga (March 1935);

"Shiga Naoya Tokushū," *Bungaku Kaigi,* special issue on Shiga, 7 (April 1949);

"Shiga Naoya to Nihonjin—Symposium *An'ya kōro* o megutte," *Kokubungaku,* special issue on Shiga (March 1976);

"Shiga Naoya tsuitō," *Bungei,* special issue on Shiga (December 1971);

"Shiga Naoya tsuitō," *Shinchō,* special issue on Shiga (December 1971);

"Shiga Naoya tsuitō Tokushū," *Minshū Bungaku,* special issue on Shiga (January 1972);

Shigetomo Takeshi, *Shiga Naoya kenkyū* (Tokyo: Kasama Shoin, 1979);

Shindō Junkō, *Shiga Naoya ron* (Tokyo: Shinchōsha, 1970);

"Shirakaba gojisshūnen kinengō," *Arano,* special issue on Shiga (April 1960);

"Shirakaba-ha no sōgō kenkyū," *Kokubungaku,* special issue on Shiga (February 1959);

William F. Sibley, *The Shiga Hero* (Chicago: University of Chicago Press, 1979);

Sudō Matsuo, *Shiga Naoya kenkyū* (Tokyo: Meiji Shoin, 1977);

Sudō, *Shiga Naoya no shizen* (Tokyo: Meiji Shoin, 1979);

Takada Mizuho, *Shiga Naoya* (Tokyo: Gakutōsha, 1955);

Takii Kōsaku, *Shiga Naoya taidan nisshi* (Tokyo: Zenkoku Shobō, 1947);

Tanigawa Tetsuzō, ed., *Shiga Naoya no sakuhin*, 2 volumes (Tokyo: Mikasa Shobo, 1942);

"Tokushū Shiga Naoya," *Gunzō,* special issue on Shiga (January 1972);

"Tokushū Shiga Naoya no bungaku II," *Kaishaku to Kanshō,* special issue on Shiga (April 1976);

Yasuoka Shōtarō, *Shiga Naoya shiron* (Tokyo: Ōfūsha, 1968).

Shimazaki Tōson
(25 March 1872 – 22 August 1943)

Cecilia Segawa Seigle
University of Pennsylvania

BOOKS: *Wakanashū (Tokyo: Shun'yōdō, 1897);*
Hitohabune (Tokyo: Shun'yōdō, 1898);
Natsukusa (Tokyo: Shun'yōdō, 1898);
Rakubaishu (Tokyo: Shun'yōdō, 1901);
Utatane (Tokyo: Shun'yōdō, 1901);
Tōson shishu (Tokyo: Shun'yōdō, 1904);
Hakai (Tokyo: Ryokuin Sōsho, 1906); translated by Kenneth Strong as *The Broken Commandment* (Tokyo: University of Tokyo Press, 1974);
Ryokuyōshu (Tokyo: Shun'yōdō, 1907);
Haru (Tokyo: Ryokuin Sōsho, 1908);
Tōsonshu (Tokyo: Hakubunkan, 1909);
Shinkatachō yori (Tokyo: Sakura Shobō, 1909); enlarged and republished as *Asakusa-dayori* (Tokyo: Shun'yōdō, 1924);
Ie, 2 volumes (Tokyo: Ryokuin Sōsho, 1911); translated by Cecilia Segawa Seigle as *The Family* (Tokyo: University of Tokyo Press, 1976);
Shokugo (Tokyo: Hakubunkan, 1911);
Chikumagawa no suketchi (N.p., 1912); translated by William E. Naff as *Chikuma River Sketches* (Honolulu: University of Hawaii Press, 1991);
Osanaki hi (N.p., 1912);
Asameshi (Tokyo: Shun'yōdō, 1913);
Bifu (Tokyo: Shinchōsha, 1913);
Suisaigaka (Tokyo: Shun'yōdō, 1916);
Sakura no mi no jukusuru toki (Tokyo: Shun'yōdō, 1919);
Shinsei, 2 volumes (Tokyo: Shun'yōdō, 1919);
Heiwa no Pari (Tokyo: Shun'yōdō, 1919); revised and enlarged as *Furansu dayori,* 2 volumes (Tokyo: Shinchōsha, 1924);
Aru onna no shōgai (N.p., 1920);
Sensō to Pari (Tokyo: Shinchōsha, 1923);
Furansu kikō (Tokyo: Shun'yōdō, 1924);
Tōson-dokuhon, 6 volumes (Tokyo: Kenkyusha, 1926);
Arashi (Tokyo: Shinchōsha, 1927);

Shimazaki Tōson

Shinsen Shimazaki Tōson shu (Tokyo: Kaizōsha, 1929);
Osanaki mononi (Tokyo: Jitsugyō no Nihonsha, 1931);
Furusato (Tokyo: Jitsugyō no Nihonsha, 1931);
Osana-monogatari (Tokyo: Kenkyūsha, 1931);
Chikaramochi (Tokyo: Kenkyūsha, 1931);
Yoakemae, 2 volumes (Tokyo: Shinchōsha, 1932–1935); translated by Naff as *Before the Dawn* (Honolulu: University of Hawaii Press, 1987);
Shimazaki Tōson shishu (Tokyo: Shinchōsha, 1935);
Tōson bunko, 11 volumes (Tokyo: Shinchōsha, 1935–1939);
Mebae (Tokyo: Mikasa Shobō, 1937);
Junrei (Tokyo: Iwanami Shoten, 1940);
Shimazaki Tōson shu (Tokyo: Kawade Shobō, 1941);
Tōhō no mon (Tokyo: Shinchōsha, 1946).

Collections: *Tōson zenshu,* 12 volumes (Tokyo: Kokumin Tosho Kankōkai, 1922);
Shimazaki Tōson shu, 9 volumes (Tokyo: Shinchōsha, 1925);
Shimazaki Tōson shu, 16 volumes (Tokyo: Kaizōsha, 1927);
Shimazaki Tōson shu, 24 volumes (Tokyo: Shun'yōdō, 1928–1929);
Shimazaki Tōson shu, 19 volumes (Tokyo: Shinchōsha, 1948–1951).

Shimazaki Tōson is one of several writers who laid the foundation of modern poetry and fiction in the development of modern Japanese literature. During his long career he produced representative works of Japanese Romanticism, Japanese Naturalism, and *shi-shōsetsu* (the I-novel) in addition to historical works. Writing primarily from autobiographical material, Tōson expanded the scope of literature at each stage of his literary development. Although Tōson's preeminence is solidly recognized in the canons of modern literature, certain enigmatic features of his style and persona elicit mixed emotions in readers.

He was an honest and sincere writer, but at the same time he was equivocal and reticent. He was educated in Tokyo and was sophisticated in his taste and thinking, but his love for his home province stayed with him throughout his life, and he had a rural, unurbane side to his character. He was proud of his national heritage, and some of his writings represent the soul of the Japanese, but his approach to literature and his liberal thinking were basically Western. He was confident and bold, but at the same time no one was more humble, hesitant, and shy. He was sometimes mysteriously inarticulate, but he did not hesitate to disclose matters that other writers would have kept to themselves. Every feature of his persona incorporated some contradictions, and his personal traits closely shaped his literature.

Tōson, whose real name was Shimazaki Haruki, was the youngest of seven children. He was born on 25 March 1872 in a small village of Magome, West-Chikuma County, Nagano Prefecture. His samurai ancestor had come to the Kiso Valley from the Miura Peninsula in 1513 and had served the lord of the Kiso clan. By the late sixteenth century Shimazaki descendents were half-samurai, half-farmer magistrates. The eighth-generation Shimazaki lost his samurai status and served as a commoner *shōya* (village headman and mediator), *honjin* (official host) for dignitaries traveling between Kyoto and Edo, and *toiya* (post station provider of horses). Shimazaki Masaki, Tōson's fa-ther and the seventeenth head of the family, also served in these hereditary capacities.

The Nakasendō, the main turnpike of the Edo Period, deteriorated after the Meiji Restoration because the *daimyōs* (lords) ceased their routine traveling, and the economy of post stations, including that of Magome, suffered. The pre-Restoration turmoil left the unpragmatic, visionary Masaki unable to maintain the land that he had inherited, and it transformed his main interest in life, the study of Japanese thought and literature, into a passionate aspiration to restore ancient Japan under the reign of the emperor. From his exhaustion and frustration with the great disparity between his ideals and his ability to hold back the onslaught of modern times his mental balance finally collapsed. Masaki's activities and insanity are touched on in many of Tōson's works and are the main theme of *Yoakemae* (1932–1935; translated as *Before the Dawn,* 1987). Masaki died in 1886 while Tōson was studying in Tokyo.

Tōson's mother, Nuiko, was the daughter of a Shimazaki, a related *honjin* family of neighboring Tsumago. She was an obedient wife to her husband and a cheerful, good mother to her children. Two of her daughters died in infancy, and a daughter and four sons survived to adulthood.

Tōson's strict father and his paternal grandmother, the daughter of a samurai, inculcated a love of learning in the young boy. In April 1881 his father decided to send the nine-year-old Haruki and Tomoya, his twelve-year-old brother, to Tokyo for studies. The trip, which they made in part on foot and in part by horse-drawn carriage, took seven days.

Haruki and his brother first stayed at the home of Sonoko, their oldest sister, who was married to Takase Kaoru, the son of an old samurai and pharmacist family in Kiso Fukushima. Sonoko and her family appear in *Ie* (1911; translated as *The Family,* 1976): Sonoko as Otane; Kaoru as Tatsuo; their son Chikao as Shōta; and Tazuko, their retarded daughter, as Osen. When Kaoru failed in business and had to return to his family business in the Kiso Valley, Haruki first lived with a family acquaintance and then moved to the home of the Yoshimuras, other acquaintances from Kiso, who treated him as a member of the family throughout his adolescent years.

Tōson's early childhood in Magome and in the Yoshimura household is recounted in *Osanaki hi* (Childhood Days, 1912). This boyhood experience of living in strangers' homes reinforced Haruki's reserved personality, and in later years he used this early experience to excuse his shyness

Tōson in November 1903

and reticence, traits that others often misinterpreted as coldness. Haruki graduated from Taimei Elementary School of Ginza in 1886 and entered Mita English School. In November his father died. He transferred to Kyōritsu School in Kanda a year later and then entered Meiji Gakuin, a Presbyterian school that was headed by James Curtis Hepburn, a missionary and physician who contributed much to the Westernization of Japan. Meiji Gakuin was staffed by six or seven American instructors along with Japanese teachers, and most courses were taught in English. Haruki's class had twenty-six students; the entire college division had eighty students.

Tōson enjoyed the free, cultured atmosphere of this school, and at first, like every young man of the era, he aspired to be a great politician or businessman. He was at the head of the class and a favorite of teachers. Sociable and dressed as a dandy, he became a conspicuous figure on campus. He was baptized a Christian in 1888 at the church pastored by Kimura Kumaji, his former English teacher at the Kyōritsu School. Kumaji later invited Tōson to teach at his school in Komoro.

Two years after being baptized Haruki suddenly changed from a cheerful, friendly student into a gloomy young man. After a classmate advised him against frivolous socializing, Haruki became totally withdrawn: he did not attend classes, spoke to almost no one, and avoided even his friends. He was under several new sources of stress. One was the tension between his worldliness and the Christian spirituality he had come to embrace in a school community that preached morality and ignored humanity. Another was his discovery of sex. He had become painfully conscious of his own body and of his longing for women. As he recalls in *Sakura no mi no jukusuru toki* (When the Cherries Ripen, 1919), his ambivalence about sex made him act in a contradictory manner: one moment he would tear up the novels of Ihara Saikaku (whose work he admired) for being lewd, and the next moment he would seek out lascivious passages in the Old Testament.

Yet another source of stress was in the reality around him, in the contrast between Western civilization and his own background. It is easy to attribute his pain to the disharmony he felt between Christianity and the traditional Japanese identity, but he probably felt greater discomfort in being torn between the idealized freedom he longed for and the repressive reality around him—another conflict between the soul and the flesh. Many writers of the period who came into contact with the West felt this conflict, especially through the fervent proselytizing of Christianity. Kitamura Tōkoku suffered from it, as did Shiga Naoya, Masamune Hakuchō, and Arishima Takeo.

Haruki abandoned his classwork but frequented the new library, Harris Hall (dedicated in 1890), where he read works by every writer he could find: William Shakespeare; Dante; Johann Wolfgang von Goethe; George Gordon, Lord Byron; William Wordsworth; Robert Burns; Jonathan Swift; and Japanese masters such as Saigyō (Satō Norikiyo), Matsuo Bashō, Saikaku, and Chikamatsu Monzaemon.

By 1891, when he graduated from Meiji Gakuin, Tōson had discarded the idea of becoming a politician or an industrialist. His grades had plummeted; he was ranked next to the lowest in his class; and he had failed the entrance examination to the elite First High School. This failure left a bitter aftertaste, and he was now determined to pursue a literary career as a poet or critic. He had come to know Iwamoto Yoshiharu, an elder in the Japanese Christian Church and Dean of Meiji Girls High School, who with his wife,

Wakamatsu Shizuko, published *Jogaku Zasshi*, a magazine for young Christian women. Tōson was given the task of introducing famous American and European women to the magazine, and the first small remuneration he received was from these translations of educational essays.

In the fall of 1892 Tōson began to teach Japanese literature (*The Tale of Genji*) at the post–high school division of Meiji Girls High School, and there he almost immediately fell in love with Satō Sukeko, a student who was a few months older than he and was the daughter of a member of the diet from Miyagi Prefecture. Deeply affected yet unable to express his love, he maintained a stern, unfriendly attitude toward her and within a year abruptly left his teaching post. He sent a letter of resignation to the school and church, but he did not let his family or the Yoshimura family know of his intentions. In January 1893 he went on a wandering trip, an extraordinary action that caused much consternation for his mother and the Yoshimuras.

Expenses for his trip were paid by Hoshino Tenchi, his friend who was the sponsor of the magazine *Bungakkai* (World of Literature), launched in January 1893 as a combination of Iwamoto's *Jogaku Zasshi* and another magazine for young women, *Jogakusei*. Iwamoto envisioned *Bungakkai* as a literary magazine with an emphasis on women's literature. It quickly became devoted to literary works and criticism and was handed over to Hoshino. Kitamura Tōkoku was asked to be on the editorial board, but he preferred to remain a contributor. The staff of the magazine included the twenty-two-year-old Tōson; twenty-five-year-old Sekiei, the younger brother of Hoshino Tenchi; twenty-year-old Hirata Tōboku; and twenty-four-year-old Togawa Shukotsu, with whom Tōson had become friends at Meiji Gakuin. Baba Kochō, another school friend, and Ueda Bin, the elitist translator of European poetry, later joined the staff of this leading Meiji literary magazine.

As though driven out of Tokyo, Tōson traveled to the Kansai region, where he first visited Hoshino's and Sukeko's friend who had graduated from Meiji Girls High School the previous year. Longing after poets of old—such as Saigyō and Bashō—who reached the apex of poetic art by rigorous wanderings, he wrote poems and did eccentric things such as making an offering of a copy of Shakespeare's *Hamlet* (1604) to the Temple of Ishiyama, where, according to legend, Murasaki Shikibu had written parts of *The Tale of Genji*.

Tōson's feelings were conveyed to Sukeko, and he found out that she returned them but was to be married soon. In the fall when he came back from his trip he saw her twice but was unable to say much to her. She followed his advice and went home to the north to marry the agronomist whom her parents had chosen for her. Tōson fell into a deep melancholy and seriously contemplated suicide, but in the end he decided that he had yet too many things to learn in life. He shaved his head, begged a priest with whom he was acquainted to provide him with a monk's robe, and went wandering again while fasting for a few days.

This rejection of death as a resolution had come not from his Christian faith but from a desire to live, and before setting out he dressed as a Buddhist monk. Tōson was fortunate in having friends—Hoshino, Togawa, Hirata, Baba, and Kitamura—who sustained him financially and spiritually, and the suicide of Kitamura was a tremendous shock to him.

Kitamura was a passionate poet-critic who in 1892 wrote "Ensei shika to josei" (The Misanthropic Poet and Woman), advocating unadulterated "pure romantic love as the solace for poetics" and "the hermitage for the defeated hero in the battle between the ideal world and the real world." The declamatory style and romantic content of his essays stirred the sensibilities of young men in Japan. He had a brilliant analytical mind and became the ideologue of the literary group around *Bungakkai*. Kitamura was also an early political writer, a member of the Japan Peace Association, and a humanist who proclaimed that the search for human truth was central to literature. But in 1894, after suffering from neurosis, he committed suicide.

Yet in spite of the brief association that he and Tōson had enjoyed, Kitamura remained a powerful and lasting influence on him. In "Kitamura Tōkoku 27-kaiki ni," on the twenty-seventh anniversary of Kitamura's death, Tōson wrote: "Among our contemporaries, he was one who cast his eyes the highest and the farthest [into the future]. And I feel that he made preparations far in advance for us [latecomers]."

In 1894 and 1895 misfortunes for Tōson followed one after another. Hideo, his oldest brother, was imprisoned for forgery and his properties seized. He had earlier sold the Shimazaki house and invested the proceeds foolishly, so the financial burden of supporting his family and Tomoya, the third of Tōson's brothers and an invalid from syphilis, fell on Tōson—whose income was the ten yen per month that he earned after returning to teaching at Meiji Girls High

*Tōson (second from left in back row) with fellow faculty members and the
graduating class of Komoro Gijuku in 1904*

School. Moneylenders hounded the family, and Tōson had to write difficult letters to borrow money and apologize for not being able to pay debts. In August 1895 he heard news that Satō Sukeko had died of heart failure during pregnancy. A month later a fire in Magome burned down the Shimazaki home. His mother was hospitalized with cancer. He could not endure his teaching duties, which had lost all meaning for him (his students nicknamed him *Cinder,* "burned out"), and he finally resigned from the school in December. Two months later the school burned down. The tragedies, catastrophes, and money pressures left Tōson totally numb. In need of money, he tried ceramic painting, but he had imagined much more artistic work and quit, totally frustrated, after one day. His novel *Haru* (Spring, 1908) recounts this period accurately.

In fall 1896 he obtained a position teaching writing at Tōhoku Gakuin in Sendai, a job for which he was recommended by a Kiso acquaintance who had taught at Meiji Girls High School. At the same time his brother Hirosuke sent word from Korea that he could help the family financially. This diminishing financial pressure signaled a turning point for Tōson. His stay in Sendai was only a year long, but he later called it a "dawn," the beginning of his real literary career. In the quiet old northern city he enjoyed freedom of movement, thought, and observation, and fresh poems began to flow.

In exhilaration he wrote, "It's good to speak; it's good to speak out without hesitation." The inspiration he had received from his friend Kitamura finally took shape. When Tōson had first read Kitamura's essay "The misanthropic poet and woman" in 1892, he felt galvanized and thought, "Was there ever a man who has spoken out so boldly what I have always wanted to yet was unable to say!" He had retained the passion, unable to speak or express it in any way, but after he had lost the object of his love he was able to find lyrical, romantic words. His contribution to modern poetry is not revolutionary but epoch-making; the paradigm of his poetics represented a new era of humanity and romanticism.

First published in *Bungakkai* and then collected in *Wakanashu* (Collection of Young Herbs, 1897), his poems revitalized the genre of poetry. They breathed life into simple words by new arrangements, offering fresh images and music totally unlike those of familiar aesthetics and sentiments. Tōson's verses combined sensuality and a pure lyricism hitherto unknown to the Japanese poetic tradition, and his *Collection of Young Herbs* became a romantic Bible for young, aspiring poets.

His days in Sendai were full of creativity and vitality. He enjoyed associating with poets and writers and voraciously read European literature. He began to translate the works of John Ruskin, whose influence on Tōson appeared a few years later.

By the time *Bungakkai* ceased publication with its January 1898 issue, Tōson was an established poet, although this status promised him no financial security. He received fifteen yen for each of his first two books of poetry, *Collection of Young Herbs* and *Natsukusa* (Summer Grass)–the latter of which Tōson wrote and published in 1898 following his summer visit that year with his sister, Sonoko, in Kiso-Fukushima.

On his way back to Tokyo he went to Komoro at the foot of Mount Asama to visit Kimura Kumaji, his former teacher, who had founded a private school there. Tōson was impressed with Kimura's life, dedicated to teaching in the beautiful natural environment. When Kimura asked Tōson if he would also like to teach at his Komoro Gijuku, Tōson accepted his offer.

In April 1899 Tōson returned briefly to Tokyo to marry Hata Fuyuko, the daughter of Hata Keiji, a prosperous wholesale fishnet dealer. As a graduate of Meiji Girls High School, she had been recommended by Iwamoto Yoshiharu. Tōson's marriage and the move to Komoro were in part moves to break away from Tokyo and his brother Hideo, who was again involved in a hopeless business scheme. Tōson had criticized the false values that Hideo embraced and his arrogance as head of the family, but Tōson had always been intimidated by him. An even more fundamental reason for the move, however, was that Tōson needed, and was determined to start, a new life in order to create a new literature.

Some of the *Bungakkai* members had become romantic dilettantes after they lost the leadership of Kitamura Tōkoku. Tōson had psychologically parted company with them and was in search of a new medium and style to express his feelings. The writing of the early Meiji Period had been in the style of the late Edo Period, a mixture of ancient literary style and Chinese vocabulary. Many writers had tried new venues: the most successful was Futabatei Shimei, who had created a basis for a contemporary prose style with *Ukigumo* (The Drifting Clouds, 1887–1888; translated as *Ukigumo*, 1967) and with his translations of Ivan Turgenev's short stories. For Tōson the issue was not just a new style but a new literature, and his own spiritual survival. He had matters he wanted to express, and he could not do so in his suffocating home and social environment of Tokyo. He believed that the new age required a new literature, which in turn would be possible only with the creation of new expressions, even a new language. To regenerate his language, he had to renew himself by shedding all extraneous conventions, and so he left Tokyo in April 1899.

Attempting to turn from poetry to prose fiction, Tōson in Komoro began with word sketches modeled after the work of John Ruskin. To train himself to look at his environment from new perspectives, he went to the fields of Komoro with an artist colleague. He obtained reproductions of paintings by Alfred Sisley, Claude Monet, and Camille Pissarro and studied the Impressionists' ways of depicting nature. He also admired the work of Charles Darwin and the uncompromising "scientific spiritualism" that dictated his grasp of the laws of nature. In his view Darwin's rigorous scientific discipline verged on spiritualism, which opened his eyes to an approach to nature entirely different from that of the traditional Asian. The clean, simple, linear word sketches he made in Komoro were later published as *Chikumagawa no suketchi* (1912; translated as *Chikuma River Sketches*, 1991).

Launching himself into the new genre of prose fiction, however, Tōson found that his earlier conviction–"It's good to speak; it's good to speak out without hesitation"–was not easy to practice. He depended heavily on the method he had learned from Ruskin and Darwin–observation and objective descriptions–and on Gustave Flaubert's emphasis on detail and precision. In the early days in Komoro he used in his short stories everything he had observed and heard, and as a result he offended some of his friends, from whom he acquired a reputation for using them as guinea pigs.

The result of sharpening his powers of perception and observation led him to what he later called "the hell of scrutiny." He had to reap the fruit of his artistic self-discipline: an inability to find simple pleasure in the environment, people, and friends. But he believed that the writer must be able to see things accurately and capture the essence of things, so he developed a style in which he chose words carefully, to give information selectively. In "Harushippitsu-chu no danwa" he offered this rhetorical rationalization for his method: "Who would be a better writer? The one who describes everything he knows even though he knows very little, or the one who reveals sparingly only the essense of what he knows thoroughly?"

Tōson's life in Komoro, which his friend Tayama Katai described as "a head-on collision of art and life," was necessarily frugal. Tōson and Fuyuko had three daughters in four years, and he had to support this family on his salary of twenty-five yen a month. Although Fuyuko had come from a comfortable home with many servants and the fashionable atmosphere of Meiji Girls High School, she stayed by her husband and endured the hardship. Life would have been more tolerable for both Tōson and Fuyuko if their marriage had managed to approximate their expectations more closely. But he felt disillusioned by her lack of intellectual interests and she by his seeming coldness. His accidental discovery of a letter she had written to a former boyfriend became for Tōson a source of bitter disappointment in and distrust for women for the rest of his life. Some of his early short stories written in Komoro are variations on the theme of a woman's infidelity and her husband's suspicion and jealousy. He also made Fuyuko resent his association with his former piano teacher at the Ueno Conservatory. Tōson faithfully describes the psychological quadrille of love and jealousy in *The Family* and, in a modified form, in "Suisai gaka" (Watercolor Artist, 1904), an earlier short story. Tōson's artist colleague at the Komoro school, who accused Tōson of using him as a model, could not have been more mistaken. Tōson was so preoccupied with his own marital difficulties that he had no need to speculate on others. In the end, however, his fortitude transformed his sufferings into strength.

In Komoro, Tōson read everything he could obtain: the works of Fyodor Dostoyevsky, Count Leo Tolstoy, Ivan Turgenev, Dmitri Merezhkovsky, Henrik Ibsen, Guy de Maupassant, Gerhart Hauptmann, Émile Zola, and especially Flaubert. His pragmatic and controlled reading of foreign literature was certainly unlike that of Tayama Katai, who was totally overwhelmed and enthralled by it. But the egocentric and utilitarian reading of foreign literature that Nakamura Mitsuo accuses him of doing in "cutting its influences to fit his needs" is not a sin of Tōson alone. Emulating existing literature according to one's taste and capacity is not unusual for a young writer emerging from his chrysalis. Tōson was striving to find and establish an identity, to reach his goal of nurturing, developing, and completing himself as a writer in the only way he knew, and he was second to none in his devotion and struggle to do these things.

In 1905 Tōson emerged from six years in the mountains ready to tackle fiction writing. He had begun a novel and now decided to return to Tokyo to concentrate on finishing it. His realistic—later labeled naturalistic—approach to his material had been established, and he had a reservoir of strength to overcome psychological, physical, and financial difficulties. He first borrowed four hundred yen from his father-in-law to publish the novel; then he borrowed living expenses from a wealthy acquaintance, Kōzu Takeshi.

The next seven months of 1905 was a time of veritable warfare. Nothing swayed Tōson from his determination to finish his novel *Hakai* (1906; translated as *The Broken Commandment,* 1974), but his effort imposed devastating sacrifices on his family. One after another his three little daughters died from diseases. Fuyuko developed nightblindness from malnutrition, and her grief at the deaths of her daughters must have been incomparably severe. The sources of these tragedies lay at least partly in the extremely frugal living that Tōson forced on his family, and other writers have criticized him for imposing such sacrifices. Shiga Naoya, for example, wrote in his "Kuniko," "Was *The Broken Commandment* a work worthy of such [sacrifices]? I was terribly angry." In *Aru ahō no isshō* when Akutagawa Ryunosuke labeled Tōson as "the most cunning hypocrite I have seen," he was referring to the incestuous incident that Tōson later recounted in *Shinsei* (A New Life, 1919), but the deaths of Tōson's three girls were undoubtedly at the root of his criticism.

The Broken Commandment won critical acclaim as the first European-scale novel with a strong message about social issues hitherto unexpressed in Japanese literature. The fact that Tōson himself had financed its publication in order to maintain artistic freedom and integrity (and had put the lives of his family and himself at risk to complete it) was acknowledged by the world.

Its protagonist—the intelligent, serious-minded schoolteacher Segawa Ushimatsu—is admonished by his father never to disclose his socially "untouchable" background. The father wishes to protect his son from being persecuted as an outcast *burakumin,* a fate that the father has already suffered. Ushimatsu respects Inoko Rentarō, a burakumin politician and social reformer who is eventually killed in a vicious assault by the hired thugs of a political enemy. The same hypocritical enemy, married to a rich burakumin woman, initiates a rumor about Ushimatsu's background to retaliate for his unwillingness to collaborate in keeping the marriage secret. Ushimatsu is forced to break his father's dying command and confess his

*Tōson's oldest sister, Sonoko (standing), with his wife Fuyuko and his first three
daughters—Midori, Takako, and Nuiko—in 1904*

background. He leaves to start a new life on a Texas farm, where the girl he loves will join him in the future.

Whether *The Broken Commandment* was truly a socially conscious European-style novel has been a source of polemics for some time. Many critics pointed out imperfections in this novel, but most of Tōson's contemporaries called it a breakthrough from the stagnant conventions of traditional plot, characters, and style. However, since the early Shōwa era Tōson's discriminatory feelings and the weakness of Ushimatsu have been criticized, and the validity of the novel as a work of social criticism has been questioned. The critics see Ushimatsu as an abject figure, though upright and idealistic. In their eyes he is weak and passive, fraught with fear and guilt, and brought nearly to a breakdown by his mounting discomfort and stress. His confession is motivated not by his inner strength but by external pressures from

the school administration and prefectural board. When the respected schoolteacher kneels on the floor and apologizes to his pupils, the reader sees Tōson's psychological double, an image of Tōson's pains superimposed on a victim of discrimination.

It is true that Ushimatsu's torment, self-deprecation, and abject posture are externalizations of Tōson's psyche. His personal torment is inseparably entangled with his attempts to call society's conscience to deal with evil and injustice in the treatment of the poor and the socially outcast. His personality and his problem with secrecy were embodied in the principal character. But Tōson's achievement should be recognized and credited with due respect. In the fictional character to whom he attributed weakness and hesitancy, he was describing the realities of his day. By depicting the protagonist as a tormented young man and surrounding him with characters such as the despicable political candidate, the hypocritical school principal, and a malicious colleague, Tōson was clearly castigating the values of late Meiji society. He was the first to bring such problems to public attention through the medium of fiction, regardless of the schema of the novel.

In addition Tōson presents, as a subplot, the problem of the sexual harassment of a young girl by her foster father, a Buddhist priest. Her real father is Ushimatsu's drunken, henpecked, pathetic colleague, who had the daughter by his first wife and has many other children by his present wife. The girl, who eventually becomes Ushimatsu's wife, is inextricably trapped because of the poverty at home and the hostility of her stepmother. The realities of the exploited female sex, especially in the face of poverty, are other aspects of contemporary life that Tōson presents, not with the sentimentality of the traditional Edo romance but with social indignation.

The unnecessary humility of the confessing hero is attributable to the fact that this was Tōson's image of himself. His writings indicate clearly that he had long been tormented either by some secret at the bottom of his heart or simply by his inability to express what he felt profoundly. A love poem that he wrote in Komoro begins, "Here in the depth of my heart, lives a secret that cannot be recounted in words." Many years after Tōson's death his grandnephew disclosed the family secrets that Tōson's father had conducted an incestuous affair with Tōson's younger half-sister and that the adultery of Tōson's mother had produced the third brother, Tomoya. These facts, which are today well known, troubled Tōson deeply. Whether or not these were the secrets which he guarded and from which he suffered cannot be determined. Yet in Komoro he had been moved by Jean-Jacques Rousseau's *Les Confessions* (Confessions, 1781–1788), and the protagonist's confession in *The Broken Commandment* was clearly inspired by that method of purging and renewing oneself.

While writing this novel Tōson thought of the theme for his next book, *Spring,* an autobiographical novel about his youth and his friends on the *Bungakkai* staff. The title was taken from Sandro Botticelli's *La Primavera* (1477–1478), and his plan was to portray a "young man who dies deceived by the 'Spring of the Ideal,' and about one who seeks and fails to find the 'Spring of the Arts' but in the end attains the 'Spring of Life.'" The hero, Kishimoto Sutekichi, returns from his wandering trips and meets with his literary colleagues. With a friend's help he has fleeting meetings with Katsuko, the love of his life, who is going to be married soon, but he cannot say any of the things that he wants to say. Frustrated with this unrequited love, he visits a brothel and is filled with self-loathing. While he wanders, seeking some way to regain self-confidence and earn a living, his friend Aoki (Kitamura Tōkoku) is also suffering from poverty and a loss of faith and hope (Tōson uses passages from Kitamura's diary to reconstruct his mental state). Aoki had fallen in love and, against objections from both families, had married young, and he is unable to support his wife and little daughter. After a bout of insomnia, he attempts suicide by cutting his throat, but he survives.

Meanwhile, Sutekichi's oldest brother is incarcerated for fraud, and the financial burdens of the family fall on Sutekichi's shoulders. He returns to teaching, but his salary does not begin to cover his financial obligations, and the bailiff and loan sharks torment him. A postcard from Aoki's wife announces her husband's suicide: he had escaped from his wife's care and hanged himself in Shiba Park. Sutekichi is still in shock when he learns of Katsuko's death during her pregnancy. In despair, he quits his teaching job and decides to concentrate on writing. Finding one's life, he insists, is more important than taking care of his family. But writing does not come easily to him: "Kishimoto became more and more laconic. What he could not say verbally, he wanted to express at least in writing. He tried all genres: novel, play, essay, even modern poetry. There was not a single way he could express himself freely." Sinking deeper in despair, he learns about a teaching position in Sendai. "Even a man such as I wants to manage to live somehow," he says to himself, and he prepares to leave for Sendai.

Spring was a different novel from *The Broken Commandment,* a much more introspective, subjective, almost reticent work. The degree to which it was influenced by the style of the personal confession in the work of a fellow Naturalist writer such as Tayama Katai is still debated. Katai's *Futon* (1907; translated as *The Quilt,* 1981) is a thinly disguised description of his thoughts and sexual desires for his wife's ward, a high school girl; this baring of his soul and carnal desires shocked readers. The subjective paralleling of protagonist and author made the work a sincere and successful, if awkward, I-novel. Nakamura Mitsuo argued that *The Broken Commandment* was the starting point for an authentic development of Japanese Naturalism, "the first attempt to transplant a modern frame to the Japanese novel," but that the success of *The Quilt* made Tōson write the pure I-novel *Spring,* which distorted the course of Japanese literature.

This theory has been widely accepted, but it has also been opposed by the theory that Tōson had begun his preparations to write *Spring* long before the appearance of *The Quilt.* Tōson states that he had planned to write the novel as early as 1905. At any rate, to ascribe the development of modern Japanese literature to Tōson's *Spring* oversimplifies literary history by ignoring complex social and political details.

By 1908 Tōson was the father of three sons and was still facing financial difficulties. His brother Hideo had been imprisoned a second time for business failure and had subsequently moved to Taiwan to reconstruct his life, and his departure again left Tōson responsible for the support of the family. The family of his sister Sonoko was also in upheaval: her husband, a bank board member, had absconded with the bank funds and taken his geisha mistress with him. These continuous pressures from relatives made Tōson question the validity of the traditional virtue of mutual help within a family. His idea of writing *The Family* evolved while he was writing *Spring.*

The two-part *The Family* covers the twelve years from 1898 to 1910, and Tōson began writing about events that had taken place a dozen years earlier. Time in the novel, of course, moved at a different rate from that in real life, so an unexpected turn in his life might lead to changes in the plot. One such event was the death of Sonoko's son, Takase Chikao, from tuberculosis and mental stress, shortly after Tōson had finished part one of the novel. Two months later Tōson's thirty-one-year-old wife died of a hemorrhage following the birth of Ryuko, their seventh child. Tōson resumed writing five months later, although he was in no condition to do so.

Tōson and Fuyuko had come quietly to accept and enjoy each other, and her death was a blow to him. He could not take care of the four small children, and all but the oldest were sent to various relatives and friends, but the children were of great concern to him. Part two of *The Family,* a section headed "Sacrifices," was written under these conditions between fall 1910 and summer 1911.

The Family is the most important work of the middle of Tōson's career. He never claimed

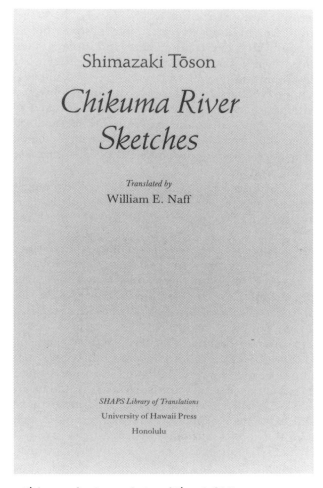

Title page for the translation of Tōson's Chikumagawa no suketchi, *a series of impressionistic sketches of the Komoro area*

to be writing a Naturalist novel in working on the piece, but his approach and style, the material treating Japanese family life, and the theory on which he was working made the book a masterpiece of Japanese Naturalism. Along with a critical subtext on traditional values, the narrative recounts a series of domestic troubles as a family disintegrates, and it presents the story simply and with more stylistic maturity than his earlier works.

The novel has been criticized for its lack of contact with historical and social events, or for not relating the darkness of *The Family* to social realities. But excluding the world outside the family was part of Tōson's intention and a means of conducting his experimental approach. He was much aware of the societal sources of evil and unhappiness, and of events of historical magnitude such as the Russo-Japanese war, but through the stories of his own family he was examining the institution of the family, its structural weight, and its restrictive system. So he symbolically excluded events and broader settings outside that institution and concentrated on developing his novel within the physical boundaries of familial structures. He did break this pattern occasionally, but in the main he adhered to his self-imposed boundary, and this method enabled him to re-create the sense of unalleviated restrictions and oppressiveness of the Japanese family system.

He also had another reason for excluding external events. While the breakdown of the family system was very much caused by rapid changes that were occurring in Japanese society, the collapse of the two old families about which he was writing also resulted from internal changes, and Tōson successfully shows the intrinsic ills infesting the families. For example, his personae display traits that he finds characteristic of old families: arrogance, egocentricity, vanity, and the dichotomies of charm and detachment, authoritativeness and irresponsibility. He also shows in old lineages the blood corruption manifested in unsavory traits such as incestuous impulses, insanity, retardation, chronic melancholy, and moral bankruptcy. The heavy responsibilities that the family system imposes on its stronger members result in the eventual downfall of those members.

From observations of his own family, Tōson had arrived at a form of Darwinism, a theory that the Japanese family system was pervasively destructive and unproductive because the weaker members of the clan fed on the stronger and drained what little strength the latter might have. Such developments are some of the reasons for the collapse of the Koizumis and the Hashimotos. Convinced that one would eventually be drawn into financial and spiritual bankruptcy in such a situation, Tōson/Sankichi advocated severing family ties and building new families.

However, the novel sustains contradictions in exposing Tōson's own contradictions. Sankichi suffers as a victim of the family system, but he imposes sacrifices on his own flesh and blood. He breaks away to establish a new, tradition-free family, but he never succeeds in disengaging himself from a sense of obligation to his family and never ceases to help the families of his brothers. Furthermore, his recognition of the family head and his pride in his prestigious lineage are obvious. In recognizing such features of family life in his novel, Tōson demonstrates the tenacious hold

of blood, which he begins to see with an increasing clarity.

In his private life Tōson's advocacy for discarding the extraneous provided a means of survival; his cheerful sociability that verged on obtrusiveness during his first two years at Meiji Gakuin was gone. He manifested stoic taciturnity from his long ascetic discipline to seek out solitude. Coming from a large family, he longed for close, warm, intimate relationships, and he had friends who were close to him, but he was incapable of allowing himself the luxury of his natural desires. As he approached middle age he was entering a period of life when he most needed support and companionship, but he was incapable of forming relationships. After finishing *The Family* in 1911, he was left desolate by Fuyuko's death and could not work on another novel for a long time.

At age forty Tōson's situation as a widower marked a midlife crisis. He was a man of tremendous self-restraint but also strong sexuality and passion. As early as the summer of 1906, when his wife had traveled to Hakodate, he had felt a strong attraction toward his niece Isako (Oshun in *The Family*), the eldest daughter of his brother Hideo. Tōson was mindful of his father's incestuous love for his half-sister, and the dark secrets of his family put him on guard against his own potential decadence. When he acknowledged his feelings toward his niece, he had grown overly stern and she had remained completely unaware of his feelings. But after his wife died six years later, Tōson was suffering from loneliness and from being denied love. Both from deference to his children's memories of their mother and from his continued distrust of women, he refused to remarry. Two nieces, the daughters of his brother Hirosuke, came to keep house for him shortly after Fuyuko's death, and Komako, the younger, remained with him after Hisako, her sister, left to be married in June 1912. In their mutual loneliness and need Tōson and Komako fell into each other's arms.

Six months after her sister's marriage Komako told Tōson that she was pregnant. In despair he left abruptly for Europe, explaining the suddenness of the trip as an effort to escape his stagnant life. Aboard the French ship *Ernest Simon* he wrote to Hirosuke to acknowledge his relationship with Komako. His actions might appear cowardly and hypocritical: he waited until he left Japan to contact Hirosuke, tried to settle the matter with money, left Komako in the care of her father, and never told her mother that he was the father of Komako's baby. His guilt was almost more than he could bear, but he could do nothing but escape.

In Paris, Tōson concentrated on forgetting Komako. He met many Japanese artists and writers, and as he mingled with the French he studied their language. He had written *Childhood Days* and had begun to write *When the Cherries Ripen*—both autobiographical novels, one about his childhood and the other about his Meiji Gakuin days before he had begun his wandering. For the Tokyo *Asahi* he also wrote "Letters from France," later collected as *Heiwa no Pari* (Paris in Peace, 1919). These letters and those in *Sensō to Pari* (War and Paris, 1923) offer observations of the people and culture in prewar and wartime France. As he met French people and experienced their art, music, and civilization in general, Tōson was rediscovering Japan, for France gave him new perspectives on both French and Japanese culture, and his ideas for *Before the Dawn* were gradually developing.

He saw the burial places of Héloïse and Peter Abelard at the Père Lachaise cemetery and remembered François Villon's poem on the two lovers, a poem that he and his friends had recited in an English version at Meiji Gakuin. He appreciated the works of artists such as Paul Cézanne, Jean Renoir, Camille Pissarro, Édouard Manet, Edgar Degas, Maurice Denis, Claude Monet, Pierre-Cécile Puvis de Chavannes, Auguste Rodin, Aristide Maillol, and Emile Antoine Bourdelle. He was deeply moved by Claude Debussy's performance of his piano music; he heard Camille Saint-Saëns conduct an orchestra for the last time and listened to Eugène Ysaōe play the violin. He heard Stéphane Mallarmé's poems read and saw Vaslav Nijinsky and Calsavina dance. He realized the efficacy of the arts in bringing about mutual understanding of people from various nationalities:

"There was a time when Europe appeared to our forefathers as ghoulish 'Black Ships,'" he wrote; if [European] materialist power had been forced upon us without Russian literature, German music, or French painting, how would Europe appear to us now? Isn't it after the arts were made known to us that we really began to understand the Europeans?. . . [W]hile Japan is introduced to them only by war, and while many of our own people take pride in war, we will still be ghouls in the eyes of Europe.

In July 1914 World War I broke out, and Tōson fled to Limoges in late August, returned to Paris in November, and, with the encourage-

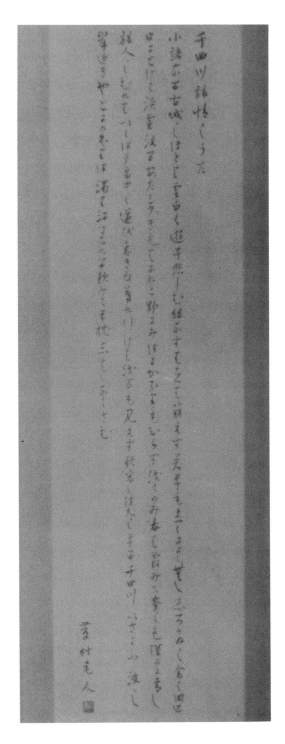

Calligraphy copy that Tōson made of "Chikuma River Travel Song" (from Chikuma River Sketches, *translated by William E. Naff, 1991)*

ment of writer friends who formed a support group, stayed for two more years. He continued to work on *When the Cherries Ripen* and wrote reports on France under fire. Eventually financial aid from the support group was discontinued, so he left Paris on 29 April 1916 and returned to Japan on 4 July by way of London and the Cape of Good Hope.

Meanwhile, after Tōson had left for Europe, Komako developed clinical hysteria that verged on insanity, and when she gave birth to a boy, the infant was handed over to foster parents. When he finally returned, Tōson found Komako almost dysfunctional; Hirosuke was suffering from an eye ailment and was almost blind; and Sonoko was in a mental hospital, where she was in the advanced stages of schizophrenia. So he was again under heavy financial pressures to support his extended family.

He decided to hire Komako as his assistant for ten yen a month to help out Hirosuke's family, and, despite Tōson's earlier contrition he had expressed to Hirosuke from France, he resumed his relationship with his niece. This second affair arose from his pity for the semi-invalid young woman, but Tōson was again entrapped in carnal desires, guilt, and obligations. Komako was twenty-six, still much in love with her uncle, and unrealistically hopeful of marrying him. Tōson had brought back Ryuko, his youngest daughter, from her foster family, and he now lived with three of his surviving children, whose eyes had to be shielded from his illicit affair. He was caught in multiple nooses of his own making and finally decided to free himself from all the obligations and guilt.

Hirano Ken's *Shinseiron* (*A Discourse on A New Life*, 1945) concludes that *Shinsei* (A New Life, 1919), Tōson's confession novel, was the only solution for Tōson, who wished to obtain freedom from the hell of love and money and to survive. In *The Broken Commandment* Tōson had made Segawa Ushimatsu catapult himself into a new life through a public confession, and even before he had left for Europe, Tōson knew that the only way he might renew his life was through an action that required courage. He had to use confession as a means of sloughing off his past and cleansing and regenerating himself. After agonizing about this decision, he asked Komako's permission to write about their affair, and she consented. Her eyes were only on him, and she believed him to be her savior. He had contemplated the decision for more than a year, and in April 1918, when Komako's mother died, he

began to write *A New Life,* which began its serial publication in the *Asahi* newspaper on 1 May.

It was an unprecedented confession of a man's incestuous love, anguish, repentance, and now supplication for redemption—a model *shishōsetsu,* or I-novel. Confession of his sins was not easy for Tōson, and he had difficulty articulating his feelings. He was fearful of what might happen to his reputation and his future as a writer: fearful of becoming the object of sneers, contempt, and denunciation from the public. The novel could destroy him professionally and spiritually and rob him of the courage to live. He said that, as he began to write, he was prepared to be buried socially and to go to prison.

At first the text was extremely inarticulate about the central occasion for the confession. The introduction explains the widowed state of the protagonist, Kishimoto Sutekichi, and not until the thirteenth segment of the novel does the heroine, Setsuko, say to her uncle Kishimoto, "You know about my condition, don't you?" The reader can only surmise that she is pregnant and that her uncle has caused her pregnancy. No love scenes and no descriptions of the beginning or developing stages of love are presented. In the twenty-eighth segment Kishimoto holds Setsuko briefly and tells her that he has good news: he has decided to go abroad.

A plot summary to this point conveys Kishimoto's utter self-centeredness and his lack of sensitivity for Setsuko's feelings, but the context of his words and actions creates compassion and understanding for him and belief in his sincere remorse and repentance. Indeed, Tōson's unadorned confession generally touched the public, although the text does not support a conjecture that Tōson had written the novel in a way calculated to win such sympathy. His strictness with himself in maintaining ethical conduct and his tortured inability to reveal himself would seem to preclude such calculations on his part. His literary spirit forced him to disclose his secret for the salvation of Komako and himself—for, indeed, he seemed to have sincerely believed that they would be saved through such public disclosure. This, at least, was Tōson's logic.

Part one of *A New Life* was completed in October 1918 and was a great success. Society neither buried Tōson nor sent him to prison. As might have been expected, however, his brother Hirosuke was deeply angry. He sent Komako out of Japan with his brother Hideo, who was returning to Taiwan, and severed all communication with Tōson. This response naturally ended all of

Tōson's financial aid to Hirosuke's family, but Tōson should not bear all the blame for terminating the financial assistance that Hirosuke's family needed. In fact, Hirosuke had often assumed a blackmailer's stance about Tōson's behavior with Komako, and Tōson had sought to aid his brothers and sister, nieces and nephews throughout his adult life. Part one of the novel, which ends with the protagonist's last days in France, thus reflected Tōson's desperate wish to escape from carnal decadence and find a "spacious, free open world" where he could live as a human being.

Part two appeared in *Asahi* from April to October 1919. The narrative begins with Kishimoto's return from France, the resumption of his relationship with Setsuko, his decision to write about their affair, and the result of his publishing part one. After resuming the illicit relationship, Kishimoto Sutekichi becomes a rather self-centered, complacent figure as he attempts to sublimate the relationship and present some ethical bases for it. He assumes a quasi-religious posture toward an idealized love affair and leads Setsuko to believe that a spiritual love is the only salvation for them. At this point the book manifests a tone of hypocrisy and self-congratulation, and Tōson, when he realized this, wished to expurgate part two of *A New Life* from his collected works. This, however, was not done.

After completing *A New Life* Tōson lived quietly and modestly, seeking to be a good father to all four children. He had written many stories for and about his children—*Osanaki mononi, Ko ni okuru tegami, Atami miyage, Haru o machitsutsu, Nobijitaku, Arashi, Bunpai*—and he traveled with his children to his home village and other parts of Japan. He sent Kusuo, his oldest son, to Meiji Gakuin, and when Kusuo later became a farmer in Magome, Tōson purchased a farmhouse and moved it to the site of the ancient *honjin,* the home of his ancestors and now the site of a museum. His second and third sons studied art; the older son, Keiji, went to France in 1929, and the younger one, Osuke, went to Germany in 1930 to do so.

In 1920 Tōson's sister, Takase Sonoko, died after years of mental torment. Tōson had loved his sister very much, and he wrote the novella *Aru onna no shōgai* (A Woman's Life, 1920) to memorialize her. For the next ten years he limited his writing to short works, essays, and children's stories, and he published his collected works while preparing to write his final masterpiece. In 1928 Tōson, at age fifty-six, ended eighteen years

of bachelorhood by marrying Katō Shizuko, his thirty-three-year-old assistant. Tōson had first met her as a member of the editorial staff of *Shojochi,* a magazine that he had begun in 1922 and that advocated the emancipation of women from subordinate positions. At least fifteen women had joined the board to work on the magazine, which had ceased publication after its tenth issue.

In April 1929 Tōson began to write his greatest work, *Before the Dawn*—a monumental work based on the life of his father. While Tōson was in Paris he had thought much about his father's life, about the turbulent historical transition that Masaki had lived through and the insanity that he suffered when he could no longer cope with those changes. On foreign soil Tōson had been able for the first time to reflect on and begin to interpret Japan's past, to reassess the accomplishments of the great scholars of Japanese studies to which his father had been devoted, and to begin to appreciate his father's spiritual legacy. He wanted to gaze at the historical crossroads of Meiji, when the old collapsed and the new had not yet dawned. The French civilization that he observed made him contemplate and look back on its course of historical development, as it seemed to provide a logical basis for anticipating developments in his own culture. Wishing to know more about his culture, he turned his eyes toward the past hundred years, to the days of Motoori Norinaga, to seek the origins of nineteenth-century Classicism. He explored the revival of the ancient spirit of the *Man'yōshu,* the earliest collection of Japanese poetry, and of love and respect for the Japanese language. These thoughts were directly related to a longing to know his father, a longing that ultimately was one of coming to know himself, for he was becoming increasingly aware of the imprint of the Shimazaki blood.

In the past Tōson had written almost entirely about his own experiences and those of his contemporaries. To take a historical perspective on events more than one hundred years earlier and see them through the eyes of his father's generation required a long and thorough preparation.

Tōson decided to use clear, simple language to write *Before the Dawn* and to keep his narrative close to the personal history of his father rather than present an overview of Japan in transition. The main part of the story covers the period from 1853, when his father was twenty-three years old, to 1886, when he died at age fifty-six. Major historical events are presented only as a

Cover for Tōson's novel Yoakemae *(1932–1935), which begins with news of the arrival of Commodore Matthew Perry's ships in Edo harbor in 1853*

backdrop that constantly affects the mood of the protagonist, Aoyama Hanzō. Produced partly from Tōson's memory, Hanzō's image becomes more vivid and touchingly real as the narrative progresses.

In part one Hanzō is the son of the village head and honjin in Magome, Kiso Valley, but his heart yearns for the restoration of Japan to its ancient ways under the sovereignty of the emperor. He goes to Edo with his brother-in-law to become a disciple of Hirata Kanetane, a noted scholar of national studies. The world outside the Kiso Valley begins to change with the coming of the Black Ships, and back in the mountains Hanzō hears news about the assassination of Chancellor Ii Naosuke, the rebellions of samurai groups, and disputes between proshogunate and proemperor factions. He frets at his inability to serve his country, and as a village head he feels helpless before the peasant uprisings raging throughout the land. He is a righteous, compassionate man whose heart is with the people. Incapable of doing anything about the famine affecting the village, he only repeats the words of the great master, Hirata Atsutane: "All is according to God's will." Finally the news reaches him that the shogun has voluntarily abdicated and yielded sovereignty to the emperor. Hanzō and his friends in the national studies group are exhilarated, for they think that the government will now return to traditional ways and rebuild the country.

In part two the exotic civilizations of the West invade Japan, and capitalism sweeps through the country. Formerly patriotic samurai terrorize foreign traders and their legations, and the peasants waiting for emancipation instead suffer new oppression from the government. Distressed that his studies are now totally out of fashion, unappreciated, and misunderstood by the peasants of his village, Hanzō is unable to cope with his daily duties as the head of the family. He yields his position as head to his oldest son and becomes a shrine priest in the Hida mountains for four years. When he returns, he finds his home in financial shambles and is blamed for having been negligent for years. In 1874, when he approaches the carriage of the traveling emperor with his appeal, he is arrested and declared insane. Imprisoned at home, he spends his unhappy last years in paranoid ranting.

The work presents a broad historical tableau in portraying a passionately patriotic, tormented man in the foreground. The controlled narrative style, while lacking in dramatic excitement, adds the weight of historical reality. Unlike the authors of conventional historical novels, Tōson exercises strict restraint by not allowing any imaginary reconstruction of scenes and dialogues. Focusing on a small community at one of the main trunkways where "history was made and the map was redrawn," Tōson gazes into the soul of his father and scrutinizes his legacy.

In six years Tōson completed this work, for which he received the highest praise from the reading public. The writing drained him to exhaustion, body and soul. In November 1935 he was appointed chairman of the new Japan P.E.N. Club in recognition of his work in founding the organization. With his wife and an old friend, the artist Arishima Ikuma (vice chairman of the club), he sailed on 16 July 1936 on the *Rio de Janeiro* from Kōbe to attend the fourteenth International P.E.N. Club meeting in Buenos Aires. After the September conference he visited the United States and then went to France before returning to Japan on 24 January 1937.

In the same year he was named a founding member of the Japanese Academy, but he declined this honor, saying that he had created his own art and destiny and had never received help from the government. After forty years of struggle, national recognition meant nothing to him, and he preferred to maintain his independence and freedom. For the next three years, while he recovered from an illness, he concentrated on writing a travelogue, *Junrei* (Pilgrims, 1940), and on editing old works. He wrote more stories for children and published them, along with some earlier stories, in four volumes. In 1940 he was again urged to join the Japanese Academy, and this time he accepted the invitation.

Living in a new house in Oiso in August 1942, Tōson began to write his final work, *Tōhō no mon* (The Gates of the East, 1946). The title was inspired by Chavannes's *Gate of the East* in the Longchamps Art Museum in Marseilles, where he had stopped on his second trip to France. He planned to write another long novel—about such cities as Colombo, Malacca, Batavia, and Hong Kong and about historical figures who had brought the West to Japan—but he completed only the first two chapters. On 22 August 1943 Tōson died while listening to his wife read from his *The Gates of the East*.

As a writer tormented by secret demons that he harbored in his heart for much of his life, Tōson never abandoned his fight to achieve what his heart dictated. In *Spring* he describes the hero (a figure modeled after himself) as being "at the same time arrogant and effete, radical and timid, sensitive and dull." Others described him in similar terms, in addition to being madly passionate and youthful. "There was no one who was as cautious as he was (like the man who struck a stone bridge before crossing)," wrote Hirano Ken, "but there was no one who took a bolder step when turning a corner of his life."

The dichotomy in Tōson's character must have been a source of his suffering, and the fact that he had inherited a manic streak from his father was probably a source of great anxiety for him. Evaluations of Tōson as a human being rather than as a literary figure range from unfair estimations that he was a hypocrite and an egoist to those of respect for his honesty, humility, and sincerity. That critics fall into such different camps attests to the complexity and opaqueness of a character that defies simple interpretation. Itō Kazuo, who studied the psychoanalytic dimensions of Tōson's character from hereditary circumstances, points out that the two sides of Tōson constantly negated each other. In vying for control of him, reality and idealism enriched each other and made him an increasingly individual and integrated personality as he matured. He was able to control his two opposing egos not by completely subjugating one of them, but by achieving a harmony between them through compromise and acquiescence. Itō concludes that Tōson thus barely avoided the crisis of a schizoidal breakdown.

Tōson's perseverence helped him survive where others might have had such breakdowns. His growing self-knowledge and the latitude he acquired as he matured permitted him to plan his life carefully and helped him avoid the pitfall of hereditary schizophrenia, but this same cautiousness appeared to be hypocrisy to outsiders. In pursuing his writing career he certainly had to make superhuman efforts at mental survival.

Tōson was a survivor who developed various skills to face many problems; the most important of these skills was his writing. At times, when he suffered from inarticulateness, he could live only through his writing. This relationship that Tōson maintained with his writing is the basis of his enigmatic writing style, which is simultaneously clear and ambiguous, reticent and forceful. Through his constant efforts he reached a height that only a few could attain in modern Japanese literature.

Letters:

Tamazaki Takeshi, ed., *Tōson no tegami* (Tokyo: Shin'eisha, 1935);

Shimazaki Kusuo and Kōzu Tokuichirō, eds., *Hakai o meguru Tōson no tegami* (Tokyo: Haneda Shoten, 1948).

Biography:

William E. Naff, *Shimazaki Toson: A Critical Biography* (Seattle, Wash., 1965).

References:

Bungaku, special issue on Tōson (August 1936);

Bungaku Kenkyū, special issue on Tōson, 2 (October 1953);

Bungakushi, special issue on Tōson, 1 (June 1954);

Bunshō Ōrai, special issue on Tōson (April 1926);

Chuō Kōron, special issue on Tōson (November 1908);

"*Hakai* o hyōsu," *Waseda Bungaku,* special issue on Tōson (May 1906);

Hikaku Bungaku Kenkyū, special issue on Tōson, 1 (June 1954);

Hirano Ken, *Shimazaki Tōson* (Tokyo: Chikuma Shobō, 1947);

Hyōron, special issue on Tōson (October 1934);

Ino Kenji, *Shimazaki Tōson* (Tokyo: Shinnō Mainichi Shinbunsha, 1949; revised and enlarged edition, Tokyo: Yushindō, 1963);

Itō Kazuo, *Shimazaki Tōson kenkyu—Kindai bungaku kenkyu hōhō no shomondai* (Tokyo: Meiji Shoin, 1969);

Itō Shinkichi, *Shimazaki Tōson no bungaku* (Tokyo: Daiichi Shobō, 1936; revised, 1947);

Kaishaku to Kanshō, special issue on Tōson (November 1943);

Kaishaku to Kanshō, special issue on Tōson (April 1990);

Kamei Katsuichirō, *Shimazaki Tōson—Ichi hyōhakusha no shōzō* (Tokyo: Kōbundō, 1939);

Kawazoe Kunimoto, *Shimazaki Tōson* (Tokyo: Meiji Shoin, 1965; revised and enlarged edition, Tokyo: Shinchōsha, 1984);

Kieda Masuichi, *Shimazaki Tōson* (Tokyo: Sanseidō, 1943);

Edwin McClellan, *Two Japanese Novelists, Soseki and Toson* (Chicago: University of Chicago Press, 1969);

Meiji Taishō Bungaku Kenkyū, special issue on Tōson, 13 (July 1954);

Miyoshi Yukio, *Shimazaki Tōson ron* (Tokyo: Shibundō, 1966);

Nihon Bungaku, special issue on Tōson (March 1956);

Nihon Shijin, special issue on Tōson (June 1925);

Ningen, special issue on Tōson (April 1915);

Nishimaru Shihō, *Shimazaki Tōson no himitsu* (Tokyo: Yushindō, 1966);

Sasabuchi Tomoichi, *Shōsetsuka Shimazaki Tōson* (Tokyo: Meiji Shoin, 1990);

Senuma Shigeki, *Shimazaki Tōson* (Tokyo: Kadokawa Shoten, 1958);

Shibungaku Kenkyu, special issue on Tōson (September 1943);

Shimazaki Osuke, *Tōson shiki* (Tokyo: Kawade Shobō, 1967);

Shimazaki Shizuko, *Hitosuji no michi—Tōson to tomo ni* (Tokyo: Meiji Shoin, 1969);

"Shimazaki Tōson Issue: Sakkaron to Sakuhinron," *Kaishaku to Kanshō,* special issue on Tōson (March 1958);

"Shimazaki Tōson to Nihon no kindai," *Kokumingaku,* special issue on Tōson (April 1971);

Shinchō, special issue on Tōson (November 1943);

Shinchō, special issue on Tōson (November 1948);

Usui Yoshimi, ed., *Shimazaki Tōson* (Tokyo: Chikuma Shobō, 1954);

Wada Kingo, *Shimazaki Tōson* (Tokyo: Meiji Shoin, 1966; revised edition, Tokyo: Koyama Shobō, 1993);

Janet A. Walker, *The Japanese Novel of the Meiji Period and the Ideal of Individualism* (Princeton, N.J.: Princeton University Press, 1979);

Yoshida Seiichi, "Shimazaki Tōson," in his *Yoshida Seiichi chosaku-shu* (Tokyo: Ōfusha, 1981).

Tanizaki Jun'ichirō

(24 July 1886 – 30 July 1965)

Ken K. Ito
University of Michigan

BOOKS: *Shisei* (Tokyo: Momiyama Shoten, 1911);

Atsumono (Tokyo: Shun'yōdō, 1913; revised, 1918);

Akuma (Tokyo: Momiyama Shoten, 1913);

Koi o shiru koro (Tokyo: Uetake Shoin, 1913);

Iraka (Tokyo: Hōmeisha, 1914);

Kirin (Tokyo: Uetake Shoin, 1914);

Himitsu (Tokyo: Suzuki Miekichi, 1915);

Otsuya goroshi (Tokyo: Senshōkan, 1915; enlarged, 1916); translated by Zenchi Iwado as *A Spring-time Case* (Tokyo: Japan Times, 1927?);

Osai to Minosuke (Tokyo: Shinchōsha, 1915);

Shōsetsu nihen (Tokyo: Yanagi Shobō, 1915);

Konjiki no shi (Tokyo: Nittōdō, 1916);

Shindō (Tokyo: Subara Keikōsha, 1916);

Oni no men (Tokyo: Subara Keikōsha, 1916);

Shisei hoka kyūhen (Tokyo: Shun'yōdō, 1916);

Ningyo no nageki (Tokyo: Shun'yōdō, 1917);

Itansha no kanashimi (Tokyo: Oranda Shobō, 1917);

Futari no chigo (Tokyo: Shun'yōdō, 1918);

Kin to gin (Tokyo: Shun'yōdō, 1918);

Chiisana ōkoku (Tokyo: Ten'yūsha, 1919);

Norowareta gikyoku (Tokyo: Shun'yōdō, 1919);

Ningyo no nageki-Majutsushi (Tokyo: Shun'yōdō, 1919);

Kindai jōchi shū (Tokyo: Shinchōsha, 1919; revised, 1924; enlarged, 1929);

Jigazō (Tokyo: Shun'yōdō, 1919);

Nyonin shinsei (Tokyo: Shun'yōdō, 1920);

Kyōfu jidai (Tokyo: Ten'yūsha, 1920);

Birōdo no yume (Tokyo: Ten'yūsha, 1920);

Jun'ichirō kessaku zenshū, 5 volumes (Tokyo: Shun'yōdō, 1921);

Hōjōji monogatari (Tokyo: Shinchōsha, 1921);

A to B no hanashi (Tokyo: Shinchōsha, 1921);

Kirin hoka nihen (Tokyo: Shun'yōdō, 1922);

Konjiki no shi hoka sanpen (Tokyo: Shun'yōdō, 1922);

Aisureba koso (Tokyo: Kaizōsha, 1922);

Tanizaki Jun'ichirō

Shindō (Tokyo: Kinseidō, 1922);

Okuni to Gohei hoka nihen (Tokyo: Shun'yōdō, 1922);

Ai naki hitobito (Tokyo: Kaizōsha, 1923);

Ave Maria (Tokyo: Shinchōsha, 1923);

Jun'ichirō gikyoku kessaku shū (Tokyo: Kinseidō, 1923);

Nikkai (Tokyo: Shun'yōdō, 1924);

Mumyō to Aizen (Tokyo: Puratonsha, 1924);

Geijutsu ikka gen (Tokyo: Kinseidō, 1924);

Shinsen Tanizaki Jun'ichirō shū (Tokyo: Kaizōsha, 1924);

Kami to hito to no aida (Tokyo: Shinchōsha, 1925);

Chijin no ai (Tokyo: Kaizōsha, 1925); translated by Anthony H. Chambers as *Naomi* (New York: Knopf, 1985);

Tanizaki Jun'ichirō hen (Tokyo: Kokumin Tosho, 1925);

Kōjin (Tokyo: Kaizōsha, 1926);

Jun'ichirō kigeki shū (Tokyo: Shunjūsha, 1926);

Akai yane (Tokyo: Kaizōsha, 1926);

Aisureba koso-Ai naki hitobito (Tokyo: Kaizōsha, 1927);

Jun'ichirō hanzai shōsetsu shū (Tokyo: Shinchōsha, 1929);

Tanizaki Jun'ichirō shū (Tokyo: Kaizōsha, 1929);

Jōzetsuroku (Tokyo: Kaizōsha, 1929);

Tade kuu mushi (Tokyo: Kaizōsha, 1929); translated by Edward G. Seidensticker as *Some Prefer Nettles* (New York: Knopf, 1955; London: Secker & Warburg, 1956);

Tanizaki Jun'ichirō zenshū, 12 volumes (Tokyo: Kaizōsha, 1930–1931);

Manji (Tokyo: Kaizōsha, 1931); translated by Howard S. Hibbett as *Quicksand* (New York: Knopf, 1993);

Mōmoku monogatari (Tokyo: Chūō Kōronsha, 1932);

Ishōan zuihitsu (Tokyo: Sōgensha, 1932);

Jun'ichirō jippitsubon Ashikari (Tokyo: Sōgensha, 1933);

Seishun monogatari (Tokyo: Chūō Kōronsha, 1933);

Shunkinshō (Tokyo: Sōgensha, 1933);

Bunshō tokuhon (Tokyo: Chūō Kōronsha, 1934);

Setsuyō zuihitsu (Tokyo: Chūō Kōronsha, 1935);

Bushūkō hiwa (Tokyo: Chūō Kōronsha, 1935);

Jun'itsurō zassan (Tokyo: Nihon Hyōronsha, 1935);

Neko to Shōzō to futari no onna (Tokyo: Sōgensha, 1937); translated by Paul McCarthy as *A Cat, a Man, and Two Women* (Tokyo & New York: Kodansha International, 1990);

Yoshino kuzu (Tokyo: Sōgensha, 1937);

In'ei raisan (Tokyo: Sōgensha, 1939); translated by Seidensticker and Thomas J. Harper as *In Praise of Shadows* (New Haven: Leete's Island Books, 1977);

Hatsumukashi-Kinōkyō (Tokyo: Sōgensha, 1942);

Kikigakishō (Tokyo: Sōgensha, 1943);

Sasameyuki, volume 1 (Osaka: Privately printed, 1944); enlarged, 3 volumes (Tokyo: Chūō Kōronsha, 1948); translated by Seidensticker as *The Makioka Sisters* (New York: Knopf, 1957);

Sannin hōshi (Tokyo: Sōgensha, 1946);

Hōkan hoka nihen (Tokyo: Sōgensha, 1946);

The author, aged four.

Tanizaki at age four

Gikyoku Okuni to Gohei hoka nihen (Tokyo: Kokusai Joseisha, 1947);

Tanpenshū–Watakushi (Tokyo: Zenkoku Shobō, 1947);

Aoi hana (Tokyo: Shinseisha, 1947);

Nigatsudō no tsuki (Tokyo: Zenkoku Shobō, 1947);

Isoda Takajo no koto (Tokyo: Zenkoku Shobō, 1947);

Miyako wasure no ki (Tokyo: Sōgensha, 1948);

Uguisuhime (Tokyo: Seiryūsha, 1948);

Eien no gūzō (Tokyo: Fusō Shobō, 1948);

Tomoda to Matsunaga no hanashi (Tokyo: Usui Shobō, 1949);

Rangiku monogatari (Tokyo: Sōgeisha, 1949);

Tsuki to kyōgenshi (Tokyo: Umeda Shobō, 1949; enlarged edition, Tokyo: Chūō Kōronsha, 1950);

Kyō no yume, Osaka no yume (Tokyo: Nihon Kōtsūkōsha, 1950);

Hyōfū (Tokyo: Keimeisha, 1950);

Tanizaki Jun'ichirō sakuhin shū, 9 volumes (Tokyo: Sōgensha, 1950);

Tanizaki's mother, Seki

Shōshō Shigemoto no haha (Tokyo: Mainichi Shinbunsha, 1950);

Shinzei (Tokyo: Asahi Shinbunsha, 1950);

Zenkamono—Tanizaki Jun'ichirō suiri shōsetsu shū (Tokyo: Sansaisha, 1951);

Tanizaki Jun'ichirō zuihitsu senshū, 3 volumes (Tokyo: Sōgensha, 1951);

Tanizaki Jun'ichirō bunko, 10 volumes (Tokyo: Chūō Kōronsha, 1954);

Kasankamangansui no yume (Tokyo: Chūō Kōronsha, 1956);

Kagi (Tokyo: Chūō Kōronsha, 1956); translated by Hibbett as *The Key* (London: Secker & Warburg, 1960; New York: Knopf, 1961);

Yōshō jidai (Tokyo: Bungei Shunjusha, 1957); translated by Paul McCarthy as *Childhood Years: A Memoir* (Tokyo & New York: Kodansha International, 1988);

Kakahangakan (Tokyo: Hōbunkan, 1957);

Tanizaki Jun'ichirō zenshū, 30 volumes (Tokyo: Chūō Kōronsha, 1957–1959);

Yume no ukihashi (Tokyo: Chūō Kōronsha, 1960); translated by Hibbett as *The Bridge of Dreams* (New York: Knopf, 1963);

Mittsu no baai (Tokyo: Chūō Kōronsha, 1961);

Tōsei shika modoki (Tokyo: Chūō Kōronsha, 1961);

Fūten rōjin nikki (Tokyo: Chūō Kōronsha, 1962); translated by Hibbett as *Diary of a Mad Old Man* (New York: Knopf, 1965);

Daidokoro taiheiki (Tokyo: Chūō Kōronsha, 1963);

Tanizaki Jun'ichirō zenshū, 28 volumes (Tokyo: Chūō Kōronsha, 1966–1970; enlarged, 30 volumes, 1981–1983).

Editions in English: *Ashikari and The Story of Shunkin: Modern Japanese Novels,* translated by Roy Humpherson and Hajime Okita (Tokyo: Hokuseido, 1936; Westport, Conn.: Greenwood Press, 1970);

Seven Japanese Tales, translated by Howard G. Hibbett (New York: Knopf, 1963; London: Secker & Warburg, 1964)—comprises "A Portrait of Shunkin," "Terror," "The Bridge of Dreams," "The Tattooer," "Aguri," and "A Blind Man's Tale";

The Secret History of the Lord of Musashi, and Arrowroot, translated by Anthony Hood Chambers (New York: Knopf, 1982; London: Secker & Warburg, 1983);

A Cat, a Man, and Two Women, translated by Paul McCarthy (Tokyo & New York: Kodansha International, 1990)—comprises "The Little Kingdom," "Professor Rado," "A Cat, a Man, and Two Women";

The Reed Cutter and Captain Shigemoto's Mother, translated by Chambers (New York: Knopf, 1994).

PLAY PRODUCTIONS: *Shinzei,* Tokyo, Yūrakuza, 6 September 1918;

Haru no umibe, Tokyo, Yūrakuza, 1 December 1919;

Jūgoya monogatari, Tokyo, Yūrakuza, 1 December 1919;

Hōjōji monogatari, Tokyo, Shintomiza, 25 October 1920;

Kyōfu jidai, Tokyo, Yūrakuza, 5 March 1921;

Okuni to Gohei, Tokyo, Teikoku Gekijō, July 1922;

Ai naki hitobito, Tokyo, Hongōza, March 1923;

Shirogitsune no yu, Tokyo, Teikoku Gekijō, May 1923;

Honmoku yawa, Tokyo, Asakusa Kōen Gekijō, July 1923;

Mumyō to Aizen, Tokyo, Hongōza, March 1924;

Udezumō, Osaka, Osaka Naniwaza, 1 April 1924;

Eien no gūzō, Tokyo, Kokumin Kōdō, 25 March 1927;

Aisureba koso, Tokyo, Teikoku Hoteru Engeijō, 31 May 1932;

Suminuri Heijū, Kyoto, Gion Kaburenjō, April 1953.

MOTION PICTURES: *Amachua kurabu*, scenario by Tanizaki, Taishō Katsuei, 1920;

Katsushika Sunago, scenario by Tanizaki, from a story by Izumi Kyōka, Taishō Katsuei, 1920;

Hinamatsuri no yoru, scenario by Tanizaki, Taishō Katsuei, 1921;

Jasei no in, scenario by Tanizaki, from a story by Ueda Akinari, Taishō Katsuei, 1921.

OTHER: Oscar Wilde, *Lady Windemere's Fan*, translated by Tanizaki as *Windemia fujin no ōgi*, (Tokyo: Ten'yūsha, 1919);

Murasaki Shikibu, *Genji monogatari*, 26 volumes, translated into modern Japanese by Tanizaki (Tokyo: Chūō Kōronsha, 1939; revised, 12 volumes, 1951; revised, 10 volumes, 1964).

During a career that extended for more than half a century, from the end of the Meiji era in 1912 to the high-growth era of the 1960s, the novelist Tanizaki Jun'ichirō was a champion of the imagination. In a literary milieu dominated by the autobiographical ruminations of the naturalists and later of the *shishōsetsu* (personal fiction) writers, he upheld fiction founded on invention. For Tanizaki, who once said that only lies interested him, truth existed in the reification of the imaginary through language that declared its own primacy and materiality. A grand old man of letters, he accumulated a body of work—comprising a dozen major novels, scores of short stories and novellas, and many plays and essays—that fills thirty substantial volumes in the standard edition of his works. Each of his pieces attests to his undying faith in artifice as the cornerstone of art; his tightly constructed plots and ingenious narrative schemes reveal his conviction that stories exist only in the alchemy of their telling.

Yet, for all of its inventiveness, Tanizaki's fiction shows a decided connectedness to the larger world. A writer preternaturally sensitive to the cultural currents swirling around him, he mirrored in his fiction the fascinations of his society. Thus, in the 1920s his stories displayed the craze for Western things that marked the *Taishō*

Period of 1912 to 1925, and in the increasingly conservative 1930s they showed a conscious embrace of tradition. His post–World War II work reflected both a nostalgia for a gentler culture that had been destroyed by the war and a recognition of the freedom brought by defeat. With a relentless focus on sexuality, Tanizaki explored such cultural twists and turns through stories about the male pursuit of the feminine. The most frequently encountered motif in his fiction is that of a man remaking a woman to accord with his desires. While there is clearly an element of fantasy in these transformations, there is also a persistent analytical counterpoint, expressed through a consideration of the power dynamics that make women subject to the fantasies of men, and of the limits of subjectivity in imposing its will on the exterior world.

There has been a certain ambivalence in the Japanese critical evaluation of Tanizaki. Because of his rejection of *shishōsetsu* (personal fiction) ideology, his embrace of playful narrative strategies, and, perhaps, even his idiosyncratic expressions of sexuality, a certain faction of Japanese critics have labeled Tanizaki a writer *shisō no nai sakka* (without serious philosophical concerns). But Tanizaki has always had his supporters, and his focus on the cultural dimensions of desire has been recognized as nothing if not serious. His love for highly plotted fictional narratives has also come up for reevaluation, with some critics now seeing him as an inheritor of the diegetic tradition of the classical *monogatari* (tale). Today few would dispute the assessment of Tanizaki as a writer of the first magnitude, one whose work figures large in the literary history of modern Japan.

Tanizaki was born on 24 July 1886 in the Nihonbashi section of Tokyo, when the city still retained many of the features and customs of the old city of Edo. Two aspects of his background, which the writer himself emphasizes in his *Yōshō jidai* (1957; translated as *Childhood Years: A Memoir*, 1988), were to be of special consequence for his later writing. First, he was a true *Edokko*, a child of Edo, whose merchant-class family had lived for generations in the *shitamachi*, the merchants' and artisans' quarter of the city. The majority of modern Japanese writers, in contrast, came from the provinces. Tanizaki was a descendant of the *chōnin* (urban commoner), who during the Edo period from 1600 to 1867 had evolved a vibrant culture that valued verve and style and reveled in the merchant's frank enjoyment of material comforts. As a child, Tanizaki came to love

Tanizaki at the Rokkō Hotel in Hyogo Prefecture, 1924

second year; for a while the Tanizakis were able to live in relative comfort on what Kyūemon had left, but with Kuragorō's mounting failures the family's fortunes slid downward. It did not help that Jun'ichirō was followed by three brothers and three sisters. Although a brother and two of the sisters were sent away to foster families, the remaining children strained the precarious family finances.

Despite his family's troubles, Tanizaki did well at school. He was consistently at the top of his class once he got past the first grade, which he was required to repeat because of his infantile behavior—a notorious crybaby, he had initially refused to go to school without his nursemaid. While still a primary-school student he also attended private academies to study English and classical Chinese. He won admission to the First Metropolitan Middle School and the First Higher School, which were among the best secondary schools in the country. By the time he entered middle school his family was living from hand to mouth, and there was talk of taking him out of school and apprenticing him in a trade; only by working as a live-in houseboy for a wealthy family was he able to continue his education. As a result of these experiences, Tanizaki felt forever deprived of his birthright: the comforts and pleasures that he had known as the scion of a shitamachi merchant family had been snatched away and replaced by the petty indignities of domestic service. Soon the shitamachi itself would be physically transformed by industrialization and overrun by migrants from other areas of Japan.

In 1907 Tanizaki moved back into his parents' home, having been dismissed from his houseboy position for becoming romantically involved with a maid. He matriculated at Tokyo Imperial University the following year.

Tanizaki's literary inclinations surfaced early: in primary school he and some friends started a hand-copied magazine, and during his middle- and high-school years he contributed frequently to school literary journals. But it was as a university student that Tanizaki began to write fiction in earnest. He chose Japanese literature as his major because the requirements were undemanding and would leave him the most time for his own writing. Initially, however, he had difficulty in getting his work published; starting his career at the height of the naturalist domination of the literary world, Tanizaki could not find an outlet for his flamboyant, highly crafted stories. He and a group of like-minded Imperial Univer-

the urban pleasures of going to the Kabuki and participating in the shitamachi's many seasonal observances.

The second important factor in Tanizaki's background is that his family, which was prosperous during his earliest years, suffered a considerable decline in its fortunes during his childhood. The family's prosperity had been established by Tanizaki's grandfather, Kyūemon, who had started out working in a kettle-making shop but had parlayed a small real estate investment into many other enterprises. Kyūemon arranged the marriage of two of his daughters to a pair of orphaned brothers whom he adopted; Jun'ichirō was the eldest son of the younger of these couples, which consisted of Seki, a renowned neighborhood beauty, and Kuragorō. Kuragorō, however, proved to be nowhere near the merchant that Seki's father had been. He quickly ruined the Western-style liquor shop that he was given to run at the time of his marriage, and, though he was subsequently set up in several other family businesses, he never succeeded at anything. Kyūemon died during Jun'ichirō's sity students finally started a coterie magazine as a way of getting themselves into print. It was in this magazine, *Shinshichō* (New Currents), that in 1910 Tanizaki published "Shisei" (translated as "The Tattooer," 1963), the story that launched his career.

"The Tattooer" is a manifesto for a certain kind of artistic sensibility—a glove slapped across the face of Japanese naturalism and its sober autobiographical realism. Blending the flash and decadence of late-Edo Kabuki with the flash and decadence of Western fin-de-siècle literature, it is a celebration of craft and artifice. This characterization applies to the story's finely wrought language and skillful storytelling, but it is most evident in its plot, which exalts the artist's capacity to create his own transcendent ideal. Set in an Edo reconstructed as a hotbed of aestheticism, "The Tattooer" is the tale of a gifted tattoo artist who has one wish: to find a beautiful woman to become the perfect canvas for his artistry so that he could create his masterpiece on her body. After years of searching the tattooer discovers the appropriate girl, whom he recognizes by the loveliness of a milk-white foot peeping out from within a palanquin. When the girl falls within his grasp he drugs her and stipples on her back the image of a gigantic black widow spider. When the tattoo is complete, after a day and a night of exhausting labor, more than the girl's appearance has been transformed: made incomparably beautiful in a world where beauty equals strength, she now glares down at the tattooer, who must beg to see what he has created. The story ends as she disrobes and bares a body made luminous by the power of art: "Just then her resplendently tattooed back caught a ray of sunlight and the spider was wreathed in flames."

This brief and brilliant story epitomizes Tanizaki's early work. His archetypal plot of a man laboring to transform a woman into the object of his desires makes its first appearance here, as does the femme fatale. It is noteworthy that in "The Tattooer" the femme fatale is literally a male construction, brought into being through the exercise of the artist's mastery over a helpless girl. The parading of an idiosyncratic sexuality is also characteristic: foot fetishism and masochism are the favorite perversions of his heroes, but Tanizaki, a reader of the works of Sigmund Freud and Richard von Krafft-Ebing, was capable of writing about a cornucopia of erotic delights. Nor was his striving to re-create extraordinary sensual experiences based solely on Western

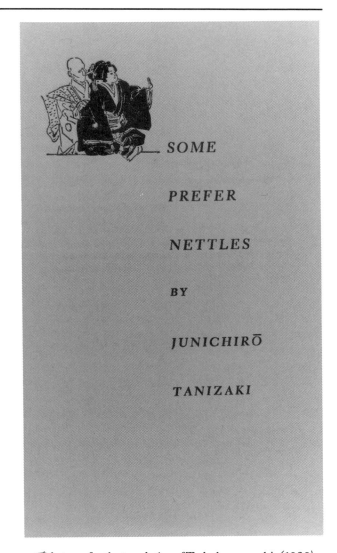

SOME

PREFER

NETTLES

BY

JUNICHIRŌ

TANIZAKI

Title page for the translation of Tade kuu mushi *(1929)*

writings on sexuality: a cultural syncretist of a high order, Tanizaki could combine, with flair and imagination, images from various cultures. The femme fatale in "The Tattooer" derives as much from the sanguinary sensibilities of late-Edo Kabuki and wood-block prints and the early-Meiji fascination with *dokufu* (poisonous women) as she does from Tanizaki's avid reading of Oscar Wilde, Edgar Allan Poe, and Charles Baudelaire. Finally, there is a love for the exotic setting. In "The Tattooer" the shitamachi of Edo is hardly a historically accurate locale; it functions as an alternative world supporting possibilities unavailable in the dessicated present.

These elements appear in various permutations in Tanizaki's early stories. In "Himitsu" (1911; translated as "The Secret," 1993), the protagonist, who disguises his identity by dressing

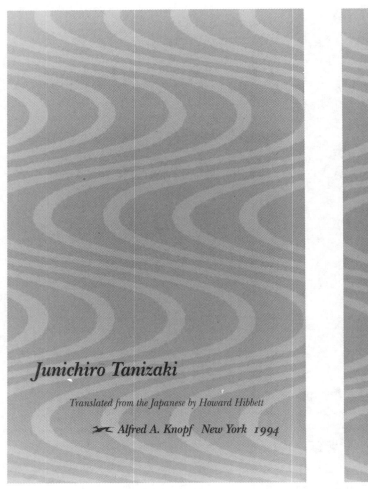
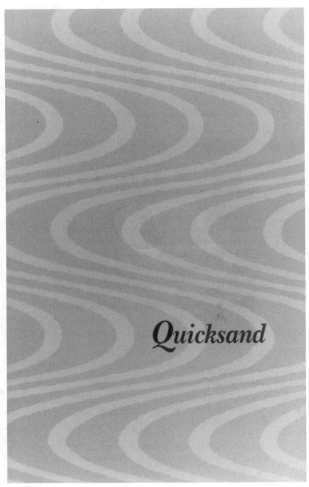

Double-truck title page for the American edition of the translation of Manji *(1931)*

as a woman, is beguiled by a lover who hides the location of her shitamachi love nest. In "Shōnen" (Children, 1911) a mansion that stands apart from the surrounding shitamachi becomes the setting for sadomasochistic games played by a group of children in which a girl emerges as the victor by taking on the guise of a Western temptress.

These early stories established Tanizaki as a promising newcomer to the late-Meiji literary scene. The respected writer Nagai Kafū, who singled out "The Tattooer" as Tanizaki's best story, gave the younger man's career a mighty boost with a glowing review that portrayed him as an urban stylist in search of the heightened sensuality of decadence. Immediately thereafter, Tanizaki's stories began to be carried in the leading literary journals, and his first collection of stories was published under the title *Shisei* in 1911.

As his career took hold, Tanizaki's personal life became increasingly unsettled. He was ex-

pelled from the Imperial University in 1911 for failing to pay his fees. For the next several years he lived in a succession of inns and boardinghouses, sometimes leaving behind a pile of debts when he moved on. During this period he was linked with a succession of women, including the wife of a cousin. In 1915 he married Ishikawa Chiyo; he makes clear in his later writings that he married not for love but for stability, calling his wife "an implement for forming my own household." He rationalizes his attitude by saying that his art required a change in his life, and that life is subordinate to art. This radical self-absorption also characterizes his pronouncements on his only child, his daughter Ayuko, who was born the year after his marriage: "Why did I dislike having a child so much? To put it briefly, it was because I was a singular egoist. It was because I was a person who had only taken care of himself." Though the chilling bluntness of such declarations must be partially attributed to

Tanizaki's love of posing, there is some truth in his statement.

Needless to say, the marriage was not happy. Tanizaki soon grew tired of Chiyo; he had hoped that she would have something in common with her brash and lively older sister, who had initially attracted his attention but had been unavailable. Chiyo, however, proved to be a gentle, retiring woman, and it was not long before Tanizaki began to look elsewhere for companionship. Within two years of his marriage he had placed Chiyo and Ayuko in the care of his father so that he would have more freedom for his pursuits, artistic and otherwise. His foremost quarry at this time was Chiyo's younger sister Seiko, in whom he found something of the eldest sister's sauce and brass.

Aside from Tanizaki's marriage, the other event that stands out in these years is the death of his mother in 1917. Because a man's longing for the maternal is a recurring theme in Tanizaki's fiction, his critics and biographers tend to emphasize the writer's relationship with his mother. But Tanizaki's stories and his psychology are complex, and a facile equation between fiction and biography is misleading. The "mother" who is the object of so much yearning in Tanizaki's fiction tends to be an abstraction, often identified with the shitamachi and defined by her "whiteness," a color that signifies transcendent beauty in the symbolic vocabulary the writer developed over the course of his career. Two stories that Tanizaki published in the years immediately following his mother's death suggest some of the problems with attempting to anchor the longing for "mother" in his biography. The portrait of the mother is decidedly unflattering in *Itansha no kanashimi* (A Heretic's Grief, 1917), an autobiographical piece set at a time when the Tanizaki family fortunes were at their lowest ebb: the embittered old woman who berates her husband over the loss of her inheritance and drives her son away with her ceaseless complaints is hardly an object of longing. Tanizaki says in the foreword that this story, which he had written previously but did not publish until two months after his mother's death, was his "only confessional work." A quite different mother appears in "Haha o kouru ki" (1919; translated as "Longing for Mother," 1980), an eerily effective re-creation of the skewed reality of dream. The first Tanizaki story about the yearning for the maternal, it tells of a meeting in a dream of a son and his mother, the latter a pale

Tanizaki at his writing desk

erotic apparition who takes the guise of a wandering singer of *shinnai* ballads.

The fiction that Tanizaki wrote in the late 1910s and early 1920s is greatly varied. His febrile imagination continued to produce decadent, sensually heightened celebrations of femmes fatales and sadomasochistic thrill seekers in exotic locales. After a trip to China in 1918 he wrote a group of stories set there, and China proved to be as open to the play of his imagination as the shitamachi had been. He also wrote mysteries and crime stories that are considered to be among the progenitors of these genres in Japan. But perhaps the most consequential strain in his writing was that dealing with the West. Like many other writers in a developing Japan, Tanizaki viewed the West as a land of freedom, prosperity, and beauty, but he was unique in the degree to which he was aware that this "West" was largely a creation of the Japanese imagination. Thus, such stories as "Aoi hana" (The Blue Flower, 1922; translated as "Aguri," 1963) and "Ave Maria" (1923) are set not in the West but in Japan and deal with the efforts of Japanese men to secure Western women.

Tanizaki was quick to recognize the new Western medium of film. While other Japanese authors considered movies nothing more than popular entertainment, Tanizaki realized that film was a form of narrative with its own possibilities.

In 1920–1921 he put much of his energy into writing scenarios for the Taishō Katsuei production company. Late in 1921 he moved his family to the port city of Yokohama, a point of entry for all things Western. There they rented a Western-style house, wore Western clothes, ate Western food, took ballroom dancing lessons, and made friends with members of the large foreign community. In early 1923 Tanizaki announced that he intended to travel to the West by the fall, but the plan was never to be carried out: on 1 September Tokyo and Yokohama were leveled by the Kantō earthquake. Tanizaki was away from Yokohama at the time; rushing back, he found that his wife and daughter were safe but that his house and the city that had supported his Westernized way of life were in ruins. He and his family took refuge in the Kansai region, staying briefly in Kyoto and then settling in the Hanshin suburbs between Osaka and Kōbe.

It was in Kansai that Tanizaki wrote *Chijin no ai* (A Fool's Love, 1925; translated as *Naomi*, 1985). This work is a milepost in Tanizaki's career: it is his first true novel; it is the work in which he combines social observation and imagination; and it both celebrates and coldly analyzes the phenomenon of cultural aspiration. *Naomi* is narrated by a man in the grip of an obsession. Jōji, an otherwise humdrum engineer, has "imitated the Western style in everything." He sees an opportunity to acquire a mate appropriate to his desires when he encounters Naomi, a fifteen-year-old waitress who resembles the actress Mary Pickford. Jōji takes Naomi from the café where he found her, installs her in a Western-style cottage decorated with the iconic images of American movie actresses, and endeavors to Westernize her through English, piano, and dancing lessons. He succeeds so well that she soon starts to despise him for being too Japanese. Before long she is having affairs, first with upper-class Japanese and later with Western men. Jōji tries to banish Naomi from his life, but his obsession with the woman he has created is too powerful to resist. By the end of the novel he has acceded to Naomi's demand that they move to Yokohama, where he supports her dalliances with a string of Western lovers who call him "George."

The novel has been read as a warning against losing one's cultural moorings; Jōji himself says, "If you think that there's a moral in it, then, please let it serve as a lesson." But even when she has apparently gained the upper hand, Naomi remains Jōji's creation; thus, her story is that of an invented West brought into being to fulfill Japanese fantasies. Tanizaki is all too aware of the hierarchies of class and gender that allow the transformation of a waitress into a temptress. His novel is laced with the ironic insight that a man can only be possessed by what he already owns.

After the publication of *Naomi* Tanizaki wrote a series of essays tracing his gradual conversion from a typical Edokko, harboring an inborn discomfort in an alien land, to a devotee of Kansai, a "second homeland" where he found traces of the merchant quarter of his youth. As he felt the pull of this older part of Japan, Tanizaki sought to define for himself what was essentially "Japanese." In his essays he struggles with the notion of Japanese cultural identity, taking note both of the desperate need to absorb Western knowledge and technology and of the losses incurred in the process. These concerns led to Tanizaki's reconstruction of "traditional" Japanese aesthetics in *In'ei raisan* (1939; translated as *In Praise of Shadows*, 1977), an essay that is both playful and lovingly lyrical in its delineation of a unique Japanese sense of beauty based on the appreciation of shadows and darkness.

Apart from the notion of cultural identity, the key issue that engaged Tanizaki as an essayist during these years was the nature of fiction. In the collection of essays titled *Jōzetsuroku* (Garrulous Jottings, 1929) Tanizaki carried on his side of a debate with his friend and fellow writer Akutagawa Ryūnosuke over what the latter called *hanashirashii hanashi no nai shōsetsu* (fiction without plotlike plots). Akutagawa, who had once produced his share of ingenious, tightly constructed stories, felt in his last years the attraction of writing that avoided the "vulgar interest" of artifice by practicing a kind of autobiographical lyricism. In the face of his friend's defection, Tanizaki held firm to fiction that was unabashedly fictional. He argued that imaginatively conceived and artfully constructed plots graced fiction with "architectonic beauty" and were indispensable.

The concerns addressed in Tanizaki's essays recur in various combinations in the fiction he produced in the late 1920s, particularly the two important novels that he wrote nearly simultaneously: *Tade kuu mushi* (1929; translated as *Some Prefer Nettles*, 1955) and *Manji* (1931; translated as *Quicksand*, 1993). In *Some Prefer Nettles* Kansai assumes the contours assigned to the region in Tanizaki's essays. It is a land with a lingering past, where the work's protagonist, the superficially modern Kaname, feels the pull of an older

Japan. Kaname's search for cultural identity is set into motion by his failed marriage, which is portrayed with chilling precision. All passion has gone out of Kaname's marriage to Misako, a woman who is superficially modern in much the same way that he is. Unwilling to act decisively, yet wanting to end the marriage, Kaname pushes Misako into a relationship with another man in the hope that the affair will lead to a painless divorce. As he pulls away from his wife, however, Kaname is paradoxically drawn to her father, who seems to have achieved a life in tune with the Japanese past. The assurance that the old man exhibits in his traditional tastes and in his relationship with his doll-like mistress fills Kaname with envy. In the closing scene of the novel, which takes place in his father-in-law's old-fashioned house in Kyoto, Kaname seems to be on the verge of indulging himself in a replacement fantasy by becoming involved with the older man's mistress.

On one level, the novel appears to depict a man being pulled to his own cultural roots. Yet the work resists a simple reading because, like all of Tanizaki's novels, it attends to the contradictory and subversive dynamics of desire. These dynamics are apparent in the portrayal of the old man, who engaged during his earlier years in "foreign tastes of the most hair-raising variety." Since then he has embarked on a painstaking program of reconstruction, remaking himself into a cultural type from the past—a retired man of taste—and forcing his mistress into antique kimonos in an effort to turn her into an appropriate partner. The relationship of a puppeteer to a *bunraku* puppet—a figure in a Japanese puppet play that dates back to the seventh century—recurs as a leitmotiv throughout the work to underscore the older man's manipulative relationship with his mistress. Kaname, it turns out, has been attracted by another man's carefully crafted fantasy about the past. *Some Prefer Nettles* is as much about the constantly mediated and constructed nature of cultural desire as it is about the rediscovery of cultural identity.

Kagi (1956; translated as *The Key,* 1960) highlights the essential inventiveness and arbitrariness of fiction by organizing its narrative as a succession of lies. The narrator, Sonoko, relates an escalating series of tricks and deceptions that she, her lesbian lover, and her husband put over on each other in carrying out the suicide pact in which the lover and the husband die. Sonoko is telling her story retrospectively, after all the deceptions have been unmasked; but she

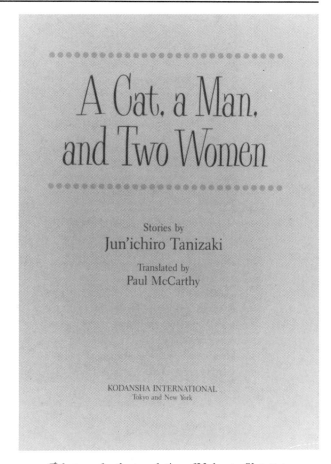

Title page for the translation of Neko to Shōzō to futari no onna *(1937)*

insists on conveying only information that was known to her at the time of the events—in effect, practicing on the reader the deceptions that others practiced upon her. The reader of *The Key* soon learns that the "truth" is only provisional and is likely to be revised by the next revelation. The result is an elaborately plotted text that constantly flaunts its own status as a fabrication and challenges the notion that writing can ever be sincere. *The Key* also exhibits Tanizaki's growing fascination with Kansai. Here the value of the region lies not in its association with the past but in its exoticism, an exoticism that is embodied in the Osaka dialect in which Sonoko tells her story and that is heightened by descriptions of her showy Kansai dress and mannerisms. The distance from the Tokyo standard renders alien everything that Sonoko says and does, and it establishes Kansai as a landscape of possibility that can support the exotic sexuality and behaviors related in the story.

The portrait of the failed marriage in *Some Prefer Nettles* may well have been drawn from life,

Nezu Matsuko, Tanizaki's wife, with her three sisters — the models for his Makioka sisters in
Sasameyuki (1944–1948)—and her daughter

for in 1930 Tanizaki divorced Chiyo, who immediately married the writer Satō Haruo. The three
principals scandalized the Japanese press by sending out a jointly signed announcement of the divorce and remarriage. The triangle that was resolved in this fashion went back many years to
what was called the "Odawara Incident." Named
for the seaside town where the Tanizakis had
lived for a few years before moving to Yokohama in 1921, the incident had involved an intense, but reportedly chaste, love affair between
Satō and Chiyo. The younger writer, who had
been a close friend of Tanizaki's, had initially
pitied Chiyo because of her husband's brutish
treatment of her, but his feelings had gradually
turned to love. Tanizaki had encouraged the relationship because he saw it as a way to dissolve
the marriage; but, after agreeing to a divorce, he
had suddenly changed his mind, saying that his
friend and his wife had failed fully to understand
his motives. Chiyo and Satō were dumbfounded,
but they had no choice except to end their relationship. Incensed by Tanizaki's reversal, Satō
declared that he wanted nothing more to do with
him and went on to attack his behavior in a
thinly veiled roman à clef. The chill between the
two writers did not ease for many years. Mean-

while, the Tanizakis' marriage was no better than
before, and in the spring of 1930 the older writer
approached Satō about marrying Chiyo. After
some understandable hesitation, Satō had accepted the proposition. This time the arrangements for the divorce and the subsequent marriage proceeded smoothly.

In the year following his divorce Tanizaki
married Furukawa Tomiko, a reporter twenty-
one years his junior. Tanizaki initially crowed
over his good fortune: "I have finally learned, at
the age of forty-six, the blessings of a marriage
where there is a true spiritual and physical union." Yet the marriage was over almost as soon
as it had begun. Tanizaki and Tomiko were living apart a year after their wedding, and a divorce followed soon thereafter.

The marriage's quick demise was tied to
Tanizaki's relationship with the woman who became his greatest muse: Nezu Matsuko, who,
when she first met Tanizaki in 1927, was married to the scion of an old Osaka wholesaling
firm. Matsuko represented to Tanizaki all that
was graceful and refined about women of the upper reaches of the Osaka merchant class. Although Tanizaki was smitten with Matsuko from
the start, the presence of her husband and her

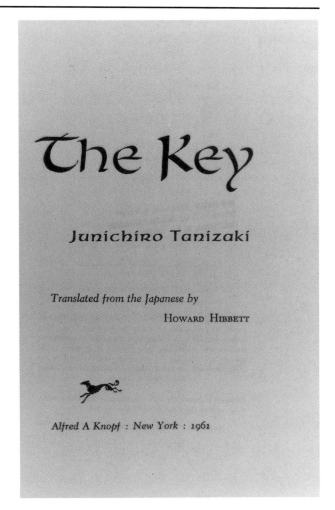

Frontispiece and title page for the translation of Kagi *(1956)*

wealth initially stopped him from considering her as anything more than a friend. These circumstances changed, however, as Matsuko's wealth evaporated with the failure of the family business and her marriage disintegrated because of an affair between her husband and her youngest sister. Despite his recent marriage to Tomiko, Tanizaki was soon declaring his love for Matsuko. In these declarations he was careful to preserve the illusion of hierarchy; a letter he wrote on 7 October 1932 shows how he delighted in playing the role of Matsuko's slave: "My lady, you once had chambermaids ten and more to do your bidding. From here on, all by myself I will take the place of your manservant, your steward, and your chambermaids." Waiting on Matsuko's needs, Tanizaki claimed, helped him "overcome an impasse in my art" and made him "brim with limitless creativity."

The works that Tanizaki professed to have written under Matsuko's influence are notable for two characteristics: they feature male protagonists' worshipful treatment of distant mistresses, and they exhibit a connection with the Japanese past. The tie with the past is established either through the use of a historical setting, as in *Mōmoku monogatari* (1932; translated as *A Blind Man's Tale,* 1963), which retells the history of the late-sixteenth-century civil wars from the point of view of a blind masseur who serves the ladies of the warring lords, or through the deliberate evocation of traditional Japanese literature, as in *Jun'ichirō jippitsubon Ashikari* (The Reed Cutter, 1933; translated as "Ashikari," 1936), a tale about a man's yearning for a ghostly mother that makes skillful use of the structure and conventions of the Nō play.

The masterpiece of this period is undoubtedly *Shunkinshō* (1933; translated as *The Story of Shunkin,* 1936), a chilling novella set in the late

Title page for the translation of Yōshō jidai *(1957)*

Edo period about the relationship of a blind musician and her manservant. From childhood on, Sasuke strives to satisfy the cruel and demanding Shunkin's every whim. Held in thrall by the erotics of distance, whereby a man's desire is fanned by the remoteness of its object, Sasuke grovels before his mistress's surpassing beauty, wealth, and social superiority. His self-abasement reaches its extreme when Shunkin's face is disfigured by a mysterious attacker; to continue serving his mistress without gazing on her ruined features, Sasuke puts out his own eyes with a needle. Thus transformed, he attends to Shunkin's needs until her death. On the surface, then, *The Story of Shunkin* is a story of monstrous devotion. But it can also be read as the record of another kind of monstrousness, for it reveals the mastery underlying Sasuke's seeming servility: Sasuke has used his acquiescence to make Shunkin totally dependent on him, thereby ensuring that she will continue to play her assigned role. When he puts out his eyes, Sasuke secures his idealized inner

vision of Shunkin against the encroachments of time and reality. There is even a suggestion, though it is never confirmed, that Sasuke may have disfigured his own mistress before age destroyed her beauty.

In a postscript to the novella Tanizaki says that in writing it he had sought to "find the form that would convey the greatest feeling of reality," and that he had finally "settled on the laziest, easiest method for a writer." The narrator is an antiquarian researcher who pieces together the story and retells it through quotations from various sources, as well as providing his own interpretations. So successful was this multilayered narrative that some readers initially mistook the unlikely story for a factual account.

In the late 1930s Tanizaki's fascination with the past and with traditional literature reached its apex when he set out to translate into the modern Japanese the greatest fictional narrative of classical Japanese literature, the eleventh-century *Genji monogatari* (The Tale of Genji). He devoted three years to the project, completing it in 1939, and would undertake two complete revisions (1951, 1964) before his death. His first effort reflected the ideological currents of the times. Sensing that the authorities would object to even a fictional representation of an act of lèse-majesté, Tanizaki excised all references to Genji's relationship with Fujitsubo, the emperor's consort, and illicit fathering of a future emperor. He also allowed drafts of his work to be checked by a leading right-wing scholar. Though Tanizaki was quick to restore the excised sections in his postwar revisions, it remains true that he was all too ready to sacrifice the integrity of a text that he loved.

Should his work on *The Tale of Genji* leave the impression that Tanizaki was an ideologically accommodating writer, one should keep in mind his paradoxically determined stand during the writing of his next major work of fiction, *Sasameyuki* (Light Snow, 1944–1948; translated as *The Makioka Sisters*, 1957). A loving evocation of the refined domestic life of an Osaka merchant family, *The Makioka Sisters* was inspired by the atmosphere of Kansai manners Tanizaki created during the late 1930s when he established a household with Matsuko, whom he had married in 1935, and her younger sisters. After a few installments of the novel appeared in serial form in early 1943, the military authorities forbade further publication on the grounds that the work's celebration of bourgeois comforts was inappropriate for a nation at war. Tanizaki continued to write, with no immediate prospect of publication, until bombs began to fall around his house in the Hanshin suburbs, and he carried the manuscript with him when he fled with his family to the seaside resort of Atami and, later, to rural Okayama Prefecture. He continued to add to the work after the surrender and completed it in 1948.

The Makioka Sisters was a major publishing phenomenon of the late 1940s. The novel allowed the postwar reader to enter, if only in fiction, a gentler, more graceful world, unspoiled by war and defeat, where the traditional and the cosmopolitan seamlessly combined in the service of good taste. The elegiac atmosphere of the novel is heightened by its focus on a once-prosperous merchant family in decline and by its setting in the late 1930s, when Japan had already embarked on the war in China. A sense of an approaching end suffuses the work as Sachiko endeavors to uphold the sagging status of the Makioka family by finding an appropriate match for her younger sister, Yukiko. These efforts are set against a background of lyrically rendered family rituals and seasonal observances that unfurls like a picture scroll. *The Makioka Sisters* is the most beautiful of Tanizaki's novels, but its elegiac thrust also makes it the most conservative work in his oeuvre. Anyone who violates the family's nearly religious belief in the maintenance of appearances—including a black-sheep sister who attempts to establish a life for herself as a workingwoman—is roundly punished. The work's beauty is purchased at the price of rejecting all human aspiration that exceeds the bounds of class and tradition.

Once the uncertainties and deprivations of the immediate postwar years were over, Tanizaki's last two decades proved to be the most comfortable of his life. Untainted by the stigma of having been a supporter of the war, he found it relatively easy to reestablish his career. With the success of *The Makioka Sisters* he achieved the status of a respected literary elder, and in 1949 he received the Imperial Order of Culture, his country's highest award for writers and artists. In 1964 he became the first Japanese to be made an honorary member of the American Academy and the National Institute of Arts and Letters. The popularity of *The Makioka Sisters* and the subsequent republication of many of his earlier works gave him financial security and enabled him to purchase a series of graceful houses in Kyoto, where he lived for some years after the war, and, beginning in the early 1950s, in Atami, a resort on the Izu peninsula whose warm climate was more comfortable to him in his old age. Tanizaki's final decades were also a time of domestic tranquillity: advancing age had brought to an end the elaborate role-playing that had characterized his marriage in the early years, and Matsuko became a helpmeet to her husband. As he grew older Tanizaki suffered intermittently from severe high blood pressure and a stroke in 1958 partially paralyzed his right hand, forcing him to dictate his works. But his imagination and creativity only seemed to expand, and he produced some of his most distinctive fiction when he was in his sixties and seventies.

In this period Tanizaki's characteristic concern with sexuality began to be colored by an absorption with the deprivations and opportunities of aging. He examined the exigencies of desire in a stage of life marked by diminishing physical powers and explored the satisfactions available through suggestion and control. In particular, he considered the possibilities of fatherhood as a relationship whereby one's desires could be made to live on within another human being. While Tanizaki's engagement with the past and with classical literature continued, there was also a regeneration of his interest in modernity and in the West. He was quick to recognize the modern comforts made available to the Japanese by the postwar recovery, and he once again began to attribute to Western material goods—such as Courvoisier brandy and Polaroid cameras—the power to excite Japanese passions. Also evident in Tanizaki's writing of this period is a more cerebral turn. In his later works desire is analyzed as a function of individual subjectivity that is both cursed and blessed by its uncertain relationship with exterior reality. Writing comes to dominate the foreground as a means of expressing subjective desire and obtaining its fulfillment.

Two masterful novellas emerged from Tanizaki's later years. *Shōshō Shigemoto no haha* (1950; translated as *Captain Shigemoto's Mother,* 1994), set in the Heian period, is perhaps the zenith of Tanizaki's stories dealing with a yearning for "mother." Here the longing for the mother is linked to the actions of the father, an aged courtier who, in a drunken moment of self-contempt and madness, gives his wife to a younger, more powerful nobleman. This impulsive and disastrous action plunges the courtier and his son into depths of loneliness that neither can escape. After the death of his father the son suffers an increased yearning that is only relieved at the end of the story when, well along in years, he is finally reunited with his mother. The tale is "re-

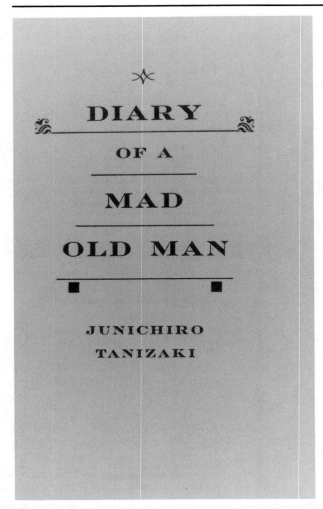

Title page for the American edition of the translation of Tanizaki's Fūten rōjin nikki *(1962)*

told" by a narrator who has found the story in other sources. The technique is similar to that of *The Story of Shunkin,* except that here the sources are actual well-known historical and literary texts. After liberally citing these sources to emphasize the authenticity of the story, however, Tanizaki does not hesitate to introduce a "source" of his own creation. Such an action shows that, despite his professed fascination with tradition, for Tanizaki the past was fundamentally a receptive milieu for his imagination.

The past is again invoked in the other great novella of Tanizaki's later years, *Yume no ukihashi* (1960; translated as *The Bridge of Dreams,* 1963). Though set in modern times, the work repeatedly alludes to the Heian classics, particularly *The Tale of Genji. Genji's* yearning for his mother and his quasi-incestuous coupling with his father's concubine are echoed in the novella by the protagonist's relationship with his stepmother,

which results in the birth of a son who is socially regarded as his brother. Tanizaki's story departs from the earlier classic tale by emphasizing the role of the protagonist's father, who has methodically reconstructed his second wife to resemble his dead first wife, even making her take her predecessor's name. Having executed one substitution, the father sets out to engineer another by designating his son as his own replacement when he becomes terminally ill. In contrast to the Heian tale, which plays with the unwitting reduplication of feminine identities, Tanizaki's novella fastens on a man's power to reconstruct deliberately not only an object of desire but also a second desiring self. The father's authority is not absolute, however, for the son is the narrator of the novella, and he emphasizes his power to tell his story in any way that he sees fit: "Of course, all that I record here is true: But there are limits even to telling the truth; there is a line one ought not to cross. And so, although I certainly never write anything untrue, neither do I write the whole of the truth." The narrator/protagonist of *The Bridge of Dreams* here says explicitly what is implied in every Tanizaki work: that writing and narrating are invariably selective and willful acts.

The essentially inventive nature of writing is the focus of the most challenging works of Tanizaki's last years, the two novels in diary form that are his most concentrated analyses of human sexuality: *The Key,* and *Fūten rōjin nikki* (1962; translated as *Diary of a Mad Old Man,* 1965). The former work consists of two sexual diaries kept by an aging college professor and his wife. While maintaining the pose that the diaries are private documents, the protagonists use them as a means of communication by reading each other's entries. This technique makes the work a combination of the diary novel and the epistolary novel. The diarists use their writing as a weapon of sexual gamesmanship: the professor, whose desires are inflamed by jealousy, encourages his wife to have an affair with a younger colleague; the wife reports on her encounters and thus invigorates her husband's diminishing virility. With the diaries as a catalyst, the characters turn up the sexual intensity in their marriage until the professor dies of a stroke brought on by overindulgence. The uses to which the diaries are put reveal the manipulative dimensions of writing; moreover, the many lies that the characters set down to achieve their ends, as well as the frequent inconsistencies in their descriptions of the same sexual encounters, point to the arbitrariness of writing. The manipulativeness and illusoriness assigned here to writing are also inherent in sexuality as it is depicted in the novel.

The isolated peregrinations of human subjectivity pursuing its desires is nowhere more poignantly captured in Tanizaki's works than in *Diary of a Mad Old Man*. In his diary an old man chronicles both the physical toll exacted by aging and the pleasures still possible for a septuagenarian—with the emphasis decidedly on the latter. An inveterate plotter, the old man gains vicarious satisfaction by pushing his daughter-in-law into an extramarital affair. All in all, the old man, as depicted in his diary, is thoroughly alive, continuously galvanized by the stirrings of desire. A quite different picture emerges, however, when he suffers a stroke during one of his sexual adventures and is no longer able to write. The novel is brought to a close through extracts from journals and medical records kept by a nurse, a doctor, and the old man's daughter, who attend him during his illness. In the words of these external observers the old man is reduced to a mere collection of symptoms and pathologies.

It is an insight into the contingency of writing, then, that brings to a close the written record of a thoroughly vital and exuberant spirit. Though Tanizaki continued to write almost to the day of his death—the notes for yet another work, set down in a shaky hand, were found on his desk the morning after he was struck down by kidney failure—*Diary of a Mad Old Man* makes a fitting coda to his career, for it embodies what animates Tanizaki's fiction from beginning to end: the exploration of desire from a perspective at once celebratory and ironic. An indefatigable searcher, Tanizaki pursued the source of his yearnings in various cultural topographies; he located it finally in human subjectivity and in writing. When he died on 30 July 1965, Tanizaki left behind a body of work that marks his culture's most sustained engagement with the power and the insubstantiality of the imagined.

Letters:

Kami to gangu to no aida, edited by Hata Kōhei (Tokyo: Rokkō Shuppan, 1977);

Tanizaki Sensei no shokan, edited by Minakami Tsutomu (Tokyo: Chūō Kōronsha, 1991).

Interview:

Kōno Toshirō and Chiba Shunji, eds., *Shiryō Tanizaki Jun'ichirō* (Tokyo: Ōfūsha, 1980).

Bibliographies:

Tachibana Hiroichirō, *Tanizaki Jun'ichirō Sensei chosho sōmokuroku* (Tokyo: Gallery Gohachi, 1965);

Nagae Hironobu, *Tanizaki Jun'ichirō–shiryō to dōkō* (Tokyo: Kyōiku Shuppan Center, 1984).

Biographies:

Tanizaki Matsuko, *Ishōan no yume* (Tokyo: Chūō Kōronsha, 1967);

Nomura Shōgo, *Denki–Tanizaki Jun'ichirō* (Tokyo: Rokkō Shuppan, 1974);

Watanabe Taori, *Sofu: Tanizaki Jun'ichirō* (Tokyo: Rokkō Shuppan, 1980).

References:

Ara Masahito, ed., *Tanizaki Jun'ichirō kenkyū* (Tokyo: Yagi Shoten, 1972);

Anthony Hood Chambers, *The Secret Window: Ideal Worlds in Tanizaki's Fiction* (Cambridge, Mass.: Council on East Asian Studies, Harvard University, 1994);

Chiba Shunji, ed., *Tanizaki Jun'ichirō: Monogatari no hōhō,* volume 18 of *Nihon bungaku kenkyū shiryō shinshū* (Tokyo: Yūseidō, 1990);

Van C. Gessel, "An Infatuation with Modernity: Tanizaki Jun'ichirō," in his *Three Modern Novelists: Sōseki, Tanizaki, Kawabata* (Tokyo: Kodansha International, 1993), pp. 68–132;

Ken K. Ito, *Visions of Desire: Tanizaki's Fictional Worlds* (Stanford, Cal.: Stanford University Press, 1991);

Sumie Jones, "How Tanizaki Disarms the Intellectual Reader," *Literature East and West,* 18 (March 1974): pp. 321–329;

Donald Keene, "Tanizaki Jun'ichirō," in his *Dawn to the West: Japanese Literature in the Modern Era–Fiction* (New York: Holt, 1984), pp. 720–785;

Nihon Bungaku Kenkyū Shiryō Kankō Kai, ed., *Tanizaki Jun'ichirō* (Tokyo: Yūseidō, 1972);

Noguchi Takehiko, *Tanizaki Jun'ichirō ron* (Tokyo: Chūō Kōronsha, 1973);

Edward G. Seidensticker, "Tanizaki Jun-ichirō, 1886–1965," *Monumenta Nipponica,* 21 (1966): pp. 249–265.

Tokuda Shūsei
(1 February 1872 – 18 November 1943)

Richard Torrance
Ohio State University

BOOKS: *Kumo no yokue* (Tokyo: Shun'yōdō, 1901);

Kyōmanji (Tokyo: Shinseisha, 1902);

Kaede no shitakage (Tokyo: Dai-Nihon Jogakukai, 1904);

Shōkazoku, 2 volumes (Tokyo: Shun'yōdō, 1905);

Hanataba (Tokyo: Hidaka Yūrindō, 1905);

Shūsei shū (Tokyo: Ekifūsha, 1908)–includes "Zetsubō," "Shoiage," and "Nirōba";

Arajotai (Tokyo: Shinchōsha, 1909);

Waga ko no ie (Tokyo: Shun'yōdō, 1911);

Ashiato (Tokyo: Shinchōsha, 1912);

Jinbutsu byōsha hō (Tokyo: Shinchōsha, 1912);

Kabi (Tokyo: Shinchōsha, 1912);

Tadare (Tokyo: Shinchōsha, 1913);

Zetsuen (Tokyo: Shun'yōdō, 1913)–includes "Tabi no soko";

Meiji shōsetsu bunshō hensenshi (Tokyo: Waseda Bungakusha Bungaku Fukyūkai Kan, 1914);

Arakure (Tokyo: Shinchōsha, 1915);

Honyrū (Tokyo: Shinchōsha, 1916);

Gisei (Tokyo: Heiwa Shuppansha, 1917);

Shōsetsu no tsukurikata (Tokyo: Shinchōsha, 1918);

Aru baishōfu no hanashi (Tokyo: Nihon Hyōronsha, 1920);

Dangai (Tokyo: Nihon Hyōronsha, 1921);

Doko made (Tokyo: Shinchōsha, 1922);

Kago no kotori (Tokyo: Bungei Nihonsha, 1925)–includes "Fuaiyagan";

Sugiyuku hi (Tokyo: Kaizōsha, 1926)–includes "Sōwa";

Machi no odoriba (Tokyo: Kaizōsha, 1934)–includes "Shiroi tabi no omoide";

Kunshō (Tokyo: Chūō Kōronsha, 1936)–includes "Kanojotachi no mi no ue," "Chibi no tamashi," and "Raz";

Kasō jinbutsu (Tokyo: Chūō Kōronsha, 1938);

Hikari o ōte (Tokyo: Shinchōsha, 1939);

Sōwa (Tokyo: Sakurai Shoten, 1942);

Sandai meisaku zenshū: Tokuda Shūsei (Tokyo: Kawade Shobō, 1942);

Shukuzu (Tokyo: Oyama Shoten, 1946);

Tokuda Shūsei

Kan no bara (Tokyo: Tokyo Shuppan Kabushiki Kaisha, 1948).

Collections: *Shūsei zenshū,* 15 volumes (Tokyo: Hibonkaku, 1936–1937)–includes "Yabukōji," *Shunko,* and "Oshina to Oshima no tachiba";

Shūsei zenshū, 6 volumes (Tokyo: Sekkasha, 1961–1962);

Tokuda Shūsei shū, Meiji bungaku zenshū, volume 68 (Tokyo: Chikuma Shobō, 1971)–includes "Zetsubō," "Shoiage," and "Nirōba";

Tokuda Shūsei shū, Nihon kindai bungaku taikei, volume 21 (Tokyo: Kadokawa Shoten, 1973);

Shūsei zenshū, 18 volumes (Kyoto: Rinsen Shoten,

1974–1975)–includes "Nijū-shi-go."

SELECTED PERIODICAL PUBLICATIONS–
UNCOLLECTED: "Shajitsu-ha," *Waseda Bungaku*
(1895): 242;
"Kawanami," *Shinshōsetsu* (1899): 68–145;
"Kimaguremono," *Bungei Kurabu,* 6 (1900):
76–117;
"Yakōbune," *Shinchō* (1906): 9–15;
"Shin no shakai shōsetsu," *Bunshō Sekai* (1906):
15–19;
"Mienu tokoro wakaranu oku," *Waseda Bungaku*
(1908): 85–86;
"Kansō futatsu mitsu," *Bunshō Sekai* (1908):
93–94.

Tokuda Shūsei was an important Japanese
writer from the turn of the twentieth century until
his death in 1943. The history of the modern ur-
banization of Japan is that of many people whose
lives were uprooted, and perhaps no other prewar
Japanese writer has so faithfully and realistically
portrayed the sheer chaos, indeterminacy, and
breathless excitement that characterized this ur-
banization.

Any consideration of the history of the modern Japanese novel has to acknowledge Shūsei's
literary career for at least three reasons. First, an
examination of how Shūsei's narrative prose developed during his long career provides a stylistic
history of the novel in modern Japan before
World War II. Lacking affiliations with political,
religious, or educational institutions for almost
fifty years, Shūsei survived as a professional novelist. Supporting himself and a large family of at
times eight dependents almost solely on the income he earned from writing fiction required that
he adapt to or stay ahead of the changing literary
stylistics of the marketplace. Second, since he remained committed to realism and to portraying
his contemporary society, his works provide compelling chronicles of common life in Japan during
the prewar modern period. Third, many Japanese
critics and novelists have praised Shūsei as the
master of the Japanese novel. This is in part because he deployed many narrative techniques acquired during years of training as a novelist to
portray everyday life and inarticulate people of no
particular social distinction. The result was a
genre of realism unique to Japan, a realism that
continues to defy efforts of literary critics to categorize it, except with superlatives. To paraphrase
Takami Jun, a noted Japanese critic and novelist,
reading Shūsei is like entering a vast sea; there is
nothing to grasp, and all one can do is float.

Tokuda Shūsei was born Tokuda Sueo to a
respectable *bushi,* or samurai family, retainers to
the Yokoyama house in the Kaga domain, the
present Ishikawa Prefecture. The samurai population of the domainal capital Kanazawa was ad-
versely affected by the political changes brought
about by the Meiji Restoration of 1868, an event
that, shortly afterward, deprived the hereditary
samurai class of its social status. Shūsei remembered armed camps of young men forming
throughout the city, the mass emigration of
déclassé samurai to become policemen in Pacific
coastal cities, and the widespread sale of young
women, especially daughters born of the gentry,
into the urban demimondes.

But according to his autobiographical fiction
and memoirs, Shūsei did not experience much
deprivation or want as a child; instead, his immediate family–his indulgent elderly father, his
mother who seemed to possess an "infinite love"
for her only son, and his elder half brothers and
sisters–protected and raised Shūsei, the youngest
male in the family. Even after the death of his father in 1891, his mother, half brother, sisters,
and half sisters somehow managed to scrape together the funds to support him through his second year of Fourth Higher School in Kanazawa,
and this schooling left him far better educated
than the majority of people with whom he associated during his life. Yet because these economic
resources were limited, Shūsei dropped out of the
elite educational system before he reached the
university and thus never enjoyed an extensive
exposure to Social Darwinism or other Western
intellectual systems. Though he never claimed to
be an intellectual, neither was he intimidated or
much impressed by those who had received better formal educations than he.

Like many young ex-samurai, Shūsei was a
supporter of the People's Rights movement, and
from 1892 to 1894 worked at jobs in Tokyo,
Osaka, Nagaoka, and Kanazawa, often as a reporter for newspapers associated with the Liberal
Party, which was agitating for greater popular
representation in government. His first patron
among Tokyo literati was the utopian socialist
Taoka Reiun, and Shūsei's earliest published fiction was a political polemic denouncing the rich
and powerful in Japanese society. In 1895 he became an apprentice to Ozaki Kōyō, the most
popular writer of the day and the founder of a
series of guilds that promoted and protected novelists during a remarkable period of economic
growth for those involved in publishing. Shūsei,
through the help of fellow Kanazawa native

Shūsei (seated at center) and his children—Momoko, Masahiko, Kazuho, Jōji, and Kiyoko—in 1935

Izumi Kyōka, became a live-in student in the craft of the novel in a "school" at the back of Kōyō's house. He remained a member of Kōyō's guild of writers until Kōyō's death in 1903, and the public continued to associate him with Kōyō even after the Russo-Japanese War in 1904–1905.

The first thing Shūsei learned from Kōyō was that it is necessary to write quickly in order to make a living. Throughout his career Shūsei published under his name an estimated two thousand or more titles (some of which may have been written by others), and bibliographically undocumented works by him are still coming to light. From 1895 to 1915 he wrote and published approximately 285 short stories and novellas, sixteen children's stories, twenty-two translations, 110 haiku, forty-four novels serialized for a popular audience, and five major experimental novels that have been acclaimed as masterpieces of modern Japanese Naturalism.

His long years of tutelage under Ozaki Kōyō also taught Shūsei to write for specific readerships. Although in later years he resented having to waste his time in pandering to a popular audience, he never really stopped writing popular fiction, at least when he needed the money, and even his serious fiction is remarkably modulated

for the audiences of the periodicals in which he published. But even as the perimeters of the literary marketplace changed with fashion during the decades, Shūsei concentrated on finding ways to give narrative voice to segments of society that were normally silent. "Yabukōji" (Spearflower, 1896), his first literary work well received by Tokyo critics, concerns the tragic fate of a young girl of *burakumin* (outcast) birth; his first major literary success was through *Kumo no yukue* (Where the Clouds Go, 1900), a long serialized novel that describes the struggles of the weak and those of illegitimate birth against the corrupt rich and high-born. The popular *Shunkō* (Spring Light, 1902) has as its protagonist a progressive feminist who has been deceived by a rich young man, has been forced to bear his child after he deserted her, and has become determined to remain independent of men, family, and marriage.

When Naturalism became embraced by Japanese writers and readers from 1906 to 1910, Shūsei was already a writer firmly identified with *shajitsu* (realism). Reticent about making theoretical pronouncements, he was not particularly associated with naturalism during this period, when polemicists such as Tayama Katai and Hasegawa Tenkei propagandized for Japanese writers to break with the heavily plotted, ornately worded fictions of the past; adopt a scientific spirit; and *ari no mama byōsha* (portray reality objectively). However, if the crucial distinction between realism and Japanese Naturalism is defined in terms of how this Naturalism resolved technical literary problems of objectively representing the extraliterary dialects of the lower strata of society and incorporating the tangible, documentary facts into the novel, then Tokuda Shūsei can probably be said to have solved these problems in the most brilliant and original ways that make him worthy of recognition as the most accomplished Japanese Naturalist.

The years from 1908 to 1915 constituted Shūsei's most productive and experimental period. The opening of *Arajotai* (The New Household, 1908) provides perhaps the most penetrating understanding of the difficult struggles and frustrating expectations involved in trying to establish, on one's own, an independent household in a major Japanese city:

> Shinkichi took Osaku as his wife during the winter four years ago, when he was twenty-five and she twenty.
>
> At the age of fourteen, the impressionable adolescent had been inspired by a success story in some biography of a rich entrepreneur, and he had dashed off from the provinces to Tokyo, where he labored with extraordinary diligence as an apprentice to a wine wholesaler in Shinkawa. After eleven years of working like hell, he managed to start his own business, renting a small shop in Omote-chō, there selling sake and soy sauce, firewood and charcoal, salt and other necessities. He worked all the harder, even begrudging himself the time spent for eating his meals; he would hastily gulp down his food at the front of his shop, not pausing to untie the cords holding up his sleeves or to put on his sandals.

No other novel so vividly represents the cold, harsh winds that even today threaten to blow away the lives of ordinary "salary men" doing business in Japanese cities.

Ashiato (Footprints, 1910) is an extraordinary exercise in narrative control. The novel is based on the life of Hama (1881–1926), Shūsei's wife, and the narrative is structured through flashbacks and digressions within digressions. Every word in this complex work belongs to the novel's heroine, Oshō, a woman of status comparable to the next-door maid, but she rarely speaks throughout the rather long novel. *Kabi* (Mold, 1911), an autobiographical novel in which Shūsei displayed not the slightest interest in dramatizing his alter ego,

Sasamura, can be read as a mere continuation of *Footprints*. The protagonist's wife, Ogin (another character based on Hama), emerges as the most sympathetic and engaging character by far. On another level, as critic Terada Tōru concluded in 1948, perhaps no literary work written since the end of World War II presents the reader with an existential vision as stark as does Shūsei's *Mold*.

In *Tadare* (Festering, 1913) Shūsei creates a mood charged with eroticism and decadence. The main character of the work is Omasu, a former prostitute who has used her body and wiles to ensnare Asai, a slightly unscrupulous businessman. Despite the seedy backgrounds of the main characters, Shūsei invests Omasu and her commonplace aspirations for respectability with a complexity and psychological depth that make her an appealing character.

In some respects *Arakure* (Rough Living, 1915) is the culmination of the "novel of common life" that Shūsei was creating from 1908 to 1915, and it remains the most popular of his works. Through the eyes of Oshima, a success-starved woman who finds a field for her ambition in the tailoring of Western-style clothing, it presents a fascinating picture of Japanese entrepreneurship. Shūsei again uses an odd perspective—that of a woman in a man's business—to keep up with new developments in society and to incorporate in the experiences of one woman those of many living in the city. Embedded in the novel are representations of the great structural transformations Japan underwent near the turn of the century: industrialization, the decline of an older landowning class, imperialistic expansion abroad, and the Westernization of native customs and manners. But these are disassembled and reconstituted in Oshima's field of vision. Of all of Shūsei's remarkable woman characters, Oshima is his most obvious "economic animal," as she exploits for profit the waves of the economy on which she rides and yet also yearns most fervently for love and human affection. She is one of the great literary creations of modern times, a ubiquitous character whose life and ethos are familiar and come to stand as touchstones or standards by which Japanese society at the end of the twentieth century may be measured or judged.

In an October 1915 interview Shūsei stated that if he were so inclined, he could write two or three more novels such as *Festering* or *Rough Living* but that he was tired of "that kind of thing," and he did not intend to write other works like them. He was true to his word. *Rough Living* marked an abrupt end to the phase of Shūsei's career that had begun in 1908 with *The New Household*. It is curious that Shūsei should declare so forthrightly that he was going to change the direction of his writing, for the works that he wrote from 1908 to 1915 had earned him a reputation as the finest realistic writer in Japan at that time.

Yet by the end of 1915 Shūsei must have been exhausted. He was forty-three years old and had been supporting himself, a wife, and up to six children almost solely by writing fiction for fifteen years. In addition to those five major novels, during the almost seven-year period from October 1908 until July 1915 he had written some twenty serialized novels for a popular audience. Two of these serially published works, "Nijū-shi-go" (Twenty-four or Twenty-five, 1909) and "Honryū" (The Torrent, 1916), were well received. It would be difficult to underestimate the linguistic effort to remain original that Shūsei expended to maintain his literary career from the turn of the century until 1915. These novels present the voice of the author refracted through an enormous diversity of language involving a highly original sound symbolism (conventionally held to be not literary); regional and urban dialects; nonstandard, pseudoclassical narrative forms; beautiful seasonal imagery; and dialogue in mixed dialects. This extraordinary linguistic diversity is, in all of these works, woven into extremely dense configurations of common voices.

By 1915, however, literary fashions and the character of Japanese society were changing. For the next twenty years Shūsei, always the professional novelist, responded to the growing urban mass culture of the Taishō and Shōwa periods and to the popularity of autobiographical fiction among the intelligentsia by changing the emphases of his writing to concentrate on autobiographical and purely fictional short stories, novellas, and popular serial romances. Postwar critics have cited this change in the direction of Shūsei's career as signaling the devolution of the Japanese novel to become merely a record of trivial personal experience, but for most of his career the majority of Shūsei's works were pure fiction. His ability to alter his style according to different readerships was remarkable, and for audiences that appreciated more complex, psychological fiction, he produced many autobiographical short stories that maintained his standing as a serious writer.

These works include "Kanshō-teki no koto" (A Sentimental Story, 1921), an account of his mother's death; "Sōwa" (An Episode, 1925), a

story of the love that arises between the middle-aged author and a provincial geisha; "Sugiyuku hi" (The Passing Days, 1925), partly an account of the death of Shūsei's wife; "Machi no odoriba" (The Town's Dance Hall, 1933), about a journey home to Kanazawa; and "Shi ni shitashimu" (Growing Accustomed to Death, 1933), about the death that Shūsei's own physician suffered from cancer. His reputation as a fine short-story writer also rests on his more purely fictional works, such as "Zetsubō" (Despair, 1907), "Niroba" (Two Old Women, 1908), "Tabi no soko" (At the Bottom of His Tabi, 1913), "Oshina to Oshima no tachiba" (The Positions of Oshina and Oshima, 1923), "Fuaiya gan" (Fire Gun, 1923), "Kanojo-tachi no mi no ue" (The Women's Circumstances, 1935), "Razō" (A Nude Figure, 1935), "Kunshō" (1935; translated as "Order of the White Paulownia," 1962), and "Senji fūkei" (Scenes from Wartime, 1937).

In 1924 Shūsei met Yamada Junko, then Masukawa Junko, who had visited Shūsei to request his help in publishing a novel that she had written. After Junko's divorce from her husband and the death of Shūsei's wife, Shūsei and Junko began a love affair that her infidelities and his age transformed into a public scandal. By 25 April 1927 the newspaper *Asahi Shinbun* published a story under the following headline: "Yamada Junko Going from One Man to the Next / As if Jumping from One Stepping Stone to Another / She suddenly betrays her lover Shūsei / Promises marriage to a student at Keiō University / A hateful woman, a pitiable woman, a poison flower, Shūsei states." This sensational love affair with his literary disciple had made Shūsei's name a household word even among those who did not read novels.

As a result of the scandal, his career went into eclipse from 1929 to 1932, but he regained the esteem of readers in 1933 when he published "The Town's Dance Hall." In 1935 he began rewriting his love affair as a chronicle and critique of modern customs and manners in *Kasō jinbutsu* (In Disguise, 1935–1938), perhaps his most distinguished novel. Donald Keene compares Shūsei's style in this long work to that of Marcel Proust, and in the late 1930s and early 1940s Shūsei's work had made him the preeminent writer of Japanese realism. Writers formed study groups to read his novels. A literary journal, *Arakure*, was established in the name of one of his novels, and he was said to personify the *sanbun seishin* ("Spirit of Prose Literature"), a slogan identifying writers associated with the "Popular Front" against fascism and united in defense of the freedom of expression that they regarded as the sine qua non of novelistic prose.

In 1941 Shūsei began and ended serialization of *Shukuzu* (The Microcosm), his last substantial novel. After almost fifty years of grappling with the problem of how to represent the voices of common characters, Shūsei created perhaps his most complexly structured novel around a character from the lowest class that he had ever treated in a sustained manner. The work is based on the life of Kobayashi Masako, Shūsei's lover and the owner of a geisha house that he helped manage in the last years of his life. The novel presents a microcosm of Japanese society from about the turn of the century until 1941. The Cabinet Information Bureau was displeased by this book, probably by the frank descriptions of poverty it presents, and ordered Shūsei to make major revisions. Refusing to compromise with the state censors, he ended serialization of the novel in mid sentence. It remains unfinished.

Tokuda Shūsei died of cancer of the pleura on 18 November 1943. He will probably be remembered as a master stylist of modern Japanese prose. Kawabata Yasunari, for example, has written that there are three pinnacles in the history of the Japanese novel: Murasaki Shikibu, Ihara Saikaku, and Tokuda Shūsei. But Shūsei should also be remembered as the novelist who managed to portray the chaos and disorientation of modernity for the urban masses, that protean middle stratum of urban immigrants who were to become the new middle class of Japan in the postwar era.

Bibliography:
Matsumoto Tōru, "Chosaku shoshutsu nenpu," in his *Tokuda Shūsei* (Tokyo: Kasama Shoin, 1988), pp. 413–459.

References:
James Fujii, *Complicit Fictions* (Berkeley & Los Angeles: University of California Press, 1993);

Funabashi Seiichi, *Tokuda Shūsei* (Tokyo: Kōbundō Shobō, 1941);

Shūsei near the end of his life

Kawabata Yasunari, "Kaisetsu," in his *Tokuda Shūsei, Nihon no bungaku,* volume 9 (Tokyo: Chūō Kōronsha, 1973), pp. 512–526;

Donald Keene, *Dawn to the West,* 2 volumes (New York: Holt, Rinehart & Winston, 1984), I: 271–281;

Kōno Toshirō, ed., *Ronkō Tokuda Shūsei* (Tokyo: Ōfūsha, 1983);

Matsumoto Tōru, *Tokuda Shūsei* (Tokyo: Kasama Shoin, 1988);

Noguchi Fujio, *Tokuda Shūsei den* (Tokyo: Chikuma Shobō, 1965);

Noguchi, *Tokuda Shūsei no bungaku* (Tokyo: Chikuma Shobō, 1979);

Richard Torrance, *The Fiction of Tokuda Shūsei and the Emergence of Japan's New Middle Class* (Seattle: University of Washington Press, 1994).

Tsubouchi Shōyō
(22 May 1859 – 28 February 1935)

J. Scott Miller
Brigham Young University

BOOKS: *Eibun shōgaku tokuhon makinoichi* (Tokyo: Kōun Shoya, 1885);

Shōsetsu shinzui (Tokyo: Shōgetsudō, 1885–1886), translated by Nanette Twine as *The Essence of the Novel* (Brisbane: University of Queensland, Department of Japanese, 1983);

Tōsei shosei katagi (Tokyo: Banseiō, 1885–1886);

Imotose kagami (Tokyo: Kaishin Shoya, 1885–1886);

Mirai no yume (Tokyo: Banseiō, 1886);

Kyō waranbe (Tokyo: Hino Shoten, 1886);

Karen jō (Tokyo: Ginshōdō, 1887);

Matsu no uchi (Tokyo: Shinshindō Honten, 1888);

Ronri jisshū (Tokyo: Tokyo Senmon Gakkō Shuppanbu, 1889);

Saikun (Tokyo: Kokumin no Tomo, 1889);

Harunoya manpitsu (Tokyo: Shun'yōdō, 1891);

Kohitsuji mangen (Tokyo: Yūhikaku Shobō, 1893);

Kiri hitoha (Tokyo: Shun'yōdō, 1896);

Bungaku sono oriori (Tokyo: Shun'yōdō, 1896);

Rien no ochiba (Tokyo: Shun'yōdō, 1896);

Maki no kata (Tokyo: Shun'yōdō, 1897);

Kiku to kiri (Tokyo: Shun'yōdō, 1898);

Jinjō shōgakkō yō kokugo tokuhon, 8 volumes (Tokyo: Fuzanbō, 1900);

Chikamatsu no kenkyū, by Shōyō and Amijima Eiichirō (Shun'yōdō, 1900);

Eibungaku shi (Tokyo: Tokyo Senmon Gakkō Shuppanbu, 1901);

Bungei to kyōiku (Tokyo: Shun'yōdō, 1902);

Eishibun hyōshaku (Tokyo: Tokyo Senmon Gakkō Shuppanbu, 1902);

Tsūzoku rinri dan (Tokyo: Fuzanbō, 1903);

Shin gakugeki ron (Tokyo: Waseda Daigaku Shuppanbu, 1904);

Shinkyoku Urashima (Tokyo: Waseda Daigaku Shuppanbu, 1904); republished as *Chōsei shin Urashima* (Tokyo: Jitsugyō no Nihonsha, 1922), translated by Kwanshu M. Furukawa as *Urashima* (Urawa: Furusawa, 1936);

Ōunabara (Shūbunkan, 1905);

Tsubouchi Shōyō

Shinkyoku Kaguyahime (Tokyo: Waseda Daigaku Shuppanbu, 1905);

Chūgaku shūshin kun, 5 volumes (Tokyo: Sanseidō, 1906);

Tokoyami (Tokyo: Shūbunkan, 1906);

Hachikatsugi hime, Niwaka sennin (Tokyo: Saiunkaku, 1907);

Bungei sadan (Tokyo: Shun'yōdō, 1907);

238

Chūgaku shin tokuhon, 10 volumes (Tokyo: Meiji Tosho Kabushiki Kaisha, 1908);

Rinri to bungaku (Tokyo: Fuzanbō, 1908);

Shinkyoku kinmōko (Tokyo: Shun'yōdō, 1908);

Saku to hyōron (Tokyo: Waseda Daigaku Shuppanbu, 1909);

Futabatei Shimei, by Shōyō and Uchida Roan (Tokyo: Ekifūsha, 1909);

Geki to bungaku (Tokyo: Fuzanbō, 1911);

Shinsen kokugo tokuhon, 10 volumes (Tokyo: Fuzanbō, 1911);

Iwayuru atarashii onna (Tokyo: Seibidō, 1912);

Kyōka to engeki (Tokyo: Shōbundō, 1915);

Reigen (Tokyo: Kinkōdō, 1915);

Datennyo (Tokyo: Kinkōdō, 1915);

Sametaru onna, Gendai otoko (Tokyo: Kōbundō, 1915);

Hototogisu kojō no rakugetsu (Tokyo: Shun'yōdō, 1916);

En no gyōja (Tokyo: Genbunsha, 1917);

Gekidan no saikin jūnen (Tokyo: Komeyamadō, 1917);

Nagori no hoshizukiyo (Tokyo: Shun'yōdō, 1918);

Yoshitoki no saigo (Tokyo: Shun'yōdō, 1918);

Shōyō gekidan (Tokyo: Ten'yūsha, 1919);

Hōnan (Tokyo: Jitsugyō no Nihonsha, 1920);

Shibaie to Toyokuni oyobi sono monka (Tokyo: Shun'yōdō, 1920);

Kabuki no tsuioku (Tokyo: Nihon Engei Gōshigaisha Shuppanbu, 1920);

Kabuki kyakuhon kessakushū, by Shōyō and Akubi Seitarō, 12 volumes (Tokyo: Shun'yōdō, 1920–1921);

Sorekara sore (Tokyo: Jitsugyō no Nihonsha, 1921);

Waga peejentogeki (Tokyo: Kokuhonsha, 1921);

Kateiyō jidōgeki, 3 volumes (Tokyo: Waseda Daigaku Shuppanbu, 1922–1924);

Geijutsu to katei to shakai (Tokyo: Jitsugyō no Nihonsha, 1923);

Buyōron (Tokyo: Kindai Meichō Bunko Kankōkai, 1923);

Jidō kyōiku to engeki (Tokyo: Waseda Daigaku Shuppanbu, 1923);

Tōzai no senjōteki higeki (Tokyo: Shunjūsha, 1923);

Gakkōyō shōkyakuhon (Tokyo: Waseda Daigaku Shuppanbu, 1923).

Atami peejento (Tokyo: Hakubunkan, 1925);

Kaioku mandan (Tokyo: Waseda Bungaku, 1925–1926);

Sheekusupiya kenkyū shiori (Tokyo: Waseda Daigaku Shuppanbu, 1928);

Ryōkan to komori (Tokyo: Waseda Daigaku Shuppanbu, 1929);

Kinsei kijin den sono ta (Tokyo: Tōkyōdō, 1931);

Kabuki gashōshiwa (Tokyo: Tōkyōdō, 1931);

Kaki no heta (Tokyo: Chūō Kōronsha, 1933);

Anan to Kishimo (Tokyo: Shomotsu Tenbōsha, 1934).

Collection: *Shōyō senshū,* 15 volumes (Tokyo: Shun'yōdō, 1926–1927); revised edition, 17 volumes (Tokyo: Daiichi Shobō, 1977–1978).

PLAY PRODUCTIONS: *Kiri hitoha,* Tokyo, Tokyo-za, February 1903;

En no gyōja, Tokyo, Tsukiji Shōgekijō, March 1926;

Ryōkan to komori, Tokyo, Teikoku Gekijō, June 1929;

Datennyo, Tokyo, Kabuki-za, December 1929;

Hototogisu kojō no rakugetsu, Tokyo, Shinbashi Enbujō, February 1934.

TRANSLATIONS: Sir Walter Scott, *Shunpū jōwa* (Tokyo: Nakajima Seiichi, 1880);

Scott, *Shunsō kiwa,* 2 volumes (Tokyo: Sakanoue Hanshichi, 1884);

William Shakespeare, *Jiyū no tachi nagori no kireaji* (Tokyo: Tōyōkan, 1884); republished as *Juriasu Shiizaa* (Tokyo: Waseda Daigaku Shuppanbu, 1913);

Edward Bulwer-Lytton, *Gaiseishi den* (Tokyo: Banseidō, 1885);

Grace and Phillip Watson, *Rōran fujin den* (Tokyo: Teikoku Insho Kaisha, 1886); republished as *Kōsai no joō* (Tokyo: Kin'ōdō / Jiyūkaku, 1887);

Anna Katherine Green, *Rōran fujin den* (Tokyo: Shinshindō Honten, 1888);

John Vanbrugh, *Futagokoro* (Tokyo: Shun'yōdō, 1897);

Shakespeare, *Hamuretto* (Tokyo: Waseda Daigaku Shuppanbu / Fuzanbō, 1909);

Shakespeare, *Romeo to Jurietto* (Tokyo: Waseda Daigaku Shuppanbu / Fuzanbō, 1910);

Shakespeare, *Oserō* (Tokyo: Waseda Daigaku Shuppanbu / Fuzanbō, 1911);

Shakespeare, *Riya-ō* (Tokyo: Waseda Daigaku Shuppanbu / Fuzanbō, 1912);

George Bernard Shaw, *Wōren fujin no shokugyō* (Tokyo: Waseda Daigaku Shuppanbu, 1913);

Shaw, *Buki to hito,* translated by Shōyō and Ichikawa Matahiko (Tokyo: Waseda Daigaku Shuppanbu, 1913);

Shakespeare, *Venisu no shōnin* (Tokyo: Waseda Daigaku Shuppanbu, 1914);

Shakespeare, *Tempesuto* (Tokyo: Waseda Daigaku Shuppanbu, 1915);

Shakespeare, *Antonii to Kureopatora* (Tokyo: Waseda Daigaku Shuppanbu, 1915);

Shakespeare, *Manatsu no yoru no yume* (Tokyo: Waseda Daigaku Shuppanbu, 1915);

Shakespeare, *Makubesu* (Tokyo: Waseda Daigaku Shuppanbu, 1916);

Shakespeare, *Ishaku hōshaku* (Tokyo: Waseda Daigaku Shuppanbu, 1918);

Shakespeare, *Fuyu no yobanashi* (Tokyo: Waseda Daigaku Shuppanbu, 1918);

Shakespeare, *Richaado sansei* (Tokyo: Waseda Daigaku Shuppanbu, 1918);

Shakespeare, *Henrii yonsei* (Tokyo: Waseda Daigaku Shuppanbu, 1919);

Shakespeare, *Henrii yonsei* (Tokyo: Waseda Daigaku Shuppanbu, 1919);

Shakespeare, *Oki ni mesu mama* (Tokyo: Waseda Daigaku Shuppanbu, 1920);

Shakespeare, *Jajauma narashi* (Tokyo: Waseda Daigaku Shuppanbu, 1920);

Shakespeare, *Jūniya* (Tokyo: Waseda Daigaku Shuppanbu, 1921);

Shakespeare, *Korioreenasu* (Tokyo: Waseda Daigaku Shuppanbu, 1922);

Shakespeare, *Shimuberin* (Tokyo: Waseda Daigaku Shuppanbu, 1923);

Shakespeare, *Koi no honeorizon* (Tokyo: Waseda Daigaku Shuppanbu, 1926);

Shakespeare, *Richaado nisei* (Tokyo: Waseda Daigaku Shuppanbu, 1926);

Shakespeare, *Uinzaa no yōki na nyōbō* (Tokyo: Waseda Daigaku Shuppanbu, 1926);

Shakespeare, *Machigaitsuzuki* (Waseda Daigaku Shuppanbu, 1926);

Shakespeare, *Taitasu Andoronikasu* (Tokyo: Waseda Daigaku Shuppanbu, 1926);

Shakespeare, *Azensu no taimon* (Tokyo: Waseda Daigaku Shuppanbu, 1926);

Shakespeare, *Verōna no ni shinshi* (Tokyo: Waseda Daigaku Shuppanbu, 1926);

Shakespeare, *Karasawagi* (Tokyo: Waseda Daigaku Shuppanbu, 1927);

Shakespeare, *Toroirasu to kureshida* (Tokyo: Waseda Daigaku Shuppanbu, 1927);

Shakespeare, *Henrii gosei* (Tokyo: Waseda Daigaku Shuppanbu, 1927);

Shakespeare, *Sue yokereba subete yoshi* (Tokyo: Waseda Daigaku Shuppanbu, 1927);

Shakespeare, *Jon-ō* (Tokyo: Waseda Daigaku Shuppanbu, 1927);

Shakespeare, *Perikuriizu* (Tokyo: Waseda Daigaku Shuppanbu, 1927);

Shakespeare, *Shihen sono ichi* (Tokyo: Waseda Daigaku Shuppanbu, 1927);

Shakespeare, *Henrii hassei* (Tokyo: Waseda Daigaku Shuppanbu, 1928);

Shakespeare, *Henrii rokusei* (Tokyo: Waseda Daigaku Shuppanbu, 1928);

Shakespeare, *Henrii rokusei* (Tokyo: Waseda Daigaku Shuppanbu, 1928);

Shakespeare, *Henrii rokusei* (Tokyo: Waseda Daigaku Shuppanbu, 1928);

Shakespeare, *Shihen sono ni* (Tokyo: Waseda Daigaku Shuppanbu, 1928);

Shakespeare, *Shinshō Sheekusupiya zenshū*, 40 volumes, revised edition (Tokyo: Chūō Kōronsha, 1932–1935).

OTHER: San'yōtei Enchō, *Kaidan botan dōro*, foreword by Shōyō (Tokyo: Haishishuppen, 1884).

In summarizing his life by recounting the various occupations he had pursued, Tsubouchi Shōyō once said that he had been first "a pathetic novelist, then I became an instructor of English literature, then a middle school director of moral education, next a scriptwriter promoting theater reform. After that, a proponent for new musical drama in Japan." Yet he also could have added two more hats to this hat rack that defines the course of his career—those of literary critic and Shakespeare translator. The characteristically modest tone Shōyō uses to list his diverse contributions to modern Japanese letters belies his significance and widespread importance, but behind Shōyō's modesty is also his awareness that his literary works—both narrative and dramatic—failed to reach the high critical standards that he proposed. Yet his bold, articulate critical writings, combined with his encouragement of budding novelists, first redefined and then reformed Japanese literature at the beginning of the twentieth century.

As a novelist, Shōyō was just slightly ahead of his time. In both his theoretical writings and his novels he sought to define concepts and demonstrate new techniques for which the Japanese language of his day had neither the vocabulary nor the stylistic conventions for anything more than a rough approximation of his grand designs. Although critics agree that Shōyō was more successful in theory than in practice, from a historical and literary perspective it is not so much a single magnum opus that secures his place among the major figures of modern Japanese literature as it is the fact that, throughout his long life, he was constantly seeking to revise, modernize, empower, and reinvest Japanese literature with both the seriousness of purpose he found in Western culture and the strength of tradition that he recognized in Japanese culture.

Thus, Shōyō emerges as a blemished patron saint of modern Japanese literature. His overwhelming influence on the course of developments in Japanese literary art sets him apart despite the fact that he wandered from one field to another or that his greatest works are translations rather than original creations. If his achievements merit nothing else, the sheer breadth of those accomplishments and their subsequent import have earned for him a place in the literary canon.

Tsubouchi Shōyō, whose given name was Yūzō, was born in Ōta, a small town in present-day Gifu Prefecture. Heinoshin, his father, was an austere man and a functionary for the Owari domain; Michi, his mother, was the eldest daughter of a sake producer from Nagoya. Shōyō was the youngest of six surviving children, and at an early age he gained an appreciation for novels, theater, and the arts from his mother and his elder sisters. His early exposure to the works of Edo-period *gesaku* (comic fiction) and drama gave Shōyō a solid grounding in the traditional arts that permeated all of his future work. Through age eleven he was educated at home in both the literary and martial arts, and then, after the Meiji Restoration, his father retired and the family moved to a farm on the outskirts of Nagoya. There young Shōyō was enrolled in a temple-affiliated school, and his proximity to Nagoya allowed him to attend the Kabuki theater, with which he quickly became enamored. A prodigious reader, he also frequented the Daisō lending library in Nagoya and deepened his reading in Edo-period fiction.

At the age of fourteen Shōyō and his elder brother, Yoshie, studied Chinese poetry composition at a private academy and also English at the Nagoya Prefectural English School. He continued to be devoted to Kabuki and pursued his English studies in public schools during the early 1870s. By the age of sixteen he was enrolled in the Aichi English School, where he studied elocution as well as the works of William Shakespeare under the guidance of an American named Latham. In 1876 Shōyō was selected by the prefecture as one of eight students to go to Tokyo to continue studies at the Kaisei Gakkō, which later became Tokyo University. At first he lodged with Yoshie, who was heir to the family line and worked for a Tokyo bank, but after Shōyō suffered an attack of beriberi for which he was hospitalized, he moved into student lodgings. His experiences there became the basis for his first novel, *Tōsei shosei katagi* (The Character of Modern Students, 1885–1886).

In 1877 Kaisei Gakkō was restructured and renamed, and Shōyō, at age nineteen, was chosen to be in the top echelon of his class in the Tokyo University Preparatory School. Although his attitude toward studying was casual, Shōyō was a brilliant student, and he plunged into literary studies. He adopted several pen names, formed a coterie magazine with his roommates, and, along with a friend named Takada Sanae, founded a literary association called the Banseikai (Latebloomers Club).

The following year he entered Tokyo University, where he enrolled in literary and legal studies. In October 1878, when the health of his brother Yoshie declined following his wife's death, Shōyō left student lodgings and moved back with his brother to offer assistance. As Shōyō's university studies continued, he developed a passion for Western literature, particularly for British novels. While accompanying Yoshie on a convalescent journey to the coastal resort town of Atami, Shōyō began working on his first translation, an excerpt from Sir Walter Scott's *The Bride of Lammermoor* (1819), that he later published as *Shunpū jōwa* (Romance of the Spring Breeze, 1880). During summer break Shōyō began translating Scott's *The Lady of the Lake* (1810), but he soon suspended this effort. On an English literature examination in which he had been asked to discuss the character of Gertrude in Shakespeare's *Hamlet* (1604–1605), Shōyō instead had written an evaluation of her behavior and failed his exam. As a consequence of this failure, Shōyō sequestered himself in the library, where he intensively read Western literary criticism and histories in order to improve his comprehension of literary theory.

During this highly charged time his mother died, and in June 1881 Shōyō failed a course that Ernest Fenollosa taught in political science. This failure meant that Shōyō did not pass his third year, and he lost his scholarship. Chagrined, he went home to Nagoya to celebrate his father's seventieth birthday before returning to Tokyo, where he taught English to support himself, attended school, and continued to translate Scott's work. His father died the following year, and, to underscore his desire to be independent, Shōyō declined his share of the inheritance.

In September 1882 Shōyō (under the name of Harunoya Oboro) published his first short pieces of allegorical fiction in newspapers such as the *Tokyo Eiri Shinbun* and the *Naigai Seitō Jijō*. Many of these early works were patterned after the traditional *gesaku* parodies that Shōyō had enjoyed as a child. He contributed many articles to newspapers in Tokyo and Nagoya in 1883, and that year he graduated from Tokyo University. Eschewing government employment, Shōyō worked as an instructor in charge of foreign history and constitutional theory at the newly founded Tokyo Senmon Gakkō (later Waseda University) through the recommendation of his friend Takada.

That autumn he published "Shōsetsu buntai" (Narrative Style), a short essay that was a precursor to what became *Shōsetsu shinzui* (1885–1886; translated as *The Essence of the Novel*, 1983), and completed *Jiyū no tachi nagori no kireaji* (The Sharp Edge of Freedom's Sword, 1884), a manuscript translation of Shakespeare's *Julius Caesar* (1623). This last piece, written in *jōruri* style, was published the following May, shortly after his two-volume translation of Scott's *The Lady of the Lake*. Both of these rather free translations were apparently undertaken to illustrate contemporary political positions, not necessarily to make their literary value accessible to Japanese readers.

Following the publication of these works Shōyō moved into new, larger quarters, as he was developing a small entourage of boarders whom he favored with lectures and discussions in the evenings. He continued to publish short pieces in newspapers and began to translate Edward Bulwer-Lytton's *Rienzi, the Last of the Roman Tribunes* (1835).

In October 1884 he agreed to write a foreword to the groundbreaking transcription of storyteller San'yūtei Enchō's oral ghost tale "Botandōrō" (The Peony Lantern). In his foreword Shōyō praises the novelty of Enchō's colloquial style and condemns the mediocrity of contemporary written narrative: "Considering the extent to which Enchō's narrative faithfully reveals the heart and soul of human feeling and evokes great sympathy within us, the shallow and inferior men of letters today, whose depiction of human feeling is superficial, whose style seems to come from the grave itself, and who do little more than try to flatter women and children, should feel great shame." Shōyō was beginning to exercise his critical voice, and he had found his targets.

Soon after "The Peony Lantern" appeared Shōyō published *Gaiseishi den* (Biography of a Patriot, 1885), his translation of the first part of *Ri-

enzi*, in addition to many articles on manners as well as on the reform of narrative and lyric modes of writing. He also published *The Essence of the Novel*, the first manifesto of modern literary criticism in Japan, and his first novel, *Tōsei shosei katagi* (The Character of Modern Students, 1885–1886), which he intended to compose as a practical demonstration of a narrative written according to those critical precepts.

Shōyō's disdain that he had expressed for contemporary writers in his foreword to *The Peony Lantern* was articulated in greater detail in *The Essence of the Novel*. Shōyō had been formulating these theoretical principles ever since being humiliated in failing adequately to discuss Gertrude from *Hamlet*. A somewhat uneven but eclectic work, *The Essence of the Novel* incorporates both Western and traditional Japanese approaches to prose narrative. It derides contemporary writers for adhering to didactic tendencies and idealistic portrayals of character, and it advocates the adoption of more realism and moral neutrality. Little evidence suggests that Shōyō's theoretical study was widely read at the time, but literary historians often use the publication of *The Essence of the Novel* to mark the origins of modern Japanese literature. In any event, many of the reforms that Shōyō advocates in this work were realized during the following two decades.

Although *The Character of Modern Students* was intended to illustrate some of the reforms that Shōyō was seeking, it is in fact much more akin to Edo-period fiction than any work of innovative narrative. The novel presents the life of contemporary college students and the young women of the pleasure quarters. Focusing on the love between Komachida Sanji, a university student, and Tanoji, a geisha of mysterious parentage, as well as on the romance between Moriyama, Sanji's friend, and Kaodori, another courtesan, the plot develops through a complex arabesque of hidden identities, forbidden liaisons, and suspense.

In narrating this tale Shōyō uses some realistic description, including detailed scenes from contemporary student life, and he introduces new narrative techniques such as flashbacks and summarization as well as dialogue filled with intellectual tangents. It also includes a hint of autobiography, another nod to realism, because at the time he was writing *The Character of Modern Students* Shōyō had fallen in love with his future wife, Sen, a low-ranking courtesan who was six years younger than he and whom he had met in the pleasure quarters. In a few respects this novel served to illustrate some of the ideas Shōyō had set forth in *The Essence of the Novel,* but it offered only slightly more novelty than traditional ge-saku, and it was quickly eclipsed the next year by the more provocative colloquial narrative in Futabatei Shimei's *Ukigumo* (Drifting Clouds). Yet *The Character of Modern Students* was well enough received by readers to establish Shōyō as a nov-elist.

The relative success of this first novel and the attention he garnered from young writers for *The Essence of the Novel* sparked a prolific outpour-ing from Shōyō during the next three years. *Imo-tose kagami* (A Mirror of Marriage, 1885–1886) demonstrated his improving skill at characteriza-tion. Shōyō also published two lesser works of fiction, *Mirai no yume* (Dream of the Future, 1886) and *Kyō waranbe* (Children of the Capital, 1886).

In addition to these works Shōyō published many articles in newspapers and literary journals to elucidate his narrative theories. He also wrote on drama, on aesthetics and on theater reform, and he became acquainted with Aeba Kōson, Sa-ganoya Omuro, and Futabatei Shimei—the last with whom he formed a particularly close friend-ship. In the midst of his frenetic writing Shōyō also married Sen in October 1886. The two had already known each other for more than three years, and they remained together until Shōyō's death. The couple had no children, but they raised two foster daughters and cared for two of Shōyō's nephews.

In 1887 Shōyō lectured on aesthetics and republished, in *Kōsai no joō,* a translation of Grace and Phillip Watson's *The Queen of Society.* Focus-ing his writing on topics such as the future of narrative and standards of criticism, Shōyō con-tinued to contribute essays to newspapers and journals, and his frequent contributions garnered him a visiting position as a writer for the *Yomiuri Shinbun.* He also published *Karen jō* (Beautiful Daughter, 1887), a work that he adapted in translation from an unknown author, but Shōyō began to suffer headaches and other neural problems from overexertion. He took a therapeu-tic trip to Kansai during the summer and subse-quently resigned from some of his part-time En-glish-teaching positions.

He took another trip to Kansai the follow-ing year when he continued to suffer with his ill-ness, and he still managed to publish a series of articles on theory, drama, and humor, as well as two more novels experimenting with the *shasei* (sketch) style currently in vogue: the incomplete "Gaimu daijin" (Minister of Foreign Affairs,

1888) and his better-known novel, *Saikun* (Wife, 1889). Both of these works emphasize the role of *ninjō* (human feelings) in society; the latter, in particular, has been regarded as Shōyō's finest novel.

Wife is the tragic tale of Otane, an unhap-pily married upper-class woman who is forced to pawn her kimonos to supply money to her step-mother, and of Osono, Otane's apprentice maid who is apprehended when the money is stolen and who commits suicide. Otane eventually leaves her husband, who then marries his French mistress. As in *The Character of Modern Students,* certain features of the plot appear to be appropri-ated straight from gesaku, but the novel presents several contemporary women whose points of view provide much of the narrative. *Wife* is di-vided into four chapters, each of which blends classical and colloquial narrative styles, as though Shōyō were experimenting with new forms of written language. In addition, the novel reveals the hearts and minds of the characters and thereby lets these characters tell their own tales. It also avoids melodrama and limits the focus in a way that holds the attention of the reader with-out relying on traditional plot complexities or twists of fate.

Written just four years after *The Character of Modern Students,* this novel reflects Shōyō's growth as a writer. As Marleigh Grayer Ryan notes, it was one of the best novels of the 1880s and "should have received considerable critical attention." However, it was published in an issue of *Kokumin no Tomo* (The People's Friend) that contained a provocative seminude illustration for a new story by Yamada Bimyō. Public and criti-cal attention zoomed in on this illustration, and *Wife* went relatively unnoticed. Considering Shōyō's sympathetic treatment of women in his novel, this is both ironic and unfortunate.

Shortly after the publication of *Wife,* Shōyō wrote in his diary, "From today I will no longer write novels to sell." Writing fiction for profit was uncomfortable for him, as he had been raised during a time when writing fiction was not a respectable profession. In addition to this stigma, Shōyō may also have been intimidated by the success and talent of his friend Futabatei, whose novels had garnered much more attention and praise than had his own. For whatever rea-sons, Shōyō's novel writing ended in 1889. Al-though he wrote thousands of pages during the rest of his life and some of the techniques he had used in *Wife* (especially in his efforts to portray the emotions of his characters) became conventions for modern Japanese fiction, he never again attempted to write a novel.

During the next three years Shōyō immersed himself in translating the works of Emile Zola and William Makepeace Thackeray, writing critical articles for the *Yomiuri Shinbun* and other periodicals, and settling into a new home. He also tried writing drama and assisted in establishing a department of literature at Waseda University. In 1891 Shōyō published *Harunoya manpitsu* (Random Notes from Harunoya) and contributed "Sheekusupiya kyakuhon hyōchū chogen" (Preface and Commentary on Shakespeare Texts), an important essay on the manifestations of ninjō in Shakespeare, in the inaugural issue of the literary journal *Waseda Bungaku*.

Soon after, in another journal, *Shigarami Zōshi*, Mori Ōgai wrote an essay that criticized the attitude that writers in *Waseda Bungaku* had taken toward realism, and Shōyō immediately retaliated with a series of rebuttals that generated a debate between the two men. This debate, which centered on the term *risō* (ideal), was more an explication of two divergent definitions than a true debate. Shōyō argued against the tradition of idealism, while Ōgai proposed the philosophical notion of Platonic ideals. Never finding a common ground, the debate eventually subsided in mid 1892, after which Shōyō published *Shōyō mangen* (Digressions of a Lamb, 1893), an essay collection in which the title characterizes him as a lamb, and then devoted his attention to writing about Shakespeare and Elizabethan drama.

Later that year Shōyō traveled with his wife to Nagoya to worship at their ancestral graves. While visiting their family, they agreed to adopt Shikō, Shōyō's nephew, as heir. Shōyō's writings began to examine the traditional historical dramas of Japan, and the following year his interests shifted from fiction toward drama and musical theater. He directed an outdoor performance by his students at Waseda, lectured on Shakespeare to the Chikamatsu Study Group, and, in *Waseda Bungaku*, published the scripts of two historical dramas that he intended to be used for elocution practice. These scripts were subsequently revised and published as *Kiri hitoha* (Catalpa Leaf, 1896) and *Maki no kata* (The Lady Maki, 1897). The former, a sequel to his earlier drama *Hototogisu kojō no rakugetsu* (Moonset at Mockingbird Castle, 1897), is a tragedy about the fall of Osaka Castle. *The Lady Maki,* also a tragedy, is set in the early Kamakura period and became the first part of a dramatic trilogy that Shōyō completed nearly two decades later with *Nagori no hoshizukiyo*

(Reluctant Departure on a Starlit Night, 1918) and *Yoshitoki no saigo* (Yoshitoki's Farewell, 1918).

Shōyō spent the rest of the 1890s working on new books and plays, including *Bungaku sono oriori* (Occasional Literary Pieces, 1896), *Rien no ochiba* (Footlight Gleanings, 1896), the plays *Moonset at Mockingbird Castle* and *Kiku to kiri* (Chrysanthemum and Catalpa, 1898), as well as *Futagokoro* (1897), an adapted translation of Sir John Vanbrugh's *The False Friend* (1702). To pursue his interest in the aesthetics of Kabuki dance, he constructed a stage in his house and encouraged his nephews and adopted daughters to study dance. Between 1897 and 1900 he entered into another debate, this time in the journal *Taiyō* with writer Takayama Chogyū, concerning the use of history in drama. Chogyū argued for a freehanded approach, while Shōyō, emphasizing realism, expounded on the aesthetic beauty of history.

In 1896 Shōyō was appointed head teacher at the newly founded Waseda Middle School, and in 1899 he was awarded the rank of Doctor of Letters. Shortly thereafter he became principal of the school, and in this new role he traveled extensively throughout northern and central Japan. During the first three years of his tenure he published two eight-volume anthologies of literary readings for young students, a history of British literature, a study of British poetry, and a monograph on literature and education. He also published a work on public morality and gave a series of ten lectures on Shakespeare's *King Lear* at the Japan Women's University. Through this wide-ranging program of writing Shōyō articulated his beliefs that the values of a culture are rooted in the literary arts and that moral education should include works of literature and drama.

The stress of his work and his grief at the death of writer Ozaki Kōyō soon overcame Shōyō, who collapsed and, citing health reasons, resigned from his post as principal in December 1903. He and his wife also suffered a loss when Toshio, Shōyō's nephew, died in the Russo-Japanese War. After a period of recuperation Shōyō again turned his attention to drama, as he attended the performance of his *Catalpa Leaf* at the Tokyo-za Theater in February 1904. He also published *Shin gakugeki ron* (A New Approach to Musical Drama, 1904), a work that introduced some of Richard Wagner's philosophy of opera to Japan. Through adapting the Japanese legend of Urashima Tarō as *Shinkyoku Urashima* (The New Urashima Tarō, 1904) and another popular legend as *Shinkyoku Kaguyahime* (A New Kaguyahime, 1905), he demonstrated his growing belief, derived from his study of Shakespeare and Wagner, that the greatest source of material for Japanese drama was to be found in various forms of traditional Japanese narrative—including legends, folk tales, and children's stories. *The New Urashima Tarō,* which is seen as his most successful dramatic work, reflects Wagner's eclectic approach to opera, as Shōyō's adaptation includes classical Japanese music and drama as well as folk songs, ballads, and Western music.

In 1905 Shōyō published two books and two plays, and helped establish two scholarly societies: one, the Ekifūkai, was organized to study folk melodies, and the other, Bungei Kyōkai (the Literary Association), was dedicated to promoting new literary movements. The latter, which he chaired, frequently met at his house. In 1906 he published a five-volume textbook series on morality as well as *Tokoyami* (Eternal Darkness), a new drama, and started translating Shakespeare's *The Merchant of Venice* (1600). At the first exhibition of the Literary Association held at the Kabuki-za Theater in November, Shōyō presented excerpts from *Catalpa Leaf, Eternal Darkness,* and *The Merchant of Venice.*

During the next two years Shōyō published critical articles on theater, morality, and literature as well as several new works for the stage and another ten-volume student reader. On the twenty-fifth anniversary of the founding of Waseda University, in 1907, Shōyō was awarded a lifelong annuity. In 1909 he introduced the plays of Henrik Ibsen to Japan, both by having *A Doll's House* (1879) performed at the second exhibition of the Literary Association and by publishing a bibliographical article and an essay comparing the Norwegian dramatist with Chikamatsu Monzaemon and Shakespeare. After nearly a quarter of a century Shōyō published the second of what later became his complete Shakespeare translations, *Hamuretto* (The Tragedy of Hamlet, Prince of Denmark, 1909). For the next thirteen years he published translations of roughly one or two Shakespeare plays per year.

In 1910, influenced by his study of Ibsen's female protagonists and the great success of the Literary Association production of *A Doll's House,* Shōyō gave a series of lectures in Tokyo, Kobe, Osaka, and Kyoto on the "new women" of modern drama. These lectures were later published in various periodicals and were finally collected in *Iwayuru atarashii onna* (The So-called New Women, 1912), a collection that reflects Shōyō's

awareness of changing attitudes and behaviors—particularly a growing desire for independence—among Japanese women. His lecture series and publications initiated public discussion about the role of women in modern Japan, and although Shōyō did not participate in these subsequent discussions, he is credited with having raised the topic.

In 1911 Shōyō and his wife moved into a new house, and in 1912 they built a villa in Atami, where he often retreated to complete his writings. His translation of *Hamlet* appeared on stage in Tokyo in June 1911, and the following year the Literary Association produced a version of Hermann Sudermann's *Heimat* (1893; translated as *Magda,* 1895) that was also taken on the road to Osaka and Nagoya. The Nagoya performances were canceled because of the death of Emperor Meiji, but the trip allowed Shōyō to visit his birthplace for the first time in forty years. Later that year a scandal erupted over an affair between Shimamura Hōgetsu, a prominent member of the Literary Association, and Matsui Sumako, who became known as Japan's first modern actress following her performance as Nora in *A Doll's House.* Shōyō resigned as a member of the Literary Association after the scandal, and the organization disbanded the following year. Despite the short existence of the association, its members became some of Japan's premier playwrights.

Shōyō completed the draft of *En no gyōja* (En the Ascetic, 1917), one of his most notable plays, in late 1912, and as he expanded his interests in Ibsen and modern drama he translated two plays by Bernard Shaw in 1913: *Wōren fujin no shokugyō* (Mrs. Warren's Profession) and *Buki to hito* (Arms and the Man). When Shōyō became ill again, he spent much of early 1914 in Atami, where he recuperated under the care of his wife. Feeling better in March, he accepted a position to oversee the publication of a multivolume series on world history for Waseda University Press, and he spent April traveling with his wife in Shikoku.

In 1915 he returned to his Shakespeare translations, as he published *Manatsu no yoru no yume* (A Midsummer Night's Dream), *Antonii to Kureopatora* (Anthony and Cleopatra), and *Tempesuto* (The Tempest), along with several works of his own. Through the next three years he published his biographical dramas *En the Ascetic* and *Yoshitoki no saigo* (Yoshitoki's Farewell, the third work of his Kamakura trilogy) in addition to *Kyōka to engeki,* a history of recent Japanese drama. His Shakespeare translations during these years include *Macbeth, Measure for Measure, A Winter's Tale,* and *Richard the Third.* In June 1918 Shōyō was offered the position of president of Waseda University, but he declined; the bulk of his translations of Shakespeare's works into Japanese had yet to be completed, and Shōyō's enthusiasm for drama was unwavering.

In late May 1919 his heir, Shikō, caused a romantic scandal, and Shōyō and his wife therefore sent him back to his family. During the next two years Shōyō's writing focused on drama, particularly Kabuki, and he translated the first and second parts of *Henry IV, The Taming of the Shrew,* and *As You Like It.* He also tried his hand at writing *waka.* In 1921 his interests turned to open-air theater, children's stories, and plays, and during the next four years he wrote numerous essays on children's drama and compiled a textbook and a three-part collection of children's plays. He also produced an outdoor pageant in Atami and assisted in the production of his revised *Urashima* in Osaka, in addition to translating *Twelfth Night, Coriolanus,* and *Cymbeline.*

In early 1925 Shōyō developed pneumonia, and for a while he was in critical condition. This illness gave him a chance to consider his life work and decide that he wished to translate all of Shakespeare's works. After he recovered Shōyō spent part of the year sorting through his old manuscripts and, the following July, published his own complete works in *Shōyō senshū,* a fifteen-volume collection, in 1926–1927. He channeled all royalties from the sale of this collection into a fund supporting children's theater in Kansai. Shōyō devoted summer 1925 to translating Shakespeare's works, and he also wrote a memoir, *Kaioku mandan* (Random Memories, 1925–1926), that was published serially in *Waseda Bungaku.*

In January 1926 he published an article in *Shin Shōsetsu* announcing his resolution to refrain from writing original works, forewords, and journal articles in order to focus all his energies on completing the translations of Shakespeare's works. In a concentrated burst of energy he published translations of seven Shakespeare plays between February and December 1926; six plays and half of the poems in 1927; and four plays, the remaining poems, and a guide to Shakespeare in 1928. At the age of seventy Shōyō finally completed his monumental, one-man translation of the entire works of Shakespeare into Japanese.

He gave his last formal Shakespeare lecture, on *King Lear,* in December 1927, and after completing his great translation effort he donated all his Tokyo property to Waseda University. For his efforts he was invited to attend the Imperial Accession Ceremonies, but he politely declined. In Shōyō's honor Waseda University erected a museum patterned after Shakespeare's Fortune Theater and named it the Tsubouchi Memorial Theater Museum.

The pressure of translating the works of Shakespeare now past, Shōyō returned to writing his own works for the stage, and two of these, *Ryōkan* (Ryōkan) and *Datennyo* (Fallen Angel), were produced during 1929. Commendations continued. In 1930 he was awarded the Asahi Prize and was made honorary chairman of the Japanese Shakespeare Association. In 1930 three of his children's dramas appeared on stage; *Moonset at Mockingbird Castle* was produced as a sound recording; and Shōyō gave his remaining property in Atami to the Society for the Promotion of National Drama. The following year he also donated his retirement honorarium to the same society.

Between 1932 and 1934 Shōyō continued to write drama and revise his earlier work. His new plays included *Kaki no heta* (Persimmon Stem, 1933) and *Anan to Kishimo* (Ananda and Harsiti, 1934). In 1933 Chūō Kōronsha published his revised Shakespeare translations in a forty-volume set, and at a commemoration ceremony for the Theater Museum he presented selections from Shakespeare on a radio broadcast.

In June 1934 Shōyō once again developed pneumonia and was confined to bed. His condition grew worse through the rest of the year, and in early February 1935 Shōyō realized that he would not recover and began to put his affairs in order. He became increasingly despondent and once tried to take an overdose of sleeping pills before he died on the last day of February. After a funeral in Atami his remains were placed in the Kaizōji Temple at Atami.

Three months after Shōyō's death the final volumes of his revised translations of Shakespeare were published, a fitting memorial to a man whose life was devoted to the reformation of Japanese literature. His voice was one of the earliest to articulate specific directions for Japanese narrative, and his observations helped guide several generations of writers. Through warm and enthusiastic encouragement he also spurred writers such as Futabatei and Yamada Bimyō to experiment with new narrative forms, on which the birth of the modern Japanese novel depended. Furthermore, as an outspoken proponent of reform, he willingly entered into public debates that helped define and articulate crucial literary issues. As an educator, he championed the belief that narrative and drama were vital components of moral education, and his anthologies encouraged an entire generation of students to take literature seriously. Finally, through his prolific writing and translating he awakened others to the broader spectrum of possibilities for literary and dramatic arts.

Bibliographies:

"Bessatsu," in *Shōyō senshū,* volume 3 (Tokyo: Shun'yōdō, 1926–1927);

Inagaki Tatsurō, *Tsubouchi Shōyō shū,* volume 16 (Tokyo: Chikuma Shobō, 1969).

Biography:

Kawatake Shigetoshi and Yanagida Izumi, *Tsubouchi Shōyō* (Tokyo: Fuzanbō, 1939).

References:

Karatani Kōjin, *Origins of Modern Japanese Literature,* translated by Brett de Bary (Durham, N.C. & London: Duke University Press, 1993);

Peter F. Kornicki, *The Reform of Fiction in Meiji Japan* (London: Ithaca Press, 1982);

Nakamura Toshiko, "Ibsen in Japan: Tsubouchi Shōyō and His Lecture on New Women," *Scandinavian Journal of Literary Research (Edda),* 5 (1982): 261–272;

Marleigh Grayer Ryan, *Japan's First Modern Novel: "Ukigumo" of Futabatei Shimei* (New York: Columbia University Press, 1965);

Ryan, *The Development of Realism in the Fiction of Tsubouchi Shōyō* (Seattle: University of Washington Press, 1975);

Tsubouchi Kyōkai, ed., *Tsubouchi Shōyō jiten* (Tokyo: Heibonsha, 1986);

Yanagida Izumi, "Tsubouchi Shōyō," *Japan Quarterly,* 11 (1964): 352–360.

Papers:

Most of Shōyō's manuscripts and papers are located in the Tsubouchi Shōyō Memorial Theater Museum on the campus of Waseda University, Tokyo.

Uno Chiyo

(28 November 1897 – 10 June 1996)

Rebecca L. Copeland
Washington University in Saint Louis

BOOKS: *Shifun no kao* (Tokyo: Kaizōsha, 1923);
Kōfuku (Tokyo: Kinseidō, 1924);
Shiroi ie to tsumi (Tokyo: Shinchōsha, 1925);
Banshō (Tokyo: Bungei Nihonsha, 1925);
Nihon shōsetsu shū, 6 volumes (Tokyo: Shinchōsha, 1925–1930);
Shinsen Uno Chiyo shū (Tokyo: Kaizōsha, 1929);
Keshi wa naze akai (Tokyo: Chūō Kōronsha, 1930);
Otona no ehon (Tokyo: Shiromizusha, 1931);
Operakan sakuraza (Tokyo: Kaizōsha, 1934);
Irozange (Tokyo: Chūō Kōronsha, 1935); translated by Phyllis Birnbaum as *Confessions of Love* (Honolulu: University of Hawaii Press, 1989; London: Peter Owen, 1990; Tokyo: Tuttle, 1990);
Aibiki (Tokyo: Shin'yōsha, 1936);
Wakare mo tanoshi (Tokyo: Daichi Shobō, 1936);
Ren'ai tokuhon (Tokyo: Chūō Kōronsha, 1937);
Hito no otoko (Tokyo: Hangasō, 1937);
Tsukiyo (Tokyo: Chūō Kōronsha, 1938);
Koi no tegami (Tokyo: Chūō Kōronsha, 1939);
Onna no aijō (Tokyo: Masu Shobō, 1940);
Aru kyakuma de no monogatari (Tokyo: Sutairusha Shuppanbu, 1941);
Tsuma no tegami (Tokyo: Kōchō Shorin, 1942);
Ningyōshi Tenguya Kyūkichi (Tokyo: Buntaisha, 1943); republished as *Ningyōshi Tenguya Hisakichi* (Tokyo: Shūeisha Bunko, 1978); translated by Rebecca Copeland as "The Puppet Maker," in her *The Sound of the Wind: The Life and Works of Uno Chiyo* (Honolulu: University of Hawaii Press, 1992), pp. 105–137;
Nichiro no tatakai kikigaki (Tokyo: Buntaisha, 1943);
Onna no aijō (Tokyo: Kobarutosha, 1946);
Wakare mo tanoshi (Tokyo: Minpūsha, 1946);
Watashi no seishun monogatari (Tokyo: Kanchōsha, 1947);
Gendai bungaku daihyō senshū (Tokyo: Banrikaku, 1949);

Uno Chiyo in 1932

Gendai Nihon shōsetsu taikei (Tokyo: Kawade Shobō, 1950);
Watashi no okeshō jinsei shi (Tokyo: Chūō Kōronsha, 1955);
Uno Chiyo kimono tokuhon (Tokyo: Nagashima Shobō, 1957); republished as *Kimono tokuhon* (Tokyo: Dabuiddosha, 1958);
Ohan (Tokyo: Chūō Kōronsha, 1957); translated as "Ohan" by Donald Keene in his *The Old*

248

Woman, The Wife, and The Archer, Three Modern Japanese Short Novels (New York: Viking, 1961; London: Constable, 1962), pp. 51–118;

Onna no nikki (Tokyo: Kōdansha, 1960);

Sasu (Tokyo: Shinchōsha, 1966); translated by Kyoko Iriye Selden as "To Stab," in *Stories by Contemporary Japanese Women Writers,* edited by Noriko Mizuta Lippit and Kyoko Iriye Selden (New York: M.E. Sharpe, 1982), pp. 92–104;

Kaze no oto (Tokyo: Chūō Kōronsha, 1969); translated by Copeland as "The Sound of the Wind," in her *The Sound of the Wind: The Life and Works of Uno Chiyo,* pp. 138–207;

Teiketsu: Uno Chiyo tanpen shōsetsu shū (Tokyo: Kōdansha, 1970);

Shitashii nakama: Uno Chiyo zuihitsu shū, 3 volumes (Tokyo: Kōdansha, 1970);

Tempū sensei zadan (Tokyo: Futami Shobō, 1970);

Aru hitori no onna no hanashi (Tokyo: Bungei Shunjū, 1972); translated by Rebecca Copeland as *The Story of a Single Woman* (London: Peter Owen, 1992);

Watakushi no bungakuteki kaisōki (Tokyo: Chūō Kōronsha, 1972);

Kōfuku (Tokyo: Bungei Shunjū, 1972);

Ame no oto (Tokyo: Bungei Shunjū, 1974);

Koi wa tanoshii ka (Tokyo: Yamato Shobō, 1974);

Gendai no joryū bungaku (Tokyo: Mainichi Shinbunsha, 1974);

Usuzumi no sakura (Tokyo: Shinchōsha, 1975);

Yaeyama no yuki (Tokyo: Bungei Shunjū, 1975);

Ōfuku shokan, by Uno and Nakazato Tsuneko (Tokyo: Bungei Shunjū, 1976);

Mama no hanashi (Tokyo: Chūō Kōronsha, 1976);

Suisei shoin no musume (Tokyo: Chūō Kōronsha, 1977);

Aru nikki (Tokyo: Shūeisha, 1978);

Nokotte iru hanashi (Tokyo: Shūeisha, 1980);

Kōfuku jinsei masshigura (Tokyo: Chūkō Bunko, 1980);

Akutokumo mata (Tokyo: Shinchōsha, 1981);

Rikonjutsu: sayonara "shinda kekkon" (Tokyo: Kawade Shobō Shinsha, 1981);

Kōfuku wo shiru sainō (Tokyo: Kairyūsha, 1982);

Zoku kōfuku wo shiru sainō (Tokyo: Kairyūsha, 1983);

Ikite yuku watakushi, 2 volumes (Tokyo: Mainichi Shinbunsha, 1983);

Aoyama Jirō no hanashi (Tokyo: Chūkō Bunko, 1983);

Hana (Tokyo: Sakuhinsha, 1983);

Jidenteki ren'ai ron (Tokyo: Daiwa Shobō, 1983);

Aru otoko no danmen (Tokyo: Kōdansha, 1984);

Aru toki totsuzen (Tokyo: Chūkō Bunko, 1984);

Shiawase no tsukurikata (Tokyo: Shōgakkan, 1984);

Watashi wa itsudemo isogashii (Tokyo: Chūkō Bunko, 1984);

Watashi no otogibanashi (Tokyo: Chūō Kōronsha, 1985);

Watakushi wa kōfuku, mukashi mo ima mo kore kara mo: jinsei taidan (Tokyo: Kairyūsha, 1985);

Watashi no tsukutta osōzai (Tokyo: Kairyūsha, 1986);

Shiawase na hanashi (Tokyo: Chūō Kōronsha, 1987);

Shiawase wo motomete ikiru: watashi no jinsei arubamu (Tokyo: Kairyūsha, 1987);

Kōfuku wa kōfuku wo yobu (Tokyo: Kosaidō Shuppan, 1987);

Kōdō suru koto ga ikiru koto de aru: ikikata ni tsuite no 343 no chie (Tokyo: Kairyūsha, 1988);

Ippen ni haru kaze ga fuite kita (Tokyo: Chūō Kōronsha, 1989);

Uno Chiyo furisode-zakura chotto jiden (Tokyo: Magajin Hausu, 1989);

Ikite iku ganbō (Tokyo: Shūeisha, 1989);

Watakushi no shiawase jinsei (Tokyo: Mainichi Shinbunsha, 1990);

Fudangi no ikite yuku watashi (Tokyo: Shūeisha, 1990);

Ren'ai sahō ai ni tsuite no 448 no danshō (Tokyo: Kairyūsha, 1991);

Ikiru kōfuku oiru kōfuku (Tokyo: Kairyūsha, 1992);

Watashi wa yume wo miru no ga jōzu (Tokyo: Chūō Kōronsha, 1992);

Kōfuku ni ikiru chie (Tokyo: Kōdansha, 1993);

Watakushi no kōfukuron: Uno Chiyo jinsei zadan (Tokyo: Kairyūsha, 1993).

Collections: *Junsui shōsetsu zenshū* (Tokyo: Yūkōsha, 1937);

Uno Chiyo zenshū, 12 volumes (Tokyo: Chūō Kōronsha, 1977–1978).

Uno Chiyo's career spanned four imperial eras, more than seventy years. Celebrated in her youth as a daring Jezebel, she came to be recognized in her later years for the skillful crafting and evocative depth of her narratives. Her stories ultimately reveal the "vulnerable strength" of women who have come to recognize the wonder of their own passions and desires. In this regard her work has been linked by critics with the sensual lyricism of Ono no Komachi, Izumi Shikibu, and earlier writers in the female literary tradition of Japan.

Uno Chiyo was born in Iwakuni, then a sleepy castle town on the Inland Sea. Her mother died when Uno was two, and her father, the

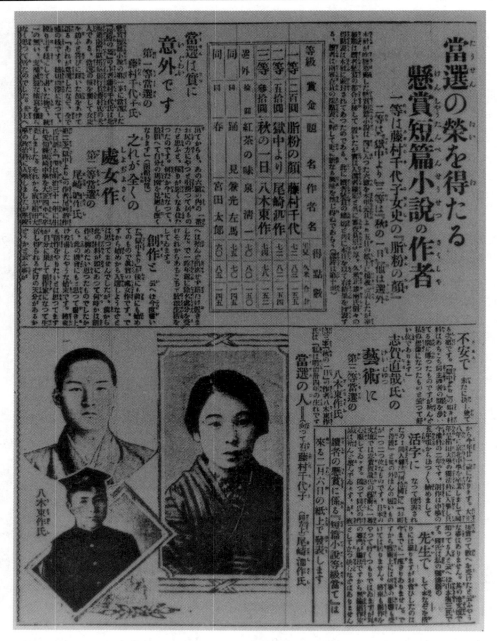

Announcement in the 21 January 1921 issue of Jiji Shimpō *that Fujimura Chiyoko (Uno Chiyo)
won first prize in its annual short-story contest*

ne'er-do-well second son of a wealthy sake brewer, was so profligate that Uno and her five stepsiblings were raised in near poverty and in constant fear of their father's explosive temper. But her stepmother, a paragon of female servitude, favored Uno among her many siblings and instilled in her a sense of self-importance.

Uno's father died of tuberculosis when she was sixteen, and just prior to his death he had tried to secure her future by marrying her to her maternal cousin, but she refused to submit to the arrangement. Her father's death freed her from his tyranny but not from her almost obsessive need for his recognition and affection, a need that surely underlies the unsuccessful relationships that both she and her fictional women characters had with men.

Left in financial straits by the death of Uno's father, her stepmother went to work at a spinning factory. Uno took a position as a teacher's assistant, but she was soon released when it was discovered that she was having an affair with a colleague. Intent on becoming a "significant woman," Uno left her hometown and eventually made her way to Tokyo, where a stint as a café waitress brought her into contact with the influential editor of the *Chūō Kōron* journal and with fashionable young writers: Akutagawa Ryūnosuke, Satō Haruō, and Kume Masao. Soon afterward she left Tokyo for Hokkaidō, where she married a different maternal cousin from the one with whom her father had tried to arrange her future.

Uno called her sojourn in Hokkaidō the only time she lived the life of a "normal woman," but she could not abide normalcy. She began to write to occupy her time, and when her "Shifun no kao" (Painted face) won first prize in a short-story contest in 1921, Uno found her ticket out of Hokkaidō. She busily set to work on another, even longer work and sent it optimistically to *Chūō Kōron*. Shortly thereafter she left for Tokyo and, upon learning that her "Haka wo abaku" (Opening the Grave, 1922) had been published, she pledged to remain in Tokyo, where she could continue writing.

She seems to have intended to return to her husband eventually, but months passed and soon Uno was involved with Ozaki Shirō, a young writer. Tired of waiting for her unlikely return, Uno's husband divorced her in 1924, and she then married Ozaki. The two moved to a small hamlet on the outskirts of Tokyo, where they counted among their neighbors the writer Kawabata Yasunari and the poet Hagiwara Sakutarō. Soon thereafter jazz music, dancing, and Marxism infiltrated the sleepy hamlet. Uno bobbed her hair and put away her kimonos for Western dresses.

Her beauty and her propensity for sensationalism attracted attention, and, as she published frequently and widely, she became a writer in demand. Many of her stories from this period describe country waifs who search for fame and fortune in Tokyo only to have their dreams scuttled by indigent brothers or lovers whose desperate situations demand female self-sacrifice. By the late 1920s her works became more personal than these stories, as she began to relate the frustrations and uncertainties of a woman whose successful career overshadows her husband's. Ozaki, whose career was floundering at this time, described a marriage between two writers as tantamount to having a thief and a detective living in the same house. He was jealous of Uno's literary

Cover for the 1 January 1937 issue of Sutairu *(Style), the first Japanese fashion magazine, which Uno edited*

success, her carefree energy, and her lovers whom she was reputed to have. Unable to endure the tension, he divorced Uno in 1929.

Following this divorce Uno vowed to live alone, but she was soon involved with the Western-style artist Tōgō Seiji, whose attempted love-suicide had rocked Tokyo in 1930. Her tempestuous five-year relationship with him inspired what many consider to be her first literary success: *Irozange* (1935; translated as *Confessions of Love*, 1989). Having been a writer whose works heretofore had delineated the subtle nuances of her own relationships, Uno was surprisingly successful in this novel-length work, for it is not about her at all. Instead, it recounts the series of affairs that a self-centered male painter enjoys before finally making a failed love-suicide attempt. Told by a first-person male narrator, the story is so closely based on Tōgō's experiences that Uno credited the success of the work to Tōgō's skill as a narrator, but later critics have suggested that the work's greatest achievements are in Uno's ability to delineate so artlessly the sexual malaise of the times and to capture so thoroughly the self-consciousness of the male narrator. The work

Uno with her third husband, Kitahara Takeo, on their wedding day, 1 April 1939

was heralded as the finest romance written in the prewar period, and Uno Chiyo earned distinction as "a writer of illicit love."

Japan was about to enter the Pacific War when *Confessions of Love* was published, and, because love stories such as this were soon in disfavor with the militaristic government, Uno had to curb her tastes. Her next important work, *Ningyōshi Tenguya Kyūkichi* (The Puppet Maker Tenguya Kyūkichi, 1943; translated as "The Puppet Maker," 1992), although also based on the stories told to her by another male narrator, is decidedly more subdued. Framed around a monthlong interview with a master Bunraku puppet carver, the story is more a rumination on life and art—or on life as art—than it is a cohesive narrative. Told in the rustic dialect of Shikoku, the island home of the puppet maker, the work is quietly poignant, at times mournful. But the tale is also imbued with a gentle humor, as Kyūkichi reveals his secrets for a life well lived.

Kyūkichi's tireless dedication to an art that was destined to perish was something of a revelation for Uno, an exuberant woman writer who could hardly stay in one house or with one man for more than a few years. She became determined that she would devote herself similarly to her art, and this determination culminated in *Ohan* (1957; translated, 1962), which many consider to be her masterpiece.

This novella-length work of barely one hundred pages took Uno more than ten years to write, although she had been involved in other projects. She had married again in 1939, and her new husband, writer Kitahara Takeo, persuaded Uno to launch the journal *Buntai* (Literary Style). Just prior to this marriage Uno had embarked on the publication of *Sutairu* (Style), which was the first woman's fashion magazine in Japan. She and Kitahara also had opened a boutique bearing the same name and featuring kimonos that Uno designed. That her literary work slowed is therefore understandable. Yet by diverting her frenetic energies in various directions, Uno was able to focus on her writing more intensely as works of art than as sources of income.

Ohan is meticulously crafted. Borrowing from *Confessions of Love* the strategy of a male narrator who "confesses" to an unseen interlocutor and incorporating the old-fashioned flavor and melancholy mood of *The Puppet Maker Tenguya Kyūkichi*, Uno creates a storybook world of yesteryear. Critics in a publishing marketplace dominated by self-referential works were quick to appreciate Uno's foray into more creative fiction. *Ohan* earned her the Noma Prize for Literature in 1958 and the Japanese Women Writer's Award in 1959.

Narrated by an irresolute, effeminate man who is caught between his love for his gentle, sacrificing wife and his need for his brash, domineering geisha, the plot of *Ohan* is familiar, even hackneyed. The story has been enacted timelessly on the puppet stage. But Uno deftly delves into the psychology of her narrator and at the same time uses him as a path to explore the unvoiced psyches of the wife and the geisha, both of whom are presented with poignancy and humor. In her essays Uno called *Ohan* an "autobiography," a metaphorical portrayal of her own rootlessness, her uneasiness with the contradictory and essentialist roles that women have been made to play.

She explored similar female roles in *Kaze no oto* (1969; translated as "The Sound of the Wind," 1992), a story she claimed to have based on the life of her father. *The Sound of the Wind* again presents a man caught between two disparate female characters, but the story lacks the lyrical simplicity of *Ohan* and presents the dark despair of women forced to conform to feudal ideals more prominently than does that earlier work.

Uno continued to examine the binary roles of the wife and the mistress–proper woman as well as the roles of social misfits in later fiction such as *Usuzumi no sakura* (The Ink-Wash Cherry Tree, serialized in *Shinchō*, 1971–1974; published in book form, 1975) and *Suisei shoin no musume* (The Daughter of Westshore Hall, serialized, 1976; published in book form, 1977). Yet she also dealt with these roles in autobiographical fiction, where she presents herself as a winsome coquette who is nevertheless expected to numb herself into asexuality once she has married. Her stories describe the tension, frustration, and vulnerability of a woman who wants the security and social acceptability of marriage but who cannot abide the loss of self that it engenders. More often than not, therefore, Uno's autobiographical works were inspired by separations and divorces. In fact, all of her divorces influenced her fiction so forcefully that Uno quipped, "No one is as fortunate as a woman writer. No sooner does she break up with a man than she can write about it all without the slightest sense of shame."

Uno wrote about her relationship with Ozaki in "Tanjōbi" (Birthday) and "Shitsuraku no uta" (Song of Lost Happiness), both written in 1929. When she and Tōgō separated, she wrote "Wakare mo tanoshi" (Parting Pleasure, 1935) and "Miren" (Lingering Attachment, 1936), and, after her twenty-five-year marriage to Kitahara ended in divorce, Uno wrote a spate of personal narratives. Most of these–such as *Sasu* (To Sting, 1966; translated in part as "To Stab," 1982), "Kono oshiroi ire" (1967; translated as *This Powder Box*, 1992), "Kōfuku" (1970; translated as *Happiness*, 1982), *Aru hitori no onna no hanashi* (1972; translated as *The Story of a Single Woman*, 1992), and *Ame no oto* (*The Sound of the Rain*, 1974)–concern her marriage to Kitahara, but others look back to her earlier relationships with Tōgō, Ozaki, her first husband, and even her father, as if Uno were trying to comprehend the directions her life had taken. As personal as these stories are, they have been admired by critics for their "objectivity" and for the willingness of their implied author to assume responsibility for her own fate.

To Sting, a novella-length work in five parts

Title page for the translation of Irozange *(1935), a narrative that brought Uno renown as a prewar "writer of illicit love"*

(the third of which is translated), recounts the collapse of the narrator's magazine enterprise, which parallels the collapse of her marriage and brings her to realize that her youth and sexuality are lost. The strength of the story lies in its delineation of the narrator's growing self-awareness and her struggle to accept a life beyond sexual desirability. By the conclusion the narrator has convinced herself that she is happy to let her husband go: knowing that he will not come back, she busily, almost gaily, helps him pack and then sends him out the door.

"Happiness" continues the narrator's resolve to see her life in a positive light. No matter what disappointments she may have met, she is determined to participate actively, even aggressively, in life. Both this work and *To Sting* were written while Uno was involved in the Tempū Society, a therapy group run by a prominent doctor and psychologist whose holistic approach to both

Uno with the puppet head that Tenguya Kyūkichi carved for her in 1943, at the time of her
Ningyōshi Tenguya Kyūkichi *(The Puppet Maker Tenguya Kyūkichi)*

mental and physical health emphasized the benefits of positive thinking. The influence of this society can be seen in the narrator's insistence on viewing even her lowest moments in a "happy" light. Uno's story approaches self-satire as its third-person narrator looks back over her life of mishap and adventure—and concludes that it was a life well-lived. The gentle self-mockery, tempered nevertheless by an undercurrent of melancholy, earned this work high critical acclaim, and Uno won her second Women Writer's Award for it.

"This Powder Box," although written shortly after Uno's divorce from Kitahara, concerns her relationship with Tōgō Seiji. Far more detached than earlier stories that treat her relationship with this artist, "This Powder Box" is double-voiced: the narrator, having gained the wisdom of age, recounts the actions of a younger self, indulges in a near dialogue with that younger self, and challenges her to explain why she acted as she did.

The Story of a Single Woman takes Uno even further back to her childhood and her relationship with her irascible father. Again the narrative is double-voiced, and again the aim of the narrator's inquiry seems to be that of achieving some self-understanding and self-legitimacy.

The Sound of the Rain, perhaps the most evocative and lyrical of Uno's autobiographical works, returns to her relationship with Kitahara. In this piece the narrator tells of the death of her former husband and tells how she accepts her own frailty and loneliness. The quiet, almost mournful tone of this story—induced by the sound of the rain—has led critics to call it a requiem. In her review of *The Sound of the Rain,* however, writer Nogami Yaeko notes that, although Uno wrote repeatedly of her love for Kitahara, the one whom she really loved was Uno herself. Nogami is suggesting not that Uno was narcissistic but that she was seeking a positive, self-affirming love. At the end of the narrator's marriage, as she faces old age and the prospects of life alone, she is not defeated by her circumstances but ready to go forward on her own.

By the early 1980s Uno had stopped writing fiction for the most part and was concentrating instead on writing essays that explored both her past experiences and present observations, and she eventually began serializing a collection of memoirs in the *Mainichi Shinbun.* When published in book form in 1983, this two-volume collection, *Ikite yuku watashi* (I Will Go on Living), became a runaway best-seller that was subsequently made into a thirteen-part television drama as well as a stage play. The success of *I Will Go on Living* aroused an Uno Chiyo revival, as most of her earlier works were reprinted and displayed prominently on bookstore shelves. *Ohan* was produced as a commerical film under the direction of Ichikawa Kon in 1985. Magazines and television talk shows vied with one another for interviews with Uno, and the *Mainichi Shinbun* asked her to write an advice column like that of American journalist Ann Landers.

Readers, mostly women, were enthralled by Uno's carefree, optimistic approach to life. Many who sent letters to her column sought advice on love matters, but more than a few posed questions about child-rearing, etiquette, and culinary skills. In 1986 Uno's talent in the kitchen eventually culminated in a cookbook, *Watashi no tsukutta osōzai* (My Favorite Dishes), a potpourri of reminiscences as well as recipes. In the midst of this flutter Uno was still able to manage her small kimono boutique and to continue writing, and she published her last volume of fiction, a collection of short stories, in 1989: *Ippen ni haru kaze ga fuite kita* (Suddenly a Spring Wind).

Time has tempered assessments of Uno Chiyo's contribution to the Japanese literary tradition. Her writings first catapulted her into the public eye as a seductive femme fatale, the value of her work depending on the interest that her love life could generate. Yet as she matured, Uno proved that she was not just a sensationalist but a writer of worth. To her credit she has received the twenty-eighth Academy of Arts Award

(1972), the Third Order of the Sacred Treasure (1974), and the thirtieth Kikuchi Kan Prize for Literature (1982)—and in 1990 she was named a "Person of Cultural Merit."

Biography:

Rebecca Copeland, *The Sound of the Wind: The Life and Works of Uno Chiyo* (Honolulu: University of Hawaii Press, 1992).

References:

Phyllis Birnbaum, "Profiles," *New Yorker,* 64 (31 October 1988): 39–59;

Rebecca Copeland, "The Madeup Author: Writer as Woman in the Works of Uno Chiyo," *Journal of the Association of Teachers of Japanese,* 29 (Spring 1995): 2–25;

Copeland, "Needles, Knives, and Pens: Uno Chiyo and the Remembered Father," *U.S.-Japan Women's Journal,* no. 11 (September 1996): 3–22;

Copeland, "Uno Chiyo: Not Just 'A Writer of Illicit Love,'" *Japan Quarterly,* 35 (1988): 176–182;

Donald Keene, "The Revival of Writing by Women," in his *Dawn to the West,* 2 volumes (New York: Holt, Rinehart & Winston, 1984), I: 1113–1167.

Appendix:
The Development of Meiji Japan

"The Development of Meiji Japan"

from *East Asia: The Modern Transformation,* by John K. Fairbank,
Edwin O. Reischauer, and Albert M. Craig
(Boston: Houghton Mifflin, 1965)

EARLY INDUSTRIALIZATION

The new regime, within a decade of its coming to power, had established a firm grip on the whole nation. But a great deal more had to be done if Japan were to win security from external aggression and equality with the West. These would depend ultimately on the economic strength of the nation and the knowledge and technological progress of its people.

The young leaders saw clearly the broader aspects of the problems they faced. Their breadth of understanding and openness of mind show what remarkable men had been propelled to national leadership by the turmoil of the preceding two decades. The elimination of the *han,* the balancing of the budget, and the suppression of samurai resistance presented them with crises demanding immediate action. Yet they did not overlook the long-range problems of modernization.

The success of the Meiji leaders was probably greater and more rapid than even they had expected. In a mere half century, they built a powerful modern nation out of a feudally fragmented and technologically backward country, thereby winning the national security and equality they longed for. In terms of their own objectives, their achievements constitute the national Cinderella-story of modern times, even though, as in Bismarckian Germany, their emphasis on national strength and military power bequeathed serious problems to later generations.

The development of Meiji Japan has particular relevance today, as a nineteenth-century counterpart to the twentieth-century theme of the modernization of underdeveloped countries. But the circumstances were in many ways different. The Japanese could expect no foreign economic aid, though they were surprisingly free from prejudice against foreign expert advice. They were threatened by rampant nineteenth-century imperialism but were not subjected to some of the pressures that are common today. For example, they were not seriously affected by foreign ideological conflicts or menaced by ideological subversion at home. Since no non-Western nation had as yet completely modernized, there was little expectation in Japan and less elsewhere that a great transformation would take place overnight. In contrast with the sometimes unrealistic expectations of the twentieth century, no one assumed that the Japanese should or could suddenly convert their feudal society into a full-fledged democracy or their backward economy into a fully industrial one. Thus they could move step by step toward their objectives, instead of attempting them in one great leap.

The background of the Japanese people was also quite different from that in most of the present underdeveloped nations. We have noted the many unusual features of their economy, society, and intellectual attitudes in the early nineteenth century that facilitated the subsequent transformation. It was the people as a whole, not merely the political leaders, who made possible Japan's rapid modernization.

The question of the respective roles of government and people in the development of Meiji Japan is of special interest today, when the proper balance between the two is an issue in many underdeveloped countries. Undoubtedly the government gave clear and strong leadership. It was the chief modernizing force in many fields. In others it created the necessary conditions of law and order. But strong leadership would have meant little if the people had not been prepared to follow and to exploit the new opportunities provided by the government.

Industrialization, which was so important an aspect of Japan's modernization, is a case in point. The story is complex; but in essence, the government provided political stability and sound monetary institutions, which were prerequisites for industrialization. The government also did the pioneering work in many industrial fields and sponsored the development of others, but it was private initiative that produced most of Japan's industrial development.

Strategic Industries and Communications. The government leaders sought particularly to develop the strategic industries on which modern military power depends. This need had been evident to the shogunate and some of the stronger *han,* which had made progress in this direction even before 1868.

For example, the Hizen domain, which had responsibility in alternate years for the defense of Nagasaki, succeeded with the aid of a Dutch book in building a reverberatory furnace for smelting iron in 1850 and three years later in casting cannon, from the iron it produced, to take the place of outmoded bronze ordnance. Within five years, the shogunate, Mito, and Satsuma followed Hizen in building reverberatory furnaces. Satsuma became the center of a thriving iron industry. The shogunate expanded its activities in this field by employing Dutch experts to set up an imported iron foundry at Nagasaki in 1857 and by establishing other foundries with French aid at Yokohama and Yokosuka in 1865.

Shipbuilding was an equally strategic industry. The shogunate built a Western-style barkentine in 1855 and a teamer at Nagasaki in 1857, apparently without Western technical aid, and constructed a shipyard at Yokosuka in 1865 with French aid. Some fourteen *han* also set up facilities for the construction or repair of Western-style ships. Satsuma had built model steamers as early as 1852, and subsequently constructed full-scale steamers, as did Mito and Hizen. By the time of the Restoration, the shogunate and *han* together owned 138 Western-style ships which they had either constructed themselves or bought from abroad. The Japanese had also acquired considerable knowledge of Western navigational techniques, and as early as 1860 the shogunate sent an entirely Japanese-manned steamer, the *Kanrin-maru,* across the Pacific to accompany the embassy to the United States.

The participants in the struggle for power during the closing years of the Tokugawa found it more practical to buy foreign ships and guns than to make them. But once the crisis was past, the new government set about building up these strategic military industries so as not to be dependent on foreign sources of supply. It set up a shipyard at Hyōgo (the modern Kōbe) to add to the two it had inherited from the shogunate at Nagasaki and Yokosuka. The Yokosuka yard built two naval vessels of more than 1000 tons during the 1870's, and by 1883 the Nagasaki yard had produced 10 steamers for the new regime and the Hyōgo yard 23. In addition, the government operated large works in Tōkyō and Ōsaka for making cannon, rifles, and ammunition and also three small gunpowder factories. The Ōsaka plant alone employed some 1100 workers. Though foreign models were used, foreigners themselves were not employed in these five arsenals for reasons of security.

The government took the lead in developing modern communications, both because of the public nature of this undertaking and because of the great capital sums required for it. A major reason for the economic backwardness of Japan, as compared with the West, was the high cost of internal transportation. There were few navigable rivers, and most goods moved on the backs of horses and men. It was said to cost as much to transport a ton of goods 50 miles within the country as all the way from Europe to Japan. Consequently, railways, once built, proved immensely profitable ventures. The 19-mile line from Tōkyō to Yokohama, completed in 1872, carried almost 40,000 tons of freight in 1877 at one-seventieth the cost of earlier transportation, and 2,000,000 passengers traveled on it in 1880. A second line had been built between Kōbe and Ōsaka by 1874 and was extended to Kyōto in 1877. But railway construction was difficult and costly in mountainous Japan, and by 1881 there were still only 76 miles of track. Telegraph lines, cheaper to construct and important for administrative control of the nation, spread more rapidly. By 1880 most of the major cities had been linked by government lines.

Other Government Industries. Industrialization could not be limited to strategic industries and communications. The production of consumer goods, especially textiles, had to be mechanized if Japan were to compete successfully with the West and eliminate the dangerous imbalance that had developed in its foreign trade.

Although there had been a serious outflow of gold (in exchange for silver) ever since trade had started in 1859, the initial lack of demand by the Japanese public for foreign goods and the strong demand for Japanese silk and silkworm eggs, occasioned by a silk blight in Europe, had created a small favorable balance of trade during the first decade. But the recovery of the European silk industry, the rising local demand for

Western goods, and the fixing of import duties at lower rates in 1866 produced large trade deficits after 1869. This unfavorable situation was heightened by charges for shipping, insurance, and other services, which because of Japanese inexperience were almost entirely in foreign hands until well into the 1880's.

Meanwhile the import of cheap foreign manufactured goods was injuring domestic textile production and other handicraft industries on which the peasants depended for much of their livelihood. The draining of specie led to a rapid depreciation of the value of paper money and credits, which, while easing the burden on the heavily indebted government, contributed to the financial collapse of the samurai, especially after their stipends had been commuted into bond payments. New industries were desperately needed to give employment to peasants in certain areas and to samurai everywhere.

The government established a Ministry of Industry in December 1870. The next year Itō took charge of it as vice-minister, and in 1873 he became minister of industry, remaining in this key post until 1878. Under Itō and his successors, the government sought to develop the nonstrategic industries, both directly by starting government enterprises and indirectly by encouraging private industrial development through technical assistance, easy credit, and subsidies.

Even with government aid, however, private industrial ventures met with little initial success. Among their various difficulties were the relative scarcity of private capital and the resulting high interest rates, which were usually above 10 per cent. Hampered by Japanese inexperience with machinery, the need for high-priced foreign experts, and exorbitant transportation costs within Japan, industrial ventures could hardly bring such high returns in their early years. Several promising starts at private industry went bankrupt because of insufficient initial profits. As a result, government subsidies to private industries were felt by some to have been largely wasted.

The government devoted special efforts to mining, as an industry that would reduce the unfavorable balance of trade. By 1873 the Bureau of Mines already employed thirty-four foreigners. The Hizen domain, with English technical and financial aid, had put a modern coal mine into operation in 1869. This was taken over in 1874 by the new government, which bought out the English interests. By 1880 the government had developed eight other modern coal mines. It made a large investment in a modern iron mine in

1881 and in that year was producing 90 per cent of the gold and silver mined in Japan.

The government also built a machine tool factory in 1871, a cement factory in 1875, a glass factory in 1876, and a white brick factory in 1878, all in Tōkyō. The last three were to provide materials for Western-style buildings, since it was official policy to construct government buildings as much as possible in Occidental style, chiefly to impress the West with Japan's modernization.

The most important industrial field was textiles, because these made up more than half of Japan's imports between 1868 and 1882, and the best way to balance trade was to stem this inflow of foreign goods by the development of cheap, machine-made domestic textiles. The role of the government was somewhat different in each major sector of the textile industry. Woolens had become important for the first time in Japan because many men had adopted Western dress and soldiers and government functionaries wore woolen uniforms. Since woolen textiles constituted an entirely new industry, private capital made no effort to develop it, and a government mill, built in 1877–78 by German technicians, remained the chief producer until after 1900.

Cotton yarn and goods were a more important field. Foreign cotton fibers were cheaper and better than those grown in Japan and during the 1890's eliminated Japanese cotton almost completely. Thus the local industry at first depended on relatively costly local fibers and later had to purchase its raw cotton abroad. It had to operate on a very large scale to compete with cheap foreign imports, and naturally found itself handicapped by local inexperience with machinery. Because of these difficulties, it took much capital and a long time before Japanese cotton yarn and goods could match Western products in quality and price, and considerable government aid was necessary in the early stages.

The first modern textile plant was set up by the Satsuma domain in 1868, with 100 looms and 2640 spindles imported from England. Satsuma built a second mill in the Ōsaka area in 1870, but this was taken over two years later by the central government, which added two other government mills in 1881 and 1882. The government raised a 10,000,000-yen loan in 1878 in order to provide imported spinning machinery on easy terms to private companies.

In contrast with the cotton industry, silk reeling was mechanized with relative ease, and the government's role was limited to providing technical advice and operating a few pilot plants. This was because turning the silk reel by steam or water power, which produced much finer silk than reeling by hand, was a simple process requiring only modest capital, while all the other steps in silk filature remained hand processes at which the Japanese were already expert. After the European silk industry recovered in 1869 and the world market again became competitive, the Japanese began to shift to machine reeling. The first mechanical silk-reeling plant was established in 1870 by a "collateral" daimyo in the silk-producing area of central Honshū, and the government established three pilot plants between 1872 and 1877. The first used French technicians until 1875. The last specialized in a new technique—utilization of waste scraps from other mills.

Private Enterprise. Government plants accounted for only a tiny fraction of mechanical silk reeling in Japan. The rest was developed by private entrepreneurs. The house of Ono, which had developed as silk importers in the late seventeenth century and had then branched into banking, built a silk-reeling plant in Tōkyō late in 1870 and seven more in 1872–73. Others, particularly the local businessmen in the silk-producing areas of central Honshū, continued to develop the industry. By 1880 some 30 per cent of Japanese silk exports were machine-reeled products which outclassed the hand-reeled silk of the rest of Asia and competed well with European silk. At this time silk accounted for some 43 per cent of Japanese exports, about double the figure for the next item, tea. Chiefly because of the brisk demand abroad for Japanese silk, foreign trade began to show a favorable balance in the mid-eighties. Thus the industry that contributed most to the balancing of Japan's foreign trade was developed largely by private capital and enterprise.

Private capital moved into the cotton industry more hesitantly. An Edo merchant had ordered spinning machinery from America as early as 1864, but because of slowness of delivery, lack of capital, and technical inexperience, it was not put into operation until 1872, and in 1878 was still bringing in only a 5 per cent return on the original investment. Two plants built by the Satsuma domain were sold to a private firm in 1878. Mainly because of the government financial aid that became available in 1878, fifteen more private plants were established in the next seven years. Thereafter the growth of private spinning firms was more rapid. Thus cotton spin-

ning, which was to be Meiji Japan's largest industry, was also developed, except in its early stages, almost entirely by private enterprise.

There were other industries besides textiles in which private enterprise was important from the start. Relatively simple processes, such as match and paper making, were well developed by private capital as early as the 1870's. Most mining also was in private hands, though much of it was done in small mines by nonmechanized processes. In 1881, 99 per cent of the coal, 94 per cent of the iron, and 77 per cent of the copper production of Japan came from privately owned mines.

THE DEVELOPMENT OF THE BUSINESS COMMUNITY

The introduction of Western industrial technology was the most spectacular economic innovation after the coming of Perry, but it was on a small scale at first. Meanwhile the growth of other sectors of the economy, such as agriculture, trade, and those traditional handicraft industries that were not destroyed by Western imports, was actually much greater. For example, agricultural acreage increased 7 per cent and average yields per acre about 21 per cent in the 1880's, and total agricultural production doubled in the next 25 years. Although private capital was at first reluctant to enter the unfamiliar and financially hazardous field of machine industry, there was no dearth of capital or enterprise in the more traditional fields of economic activity. New commercial opportunities were enthusiastically exploited, and there was a rush of eager businessmen to the treaty ports when these were opened.

The result was a steady and rapid growth of the whole Japanese economy, and not merely the development of modern industry fostered by the Meiji government. In fact, the success of the government and private interests in industrialization can be explained only by this growth of the rest of the economy, which developed a sound foundation for the industry that the government was trying to construct from the top. This was probably one of the chief differences between Japan's rapid industrialization and the less successful efforts in China and other Asian countries, where modern industry initiated from the top often sank into the quagmire of a stagnant local economy.

The Government and Private Business. Government policies, as well as the opening of Japan, helped to account for this almost explosive growth of the Japanese economy. It could never have happened without the stimulus of foreign trade, the creation of political stability by the government, the economic unification of the country, the reform of the currency system, and the removal of feudal restrictions. The government's development of railways, ports, roads, and, in time, such urban services as water systems and street railways also contributed greatly to economic growth.

The government, having originally led the way in many fields of industry, later withdrew from most of its economic activities, but individual government leaders continued to act as the prime movers in developing certain new industries or enterprises. In their eagerness to see Japan grow economically, they cajoled reluctant businessmen into new and still risky fields of activity; they helped them assemble the necessary capital, sometimes by putting pressure on other businessmen, sometimes by providing government subsidies of a type that would now be considered examples of corruption; they helped enterprising younger men to advance at the expense of their more conservative elders; and they forced weak companies to merge into stronger units. Inoue of Chōshū, who became a sort of arbiter in the affairs of the great Mitsui interests, was the most prominent of the government leaders in such economic activities, but others played similar roles. They were probably aided by the well-established Tokugawa tradition that businessmen depended not only on the tolerance of government leaders but on their business patronage as well.

Thus government leaders individually, as well as the government itself, played a large role in industrialization. Yet the fact remains that the great bulk of the economic development of Meiji Japan was the work of private individuals acting largely on their own initiative. It was they who built up agriculture and the small and more traditional lines of enterprise. They also played the major role even in industry.

The immediate political response by large numbers of Japanese has already been noted as an unusual feature of Japan's reaction to the Western menace. The response of an equally large number of private entrepreneurs was even more unusual in modern Asian history. Some of these men broke with the stable, orthodox, Tokugawa patterns to seize new opportunities in the period between 1853 and 1868. Others emerged only afterward in response to the radically new climate created by the early Meiji government. Even though most people clung with bewildered desperation to the old ways of life, a few exceptional persons had the daring to introduce large-scale enterprises based on Western models.

Patriotism often was as much of a motive for these entrepreneurs who industrialized Japan as for the political leaders who reorganized its government. They realized that they too were strengthening the country and establishing its security. In return, Japanese society gave them respect and prestige. As with the political leaders, their dreams of a strong and economically modernized Japan merged indistinguishably with personal ambitions, inducing them to plunge into risky industrial ventures when much higher and more certain profits were to be had in money-lending or in traditional lines of commerce.

The Role of the Merchant Class. The urban merchants, who had dominated much of the culture of Tokugawa Japan as well as its economy, naturally contributed to economic growth in the Meiji period, but in comparison with their former economic role their share was surprisingly small. Their past experience, instead of aiding them, seems to have inhibited their developing new entrepreneurial skills. Their outlook was conservative, conditioned by their long dependence on and subservience to the shogunate and *han*. The house laws of most of the large merchant firms explicitly enjoined their members from entering new lines of business. Thus for the most part they stuck to traditional banking and merchandising activities, waiting until others had pioneered in the new industries and proved their profitability before investing their own considerable capital.

Some of the larger firms that attempted in the early years to branch out into new fields failed during the financially chaotic 1870's. For example, the houses of Shimada and Ono, which with the Mitsui served at first as the bankers for the new government, went bankrupt within a decade after the Restoration. The Kōnoike firm, which had been important in *sake* brewing in the Ōsaka area in the early seventeenth century and had switched to banking toward the end of that century, did manage to survive but gradually lost ground as a leading financial institution.

The house of Mitsui was an outstanding exception among the large old merchant firms. Under the aggressive leadership of Minomura Rizaemon (1821–1877), it made the transition to modern banking methods and subsequently branched out into a variety of new enterprises, becoming in time the largest of the great financial and industrial giants later known as the zaibatsu, a term meaning "the financial clique."

Minomura was an unusual merchant leader, having started as a poor orphan of obscure origin, and his appointment as general manager was unprecedented in Mitsui history. Having shown his ability by successfully conducting the firm's relations with the authorities during the last years of the shogunate, he was equally skillful in dealing with the new government, establishing a particularly close relationship with Inoue. Minomura moved the headquarters of the firm from Kyōto to Tōkyō, sent five members of the Mitsui family and two employees to study in the United States in 1872, and separated the rest of the firm from its merchandising branch. The latter, forced to stand on its own feet, modernized its procedures and eventually developed into Mitsukoshi, the first of those great modern department stores so important in Japanese urban life.

The third largest of the later zaibatsu also grew out of an old merchant company, the Sumitomo firm, which dated back to the early seventeenth century. After the Restoration, an able employee modernized its copper-mining activities and then launched it in banking, foreign trade, and other enterprises. Another great zaibatsu firm was founded by Ōkura Kihachirō (1837–1928), who came from a prosperous merchant house in Niigata on the west coast of Honshū. Abandoning his hereditary business, he traded in rifles during the disturbed period preceding the Restoration and then came to Tōkyō, where he succeeded in foreign trade and branched out into industry.

Samurai Businessmen. In general, entrepreneurial ability emerged from the samurai class more than from the townsmen. This may seem strange in view of the traditional samurai contempt for economic activity and the profit motive, but it is explained by samurai traditions of leadership, their high standards of education, the tremendous interest in economic problems among samurai intellectuals during the second half of the Tokugawa period, the managerial skills some samurai had developed as *han* or shogunate officials, and the severe financial difficulties in which most samurai found themselves in the 1870's.

In the large samurai class as a whole, however, it was only a few rather untypical figures who distinguished themselves as entrepreneurs.

The great majority found themselves unprepared, by their inexperience in business and their traditional contempt for the profit motive, to succeed in business life. Samurai did provide almost a third of the capital for the 148 national banks founded in the first two years after the reform of the banking law in 1876. Their capital came from the bonds paid them in 1876 in lieu of their former annual stipends (as was also the case with the 44 per cent of the capital provided by former daimyo). The organization of these banks, however, was supervised by the government and did not represent a very significant entrepreneurial activity on the part of samurai or daimyo. Moreover, almost all of the hundreds of business companies formed by samurai groups during the decade after 1876 failed completely. It was thus only a very small per centage of the men of samurai origin who succeeded in business and still fewer who became important entrepreneurs in industry.

The most outstanding of the new business magnates of samurai origin was Iwasaki Yatarō (1834–1885). He came from the Tosa domain, where he had been a "rural samurai" but had become the supervisor of the *han*'s mercantile operations in Nagasaki before the Restoration. After the dissolution of the *han*, he transformed the *han*'s commercial and shipping interests into his own private concern, which he subsequently named the Mitsubishi Company.

Iwasaki was greatly helped by the government, which saw him as a promising person to develop a Japanese shipping line that would eliminate dependence on foreign ships and reduce payments for haulage in foreign bottoms. The government bought thirteen foreign ships for the Formosan expedition in 1874. It entrusted these to Iwasaki to operate and subsequently gave them to him. He again was put in charge of marine transportation during the Satsuma Rebellion in 1877, being provided by the government with nine more ships and a large subsidy. With this sort of aid and continuing subsidies, he was able to develop a large fleet, which began to operate abroad in 1879. From these beginnings the Mitsubishi Company moved out into other fields, eventually becoming the second largest zaibatsu concern and the major rival of the Mitsui interests.

Peasant Entrepreneurs. Men of peasant origin had an even more remarkable role than the samurai businessmen. Since Japanese agriculture was already quite commercialized by the early nineteenth century, the wealthy peasant class had developed entrepreneurial skills in the processing and sale of local agricultural products. It was not strange, therefore, that these men were able to invest in technological improvements in agriculture and develop their other economic interests. In this they were aided by the prosperity that came to rural Japan in the late 1870's. Though partially a result of the general development of the economy this also came from the lowering of the land tax in 1876 and the inflation that hit Japan in these years, further reducing the real value of taxes. During the next few years, agriculture bore, by traditional standards, only a modest tax burden, so that the richer and more enterprising peasants were able to invest heavily in agricultural improvements and in commercial and industrial undertakings. The mechanization of silk reeling was mainly the work of wealthy peasants, and many other traditional local enterprises were expanded and modernized by them in much the same way.

The most spectacular of the peasant-born entrepreneurs was Shibusawa Eiichi (1890–1931). Born near Edo into a rich peasant family in the indigo-dyeing business, Shibusawa was given a good education and developed great ambitions. He left home in 1863, determined to achieve samurai status and make a name for himself. He plotted an armed uprising to expel the foreigners, became enrolled as a samurai under Keiki, the future shogun, and accompanied Keiki's younger brother to Europe on an official mission in 1867.

After Keiki's abdication, Shibusawa started a banking and trading company for his former lord but was soon drafted to serve in the new central government. Under the patronage of Ōkuma and Inoue he rose rapidly, becoming one of the major figures in the Treasury and leading the way in establishing the government's first silk-reeling plant. However, he resigned from the government in 1873, after a budgetary disagreement, and then became president of the First National Bank, which he had helped found by forcing Mitsui and Ono banking interests into a merger. In 1880 he organized the Ōsaka Spinning Mill, which soon became Japan's first major industrial success. From this beginning he went on to become one of the nation's greatest entrepreneurs, having a hand in the founding and management of more than a hundred companies spread throughout the major fields of industry and finance.

Another man of rural origin who founded an important zaibatsu firm was Asano Sōichirō (1848–1930), son of a village physician. He ran away from home, came to Tōkyō in 1871, got into the making of cement, acquired control and then ownership of the cement factory that the government had built, turned his hitherto financially disastrous undertaking into a great success, and then launched out into other industries.

The fourth largest of the later zaibatsu firms was founded by still another man of humble origin. This was Yasuda Zenjirō (1838–1921), who in his youth ran away from his home on the west coast of Honshū to Edo where he became a money-changer. After the Restoration he founded a modern banking empire that bore his name and then branched out into railways and other business.

These six men are merely a few outstanding examples among the thousands of individuals of all classes who helped to develop the modern Japanese economy. Many of the most important figures were uprooted men who had fearlessly turned their backs on the past, determined to industrialize Japan, with unbounded faith in the magic of economic modernization. They could have done little without the favorable conditions for economic growth created by the government; for some, direct government aid was crucial to success. But if thousands of private entrepreneurs had not spontaneously appeared, the government's economic efforts might have failed completely or at best would have progressed slowly.

THE GROWTH OF THE ECONOMY

The Development of Hokkaidō. While improved technology permitted some expansion of agricultural acreage throughout Japan, the only large unexploited area was the northern island of Hokkaidō. Since development of this cold, inhospitable region required long-range investment and had important strategic implications, the government took the lead.

The Japanese had exercised some control over Hokkaidō since about the eleventh century, but in the early nineteenth century the Japanese population was still limited chiefly to the coast and the extreme south, while the rest of the island and the smaller ones to the north were inhabited for the most part by the hairy Ainu aborigines. The Matsumae domain in southern Hokkaidō had established fishing settlements as far north as Sakhalin by the late seventeenth century, and the southern Kuril Islands had been developed into rich fishing grounds. Japanese cartographers surveyed and mapped the coasts of this whole northern area in the early nineteenth century. The explorer Mamiya Rinzō (1780–1845) in 1808 proved that Sakhalin was an island and the next year ventured up the Amur River.

Because of the opening of Hakodate to foreign ships through the Treaty of Kanagawa in 1854, the shogunate took over direct control of Hokkaidō from the Matsumae daimyo, as it had on certain previous occasions. This time a serious attempt was made to colonize the island, but with little success. When the shogunate signed its first treaty with the Russians at Shimoda in February 1855, it also agreed to Russian demands for a rough delimitation of the northern boundary. Kunashiri and Etorofu, the two large southern islands in the Kurils, were assigned to Japan and the rest to Russia, while the two countries agreed to continue their joint occupation of Sakhalin.

This settlement of the boundary question did not please the Russians, who kept pressing Japan to modify it. For this purpose, Muraviev, the governor-general of Siberia, went to Kanagawa in 1859 with seven ships but obtained nothing from his show of naval power. In 1861 a Russian naval expedition occupied the island of Tsushima in the straits between Japan and Korea, but soon withdrew from this ill-considered effort to annex Japanese territory. A clear settlement of the Russo-Japanese border was finally reached at St. Petersburg on May 7, 1875, with Admiral Enomoto, the former shogunal naval commander, acting for Japan. The Japanese ceded their interests in Sakhalin to Russia in return for Russia's giving up her claims to the central and northern Kuril Islands.

The Tōkyō government was much more interested in Hokkaidō than in the islands to the north, because of its greater economic potentialities and its strategic value as a bulwark against Russia. As early as 1868 the government had been laying plans for the development of the island. In 1869 the name of the island was changed from Ezo to Hokkaidō, meaning "Northern Sea Circuit," and its development was put in the hands of a Colonization Office (*Kaitakushi*). In 1870 Kuroda Kiyotaka (1840–1900), a Satsuma samurai who had commanded the government forces against Enomoto, assumed charge of this office, serving until a month before it was dissolved in 1882.

Kuroda went to the United States, where, on President Grant's advice, he hired the United States Commissioner of Agriculture, Horace Capron, at the princely salary of $10,000 plus ex-

penses, and a staff of American experts to advise on the development of Hokkaidō. Capron and his group remained in Japan until 1875. The next year William S. Clark, president of the Massachusetts Agricultural College, arrived to take charge of the newly founded Sapporo Agricultural College. Clark left a lasting influence on this institution, which grew eventually into Hokkaidō University. Through the work of such men, the agriculture and rural landscape of the island were given a somewhat American cast. Silos, for example, are a common feature of Hokkaidō farms.

Under government sponsorship, subsidized farmer immigrants came into Hokkaidō, reaching a high point of 13,784 in 1872. Some 2139 colonist militia were settled on the soil in 1875–76. Thus between 1869 and 1881 the total population of the island more than quadrupled, reaching 240,391. Agricultural acreage increased more than tenfold, the fishing industry more than doubled, and many other new industries got started. In these ways, foundations were laid for still greater economic exploitation of this frontier region in the following decades and a further tenfold increase in population by 1918. More important, Hokkaidō was made fully Japanese and secure from Russian penetration. In 1883 it was given a normal prefectural system of local government, though it continued to be called a "circuit" (*dō*) rather than a prefecture (*ken*).

Economic Retrenchment under Matsukata. The development of Hokkaidō, though valuable in the long run, added to the financial drain on the central government during the 1870's. Meanwhile the government's many industrial enterprises for the most part were losing money; even when they were successful, they rarely brought in profits on investment equal to the current rates of interest. This situation was not unexpected, since the government had concentrated on strategic industries and the fields in which the risks were so great and the returns so slow in materializing that private capital was reluctant to enter them. In any case, the ambitious program of economic development in the 1870's helped produce a serious financial crisis in the last years of the decade.

The costs of liquidating the old regime—payments to the daimyo and samurai, repayment of shogunal and *han* debts, and costly military campaigns—were a heavy financial burden, which was augmented by the broad program of modernization. As a result, the government was living beyond its means. It had been able to do all these things through deficit financing, but the rapid increase of its liabilities because of the conversion of daimyo and samurai payments in 1876 and the Satsuma Rebellion the next year overstrained its credit. Its specie coverage for outstanding notes and paper currency fell to less than 5 per cent; by 1880 paper currency depreciated to hardly more than half its face value; a serious inflation set in, with the price of rice more than doubling between 1877 and 1880; and inflation cut the real value of the land tax on which the government largely depended.

In the face of this financial crisis, Ōkuma proposed floating a huge loan in London, but more conservative opinion prevailed, and a policy of economic retrenchment and deflation was adopted. The first major step, announced on 5 November 1880, was the sale of government industrial enterprises. A prime advocate and the chief executor of this retrenchment policy was Matsukata Masayoshi (1835–1924), a Satsuma man of humble samurai origin who had risen rapidly in the new regime because of his financial genius. In 1880 he had been appointed home minister and in 1881 was shifted to be minister of finance, remaining in this key position without interruption until 1892.

At first, because of the weakness of private capital and the unprofitability of most of the government industries, the government could find no buyers at the prices it was asking. Not until 1884 were most of the enterprises sold, and then only at very low rates. Among the major plants and mines for which figures are known, the sale prices ranged between 11 and 90 per cent of the original investment. Almost all were sold, sometimes without competitive bids, to insiders, that is, to businessmen or public servants already closely associated with leading officials. In some cases there was obvious collusion. For example, the proposal to sell the government's assets in Hokkaidō to a group of businessmen and former Colonization Office incumbents for about 3 per cent of the original investment became a major scandal and had to be abandoned.

The sale of the government industries put the development of most sectors of the economy—except for war industries, communications, and public services—entirely into the hands of private enterprise and contributed to the eventual concentration of much of Japanese industry in the hands of a small group of giant corporations. Since the government enterprises formed a large proportion of all the modernized industries of Japan, the rather few firms that acquired them at

low prices in the 1880's ultimately found themselves in an advantageous position. As Japan's industrialization overcame its initial handicaps and began to pay off handsomely a few years later, some of these firms got such a head start on possible competitors that they were able to develop into the great zaibatsu combines of the twentieth century.

This outcome of the retrenchment policy has given rise to Marxist interpretations that the chief motive in the sale of government industries was the commitment of the government leaders to large-scale capitalism. There is no real evidence for this theory, however, and it assumes an understanding by the Japanese leaders of the long-range effects of their action and a preference for capitalism over government ownership that seem altogether improbable. Another theory, that the sale was an economic concession by the government to the forces of opposition within Japanese society, appears to have even less basis.

The obvious explanation for the sale of the industries, made amply clear by all contemporary documents, was the financial crisis. Curtailment of government expenses seemed a safer course than large foreign loans. The sale of enterprises was merely one aspect of this budgetary cutback. The funds of almost all branches of government, including the military, were also reduced; costly foreign experts were dismissed, and students were recalled from abroad.

The government leaders probably saw nothing reprehensible in selling industries to insiders at bargain rates. They had been trying to modernize the national economy by all available means, encouraging and assisting private enterprise whenever possible as well as founding government industries when this seemed necessary. Selling the industries at reasonable prices to men they felt were competent seemed the best way to ensure their continued development. This was far more important to the national interest than the payment the government received. As it turned out, most of the industries sold did not for a decade or more make profits comparable to the return in other economic fields. The purchasers' faith in the future of industry in Japan is, in fact, more surprising than the low prices they paid.

Matsukata's retrenchment policies were successful, and by 1886 he had the government back on an even financial keel. New taxes were instituted; a centralized, European-style banking system, under the newly founded Bank of Japan, was substituted in 1882 for the earlier American system; paper currency in circulation was reduced about one-quarter; interest rates dropped; specie reserves were increased to 35 per cent of notes outstanding; and by 1886 paper money had been restored virtually to face value. As a result, the real income from the land tax had also been restored.

The Success of Industrialization. Once back on a sound fiscal basis, the Meiji government thereafter remained financially much stronger than during its first two decades. The general economy, too, though temporarily depressed by Matsukata's deflationary policies, soon recovered and surged ahead even more rapidly than before.

Deflation had weeded out the unsound speculative ventures that had flourished under the inflationary conditions of the late 1870's, leaving only the sounder enterprises. These profited from the return to hard money and the drop in interest rates from around 15 per cent to around 10. Private management of the former government industries, being free from cumbrous bureaucratic control, seems also to have been more efficient. Thus Matsukata's financial policies appear to have provided the last of the prerequisites needed before industrialization could really begin to pay. Political stability, with its assurance of continued law and order, had helped to create adequate domestic capital based in large part on government credit. The Japanese were also beginning to overcome initial handicaps, such as the high cost of internal transport and inexperience with machinery. Long-term investment in industry was short, Japan was ready for an industrial "breakthrough" or "takeoff"—at least in certain fields of industry.

Shibusawa's Ōsaka Spinning Mill spearheaded the new industrial development. It was much larger than earlier mills, thus cutting overhead costs, and Shibusawa had a highly educated young man specially trained in England to run it with the most up-to-date techniques. The mill had already proved a great financial success by 1884, in the midst of the deflationary depression. In the next few years there was a rush of entrepreneurs into the spinning industry, particularly in Ōsaka, the old center of the cotton trade, and a large number of new firms were founded, including such later giants as the Kanegafuchi Company (Kanebō).

The spinning boom was followed by a more general boom in other industries. New firms prospered in such diverse fields as mining, weaving, cement, beer, chinaware, gas, and electricity, but the greatest growth came in cotton spinning and railway transportation. Between 1883 and 1890, government railways expanded from 181 to 551 miles and private railways from 63 to 898 miles. Cotton spindleage almost tripled between 1882 and 1887 and production grew tenfold in the next five years. In the early 1880's Japan was still importing more than 90 per cent of the cotton yarn it consumed, but after 1889 imports dropped off sharply, and within five years the Japanese spinning industry had become so efficient that its products began to venture into the world market on a significant scale. By 1897 Japan had become a net exporter of cotton yarn, and by the end of the century cotton spinning and weaving employed 247,117 persons, or 63 per cent of all factory workers.

The mid 1880's, which saw the transfer of most government enterprises to private hands and the first industrial boom, also saw the emergence of a pattern of cooperation and cartel-like organization among big business concerns, in place of sharp competition. This was to become a worldwide trend in mature industrial economies, but in Japan's industrialization it appeared at an earlier stage and in greater strength than might have been expected from the experience of Western countries. Perhaps this was partly a result of the old Japanese preference for collective leadership and the long tradition among Tokugawa businessmen of establishing monopolistic associations under official sponsorship. There was also pressure from government authorities, particularly Inoue, for joint business enterprises that would create strong companies. Cooperation between big businessmen does not seem to have stunted Japan's industrial growth; on the contrary, it produced a pooling of resources that facilitated the financing of large-scale new enterprises.

The first clear sign of the new tendency was the merger in 1885 of competing steamship lines owned by the two emerging business giants, the Mitsubishi and Mitsui interests. The resulting Japan Mail Line (Nippon Yūsen Kaisha, commonly known as the N.Y.K.), which was under Mitsubishi domination, has remained ever since the largest component in Japan's merchant marine.

Another example was the development under Shibusawa's leadership of a tight cotton-spinning cartel. The cartel allocated the inadequate supply of skilled labor, organized joint noncompetitive efforts for the purchase of foreign raw cotton and the sale of cotton yarn abroad, assigned quotas in times of overproduction, and lobbied for favorable legislation such as the elimination of duties on raw cotton imports and cotton exports. It also made mutually advantageous compacts with the Mitsui foreign trade network and with Mitsubishi's Japan Mail Line, which brought the spinners their raw cotton and exported their products. Thus by the 1890's the pattern had been set for the development of industry-wide cartels and of "combines" of interlocking business interests in finance, commerce, and manufacturing.

Industrial growth in Japan, as in other countries, was not a straightline development. The boom years of the 1880's were followed by a period of slower expansion of factory capacity, but Japan's victory in the Sino-Japanese War in 1895 set off another sudden upsurge in all the established industrial fields and in certain new ones such as chemical fertilizers. Not only did the war stimulate the demand for a wide variety of goods, but it proved no financial strain, since the Chinese indemnity of 230 million taels (414 million yen) more than paid for all direct war costs. Subsequently the development of new factories again slowed down, but this was a constructive period of amalgamation of existing companies into a few large and strong units.

Then in 1905, after the Russo-Japanese War, came a third and bigger boom. Cotton weaving began to catch up with cotton spinning; the electric industry grew as railways were electrified and cities installed street lighting; shipping tonnage and services abroad expanded rapidly; the production of coal almost tripled in the decade after 1904; the Yawata Iron Works, founded by the government in 1901 at the northeastern tip of Kyūshū, helped Japan to meet a significant proportion of its iron and steel needs; and a few other heavy industries began to join the simpler light industries as important components of the economy. The scale of the boom can be seen from the increase between 1902 and 1912 of capital invested in various industries: fivefold in sugar refining, eightfold in fertilizer plants, ninefold in the production of machinery, elevenfold in gas companies, and fifteenfold in electricity. Thus, during the two and a half decades following Matsukata's financial reforms, one industry after another came of age, and Japan, with its industrial base now diversified and soundly established, entered a period of sustained industrial growth.

THE TRANSFORMATION OF SOCIETY

Industrialization as well as political and military modernization depended on new skills, new attitudes, and broader knowledge among the leaders and other men in the cities also adopted the Western fashion. Even the then-current occidental style of wearing heavy beards was followed by many prominent men, aided in this endeavor by the relative hairiness of the Japanese as compared with other Mongoloid peoples. Photographs of the Meiji emperor, Itō, and many other leaders show them adorned with very fine mustaches and beards.

Similarly, Western-style uniforms were adopted by military and government functionaries, while government leaders and other progressive-minded men shifted to Western civilian attire for general public use. Western dress was prescribed in 1872 for all court and official ceremonies. The emperor always appeared in public dressed in the military manner of the crowned heads of Europe. In the latter part of the Meiji period, the cutaway (called *mōningu* for "morning coat") became so firmly entrenched that it is still widely used in Japan for formal occasions, and *haikara,* meaning "high collar" and referring to the Western styles of the early twentieth century, became the common term for "fashionable" or "swanky." Since the Japanese understood that Englishmen were considered the best-dressed civilians of Europe, they sought to follow English styles. One curious result was the adoption of *sebiro,* a corruption of Saville Row, the street of fine tailors in London, as the Japanese word for the modern business suit.

The dress and style of women were less affected, since they lived more in seclusion. In 1873, however, the empress set an example by giving up the ancient custom for married women of blackening the teeth and shaving the eyebrows. She and the other court ladies adopted Victorian styles of dress, which are still followed by the court in modified form.

The Swing of the Pendulum. The craze for Westernization reached its height in the 1880's. There was even talk in responsible circles of adopting an official policy of intermarriage with Caucasians to "improve" the Japanese race. There were efforts to make social relations between the sexes conform to Western practice. Women of good families were taught foreign languages and ballroom dancing. In 1883 the government erected in Tōkyō at great expense an elaborate social hall, called the Rokumeikan, where dances were held every Sunday night for the political elite and the diplomatic corps. A great fancy-dress ball was held there in 1887, attended by the chief government dignitaries.

The fancy-dress ball, however, proved to be the last straw for more-conservative Japanese. This and other excesses led to a general revulsion against unnecessary imitation of the West, accompanied by a re-emphasis against unnecessary imitation of the West, accompanied by a re-emphasis of native values and traditions. The resultant slowing down of Westernization proved to be a useful phase in the general process of modernization. Many superficial aspects of Western culture, such as ballroom dancing, were dropped; thus the significant technological innovations lost the onus of being associated with useless and irritating peculiarities.

The same cycle of enthusiastic and somewhat indiscriminate adoption of Western ways, followed by the rejection of certain less-essential aspects of these innovations, was to repeat itself more than once in subsequent Japanese history. Such cycles can also be discerned in other Asian countries. They seem to be a fundamental pattern in the whole process of modernization through borrowing.

Legal Reforms. To win acceptance by the West, it was essential that the Japanese reform their legal institutions along occidental lines. Extraterritoriality was among the most galling features of the unequal-treaty system, but there was no hope of eliminating it until the Western powers had full confidence in Japanese legal processes.

Legal renovation was also fundamental to technological modernization and was necessitated by the abolition of the old class structure and the other great changes taking place. For example, the Western concept of individual rather than family ownership of property had to be adopted, since it fitted the new economic system and the individual initiative so important in Japan's transformation. On the other hand, for purposes of formal registration of the population, the laws continued to recognize the old extended family, or "house," consisting of a patriarch and those of his descendants and collateral relatives and their wives who had not legally established a new "house." The Western practice of publishing all laws was also necessary, and the Occidental emphasis on legal rights, as opposed to the East Asian emphasis on social obligations, came to permeate the new system. Torture as an accepted legal practice was abolished in 1876, while the structure and procedures of the law courts were made to conform with those of the West.

Most of these legal reforms were instituted in the same piecemeal fashion as the reforms in other fields. Some of the early innovations were obviously designed more to placate Western moral prejudices than to meet the recognized needs of Japanese society. For example, abortion and mixed bathing of the sexes were banned in 1869; pornography, tattooing, and exposure of the body by workers in Tōkyō were proscribed in 1872; and the next year all indentured geisha and prostitutes were ordered freed. Since laws of this type were not essential to the technological changes of the time and rested on no popular support or understanding, they naturally proved ineffective and for the most part were later abandoned.

The new legal system did not reach maturity until the 1890's, by which time the Japanese no longer felt the need of catering to every Western notion. A committee to compile a new civil code had been appointed in 1875. Aided by a French jurist, Boissonade, it submitted drafts in 1881 and 1888. The draft of 1888, which showed strong French influence, was subsequently revised, in part on the basis of German legal precedents, and finally went into effect in 1896.

THOUGHT AND RELIGION

One prominent feature of Western civilization which the Japanese government made no move to borrow was Christianity, even though Westerners would have been more favorably impressed had the Japanese adopted their religion rather than their costumes. This failure and the superficiality of much that was borrowed gave rise to the impression that only the externals of Western civilization were accepted and that native traditions were impervious to the ideas and ideals of the West. Sakuma's old slogan of "Eastern ethics and Western science," which many of the Meiji leaders endorsed, strengthened this interpretation.

In practice, however, no clear line could be drawn between the external aspects of Western civilization and its internal value system. The legal forms of the West, for example, inevitably brought with them the concepts and value judgments on which they were based. Moreover, the Japanese of the early Meiji period, though naturally influenced by the feudal and Confucian elements in their past, remained nonetheless open to the ideas and institutions of the West. Although scientific techniques and external fashions were easier to understand and adopt than were Western ideas and values, no distinction could be made between them in practice.

The Outlook of the Leaders. It would be a mistake to view the Japanese of the early Meiji period, particularly the political leaders, as either ideological traditionalists or intellectual and spiritual followers of the West. They were at the same time both and neither. Any of the leaders—including even those who seem today the most conservative—would champion Western ideas if they seemed useful or an inevitable trend. On the other hand, all of them, even the most Westernized, would defend traditional points of view that seemed of continuing value.

Hence the Meiji leaders might best be described as pragmatists and utilitarians, ready to adopt whatever techniques, institutions, or ideas seemed useful. They had the advantage of being in complete agreement on their ultimate objective and of having the support of most thinking Japanese. The country was to be made strong enough to withstand foreign domination and to win equality. The trial-and-error experience of the late Tokugawa period had shown that the best way to create "a rich country and a strong military" was to centralize Japan politically by means of the convenient imperial symbol and to modernize it by borrowing from the West. But no one as yet had a formula for modernizing an underdeveloped nation, and the leaders, faced with a confused and rapidly changing situation, were flexible rather than doctrinaire about the best way to achieve their ends.

This attitude on the part of the Meiji leaders was perhaps a natural product of the growing pragmatism in Tokugawa thought. They were an extreme expression of this trend, since they had risen to power largely because of their unusual flexibility of mind and ability to meet rapidly changing circumstances. And they found in the West strong encouragement for this point of view. The utilitarian doctrines of Jeremy Bentham and John Stuart Mill clearly supported their own outlook, and Herbert Spencer, as the great popularizer of liberal thought, became the idol of many Japanese intellectuals.

The objectives of the Meiji leaders were entirely secular and largely political, for their primary concern was the future of the nation as a whole. These qualities reflected the growing secularism of Tokugawa society and the agnosticism of the Confucian heritage and at the same time did not conflict with the dominant secularism, materialism, and nationalism that most appealed to them in the nineteenth-century West. Thus the guiding philosophy of Meiji Japan was a natural and easy blend of the Confucian concept of the perfectibility of society through the proper ethico-political organization and leadership, and Western confidence in science as leading to unlimited progress.

This pragmatic, utilitarian approach helps explain the extraordinary moderation of the revolutionary changes in Meiji Japan. The virulent "expel the barbarians" doctrine, which most leaders had supported in their younger days, and the use of assassination during those years as a common political weapon had shown how extreme the Japanese could be. Yet none of the Meiji leaders was a doctrinaire idealist. In typical East Asian fashion, they could see that practical optimums usually lay far short of logical extremes.

Their moderation was also due to their typical Japanese skill at teamwork. They were all strong personalities, yet most of them showed a great capacity for effective cooperation. In contrast with political patterns in many countries, not even the most powerful and influential of these men ever sought to monopolize authority by eliminating the others. When one found that his policies had failed or lost support, he usually stepped aside in favor of someone else who better represented the consensus. The result was extraordinary flexibility in policy for a government that had no formal mechanism for deciding differences of opinion. This flexibility in turn made it easy for the government to retreat from unnecessarily extreme positions and maintain a middle course.

The Native Religions. The Meiji leaders, because of their early Confucian training and entirely secular outlook, were not interested in religion, except as a possible handmaiden of the state. Nor were they particularly interested in Confucianism. They had grown up under its influence, and many of its attitudes persisted in their minds. But as the organized orthodoxy of the Tokugawa system they were destroying, it stood discredited in their eyes. Confucianists were the most effective critics of Christianity, and in time Confucian thinkers managed to win acceptance from government leaders for some of their ideas, but many of the fundamental ideas of Confucianism were obviously not suited to the new situation, and it was unable to provide the guiding philosophy for the new Japan.

Since a revived interest in Shintō had figured among the intellectual trends that had raised the prestige of the imperial house during the late eighteenth and early nineteenth centuries, some of the participants in the Restoration movement had expected the establishment of a Shintō-oriented government, modeled on the semitheocracy of the Japanese state of more than a millennium earlier. Such ideas lay behind the placing of the Office of Shintō Worship above the organs of civil government in 1869. They also help account for the somewhat violent disestablishment of Buddhism in the first years of the new regime.

The Buddhist clergy, through the system known as Dual Shintō, had gained administrative control over a large proportion of the Shintō shrines almost a thousand years earlier. Under the Tokugawa most Japanese had been forced to register for census purposes as members of Buddhist parishes. Now this latter practice was discontinued; the administrative association of Buddhist and Shintō institutions was dissolved; and Shintō properties were restored to their own priests. These measures inspired a general anti-Buddhist outburst, in which church property and many artistic treasures were destroyed.

Despite the official favor shown to Shintō, the attempted revival had very little inner life and soon faded away completely. Neither institutionally or intellectually did this simple nature worship have much to offer the men of the new age. The Office of Shintō Worship was downgraded in 1871 and the next year replaced by a religiously neutral Board of Religious Instruction, which was abolished four years later. The government continued to control and support most Shintō shrines, but the Shintō cults themselves lapsed into their traditional passive state, forming no more than a quiet groundswell in the emotional life of the people. Only the so-called popular Shintō Sects, such as Tenrikyō, which were recently founded, eclectic religions, popular among the lower classes, continued to show much vigor.

Buddhism was hard hit by the violent reaction against it in the early years after the Restoration. These attacks indeed shook it from its lethargy of recent centuries. Christianity also proved a stimulating challenge. There was a gradual revival of Buddhist scholarship. The large Shinshū, or True (Pure Land) Sect, showed particular vitality. In time it even adopted some of the organizational techniques of the Christian churches, including foreign missions to the nearby continent, Hawaii, and the West Coast of the United States.

The Reintroduction of Christianity. Both Shintō and Buddhism labored under the handicap of being too closely associated with the feudal past, whereas Christianity had the advantage of being part of the Western civilization that seemed to many Japanese the obvious wave of the future. This assumption contributed to what success Christianity had in Japan, but at first it was offset by strong anti-Christian prejudices inherited from the past.

The new government in 1868 actually reestablished the old Tokugawa bulletin boards proscribing Christianity. In the same year it aroused a storm of protest from the foreign diplomats by rooting out a clandestine community of some three thousand Christians which had remained in the Nagasaki area from the period of Catholic missions in the sixteenth and seventeenth centuries. Not until the members of the Iwakura Mission had seen how strongly the Western nations felt about their religion did the government in 1873 drop the old ban on Christianity, and even then only indirectly by removing the public bulletin boards on the grounds that their content was already well known.

But Christianity had in the meantime reentered Japan. As early as 1859 American Protestant missionaries had taken advantage of the Harris treaty to come to the open ports. One of the first was Guido Verbeck of the Dutch Reformed Church, who, coming to Nagasaki, taught English to Ōkuma and other men who later had important roles in the Meiji government. After the Restoration, Verbeck became a teacher in the forerunner of Tōkyō University and a government adviser. Another early figure was Dr. J. C. Hepburn, a medical missionary of the American Presbyterian Church. He compiled a Japanese-English dictionary, published in Shanghai in 1869, which established the standard system for romanizing Japanese that still bears his name. Catholic missionaries also started to regather their remaining flock in the Nagasaki area, while a French priest established a church in Yokohama in 1862.

The most remarkable of the missionaries was the Russian Orthodox monk Nikolai (1836–1912). He came to Hakodate in 1861 as chaplain of the local Russian community and moved in 1872 to Tōkyō, where he became the bishop and later the archbishop of a flourishing missionary church. In 1884 he started construction of a great cathedral which is still a landmark of the city.

By 1873 there were fifty-three Protestant, Catholic, and Orthodox missionaries in Japan. The prejudice against Christianity subsided only slowly, and occasional acts of overt hostility still occurred. But there was relatively little resistance from the native religious communities, which themselves had been thrown into confusion by the changes sweeping the country. Moreover, during the 1880's the government, partly because of religious indifference and partly to please the Western nations, adopted a policy of complete religious toleration, which was formally written into the new constitution in 1889. Christianity was tacitly accepted, along with Buddhism and Shintō, as one of the three recognized religions.

Although Christianity has never had much mass appeal in modern Japan, it did attract certain inquiring intellectuals. One example was Niishima Jō (1843–1890; also known as Joseph Neesima), a samurai from central Honshū. He managed to leave Japan on an American vessel in 1865, was financed through Amherst College by an interested American ship's captain, and served as an interpreter for the Iwakura Mission. Subsequently he became an ordained Congregational minister. Returning to Japan, he founded in Kyoto in 1875 a private Christian school, which grew into Dōshisha University. A group of young samurai, known as the Kumamoto Band, who had been converted by an American teacher of English at Kumamoto (Captain Janes), transferred to this institution in 1876 and later became prominent Christian leadership.

Similarly Dr. Clark, who came in 1876 to the Sapporo Agricultural College in Hokkaidō, converted several able young Japanese of samurai origin. Among these were Nitobe Inazō (1862–1933), who became a leading scholar and educator, and Uchimura Kanzō (1861–1930), who reacted to the sectarian divisions and close national affiliations of the Protestant missionary societies by founding a "No Church" (Mukyōkai) movement. This, though lacking all formal church organization, won the support of many leading Christian intellectuals. Uemura Masahisa (1857–1925), who was born a shogunal retainer, became the leading clergyman of the Church of Christ in Japan (Nihon Kirisuto Kyōkai), the Calvinist branch of the Protestant movement.

By 1888 the Protestants had translated the Bible into acceptable Japanese and were founding schools all over the country. In Tōkyō alone, American missionary societies founded three institutions—Rikkyō in 1874, Aoyama Gakuin in 1883, and Meiji Gakuin in 1886—all of which later grew into universities. But in spite of its strength among intellectuals, the Christian movement remained numerically very small. Although

Christians had constituted close to 2 per cent of the Japanese population in the early seventeenth century, in 1889 they numbered less than a quarter of 1 per cent, divided among forty thousand Catholics, twenty-nine thousand Protestants, and eighteen thousand Orthodox.

EDUCATION

New knowledge was essential for everything that the Meiji leaders hoped to achieve. Their clear realization of this point was evident in the statement in the "Five Articles Oath" of 1868 that "knowledge shall be sought throughout the world so as to strengthen the foundations of imperial rule," as well as in the emphasis they placed on developing a modern educational system.

Study Abroad. The first need was to acquire the necessary new knowledge from the Occident. One obvious way was by study abroad. The shogunate and some of the *han* had started this before the Restoration. Among the first students sent by the shogunate to the Netherlands in 1862 had been Enomoto, the later naval commander, along with others who were to play important roles in modernizing Japan. Itō and Inoue were sent by Choshu to England in 1863, and in 1865 Mori Arinori (1847–1889), who was to be another important government leader, was sent there by Satsuma.

The sending of students abroad was continued and expanded by the new government to the limit of its financial abilities. Young men and even some young women were sent to Europe and the United States. As noted above, no less than fifty-four students accompanied the Iwakura Mission in 1871.

Students returned from the West played a critical role in the modernization of Japan. Several of them, such as Itō, Inoue, and Yamagata, were among the chief architects of the Japanese state. Others, such as Saigō Tsugumichi, Enomoto, Mori, and Inoue Kowashi (or Ki; 1844–1895), a samurai from Kumamoto, were only slightly less important as statesmen or advisers to the top leaders. Many others have careers as political, intellectual, and economic innovators and leaders.

A large proportion of the important leaders of the Meiji period studied in the West during their early, formative years, and most of the others traveled in the Occident and observed its institutions at least in a superficial manner. It is significant that, of the top dozen figures, only two never went to Europe or America. These were Ōkuma, who was enough of an iconoclast not to need to see the West, and the elder Saigō, who failed to make the full transition to the new age and became instead the last dangerous opponent of Japan's modernization.

Foreign Experts. Importing foreign experts was another way to get knowledge of the West and mastery of its technology. In the closing years of the old regime, foreign experts had been used in various industrial undertakings. The new government greatly expanded the use of such hired talent. We have already noted the role of Americans in the development of Hokkaidō, the employment of thirty-four foreigners by the Bureau of Mines in 1873, and the use of various European experts in setting up factories. Between 1868 and 1874 an Englishman, R. H. Brunton, supervised the costly task of installing lights and buoys for navigation. By 1879 the Ministry of Industry employed 130 foreigners, whose salaries accounted for nearly three-fifths of the ministry's fixed expenditures.

Since the "Dutch learning" of the late Tokugawa period had proved to be a half century or more out of date, a new start in Western science and scholarship was made through the use of foreign scholars. A series of German doctors, starting in 1871, gave Japanese medicine a strong German cast that still persists. English and American scholars were more important in other sciences. Professor E. S. Morse of Harvard, who arrived in 1877, is remembered as the founder of modern zoological, anthropological, archaeological, and sociological studies, and the Japanese still feel a strong sense of debt to Ernest Fenollosa of Boston, who came as a professor of philosophy in 1878 and by his own enthusiasm helped to revive an interest in the native artistic tradition.

In the present day, underdeveloped nations can usually secure experts and scholars on easy terms from foreign nations or international agencies, but in the nineteenth century the Japanese had to make a much greater effort to get them and had to pay for them entirely out of their own funds. Perhaps because the foreign experts were hired on Japanese terms, they seem to have been more esteemed and put to better use than is sometimes the case today.

The foreign experts and scholars were inordinately expensive, because they required what were by Japanese standards fabulous salaries and a luxurious style of living and so they were replaced as quickly as possible by their Japanese students and assistants or by Japanese returned from study abroad. For example, the number of foreign employees in the Bureau of Mines was reduced by a third between 1873 and 1880. Subsequently, as a result of Matsukata's retrenchment policy, foreign experts in all fields were eliminated at an even more rapid rate. By the turn of the century few hired foreign experts remained, except as language teachers.

There was, however, one category of foreign teachers that constituted no drain on the Japanese economy and actually grew in numbers. These were missionaries, who though not usually important scholars nevertheless made a tremendous contribution as transmitters of knowledge about the West and as teachers of English.

Writers and Translators. The printed word had been the chief source of knowledge for the "Dutch scholars" of the Tokugawa period. The shogunate, as we have seen, had founded in 1811 a bureau for the translation of Western books, and this work was continued under the new government by its Translation Bureau. Many private individuals, responding to the challenge of the time, also took up the task and became more effective spreaders of Western knowledge through books than the government itself.

The leading popularizer of knowledge about the West was Fukuzawa Yukichi (1835–1901), probably the most influential man in Meiji Japan outside of government service. His autobiography, which has been translated into English, gives a fascinating account of his early life.

Fukuzawa, by origin a samurai of a North Kyūshū *han,* went in 1854 to Nagasaki to study Dutch and gunnery and the next year moved to Ōsaka to take up Western medicine. Brought in 1858 to the *han* residence in Edo as a teacher of Dutch, he discovered to his consternation that most of the foreign merchants settling in Yokohama spoke not Dutch but English. He therefore shifted his attention to English and in 1860 accompanied the shogunal mission to the United States and in 1862 the mission to Europe.

After returning from Europe, Fukuzawa developed his teaching facilities into a private school devoted largely to the teaching of English and useful knowledge about the West. Named in 1868 the Keiō-gijuku, this school eventually grew into Keiō University, one of Japan's two leading private universities and the source of many business leaders.

Fukuzawa's first fame came from his writings. He published in 1869 a book called *Conditions in the West (Seiyō jijō)*, in which he described in simple and clear terms the political, economic, and cultural institutions of the Occident, making plain his preference for the British parliamentary form of government. This work sold 150,000 copies in its first edition and had a tremendous influence on Japan. Fukuzawa followed it in the next decade with a number of others, including *The Encouragement of Learning (Gakumon no susume)*, which is said to have sold over 700,000 copies.

Fukuzawa also encouraged the development of a simple style of written language, in which the number of Chinese characters would be limited to two or three thousand. In 1873 he and fifteen other intellectual leaders, including returned students such as Mori, founded a society known as the Meirokusha ("Sixth Year of Meiji Society"), which through lectures and publication of a magazine popularized many Western ideas. The Meirokusha had only a brief existence, succumbing in 1875 when most of its members deserted it for government service.

Many other private scholars joined Fukuzawa in the task of introducing knowledge about the West to the reading public, often by translating serious works on politics and economics. Two early and influential books translated were Samuel Smiles's *Self-Help* and John Stuart Mill's *On Liberty,* in 1870 and 1871 respectively. Translations of novels and other lighter works were probably just as important in spreading an understanding of Western attitudes. *Robinson Crusoe,* translated in 1859, was followed by a flood of Western classics and popular works of the nineteenth century (works not originally in the English language were usually translated from their English versions). The pseudo-scientific tales of Jules Verne were immensely popular. Translation was the great literary activity of the first decades after the Restoration and overshadowed creative work, which was at a low ebb during these years.

The New Educational Pattern. In building up an organized school system, the government leaders naturally were influenced by Western theory and practice, but they were not merely imitative. In fact, they proved to be in the forefront of some of the modern educational tendencies.

The Japanese government had some advantages over Western regimes in developing an educational system to meet the needs of a modern state. For one thing, Japanese education, starting almost entirely afresh, was free to apply the latest educational concepts. Not having to contend with the entrenched relationship between religion and education that existed in many Western countries, the government leaders found it easier to standardize education and to shape it to the needs of the nation as they saw them. As a consequence, the lower levels of the Japanese educational system by the early twentieth century showed signs of the complete uniformity and the effective utilization of education for official indoctrination that later in the century were to characterize totalitarian regimes of the West.

During the Tokugawa period, Buddhist "temple schools" (*terakoya*) and private teachers had taught many commoners to read, while the samurai had been given a strongly Chinese Confucian education at the schools maintained by the shogunate and *han* or at small private schools conducted by individual scholars. Almost all of these educational institutions withered away after the Restoration, except for the chief shogunal schools. The Confucian "University" in Edo, the shogunal medical school, and the language programs at the Institute for the Study of Foreign Books were combined in 1869 into a new government university, renamed Tōkyō University in 1877.

During the early years of the new regime, scholars of Shintō orientation hoped to make traditional Japanese culture the core of education at the government university and to relegate Chinese Confucian studies and Western science to a subordinate status. However, this attempted Shintō revival was no more successful in education than in religion. The old Confucian orientation of education was also largely discarded under the vigorous attack of men like Fukuzawa, who championed not only a utilitarian concept of education but specifically the liberal Anglo-Saxon ideal of education as a means of developing independent, self-respecting individuals.

In 1871 the government dropped all but the Western aspects of the work at its university and established a Ministry of Education on occidental models. The next year this ministry adopted the highly centralized French system, with the country divided into eight university districts, and subdivided into middle-school and elementary-school districts. Sixteen months of schooling were made compulsory for children of both sexes. Compulsory education was extended to three years in 1880 and later to six years.

It was no easy matter to carry out such a plan because of the insufficiency of both funds and teachers. As late as 1886 only 46 per cent of the children of statutory school age were in school. But by 1905 the figure had risen to 95 per cent, and subsequently it crept up still further, until Japanese literacy rates were among the highest in the world.

In the meantime the original centralized French plan had undergone more than one fundamental change. It had hardly been adopted when more liberal American concepts of education began to dominate the Education Ministry as the result of the influence of men like Fukuzawa and Mori, then stationed in Washington. Dr. David Murray of Rutgers College was brought to Japan in 1873 and for the next six years served as an influential adviser in the Ministry of Education. Elementary education was modeled on that of America, control over the newly founded normal schools was handed over to the prefectural governments, and in 1879 a plan for the complete decentralization of control over education was adopted, though never put into effect.

The liberalization of education was also fostered by private schools. Mention has already been made of Fukuzawa's Keiō-gijuku and of Dōshisha and other Christian schools. Ōkuma, who, as we shall see, was forced out of the government in 1881, answered his political rivals partly by founding in 1882 an institution that grew into Waseda University. Waseda, which is ranked with Keiō as one of the two leading private universities of Japan, became an important source not only of business leaders but also of democratic politicians. During these years many other private schools were founded, and some grew into large universities.

Under Christian auspices a start was also made in women's education. Missionary societies founded many of the early secondary schools for girls, and Chirstian leaders subsequently introduced higher education for women. Tsuda Umeko, one of the first five girls sent as students to the United States in 1871, founded Tsuda College in 1900 as an institution specializing in the English language. Japan Women's University (Nihon Joshi Daigaku) and Tōkyō Women's University (Tōkyō Joshi Daigaku) were founded under Christian auspices in 1901 and 1918. Though most private schools for men were in time overshadowed by the prestige of government institutions, private schools still remain in the forefront of women's education.

The Perfected Educational System. A great shift in educational policy came during the 1880's. By that time the new leaders, having successfully weathered the grave political and economic crises of their first decades of rule, could turn to the consolidation and rationalization of the system they were creating. A highly centralized, strictly controlled educational system probably appealed to them as being more in keeping with the Confucian concept of the close relationship between education, morality, and government, and better adapted to building a strong and prosperous state than the decentralized and freer American system. The shift in educational policy was also part of the general swing during the 1880's away from unnecessarily close imitation of the West and back toward more-traditional values.

The first sign of change was a decision in 1882 to put a greater emphasis in elementary education on courses in morals, through which undesirable occidental influences could be combated and proper attitudes inculcated in the masses. The same tendency was manifest in the issuance in 1890 of a brief document, known as the Imperial Rescript on Education, on which the government laid great emphasis.[1] This document makes only passing reference to education but stresses the ideals of social harmony and loyalty to the throne. Its strongly Confucian tone, reminiscent of the Sacred Edict of the K'ang-hsi Emperor in China, resulted from the influence of Motoda Eifu (1818–1891), the emperor's venerable Confucian tutor. But the concept of mass indoctrination through formal education, which lay behind the issuance of the document, was entirely modern.

Traditionalists were by no means the primary architects of the new educational policy. The most important figures were men like Mori who were earnest students of the West. Mori, who became minister of education in 1885, was one of the most iconoclastic and Westernized of all the Meiji leaders. He was, in fact, assassinated by a fanatic in 1889 for allegedly desecrating the Ise Shrines, greatest of Shintō holy places. Yet Mori felt strongly that an educational system should operate "not for the sake of the pupils but for the sake of the country."

Another student of the West who followed the same line of thought was Katō Hiroyuki (1836–1916), who had been an instructor of Dutch in the old Institute for the Study of Foreign Books and served for many years as president of Tōkyō University. Katō had entertained very liberal political views, but a knowledge of German brought him under the influence of the more authoritarian German tradition, and he came increasingly to emphasize the supremacy of the state in all matters, including education. This German influence was further heightened by Professor Emil Hausknecht, who came to Tōkyō University in 1887 to lecture on pedagogy.

Part of the new educational policy was an entirely healthy emphasis on Japanese and Chinese literature, history, and thought, to balance the hitherto almost exclusive concern with Western subjects. Other aspects of the new policy were an increasing emphasis on indoctrination in education, the standardization of the curriculum, and increased government control over private institutions, especially at the lower educational levels. Still another aspect was the expansion of the government school system and the enhancement of its prestige over the private schools. As a result, private elementary and secondary schools shrank to relative insignificance. In 1896 higher schools were added as a new educational level between the middle schools and universities. In 1903 these were divided between technical schools, which gave terminal training, and academic higher schools, which led on to the universities and, in the case of the government higher schools, enjoyed much prestige.

Tōkyō University was reorganized into a genuine multifaculty university in 1886 and became the principal training center for future government officials. For a while its graduates were accepted directly into government service without examination. An inevitable result of this policy was the domination of the higher ranks of the bureaucracy by graduates of the Law Faculty of Tōkyō University, a tradition which still persists. Other government universities were subsequently added—Kyōto in 1897, Tōhoku (in Sendai) in 1907, Kyūshū (in Fukuoka) in 1910, Hokkaidō (in Sapporo) in 1918, and others later. Starting with Kyōto University in 1897, the government universities were all named Imperial Universities. In prestige, these Imperial Universities (the "Imperial" was dropped from the name after the Second World War) have usually ranked more or less in the sequence of their founding, and most of them far outrank the private universities.

Early in the twentieth century, the new Japanese educational structure was almost complete. At the bottom were compulsory six-year coeducational elementary schools, designed to produce a literate citizenry for efficient service in the army, factories, and fields. On the level above these were three types of institutions: (1) five-year academic middle schools for boys, (2) various lower technical schools, which produced the lower levels

of technical skills, and (3) the girls' higher schools, which were supposed to provide all the education needed even by girls from better families. Above this level stood the three-year academic higher schools and the higher technical schools. And at the top of the pyramid were the three-year government universities (four-year in medicine), which produced the elite.

This was a beautifully logical system, and on the whole it worked very well. The unchallenged prestige of the government institutions, which had the lowest tuition rates, gave Japanese education a more egalitarian flavor than the schools of the English-speaking countries. But the whole seventeen-year educational program was so carefully tailored to fit the needs of the state, as these were envisioned by its leaders, that it did not adequately meet all the educational needs of Japanese society. Women's higher education, for example, grew up largely outside the official educational structure, and the continued rapid growth of private universities showed that there was a demand in Japanese society for much more higher education than that deemed adequate by the government.

THE INTRODUCTION OF REPRESENTATIVE INSTITUTIONS

Universal elementary education and the great expansion of higher learning eventually had a profound impact on Japan, creating social and intellectual conditions comparable to those that contributed to the rise of modern democracy in the West. But long before the new education had produced these results, the Japanese were beginning to experiment with representative government and had decided to create a parliament.

The introduction of democratic institutions was perhaps the most surprising innovation of the Meiji period, because the Japanese had in their background no trace of representative government either in theory or in practice. The group in charge of the government had demonstrated its ability to control the nation without sharing its authority through democratic procedures. But the effort at democracy in Japan was part of a worldwide trend. All countries admired the power of Europe. Constitutional government appeared to be one source of this power. Therefore, several non-European countries that had not become European colonies attempted in the last nineteenth or early twentieth century to imitate the Occident and set up constitutional governments. Turkey, Egypt, Persia, and others tried this, but most of them failed.

If one assumes that democracy is the modern political norm, then the limited progress the Japanese made toward democracy during the Meiji period might be described as a failure. But such an assumption is anachronistic because it reads back into the nineteenth century aspirations and conditions more typical of the twentieth. In nineteenth-century terms, the progress of Meiji Japan toward democracy was a significant and surprising success, for it was the first demonstration that elements of democracy could be transplanted and live in a society with neither a native democratic heritage nor a strong belief in democratic ideals.

The Intellectual Background. The successes of democracy in Japan in the twentieth century were no doubt due to the modernization of the society as a whole, but the introduction of democratic ideas and institutions in the nineteenth century must be attributed to other factors. One was the existence at the time of the Restoration of a relatively broad stratum of society that was not only well educated but also politically conscious. The new government was not dealing only with illiterate peasants and unthinking townsmen. A large per centage of the samurai were men of education, and they had strong traditions of political leadership, fostered by the feudal division of the country into 265 autonomous units. Many townsmen and richer peasants were well educated and capable of independent thinking. Influenced by new ideals from the West and by changed conditions at home, they too, quickly developed an interest in politics.

Although a small group of men had won firm control over the nation, these other politically conscious Japanese did not all meekly acquiesce in their rule, as the samurai revolts of the 1870's clearly showed. Among the thousands of Japanese who rushed into new fields of economic or intellectual endeavor, many were subsequently drawn into the government; a few remained proudly aloof—like Fukuzawa, who preferred to make his contribution from outside the government, even though its leaders accepted him as their equal. Others who felt they deserved to be in the government but had found no place in it demanded a share in political leadership.

Demands for the sharing of political power, though a major historical source of democracy in the West, did not force democratic institutions on a reluctant government in Meiji Japan. The governing group had gained such complete and rapid mastery over the nation, and the whole concept of democracy was so unfamiliar to most Japanese, that the new regime at first did not have to worry about such outlandish ideas.

Rather, democratic institutions were introduced chiefly because many government leaders felt that Japan had something to gain from them. They were influenced by prevalent Western beliefs in the triumph of democracy as part of the inevitable course of progress. They saw the specter of the French Revolution as the fate of any too-autocratic regime. They also noted that strong and advanced countries like Great Britain, France, and the United States based their national strength on democracy, while democratic ideas had some currency in all of the more-modernized nations. Assuming that representative institutions, like machine production, were among the reasons for the power and dominance of the Occident, most of the government leaders felt impelled to introduce at least some aspects of parliamentary government as a means of modernizing and strengthening the nation. The introduction of democratic institutions, they also felt, would help win the esteem of the West and bring nearer the day of Japan's acceptance as an equal.

If the Japanese leadership, both within and outside the government, had not been as pragmatic and moderate as it was, the experiment with democratic institutions might have been rashly attempted and hastily abandoned. Instead, the Japanese felt their way cautiously and slowly. In this they had the advantage of the nineteenth-century setting for their experiment. Few expected that democracy would be achieved in one giant leap, as is the common twentieth-century assumption. Even in Europe at that time, electorates were usually limited and parliaments circumscribed in their powers. Neither the Japanese nor their foreign advisers expected more for Japan. Former president Grant of the United States, when consulted during this trip to Japan in 1879, advised the emperor to adopt parliamentary institutions only gradually and with great caution.

The introduction of representative government, then, was a slow process—so slow that most critics have described it as a series of failures. But its very slowness helped ensure its success. For a half century, democratic institutions steadily expanded their scope and power, until by the 1920's Japan had become much more democratic than most Meiji Japanese would have desired.

Early Agitation for Representative Government. In the last years of the Tokugawa, a few men had shown interest in the representative political institutions of the West, and had made some proposals. A council of *han* representatives, for example, seemed one way to have the shogunate share its former monopoly of national leadership. It also seemed a way to avoid the transfer of the shogunate's full powers to a single *han,* or to some small group of leaders, which many feared would be the result of the Restoration. Because of such fears the new regime promised in the "Five Articles Oath" of 1868 that "deliberative assemblies shall be widely established and all matters decided by public discussion."

However, both "deliberative assemblies" and "public discussion" were quite unfamiliar to the government leaders and to the would-be participants. The four attempts between 1868 and 1870 to create a deliberative assembly made up partly of *han* representatives seemed to add nothing of value, and there was no great outcry when the effort was quietly dropped. Attempts at local assemblies, first within some of the *han* and later in various new units of local government, proved no more successful. The concepts of representation, majority decision, and a loyal opposition were simply too foreign to the whole Japanese political background.

Interest in representative institutions reached a new level in the autumn of 1873, when the split in the government ranks over Korea brought to a head two very different types of samurai opposition. These were led, respectively, by Saigō and Itagaki, two of the triumvirate that had dominated the government during the absence of the Iwakura Mission. As we have seen, Saigō retired in dudgeon to Satsuma, where he became the focal point of the major military effort to overthrow the government. In contrast, Itagaki of Tosa chose the method of peaceful political agitation in favor of democratic institutions.

In the autumn of 1873 Itagaki, with Etō of Hizen and Gotō and other Tosa leaders, founded a political club, which the next January they named the Public Party of Patriots (Aikoku Kōtō). This was a daring departure from political precedent, because political parties or factions of any sort had usually been regarded in East Asia as disruptive of good government, if not openly subversive. The new "party" included several students returned from the West. Itō presented the government with a memorial, denouncing its

arbitrariness and calling for the establishment of "a council-chamber chosen by the people."

Shortly afterward, Itagaki left Tōkyō and returned to Tosa, where he flatly refused to become involved in Etō's revolt in Saga. Instead he founded a new political organization. In this he was joined by Kataoka Kenkichi (1843–1903), a Tosa samurai who had withdrawn with him from the government. Kataoka served as president of the new organization and in time became a parliamentary leader and a prominent Christian layman. The new group was called the Risshisha, or "Society to Establish One's Moral Will," a name based on the Japanese translation of the title of Samuel Smiles's widely read book, *Self-Help.*

One aim of the Risshisha was the economic rehabilitation of the samurai class, a problem that weighed heavily on Itagaki's mind. The organization, however, was more successful as a political movement devoted to the creation of a popular assembly. It spread rapidly throughout Tosa and from the samurai down to the commoners. To make the movement nationwide, Itagaki founded still another organization, called the Society of Patriots (Aikokusha) in Ōsaka in January 1875.

It is hard to say why Itagaki among the early political leaders took this unusual turn toward popular democratic agitation or why the samurai and commoners of Tosa were so very responsive and produced such a large share of the early leaders of the democratic movement. Tosa does not seem to have been more advanced economically or socially than many other parts of Japan and was probably well behind the more-urbanized central regions of Honshū. And Itagaki, like Saigō, was more of a military man than some of the more politically minded new leaders, such as Kido and Itō.

One explanation for the prominence of Tosa men in the democratic movement was their strong resentment over the dominance of men from Satsuma and Choshuin the new government. Although Tosa had played an important role in its founding and Tosa samurai probably ranked next in numbers in the administration to men from these other two *han,* Itagaki and his associates were disgruntled at their minority status and were quick to assume the role of a political opposition. The great responsiveness of the commoners of Tosa to Itagaki's call for a popular movement may be attributed partly to the strong position of the "rural samurai" and village headmen of Tosa and their tradition of rural opposition to the *han* government. This unusual political situation may explain why Tosa, under the leadership of Itagaki and Got, led the rest of the country between 1868 and 1871 in wiping out class distinctions and why after 1873 Tosa men took the lead in demands for a parliament.

Government Experiments with Representative Institutions. The government leaders were not particularly shocked by Itagaki's proposals for a representative body, since they still regarded him as one of their own group and were themselves in favor of experiments along this line. Kido on his return from abroad in 1873 had argued that despotic government was essentially weak, whereas a government based on a constitution with reasonable guarantees of popular rights would be stronger. He also implied that, although Japan was not yet ready for even a limited parliamentary government, the people should be guided toward this enlightened end. Between 1872 and 1874, the Left Chamber of the government brought up several proposals for a constitution, and various private study groups, made up largely of officials, began to inquire into the problem of creating a constitution and a parliament. In 1875 the government issued a promise in the emperor's name that in due time a national assembly would be formed.

Itagaki was not committed to an extreme stance in opposition to the government. When the scholar Katō attempted to refute his 1874 proposal by arguing that it was still too early for a national assembly and that Prussia's case showed that national strength did not depend on such an institution, Itagaki made clear that he had only a limited suffrage in mind. In February 1875 he came to a reconciliation with his political foes.

Kido had followed Itagaki out of the government in 1874, when Ōkubo overrode his opposition to sending an expedition to Formosa. Inoue and Itō, distressed at the resignation of Kido, who was the leading figure from their own former *han* of Choshu, helped arrange meetings between him and Ōkubo early in 1875. At these conferences, which took place in Ōsaka, a four-point program of cooperation was worked out between Kido and Ōkubo; Itagaki, agreeing to these same terms, then disbanded the Society of Patriots he had just founded and together with Kido rejoined the government in March.

Two of the points agreed on at Ōsaka were speedily put into effect. These were the abolition of the Left and Right Chambers and their replacement by a Supreme Court (*Daishin-in*), designed to protect the independence of the judici-

ary, and a Senate, or more literally a Chamber of Elders (*Genrō-in*). The latter was given the task of preparing for a national assembly. In 1876 it set about drafting a constitution with the aid of a book on English parliamentary government. When the fruits of its labors were finally presented in 1880, however, Itō and Iwakura, then the chief powers in the regime, found the draft too closely modeled on English institutions and shelved it.

A third point agreed on at Ōsaka had been the calling of a conference of prefectural governors as a modest start toward a representative assembly. The conference convened in June 1875 under Kido's chairmanship and engaged in vigorous debates. Subsequent conferences were held in 1878 and 1880, but thereafter this attempt at representation through local officials was allowed to lapse.

The fourth point agreed on at Ōsaka—separation of the functions of Councilors from those of the heads of ministries—was not put into effect. The idea was that ministers should serve purely as administrative officers, while the Councilors should constitute a sort of cabinet to advise the emperor. Piqued by the failure to carry out this agreement and jealous of kubo's continuing domination of the administration, Itagaki again resigned from the government in October 1875.

The government continued with its experiments in representative institutions. The second conference of prefectural governors decided in July 1878 on the establishment of elected prefectural assemblies. This had been under discussion for some time and was put into effect the next March. The franchise was restricted to males who paid five yen or more in land taxes, and the powers of the assemblies were limited to discussing tax and budgetary matters. The local governor had the right to initiate all legislation, to veto the assembly's decisions, and to dissolve it. Nevertheless, these prefectural assemblies constituted a significant step toward democracy, for they were the first successful elected political bodies anywhere in the non-Western world. Similar assemblies were established in 1880 in towns and the other smaller units of local government.

THE CLAMOR FOR PARLIAMENTARY GOVERNMENT

Itagaki, after resigning from the administration a second time, returned to organizing a popular opposition. Some members of the

Risshisha in Tosa took advantage of the Satsuma Rebellion in 1877 to plot with a few members of the government an armed uprising in behalf of liberal principles. This led to the imprisonment of the Risshisha president, Kataoka, and a few others. Itagaki and the more moderate elements in the Risshisha decided to avoid all violence, but they did submit a memorial to the government, condemning its despotic nature and demanding that it heed "the will of the people," respect their "rights and privileges," and establish a national assembly. This manifesto was not entirely democratic, however, since it also reflected traditional samurai attitudes in its condemnation of the government for disregarding the emperor's will and for equalizing the status of samurai and commoners.

The "People's Rights" Movement. The next year Itagaki and his associates tried again to make their movement nationwide by reviving the Society of Patriots. The response this time was tremendous. The movement spread rapidly, and similar political associations sprang up all over Japan, particularly in the cities and the economically advanced and prosperous farming areas of central Honshū northwest of Tōkyō.

The burgeoning of political organizations led to some violence, because meetings often resulted in clashes with the overly jealous police. The line between opposition through rebellion and through political agitation was by no means clear to the Japanese at this time. Even assassination seemed a legitimate weapon to some would-be champions of democracy. In one "people's rights" newspaper in 1876 there were articles with captions such as: "Freedom must be bought with fresh blood," and "Tyrannical officials must be assassinated." Indeed kubo, the most powerful figure in the government, was killed in May 1878 by extremists who had the curiously mixed motives of avenging Saigō's death and defending "people's rights."

Itagaki attempted to coordinate the mushrooming political movement through national conventions of the Society of Patriots. The first was held in September 1878. The second one the following March was attended by representatives of twenty-one societies from eighteen prefectures. The fourth convention in April 1880 was attended by representatives of societies claiming eighty-seven thousand members, more than half from Tosa. The convention uniformly demanded the creation of a national assembly. At the fourth meeting, the Society of Patriots adopted a new

name—the League for Establishing a National Assembly (Kokkai Kisei Dōmei).

Two factors lay behind the rapid spread of the demand for parliamentary government, which was now beginning to be known as "the movement for freedom and people's rights" (*jiyū minken undō*). One was its development from a protest movement of disgruntled samurai into a much broader political groundswell, in which men from all classes participated. The most numerous and enthusiastic new members were the prosperous peasant landowners, probably because they, rather than the impoverished samurai, constituted the chief taxpaying group. Men of samurai origin usually remained the top leaders and intellectual guides, but rich peasants provided the chief financial support and the bulk of the members of the new political associations.

Another reason for the spread of the parliamentary movement was the growing knowledge of democratic institutions among Japanese intellectuals. Fukuzawa's *Popular Account of People's Rights (Tsūzoku minken ron),* as well as some of his other writings, contributed to this. So also did the works of other writers—for example, those of Ueki Emori (1857–1892), a Tosa samurai by origin, who acted as a political adviser to Itagaki, and Nakae Chōmin (1847–1901), another Tosa samurai, who was even more important. He had studied Dutch and French in his youth, served as an interpreter for the French minister, Roches, during the last years of the shogunate, was sent abroad to study in 1871 on Itagaki's recommendation, and served briefly in the government after his return in 1874. His chief work was the popularizing of the ideas of Rousseau, whose *Contrat social* was first translated into Japanese by another scholar in 1877. By championing Rousseau, Nakae became the spiritual father of the radical intellectual wing of the democratic movement, which looked to French rather than British political philosophy.

Nakae's help in founding the *Oriental Free Press (Tōyō Jiyō Shimbun)* in 1881 illustrates the role of newspapers in the parliamentary movement. The shogunate in 1862 had started publishing for its own use translations from the *Batavia Nieuws.* English-language newspapers, published by the foreign port communities, also appeared and were followed by less regular publications in Japanese. The first real Japanese daily, the *Yokohama Daily Newspaper (Yokohama Mainichi Shimbun)* was started in 1870. By 1875 there were more than a hundred Japanese periodicals.

None of the newspapers or other periodicals had wide circulation. Most were journals of opinion, reflecting the political views of their backers. Some were sponsored by men in the government but most by political outsiders, like Nakae or Fukuzawa, who founded the *News of the Times (Jiji Shimpō)* in 1882. Unemployed samurai flocked into journalism and created a strong tradition of protest against the government. This tradition has persisted to the present, despite many decades of efforts by the authorities to bring newspapers into line with official views. As a result, the vigorous, expanding press has tended to be on the side of the government's critics and has thus played a large role in popularizing democratic ideas.

Government Countermeasures. The government leaders, apprehensive of the growing popular demand for a parliament, were determined to keep the movement under control. In 1875 they adopted new press, publication, and libel laws, designed to prevent newspaper attacks on the government. A running fight resulted between journalists and officials, with the government imprisoning and fining editors, and the newspapers setting up dummy editors as a defensive tactic. Alarmed by the national conventions of the Society of Patriots, the government adopted in 1880 a stringent law on public gatherings. This law required police permission for any public meeting, prohibited soldiers, policemen, teachers, and students from participating in political activities, and gave the authorities such general and vague powers that they could suppress almost any form of political agitation.

The government leaders kept warning one another that firm and speedy action was necessary to keep the "people's rights" movement under control. They were not so much opposed to what was being demanded as they were determined to make the decisions themselves and not be coerced by men they considered irresponsible outsiders. Most of the leaders were convinced that adopting a fixed system of government under a written constitution, with provision for some sort of parliament, would be a decided forward step. But they did not agree as to what sort of constitution or parliament should be created or how rapidly. Opinions were divided in two ways: between those who looked toward Prussian political precedents and those who admired British institutions, and between gradualists and those who felt that the step should be taken at once.

To clarify the situation, all the Councilors were asked in 1879 to submit to the emperor in writing their individual views regarding a constitution and a national assembly. By this time the original composition of the government had changed considerably. Ōkubo and Kido, for long the two most powerful men in the regime, had disappeared from the scene, Kido dying of tuberculosis in 1877 and Ōkubo at the hands of assassins the following year. This left the former second line of samurai leadership, men like Itō, Yamagata, and Ōkuma, in control under the general supervision of the court noble Iwakura.

The responses of the Councilors to the request for their views were predominantly cautious. Yamagata, the army builder, replying in December 1879, decried the popular demands for "freedom" and the decline of traditional virtues such as loyalty, but even he felt that some sort of national assembly should be formed. His specific proposal was to select the better men from the prefectural assemblies as a start and, through this body, work slowly by trial and error toward a real national assembly. Most other leaders took similar stands for the creation in due time of an assembly with strictly limited powers. Only Kuroda, the head of the Hokkaidō Colonization Office, felt that all talk about an assembly was premature.

Most of the men in authority, in power for a decade or more, felt they knew better how to strengthen Japan and persuade the West to grant it equality than did undisciplined, inexperienced political agitators outside the administration. Moreover, they had already put into effect the revolutionary ideas of their youth, such as the abolition of feudalism, legal equality for all classes, universal education, and universal conscription. Now entering their forties, they could hardly be expected to embrace with enthusiasm so new and foreign a concept as democracy. Only a new generation with a different background could do this.

The Crisis of 1881. Consequently it is rather surprising that almost all the government leaders were willing to experiment with a limited national assembly and that one of them, Ōkuma, joined Itagaki, the self-ostracized member of the ruling group, in advocating almost complete democracy. Ōkuma's memorial, not submitted until March 1881, showed the influence of one of his advisers, a student of the British parliamentary system. Itō suggested that elections be held in 1882, parliament be convened the next year, and the British system of a cabinet responsible to Parliament be adopted.

Itō was thunderstruck by the extremism of Ōkuma's proposals. Since kubo's death, he and Ōkuma had emerged as the two strongest contenders for leadership, and he seems to have regarded Ōkuma's proposals as an attempt to get ahead of him by jumping on the bandwagon of the "people's rights" movement. This impression was heightened by the subsequent outbreak of clamorous protests in the press against the proposed sale of the assets of the Hokkaidō Colonization Office—a policy which Ōkuma, among others, had opposed in the government. Ōkuma, it was suspected, was conniving with such powerful outsiders as Fukuzawa and Iwasaki, founder of the Mitsubishi interests, against his colleagues in the government.

These suspicions were probably not justified. Ōkuma seems only to have been trying to tip the scales within the government in favor of his own rather liberal ideas by taking an extreme bargaining position. If this was so, he made a colossal political blunder, though one consistent with his impetuous temperament, for he seriously misjudged the reaction of his colleagues to his provocative proposals. Itō, a consummately skillful politician, may have wanted to seize this opportunity to oust his most formidable political rival. In any case, he and the other leaders decided that Ōkuma must go. The day after the emperor returned from a tour of inspection of the north, on 11 October 1881, Ōkuma was dismissed from office. At the same time, the Hokkaidō sale was canceled as a sop to the opposition, and an Imperial Rescript was issued, promising a national assembly in 1890.

This incident, known as "the crisis of 1881," was a turning point in modern Japanese history. Ōkuma joined Itagaki in the opposition, taking with him a number of able young officials, including Inukai Tsuyoshi (or Ki; 1855–1932) and Ozaki Yukio (1859–1954), two men of samurai origin who became important democratic politicians. Thus the popular democratic movement was strengthened while the liberal element within the government was correspondingly weakened.

Ōkuma's withdrawal from the regime removed the only major leader who was not from Satsuma or Choshu. Since these two han had led the Restoration movement, their samurai had been particularly numerous and strong in the Meiji government from the start. The withdrawal of Itagaki, Etō, and other Tosa and Hizen samurai from Tōkyō in 1873 had concentrated power

still more in the hands of Satsuma and Choshu-men. Ōkuma's expulsion furthered the process. Many influential men from other han remained, but the top figures—such as Itō, Yamagata, and Inoue of Choshu, and Kuroda, Matsukata, and Saigō Tsugumichi of Satsuma—were all from these two han. This strengthened the rising complaints that the government was a two-han oligarchy or a "Sat-Chō clique," as it came to be called.

The shrinking of the ruling group through death increased its oligarchic nature. Ever since 1868 most major political decisions had been made by a group of about a dozen men, who shared their counsels and authority with a few score more. Though this oligarchy was never a clearly defined and specific group, during the two decades after "the crisis of 1881" it was probably more static in membership and more sharply defined than at any other time.

"The crisis of 1881" resulted in a definite date being set for creating a parliament. This is often regarded as a victory for Ōkuma and the whole "people's rights" movement. Certainly Ōkuma had helped force the issue, but the victory was rather Itō's, for the chosen date of 1890 represented his gradualist view. He had already induced Iwakura to appoint him the drafter of the future constitution and to issue a series of very conservative principles for it and the national assembly. These principles, largely the work of the returned student, Inoue Kowashi, who was Itō's chief "brain-truster," included a number of things later embodied in the constitution that Itō finally prepared. Among them were the provisions that the constitution was to be a gift from the emperor, the franchise was to be limited, the upper house was to be a House of Peers on the English model, the cabinet was to be entirely independent of the Parliament and was to have a number of important powers reserved to it in the name of the emperor, and the preceding year's budget was automatically to be continued in effect if parliament failed to vote a new one. This last concept, borrowed from the Prussian constitution, was considered a trump card that would keep the purse strings from falling into the hands of parliament.

PREPARATIONS FOR THE CONSTITUTION

Although the general outline of the constitution and the parliament that would operate under it had already been established, Itō and his colleagues spent the next eight years in careful preparation for this new stage in Japan's political development. So also did Itagaki, Ōkuma, and their associates among the opposition forces. In fact, the first response to the imperial promise to create a national assembly in 1890 was an outburst of organizational activity among the political outsiders.

The Founding of Political Parties. In October 1881 Itagaki, with Gotō and his other political henchmen, reorganized the League for Establishing a National Assembly into a new party, boldly called the Liberty Party (Jiyūto)—though the accepted English translation of its name has always been Liberal Party, a title more consonant with its later history. Drawing on radical French doctrines, the party proclaimed that "liberty is the natural state of man" and its preservation his "great duty." Itō advocated popular sovereignty and a constitution decided upon at a national convention. While the Tosa samurai around Itagaki took the lead in this party, most of its strength came from the landowners and petty entrepreneurs such as *sake* brewers who, aroused by new government taxes, constituted an important part of its early support.

Ōkuma and his followers founded in March 1882 a less radical party, the Constitutional Progressive Party (Rikken Kaishintō), oriented toward English parliamentary concepts. It initially drew its chief support from urban intellectuals and businessmen. Fukuzawa and the products of his Keiō University were among its most important supporters, as was Iwasaki, head of the great Mitsubishi interests.

Both the Progressive and Liberal Parties supported the imperial institution as the symbol of Japan's political unity. There was no dispute on this point at all. But the parties did challenge the right of what they regarded as a Satsuma-Choshu oligarchy to speak for the emperor. To the party men it seemed that the imperial will could be better expressed by a parliament.

A third party of transient significance, the Constitutional Imperial Rule Party (Rikken Teiseitō), was also founded in March 1882 to support the government position on the constitutional problem. It was started with the encouragement of some of the government leaders, who apparently hoped to fight fire with fire, but it found little popular support and soon dissolved.

The Liberal and Progressive Parties, though repeatedly disbanded, reorganized, or merged, have continued as major political groupings until the present day. The weaknesses of their first years also persisted for many decades. Although they were able at times of political crisis to stir up enthusiastic mass support, their enrolled membership was very small—at most only a few thousand. Most people felt too close to the feudal past to commit themselves publicly by joining political parties. Moreover, despite this smallness of membership, party control over local affiliates was always tenuous.

Party organization showed strong survivals of feudal patterns. Though the parties had political programs, principles were usually subordinated to personal loyalties. Each party was regarded by the other as less interested in parliamentary government than in replacing the Satsuma-Choshuoligarchy with its own members. The Tosa leadership of the Liberal Party gave it a regional cast that hurt its cause elsewhere. Moreover, each group, dominated by one towering political figure, was in essence a leader-follower band, split up into smaller leader-follower factions. The parties, in other words, had certain similarities to the personally organized, daimyo-dominated, and clique-ridden regimes of the *han* of Tokugawa times.

The Collapse of the Party Movement. The weak new political parties faced formidable opponents in the government leaders, who were determined to exclude their noisy critics from participation in drafting the promised constitution. In 1882 the laws on public meetings were made still more stringent. Local party branches were prohibited, making it difficult to organize unified movements. The government also managed to get the chief leaders of the Liberal Party temporarily out of the country, when Inoue Karou, the foreign minister, persuaded the Mitsui firm secretly to finance a trip by Itagaki and Gotō to observe European governments. The Progressives insinuated that the Liberals had been bribed; the Liberals in reply violently attacked the Progressives for their connections with that "Sea Monster," the Mitsubishi firm with its big shipping line.

During Itagaki's absence abroad in 1882–1883, his party got into serious difficulties. Matsukata's deflationary policy had brought a sharp decline in prices, which made payment of the fixed monetary taxes very difficult for many peasants. The result was a wave of armed uprisings, some of them led by local members of the Liberal Party—thus involving it in open rebellion. The worst outbreaks were in the silk-growing areas of the mountainous fringes of the Kantō Plain around Tōkyō, an area economically more advanced than most of rural Japan and particularly sensitive to general market conditions. The first serious rising occurred in Fushima Prefecture north of Tōkyō in December 1882, when the local governor had overridden the actions of the prefectural assembly. The unrest culminated in a series of uprisings in the autumn of 1884.

The government, with its solid military backing, had no trouble suppressing these disturbances, which, in any case, soon subsided with the improvement in business conditions. But the uprisings discredited the Liberals and the whole parliamentary movement and helped to split the Liberal Party between the ideological radicals, who had encouraged the peasant unrest, and more-moderate elements, backed by the essentially conservative landowners who constituted the financial backbone of the party. This situation, together with the government's restrictive legislation, induced the party to dissolve in October 1884. The faction-ridden Progressives also soon fell apart. Ōkuma and some of his chief associates resigned from the party, which then sank into temporary insignificance.

Another effort was made in 1887 to rally the opposition political groups against the government, this time with new strength drawn from an unexpected source. Inoue as foreign minister had been attempting once again to win from the foreign powers a revision of the unequal treaties, but his terms, when prematurely revealed, aroused a storm of nationalistic protest in Japan. He had proposed the relinquishment of extraterritoriality by the foreign powers but had provided for a transition period during which mixed courts of foreign and Japanese judges would try cases involving foreigners. Both this provision and the proposed opening of all Japan to foreign residence were very unpopular. The 1880's also saw the height of the government-inspired craze for ballroom dancing and other Western customs which irked conservative Japanese. The government thus was open to attack from one side for its failure to adopt the democratic institutions of the Occident and from the opposite direction because of its pro-Westernism.

This simultaneous attack on the government from apparently contradictory points of view suggests a fundamental ambiguity in the party movement. But the party men saw nothing inconsistent in their stand. They advocated Western parliamentarianism as a superior political system that would give them a share in power, but they were not any more committed to other Western institutions or any less chauvinistic than the government leaders. Indeed, as men unencumbered by the responsibilities of national leadership, they could afford to be more extreme on both scores than could the men in power.

The lead in rallying the disparate forces of opposition was taken by Itagaki's old associate, Gotō. Large meetings were held in the autumn of 1887, but the government struck back vigorously. Yamagata, as home minister in control of the police, took strong repressive measures against the political agitators, and on 25 December the government issued a Peace Preservation Law, which gave it the right to expel from the Tōkyō area any person felt to be "a threat to public tranquility." In the next few days some 570 persons were removed from the capital.

The revived party movement was shaken by this sudden blow and soon collapsed completely when some of its members were inveigled back into the government by offers of high posts. Ōkuma became foreign minister in February 1888 and got communications minister in March of the next year. As foreign minister, Ōkuma replaced the Satsuma-Choshu oligarchs as the object of popular indignation at the failure to get revision of the unequal treaties, and in October 1889 he lost a leg when a fanatic threw a bomb at him.

Strengthening the Base of Authority: Itō and the Cabinet System. The running fight between the parties and the government leaders had not prevented the latter from going ahead with their plans for writing a constitution and inaugurating limited parliamentary government. The basic scheme had already been adopted in 1881. Itō, though annoyed by the attacks of proponents of French and English political concepts, remained determined that the new constitution should be based on sound Western political theory, with European precedents for its major features. He therefore had himself sent in March 1882 at the head of a group to study European constitutions.

Knowing what he wanted, Itō stayed first for nine months in Germany and Austria, studying with two conservative scholars—in Berlin with Albert Mosse, who had been assigned to him by Rudolf von Gneist, and in Vienna with Lorenz von Stein. These men as well as Bismarck confirmed his previous opinions and gave them the support of the latest conservative European theorizing. In contrast with his long stay in Berlin and Vienna, Itō was in London only six weeks and in the other European capitals for still briefer periods.

Since Iwakura, the court noble, died during his absence, Itō found himself on his return in August 1883 even more powerful than before and quite free to proceed with his plans. He busily set about creating strongholds of executive power against possible encroachments by the future parliament. In March 1884 he assumed the post of imperial household minister and the chairmanship of a special commission set up under this ministry to draft the constitution.

In July 1884 a new peerage was created to form the membership of the projected House of Peers. It was made up of more than five hundred persons in five ranks—prince, marquis, count, viscount, and baron (designated by the titles used in ancient Chou China). Most of the new peers were the former daimyo, graded according to the size of their former *han* and the latters' service in the "imperial restoration." A large but impoverished segment of the peerage was made up of the old court aristocracy. The oligarchs also assigned themselves modest positions among the new nobles. Itō, for example, started as a count; but he and a few others, through subsequent promotions, eventually achieved the top rank of prince.

Itō's most important innovation was the creation in December 1885 of a cabinet to take the place of the Council of State, in which a few high-court nobles had exercised an uncertain degree of control over the Councilors and the individual ministries. The cabinet was a strong executive body, made up of the heads of ministries under a prime minister. It not only brought Japanese administrative organization into line with the most up-to-date European models but also gave the oligarchs a consolidated base of power, free of supervision by the old court aristocracy and unified against the attacks of the popular opposition. At the same time Itō modernized the system of bureaucratic appointments in keeping with the new cabinet organization. Eventually in 1887 the government adopted a civil service examination system, based on the German model.

Itō and his colleagues made sure that the cabinet, as the chief bastion of executive power, would be entirely in their own hands. The first cabinet is a roster of the top oligarchs. Choshu was represented by Itō as prime minister, Inoue as foreign minister, Yamagata as home minister, and Yamada Akiyoshi (1844–1892) as justice minister. Satsuma had an equal representation: Matsukata as finance minister, Ōyama Iwao (1842–1916) as army minister, Saigō Tsugumichi as navy minister, and Mori as education minister. The only peripheral figures were Tani Kanjō

(1837–1911), a conservative general from Tosa, as minister of agriculture and commerce, and Enomoto, the former leader of the shogunal navy, as communications minister.

To emphasize the unique position of the emperor, Itō created certain posts above the cabinet to speak in the emperor's name. In 1885 he revived the ancient title of Naidaijin, or inner minister, often translated "lord keeper of the privy seal," a post the court noble Sanjō occupied until his death in 1891. Itō also placed the Imperial Household Ministry outside the cabinet, though continuing himself to serve as its minister. Most important of the supra-cabinet organs was the Privy Council (*Sūmitsu-in*), created in April 1888 to approve the constitution then being drafted. Characteristically Itō took the presidency of this new body, relinquishing the prime ministry to do so.

Itō chose Kuroda, formerly head of the Hokkaidō Colonization Office, to be the new prime minister. The choice of Kuroda was particularly appropriate, since it seemed politic to have a Satsuma man follow a Choshu man at the helm. Though selection of the prime minister was always determined by a complex of factors, the alternation in power of Choshu and Satsuma men was certainly one important consideration—and as it worked out this practice was strictly observed until 1898.

Kuroda resigned in October 1889, following a serious split in the cabinet over the revision of the unequal treaties and the bomb attack on his foreign minister, Ōkuma. The choice of prime minister fell on Yamagata of Choshu, just returned from a second trip to Europe. And after Yamagata's resignation in 1891, Matsukata of Satsuma alternated with Itō as prime minister for the next seven years. During these shifts in the premiership, the other oligarchs for the most part held their original portfolios or exchanged positions with one another. New men brought into the cabinet were mostly from Satsuma or Choshu, and even the two outsiders, Ōkuma and Gotō, were former members of the governing group.

While Itō and his colleagues were setting their proposed pattern for the development of Japanese politics, their political philosophies also gradually hardened into a mold. It was becoming increasingly clear that, to maintain their leadership in the face of mounting opposition both by chauvinists and by advocates of democracy, they would have to reserve extensive powers and prerogatives in the name of the emperor. While the "imperial restoration" had been an excellent justification for revolutionary changes, imperial prestige would have to be further enhanced in order to give the oligarchs an impregnable position. To do this, greater efforts would be needed to control and guide public opinion.

Thus the 1880's saw a definite crystallization of the official philosophy. Efforts were redoubled to build up the prestige and power of the imperial institution. As we have seen, education was again put under strict centralized controls, and the imitation of Western social custom was dropped after the fiasco of the fancy-dress ball of 1887. In many fields conservative German theories were given precedence over more-liberal theories from other Western countries, and the Confucian and feudal emphasis on loyalty and obedience also came back into fashion, finding expression in 1890 in the so-called Imperial Rescript on Education.

Strengthening the Base of Authority: Yamagata and the Military. While Itō had been planning a strong executive system in which, at least initially, the cabinet would remain almost entirely free of influence by parliament, Yamagata, who had even greater misgivings about parliamentary government, had been following a parallel but separate course of institutional innovation. Yamagata seems to have had a more literal and old-fashioned concept of imperial rule than Itō, and as the chief architect of the army, he placed more emphasis on the armed services as a bulwark of strong executive power. Despite the crushing of the Satsuma Rebellion in 1877, the army, made up largely of samurai born in various autonomous *han* and peasants new to their role as soldiers, continued to have major problems of discipline. In fact, there was a serious revolt in the Imperial Guards Division in 1878. Yamagata therefore devoted himself to building up the army's morale and technical competence and to developing a degree of autonomy for the armed services within the government.

In December 1878 Yamagata adopted the German general staff system. This not only was an important advance in military technology but also established the principle that the chief of staff in matters of military command, as opposed to financial and administrative affairs, was independent of the army minister and the civil government and acted only under the command of the emperor, with the right of direct access to him. To emphasize the importance and independence of the chief of staff, Yamagata resigned as army minister and assumed this new post.

In the same year Yamagata put out an "Admonition to the Military," emphasizing the old virtues of loyalty, bravery, and obedience, and in 1882 he had the emperor issue an "Imperial Precept for the Military" (sometimes called the "Rescript to Soldiers and Sailors"). The fact that this document was made public in the name of the emperor increased the prestige of the armed services. The text made clear that "the supreme command" of the army and navy was in the hands of the emperor and would never be delegated to others, thus strengthening the independence of the armed services from the other organs of government.

Yamagata, as home minister between 1883 and 1888, also had a chance to build up strong executive power in other fields in anticipation of the future challenge by Parliament. The police force under his control crushed the peasant uprisings of the mid 1880's and dealt severely with political agitators. The Peace Preservation Law of 1887, a prime factor in the breakup of the opposition, was largely his handiwork. Meanwhile he reorganized the police into a more centrally controlled and efficient body. With the aid of Mosse, who had been Itō's teacher in Berlin, he undertook a reorganization of local government into an efficient but highly authoritarian and hierarchic system, embodied in laws promulgated in 1888 and 1890.

The Meiji Constitution. The actual work of drafting the constitution and subsidiary legislation to accompany it did not get under way until 1886. The chief participants under Itō's supervision were Inoue Kowashi, who had helped Yamagata with the "Imperial Precept for the Military"; Itō Miyoji (1857–1934), who was a protégé of the other Itō; Kaneko Kentarō (1853–1942), who came from the Fukuoka domain in North Kyūshū and had studied at the Harvard Law School; and a German, Hermann Roessler. In May 1888 the finished documents were submitted to the newly created Privy Council, under Itō's presidency, which after long deliberation approved them with only minor modifications. The constitution, which had been kept jealously secret from the public, was promulgated on schedule on 11 February 1889, the official anniversary of the supposed founding of the Japanese state in 660 B.C.

The constitution and its subsidiary legislation made good the promise to create a national assembly by 1890—but with the limitations decided upon by the oligarchs in 1881. The constitution included an extensive series of popular rights, such as freedom of religion, freedom of "speech, publication, public meetings, and association," liberty of residence, and rights to property and due processes of law, but all of these were hedged about with such phrases as "except in cases provided for in the law" or "within limits not prejudicial to peace and order."

A bicameral parliament, called in English the Diet, was to be convened in 1890. The House of Peers was to consist of the higher ranks of the nobility, elected representatives of the lower ranks, and a few imperial appointees, who turned out usually to be men of scholarly distinction. The House of Peers was to be a conservative check on the House of Representatives, which was to be chosen by a strictly limited electorate—adult males who paid national taxes of fifteen yen or more. This category numbered 450,000 in 1890, only a little over 1 per cent of the population. But the Diet, however restricted in selection, was to exercise real powers and its consent was required for all laws.

The oligarchs, however, set up what they felt were adequate safeguards against parliamentary domination. The emperor could at any time prorogue (that is, discontinue) the Diet or dissolve the House of Representatives. When the Diet was not in session, he could issue imperial ordinances which took the place of laws until the Diet could take action on them. Moreover, the oligarchs sought to keep control over the purse strings by providing that, if the Diet failed to vote a new budget, that of the preceding year would continue in effect.

The oligarchs also saw to it that the constitution established unequivocally those imperial prerogatives which they envisaged as the chief defense of executive leadership. It would be unfair to assume that they cynically used the imperial institution to preserve their personal power. They were men who, since their youth, had been stirred by the concept of an "imperial restoration" and they no doubt believed in it strongly—at least in a mystical sense. It would be impossible to draw a line between their selfish or at least self-confident desires to perpetuate their own powers and their sincere veneration for the imperial institution.

The constitution was presented as the gift of the emperor, who reserved the exclusive right to initiate amendments—none in fact were ever made. Itō declared the person of the emperor to be "sacred and inviolable" and the locus of sovereignty, as the descendant of a dynasty "which has reigned in an unbroken line of descent for ages past." It made clear that the emperor exercised all executive authority and also "the legislative power with the consent of the Imperial Diet." It specifically stated that "the emperor has the supreme command of the army and navy," and it made the individual ministers directly responsible to him, rather than collectively responsible as a cabinet. A judiciary branch of government was created but, being controlled by the justice ministry, it was little more than an extension of the emperor's executive powers.

The Meiji constitution was a blend of many conflicting ideas. Ōkuma, once again in the government, and some of the other oligarchs had urged more-liberal principles, while Confucianists like Motoda Eifu had hoped for a more conservative policy. The final document reflected Yamagata's insistence on the theoretical autonomy under the emperor of the armed services and the parallel principle of the direct responsibility of the ministers to the throne. But clearly Itō had been responsible for the overall pattern. He had skillfully dominated the whole process of constitution writing, and the result bore the clear stamp of his particular point of view.

Itō so successfully balanced the various political forces in Meiji Japan that there was never any serious attack upon the constitution itself. Enough scope had been given to the advocates of parliamentary government to satisfy their minimal demands. At the same time enough powers had been reserved for the government to satisfy the minimal desires of those of authoritarian outlook. Moreover, the document proved more flexible than had been intended. It gave the parties greater scope than had been expected, while the fact that it was explicitly a gift from the emperor made open attack by conservatives impossible. Considering the period when it was written, the feudal background of the men in control of the government, and the nature of Japanese society and politics, it established perhaps as liberal a system of government as could have worked in Japan at that time.

On the other hand, the Meiji constitution contained inconsistencies and ambiguities which were to plague later generations who had a weaker and less unified leadership than that provided by Itō and his colleagues. The constitution left quite vague the degree of control the Diet could exercise over the administrative processes of government through its functions of voting budgets and approving laws. It left even more ambiguous the degree of control the cabinet and Diet could exercise over the army and navy through control of the purse strings. Worst of all, it assumed clear moral leadership on the part of the emperor, not only over the appointive members of government but also over the electorate and the Diet, but it failed to create a situation where emperors could give this leadership and did not provide organs which could perform this role in place of the emperors. The oligarchs themselves did perform this function of top leadership as long as they remained united and vigorous, but thereafter no other group fully took their place. The Privy Council and other high-court offices might claim to speak for the emperor, but the prime minister and his cabinet did not necessarily have to follow their lead. Meanwhile the army and navy general staffs, because of their direct access to the emperor, and the politicians in the Diet, as the representatives of the Japanese people, also could claim that they were the rightful interpreters of the "imperial will." Thus the constitution assumed the continued existence of a strong and unified political leadership that did not in fact exist once the Meiji leaders had themselves passed from the scene.

THE EARLY YEARS OF CONSTITUTIONAL GOVERNMENT

Itō, while reserving the trump cards for the government, had foreseen the possibility that the powers of the Diet might gradually increase until it would even have some share in selecting the cabinet. But development in this direction was more rapid than he had expected. The drafters of the constitution had looked upon the House of Representatives as a safety valve, which would give the advocates of parliamentary government a forum of debate and the prestige of participation in the government. They hoped this would lessen the pressure for further sharing of real power. The opposition, however, proved more obstreperous than had been foreseen.

The oligarchs also discovered that, in stacking the political deck in their own favor, they had made one serious miscalculation. Their chief trump card turned out to be almost valueless. At a time when the national economy and government expenditures were expanding rapidly, the preceding year's budget was never adequate. The national budget actually tripled between 1893 and 1903. Conservative German political theory

had proved deficient on this crucial economic point. The oligarchs, dependent upon the Diet to vote their ever expanding budgets, had to make greater concessions to it than even the more liberal of them had anticipated. They fought doggedly to preserve what they felt were the rightful prerogatives of the emperor and his advisers, but bit by bit leadership gravitated from their hands to the Diet.

The First Diet Session. The first elections were held on 1 July 1890, and the Diet was convened in November. The party politicians had acquired considerable experience, both in electioneering and in parliamentary techniques, in the prefectural assemblies that had been in existence since 1878. Some had developed strong constituencies among the local electorate, which, to the consternation of the government, consistently preferred party politicians over announced supporters of the government. Of 300 members of the first House of Representatives, 130 belonged to the newly reconstituted Liberal Party and 41 to the Progressives, while some of the independents were obviously prepared to vote with these opposition parties against the government.

The party men, wanting to establish party control over the cabinet, made immediate use of the one substantial power the constitution had given the Diet. They slashed the budget by about 11 per cent, concentrating on the salaries and perquisites of the bureaucratic followers of the oligarchs.

The government leaders faced the first Diet under the premiership of Yamagata, who was the least inclined to tolerate dictation by the Diet. They had all agreed that the cabinet should remain in a "transcendent" position—that is, unaffected by the support or opposition of the Diet. But the lack of majority support among the members of the lower house was nonetheless embarrassing. The cabinet was reluctant to resort to the extreme measure of dissolving the Diet. In particular, Itō was eager to the extreme measure of dissolving the Diet. In particular, Itō was eager to demonstrate, both to his countrymen and to Westerners, that his constitution was wise and this first experiment in parliamentary institutions a success. Yamagata tried to beat down the opposition by citing a constitutional provision that the Diet could not refuse to vote certain categories of previously fixed expenditures, and there were efforts at bribery and intimidation of the Diet members. Eventually Itagaki and some of his Tosa associates in the Liberal Party agreed to restore about a quarter of the funds cut by the

Diet, and the cabinet had to settle for this compromise.

Compromises of this sort were the main pattern of Japanese political development over the next few decades. They were a characteristically Japanese way of solving differences of opinion. Compromise was also a natural product of the somewhat ambiguous situation. The constitution had given neither the cabinet nor the Diet enough power to control the other completely. Nor was either body a fully united group. The Diet was divided between mutually hostile parties and a great many personal factions. The oligarchs also, though a smaller and more cohesive group, included men with sharp differences of attitude.

For the oligarchs, the first Diet session was hardly an auspicious start in constitutional government. It showed they had given away more than they had intended and revealed a growing division of opinion among themselves. Itō was critical of Yamagata's inflexible attitude toward the Diet. Yamagata, who considered himself a soldier rather than a statesman, resigned in May 1891.

Matsukata, who had served so ably as finance minister since 1881, was chosen as the new prime minister. Lacking the strong personal position of Itō or Yamagata and not fully supported by either of them, Matsukata proved so dependent on the group of oligarchs as a whole that his cabinet was dubbed the "puppet cabinet." The leaders who by this time were beginning to be called the Elder Statesmen, or Genrō, consisted essentially of Itō, Yamagata, Inoue Kaoru, and Yamada from Choshuand Kuroda, Saigō, Ōyama, and Matsukata from Satsuma. Though subsequently depleted by deaths and joined by occasional new recruits, they remained a fairly clear-cut and stable group over the next two decades, serving as the ultimate source of executive authority and making many of the decisions that had been reserved for the emperor. While each did his best to have his own views prevail, they all held to the Japanese ideal of collective rather than individual leadership. Any one of them, when pressed by the others to take the prime ministry, usually accepted with a show of reluctance that was not altogether feigned and, if strongly opposed by the others on any issue, would readily yield rather than bring disagreement to a head.

The Struggle Between the Diet and the Cabinet (1891–1894). Matsukata attempted to carry out the strong repressive policy against the Diet that Yamagata had advocated. When the Diet reconvened in November 1891 and again attempted to slash the budget, he dissolved it. In the following election, on 15 February 1892, the home minister, Shinagawa Yajirō (1843–1900), a Choshu henchman of Yamagata and former minister to Germany, used all the powers of bribery and force he could muster as head of the police and local government system. It was the bloodiest election in Japanese history. The official figures, probably underestimated, list 25 killed and 388 wounded in melees between the police, hired thugs, and politicians. But this frontal attack failed completely. The opposition forces again won a clear majority, of 163 seats, in the House of Representatives. Shinagawa resigned because of the public clamor, and when the Diet met in May, both houses passed resolutions condemning the government.

Matsukata ignored the vote of nonconfidence and prorogued the Diet for a week as a disciplinary measure. The lower house struck back by cutting the supplementary budget by a third. The House of Peers restored the cuts, raising a constitutional issue, which was referred to the Privy Council, thus setting a constitutional precedent. The Council decided that the two houses would have to compromise their differences on budget matters. Matsukata, however, ran into further trouble with his own colleagues. The army and navy ministers withdrew from his cabinet in August in protest at the punishments of officials who had intervened in the election earlier that year, and Matsukata thereby was forced to resign.

Itō now took his turn at trying to deal with the Diet. Where Yamagata, in his simple devotion to imperial rule, had advocated a straightforward policy of riding roughshod over the party opposition, Itō, with the flexibility of a true politician, took a more ambiguous view of the imperial prerogatives and was more inclined to compromise solutions. He had proposed in January 1892 that the policy of "transcendent" cabinets be abandoned and a government party be formed to capture the Diet, but the other Elder Statesmen had quashed this startling scheme. However, when the Diet, convened again in November 1892, attempted as usual to slash the budget, and sent a memorial to the emperor impeaching the cabinet, Itō showed he had other tricks up his sleeve. He had the emperor admonish the disputants to compose their differences and undermined opposition to the budget by having the emperor surrender some of his own income and order his civil and military officials to follow suit. This invoking of the imperial name and the voluntary reduction of a part of the budget in this dramatic way won enough votes to carry the rest of the budget.

Itō was more successful than his predecessors in dividing the opposition. When the Diet met in November 1893, he won some cooperation from the Liberals on matters of foreign policy and so brought them into conflict with the Progressives, who were concentrating their attacks on the failure of the government to obtain revision of the unequal treaties. In the resulting fight in the House of Representatives, the Progressives and their ultranationalists allies impeached Hoshi Tōru (1850–1901), president of the Liberals and speaker of the lower house, on grounds of an improper stock exchange deal, and ousted him from the Diet.

But in the long run, Itō too proved unable to control the Diet even by his more subtle and varied tactics. Itō's chauvinistic criticism of the treaty revision negotiations was extremely embarrassing, because they had reached a critical state. Itō twice prorogued the Diet and finally in January 1894 dissolved it. He insisted that the third election, held on 1 March 1894, be strictly fair, and he was justified by the results, which were more favorable to the government. But the new Diet voted to condemn the cabinet for having dissolved the previous Diet, and Itō, faced with war clouds on the continent and Western hesitation at treaty revision, dissolved it again in June, for the second time in six months.

Attempts at Oligarch-Party Coalition (1895–1898). Itō's second dissolution of the Diet was followed not by a renewed storm of protest but by a period of unusual cooperation between Diet and cabinet. A treaty signed with Britain on 16 July 1894, heralded the end in 1899 of extra-territoriality, a major aspect of the unequal-treaty system, thus removing one reason for the Diet's criticism of the government. More important was the outbreak that summer of war with China over Korea. The new Diet, elected on 1 September, reacting to a war situation in the same way as most Western parliaments, voted all the war budgets unanimously and almost without discussion.

The Sino-Japanese War was a great success from the viewpoint of the Japanese. They were delighted by the quick victory over their giant neighbor and the acquisition of new territories–Taiwan, the adjacent Pescadores Islands, and the Liaotung Peninsula in southern Manchuria. But when joint pressure by Russia, Germany, and France forced the government to give back Liaotung, the public protested bitterly, and the attack on the cabinet was resumed in the Diet.

This time Itō weathered the storm by openly allying himself with the Liberals, thus taking a long step away from the policy of "transcendent" cabinets. Itagaki, again president of the Liberal Party, had been gradually won over to Itō's foreign policy and in November 1895 pledged his support of the cabinet. Prime movers in the formation of this coalition had been Itō's old adviser, Itō Miyoji, and his able foreign minister, Mutsu Munemitsu (1844–1897), who earlier had been a strong advocate of parliamentary government. Originally of the "collateral" *han* of Wakayama, Mutsu had twice studied abroad and in 1877 had been imprisoned with other advocates of parliamentarianism for plotting against the government. To reward Itagaki for his support, Itō gave him the key post of home minister in April 1896, while Hoshi was made minister to the United States, and other party stalwarts were given other political plums.

But the coalition between Itō and the Liberals did not last long. The Progressives responded by joining with other Diet groups in an opposition party, named the Shimpotō, which also is best translated as Progressive Party. The new party, under Ōkuma's leadership, began to cooperate with Matsukata, who, unlike Yamagata, was flexible enough for this kind of political maneuvering. To counter this combination of the forces opposed to him within the Diet and the oligarchy, Itō sought to bring Ōkuma and Matsukata into his cabinet, but Itagaki objected. Itō's tenure as prime minister had already lasted an unprecedented four years, and he resigned in disgust.

Matsukata was selected to try his hand again at dealing with the Diet, and he followed Itō's lead in the new cabinet that he set up in September 1896. He publicly recognized the support of the Progressives by making Ōkuma foreign minister and giving subcabinet posts to several of the latter's followers. But the Matsukata-Progressive coalition proved no more durable than that between Itō and the Liberals. The Progressives felt that Matsukata had failed to keep some of his promises, and criticism of the Imperial Household Ministry published by the chief cabinet secretary, a party man, seriously embarrassed the oligarchs in the cabinet. Ōkuma resigned in November 1897, and in December Matsukata, now faced by overwhelming opposition in the Diet, resorted to the old technique of dissolution after a futile effort to win Liberal support. He then resigned the premiership before he would have to face another hostile Diet.

Itō, returning to the helm in January, turned first to the Progressives for their support, but Ōkuma's price of the Home Ministry and three other cabinet posts was too high. Itō also found it impossible to agree with the Liberals. Without party support, he saw his budget attacked and his tax measures voted down by the new Diet elected on 15 March 1898. He had no recourse but to dissolve the Diet again in June and to resign.

As none of the other oligarchs were ready to undertake the premiership, Itō suggested that he be allowed to organize a government party, if necessary resigning his positions in the government, or else that the cabinet be surrendered to the former oligarchs, Ōkuma and Itagaki. These two had just merged their followings into the Kenseit, or Constitutional Party, which was shortly to prove its overwhelming strength by winning 260 of the 300 seats in the lower house in the election of 10 August. The Elder Statesmen, who did not like either proposal, finally settled on the second. Thus in a mere eight years they had been forced to abandon completely their original assumption that the cabinet could remain above Diet politics.

The parties, however, were not yet ready for the heavy responsibility of executive leadership. The army and navy ministers, continued from the previous cabinet, held themselves disdainfully aloof from the party men. The bureaucrats, who usually owed personal allegiance to one or another of the oligarchs, were reluctant to cooperate fully with the politicians in charge of the various ministries, thus preventing the partymen's control of the administration. The sudden shift from opposition to leadership found the politicians agreed upon vague general principles but without a specific program. Worst of all, the old factional divisions remained strong within the new party. Itagaki as foreign minister had only two of his followers in the cabinet, while Ōkuma as prime minister had four. When one of these, the veteran Progressive, Ozaki Yukio, was forced to resign for having referred in a speech to republicanism in Japan, the cabinet broke up over the naming of his successor. Thus it failed after only a half year in office, without even having faced the Diet.

Yamagata's Efforts to Reassert Oligarchic Control. By 1898 the split between Itō and Yamagata over handling the Diet had become acute. From the start Yamagata had been more insistent than Itō that the Diet should have no control over the cabinet, and he had opposed every compromise step Itō had taken in this direction. He naturally lacked Itō's pride of authorship in the constitution and so felt less committed to its success, at times even suggesting its suspension. He saw Japan's needs primarily in military terms. Stability having been achieved at home, he turned his attention abroad, arguing that the geographic line of national advantage that Japan should defend lay far beyond the line of sovereignty. These imperialistic concepts might be traced to the ardent Choshu expansionist, Yoshida Shōin, under whom both Yamagata and Itō had studied in their youth. But wholly aside from such early influences, these ideas were natural to any military figure in the late nineteenth century. Since expansion or even a strong defense depended on ever-increasing military budgets, it seemed to Yamagata the height of folly to surrender control over the government and its purse strings to the economy-minded representatives of the taxpayers.

There was no concealing the divergence of views between Yamagata, determined to keep what he viewed as the emperor's own military forces and bureaucracy free from control by petty-minded businessmen, and Itō, the agile politician, prepared to make any compromises necessary to win the support of the parliament he had created. But neither Itō, with his strong following in the bureaucracy, nor Yamagata, with his even more powerful following in the military establishment as well as the bureaucracy, attempted to use his base of power against the other. The interests uniting them were greater than those dividing them. Both were devoted to the same dream of creating a strong and rich Japan, and Itō's hopes for a powerful military and firm leadership by the Elder Statesmen differed only in degrees from those of Yamagata. They both did their best to continue the cooperation that had started in their revolutionary youth in Choshu, making what concessions they could to each other. Itō had not objected to the autonomy Yamagata had won for the armed services within the government, and in the wave of nationalistic enthusiasm following the Sino-Japanese War, he obtained Diet approval for a great expansion of the military. The army alone was increased by six divisions and its budget more than fivefold, taking almost a third of the national budget.

Yamagata had been in Europe when Itō established his first coalition with a party by taking Itagaki into his cabinet in 1896. He naturally disapproved of this step and was even more bitterly opposed to the invitation to Itagaki and Ōkuma to form a cabinet. He insisted that the navy and army ministers be appointed separately from the rest of the cabinet. They were Saigō Tsugumichi and Katsura Tarō (1847–1913), a Choshu general who had returned from study in Germany in time to help Yamagata introduce a general staff system in 1878. Representing his patron's point of view, Katsura worked from within the cabinet to help bring about its downfall in the autumn of 1898. Thereupon Yamagata, taking advantage of Itō's temporary absence in China, took the premiership in November to try out his own concepts of constitutional government.

Yamagata was enough of a realist to know that he had to have some support in the Diet for his policies. As early as 1892 he had encouraged Saigō and the infamous home minister Shinagawa to form a Diet group to support his policies. This was the Kokumin Kyōkai, or Nationalist Association, which was still in existence, though in 1899 it changed its name to Teikokutō, or Imperial Party. This group, however, was not enough.

Fortunately for Yamagata the Constitutional Party, following the collapse of the Ōkuma-Itagaki cabinet, had split into its component elements, the Liberals retaining the name of Constitutional Party and the Progressives calling themselves the Real Constitutional Party (Kenseihontō). With Katsura's aid, Yamagata achieved an alliance, rather than a coalition, with the former. He stubbornly resisted all efforts of the former Liberals to obtain posts in the cabinet, but he worked out a joint legislative program with them. One result was the reduction in 1900 of the tax qualification for voting from fifteen yen to ten yen and the expansion of the House of Representatives to 369 members. Another result was the passage, with the aid of considerable bribery, of Yamagata's budgets and his bills for increased taxation.

Despite these concessions to Diet power, Yamagata's chief efforts were devoted to increasing the autonomy of the armed services and the bureaucracy. Half the members of his cabinet were generals or admirals, and his most important innovations were introduced as imperial ordinances while the Diet was not in session. These included new regulations, issued in 1899, regarding civil service examinations, which were aimed at excluding politicians from the higher ranks. Other measures, adopted in 1900, were the extension of the powers of the Privy Council and a ruling that only officers of the two top ranks on active service could be appointed army or navy ministers. As early as 1873 Yamagata had insisted as an efficiency measure that only professionals, not civilians, should occupy these posts. Now, by specifying their active status, he ensured that the Army and Navy General Staffs would have virtually complete control over the occupants of these two vital cabinet posts.

Itō's Party Government. The cooperation between Yamagata and the Constitutional Party was at best a union of convenience. As Yamagata busily devised ways of freezing the party men out of administrative posts, the latter wearied of supporting him and approached Itō instead. Still determined to have the constitution work according to his own interpretation rather than Yamagata's, Itō finally won approval from the Elder Statesmen and the emperor for his old scheme of organizing a political party. In September 1900 he founded the Rikken Seiyūkai, or Friends of Constitutional Government, made up of the old Liberals, now called the Constitutional Party, and his own supporters in the bureaucracy. Then in October Yamagata, who had for some months been talking of giving up the premiership, finally resigned, and Itō took his place.

Itō's cabinet was ostensibly a party one, since its members, except for the army, navy, and foreign ministers, were party members. However, only some of them, such as Hoshi, the strong man of the Constitutional Party, were real party politicians. Others, like Kaneko, who had helped Itō draft the constitution, were bureaucrats who had just become party members.

Since the Seiyūkai had a majority in the House of Representatives, the Itō cabinet had relatively smooth sailing there, despite determined opposition by the Real Constitutional Party. Overcoming opposition among the Elder Statesmen was more difficult, and Itō found his bill for increased taxes voted down, not by the lower house, but by the House of Peers. He surmounted this difficulty by turning the tables on his conservative opponents. He had the emperor instruct the Peers to pass the bill, which they then did unanimously. But Itō was unable to ride out criticism arising over his inclusion in the cabinet of Hoshi, who had been repeatedly associated with financial scandals. Hoshi was forced to resign in December and was assassinated the next year by a fanatic. Internal dissension soon added to the cabinet's troubles. A bitter dispute over financial measures led Itō, already wearying of his fourth term as prime minister, to resign in May 1901.

The Katsura and Saionji Cabinets (1901–1913). Yamagata was unwilling to resume the arduous duties of prime minister, and after much discussion among the Elder Statesmen, the choice went in June to his protégé, General Katsura. This marked the end of the original oligarchs' titular responsibility for the government. Yamagata served again as chief of the General Staff during the Russo-Japanese War in 1904–1905, and he and Itō between them occupied the post of president of the Privy Council from 1903 until Yamagata's death in 1922, but neither they nor any other men of their generation, with the exception of the former oligarch Ōkuma, ever assumed the premiership again or held a cabinet post. Instead they let their slightly younger protégés take over, retaining only indirect and gradually fading control as Elder Statesmen.

Katsura established a purely bureaucratic cabinet, in the tradition of his patron Yamagata. At first he had little difficulty with the Diet, because Itō, as both Elder Statesman and party president, made the Seiyūkai support him. But Katsura ran into trouble when Itō, whose party following represented primarily the rural taxpayers, refused to support his bill for an increased land tax to pay for further naval expansion. The Diet had for the first time lived out its term of four years without dissolution, and a new one had been elected in August 1902, with the Seiyūkai again winning an absolute majority. Katsura dissolved the Diet in December, shortly after it had convened. But the new one, elected on 1 March 1903, was again dominated by the Seiyūkai, and Katsura was forced to compromise, agreeing to pay for the naval expansion by loans rather than by increased taxes.

Yamagata, the other oligarchs, and Katsura naturally were not content to see Itō dominate political decisions through his double role as Elder Statesman and parliamentary politician. In July 1903 Katsura tried to withdraw from the prime ministry in protest. Yamagata then persuaded the emperor to request Itō to resign his party position and resume the presidency of the Privy Council. Itō complied and was joined there by Yamagata and Matsukata, thus making the Privy Council a major organ for policy decisions.

Yamagata's victory, however, was far from complete. Though Itō had withdrawn from party politics, his bureaucratic protégé remained in the Seiyūkai and took his place at its helm. The new

president was a figure whose double role was almost as ambiguous as Itō's had been. This was Saionji Kimmochi (1849–1940), a member of the old court nobility who had taken an active part in the "restoration" movement and had then studied for ten years in France, where he became deeply imbued with French and British liberalism. Returning to Japan in 1880, he threw himself into the parliamentary movement, taking the lead in 1881 in publishing with Nakae and others the *Oriental Free Press (Tōyō Jiyū Shimbun)*. Journalism, however, was considered a shocking profession for a court noble. Iwakura and Sanjō, the two leading members of the group, acting in the name of the emperor, soon forced Saionji to leave the newspaper and brought him into government service, regarded as a more fitting occupation for a man of his high social background.

In the bureaucracy, Saionji became associated with Itō and accompanied him on his trip to Europe in 1882 to study constitutions. In 1894 he joined the cabinet as education minister, and he served as president of the Privy Council between 1900 and 1903. Despite this exalted position, however, he had been one of the prime organizers of the Seiyūkai and was Itō's natural successor as party president. Thus on the one hand he was a hereditary associate of the emperor and a leading member of the bureaucracy, and on the other he was much more deeply committed to parliamentary government than Itō had ever been. This combination of qualities made Saionji's dual role almost as embarrassing to the oligarchy as Itō's.

Katsura managed to hold on as prime minister for four and a half years. He dissolved the Diet in December 1903 but was saved from the usual consequences by the outbreak of the Russo-Japanese War. As in the Sino-Japanese War, the new Diet enthusiastically supported the cabinet's war effort and budgets, and the whole nation exulted in the final victory. But once again disappointment over the terms of the treaty revived the attack on the government. In public opinion, control over Korea and South Manchuria and extension of the empire to include the Liaotung Peninsula at last and the southern half of Sakhalin did not compensate for the failure to obtain an indemnity from Russia. The government was accused of having snatched defeat from the jaws of victory. There was widespread rioting. More than a thousand police and citizens were killed or wounded in Tōkyō before order was restored through martial law. Ōkuma's faction—the Real Constitutional Party—which had always had a strong chauvinistic tinge, was particularly violent in its attacks on the government in the Diet. Katsura felt forced to resign in January 1906, and in the face of such strong popular criticism, the Elder Statesmen could only choose Saionji to be his successor.

They insisted that they were selecting Saionji not as president of the Seiyūkai but as a noble and bureaucrat, while he, being by temperament a gradualist, took a very moderate stand on party control of the cabinet. He selected for it only four men of Satsuma or Choshu origin, as opposed to the eight in Katsura's cabinet, but only two cabinet members besides himself were Seiyūkai members. Like Itō, he had no trouble in keeping support within the Seiyūkai, and it continued to have a majority in the Diet. Moreover, Yamagata's militarist faction in the oligarchy repaid Saionji's earlier cooperation with the Katsura cabinet by giving him support on many issues.

A fairly stable, though ambiguous, solution of the Diet problem had been reached—at least for the time being. The premiership was passed back and forth with relative ease between Saionji and Katsura until 1913, and neither was again forced to dissolve the Diet. The two proved able to cooperate with less open friction than had their respective patrons, Yamagata and Itō. Katsura was more flexible and conciliatory in dealing with the Diet than Yamagata had been, and Saionji, though a more genuine supporter of parliamentary government than Itō, moved only very cautiously toward party control of the cabinet. At the same time, he was as successful as Itō in maintaining the Seiyūkai's support for his own cabinets and the party's cooperation with those of Katsura.

When Saionji's cabinet ran into increasingly hostile pressure from Yamagata, and its Seiyūkai policies were voted down by the House of Peers, Saionji passed the prime ministership back to Katsura in July 1908. Katsura, caught between military demands for another large expansion program and Diet unwillingness to increase taxes, returned the post to Saionji in August 1911. This period of successful cooperation and alteration in power, begun in 1901, continued until the winter of 1912–1913, when the military faction forced Saionji to resign by withdrawing the army minister from his cabinet. When Katsura succeeded to the prime ministry for the third time, the enraged Diet almost at once forced his resignation.

THE FULFILLMENT OF THE MEIJI DREAM

Even in the period of relative political stability during the alternating Katsura and Saionji cabinets, there had been no clear solution of the constitutional problem. The Japanese government was no longer purely authoritarian nor had it become fully democratic. The Diet had proved unable to control the military and bureaucracy and had shown itself constantly subject to corruption, which undermined the confidence of the public. But the old oligarchy was fading from the scene and even in its heyday had not been able to control the Diet it had created. Saionji and Katsura, representing two irreconcilable views of Japanese politics, had shown the typically Japanese genius for cooperation and compromise. But their *modus vivendi* broke down completely in the winter of 1912–1913. That the military faction, using its autonomy within the bureaucracy, had been able to torpedo the Saionji cabinet was indeed an evil augury for the future of democracy in Japan. But the speed with which the Diet in retaliation had forced Katsura to resign showed that the authoritarian traditions of the past could not be easily reconstituted.

Japan's problems were not only political. By 1905 the economy had expanded tremendously, and the country was well on the way toward industrialization, but population growth had also been accelerating. In a mere half century the total had shot up from around 30 million to more than 46 million, eating heavily into the economic gains and raising the specter of a deficiency of food and natural resources within the home islands as the population went on increasing. Although Japan had become a strong military power, it had embarked on the unpredictable and stormy sea of world politics. And at home unrest and disunity were growing in the complex society produced by the great innovations of the Meiji period.

In the early years of the twentieth century, however, these were but clouds on the horizon. To the group piloting the Japanese state, the progress made was more obvious than the storms brewing in the distance. They had not set out to create a democracy or an autocracy, but a strong country, and this they had done with spectacular success. However hybrid and anomalous, the political system obviously worked well. Japan had won two major wars—against China and against Russia, the larger of the Western nations. Political, military, social and educational institutions had been modernized with amazing speed. The economy had been expanded almost unbelievably. Early difficulties in industrialization had been overcome. Though still poor and underdeveloped compared with the advanced nations of the West, Japan was becoming the one really modernized nation in the non-Western world.

The Meiji leaders had clearly succeeded in building the "rich country and strong military" they had dreamed of and in the process had achieved their primary aim of security from and equality with the West. Japan's military security had been unmistakably established in the wars with China and Russia. Equality had also been won. For years the efforts to revise the unequal treaties had been fruitless, despite increasingly explosive demands by the political parties and public for treaty revision. By 1888 only one nation—Mexico—had surrendered its extraterritorial privileges. But finally Britain, impressed by Japan's legal as well as military progress, relinquished extraterritoriality as of 1899, in a treaty signed in London on 6 July 1894. The United States and the other powers quickly followed. Subsequently Japan regained complete control over its own tariffs through a treaty signed with the United States on 21 February 1911.

Japan also achieved equality in another and more dramatic way. On 30 July 1902, the Anglo-Japanese Alliance was signed—the first military pact on equal terms between a Western and a non-Western nation. The British, seeing their long dominance of the eastern seas threatened by the rise of new naval powers, bolstered their position in East Asia by allying themselves with the only strong naval power in the area. The Japanese, facing war with Russia over Korea, needed the alliance to ensure that Russia would not be joined by another European power. Itō had favored instead an alliance with Russia itself, but Yamagata and Katsura, who wanted the British alliance, were in control of the cabinet at the time and had their way.

In addition to achieving security and equality, Japan had joined the Western powers in the scramble for empire. The intense nationalism that the Japanese had displayed ever since the coming of Perry had often been expressed in expansionist terms. But it would be a mistake to interpret Japanese imperialism in modern times as merely an expression of an inherent trait. The Japanese throughout their history had engaged in rather less foreign aggression than had most other peoples. Except for unorganized marauding by pirates in the medieval period, they had made only one attempt at foreign conquest in historic times—the invasion of Korea by Hideyoshi between 1592 and 1598.

Japan's recent imperialism thus seems to have been more a product of modernization than of native tradition. It was accepted theory and practice in the international Western society which Japan joined in the second half of the nineteenth century for strong nations to build empires at the expense of more-backward areas. Yamagata was not being peculiarly Japanese but merely a military man of his time when he insisted that the line of national advantage which Japan should defend lay far beyond its borders. In keeping with the nineteenth-century zeal for empire building, the Japanese were as enthusiastically commended by Occidentals for their territorial aggrandizement during the Meiji period as for the more-peaceful ways in which they emulated the great Western powers.

The demand for war against Korea in 1873 and the expedition against Taiwan the next year, which confirmed Japan's claims to the Ryukyu Islands, had been the product of internal difficulties more than of any clear policy of expansionism. But the government's subsequent efforts to dominate Korea showed clearly that it was adopting the imperialistic strategy of the contemporary West. In the resulting Sino-Japanese and Russo-Japanese wars, Japan obtained Taiwan, the Pescadores, southern Sakhalin, and Liaotung, and control over South Manchuria and Korea. The latter it annexed outright in 1910, without protest by any Western nation. Entering World War I as Britain's ally by treaty, Japan picked up the German colonial possessions in East Asia and the North Pacific and sat at Versailles as one of the Five Great Powers—the only non-Western nation to have been accepted as a full equal by the great nations of the West.

Thus even before the original leaders of Meiji Japan had fully passed from the scene, Japan had become a world power. The Meiji leaders had succeeded beyond their fondest dreams. This was clear even before Itō, after serving four years as resident-general in Korea, was assassinated by a Korean while traveling in Manchuria in 1909. It was all the more obvious by the time the last two of the group died as venerable octogenarians—Yamagata in 1922 after a long period as president of the Privy Council and Matsukata in 1924 after several years as inner minister.

[1] *The Imperial Rescript on Education*

Know ye, Our subjects:

Our Imperial Ancestors have founded Our Empire on a basis broad and everlasting, and have deeply and firmly implanted virtue; Our subjects ever united in loyalty and filial piety have from generation to generation illustrated the beauty thereof. This is the glory of the fundamental character of Our Empire, and herein also lies the source of Our education. Ye, Our subjects, be filial to your parents, affectionate to your brothers and sisters; as husbands and wives be harmonious, as friends true; bear yourselves in modesty and moderation; extend your benevolence to all, pursue learning and cultivate arts, and thereby develop intellectual faculties and perfect moral powers; furthermore, advance public good and promote common interests; always respect the Constitution and observe the laws; should emergency arise, offer yourselves courageously to the State; and thus guard and maintain the prosperity of Our Imperial Throne coeval with heaven and earth. So shall ye not only be Our good and faithful subjects, but render illustrious the best traditions of your forefathers.

The Way here set forth is indeed the teaching bequeathed by Our Imperial Ancestors, to be observed alike by Their Descendants and the subjects, infallible for all ages and true in all places. It is Our wish to lay it to heart in all reverence, in common with you, Our subjects, that we may all attain to the same virtue.

30 October 1890

Appendix:
Encounter with the West

"Encounter with the West"

from *Japanese Culture,* by H. Paul Varley
(Honolulu: University of Hawaii Press, 1984)

In 1844 King William II of Holland dispatched a letter to the shogun of Japan warning him that the quickening pace of world events made continuance of the Japanese policy of national seclusion both unwise and untenable. The development of steam navigation, for one thing, now enabled the ships of Western countries readily to penetrate the most distant waters of the world. China had already suffered military defeat at the hands of the British in the Opium War of 1839–42, and Japan could not expect to remain aloof from world affairs much longer.

Although they debated it among themselves, Tokugawa officials did nothing concrete in response to the letter of the Dutch king. The shogunate was at the time engrossed in the last of its great traditionalistic reforms, and the failure of this reform, combined with vacillation in the face of a growing need to reconsider the seclusion policy, portended trouble for the shogunate. The Edo regime was certainly under no immediate threat in the 1840s of being overthrown, but opinion was developing in the country that was eventually to be turned against it in the fervid movement for imperial restoration at the end of the Tokugawa period.

Interestingly, the seeds that gave growth to this opinion were first sown by scholars of the Mito school, whose daimyo was related to the Tokugawa family. For it is the Mito scholars who are usually credited with coining the slogan "Revere the Emperor! Oust the Barbarians!" (*sonnō-jōi*) that was to become the rallying cry of loyalists in the Meiji Restoration. As originally used by the Mito scholars, this slogan was not intended to be either an attack on the shogunate or a call for imperial restoration. "Revere the Emperor!" was a Confucian-Shinto-inspired reminder of the ethical obligations within Japan's hierarchically ordered society: by revering the emperor, subjects would automatically be loyal to the shogun (to whom the emperor had delegated governing powers) and, at a lower level, would be obedient to their immediate superiors. "Oust the Barbarians!" on the other hand, was an injunction to the shogunate to strengthen defenses against the threat of foreign aggression.

The debate over foreign defense and the seclusion policy became a national one with the arrival in Edo Bay in the summer of 1853 of Commodore Matthew Perry of the United States and his squadron of "black ships." Perry had been dispatched by President Millard Fillmore to inquire into the possibility of opening diplomatic and commercial relations with Japan, and in 1854 he achieved the first objective through the signing of a Treaty of Friendship that provided for an exchange of consular officials between Japan and the United States.

The first American consul, Townsend Harris, arrived in Japan in 1856, and it was he who finally secured a commercial pact. This pact, in addition to providing for the opening of certain Japanese ports to trade, contained a set of stipulations, previously worked out by the Western powers in their dealings with China, that became known as "the unequal treaty provisions." These included the principle of extraterritoriality, or the right of the Western signatory to try its nationals by its own laws for offenses committed on Japanese soil; the most-favored-nation clause, which provided that any additional treaty benefit acquired by one Western nation would automatically accrue to all other nations holding similar treaties; and the setting of a fixed customs levy of approximately 5 percent on all goods imported to Japan, a levy that could be altered only with the consent of both parties to a treaty. It was on the basis of the Harris agreement, and especially its most-favored-nation clause, that the principle European powers also acquired commercial treaties with Japan during the next few months.

The coming of Perry and Harris brought to an end Japan's seclusion policy of more than two hundred years, but it did not resolve differences of opinion about the policy. There was the question, for example, of the extent to which Japan should be opened. The Harris treaty specified only that a few ports be made available to foreign trade over a period of years. Should the rest

301

of Japan, even the interior, also be opened to foreign merchants, missionaries, and residents, and if so over what span of time? Some diehards continued to insist that the treaties with the Western "barbarians" be regarded simply as tactical measures valid only until Japan could strengthen itself sufficiently to drive the foreigners once again from the divine land; but other Japanese began to consider more soberly the sweeping and long-term implications of their new relations with the West.

The final, chaotic years of the Tokugawa period are fascinating for the momentous political events that led to the overthrow of the shogunate, but they are not especially important to Japanese cultural history and hence may be briefly summarized here. The first wave of opposition to the shogunate's handling of foreign affairs came primarily from certain of the larger *tozama* or outside *han* of western Japan, especially Satsuma and Chōshū. These great domains regarded as anachronistic the Tokugawa governing system whereby they were theoretically excluded from all participation in the conduct of national affairs at Edo. In the early 1860s, the shogunate sought a reconciliation by bringing some of the more important outside daimyos into its deliberative councils. At the same time, it attempted to strengthen relations with Kyoto by arranging a marriage between the shogun and an imperial princess.

With these developments, the initiative in opposition to the shogunate's policies was assumed by younger, activist samurai from Satsuma, Chōshū, and other domains, many of whom renounced their feudal ties to become *rōnin* and thus free to pursue their own political convictions. These samurai, also known as *shishi* or "men of high purpose," formed the nucleus of the loyalist movement that grew in intensity during the next few years. By the middle of the decade, the loyalists were openly calling for the overthrow of the shogunate on the grounds that, not only had it usurped the rightful ruling powers of the emperor, it had failed militarily to protect Japan against the intrusion of the Western barbarians. For them, "Revere the Emperor!" became a call for imperial restoration and "Expel the Barbarians!" a demand that the shogunate do what in fact was no longer possible: drive the foreigners from Japanese soil.

The climax to the confrontation between the shogunate and the loyalists, more and more of whom were congregating in Kyoto where they aligned themselves with anti-Tokugawa ministers

at the imperial court, came in 1866 when the shogunate attempted for the second time in two years to put down the loyalist faction in the most unruly of the domains, Chōshū. At this critical point, Satsuma, whose loyalists had already formed a secret alliance with Chōshū, refused to join the shogunate's expedition, and in the ensuing conflict the shogunate forces were defeated. Encouraged by this demonstration of military weakness on the part of the shogunate, Satsuma and Chōshū loyalists, joined by men from other domains, carried out a coup in Kyoto at the end of the year and proclaimed an imperial restoration. The shogun, realizing the futility of further resistance, capitulated; and, although there was some scattered fighting by stubborn supporters of the shogunate, the restoration was completed by early 1867 with very little loss of blood.

The Meiji Restoration, named after the Emperor Meiji (1852–1912) who ascended the throne in 1867 at the age of fifteen, was a political revolution from above carried out by younger, enlightened members of Japan's ruling samurai class.[67] These men and their supporters had called for a "return to antiquity" (*fukko*), and, in the early days following the Restoration, there was a certain heady excitement about recapturing the spirit and ways of the past, especially through temporary reinstatement of the ancient institutions of imperial government as originally set forth in the eighth-century Taihō Code. But the new Meiji leaders, who included some Kyoto courtiers along with samurai, were men of the future, not the past. They made this clear from the very outset of the Meiji period by quietly dropping the cry of "Expel the Barbarians!" which they had so recently used to embarrass the Tokugawa shogunate. They may have continued to harbor personal animosities toward the West, particularly for forcing Japan to accede to the unequal treaties; but the Meiji leaders were by and large pragmatic men who respected the material superiority of the West and wished to emulate it by undertaking modernization. Sharing an overriding concern for Japanese territorial independence, they believed that, quite apart from the obvious benefits and enjoyments it would bring, modernization was essential if Japan was to be protected against possible future threats from the outside. Accordingly, they adopted as a general statement of their policy the slogan, taken from Chinese legalist thought, of "Enrich the country and strengthen its arms" (*fukoku-kyōhei*). Japan was to be enriched through modernization for the primary purpose of strengthening it militarily.

The devotion of the Meiji leaders to modernization can also be seen in the brief, five-article Charter Oath they issued in 1868 in the emperor's name. This may be regarded as a very broad statement of purpose by the new regime, and it is significant that at least two of its articles seem to be explicit commitments to modernization:

> Article 4. Evil customs of the past shall be broken off and everything based upon the just laws of Nature.

> Article 5. Knowledge shall be sought throughout the world so as to strengthen the foundations of imperial rule.[68]

In line with their determination to make Japan a modern state, the Meiji leaders took a series of steps during their first decade in power that together constituted a radical and sweeping reform of Japanese society. These included abolition of the feudal *han* and the institution of a centrally controlled system of prefectural government; and dissolution of the samurai class and the establishment of basic legal equalities for all people. One of the most severe blows to the old, rigid class system, and particularly to the inflated samurai sense of superiority, was the adoption in 1873 of universal military conscription.

Despite the inevitable stresses caused by social change and the specific grievances of many samurai as they were dispossessed of their traditional privileges, the Japanese by the early 1870s had in general abandoned their dreams of restoring the past and were caught up in an overwhelming urge to join the march of Western progress. This was the beginning of a period of nearly two decades during which the Japanese unabashedly pursued the fruits of Western "civilization and enlightenment" (*bummei-kaika*). That the government intended to take the lead in this quest for the holy grail of foreign culture can be seen in the dispatch in 1871 of a mission to visit the United States and Europe headed by a distinguished court noble, Iwakura Tomomi (1825–83), and including a number of other leaders of the new Meiji regime. So cherished was the opportunity to journey to the West at this time that one young boy who accompanied the Iwakura Mission in order to study in the United States wrote (years later) that he and his fellow students all fervently believed that one could not become a real human being without going abroad.

Although it may be debatable whether exposure to the West was a necessary qualification for full status in the human race, there is no question that it became the surest means for advancement among Japanese in the early Meiji period. Of the many youths who went to study in Europe and the United States, the great majority were sponsored by the government as part of its civilization and enlightenment policy. Upon returning home, these youths had virtually unlimited career opportunities. Meanwhile, for those who could not make the trip abroad, the government and other institutions invited a number of foreigners to Japan as teachers and technical advisers. Offering high wages, they were able to attract generally excellent people, who provided knowledge and expertise crucial to the modernization process.

Outward signs of modernity began to appear throughout the country, but particularly in the metropolitan centers like Tokyo and Yokohama: steamships, railroads, telegraph lines, a national postal service, industrial factories, and, especially exciting to the Japanese, gas-burning streetlamps that "made the night as bright as the day." Most of these innovations were, of course, indispensable to modernization; but many others were just marginally important or were even ludicrous fads reflecting the craze among some people to "become Western."

Western-style uniforms were first adopted by the Japanese military before the Restoration and were made standard for policemen, train conductors, and other civil functionaries within a few years after the beginning of the modern era. During the 1870s, Western clothes, deemed more practical and up-to-date, were increasingly worn by men in the cities, often combined amusingly with items of native costume. Thus, it was not unusual to see men sporting kimonos over long pants or suit jackets and *hakama* skirts. Women and people in the rural areas, on the other hand, were much slower in adopting the sartorial ways of the West. Western shoes, moreover, presented a special problem, for the Japanese foot, splayed from the traditional wearing of sandals, frequently could not be fitted into footgear imported from abroad.

But whereas the shift to Western wearing attire was made erratically, and never completely, the transition to the Western custom of cropped hair for men became something of a national issue. The Japanese are by nature extraordinarily sensitive to ridicule by others. No doubt this sensitivity has been heightened by the minimal contact they have had with foreigners through much of their history. In the early Meiji period, as they sought to "catch up with the West," they also faced the practical problem that, so long as the Western nations regarded their ways as barbaric, it would be that much more difficult to secure revision of the unequal treaties and achieve complete independence. Hence, the Japanese government either banned or tried to restrict practices, such as public bathing, tattooing, and the sale of pornography, that they thought the foreigners found offensive. And the wearing of the topknot, which had been the practice of Japanese men for centuries, also came to be looked upon as primitive and unbecoming to the citizens of a modern Japan.

Again, it was the Japanese military who first cut their topknots in order to wear the hats of their Western-style uniforms. By the early Meiji period, all prominent Japanese men, including the emperor, wore their hair cropped (and often grew fine beards and mustaches, like their Western counterparts): indeed, it was very much the sign of the progressive man to wear his hair this way, and a popular jingle claimed: "If you tap a cropped head, it will play the tune of civilization and enlightenment." But the fashion was not immediately accepted by the lower classes, and the Japanese government felt constrained to issue occasional directives urging its adoption. Some headmen in rural villages are said to have walked around reading the directives while still sporting their own topknots; others cut the topknots but let their "hair of regret" hang down their backs. Not until about 1890 did the wearing of cropped hair by men become universal in Japan.

Among the many Western fads, none was more conspicuous or symbolic of the humorous side of foreign borrowing than the eating of beef. Owing to Buddhist taboos and a scarcity of game animals, the Japanese had traditionally abstained from eating meat. With the coming of foreigners, however, restaurants specializing in beef dishes, especially *gyūnabe* or beef stew, began to crop up in the cities. A contemporary author of "witty books," Kanagaki Robun (1829–94), even wrote a collection of satirical sketches entitled *Aguranabe* (Eating Stew Cross-Legged) about the conversations of customers in a beefhouse who concluded that a man could not be regarded as civilized unless he ate beef. Kanagaki's description of one customer includes the observation that

he uses that scent called Eau de Cologne to give sheen to his hair. He wears a padded silken kimono beneath which a calico undergarment is visible. By his side is his Western-style umbrella, covered in gingham. From time to time he removes from his sleeve with a painfully contrived gesture a cheap watch, and consults the time.[69]

Meanwhile, this newly enlightened man commented to his neighbor that "we really should be grateful that even people like ourselves can now eat beef, thanks to the fact that Japan is steadily becoming a truly civilized country." Perhaps it was in celebration of the glory of beef that about this time some students invented sukiyaki, now the hallmark of Japanese cuisine to most foreigners.

Some of the more fervent advocates of *bummei-kaika* at the height of the Western fever in early Meiji times even went so far as to suggest that Japan should adopt English as its national language. But the most extreme suggestion was that, since Caucasians were observably superior to the people of all other races, the Japanese should intermarry with them as quickly as possible in order to acquire their higher ethnic qualities.

One of the most ultimately profound changes wrought by modernization in Japan was the gradual adoption of Western building materials and architectural styles. Throughout their history, the Japanese had constructed their dwellings and other buildings almost entirely out of wood. With the growth in recent centuries of great urban centers like Edo and Osaka, this type of construction gave rise to the constant danger—and all too frequent occurrence—of fires that consumed large portions of the cities. For example, a devastating fire in 1657 made necessary the extensive rebuilding of Edo. In 1874, after a fire that gutted the Ginza area of central Tokyo, the government took the opportunity to order the construction of a row of some three hundred two-story brick buildings for the use of merchants on this bustling thoroughfare. Contemporary woodblock prints show how grand and exotic these buildings appeared to the Japanese of that day. The government hoped that the Ginza would serve as a model to encourage others to build these new fireproofed buildings; and the newspapers declared that people who walked down the Ginza could enjoy the enchanted feeling of being in a foreign country.

Although more and more public and commercial buildings on Western lines were built in the cities, the construction of Western private homes was undertaken much more slowly. The higher cost of such homes was one reason; but another was the continuing, overwhelming preference of the Japanese for their traditional, native-style homes. This was one area in which Westernization made little headway in Japan, and even today the Japanese continue to live, as they have for centuries, in houses consisting chiefly of sparsely furnished rooms with matted floors upon which to sit and sleep.

In intellectual circles, the great national quest for civilization and enlightenment in early Meiji gave rise to a number of study and discussion groups devoted to the question of transforming Japan into a modern state. Of these, the most influential was the Meirokusha or "Meiji Six Society" founded in the sixth year of Meiji, 1873, by some ten of the more prominent Westernizers of the day. The members of the Meirokusha met twice a month to discuss such subjects as politics, the economy, education, religion, the Japanese language, and women's rights. In 1874 they began publication of the *Meiji Six Magazine* for the purpose of publishing articles on their views. A large percentage of the Meirokusha membership comprised men who had engaged in Western learning before the Restoration and had been employed as translators and teachers by the Tokugawa shogunate in its Office for Barbarian Studies, established in 1855 after the arrival of Perry. Hence, the Meirokusha had as its legacy the venerable tradition of Dutch Studies begun nearly a century and a half earlier in Japan.

The leading figure in the Meirokusha, and indeed the most popular and widely read intellectual of the Meiji period, was Fukuzawa Yukichi (1835–1901). Fukuzawa was a low-ranking, but personally ambitious and opportunistic, samurai who began the study of Western gunnery and the Dutch language as a youth under the patronage of his feudal domain. Later, when Fukuzawa visited Yokohama shortly after the signing of the Harris treaty in 1858 and observed the newly arrived foreigners at first hand, he learned a sad fact that was to cause anguish for all students of Dutch Studies: Dutch was practically useless as a medium for dealing with most Westerners. Fukuzawa, we are told, switched the very next day to the study of English; and, two years later, in 1860, he was selected to accompany a shogunate mission to the United States in what was the first transoceanic voyage of a Japanese-manned ship.

Fukuzawa made two other trips abroad, in 1861 and 1867. In between he published *Conditions in the Western World (Seiyō Jijō)*, a book that

established him as one of the foremost interpreters of the West. Fukuzawa was more of a popularizer than a pure intellectual, and as such he made a far greater impact on the people of his time. It is no exaggeration to say that he, more than any other single individual, influenced the minds of a generation of Japanese in the early, formative years of the modern era. His most successful book, *An Encouragement of Learning (Gakumon no Susume)*, written between 1872 and 1876, eventually sold nearly 3.5 million copies. The opening paragraph sets the tone for Fukuzawa's argument:

> It is said that heaven does not create one man above or below another man. This means that when men are born from heaven they all are equal. There is no innate distinction between high and low. It means that men can freely and independently use the myriad things of the world to satisfy their daily needs through the labors of their own bodies and minds, and that, as long as they do not infringe upon the rights of others, may pass their days in happiness. Nevertheless, as we broadly survey the human scene, there are the wise and the stupid, the rich and poor, the noble and lowly, whose conditions seem to differ as greatly as the clouds and the mud. The reason for this is clear. In the *Jitsugokyō* we read that if a man does not learn he will be ignorant, and that a man who is ignorant is stupid. Therefore the distinction between wise and stupid comes down to a matter of education.[70]

Strongly influenced by British utilitarianism and by the then current Western idea of the perfectibility of man through education, Fukuzawa became a staunch advocate of modern education, with the emphasis particularly on practical subjects. He vigorously denounced the social inequities and indignities of Tokugawa feudalism and declared that all men should be free and all countries independent on the basis of "natural reason." The democratic idealism that Fukuzawa thus espoused was concurrently reflected in the new Meiji government's attitude toward education. Dedicating itself to the goal of universal primary education on the American model, the government's 1872 ordinance founding a new public school system contained the vow that "in no village will there be a family without learning and in no household will there be an uneducated person."

Unlike most of the other members of the Meirokusha, Fukuzawa steadfastly refused to enter the service of the Meiji government and insisted upon the importance of maintaining his independence as a social critic. The sensitivity of the Meiji Six enlighteners in general to changes in government attitude, however, was revealed in 1875 when, as the result of issuance by the government of a restrictive press law, they ceased publication of the *Meiji Six Magazine* and soon terminated the activities of its parent society. Amid the continuing enthusiasm for civilization and enlightenment, the government had found itself faced in the mid-1870s with a newly organized political opposition; and the predominantly government-oriented membership of the Meirokusha deemed it prudent to dissolve an organization that might be viewed as sympathetic to that opposition.

The Meiji Restoration had been carried out under the euphoric slogan of a "return to antiquity"; in fact, the restorationists do not appear to have any concrete political plan other than to wrest power from the tottering shogunate. As leaders of the new Meiji government, they launched the country on the road to civilization and enlightenment and encouraged aspirations among the Japanese people for "independence," "freedom," and "individual rights," concepts taken from British liberal democracy, which absorbed the thinking of Japanese officials and intellectuals during the first decade or so of the Meiji period. But, although a few extreme Westernizing enthusiasts suggested that Japan establish a republic, no one of importance went so far as to advocate that a "free" people should also have the right to select their own government. The new political and intellectual leadership of Meiji Japan came almost entirely from the samurai class; and, while vociferously attacking the evils of Tokugawa feudalism, they retained the feudalistic attitude that the masses were by nature inert and stupid. It was their purpose to enlighten the people, not to make them politically active but to "enrich the country" and thereby strengthen it vis-à-vis the nations of the West. Even the iconoclastic and utilitarian-minded Fukuzawa was not prepared to encourage a critical attitude on the part of the people toward the government. When political opposition did arise in the 1870s, it was the result not of a movement from without but of a factional dispute within the government itself.

The leaders of the Meiji Restoration were primarily samurai from the domains of Satsuma, Chōshū, Tosa, and Hizen. From the outset, however, the Satsuma-Chōshū men formed a separate clique, based on the pact between their two domains that had been so important in the overthrow of the Tokugawa shogunate, and increas-

ingly they monopolized real power in the new government. The dissatisfaction that this created among the samurai of Tosa and Hizen was transformed into a national issue in the so-called Korean invasion crisis of 1873. The ostensible issue in the 1873 crisis was how to deal with a rebuff by Korea to Japanese overtures to open diplomatic and commercial relations. Most of the Tosa and Hizen leaders in the government urged a hard line, including the possibility of invading Korea; but the Satsuma-Chōshū clique, with the notable exception of Saigō Takamori (1827–77) of Satsuma, counseled restraint on the grounds that Japan was still too weak to risk any foreign involvement. When the views of the "peace" party prevailed, Saigō and other members of the "war" party left the government.

Although the Satsuma-Chōshū clique had won a major victory and had further strengthened its hold on the government, it now had powerful enemies on the outside. Some of these enemies turned to open rebellion, leading armies composed of samurai who were discontented with the progressive policies of the Meiji government. The most serious of these uprisings was the Satsuma Rebellion of 1877, led by Saigō Takamori. More than any other Restoration leader, Saigō felt a continuing attachment to the ideals of the samurai class. His bellicose attitude at the time of the 1873 crisis was based largely on his belief that the samurai of Japan could and should deal with a foreign insult by taking direct military action. In assuming leadership of the Satsuma Rebellion in 1877, Saigō made a last gallant gesture for feudal privilege and became the great romantic hero of modern Japan. At the same time, the failure of the Satsuma Rebellion also marked the last attempt to oppose the Meiji government through force.

Of far greater historical significance was the demand made by other samurai leaders, who had also been members of the war party in 1873, that participation in government be expanded through the establishment of an elected assembly. In 1874 a group of samurai, led by Itagaki Taisuke (1837–1919) of Tosa, submitted a memorial to the throne attacking the absolutist Satsuma-Chōshū regime in the following terms:

Present political power does not rest with the Emperor, nor with the people. It is monopolized entirely by one group of officials. If the absolutism of these officials is not corrected, it could mean the downfall of the nation. Moreover the only means of correction would be to establish an assembly elected by the people and to expand discussion concerning the country.

The government replied that it was too soon to consider giving "the people" a voice in political affairs. Actually, it is doubtful that any of the memorialists had in mind an electorate that would include more than a small percentage of the Japanese people. The memorialists were former samurai who espoused ideas of parliamentary democracy at this time primarily as a means to attack the Satsuma-Chōshū oligarchs in the Meiji government. Although the people's rights (*minken*) movement they thus launched eventually became a campaign for full democracy, including universal manhood suffrage, it was by no means a "popular" undertaking in its origins.

One response of the government to the people's rights movement was to issue the press law in 1875 that caused dissolution of the Meirokusha. This law and others repressive of the freedoms of speech and assembly were aimed at curbing the efforts by Itagaki and his allies to form political parties. Nevertheless, the emergent party advocates continued to press their demands, and, in the same year, 1875, Itagaki formed the first national political association, the Patriotic Party (Aikokusha). But it was not until 1881 that the *minken* people received a public commitment from the oligarchs that they would eventually be given the opportunity to participate in government.

In 1881 Ōkuma Shigenobu (1838–1922), one of the last of the non-Satsuma-Chōshū statesmen still in the government, was relieved of his position as the result of disclosures he made about corruption in high office. In the wake of Ōkuma's dismissal, the government secured an imperial edict promising a constitution and the opening of a national parliament within nine years, or by 1890. Although it may appear that Ōkuma thus forced a concession from the Satsuma-Chōshū oligarchs, in fact the latter had for long been considering how and when a constitutional form of government should be established in Japan, and the action of Ōkuma in 1881 probably did not appreciably alter their plans, although they may not have wished to reveal them publicly so soon.

The Meiji oligarchs were, by any criterion, extraordinarily capable and farsighted men who took a strong pragmatic approach to problems. Once secure in power they did indeed tend toward the authoritarian in consonance with their samurai backgrounds. But one advantage of their functioning as oligarchs was that, immune from the everyday strife of elected politicians, they could concentrate on the pursuit of loftier goals for the betterment of Japan. They were committed to making Japan into a truly modern state, and national constitutions were an integral part of modernist thinking everywhere in this age. The man who assumed chief responsibility for writing the Meiji Constitution was Itō Hirobumi (1841–1909) of Chōshū. In 1882 he went to Europe to study Western constitutionalism, particularly as propounded by German theorists; and, in 1885, he became Japan's first prime minister upon the institution of a cabinet system of government.

Meanwhile, the people's rights advocates were also active, and both Itagaki and Ōkuma formed new political associations—the Liberal Party (Jiyūtō) and the Progressive Party (Shimpotō)—in preparation for the opening of a parliament (or Diet) within the decade. It is difficult to assess precisely the differences between the two major party lines established at this time. The works of Rousseau, Mill, and other Western political theorists had been translated into Japanese and were widely read and admired by the party people. French natural rights democracy seems to have appealed particularly to the Itagaki group, while Ōkuma and his followers espoused British utilitarianism. Moreover, whereas the Liberal Party came in general to represent agrarian interests, the Progressive Party tended to align itself with the emerging class of urban industrialists. Yet, far more than any political creeds, specific issues, or class alliances, it was personal allegiance to the leaders themselves that provided the basis for party unity during this preconstitutional phase of the people's rights movement.

In addition to the political parties, an important source of burgeoning opposition to the Meiji oligarchy was the press. A number of the embryonic newspapers of the early Restoration period had been staffed by former shogunate officials hostile to the new Satsuma and Chōshū leaders in the government. With the continued growth of a modern press, this opposition was taken up by journalists who were largely former samurai excluded from government by *han* cliquism. Many members of the emergent political parties, in fact, first got their start in journalism. Moreover, many newspapers founded in the early Meiji period were intended by their founders to serve as mouthpieces for specific political and social views, almost invariably of an antigovernment tone. Hence, journalism in modern Japan was in its early development distinctly a journalism of protest, and it was to a great extent for this reason that the Meiji oligarchs so readily and frequently attacked journalists through the issuance of restrictive press laws.

The temper of the 1880s in Japan was markedly different from that of the 1870s. For the first decade or so following the Restoration, the Japanese had pursued with great, and often indiscriminate, enthusiasm the remaking of their country on Western lines. In the 1880s, they not only modified their earlier, naive admiration for the West but also began to reassess and find new value in their native traditions. For the oligarchs, it became incumbent to enunciate a coherent ideology for the state they were in the process of constitutionally fashioning. The way in which they did this can be seen most clearly in their policy toward education.

In its act of 1872, the Meiji government had proclaimed the goal of universal primary education, and, during most of the remainder of the decade, it had sought to provide training to Japanese schoolchildren that stressed practical subjects and encouraged Western-style individualistic thinking. But, by the beginning of the 1880s, the official attitude had changed and the government now took deliberate steps both to reinstate traditional moral training in the schools and to redefine the aim of education to serve that state rather than the individual. The culmination of this new policy toward education was the issuance in 1890 of the Imperial Rescript on Education, a brief document that began as follows:

Know ye, Our Subjects!

Our Imperial Ancestors have founded Our Empire on a basis broad and everlasting, and have deeply and firmly implanted virtue; Our subjects ever united in loyalty and filial piety have from generation to generation illustrated the beauty thereof. This is the glory of the fundamental character of Our Empire, and herein also lies the source of Our education.[71]

From these few lines it is obvious that, after its earlier flirtation with the ideals of Western liberalism and democracy, the Meiji government in its critical education policy had determined to indoctrinate a social ideology derived mainly from the Shinto-Confucian concepts that had evolved as a new orthodoxy of thought in the late Tokugawa period. Morality was once again to be based on such hierarchical virtues as loyalty and filial pi-

ety, and the ultimate object of devotion for all Japanese citizens was to be the throne, described elsewhere in the Rescript on Education as "coeval with heaven and earth." The new Japanese state was, in short, to be conceived as a great and obedient Confucian family with a father-like emperor at its head.

Nor was the government alone in its shift to conservatism in the 1880s. Even the blatant Westernizers like Fukuzawa Yukichi began to have second thoughts about Japan's previously uncritical acceptance of everything Western in its rush to become civilized and enlightened. To a great extent, such second thoughts were simply the result of a more sophisticated view of the West. In their initial, excited response to the utopian ideals of liberal democracy, intellectuals like Fukuzawa had failed to temper their pro-Westernism by acknowledging that the Western powers themselves were pursuing baldly self-interested policies of world imperialism. Western theorists sought to justify these policies on the grounds of the social-Darwinist doctrines of Herbert Spencer: before the world could achieve a pacific stage of fully industrialized and enlightened civilization, it must continue to engage in a militant selection process that promised survival to the fittest races and nations.

It is to the credit of the Meiji oligarchs, who were usually far more realistic than their critics, that they always kept in mind the aim of enriching Japan in order to strengthen it militarily. In 1873 they had avoided armed intervention in Korea because it was too dangerous, but even then they envisioned a time when Japan would be able to compete for empire with the West. On the other hand, nongovernmental intellectuals and the public in general did not, for the most part, come to accept the need for more statist-oriented policies and the open pursuit of nationalistic goals until the 1880s.

Overridingly the most important nationalistic goal of the 1880s and early 1890s was revision of the unequal treaties, and the repeated failure of the government to achieve revision contributed not only to growing skepticism about the West but also to the spread of conservative, Japanist sentiments. In one spectacular breakdown of treaty talks in 1888, Ōkuma Shigenobu, who had been drawn temporarily back into the government as a foreign minister, lost a leg when a fanatical member of a right-wing organization threw a bomb into his carriage.

Symbolic to many Japanese of their frustrations and humiliation over treaty revision was a

Western-style building in downtown Tokyo called the Rokumeikan or Deer Cry Mansion. Constructed in 1883 for the purpose of entertaining foreign diplomats and dignitaries, the Rokumeikan was the scene of many festive and gala entertainments, the most notoriously memorable of which was a masquerade ball thrown by Prime Minister Itō in 1887. Affairs like the 1887 ball in the Rokumeikan were regarded as the most conspicuous examples of how ludicrously even high-ranking Japanese could behave in their desire to prove to Westerners that they were civilized and knew the social graces. A decade or so earlier, such conduct would probably have been hailed as enlightened and progressive: it was a sign of the changed temper of the times that Itō and his ministers were disparagingly dubbed "the dancing cabinet."

It should not be supposed that the opposition to over-Westernization and the turn to conservatism in the 1880s was either universal or unthinkingly reactionary. Some extremely radical nationalists (like Ōkuma's assailant) did appear on the scene, but many prominent people remained highly committed to Westernization; and even those who most articulately called for a reassessment of traditional values more often than not advocated that Japan discriminately select what was appropriate for it from both East and West. The debate that emerged in the late 1880s over Westernization versus traditionalism was, moreover, conducted principally by the members of a new generation whose most impressionable years of intellectual growth had been spent during the epochal, but highly unsettling, period of transition from Tokugawa to Meiji. To a far greater extent than their elders, like the Meiji oligarchs and Fukuzawa Yukichi, they felt the intense cultural uncertainty of being torn between a Japan that had always represented the past and a West that invariably stood for the future.

Among those of the new generation who most fully embraced Westernization was Tokutomi Sohō (1863–1957).[72] The son of a wealthy peasant family of the Kumamota region of northern Kyushu, Tokutomi received Western training as a youth in his native Kumamoto and later studied at the Christian university, Dōshisha, in Kyoto. In the mid-1880s, Tokutomi moved to Tokyo, where he took up a career as a writer and journalist. He organized a group called the Min'yūsha (Society of the People's Friends) and in 1887 began publication of a magazine entitled Friend of the People (Kokumin no Tomo) to express the group's views.

Tokutomi, whose magazine soon achieved an enormous circulation, forcefully advanced his own opinions in books and articles on the progress of modern Japan. He criticized the kind of Westernization advocated by Fukuzawa and other enlighteners of the early Meiji period because it was directed only toward acquisition of the material aspects of Western civilization and not its underlying spirit. At the same time, Tokutomi pointed out the futility of pursuing the pre-Meiji ideal of "Eastern morals and Western technology," which was precisely what the Meiji government seemed to be doing then in its policy of reinstituting Confucian moral training in the public schools. Under the new policy, Japanese students were expected simultaneously to learn modern, practical things and feudal morality. According to Tokutomi, the only possible choice for Japan, if it was to succeed in modernization, was to reject the Japanese past entirely and pursue wholeheartedly both the material and spiritual aspects of Western civilization.

Tokutomi, who was strongly influenced by the writings of Herbert Spencer, justified his extreme position on the grounds that progress was a universal phenomenon. Hence, Westernization was actually another term for universalization. The features of modern civilization observable in the Western countries were the same that would appear in all countries as they advanced toward modernity. Japan already had many of these modern features and should seek to acquire the remainder as speedily as possible.

The principal challenge to the views of Tokutomi and the Min'yūsha came from the Seikyōsha (Society for Political Education), founded in 1888 by another group of young writers and critics. Publishing the magazine The Japanese (Nihonjin) in competition with the Min'yūsha's Friend of the People, the Seikyōsha people attacked Westernization and called for "preservation of the national essence" (kokusui hozon). Their general position was perhaps best presented in the book Truth, Goodness, and Beauty of the Japanese (Shin-zen-bi Nihonjin) by Miyake Setsurei (1860–1945). Miyake, a student of philosophy who remained a rival of Tokutomi throughout their long, concurrent careers, asserted that although a Spencerian type of struggle among nations was unavoidable during the course of historical progress, the process of modernization did not lead inevitably to a universal kind of state. On the contrary, nations competed best by utilizing those special qualities that distinguished them from others. Like many members of the

Seikyōsha, Miyake was much interested in physical geography and placed great store in the effects of geography and climate on the molding of racial characteristics and national cultures. To his thinking, diversity among peoples and nations was fundamental to progress in the world, and any attempt to reject national customs and indiscriminately adopt the ways of others could only be harmful. It was, in any event, clear that the Western countries were clinging tenaciously to their own particularistic national cultures, even while commonly pursuing modernization.

The advocates of preserving the national essence made many effective points in their arguments against the Westernizers, and, in theory, they provided the Japanese with a much-needed feeling of cultural worth after some two decades of breathtaking change within the ever-present shadow of the more advanced and "superior" West. A concomitant to the Seikyōsha movement, for example, was a renewal of interest in Japan's classical literature even at a time, as we shall see, when Japanese writers were first beginning to produce a modern literature under the dominant influence of the West. Ancient works, including collections of *waka* poetry, were reprinted one after another, and especially great excitement was aroused over the rediscovery of Genroku literature. The prose of Saikaku, the puppet plays of Chikamatsu, and the poems of Bashō were resuscitated, annotated, and made available to a wide reading public.

Unfortunately, the concept of preserving the national essence, while emotionally stimulating, did not lend itself to very precise definition, and the Seikyōsha writers were never able to present a convincing program of action. Moreover, even though they were generally reasonable-minded people themselves, their views tended to provide fuel for the xenophobes and extreme nationalists; and, in subsequent years, as Japan embarked upon overseas expansion, preservation of the national essence became synonymous with ultranationalism.

Intertwined with the debate in the mid-Meiji period over such questions as the modern (Western?) spirit and Japan's national essence was the major problem of Christianity. The leaders of the Meiji Restoration had little if any personal interest in Christianity, although some, like Itagaki Taisuke, the pioneer in the people's rights movement, conjectured that it might be an essential element in modernization. On the other hand, many of the intellectuals of the new generation of the 1880s and 1890s, including Tokutomi

Sohō, were powerfully, and in some cases decisively, affected by Christian teachings.

The centuries-old ban on Christianity was not immediately lifted at the time of the Restoration. Not until 1873, after the Iwakura Mission observed how highly the Westerners treasured their religion, was it quietly legalized in Japan. Meanwhile, Western missionaries—particularly American and British Protestants—had already entered the country and begun their activities, including the compilation of English-Japanese dictionaries and translation of the Bible into Japanese. One field in which the missionaries performed especially valuable service was education. While the government concentrated on developing a national system of primary education, foreign missionaries and prominent Japanese independently established private schools to provide much of the higher training essential to Japan's modernizing program. Among the well-known private colleges founded about this time were the Christian university, Dōshisha, in Kyoto, and Keiō University and Waseda University in Tokyo, founded respectively by Fukuzawa Yukichi and Ōkuma Shigenobu.

Many of the youths most strongly influenced by Christianity were samurai from domains that had been on the losing side in the Restoration.[73] Restricted in the opportunities open to them in the new government, these youths sought alternate routes to advancement through the acquisition of Western training. When brought into direct contact with foreign Christian teachers, they were particularly impressed with the moral caliber and fervid personal commitment of most of these men. To the young and impressionable Japanese, the foreign teachers appeared to possess qualities of character very similar to the ideal samurai and Confucian scholars of their own traditional backgrounds. Indeed, many Japanese who converted to Christianity in the 1870s and 1880s seem to have viewed it as a kind of modern extension of Confucianism.

For their part, the American missionary and lay Christian teachers who came to Japan in the 1870s also responded with high enthusiasm toward their Japanese students. The faith of these men, who were imbued with the religious spirit of late nineteenth-century New England, was rooted in the belief that God's work on earth was to be carried out by individuals acting in accordance with a high moral code and the dictates of their Christian consciences. They were not particularly concerned with questions of dogma and abstract theology but wished to build strong characters; and they were quick to appreciate the features of good character, derived from the samurai code of conduct, that they detected in many of their students.

Tokutomi Sohō was one of a famous group of thirty-five Japanese youths, known as the Kumamoto band, who in 1875 climbed a hill in their native domain of Kumamoto in Kyushu and pledged themselves to Christianity and to propagation of the faith in order to dispel ignorance and enlighten the people. These youths were students at a school for Western studies in Kumamoto conducted by Leroy L. James, a West Point graduate and former military officer in the American Civil War, and several of them went on to become distinguished spokesmen for Christianity in Japan. Although Tokutomi himself later renounced his formal ties with the church, he retained the Protestant Christian belief in "inner freedom" and the individual's duty to use his independent conscience as a guide to social and political behavior. It was on the basis of this belief that he attacked the kind of Confucian morality the Meiji government sought to inculcate in the primary schools from the 1880s on that called upon all Japanese to give blind and unquestioning loyalty to the state.

The influence of Protestant Christianity on Japanese who came to criticize the strongly statist policies of the government in the mid-Meiji period can be seen not only in independent intellectuals like Tokutomi, but also in many individuals who entered the socialist movement after its beginnings in the 1890s. In fact, a number of the most prominent Christians in modern Japan have also been leading socialists. Still other Christians, however, were driven by the unfavorable climate for their views after the commencement of parliamentary government in 1890 to withdraw entirely from the arena of political and social criticism and to devote themselves to the private cultivation of their religion. The best-known example of these Christians was Uchimura Kanzō (1861–1930).

Uchimura, the son of a samurai, attended a Christian-influenced agricultural school in the northern island of Hokkaido and became a student of Dr. William S. Clark, an American lay teacher who, like Janes at Kumamoto, was successful in attracting young Japanese to the faith. Later, Uchimura went to the United States to study at Amherst, and it was there that he was converted to Christianity. In 1891 Uchimura created a sensation back in Japan when, as a teacher at the esteemed First High School in Tokyo, he refused to bow before a copy of the Imperial Rescript on Education. He was branded a traitor by some people, forced to resign his position for the offense of lèse majesté, and became the target of polemical attacks that charged him with possessing allegiances incompatible with the responsibilities to emperor and nation required of subjects in the educational Rescript.[74] Uchimura thus became a victim of the shift in attitude, on the part of the Japanese public and many intellectuals, from the open and naive internationalism of the 1870s to an illiberal, virulent nationalism. Although he worked for another decade or so in journalism, Uchimura eventually retired from public view to a life of private teaching and writing on religion.

Contrary to the assertions of his detractors, Uchimura did not embrace Christianity to the exclusion of national loyalty. He steadfastly proclaimed his devotion to the "two J's"—Jesus and Japan—and insisted that, just as Anglicans were essentially English Christians, Presbyterians were Scottish Christians, and Lutherans were German Christians, he was a Japanese Christian. Uchimura even founded a "non-church" (mukyōkai) movement in an attempt to deracinate Christianity from its alien institutions and traditions by eliminating its clerical organization and other ecclesiastical trappings, and to render it as much Japanese as Western. For his epitaph he wrote in English:

I for Japan
Japan for the World;
The World for Christ;
And All for God.

Even when it enjoyed its greatest popularity in the Meiji period, Christianity could never claim as its own more than a very small percentage of the population of Japan (less than one-half of 1 percent); and after the turn to conservatism in the late 1880s and 1890s, it lost any opportunity it may have had to become a major force in Japanese life. Moreover, even it if had not been seen as a threat to the statist views rendered newly orthodox in the Meiji Constitution of 1889 and the Imperial Rescript on Education, Christianity would have (and indeed has) suffered from sectarianism in Japan, a sectarianism that had been kept to a minimum by American Protestant missionaries in the palmy days of successful proselytizing during the first two decades of Meiji. Apart from its work in such fields as education and medicine and the profound influence it exerted on certain individuals, like the ones we have been examining here, Christianity has been of negligible importance in modern Japan.

The Meiji Constitution was written in secret by Itō Hirobumi and his colleagues and was presented to the Japanese people in 1889 as a gift from the emperor. It was based on a carefully considered mixture of conservative and liberal principles (with the former heavily outweighing the latter) that owed much to the constitutional theories of Germany, the Western country which the Meiji oligarchs had come increasingly to regard as most analogous to Japan in historical background and stage of modernization. The conservative character of the Constitution may, for purposes of illustration, be noted in several major areas. First, an appointive House of Peers was given equal lawmaking powers with an elective House of Representatives. Second, the personal liberties granted to the Japanese people were all made "subject to the limitations imposed by law"; in other words, such liberties were not to be inalienable but might be (and often were) restricted by government decree.

But the most strongly conservative feature of the Meiji Constitution was the great power it allowed the executive branch of government. This power derived in large part from omission: that is, from the deliberate failure to specify how the executive was to be formed and what were to constitute the precise limits of its authority. There was no provision at all, for example, for appointment of the prime minister, and no proviso about accountability of the other ministers of state in the cabinet to anyone except the emperor. Clearly, the oligarchs intended to retain firm control of the executive, and, after the opening of the first Diet in 1890, the party members in the House of Representatives found very little prospect that they would in the near future be able to participate significantly in the ruling of Japan. The oligarchs formed an extralegal body known as the *genrō* or "elders," consisting at first entirely of the highest Satsuma and Chōshū leaders in government, and it was they who selected the prime ministers (from among themselves) and continued to dominate the affairs of state.

The sociopolitical orthodoxy that the oligarchs codified in the Meiji Constitution and the Imperial Rescript on Education is commonly called *kokutai,* a term that literally means the body of the country but is usually translated as "national polity." Based on the Shinto-Confucian concept (which we observed in the Rescript on Education) of Japan as a great family-state, *koku-tai* held a special appeal for the Japanese people because of its glorification of the mystique of emperorship. The Japanese regarded their line of sovereigns—described in the Constitution as "unbroken for ages eternal" and in the Rescript on Education as "coeval with heaven and earth"—as a unique and sacrosanct institution that gave Japan a claim to superiority over all other countries in the world. For centuries, of course, the emperors of Japan had wielded no political power whatever, and during the Tokugawa period they were held virtual prisoners in Kyoto by the shogunate. Nevertheless, the throne had served as an incomparably effective rallying point for nationalistic sentiment during the difficult and dangerous transition to the modern era. Although perhaps relatively ignored during the liberal euphoria of the 1870s, it inevitably drew the renewed attention of government leaders and conservative intellectuals in the 1880s. For nothing was more venerably Japanese than the imperial institution, and anyone wishing to revive traditional values, whether moral or cultural, was almost perforce obliged to start with recognition of the throne as the font of Japanese civilization. No simple explanation, however, can be given of the throne's role in modern Japan. For the most part the emperor has been held "above politics" and, with few exceptions, his participation in governmental affairs has not been made public. But there can be no question that, as the living embodiment of *kokutai,* he was a potent symbol for radically nationalistic emotions in the period up through World War II.

A corollary to emperor glorification in the *kokutai* ideology was that, of all the peacetime occupations, government service was the most cherished because it meant, in effect, employment by the emperor. Although the Satsuma-Chōshū oligarchs continued to control the highest councils of state, a vast expansion of the bureaucracy during the final years of the nineteenth century created ample opportunities for good careers in government, careers that were avidly sought by youths of all classes. Tokyo Imperial University, moreover, was made a kind of orthodox channel for governmental preferment, further proof of the degree to which Japanese society and the aspirations of its members were subjected to state manipulation in the middle and late Meiji period.

Japanese prose literature by the time of the Meiji Restoration had sunk to an extremely low level. Tedious didacticism, bawdy comedy, and bloody adventure were the stock-in-trade of the authors of these years, and there was little prospect, in the absence of stimulation from outside, that the quality of their work would soon improve. But this remains conjecture, for the fact is that, within a few decades of the Restoration, Western influences had wrought a change in prose literature as profound as in any other area of Japanese culture during the modern era.

The most successful writer in the years immediately before and after the Restoration was Kanagaki Robun (1829–94), an *edokko* or "child of Edo" who specialized in the traditional genre of "witty books" (*kokkeibon*). One of Robun's post-Restoration works was *A Journey by Foot Through Western Lands (Seiyō Dōchū Hizakurige),* in which he attempted to give a modern twist to Jippensha Ikku's famous story of two rogues frolicking their way down the Tōkaidō from Edo to Kyoto; another was *Eating Beef Stew Cross-Legged,* the parody on the aping of Western customs that we noted earlier in this chapter. A prime example of Robun's irreverent humor can be observed in the title of still another of his books, *Kyūri Zukai.* This title was phonetically the same as Fukuzawa Yukichi's *Physics Illustrated;* but, in the Sinico-Japanese characters used by Robun, it meant *On the Use of Cucumbers.* Such punning was of course frivolous, an adjective that may be applied to much of the work done by Robun and his fellow Edo authors. Although these men continued to hold the center of the literary stage for a while, they produced almost nothing that was memorable. The future of Meiji literature lay clearly in the assimilation of powerful artistic ideas and styles then being imported from the West.

In the first decade or so of Meiji, those Japanese writers and scholars interested in foreign literature devoted themselves mainly to the translation of famous Western works. An adaptation of *Robinson Crusoe* had, in fact, been completed even before the Restoration, and a Japanese rendering of *Aesop's Fables* existed as one of the few products of the old Jesuit press that had survived the attempt by the Tokugawa shogunate to eradicate all traces of contact with the Catholic Christian countries during the century from the 1540s to the 1630s. Among the earliest Western translations to appear in print in the Meiji period was Samuel Smiles's *Self-Help,* a book of success stories whose very title suggests the kind of subject matter that Japan's passionate new devotees of civilization and enlightenment were most likely to appreciate.

One of the first modern Western novels to be translated into Japanese was Bulwer-Lytton's *Ernest Maltravers,* the tale of a modern man's ingenuity and self-motivated drive to succeed (although the translator of this work saw fit to give it the erotically provocative Japanese title of *Karyū Shunwa* or *A Spring Tale of Flowers and Willows* in the hope of boosting its sales). For most of the first two decades of Meiji, Japanese translators of Western fiction concentrated overwhelmingly on the writings of British authors, a clear reflection of the enormous prestige in Japanese eyes of British civilization compared to that of any other country of the West. In addition to Bulwer-Lytton, prominent British authors translated into Japanese during the early Meiji period included Scott and Disraeli.

The Japanese were especially taken with tales of modern and "scientific" adventures, as can be seen in the popularity of Jules Verne's *Around the World in Eighty Days* and *A Trip to the Moon.* And from about the early 1880s on, largely in response to the movement for parliamentary government, they became infatuated with political novels. The translated writings of Disraeli and Bulwer-Lytton helped make respectable the practice of prose writing, which members of the ruling samurai class of the Tokugawa period had for the most part eschewed as vulgar; and during the 1880s many prominent members of the embryonic parties tried their hands at politically oriented novels. A good many of these novels dealt with the present, but others were set in such disparate times and places as ancient Greece, Ming China, France during the Revolution, and even a hypothetical Japan in the 173rd year of Meiji (A.D. 2040, one hundred fifty years after the opening of the first Diet in 1890).

Some idea of the growing consciousness in the 1880s of Japanese achievements and the anticipation that Japan would assume a more assertive international role can be seen in a passage from one of these political novels entitled *Strange Encounters of Elegant Females (Kajin no Kigū),* written in 1885 by Shiba Shirō under the nom de plume of the Wanderer of the Eastern Seas. Far from being an account of romance and passion, as the title would seem to suggest, *Strange Encounters* is the story of the Wanderer's investigation into revolutionary activities throughout the world. At the outset, he meets two strikingly beautiful European ladies, one Spanish and one Irish (although both graced by the author with Chinese names), at the Liberty Bell in Philadelphia. The three enter into serious discussion about matters of political repression and revolution and, even after the Wanderer departs for other foreign lands, the ladies periodically reappear to meet him on his travels. Although they are obviously in love with him, the Wanderer can think only of the need for promoting freedom and justice in the world. At one point, the Spanish lady encourages him by saying:

> Now that your country has reformed its government and, by taking from America what is useful and rejecting what is only superficial, is increasing month by month in wealth and strength, the eyes and ears of the world are astonished by your success. As the sun climbs in the eastern skies, so is your country rising in the Orient. Your August Sovereign has granted political liberty to the people, the people have sworn to follow the Imperial leadership. So the time has come when, domestic strife having ceased, all classes will be happy in their occupations. Korea will send envoys and the Luchu Islands will submit to your governance. Then will the occasion arise for doing great things in the Far East. Your country will take the lead and preside over a confederation of Asia. The peoples of the East will no longer be in danger. In the West you will restrain the rampancy of England and France. In the South you will check the corruption of China. In the North you will thwart the designs of Russia. You will resist the policy of European states, which is to treat Far Eastern peoples with contempt and to interfere in their domestic affairs, so leading them into servitude. Thus it is your country and no other that can bring the taste of self-government and independence into the life of millions for the first time, and so spread the light of civilization.[75]

A major problem for both translators of Western books and writers of Western-inspired political novels was that of style. Tokugawa authors had employed several methods of writing, from the poetic use of alternating metrical lines of five and seven syllables to a style derived from Sinico-Japanese. The gap between these classical styles and the colloquial language of everyday speech was enormous, and the difficulty of devising a means to reproduce in Japanese the vernacular novels of the modern West taxed the ingenuity of the most dedicated of Meiji translators. As a result, most of the renditions of Western novels in the early Meiji period were not true translations at all, but rather were free adaptations of the original works. During the 1880s, a movement was begun to "unify the spoken and written languages" (*gembun-itchi*), and, toward the end of the decade, Futabatei Shimei (1864–1909), author of Japan's first truly modern novel, was also the first successfully to

bridge the gap between speech and writing. With continuing progress in education, growth of the mass media, and acceptance of the Tokyo dialect as the standard form of speech, the modern Japanese vernacular or *kogō* was finally evolved, although it was not used widely by novelists until after the Sino-Japanese War of 1894–95, by the authors of primary school textbooks until 1903, or by newspaper reporters in general until a decade after that.

The man who more than any other made possible the writing of a modern prose literature in Japan was Tsubouchi Shōyō (1859–1935).[76] A graduate of Tokyo Imperial University and translator of the collected works of Shakespeare, Tsubouchi published an epochal tract in 1885 entitled *The Essence of the Novel (Shōsetsu Shinzui)*. In it he attacked what he regarded as the deplorable state of literature in Japan during his day:

> It has long been the custom in Japan to consider the novel as an instrument of education, and it has frequently been proclaimed that the novel's chief function is the castigation of vice and the encouragement of virtue. In actual practice, however, only stories of bloodthirsty cruelty or else of pornography are welcomed, and very few readers indeed even cast so much as a glance on works of a more serious nature. Moreover, since popular writers have no choice but to be devoid of self-respect and in all things slaves to public fancy and the lackeys of fashion, each one attempts to go to greater lengths than the last in pandering to the tastes of the time. They weave their brutal historical tales, string together their obscene romances, and yield to every passing vogue. Nevertheless they find it so difficult to abandon the pretext of "encouraging virtue" that they stop at nothing to squeeze in a moral, thereby distorting the emotion portrayed, falsifying the situations, and making the whole plot nonsensical.[77]

Tsubouchi insisted that the novel must be regarded as art, to be appreciated soley for its own sake. He urged that Western, and particularly English, literature be taken as the model for a new kind of novelistic prose writing in Japan free of didacticism and devoted to the realistic portrayal of human emotions (*ninjō*) and the actual conditions of life. Even the supposedly enlightened authors of contemporary political novels dealt only with stereotypical characters who were motivated by the desire to "reward virtue and punish vice." Writers of the new fiction must seek to penetrate the wellsprings of individual behavior and reveal it, with candor, in all its manifestations.

Unfortunately, Tsubouchi, although a first-rate critic, was himself unable to produce the kind of modern novel that he so vigorously advocated. His book *The Character of Present-day Students (Tōsei Shosei Katagi),* written in conjuction with *The Essence of the Novel,* deals with the lives and loves of students at Tokyo Imperial University in the early 1880s; but, despite Tsubouchi's efforts to delineate the psychological complexities of the students he was portraying, the work is very similar to the superficial character sketches and witty books of Tokugawa authors.

The kind of modern novel Tsubouchi had in mind was in fact written by his friend and disciple, Futabatei Shimei. Futabatei, born in Edo the son of a samurai a few years before the Meiji Restoration, studied Russian from 1881 until 1886 at a school for foreign languages sponsored by the Meiji government. His extraordinary talent for languages enabled him to excel at the school and gave rise to his decision to become a full-time translator and writer. Futabatei's translations from the Russian of such authors as Turgenev, begun in the mid-1880s, were of prime importance in the literary history of the Meiji period; for they were the first renderings of Western literature into Japanese that can truly be called translations. In the free adaptations of other early and mid-Meiji translators, large sections were often either omitted or added and sometimes only the most essential plot of a book was retained. Beginning with Futabatei, Japanese translation of the literature of the West became a genuinely professional pursuit.

Immediately after finishing his studies at the foreign language school in 1886, the still unknown Futabatei boldly called upon Tsubouchi to discuss the literary matters raised by the latter in *The Essence of the Novel.* Thus began a warm and lasting friendship between the two men that provided, among other things, the conditions necessary for Futabatei to embark upon the writing of the first modern Japanese novel, *The Drifting Cloud (Ukigumo),* published in installments between 1887 and 1889.

The Drifting Cloud is a realistic novel, written in a colloquial style, that has a unified and sustained plot and probes the feelings and psychological motivations of its principal characters. It is the story of Bunzō, a government clerk who lives in the home of his aunt and who loves and hopes to marry his cousin, Osei. As the story opens, Bunzō has lost his job, much to the disgust of the aunt, who has never been particularly fond of him and is now convinced that he is a failure. Bunzō's apparent inability to get ahead in a generation of Japanese striving madly to achieve the fame and fortune promised by modernity stands in sharp contrast to the prospects of Noboru, a colleague who has received a promotion just as Bunzō is fired. Clearly, Noboru is the new Meiji man, while Bunzō is a pathetic example of those who inevitably fall the victims of progress. When Noboru visits the aunt's home, he predictably causes new difficulties, for the aunt sees in him the ideal match for her daughter, and Osei herself, a flighty and superficial person, responds by rejecting Bunzō and entering into a flirtation with Noboru. Unfortunately, Futabatei's handling of the later stages in the plot of *The Drifting Cloud* is clumsy and unconvincing. The Osei-Noboru flirtation peters out and, in the end, Bunzō, who has been immobilized by events, is encouraged by a mere smile from Osei to anticipate a reconciliation with her. For all its faults, however, *The Drifting Cloud* remains an epochal work that inaugurated realistic fiction writing in modern Japan.

While Tsubouchi Shōyō and Futabatei Shimei were thus taking the pioneer steps in creating a new fiction on Western lines, other writers, motivated in part by the strongly conservative, nativistic trend of the 1880s, sought to revitalize Japanese literature by means of its own tradition. The most influential of these writers emerged from a group called the Ken'yūsha (Society of Friends of the Inkstone), founded in 1885 by Ozaki Kōyō (1867–1903) and others, who were at the time still students at Tokyo Imperial University. Issuing a magazine with the facetious title of *The Literary Rubbish Bin (Garakuta Bunko),* the members of the Ken'yūsha called for a literary renaissance through rejection of the styles of writing and themes, including the didactic and the "witty," that had held sway in Japan from the Bunka-Bunsei epoch earlier in the century, and restoration of the great prose standards of Genroku, particularly as found in the works of Saikaku.

Like the contemporary scholars of the "national essence" movement, the Ken'yūsha writers were not simply blind reactionaries. Ozaki, for example, thoroughly agreed with Tsubouchi's dictum (presented in *The Essence of the Novel*) that literature should be regarded as an independent art, not requiring justification on moralistic or other grounds. Ozaki believed, moreover, that the realism Tsubouchi sought in modern Western fiction was more readily and appropriately accessible to Japanese in the realistic writing of

Saikaku. Ozaki's own novels, written in the style of Saikaku, were enormously popular and helped stimulate the rediscovery of Genroku literature that we have already noted. Yet Ozaki and the other Ken'yūsha writers, despite their appeal to readers in the 1880s and 1890s, contributed virtually nothing to the development of the modern novel in Japan. They were almost unchallengeably powerful in the literary world of the late 1880s and early 1890s, even to the point of controlling many of the most important outlets for fictional publication; but, upon the untimely death of Ozaki in 1903, their brand of "renaissance literature" quickly gave way to other kinds of modern fictional writing whose growth had been prefigured by the earlier work of Tsubouchi and Futabatei.

Japanese poetry, while subject to much the same pull between traditional and modern (i.e., Western) influences that afflicted prose literature and nearly all other aspects of culture in the Meiji period, had its own special problems. First, poetry had always been the most "serious" of Japanese literary pursuits and hence brought an infinitely more weighty tradition to the modern era than the slightly regarded practice of prose writing. Second, although constricting rules of diction and vocabulary could be broken, the special qualities of the Japanese language that so fundamentally determined what could and could not be done poetically (for example, rhyme could not be used as a prosodic device) prevented Japanese poets from emulating much of Western poetry. And finally, in Japan as in the West, poetry could not hope to compete in popularity with the novel as the dominant literary form of modernization.

To many early Meiji poets, the classical *waka*–or *tanka* (short poem), as it has been more commonly called in modern times–was so buried in the past that there was little sense in even trying to exhume it. And, at any rate, both the *tanka* and the *haiku* were forms so limited in scope as to be useless for the expression of modern ideas and sentiments. Poets should instead turn their attention to the translation of Western poetry and to the development of new kinds of verse based on Western models. The first major step in this direction was the publication in 1882 of the *Collections of Poems in the New Style (Shintaishō)*, compiled by three professors of Tokyo Imperial University and consisting of nineteen translations from English and five original pieces by the compilers themselves. Like the political novels of the same time, much of the poetry written in the new style during the next few years dealt with the subjects of governmental and social reform.

Meanwhile, as a result of the conservative winds that had begun blowing forcefully by the middle and late 1880s, devotees of the older poetic modes, and especially the *tanka,* were given something of a new lease on life. The hidebound members of the traditional *tanka* schools, who had continued composing as though the Meiji Restoration had not happened, are of no particular interest to us; but other *tanka* poets actively sought to reform and reinvigorate their art. Perhaps the most noteworthy of these reformist poets (who first came to prominence during the 1890s) was Masaoka Shiki (1867–1902), a practitioner of *haiku* who did not seriously take up the *tanka* until about this time. Shiki was employed as a reporter on the staff of *Japan (Nihon),* a magazine devoted, like Miyake Setsurei's *The Japanese,* to "preservation of the national essence"; and it was in large part because his editors began publishing *tanka* composed by members of the traditional schools as examples of a native art worth preserving that Shiki decided to speak out on *tanka* reform.

In addition to calling for freedom of poetic diction and the use of modern language, Shiki championed the concept of *shasei* or "realistic depiction." Furthermore, he deplored the fact that the *tanka,* from the time of the standard-setting tenth-century anthology *Kokinshū,* had been infused with an artificiality of wit and a fragility of emotion unsuited to the true spirit of the Japanese. Strongly endorsing the views of the Tokugawa period scholar of National Learning, Kamo Mabuchi, Shiki lauded the merits of the *Man'yōshū.* He saw in the poems of this earliest of anthologies such qualities as masculine vigor, directness of expression, and "sincerity" (*makoto*) that were in particular likely to be appreciated by his fellow countrymen in the expansive, imperialistic mood following Japan's startling military victory over China in 1894–95.

Much like the novelist Ozaki Kōyō, Shiki tried to find realism–apparently the most valued of "modern" aesthetic qualities–in the Japanese literary tradition. In fact, Shiki's advocacy of "realistic depiction" was, as Robert Brower has observed, "a quasi-scientific principle directly influenced by conceptions of illusionist realism in Western-style painting."[78] It appears that, with Shiki, we have still another example of the strong impulse on the part of so many modern Japanese scholars and artists (indeed, probably all of them during at least one phase or another of their careers) either consciously or unconsciously to relate to their own national past those features of modern culture that emerged in the West and that they admire or wish to utilize. But history is cruel to this impulse, for the unalterable fact is that the West evolved such things as modern realistic literature first and the Japanese will never know whether they could have done it independently.

In contrast to their relatively recent exposure to Western literature (that is, belles-lettres), the Japanese had had a rather long historical acquaintanceship with the visual arts, particularly painting, of the West. Unencumbered by a language barrier, the visual arts are obviously more amenable to cross-culture transmission, although in the case of Japan this in fact meant simply that the inevitable clash between Japanese tradition and Western modernity could be precipitated even more readily and with greater abandon than it could in literature. At the same time, as Sansom has suggested, it is also possible that in the visual arts Japan's aesthetic heritage was better prepared than it was in literature to stand up against Western intrusion.[79]

The Jesuits had first introduced Western visual arts to Japan in the sixteenth century and had even trained Japanese artists in contemporary painting techniques. But the anti-Christian measures of the Tokugawa shogunate had, of course, eliminated this and almost all other Western influences from the country during the midseventeenth century. Not until the rise of Dutch Studies about a hundred years later did knowledge of Western art again make its way into Japan. Subsequently, nearly all of the major, vital schools of painting in the late eighteenth and early nineteenth centuries were influenced to a greater or lesser degree by Western techniques. Some painter, like Shiba Kōkan, went over entirely to the foreign medium and learned to paint in precise technical imitation of the Western manner. Curiously, however, the work of Shiba and other pioneer Western-style painters seems to have fallen into obscurity, and some artists in the last years of the Tokugawa shogunate, after Japan had been opened by Perry, laboriously set about to learn Western painting on their own from the few foreign-language manuals they could acquire without being aware of what Shiba and his fellow proponents of Dutch Studies had already accomplished.

The most prominent person in the late Tokugawa and early Meiji efforts to develop and popularize Western art in Japan was Kawakami Tōgai (1827–81).[80] A moderately skilled artist in the *bunjin* or literati style of painting, Kawakami took up the study of the Dutch language sometime about the 1850s and soon turned his attention also to European painting. In 1857 he joined the shogunate's Office for Barbarian Studies, the organization that also employed a number of the later members of the Meiji Six Society, and within a few years was appointed to head its newly established section on the study of painting. After the Restoration, Kawakami, who was primarily interested in the practical, scientific side of Western painting, was engaged by the Ministry of Education to develop teaching methods and prepare training manuals on art for use in public schools. Among the innovations he sponsored was instruction in realistic drawing with pencils, rather than painting with the traditional Japanese ink-brush.

In 1876 the Meiji government, continuing its policy of encouragement of Western-style art, opened the Industrial Art School (Kōbu Bijutsu Gakkō) and invited several Italian artists to provide training in painting, sculpture, and general methods of art. The most important of these was Antonio Fontanesi (1818–82), who during his stay of approximately two years in Japan made a profound impression on the students he taught, several of whom became outstanding Western-style painters in later years. So popular was Fontanesi that when he left for home in 1878, at least partly owing to a difference of opinion with his employers in the Japanese government, a number of students withdrew from the school and founded a society for the furtherance of Western art, thereby inaugurating the first independent art movement of the modern era in Japan.

Fontanesi's departure was undoubtedly related to the beginning of a trend in the late 1870s and 1880s away from Western art to a revival of interest in the traditional art of Japan. Coincidentally, in the very same year that Fontanesi left, 1878, another foreigner, the young American Ernest Fenollosa (1853–1908), arrived in Japan to begin a remarkable career as one of the two leading figures in the great resurgence of native art appreciation.

Fenollosa, a recent graduate of Harvard, was originally engaged to teach philosophy at Tokyo Imperial University, but before long he became an outspoken (and highly opinionated) admirer of Far Eastern, and particularly Japanese, art. Eventually, Fenollosa evolved a grand philosophical concept along the lines of "Eastern morals and Western technology," according to which he prophesied a Hegelian-type dialectical synthesis between the spiritual East and the material West that would advance the world to a new cultural plane. On a more immediate and practical level, Fenollosa, along with one of his students, Okakura Tenshin (1862–1913), began to take stock of Japanese art and to advocate ways in which it could be repopularized and perpetuated.

Traditional Japanese art and artists had unquestionably fallen on bad times during the early Restoration period. The two leading practictioners of the ancient Kanō school of painting, for example, were reduced to menial occupations in order to earn their livings. It was also because of the almost total lack of interest in native work in these years that Fenollosa and others were able to buy up at very low prices the vast number of art pieces that still constitute the core of many major Japanese collections in foreign museums today.

Fenollosa gave lectures to private groups in Japan extolling the glories of Japanese art and even pronouncing it to be superior to the art of the West. He and Okakura also founded a Society for the Appreciation of Painting (Kangakai) and urged the Meiji government to sponsor training in the native artistic styles. Two results of their lobbying were the discontinuance of the Western-oriented Industrial Art School in 1883 and the substitution of brush painting for pencil drawing in public school art courses. But the greatest achievement of Fenollosa and Okakura was their role in the creation in 1889 of the government-backed Tokyo Art School (Tōkyō Bijutsu Gakkō), devoted exclusively to training in Far Eastern art. In 1886–87, Fenollosa and Okakura had traveled to Europe to study methods of art education and museum administration, and within a few years after their return, Okakura became head of the Tokyo Art School.

Of these two dynamic men who led the return to Japanese art in the 1880s, Fenollosa was by far the more inflexible. A transparent Japanophile so far as art was concerned, he also sought to impose on others his personal biases within the realm of Japanese art. For example, while he admired the Kanō school of painting, he viewed with distaste the literati movement of the middle and late Tokugawa period. Largely because of this preference on the part of a foreigner, it ap-

pears, no study of the *bunjin* painters was included in the curriculum of the Tokyo Art School.

Okakura, on the other hand, was very similar in sentiment to a number of his contemporaries who have been noted in this chapter, including the "national essence" intellectuals, the novelist Ozaki Kōyō, and the *haiku-tanka* poet Masaoka Shiki. All of these men were participants in the Japanist reaction of the 1880s and 1890s; and, although not all of them may have succeeded very well in their aims, they mutually aspired to revitalize Japanese culture and art by incorporating modern Western (or "international") elements into the native tradition and not by trying simply to reverse the course of progress. The tragedy for most of them was that this was no easy thing to do. A little Western "materialism" could rapidly dissipate a lot of Eastern "spiritualism."

In the case of the visual arts, the return to tradition led by Fenollosa and Okakura had been too radically launched, and within a few years the pendulum began to swing back to a position where both Western-style and Japanese art could coexist in Japan in an atmosphere of relative tranquility and equal competition. The fiery Fenollosa returned to the United States in 1890, and paintings in the Western manner were prominently displayed along with Japanese works in an industrial fair held the same year. More important, it was about this time that a number of highly promising artists returned from periods of study in France, Italy, and other Western countries. Among these, the one who was to have the greatest influence in art circles and who may rightly be regarded as the true founder of modern Western-style art in Japan was Kuroda Seiki (1866–1924). An Impressionist who had studied for ten years in Paris, Kuroda caused a minor furor by publicly exhibiting a painting of a nude for the first time in Japan (fig. 57). His influence and popularity spread rapidly, and in 1896 he was invited to join the faculty of Okakura's Tokyo Art School, a clear recognition—however reluctantly given—that Western-style art was in Japan to stay.

Since very little specific attention has thus far been given to the development of traditional Japanese music, some general remarks should be made before examining the impact upon it of Western music following the Meiji Restoration.

To a great extent Japanese music evolved through the centuries in conjunction with—or, perhaps more precisely, as an auxiliary to—literature. This was particularly true from the medieval age on, when music was used as an accompaniment both to plays of the *nō* theatre and to the recitations of itinerant storytellers, who strummed their lutelike *biwa* as they chanted excerpts from such works as *The Tale of the Heike*. Music, of course, also became an essential ingredient of the two major dramatic forms of the Tokugawa period, *kabuki* and *bunraku*. Like the earlier *nō kabuki* and *bunraku* were presentational rather than representational theatres and hence readily incorporated not only music but also miming, stunt-performing, and, in the case of *kabuki*, dancing. Although some purely instrumental, nonvocalized music was naturally performed (perhaps most notably on the *samisen* and the zitherlike *koto*, an instrument of refined taste dating from very early times), much of the music of pre-modern Japan was quite clearly subordinated to lyrical singing, acting, and dancing, and to the recitation of libretti that possessed independent literary merit.

Probably the first public performance of Western music in Japan in modern times was the playing by Perry's naval band during its visit to Edo in 1853.[81] And as in the case of the conversion to Western-style clothing, it was the Japanese military that led the way in the adoption of Western music. Military units of the early Meiji period initially formed bands simply as part of their general reorganization along Western lines. But before long, these army and navy bands began giving frequent public concerts, and they became familiar fixtures at the ballroom dances and other Western-style social affairs held at the Rokumeikan in the 1880s.

In addition to military music, Christian church music was also prominently introduced to Japan in the early Meiji period. By far the most important form here was the Protestant hymn; and, as one authority has pointed out, many Japanese songs of the Meiji period tended to have a strongly "Christian" sound, just like the early nationalistic songs of missionary-influenced countries in twentieth-century Africa.[82]

It was in the public schools, however, that the most important measures were taken to advance knowledge and appreciation of Western music among the Japanese, and the pioneer figure in implementing these measures was Izawa Shūji (1851–1917). After a period of study in the United States, Izawa was engaged by the Ministry of Education in 1879 to prepare songbooks and to plan for the teaching of music in the public schoo system. Izawa's principal aim was to find some way of blending traditional and Western music in order to produce a new kind of national music for modern Japan. To accomplish this, he worked chiefly with an American, Luther Mason of Boston, and with members of the *gagaku* school of ancient court musicians. The choice of *gagaku* musicians as the Japanese specialists in the composition of "blended" music is particularly interesting, since it meant that Izawa and his associates chose to bypass the more recent and vital forms of "vulgar" music that had evolved in the Tokugawa period and to draw instead upon the rigidly conventionalized, albeit "elegant," musical tradition of at least a millennium earlier in Japanese history.

One notable product of the mixing of music in early Meiji (although not by Izawa) was the Japanese anthem, "Kimi ga Yo" ("His Majesty's Reign"), composed in response to the desire to have a national song like the Western countries. The words for "Kimi ga Yo," taken apparently from the tenth-century poetic anthology *Kokinshū*, were first put to Western music by an English bandsman in the 1870s but were later adapted to a melody by a *gagaku* musician that was in turn harmonized and arranged for orchestra by a German, Franz Eckert.

However we may judge the efforts of Izawa to synthesize traditional and Western music, the most important result of musical training in public schools from his time on was to accustom successive generations of Japanese students to Western harmonies and modes, and thus to make possible Japanization of the classical repertoire of Western symphonic and chamber music. Today, Bach, Mozart, and Beethoven belong as much to the Japanese as they do to anyone else in the world.

Since the main orchestrated styles of native Japanese music were so closely associated with the theatre, the fate of the traditional theatrical forms after the Meiji Restoration has quite naturally determined their course as well. The *nō* theatre, a remnant of the medieval age, was antiquated even during the Tokugawa period and, despite the authorship of new plays by certain contemporary writers, remains a drama engulfed in history and aesthetic tradition to be admired primarily by connoisseurs and by students of the classical arts. Similar patronage continues to support the bourgeois puppet theatre. After a period of great flourishing in mid-Tokugawa times, *bunraku* declined steadily in popularity and, with the coming of the modern era and new demands for realistic portrayal, has had little hope of regaining any mass following.

Of chief theatrical interest in the early Meiji period was the development of *kabuki*. Much of the success of *kabuki* after the Restoration was owing to the efforts of the impresario Morita Kanya (1846–97) and the playwright Kawatake Mokuami (1816–93). After the overthrow of the Tokugawa regime brought to an end the many restrictions that the shogunate had imposed on *kabuki* over the years, Morita moved his theatre from the outlying Asakusa (formerly the Yoshiwara) region to the central Tsukiji area of Tokyo. Built first in 1872 and reconstructed in 1878 after destruction by fire,[83] Morita's theatre gave rise to a new era in which *kabuki* enjoyed social respectability and was amenable to up-to-date, modernizing ideas.

One step taken to advance *kabuki* was the production of *sangiri* ("cropped hair") plays, especially by Mokuami, that dealt with current fashions and fads (although, apart from greater topical relevance, the *sangiri* plays were structurally much like the domestic pieces—*sewamono*—of traditional *kabuki*). Another type of new play was the *katsureki* or "living history," created after the rise of the people's rights movement in the 1870s. In the politically conscious atmosphere of the times, these plays represented ann effort to stage realistic historical drama rather than the fancifully distorted quasi-history of earlier *kabuki*.

An even more significant innovation to emerge from the political ferment of the second and third decades of the Meiji period was *shimpa* or the "new school" of theater, whose founders were actual participants in the political party movement. Chief among them was Kawakami Otojirō (1864–1911), a former *kabuki* actor and fervid political liberal of the day. Using current events and material from recently written political novels (including the *Strange Encounters of Elegant Females* discussed above), Kawakami attempted to present plays of topical interest, which he further enlivened with special sound and lighting effects. The war with China in the mid-1890s provided a particularly fine opportunity for Kawakami, who was able to capitalize on heightened patriotic feelings by staging *shimpa* extravaganzas dealing with the fighting then in progress on the continent.

Books for Further Reading

Fowler, Edward. *The Rhetoric of Confession: Shishōsetsu in Early Twentieth-Century Japanese Fiction*. Berkeley: University of California Press, 1988.

Fujii, James A. *Complicit Fictions: The Subject in the Modern Japanese Prose Narrative*. Berkeley: University of California Press, 1993.

Hijiya-Kirschnereit, Irmela. *Rituals of Self-Revelation: Shishōsetsu as Literary Genre and Socio-Cultural Phenomenon*. Translated by Hijiya-Kirschnereit. Cambridge, Mass.: Council on East Asian Studies, Harvard University, 1996.

Karatani Kōjin. *Origins of Modern Japanese Literature*. Translation edited by Brett de Bary. Durham, N.C.: Duke University Press, 1993.

Kato Shuichi. *A History of Japanese Literature*. Vol. 3: *The Modern Years*. Translated by Don Sanderson. Tokyo: Kodansha International, 1983.

Keene, Donald. *Dawn to the West: Japanese Literature in the Modern Era*. Vol. 1: *Fiction*. New York: Holt, Rinehart & Winston, 1984.

Lippit, Noriko Mizuta. *Reality and Fiction in Modern Japanese Literature*. White Plains, N.Y.: Sharpe, 1980.

Miyoshi, Masao. *Accomplices of Silence: The Modern Japanese Novel*. Berkeley: University of California Press, 1974.

Mulhern, Chieko I., ed. *Japanese Women Writers: A Bio-Critical Sourcebook*. Westport, Conn.: Greenwood Press, 1994.

Pollack, David. *Reading Against Culture: Ideology and Narrative in the Japanese Novel*. Ithaca: Cornell University Press, 1992.

Powell, Irena. *Writers and Society in Modern Japan*. London: Macmillan, 1983.

Rimer, J. Thomas. *Modern Japanese Fiction and Its Traditions: An Introduction*. Princeton: Princeton University Press, 1978.

Rubin, Jay. *Injurious to Public Morals: Writers and the Meiji State*. Seattle: University of Washington Press, 1984.

Suzuki, Tomi. *Narrating the Self: Fictions of Japanese Modernity*. Stanford, Cal.: Stanford University Press, 1996.

Tsuruta, Kinya, and Thomas E. Swann, eds. *Approaches to the Modern Japanese Novel*. Tokyo: Sophia University Press, 1976.

Ueda, Makoto. *Modern Japanese Writers and the Nature of Literature*. Stanford, Cal.: Stanford University Press, 1976.

Vernon, Victoria V. *Daughters of the Moon: Wish, Will, and Social Constraint in Fiction by Modern Japanese Women*. Berkeley, Cal.: Institute of East Asian Studies, University of California Press, 1988.

Walker, Janet A. *The Japanese Novel of the Meiji Period and the Ideal of Individualism*. Princeton: Princeton University Press, 1979.

Washburn, Dennis C. *The Dilemma of the Modern in Japanese Fiction*. New Haven: Yale University Press, 1995.

Yamanouchi, Hisaaki. *The Search for Authenticity in Modern Japanese Literature*. Cambridge, U.K.: Cambridge University Press, 1978.

Contributors

Rebecca L. Copeland .... *Washington University in Saint Louis*
Joan E. Ericson .... *The Colorado College*
Van C. Gessel .... *Brigham Young University*
Sakagami Hiroichi .... *Meiji University*
Charles Shirō Inouye .... *Tufts University*
Ken K. Ito .... *University of Michigan*
Kamiya Tadataka .... *Hokkaidō University*
Hasegawa Kei .... *Women's College, Jōsai University*
Yamazaki Kuninori .... *Hanazono University*
Kyoko Kurita .... *Pomona College*
Anthony V. Liman .... *University of Toronto*
Yoko McClain .... *University of Oregon*
Eileen B. Mikals-Adachi .... *University of Notre Dame*
J. Scott Miller .... *Brigham Young University*
Leith Morton .... *University of Newcastle*
James O'Brien .... *University of Wisconsin–Madison*
Cecilia Segawa Seigle .... *University of Pennsylvania*
Tōgawa Shinsuke .... *Gakushūin University*
Hidaka Shohji .... *Kanagawa University*
Lin Shu-Mei .... *Bunkyō University*
Richard Torrance .... *Ohio State University*
Hiraoka Toshio .... *Gumma Prefectural Women's University*

Cumulative Index

Dictionary of Literary Biography, Volumes 1-180
Dictionary of Literary Biography Yearbook, 1980-1996
Dictionary of Literary Biography Documentary Series, Volumes 1-14

Cumulative Index

DLB before number: *Dictionary of Literary Biography,* Volumes 1-180
Y before number: *Dictionary of Literary Biography Yearbook,* 1980-1996
DS before number: *Dictionary of Literary Biography Documentary Series,* Volumes 1-14

G

M

Q

ISBN 0-7876-1069-0

90000